Ajax Design Patterns

D0479059

Explicit Submission   Page 227
Instead of automatically submitting upon each browser event, request it; e.g., submit upon a button click.

Fat Client   Page 317
Create a rich, browser-based client by performing remote calls only when there is no way to achieve the same effect in the browser.

Guesstimate   Page 303
Instead of requesting information from the server, make a reasonable guess.

HTML Message   Page 186
Have the server generate HTML snippets to be displayed in the browser.

HTTP Streaming   Page 113
Stream server data in the response of a long-lived HTTP connection.

Heartbeat   Page 509
Have the browser periodically upload Heartbeat messages to indicate the application is still loaded in the browser and the user is still active.

Highlight   Page 468
Highlight elements by rendering them in a consistent, attention-grabbing format.

Host-Proof Hosting   Page 493
Host sensitive data in encrypted form, so that clients can only access and manipulate it by providing a pass-phrase that is never transmitted to the server.

IFrame Call   Page 108
Use IFrames for browser-server communication.

JSON Message   Page 201
Pass messages between server and browser in JavaScript Object Notation (JSON) format.

Lazy Registration   Page 474
Accumulate bits of information on the user as he interacts while deferring formal registration until later on.

Live Command-Line   Page 376
In command-line interfaces, monitor the command being composed and dynamically modify the interface to support the interaction.

Live Form   Page 383
Validate and modify a form throughout the entire interaction, instead of waiting for an explicit submission.

Live Search   Page 368
As the user constructs and refines his search query, continuously show all valid results.

Logging   Page 534
Provide your JavaScript with log messages.

Malleable Content   Page 407
Compose the page of Malleable Content blocks—small chunks of content that can be edited in page.

Microlink   Page 416
Provide Microlinks that open up new content on the existing page rather than loading a new page.

Ajax Design Patterns

Michael Mahemoff

O'REILLY®

Beijing • Cambridge • Farnham • Köln • Paris • Sebastopol • Taipei • Tokyo

Ajax Design Patterns
by Michael Mahemoff

Editor: Simon St.Laurent

Production Editor: Mary Brady

Copyeditors: Mary Brady and Lydia Onofrei

Indexer: Julie Hawks

Cover Designer: Mike Kohnke

Interior Designer: Marcia Friedman

Illustrators: Robert Romano and Jessamyn Read

Printing History:

June 2006: First Edition.

 This book uses RepKover™, a durable and flexible lay-flat binding.

ISBN: 0-596-10180-5

[M]

CONTENTS

AJAX DESIGN PATTERNS IS A REFERENCE FOR DEVELOPERS, DESIGNERS, AND MANAGERS WHO WANT TO know how Ajax is being used in the real world. Ajax is a new label to describe rich, desktop-like Internet applications that run in standard web browsers and do not require any special plugins. Its popularity stems from high-profile Ajax applications like Gmail, Google Maps, and 37signals' Basecamp, and it is becoming popular in the enterprise as well.

The patterns in this book fall into four categories. Foundational Technology patterns overview the raw technologies required for Ajax development, such as the XMLHttpRequest object. Programming patterns expose techniques developers have been discovering to ensure their Ajax applications are maintainable and performant. Functionality and Usability patterns are about the kinds of user-interfaces you'll come across in Ajax applications and the new types of functionality that Ajax makes possible. Finally, Development patterns explain the processes being used to monitor, debug, and test their Ajax applications.

Who Should Read This Book?

You should read this book if you want to:

- Learn what's possible—and what's not—with Ajax, and see how Ajax is being used in the real world.

- Get up to speed with core Ajax technologies such as XMLHttpRequest, the DOM, and JSON.

- Discover the patterns developers are using to produce high-quality Ajax architectures, streamline performance, and improve usability.

Because of the reference-like nature of the patterns, the book is accessible to people from different backgrounds. Developers who want to ramp up on Ajax will be able to begin with the tutorial chapter and the foundational technologies. Those who already have some experience with Ajax will probably gain the most from the Programming and Development patterns. People in less technical roles will be able to take a high-level perspective, looking especially at the Functionality and Usability patterns and the Real-World Examples therein to see what's possible with Ajax.

To follow the technical discussion and code examples, programmers should have some experience with the basics of web development—HTML, form submission, server-side scripting, and so on. Ideally, you should know some JavaScript too, as this book isn't intended to teach you the language, but the writing does take into account that many readers will only have basic familiarity with JavaScript.

Ajax is mostly about what happens in the browser, so the book doesn't assume you know any particular server-side environment. On those occasions where server-side code is involved, the examples are PHP-based and always explained in language-neutral terms.

Who Should Not Read This Book?

If you haven't performed any web development work, you're probably better off looking for an introduction to the basic concepts before jumping into Ajax and these patterns.

Ajax development involves working with a broad range of technologies, including HTML, XML, CSS, JavaScript, and server-side development. This book will help you understand how Ajax relates to each of these and how they are often combined together, but if you're looking to learn any one of these in depth or you're seeking a reference on browser specifics, I'd recommend consulting a specialized text.

About the Examples

All the examples in this book—the tutorial code as well as the Ajax Patterns code examples—can be downloaded from *http://ajaxify.com/run*. They've been developed to be compatible with recent versions of Firefox and Internet Explorer (IE), and have been tested on

Firefox 1.5 and IE 6.0.* Most of the server-side code requires PHP 5 or later and was tested on PHP 5.0.4. The PHP code should run on any standard web server capable of running PHP scripts; Apache 1.3.33 was used for testing. The Wiki Demo requires MySQL and was tested on version 4.1.14-max. See Appendix B for information on installing the demos.

Browser Specifics

True to the aims of Ajax, all of the Ajax Patterns are implementable in any modern, standard browser, and the discussions focus more on issues of general architecture and usability instead of browser specifics. However, portability issues do arise in some cases and are addressed where they are critical to implementing the pattern (as in some of the topics in Part II, *Foundational Technology Patterns*). To maintain a high-level focus, most of these discussion are still limited to IE and Firefox; it's beyond the scope of the patterns to outline the idiosyncracies of each browser and version, for which a specialized reference is advisable.

Organization of This Book

Part I, *Introduction*
> The first few chapters are a prelude to the patterns. Chapter 1, *Introducing Ajax*, overviews the Ajax phenomenon and discusses current trends. Chapter 2, *A Pattern-Led Tutorial*, is a quick-start tutorial on Ajax and the Ajax Patterns. The design concepts behind the Ajax Patterns are discussed in Chapter 3, *Ajax Design: Principles and Patterns*, along with an introduction to the patterns themselves.

Part II, *Foundational Technology Patterns*
> The Foundational Technology patterns outline the "building blocks" at the heart of any Ajax application. Ajax itself is a pattern, hence the first pattern, Ajax App (Chapter 4), which acts as the root for all the Ajax Patterns. The next few chapters look at the three core technologies involved in creating an Ajax App. Display Manipulation (Chapter 5) patterns are about repainting the user interface, and Web Remoting (Chapter 6) patterns document several alternatives for communicating with the server. The Dynamic Behavior (Chapter 7) patterns are about events—those derived by users and those based on timing. Finally, Extended Technologies (Chapter 8) explain how you can extend an Ajax App with nonstandard technologies.

Part III, *Programming Patterns*
> The Programming patterns focus on technical qualities of software, in particular maintainability, robustness, and performance. The first chapter in this part, Chapter 9, provides several alternative strategies for designing Web Services. Also related to Web Remoting, the Browser-Server Dialogue (Chapter 10) patterns look at the flow of information between browser and server; e.g., synchronization techniques. The DOM Population (Chapter 11) patterns cover several strategies for handling DOM population

---

* It would have been nice to ensure full compatibility for all major browsers (e.g., Safari, Opera), and that's certainly advisable for production systems, but portability was considered orthogonal to the individual demos, each aiming to expose information about a particular Ajax concept.

following a server response. Code Generation and Reuse (Chapter 12) contains a couple of general programming patterns for maintainability and portability. Finally, the Performance Optimization (Chapter 13) patterns are about improving not only speed of updates and communication, but also optimizing the user experience in the face of inevitable delays.

Part IV, *Functionality and Usability Patterns*

The Functionality and Usability patterns are focused on usability of Ajax applications. Chapter 14 introduces a number of widgets that are being woven into many Ajax interfaces. A higher-level perspective is taken by the Page Architecture (Chapter 15) patterns, where the focus is on page layout, content breakdown, and techniques for exposing server-side content. With the popularity of Ajax, the Web is undergoing a rise in visual effects somewhat unprecedented on conventional desktop systems, and the most common effects are described in the Visual Effects (Chapter 16) patterns. The patterns in the final chapter of this part, Functionality (Chapter 17) patterns, are about new kinds of functionality that Ajax makes possible.

Part V, *Development Patterns*

The Development patterns are not "things" in the same sense as the patterns in previous patterns, but "processes" you can use to aid development. Diagnosis Patterns (Chapter 18) helps with troubleshooting and monitoring the health of an Ajax App. Testing Patterns (Chapter 19) helps with testing at various levels and is based on the agile practice of testing as the application evolves.

Part VI, *Appendixes*

There are four appendix sections. Appendix A, the largest appendix, is a listing of Ajax-related frameworks and libraries, many of which are a great aid in implementing some of the patterns described in this book. Appendix B is a set of installation notes for the code examples. Appendix C places the work here in the context of general design pattern theory. Finally, Appendix D lists texts referenced throughout the book.

Conventions Used in This Book

Italics
> Used for names of patterns

`Constant width`
> Used for code examples and fragments

`Constant width bold`
> Used for important or significant lines of code

The term "the browser" is shorthand for the entire system at the browser end—not only the browser application (e.g., Firefox), but also the web application running inside it (e.g., Google Maps). When I'm talking about the browser application, I'll usually call it a "web browser"—it's fairly obvious from the context anyway. Likewise, "the server" or "the server side" refers to everything on the server—the operating system (e.g., Linux), the web server (e.g., Apache), as well as the application-specific scripts running within.

The terms "ECMAScript" and "JScript" don't appear—"JavaScript" is meant to cover these terms.

The term "class" is used to describe JavaScript functions that are used in a manner similar to classes in object-oriented systems.

The first figure that appears in each pattern's section is an illustrated overview of that particular pattern.

Some common acronyms used throughout the book are:

- CSS: Cascading Style Sheets
- DHTML: Dynamic HTML
- DOM: Document Object Model
- HTML: Hypertext Markup Language
- IE: Microsoft Internet Explorer
- XML: eXtensible Markup Language

Conventions in Code Examples

Design diagrams are based on Universal Modelling Language (UML) notation, though less formal in most cases.

In the code examples, a `.phtml` suffix is used for PHP files that output HTML; all other PHP files (such as business logic modules) end in `.php`.

As illustrated in Chapter 2, `$( )` is aliased to `document.getElementById( )` to reduce code clutter (inspired by the prototype library—see *http://prototype.conio.net/*).

Some code examples have been reformatted for the sake of clarify.

Safari® Enabled

 When you see a Safari® Enabled icon on the cover of your favorite technology book, that means the book is available online through the O'Reilly Network Safari Bookshelf.

Safari offers a solution that's better than e-books. It's a virtual library that lets you easily search thousands of top tech books, cut and paste code samples, download chapters, and find quick answers when you need the most accurate, current information. Try it for free at *http://safari.oreilly.com*.

How to Contact Us

Please address comments and questions concerning this book to the publisher:

O'Reilly Media, Inc.
1005 Gravenstein Highway North
Sebastopol, CA 95472
800-998-9938 (in the United States or Canada)
707-829-0515 (international or local)
707-829-0104 (fax)

We have a web page for this book, where we list errata, examples, and any additional information. You can access this page at:

http://www.oreilly.com/catalog/ajaxdp/

There's also web page for this book, containing full draft text for all patterns and links to an increasing collection of audio podcasts about the patterns. In addition, you'll find information on various Ajax resources and errata for this book. The web page is located at:

http://ajaxpatterns.org

To comment or ask technical questions about this book, send email to:

bookquestions@oreilly.com

For more information about our books, conferences, Resource Centers, and the O'Reilly Network, see our web site at:

http://www.oreilly.com

Acknowledgments

Writing this book online means I received lots of excellent feedback throughout the process and have many people to thank. Which is another way of saying it's highly probable I'll leave someone out! If that's the case, please mail me any corrections.

My editor, Simon St.Laurent, has always been quick to respond to my queries and dealt admirably with a book being written in a somewhat unusual manner. Thanks also to proofreader Mary Brady for leaving no stone unturned, and illustrator Rob Romano for helping to make the content accessible at a glance. I also want to express my appreciation to O'Reilly for taking on the Ajax Patterns and especially for letting me write the book online, and blog and podcast about the content without restriction.

The book grew from a blog post on Ajax Patterns (*http://softwareas.com/ajax-patterns*), and it was the insight of Thomas Baekdal to cover Ajax usability principles that inspired to the initial patterns post (*http://www.baekdal.com/articles/Usability/XMLHttpRequest-guidelines*). I also have Brent Ashley to thank for his discussing the patterns at the initial Ajax summit and in his blog, apparently the trigger for the initial ripple of online interest in the project.

The ideas in this book also owe a great deal to Jesse-James Garrett and his seminal Ajax article, without which you would not be reading these words.

All the book reviewers provided valuable feedback on the online version throughout the writing process as well as offering many detailed comments on the book's draft version. The reviewers were: Cameron Shorter (ADI Limited, Mapbuilder) and Kevin Vinsen (ADI Limited), whose employer, ADI Limited, provided time for them both to conduct the review; Jep Castelein (Backbase), Daniel Czarnecki (Zoltak Consulting), Tony Hill (Thomson Corporation), and Alex Kirk (Blummy.com, WizLite.com). In addition, a big thanks to members of the Software Architecture Group (SAG) at the University of Illinois at Urbana-Champaign for conducting several rich discussions on the patterns and making the audio publicly available (*http://www.softwareas.com/sag-ajax-patterns-review-1*)—the comments certainly made a difference as the editing moved into its final stages. Ralph Johnson, who leads the group, nominated the Ajax Patterns for review, and Brian Foote kept me informed throughout the process. I'm also grateful to everyone who added to the public portions of the AjaxPatterns.org wiki and offered feedback on the online draft via email, blog comments, and in wiki discussions.

As the patterns were discovered from many existing applications, I would like to thank the creators of all the examples featured in the pattern descriptions, many of them true pioneers. Special thanks to those developers who explained aspects of their designs to me: Kevin Arthur (Stream), Richard Cowin and Bill Scott (OpenRico), Donovan Preston (Live-Page), Jeremy Ruston (TiddlyWiki), and Tino "Crisp" Zijdel (DHTML Lemmings). The patterns are also based on numerous writings, code dissections, ideas, proofs-of-concept, and direct suggestions. In particular, a number of patterns are only here because of the contributions of the following authors and developers (also mentioned in individual pattern descriptions): Julien Couvreur, James Dam, Abe Fettig (Twisted, Jotspot), Chris Justus, Christopher Kruslicky, Alex Russell (Dojo, Jotspot), Richard Schwartz, Mike Stenhouse, Joel Webber, and Chris Were. In addition, there were several news-focused services that made it a lot easier to locate all this content as it happened (and also helped other people find AjaxPatterns.org!). Among these resources: Niner Niner's AjaxBlog.com, Chris Cornutt's AjaxDeveloper.org (Chris is now with Ajaxian.com), Dion Almaer, Ben Galbraith, and Rob Sanheim at Ajaxian.com (disclaimer: I've since joined the Ajaxian team), Shane Witbeck's AjaxMatters.com, Mike Papageorge's FiftyFourEleven.com, Brian Benzinger's SolutionWatch.com, and Mike Arrington's Techcrunch.com.

Last but not least, heaps of gratitude to my family for their support throughout the writing process.

PART ONE

Introduction

THE FIRST FEW CHAPTERS ARE A PRELUDE TO THE PATTERNS. CHAPTER 1 OVERVIEWS THE AJAX phenomenon and discusses current trends. Chapter 2 is a tutorial on Ajax and the Ajax Patterns. The design concepts behind the Ajax Patterns are discussed in Chapter 3, along with an introduction to the patterns themselves.

CHAPTER ONE

Introducing Ajax

BY NOW, YOU'VE PROBABLY USED AJAX ON SITES LIKE GOOGLE MAPS (*HTTP://MAPS.GOOGLE.COM*) Amazon's A9 search engine (*http://a9.com*), and Flickr (*http://flickr.com*). Despite their different domains, all these web sites make heavy use of Ajax. The technology lets them take a great leap forth towards the richness of standard desktop applications, and in a manner which still respects the established conventions of the Web.

Ajax and the Usable Web

No longer are you forced to wait five seconds a web page to reload every time you click on something. Ajax applications change in real-time. They let you drag boxes around instead of clicking on arrows and typing in numbers. They keep page content fresh instead of forcing you to keep hitting Refresh. They show meaningful animations instead of verbose messages.

At the heart of all this is a growing emphasis on web usability.* Perhaps you've heard the story of the dancing bear—everyone's impressed with it even though its skills quite

---

* See Thomas Baekdal's "The Usability Revolution is Over—We Won!" (*http://www.baekdal.com/ articles/Usability/usability-revolution/*).

frankly wouldn't get the bear into a dance academy;* it makes an impression because it *can* dance and not because of *how well* it well dances. The Web felt like that at first. Suddenly you could read news from the other side of the world, find hints on some obscure game, purchase a rare book. All valuable activities, regardless of how easy or difficult to perform them. Usability? We don't need no stinkin' usability!

Here's what happened: people discovered that any coder and his dog can build the basic functionality (and you don't always need the coder); amid the rush of B2B companies hyping multimillion dollar auction systems, I recall one CTO bragging that his summer students created the same thing for a few thousand bucks. So if companies in a saturated market can't compete on raw functionality, what can they compete on? The things that matter to users. Most of the companies that have survived and prospered—companies like Google, Amazon, and Yahoo!—avoided feature bloat and promoted simple, though not dumbed-down, interfaces. It's no coincidence that each of these companies have been busy incorporating Ajax features to that end. Each of these monster dotcoms not only uses Ajax, but has actually pioneered some of the concepts described in this book. You can throw Microsoft into that list as well.

In addition, a whole new generation of companies has risen on the strength of their simple, intuitive applications. 37signals has a suite of tightly focused applications used daily by a passionate user base. With an innovative photo-sharing interface, Flickr built a community of 1 million photo-sharing users in around 18 months.† Another recent entrant is Odeo, a podcast manager that works as an easy-to-use web application rather than running in the desktop like most of the competition. Like their giant counterparts, these newcomers are big proponents of Ajax and have helped define the concepts behind many of the Ajax Patterns featured in this book.

And then there are all the systems you and I will never see firsthand: the scores of web applications sitting on closed intranets. Like the dotcoms, there remain plenty of dancing bears in this category too. Companies welcomed internal web apps, but mostly for technical reasons, such as easy deployment, monitoring, and remote access—and also because it seemed like the "cool" thing to do. Usability was rarely the driving factor. Just ask a user who's wondering where her keyboard shortcuts have gone in the "new, improved" web interface. I recall one web migration that increased an average customer transaction from 20 seconds to 2 minutes! One reaction has been to throw in the towel and retreat back to the desktop. But many companies have chosen to persist with the Web, accepting the idiosyncrasies and using whatever workarounds are necessary to get the benefits of a web

---

* The dancing bear story is used throughout *The Inmates Are Running the Asylum* (Cooper, 1999), a book decrying the obsession with everything that's "cool" at the expensive of true usability.

† The Flickr estimate is based on a projection from a June 2005 article (*http://www.internetnews.com/ec-news/article.php/3512866*) that cites the user base as 775,000 and growing at 30 percent per month, leading to over a million users in June or July. The company launched in February 2004 (*http://www.adaptivepath.com/publications/essays/archives/000519.php*) and was soon acquired by Yahoo!.

platform without the usual problems. It's this spirit that has led to Ajax features evolving in the enterprise, and the popularity of Ajax continues to fuel progress. While many usages will remain hidden, one open example we do have is work performed internally at the Sabre travel company, which led to the open source OpenRico library (*http:// looksgoodworkswell.blogspot.com/2005/06/death-to-paging-rico-livegrid-released.html*).

FINALLY, WEB APPS GIVE SOMETHING BACK

An all-too-common phenomenon in the past few years is taking a reasonable desktop application and spending lots of time and money "upgrading" it into a hopelessly unusable web application. In his podcast, software consultant Craig Shoemaker recalls one such experience (*http:// polymorphicpodcast.com/shows/architectajax/*):

> Ajax is about giving back to the user what they might have had taken away from them when their application got turned into a web app in the first place. I did some consulting for a company that had an old Powerbuilder application, and they had all kind of services for the users. They had things like multi-column dropdown lists and all this user interaction from the user-interface.
>
> What did they do? They created their application as a web app and the users hated it. A lot of the services and the interaction that they were used to were taken away because of the statelessness and the way a web application is architected. With Ajax, we can give some of that back.

In summary, Ajax aims to keep the benefits of the Web, but without sacrificing usability. Most users are now comfortable working inside the browser—meaning that, for some applications, we actually get the best of both worlds: better usability *and* better infrastructure.

The Rise of Ajax

On February 18, 2005, Jesse-James Garrett published an online article "Ajax: A New Approach to Web Applications" (*http://www.adaptivepath.com/publications/essays/archives/ 000385.php*). The Web was becoming richer and responsive, closing the gap with the desktop. Garrett introduced "Ajax" to label the architecture behind the new generation of rich web apps like Google Maps and Google Suggest. Ajax isn't a plugin, nor a proprietary technology. It's an architectural style—a high-level design pattern—composed of many related technologies and ideas.

Ajax technologies and applications were around before Garrett's article labelled them as such, but the article was a tipping point. Just like when the terms, "object-oriented," "agile development," and "postmodernism" began to be used, a converging trend had been given a buzzworthy umbrella term around which a community could form. "Ajax" gave us a label for the systems that were combining several powerful technologies. With this label established, the development community could suddenly share ideas about how the technologies fit together, debate in blogs about different design approaches, build libraries to support these kind of systems, and catalog common patterns.

Strictly speaking, the term is an acronym—"AJAX," for "Asynchronous JavaScript + XML"—although Garrett has noted that other technologies like CSS and DOM are just as important in the Ajax equation. "Ajax" just happens to roll off the tongue a whole lot easier than "Asynchronous JavaScript+CSS+DOM+XMLHttpRequest." Consistent with his original article, Ajax is generally written "Ajax," not "AJAX." That's a mindset, not mere cosmetic detail, because Ajax is a design style and attitude rather than a precise set of technologies; the technologies are whatever happen to let us build the things we want to build. Throughout this book, I refer to Ajax in terms of what it offers users and their organizations. Here's a working definition:

> An Ajax application builds on standard web technologies to deliver a rich, responsive, user experience.

If you look at the Ajax poster children like Google Maps and Gmail, it should be apparent how they fit this definition. They rely on nothing more than a standard web browser, be it Internet Explorer (IE), Firefox, Safari, Opera, or several others. The interfaces are rich in that they include input controls and display effects that go well beyond the familiar form-submission paradigm. And they're responsive in that changes happen quickly and incrementally. The definition is there to be applied pragmatically—the last thing you'll hear from me is a big argument about whether or not application X is Ajaxian or not. We'll walk through typical characteristics of Ajax apps later on, but let's now look at some examples of how Ajax is transforming the Web.

Ajaxifying the Web: The Story of Portals

If you Google for "year of the portal", you'll find ample evidence that every year since 1996 has been *the* year of the portal. It's just around the corner, really. The idea has so much promise: the first thing you see when your browser opens up is a personal home-page with "My News" and "My Mail" and lots of other boxes just about "Me." In short, a page created by Me for Me. So why have they never really taken off? One big factor is that most portal interfaces, frankly, are unusable.*

---

* There are several problems with portals that Ajax can't solve on its own. Most importantly, the fact that portal servers don't know what you're doing in the browser most of the time suggests that some kind of browser plugin is necessary. Nevertheless, Ajax remains the most obvious way to create the Web interface to any such system.

Consider the problems you face in using a legacy-style portal, using Excite.com as an example—many other conventional portals work in a similar manner (Figure 1-1).*

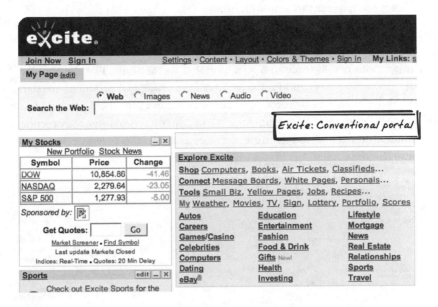

FIGURE 1-1. Excite

1. Customizing the page is the most critical task, but you have to register first; each of the customization controls on the homepage will close the portal and take you to a completely different registration page.

2. Adding new "portlets"—the blocks of content—is rather painful. You have to click on Add/Delete Content, which will whisk you off to a tabbed configuration interface. There, you add and delete portlets by updating a list of current portlets.

3. Customizing an individual portlet—e.g., setting the stocks you're watching—will close the portal and send you to a special configuration page. You've lost the context.

4. Changing layout doesn't happen directly on the page, but in the configuration area. The layout is managed on a miniature model of the real portal, with titles shown only. (Some portals require repetitive clicking on arrow buttons for layout; fortunately, Excite allows drag-and-drop on the model.)

5. Volatile content such as news and market information is present on the page, but refreshes occur only occasionally; the smallest allowed period is five minutes. Refreshes force the whole page to be reloaded, which is not only distracting, but also makes it difficult for the user to see what, if anything, just changed.

---

* I'm not picking on Excite, which gained a lot of interest and did some good things with the technology that was available at the time; its inclusion here is testimony to its status as the quintessential example of the first generation of portals.

6. You can't interact with individual portlets—for example, to perform a search. Any time you act on a portlet, such as submitting a form from it, the entire page will update or you'll be sent to a new location.

Portals are so well-suited to Ajaxification that they are probably the most widespread Ajax genre right now; editing the Ajaxian.com blog in late 2005, we reached a point where we were hearing about two or three new Ajax portals a week! Some, like the popular NetVibes (*http://netvibes.com*) and Protopage (*http://protopage.com*) products, are startups. Among the more mature portal producers are none other than Google (*http://www.google.com/ig/*) and Microsoft (*http://live.com*). An explanation follows of how Ajax rectifies each of the problems mentioned above, using NetVibes as an example (Figure 1-2).

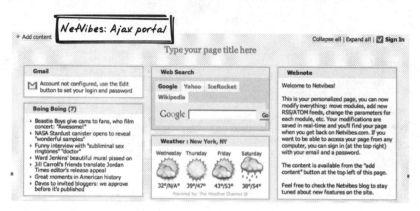

FIGURE 1-2. NetVibes

1. When a new user visits NetVibes, she is free to add and manipulate content, which will stay there for the next time she logs in from the same browser (via cookies). As explained in *Lazy Registration* (Chapter 17), this has always been possible, but Ajax makes the customizations richer and the transition to registering smoother.

2. Clicking on NetVibes' Add Content link doesn't cause a disruptive new page to be shown. It is simply the appearance of a new column (an example of the *Microlink* pattern). There, you can choose new portlet types and watch them appear instantly in the portal. Thanks to the remoting and display manipulation technologies of Ajax, a browser app can talk to the server and update elements without forcing a page refresh.

3. Portlets are customized in-page and without disrupting the other content. Clicking on an Edit link will lead to a small customization form being squeezed into the portlet (an example of *Malleable Content*). There's no page refresh involved, and you can see the effects of editing immediately.

4. Changing layout is as effortless—and fun—as dragging portlets around the page, discussed in *Drag-And-Drop* (Chapter 15).

5. Portlet content is updated directly and without page refresh. Moreover, each portlet is refreshed on its own schedule. In theory, the weather portlet could be updated once a day; the news portlet every five minutes; the stock portlet each second, as explained in *Periodic Refresh* (Chapter 10) and in *Portlet* (Chapter 15). When a portlet updates, an effect like those described in *One-Second Spotlight* (Chapter 16), can be shown for the sake of user feedback.

6. You can have a conversation with an individual portlet, clicking on controls and watching it update. It's as if the portlet is a mini-page; no page refresh occurs and no other content is affected.

The story of portals demonstrates how Ajax can radically improve the usability of a well-established web genre. Indeed, Ajax is breathing new life into many genres that, like portals, had stagnated. Flickr is an Ajax-heavy update of the old photo-sharing category. Gmail (*http://gmail.com*) reinvented webmail, Google Maps (*http://www.googlemaps.com*) reinvented maps, and Google Suggest (*http://www.google.com/webhp?complete=1&hl=en*) opened up new possibilities for search and data entry. Newer genres like RSS readers, wikis, social bookmarking and tagging are also benefiting from Ajax.

Webifying the Desktop: The Story of Office Applications

Attempts to webify office applications are almost as old as the Web itself. It's now part of computer folklore that Netscape's Marc Andreesen exclaimed, in the mid-1990s, that MS-Windows would be reduced to "a poorly debugged set of device drivers running Netscape Navigator," expecting to herald in a new era of desktop-style applications running inside the browser. The benefits of the Web over desktop apps are clear and abundant—e.g., an ability to access data from any web browser in the world, easy upgrading, no tampering of local machines, and better collaboration. However, there are serious problems too, and the most severe is interface. In the past, it's simply been impossible to produce a portable interface that's good enough to justify switching from the desktop.

This is changing quickly though, thanks to Ajax.* A new generation of Ajax office applications (*http://innerphaze.homelinux.com/blog/?p=28*) are emerging as a serious substitute for MS-Word, Excel, and their desktop contemporaries.

One such offering is Writely, a Google acquisition billed as "The Web Word Processor" (Figure 1-3). Writely rightly avoids slavishly reproducing the desktop word-processing experience and instead aims for a feature set and interface that will work on the Web. The result is something that's as much a turbo-charged wiki as a webified word processor. The list that follows describes some of its features.

---

* As with the portals, Ajax alone is no magic bullet for web-based office apps—there are other issues at stake like interoperability and security of hosted content. That said, Ajax does remove one big barrier by at least making them usable.

FIGURE 1-3. Writely

- The content under edit is What-You-See-Is-What-You-Get (WYSIWYG). As you edit, you get to see the final content—color, fonts, layout, and all. The idea is covered in *Rich Text Editor* (Chapter 14).

- Writely allows several people to collaborate on the same document at once. Using technology described in the *Periodic Refresh* (Chapter 10) pattern, it's able to keep updating the document and also the status of other authors.

- Documents are easy to manage—you can "tag" (add keywords) and "star" (mark for attention) an element with immediate effect. Again, this is an example of fitting into web conventions. The Web Remoting (Chapter 6) patterns describe making the change persistent without forcing a page refresh.

The story of office applications illustrates there's enough new substance in Ajax to contemplate serious web versions of applications that have been stuck in the desktop forever. In addition to Writely, spreadsheets are being supported by the likes of NumSum (*http://numsum.com*) and presentation managers are being supported by the likes of S5 ((*http://www.meyerweb.com/eric/tools/s5/*). Beyond the office, there are Ajax versions of instant messaging clients (see Meebo at *http://meebo.com*), terminal emulators (see Anyterm at *http://anyterm.org/*), and even programming environments (see Why the Lucky Stiff's Try Ruby at *http://tryruby.hobix.com/*). Web applications will always be more limited than their desktop counterparts, but Ajax closes the gap to a point where many of them are suddenly "good enough." Being "good enough" will trump many users' desktop alternatives, thanks to the intrinsic benefits of working inside the browser.

Characteristics of Ajax Applications

Earlier on, Ajax was defined as a technology that "builds on standard web technologies to deliver a rich, responsive, user experience." This shouldn't be seen as a binary thing, because it's useful to think of Ajax as a continuous spectrum—an application that happens to include a Flash widget, or one that avoids using any remoting technology can still be considered "partly" Ajaxian; it's useful to do so if you're designing that system as you can leverage the experience of other Ajax developers, which is the kind of experience encapsulated in the Ajax Patterns. And in documenting the Ajax Patterns, it's certainly useful to learn from applications that aren't "pure Ajax." To that end, the characteristics here are intended as a general guide, but not hard-and-fast rules, for what constitutes an Ajax application.

Applications, Not Just Web Sites

These days, you'll hear a lot more about "web applications"—or "webapps"—than about "web sites." Driving many modern web projects is the perspective of the browser as a platform and the Web as an operating system. People aren't just buying a book or browsing a manual, but are performing day-to-day work as well as socializing via the browser platform, often working on more critical, complex tasks than in the past. While Ajax can really be applied to anything running inside a browser, it comes into its own with these kinds of systems, where it helps keeps users engaged and productive.

Smooth, Continuous Interaction

Traditional web sites make you submit a form, wait a few seconds, watch the page redraw, and then start the whole cycle again. That's because the tiniest server interaction, and even the tiniest display change, requires a call to the server, and then a complete page refresh. It's a frustratingly slow and erratic sequence. Ajax changes the model in a few ways. First, JavaScript running inside the browser can manipulate the display directly—you don't have to send a whole new page from the server in order to hide an element or rearrange the page. Second, server interaction can be handled via JavaScript, so you can upload user commands and download new information without any page refresh. Third, user actions such as mouse-clicking and typing can be handled by JavaScript, so the interaction is a lot richer than just filling in a form and hitting Submit. All of these enhancements make Ajax interaction feel faster and more continuous.

Live

With browser-server interaction no longer a major ritual, it's possible to continuously poll the server for new information. Thus, an Ajax App can be programmed to always show the latest news, details on who else is online, or to send messages to the user. The content is "live."

Supportive

Ajax Apps can monitor user actions and proactively support whatever task the user's working on. Actions as small as a single keystroke can lead to a server call, where the server's knowledge and processing power can be harnessed to produce useful content a subsecond later. For example, a form might change according to the user's input, or an error message might appear as soon as a value is typed.

Visual Effects

Ajax Apps look similar to conventional web apps, but do tend to include a little more animation. Not the kind of flashy animation that's just there for the sake of it, but animation that gets across a message about what's happening and what the user can do next. For example, a deleted icon might slowly shrink and disappear.

WHY WEB APPLICATIONS?

So what's the big attraction of web apps? Why, when the desktop seems to be working just fine, are many developers targeting browsers instead? The following describes some of the reasons why people are moving towards the web platform.

- People are using different computers at home, at work, at school, in cafes, and on their phones. Hosting the data online is the most natural way to take their data and preferences with them.

- A much greater problem than having too many computers is having none at all. Many people around the world have no computer to install desktop software on and store their data. For them, a web application is the only practical way to use a particular application and safely retain all their data.

- Desktop applications suffer from something of a catch-22 situation: a user needs to be convinced an application is useful enough to bother installing, but she often can't make that call until she's installed it. In contrast, most web applications allow a user to jump in straight away and immediately begin using the application, avoiding an installation process altogether.

- Many homes and offices now have broadband, and server hardware is more powerful than ever. The infrastructure makes it possible to deliver the kind of rich, interactive, applications that were envisioned in the 1990s but weren't yet practical. Furthermore, server-side storage is cheap enough for vast amounts of data to be held online—Gmail's initial offering of 1 GB mail storage took the world by surprise, and there are now startups offering to host entire music collections online (e.g., mp3tunes.com).

- The technologies behind Ajax—JavaScript, the DOM, and web remoting—have matured and become more standard. This means web applications can now be made more portable and more usable. In addition, there's a hidden benefit of modern web applications: performance. Compared to the old days of complete page refreshes, smart developers can choose to minimize data transfer with a range of performance optimization techniques. So performance is not only boosted by bandwidth increases, but by the new school of web application architecture.

- For developers, a modern web application is often more productive than a conventional GUI alternative, especially if you want frequent releases on multiple platforms. Developers only have to code a single product for all platforms; they can upgrade the application incrementally rather than in "big bang" style. And on the server, where most of the logic lives, they can use whatever programming language and libraries they care to work with.

- Developing rich applications on the Web used to be considered a kind of rocket science. But it's actually a lot easier now to develop for the Web—arguably easier than many GUI environments. Several factors have improved the development experience: (a) developers are now comfortable with the web architecture and the various libraries and frameworks around; (b) these libraries and frameworks have improved a great deal, especially since the rise of Ajax; (c) browsers are now more consistent and standards-based, and also offer better support for development such as debugging toolkits.

—continued—

- As security concerns have heightened, companies are now quicker to lock down desktops and forbid browser plugins. Web applications hosted on a company's Intranet are often seen as more secure, and support tighter monitoring and access control.

- Application developers are usually interesting in supporting as wide a user base as possible. Those who just target MS-Windows will not only miss out on other desktop options like Apple and Linux, but also on less conventional platforms like smartphones, home entertainment systems, and game consoles. A web application is often a more flexible way to target these newer platforms.

- One of the great strengths of the Internet is the ability to communicate and collaborate with remote users. However, doing that relies on common or interoperable software. As web browsers are virtually ubiquitous on Internet-connected computers, web apps are a very attractive option for communication and collaboration.

New Widgets

Ajax widgets go beyond the standard HTML controls—text fields, selectors, buttons, and so on. Widgets such as sliders and progress indicators, built on standard HTML elements, are becoming popular. As well, we're seeing conventional widgets enhanced. Instead of a boring old table, you might see a searchable, editable data grid. In place of a textarea element, you might see a rich text editor with "What-You-See-Is-What-You-Get" qualities similar to most word processors.

New Styles of Interaction

It's not only widgets that are getting an upgrade, but styles of interaction. Here, too, Ajax developers have been borrowing from concepts in traditional desktop environments. Drag-and-drop, for example, has been a staple feature of windowing environments for two decades, but somehow didn't made it onto the Web for a long, long time. Now we're seeing it more and more, and it all makes so much sense, as the earlier portal example illustrated. Other styles of interaction are also becoming more popular. Keyboard shortcuts are being used to streamline activity. And some developers are being a bit more adventurous with mouse buttons, experimenting with double-clicking as well as the right and middle buttons. We're yet to see mouse gestures like those available in the Opera browser and other programs, but anything's possible.

Standards-Based

Ajax applications require nothing more than a standard web browser from the past few years, such as Internet Explorer 6 or Firefox 1.0. While the precise browser coverage depends on your objectives, the point is that Ajax makes the most of standard browser features and avoids browser-specific features and plugins where possible. This means more than *standard* technologies; it's also about respecting *standard* user-interface conventions of the Web.

The Ajax Technologies

Here's a quick rundown of the various technologies involved in Ajax. To begin with, there are several that have always been popular on the Web, which are relatively well-understood by the development community. They are still used in Ajax applications, though sometimes in different ways.

HTML/XHTML

As always, HTML provides the structure of a web page. An Ajax App uses an HTML document to show the initial page, and the document is continuously manipulated to change the display and set up new events. Where possible, its XML-compliant variant, XHTML, should be used in order to make manipulation more robust.

CSS

CSS enriches the display and, thanks to stylesheets, helps separate document structure from style details. Fortunately, browsers are now reasonably consistent in their support for CSS2, so the past few years have seen many web sites shift from table-based layout, which was always something of a hack, to the cleaner, more flexible, CSS-based layout. From our perspective, the great thing about all this is that CSS can easily be manipulated with JavaScript. With just one line of code, you can make an object disappear, move it around the page, or alter its appearance.

HTTP, CGI, Form Submission

As with conventional web applications, Ajax communicates via HTTP. The difference is that instead of returning full pages, the server returns concise results that are then processed in the browser script. Form submission—often with CGI-style URLs—is also used, but again is initiated programmatically, meaning that no page refresh need take place.

Server-Side Scripting

The server is still required to perform tasks like data persistence and input validation. However, in some Ajax architectures, it no longer performs any duty of display or application logic, leaving those things for the browser script to handle.

Ajax also adds a mix of newer technologies. I say "newer" with considerable reservation, because every one of them has actually been around for many years. It's just that they're only now becoming well-understood, standard across all major browsers, and combined together to produce a new style of application.

JavaScript

One thing is true about any Ajax App: stuff happens in the browser. JavaScript is the client-side programming language that coordinates browser activity. Prior to Ajax, web developers might have sprinkled a little JavaScript into their pages, but few could claim to have a thorough understanding of the language. That's now changing, with developers making an effort to master JavaScript just as they would strive to learn any given server-side language.

XML and the Document Object Model (DOM)

A DOM object is a hierarchical data structure representing an XML document, and JavaScript can read and manipulate DOM structures. One particularly important XML document is the current web page, since HTML is, loosely speaking, a dialect of XML (for most intents and purposes, browsers will treat it as such, though it's really only when you code in XHTML—an XMLicized form for HTML—that you're truly using XML). Being a kind of XML document, the current web page is exposed as a DOM object in the browser, and by manipulating it, you can affect what's on the page (see *Display Morphing* and *Page Rearrangement* [Chapter 5]). In addition, there will be other DOM objects as well if you choose to talk to the server using *XML Message*.

Event model ("DHTML")

The event model allows JavaScript to respond to events such as mouse clicks. This is the key to interactivity within the browser—a conversation between the user and the web site (see *User Action* and *Scheduling* [Chapter 7]).

Web Remoting

Web Remoting is the ability for JavaScript to talk directly with the server—no page refresh required. XMLHttpRequest dominates most of the headlines, but there are actually several viable remoting technologies (see *XMLHttpRequest Call, IFrame Call, HTTP Streaming*, and *On-Demand JavaScript* [Chapter 6]).

Anatomy of a Server Call

At a lower level, how does an Ajax interaction look? Here's a typical sequence of events. Let's begin with the application startup sequence (Figure 1-4):

1. User points browser to Ajax App. The user begins interacting with an Ajax application by visiting it in the usual way; e.g., by following a link or selecting a bookmark.

2. Browser loads initial content. The browser fills up with initial content sent out by the Ajax application. This includes the initial HTML to be displayed, the CSS to establish styling, and the JavaScript code to manage further interaction. The HTML is sometimes as raw as a general page structure, in which case the initial content will subsequently be pulled down in a second call. The code will usually set up event handlers to dictate how the system should respond to user actions.

Once the application has loaded, further activity will be triggered by events. Following is the typical sequence for each event (Figure 1-5):

1. User does something. Most events are triggered by user actions such as mouse clicks. As explained in Dynamic Behavior patterns, JavaScript functions can be registered against particular event types on particular page elements; e.g., you can arrange for the purchase( ) function to be called whenever a shopping item (the page element) is double-clicked (the event type). Thus, the user action will typically cause an event handler to be invoked.

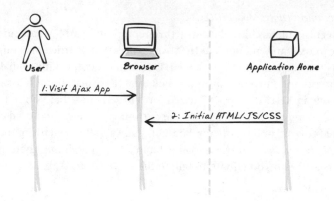

FIGURE 1-4. Typical startup sequence

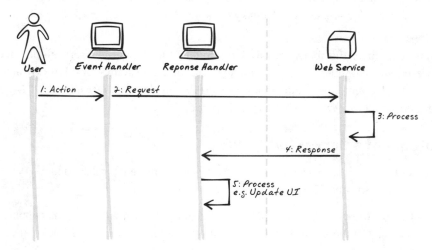

FIGURE 1-5. Typical event-handling sequence

2. **Event handler sends request to server.** Certain events require server interaction—for example, the user has just entered some information that should be validated by the server; or the user has just requested some new information. XMLHttpRequest—a key Ajax technology—is designed specifically for this purpose. It's a way for JavaScript code to directly call the server, and in doing so, the code will indicate a callback function that will be notified when the response eventually arrives. Browser-server interaction is described in Web Remoting (Chapter 6) patterns.

3. **Server processes request.** In the server, a web service (see the *Web Service* [Chapter 6] pattern) receives the request.

4. **Server responds.** The web service receives the request and outputs a response using standard HTTP techniques that will be familiar to anyone who has worked on traditional web applications.

5. **Browser callback function receives response.** Back in the browser, the callback function is notified that the call has completed and can read the server response. It's free to use the response however it wants, but the most common activity is changing the display. This relies on manipulating the DOM, a representation of the web page that can be altered with JavaScript. See the Display Manipulation (Chapter 5) patterns for more details.

The sequence gives a quick overview of the technologies—there's a hands-on introduction to each of them in the next chapter, and the first part of the patterns, Foundational Technology Patterns (Part II) covers them in more detail.

Ajax Trends

This book has certainly been a moving target. There were already quite a few Ajax applications available when the "Ajax" term was coined, and the space has since exploded, propelled by the rush of activity in what's come to be known as the "Web 2.0" movement. Each day is bringing fresh ideas to the table, as more and more Ajax applications are released. It's impossible to know where it will all lead, but this section identifies a few future trends and open questions.

Standards and Fragmentation

Better compatibility across browsers has made rich web development much easier. However, we're at a crossroads now, because the same economic boom that's fuelling Ajax application development is also fuelling innovations in the browsers themselves, leading to a serious risk of diverging technologies.

One group pushing for change is the Web Hypertext Application Technology Working Group (WHAT-WG). The key term here is "Application," as the group is pushing for the Web as a true application platform, a goal that resonates loudly with the aims of Ajax. Under current proposals, rich controls and interaction techniques such as drag-and-drop will enjoy native browser support. All this is good for Ajax developers, but will probably come at the price of compatibility. It's not clear which browsers will support which standards, and there are likely to be major discrepancies in the implementation schedules. Moreover, Microsoft is conspicuous by its absence from WHAT-WG, and it's distinctly possible IE will end up with a very different API for all this functionality. As well as standards endorsed by WHAT-WG and W3C, there will inevitably be browser-specific features to consider as well. Microsoft will continue to evolve its Atlas framework, and it's certainly possible that IE will give Atlas functionality—such as local data storage—that's not available to other browsers.

If browsers do go down the mid-1990s path of diverging APIs, developers will have to decide on appropriate strategy. The options will include: targeting a specific browser (unfortunate, but will sometimes be the most pragmatic choice), ignoring browser-specific features, and relying on compatible plugins for behavior not directly supported by a particular browser.

Browser Adoption

There may well be many browser enhancements on the horizon, but will users upgrade to take advantage of those features? Most Internet users haven't heard of Ajax and probably wouldn't care a great deal if you told them about it. They'll need a lot of convincing to upgrade their browser and even greater persuasion in order to switch to a different brand. On the other hand, there's now a large population who grew up with the Internet and are quite comfortable with frequent upgrades and browser switches. Furthermore, browsers—like a lot of desktop software—have become smarter about upgrading themselves, so for users who have installed a recent browser edition that does this, they will always have the latest browser features available.

User Acceptance

Early indications are that users appreciate most Ajax features, but it's still not clear if mainstream users will feel comfortable with features like drag-and-drop and full-blown applications like word processors running inside the browser. Another issue is the handling of URLs and the Back button. The problem is not as bad as some critics have argued, as explained in the *Unique URLs* (Chapter 17) pattern, but it's true that features like page refresh and the Back button don't work exactly the same way as in conventional applications. How will users deal with all these changes, and what tricks will developers discover to help the situation?

The Desktop

Being something of a substitute for the desktop, Ajax's future will be affected by what happens there. Some have predicted the demise of traditional desktop genres as word processors and personal information managers. Certainly, Ajax has closed the gap, and the question is whether the gap will continue to close or widen due to desktop innovation. Microsoft's Live strategy, as well as the rumored Ajax version of the Star Office product from Sun and Google, will be especially interesting to watch, as they essentially involve a hybrid approach: a rich desktop for deep, long-term activity and a lighter Ajax client with all the benefits of a web interface described earlier on.

Flash

Flash has an interesting role in the Ajax world. It's clear that Ajax is stronger from a standards perspective—you can take a regular form and sprinkle some Ajax onto it by way of effects and dynamic validation. Even better, the form can be made to work with or without Ajax technologies available. Flash, however, does many things Ajax can't, such as hardware access, rich graphics, and local file storage. And both technologies are moving targets. Will Adobe steer Flash towards being a direct replacement for Ajax or more of a complementary technology? Or might upcoming browser innovations trump Flash's main selling points?

Rich Graphics

Dynamic vector graphics are now possible. IE supports Vector Markup Language (VML), and Firefox and Safari support SVG. We'll likely see sophisticated APIs evolve and eventually 3-D graphics, opening up even more possibilities. Compatibility issues aside, there are going to be many design issues to consider. In theory, you can generate any display you like, so you could potentially ignore HTML standards altogether and build a set of controls from scratch. That's an extreme example, but developers will face day-to-day decisions between sticking with the standard or opting for a richer custom control, and libraries will likely emerge to provide such controls.

The Two-Way Web

On the Web, it's always the browser that initiates a connection. There's no way for the server to jump into the user's browser and say "Hey, your buddy just logged on!" Well, no standard way anyway; for a long time now, people have been trying every hack they can think of to enable what's known variously as "server push," "streaming," "the two-way web," and, more recently, "Comet" (*http://alex.dojotoolkit.org/?p=545*). These ideas aren't central to Ajax, but there's certainly a growing undercurrent of interest and a great deal of synergy with the core Ajax technologies. A few patterns in this book address the idea (*HTTP Streaming*, *Periodic Refresh* and *Distributed Events*), but it's still difficult to do well, fraught with compatibility issues, and certainly a challenge to scale. Solutions are emerging—servers such as Twisted (*http://twistedmatrix.com/*) that support many long-lived connections, along with browser tricks to make the hacks less intrusive.

Local Storage

As Ajax has become popular, there has become a stronger demand for local storage. Right now, the only standard way to store data inside the browser is with cookies. But people want a way to store much larger data sets—many megabytes—and also to prevent the data ever being transmitted to the server. In addition, local data storage lets users continue to work offline, thus resolving a major argument against rich web applications. Some Ajax libraries, like Dojo, now hook into Flash's local storage capabilities. In addition, there are plans ahead for Firefox to support it, and Microsoft's Atlas framework has also indicated it will do so (it's not clear if the support will be IE-specific). Is local storage really useful when Ajax makes it so easy to synchronize with the server? Will users understand what's local and what's not, and will they be able to manage their data? There will be design issues as well, such as how to handle synchronization after an offline session.

XForms

XForms is a new standard being defined by the W3C, a major upgrade of the standard web form. XForms separate data from view, offer rich widgets for data manipulation, and allow fields to respond to changes in other fields. All of this is already possible with Ajax, but XForms is a more standards-based approach. It's an interesting question as to whether XForms will really take off now that Ajax is so popular, and if it does take off, how will it coexist with Ajax technologies such as web remoting?

JavaScript

Developers have begun taking JavaScript seriously as a result of Ajax, and the language will continue to evolve. In the future, we can expect to see improved support for multi-threading, classic interface-implementation separation, and various syntax improvements (see *http://weblogs.mozillazine.org/roadmap/archives/008325.html*). In addition, server-side JavaScript might grow in popularity as it would help with Ajax applications, which often need the same logic and data structures on both sides of the network. For example, validation logic is often run in the browser for better performance, but it must be double-checked in the server for security reasons. In addition to the language evolving, design patterns will also continue to evolve as people push JavaScript to its limits and create more complex scripts.

Development Support

There's already a plethora of Ajax-related libraries and frameworks available (see Appendix A), but we'll likely see a lot more of these develop as Ajax goes mainstream and as the underlying technologies continue to evolve. IDEs and related tools will also evolve—we'll hopefully have the same kind of support for JavaScript that programs like Eclipse and IntelliJ Idea offer today for Java. This includes code refactoring, error checking as you type, and suggestions for code fixes. There are also more specialized, web-related needs, such as traffic visualization and automated web testing. Though tools for these things have been around for a while, they'll need to become a lot more sophisticated to support complex Ajax Apps.

Hardware and Bandwidth Improvements

There have already been surprises with Ajax, such as Google Suggest (*http://www.google.com/webhp?complete=1&hl=en*) showing it's possible to make a round-trip to the server on just about every keystroke. With improving hardware and bandwidth, it will be possible to do even more things previously considered impractical. And more than just bandwidth, latency will also be a critical factor. Might Ajax be practical for real-time multimedia collaboration? Networked games? Interactive data visualization? The answers will depend on the extent of hardware and bandwidth advances, as well as the ability of browser and server software to exploit them.

Conclusions

This chapter has introduced the basic technologies of Ajax, provided overviewed characteristic examples, and given some indication of where it's all going, though there will doubtless be some surprises along the way. Even if the "Ajax" name is fairly new, Ajax has been kicking around in various corners of the Net for some time now, and the rest of the book explains what we've learned so far about working with Ajax. In the next chapter, we'll dive head-first into Ajax with a "pattern-led tutorial"—a hands-on introduction to the basic technologies of Ajax as well as the Ajax Patterns that guide their usage.

CHAPTER TWO

A Pattern-Led Tutorial

THIS CHAPTER INTRODUCES AJAX AND THE AJAX PATTERNS IN A THREE-PART TUTORIAL. THE FIRST section is a whirlwind tour of the key technologies, recommended if you've never worked with Ajax before. The second section shows how the higher-level patterns work to enhance a system; if you've already tinkered with Ajax, you might like to jump straight there. The final section proposes some exercises to try on your own.

The online home for this tutorial is *http://ajaxify.com/tutorial/*, where you'll discover running demos for each example here. To work locally, you'll need a standard PHP installation (version 5 or later) with Apache or a similar web server (no database is required). If you want the completed code, you'll find a downloadable package at the above URL—consult Appendix B for more details on installation. Each section in the tutorial begins with a summary of the corresponding online demo as well as the directory within the code package where you'll find the completed code.

Ajax Technologies in a Blink

This section includes a few exercises to get up to speed with the basic Ajax technologies. Each section is independent from the others, and each corresponds to a group in the Foundational Technologies Patterns (Part II), which are patterns about the raw technologies on which all Ajax applications are based.

Preparing the Demos

Each demo should live in its own directory, so create a tutorial directory under your server's document root, and then create three fresh directories underneath that:

```
cd /apache/docroot (substitute your own document root)
mkdir tutorial
cd tutorial
mkdir display remoting dynamic
```

For Unix systems, ensure permissions are appropriate for your web server (e.g., make the directories globally readable and executable). Each directory will begin with the same "blank slate" HTML file, *index.html*. Open up your favorite editor and save the following file to *display/index.html*, *remoting/index.html*, and *dynamic/index.html*:

```
<html>

<head>
  <title>AjaxPatterns.org - Tutorial</title>
  <script type="text/javascript" src="tutorial.js"></script>
</head>

<body>

  <h1>AjaxPatterns Tutorial</h1>

  <div id="sandbox">
  </div>

</body>
```

Remember to set file permissions according to the web server's requirements. Now point your browser to one of the new files and check that you can see the above content. The URL should be *http://localhost/tutorial/display/* or, failing that, try *http://localhost/tutorial/display/index.html*.

The HTML file loads the JavaScript file *tutorial.js*, which isn't there yet. The next three demos will leave the HTML file alone and illustrate Ajax concepts with code in their respective *tutorial.js* files.

Display Manipulation and the DOM in a Blink

Hello World!

To begin, go to the working directory (tutorial/display/). Note that there's an online demo of the application we're going to build at http://ajaxify.com/tutorial/display.

The first thing we want to do with Ajax is update the display—change controls, run animations, and so on. We do that by manipulating the DOM so this tutorial will change the DOM as soon as the page loads. We'll do all our work in the working directory, *tutorial/display*, so once you're in there, save the following as *tutorial.js*:

```
window.onload = function( ) {
    var greeting = document.createElement("span");
    greeting.style.backgroundColor = "yellow";
    greeting.innerHTML = "Hello World!";
    document.getElementById("sandbox").appendChild(greeting);
}
```

Now point your browser to the *display* demo (*http://localhost/tutorial/display/index.html*) and you should see a "Hello World!" message with yellow background. As explained in *Display Morphing* (Chapter 5), the DOM is a tree structure representing the current page, and the browser will keep the display synchronized with programmatic changes to the DOM. You can, if you like, confirm this by visualizing the DOM after running the script above. There are numerous visualization tools, described in *DOM Inspection* (Chapter 18).

In the above code, greeting is a new DOM node that's appended to the existing sandbox DOM node. After creating greeting, we set its background color as a CSS style property, and we use innerHTML as a simple means of setting its content. The resulting DOM is the same as if the page had been loaded with the following HTML:

```
<div id="sandbox">
    <span style="background-color:yellow;">Hello World!</span>
</div>
```

$( ) Convenience function

Now, a quick refactoring. Since we often need the function, document.getElementById( ), all the demos here will use a convenient alias, so append the following function:

```
function $(id) { return document.getElementById(id); }
```

Now we can make the final line of the earlier code more concise:

```
$("sandbox").appendChild(greeting);
```

Verify the page works as before. The $( ) notation* is used throughout this book. In fact, it's sometimes used repeatedly to refer to the same DOM element, which is a slight performance overhead, since each reference will cause a DOM lookup. In production systems, consider using $( ) just once to assign a DOM element to a temporary variable, and then reference the temporary variable after that. You'll gain some performance at the expense of a little code clarity.

Adding a link

We'll complete this section by dynamically creating a link. Append some code to onload( ):

```
window.onload = function( ) {

    var greeting = document.createElement("span");
    greeting.style.backgroundColor = "yellow";
```

---

* The $( ) alias for document.getElementById( ) is based on the prototype library (*http://prototype.conio. net/*). Because many popular Ajax libraries build on prototype, it's becoming something of a standard idiom in Ajax scripts.

```
        greeting.innerHTML = "Hello World!";
        $("sandbox").appendChild(greeting);

        $("sandbox").appendChild(document.createElement("hr"));

        var link = document.createElement("a");
        link.href = "http://ajaxpatterns.org";
        link.appendChild(document.createTextNode("More Ajax Stuff ..."));
        $("sandbox").appendChild(link);
    }

    function $(id) { return document.getElementById(id); }
```

Reload the page and confirm it looks like Figure 2-1.

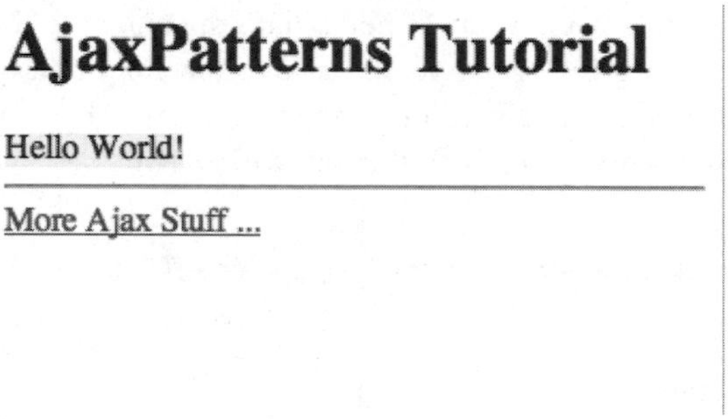

AjaxPatterns Tutorial

Hello World!
_____

More Ajax Stuff ...
_____

FIGURE 2-1. Tutorial display

We've just added two further child nodes to the sandbox. The first child is an hr element
for aesthetic purposes. Then comes the link, an anchor tag with appropriate href property
(just like an HTML <a href="..."> declaration). To set the link text, we append a new child
text node. Contrast this with the earlier example, where we used innerHTML to set an element's contents. With innerHTML, the browser will parse the HTML content and attempt
update the DOM on that basis. It's convenient, but somewhat more error-prone than the
kind of direct DOM manipulation performed with the link text.

Web Remoting in a Blink

*To begin, go to the working directory (tutorial/remoting/). Note that there's an online demo of the
application we're going to build at http://ajaxify.com/tutorial/remoting/.*

We're going to use web remoting to do something very basic: dynamically inject a server-
side HTML segment onto the page. First, create the HTML page to be injected: *message.html*:

```
    <h2>This is message.html</h2>

    and there's <strong>some markup</strong> here<br/>
    as well as an <a href="http://ajaxpatterns.org">AjaxPatterns link</a>.
```

Now we have to code *tutorial.js* to retrieve the message and put it in the "sandbox" container.
We'll perform remoting with XMLHttpRequest, detailed in the *XMLHttpRequest Call* (Chapter 6)
pattern. Since its creation is browser-specific, begin *tutorial.js* with a createXMLHttpRequest( )
factory function:

```
function createXMLHttpRequest() {
    try { return new ActiveXObject("Msxml2.XMLHTTP"); } catch (e) {}
    try { return new ActiveXObject("Microsoft.XMLHTTP"); } catch (e) {}
    try { return new XMLHttpRequest(); } catch(e) {}
    alert("XMLHttpRequest not supported");
    return null;
}
```

As in the previous demo, create the $() convenience function as well:

```
function $(id) { return document.getElementById(id); }
```

With these library functions in place, the only remaining task is to have XMLHttpRequest pull down the content and display it once loaded:

```
window.onload = function() {
    var xhr = createXMLHttpRequest();
    xhr.onreadystatechange = function() {
        if (xhr.readyState==4) { // Request is finished
            if (xhr.status==200) {
                $("sandbox").innerHTML = "Retrieved from server ...<hr/>";
                $("sandbox").innerHTML += xhr.responseText;
            } else {
                alert("Message returned, but with error status.");
            }
        }
    }
    xhr.open("GET", "message.html", true);
    xhr.send(null);
}
```

And what you'll see is the contents of *message.html* inside the sandbox, as shown in Figure 2-2.

AjaxPatterns Tutorial

Retrieved from server ...

This is message.html

and there's **some markup** here
as well as an <u>AjaxPatterns link</u>.

FIGURE 2-2. A message inside the sandbox

The code demonstrates XMLHttpRequest usage in a nutshell. Three things happen:

1. XMLHttpRequest.onreadystatechange is defined. This is a callback method that's notified several times throughout the call lifecycle, including when the call has completed. For convenience, we've assigned the property to a "closure"—an anonymous method inside function() {...}—to save creating a separate method. The closure's contents are explained below.

2. Next, XMLHttpRequest.open( ) will open up a new connection. The parameters say that a GET request should be sent, and the URL is *message.html*. [See *XMLHttpRequest Call* (Chapter 6) for details on the third argument.]

3. XMLHttpRequest.send( ) will complete the request. The argument is null because the request only has headers, but no body.

How is the XMLHttpRequest callback mechanism used here? During a call, XMLHttpRequest progresses through several stages, from 0, before the connection's open, to 4, when the response has arrived. Here, we only care about that final state, so onreadystatechange ignores any prior states. At that stage, we have a complete response, but is it valid? We have to check that the header has a successful response code, which is 200. If all has gone well, XMLHttpRequest.responseText will then hold the content that was retrieved from the server.

So, after the screening the response, responseText is a string reflecting precisely the contents of *message.html*: "<h2>This is message.html</h2>...AjaxPatterns link</a>." It can then be displayed by appending it to the sandbox's innerHTML.

A response doesn't have to be HTML. It could also be a piece of data, like "5," "OK," or "1,1,2,3,5." Also, the response handler can use it however it wants to. It doesn't have to place the response directly onto the page, and in fact, it doesn't have to change the display at all—it might just store the value for later on. Furthermore, the target URL could be any location on our server. More often that not, it's a dynamic script rather than a static HTML file like the message file used here. The URL will often contain CGI-style variables as input for the server-side script.

Dynamic Behavior in a Blink

*To begin, go to the working directory (/*tutorial/dynamic/*). Note that there's an online demo of the application we're going to build at* http://ajaxify.com/tutorial/dynamic/.

This demo shows how to handle events in JavaScript. Begin creating *tutorial.js* with the usual $( ) definition:

```
function $(id) { return document.getElementById(id); }
```

Once the page has loaded, we'll invite the user to click on the sandbox:

```
window.onload = function( ) {
   $("sandbox").innerHTML = "Click Here!<br/>";
 };
}
```

So what we want to do is catch the event of a user clicking on the sandbox. When that happens, we'll append a message to the sandbox:

```
window.onload = function( ) {

  $("sandbox").innerHTML = "Click Here!<br/>";
```

```
$("sandbox").onclick = function(ev) {

  ev = ev || window.event;
  $("sandbox").innerHTML =
  Clicked at " + new Date() + ". Event: " + ev + ";

  for (property in ev) {
    var message = "Property " + property + ": " + ev[property] + ";
    $("sandbox").innerHTML += message;
    }

  };
```

Clicking on the sandbox triggers the event handler, which outputs the event contents, shown in Figure 2-3.

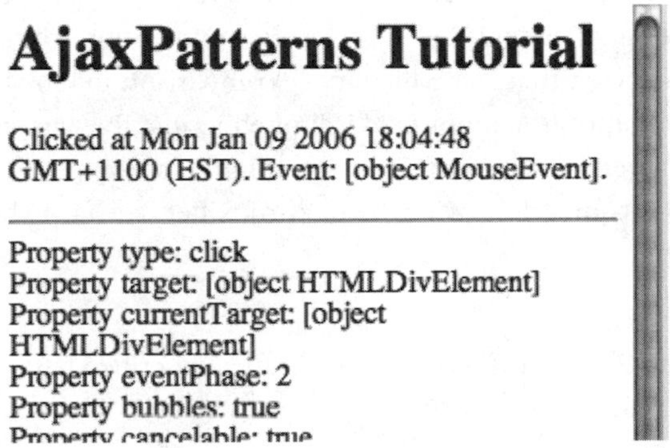

AjaxPatterns Tutorial

Clicked at Mon Jan 09 2006 18:04:48
GMT+1100 (EST). Event: [object MouseEvent].

Property type: click
Property target: [object HTMLDivElement]
Property currentTarget: [object HTMLDivElement]
Property eventPhase: 2
Property bubbles: true
Property cancelable: true

FIGURE 2-3. Event contents

We assigned $("sandbox").onclick to an anonymous function that will handle the event. That's one common way of registering an event handler. We could just as easily register $("sandbox").onmouseover if we want to capture mouse movement instead of clicking activity. Browsers usually generate an event object with information about what just happened, such as the time and mouse location. It's either passed into the callback or set as the global window.event, depending on the browser. The first line of the callback ensures ev is set to whichever of these is valid, so we can assume for the rest of the callback that ev is a proper representation of the event that took place. The handler then shows a detailed report of the event by looping across each property.

Ajaxifying a Web App: One Pattern at a Time

Patterns aren't necessarily about big upfront design; more often, they're used for refactoring and enhancing existing systems. The foundational technologies from the previous section can be seen as techniques for Ajaxifying a conventional web app in addition to being useful for building a new one. In the same way, many of the subsequent patterns can be seen as techniques for improving an existing Ajax App.

Here, we'll look at how a few patterns can be progressively applied to enhance a web app. The conventional app is initially described for comparison, but we really begin building the app at Step 1, where we produce a basic Ajax version. In all, there are four steps. In the packaged code, you'll find the complete code for each step. So if you get lost in the middle of Step 2, you can start Step 3 afresh by taking a clean copy of the completed Step 2 directory. Note that all the application files reside in just the one directory.

Background: Old-School Ajaxagram

There is no working directory (no coding required here). See the location of the completed code within the installation package at /tutorial/ajaxagram/. *There's an online demo at* http://ajaxify.com/tutorial/ajaxagram/.

Starting on familiar ground, the initial version is a conventional web app—no Ajax here. It takes a word and lists all anagrams; i.e., all possible combinations of the letters (Figure 2-4). For simplicity, there's no dictionary comparison to look for real words, and for the sake of performance, the input field is limited to just five characters. We won't actually build this conventional version, but you might want to peruse the code (in *tutorial/ajaxagram/*) for comparison with the next Ajaxified version. There are two source files:

anagram.php
> The server-side business logic for finding anagrams, described later in the section "Business logic: the anagram web service."

index.phtml
> The application's view, a query form, and the list of anagrams. The page submits back to itself; the results area always shows all anagrams arising from the previous form submission (if there was one).

FIGURE 2-4. Conventional Ajaxagram

Step 1: Ajaxagram Done Ajax-Style

Ensure you're in the working directory for this demo (/tutorial/ajaxagram/; *this is the same for all steps). Note that you'll find completed code for this step within the installation package under directory* /tutorial/ajaxagram/ajaxified/, *and an online demo for this step at* http://ajaxify.com/tutorial/ajaxagram//ajaxified.

The initial Ajax version looks and feels just like the conventional version. The only difference is that there's no page refresh as the query word is passed via web remoting [see the Web Remoting (Chapter 6) patterns], and the results updated using display manipulation [see the Display Manipulation (Chapter 5) patterns]. As an overview, we'll be creating four files inside the one directory:

anagram.php

  The server-side business logic for finding anagrams; described in the next section.

anagram.phtml

  A server-side web service; accepts a word and outputs a comma-separated list of anagrams.

index.html

  The browser-side application's view; a plain HTML file that contains the form and list of anagrams.

ajaxagram.js

  The browser-side application logic; waits for a submission, passes the query word to anagram.phtml, and alters the display accordingly.

Begin the application by creating a fresh directory; e.g., *tutorial/ajaxagram/* (you'll need to create *tutorial/* if you didn't already do so).

```
mkdir tutorial
cd tutorial
mkdir ajaxagram
```

For Unix systems, ensure permissions are appropriate for your web server (e.g., make the directories globally readable and executable). All the files throughout the four steps described next should go in this directory.

Business logic: the anagram web service

We'll begin the web service by creating a backend module that knows only the business logic related to anagrams, and nothing about HTML. Since we're talking pure business logic, I'll just show you the entire file and skim over the details. Create the following as anagram.php (or copy it from the code package):

```
<?

    /* Cleans input word and passes into findAnagramsRecursive */
    function findAnagrams($word) {
      $sorted = str_split(filterInput($word));
      sort($sorted);
      return findAnagramsRecursive(implode($sorted));
    }

    /* Convert to lowercase and only include letters */
    function filterInput($word) {
      $word = strtolower($word);
```

```
    $word = ereg_replace("[^a-z]","", $word);
    return $word;
}

/* Assumes $word is sorted */
function findAnagramsRecursive($word) {

    if (strlen($word)==0) { return array(); }
    if (strlen($word)==1) { return array($word); }

    // For each character in the word, extract it and find all anagrams
    // where it's the first character.
    $anagrams = array();
    for ($pos=0; $pos<strlen($word); $pos++) {

        $extractedChar = substr($word,$pos,1);
        // If same as previous, don't process any further as it will only
        // create duplicates (this is the only check against duplicates,
        // since the word is sorted).
        $sameAsPreviousChar =
            ($pos > 0 && $extractedChar==substr($word,$pos-1,1));

        if (!$sameAsPreviousChar) {
            $remaining = removeCharAt($word, $pos);
            $anagramsOfRemaining = findAnagramsRecursive($remaining);
            foreach ($anagramsOfRemaining as $anagramOfRemaining) {
                array_push($anagrams, $extractedChar . $anagramOfRemaining);
            }
        }
    }

    return $anagrams;

}

/* Return word without character at pos */
function removeCharAt($word, $pos) {
    return substr($word, 0, $pos) . substr($word, $pos+1);
}

?>
```

There's also a packaged test case, AnagramTest.php; it's good practice to test backend business logic in isolation. If you want to run the test, install PHPUnit2 (*http://www.phpunit.de/pocket_guide/3.0/en/index.html*) first and see its documentation for details on running tests.

With the business logic now in the server, we need a thin wrapper to expose it as a clean *Web Service*. Placing it in a separate file helps separate business logic from concerns about how it will be invoked from the browser. Thus, create the web service anagrams.phtml as follows:

```
<?
    require_once("anagram.php");
```

```
    $word = array_key_exists('word', $_GET) ? $_GET['word'] : "";
    $anagramsArray = findAnagrams($word);
    print implode(",", $anagramsArray);
?>
```

You can test the web service: point your browser at *http://localhost/tutorial/ajaxagram/*
anagrams.phtml?word=ajax, and you should see a comma-separated list of "ajax" anagrams.
Notice that this is a raw response intended for easy script processing and not the sort of
thing you'd show a user. Our script will need to parse it in order to present the results to
users.

Presentation: initial HTML

The initial HTML file contains the basic display detail—a form and a list of anagrams—and
also pulls in the required JavaScript. Create *index.html* as follows:

```
<html>

<head>
  <title>AjaxPatterns.org - Ajaxagram (Basic Ajax Version)</title>
  <script type="text/javascript" src="ajaxagram.js"></script>
</head>

<body>

  <h1>Ajaxagram (Basic Ajax Version)</h1>

  <div>
    <input type="text" id="word" size="5" maxlength="5" />
    <button id="findAnagrams">Find Anagrams!</button>
  </div>

  <div id="results">
  </div>

</body>
```

Point your browser to the HTML; you should see the heading and the form, but probably
not the results area as it's initially empty.

There are a few things to note about the HTML, and you might like to contrast it with
index.phtml packaged in the conventional version. First, the "form" is not a true HTML
<form> element because we don't need the browser to submit it to the server; our script
will issue the query manually. Second, as there's no HTML form here, a button element is
used instead of a submit control. Third, the results div is empty. It will be populated each
time our script receives a list of anagrams from the server. Finally, note the absence of any
JavaScript code here; all the application logic is isolated in a separate file, *ajaxagram.js*.

Application logic: JavaScript

The final task is coding the application logic that acts as the glue between the server-side
web service and the browser-side web page. Create *ajaxagram.js* with the following generic

methods, explained earlier in the "In A Blink" tutorials. Keep these at the end of the file as we build the rest of the JavaScript.

```
// -- Generic functions ---------------------------------------------

function createXMLHttpRequest( ) {
      try { return new ActiveXObject("Msxml2.XMLHTTP"); } catch (e) {}
      try { return new ActiveXObject("Microsoft.XMLHTTP"); } catch (e) {}
      try { return new XMLHttpRequest( ); } catch(e) {}
      alert("XMLHttpRequest not supported");
      return null;
}

function $(id) {
   return document.getElementById(id);
}
```

The JavaScript needs to handle the query lifecycle, which has three stages:

1. The user clicks the findAnagrams button.

2. XMLHttpRequest submits word input to the anagarams.phtml web service.

3. When the anagram list arrives from server, the anagrams block is updated.

We'll now create three JavaScript functions, with each function roughly corresponding to each of these stages. The first of these ensures the findAnagrams button will trigger the query:

```
window.onload = function( ) {
  $("findAnagrams").onclick = function( ) {
    submitWord( );
  }
}
```

If you like, you can test the application now. Upon submitting, you should see an error message because submitWord( ) is not there yet. We'll create submitWord( ) now, using essentially the same boilerplate code as in the earlier "Web Remoting in a Blink" tutorial.

```
function submitWord( ) {
  var xhr = createXMLHttpRequest( );
  xhr.onreadystatechange = function( ) {
    if (xhr.readyState==4) { // Request is finished
      if (xhr.status==200) {
        var anagramsCSV = xhr.responseText;
        updateAnagramsDisplay(anagramsCSV);
      } else {
        alert("An error occurred.");
      }
    }
  }
  var word = $("word").value;
  xhr.open("GET", "anagrams.phtml?word="+word, true);
  xhr.send(null);
}
```

After adding `submitWord( )`, the browser submits the query word to `anagrams.phtml`. You can check it by clicking on the Find Anagrams! button and verifying that your web server logs the call to `anagrams.phtml`. You might also monitor the browser-server traffic using a tool mentioned in *Traffic Sniffing* (Chapter 18). Once the script has returned successfully, `updateAnagramsDisplay( )` is called.

`updateAnagramsDisplay( )` receives the comma-separated list of anagrams, splits it to form an array, and outputs each anagram on a separate line:

```
function updateAnagramsDisplay(anagramsCSV) {
  $("results").innerHTML = "";
  var anagrams = anagramsCSV.split(",");
  for (var i=0; i<anagrams.length; i++) {
    $("results").innerHTML += anagrams[i] + "<br/>";
  }
}
```

Ajaxagram should now work as described earlier. Congratulations, you've built a working Ajax application! You built it using several of the patterns described in the first part of the Ajax Patterns language—the patterns of foundational technologies. Those patterns are enough to build an application, but the patterns of the latter sections consider real-world issues like usability and maintainability. Those are illustrated in the next few sections.

Incidentally, you might notice a small bug. If you search too quickly, you'll see the results for different searches blending together. This is a consequence of the asynchronous nature of Ajax, with results being processed simultaneously in the browser. We'll eventually fix the problem in Step 3, where we introduce one of several possible techniques to prevent issues like this.

Step 2: Enhancing Functionality and Usability

*Ensure you're in the working directory for this demo (/*tutorial/ajaxagram/*; this is the same for all steps). Note that you'll find completed code for this step within the installation package under directory /*tutorial/ajaxagram/ajaxified/richer, *and an online demo for this step at* http://ajaxify. com/tutorial/ajaxagram/ajaxified/richer/.

So far, Ajaxagram is impressive insofar as you can now tell your tech friends you've coded an Ajax application. Still, your boss/client/shareholder is going to have a hard time telling it apart from the conventional version. We're going to have to jazz the user interface up if we want to make a true impression. (And hopefully improve usability in the process.) We'll refactor according to Functionality and Usability Patterns (Part IV). By the way, we're only "refactoring by patterns" for demonstration purposes; in real life, it's a lot wiser to let the requirements drive the changes you make and let the patterns follow from there.

Note that the tutorial code package includes the completed files for each step. If you had any problems with the initial version, simply start from here using the files in */tutorial/ ajaxagram/ajaxified/*.

Live Search

We'll begin the UI face-lift by making the input mechanism become a *Live Search* (Chapter 14). No more pressing the Find Anagrams! button because the results will update on each keystroke. Incidentally, Live Search needs to be applied with caution in the real world, because it can sometimes be more of an annoyance than an aid.

Where we previously submitted upon button click, we now submit upon each keypress:

```
window.onload = function( ) {
  $("word").onkeyup = function( ) {
    submitWord( );
  }
}
```

And that's that! Reload the page and we now have a working *Live Search*. Frankly, there's more work required to make it production-ready, but it's pretty neat that our basic Ajax code could be modified so easily to do it. Complete the Live Search by scrapping the Find Anagrams! button, which is now obsolete. This will leave the input area as follows:

```
<div>
  <input type="text" id="word" size="5" maxlength="5" />
</div>
```

Progress Indicator

The input field is limited to five characters because long queries take a very long time. But even with five characters, the delay will be noticeable, especially in a real-world context, so we'll ease the pain with a *Progress Indicator* (Chapter 14). This is an animated GIF that's always present on the page, with its visibility toggled on and off, depending on whether we're waiting for a response.

```
<div>
  <input type="text" id="word" size="5" maxlength="5" />
</div>

<img id="progress"
 src="http://ajaxify.com/tutorial/resources/progress.gif"
      class="notWaiting"/>
```

You can leave the image URL pointing to my ajaxify.com server—you're welcome to do so and it will work fine—or alternatively, download the image (or copy it from the code package *tutorial/resources/*) to the current directory and reference it locally (using src="progress.gif").

Next, we're going to introduce a CSS file with the styles for waiting and notWaiting modes. Just as we've separated JavaScript from HTML, we'll also separate CSS. To that end, add the following line near the top of index.html:

```
<head>
  <title>AjaxPatterns.org - Ajaxagram (Basic Ajax Version)</title>
  <script type="text/javascript" src="ajaxagram.js"></script>
  <link rel="stylesheet" type="text/css" href="ajaxagram.css"/>
</head>
```

Now create the new CSS file, *ajaxagram.css*, in the same directory.

```
.waiting {
  visibility: visible;
}

.notWaiting {
  visibility: hidden;
}
```

Now we can just flip the image's CSS class between waiting and notWaiting, according to the request state. The image enters waiting mode when a query is submitted, in the submitWord( ) method, and enters notWaiting when the query returns.

```
function submitWord( ) {
  // Show progress indicator and clear existing results
  $("progress").className = "waiting";
  $("results").innerHTML = "";
  ...
}

function updateAnagramsDisplay(anagramsCSV) {
  $("progress").className = "notWaiting";
  var anagrams = anagramsCSV.split(",");
  ...
}
```

At this stage, you should see the *Progress Indicator* while waiting (Figure 2-5). If the wait is too short to see it, buy yourself a slower PC or alternatively, instrument anagrams.phtml with a delay; e.g., sleep(1);. That's a basic illustration of the Progress Indicator pattern. For a harder problem, increase the width of the input field to allow longer anagrams, and then change the Progress Indicator to show percent complete. (Hint: use a *Guesstimate* [Chapter 13] or create a monitoring channel.)

Ajaxagram (Richer UI)

ajax

FIGURE 2-5. Ajaxagram with Progress Indicator

One-Second Spotlight (Yellow Fade Technique)

Along with *Progress Indicators*, one of Ajax's great visual landmarks is the *Yellow Fade Technique*, or the more general *One-Second Spotlight* (Chapter 16) pattern. Here, we're going to fade results in each time they update. The div will suddenly become yellow and gradually settle back to white over the space of a second. It will happen frequently enough to be considered an abuse of the technique, but hey, it's nice eye candy and good enough for demo purposes.

The fade animation here is super-simplistic. In 10 steps, each 100 milliseconds apart, it pumps up the RGB value from (100%, 100%, 0%) to (100%, 100%, 100%). That is, from yellow to white. Thus, red and green components of the div color are fixed at 100 percent, while blue increases by 10 percent each iteration:

```
// Caller-friendly front-end to fadeLoop
function fade() {
  fadeLoop(0);
}

function fadeLoop(nextBluePercent) {
  $("results").style.backgroundColor = "rgb(100%, 100%, "+nextBluePercent+"%)";
  nextBluePercent += 10;
  if (nextBluePercent<=100) {
    setTimeout("fadeLoop("+nextBluePercent+")", 100);
  }
}
```

Invoke fade( ) just prior to outputting the fresh anagram list:

```
function updateAnagramsDisplay(anagramsCSV) {
  $("progress").className = "notWaiting";
  fade(0);
  ...
}
```

Now click on Find Anagrams! and enjoy the hypnotic Ajax fade effect (Figure 2-6).

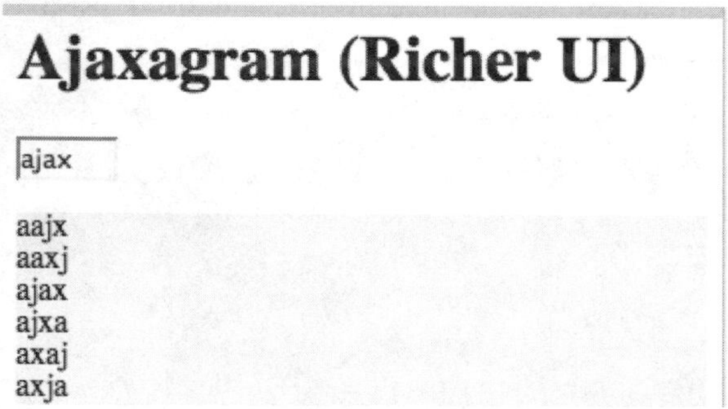

FIGURE 2-6. Yellow Fade Effect (One-Second Spotlight) in Ajaxagram

Step 3: Refactoring for Performance

Ensure you're in the working directory for this demo (/tutorial/ajaxagram/; this is the same for all the steps). Note that you'll find completed code for this step within the installation package under directory /tutorial/ajaxagram/ajaxified/richer/performant/, and an online demo for this step at http://ajaxify.com/tutorial/ajaxagram/ajaxified/richer/performant/.

The previous section shows how the Ajax Patterns go beyond foundational technologies to look at usability and functionality issues. That alone would be useful, but we still need to address the nonfunctional aspects of a rich web application, like performance, data integrity, testability, and programmer productivity. That's the domain of Programming Patterns (Part III), as well as Development Patterns (Part V). Here we'll treat the application with *Submission Throttling*, a programming pattern.

The problem we're dealing with arises from the *Live Search* capability. Responding to each keystroke is nice, but unfortunately impractical in most real-world settings. We want a way to limit—throttle—the submissions. The solution is very simple: submit only after an idle period of one second. Modify *ajaxagram.js* as follows:

```
var submitTimer;

window.onload = function( ) {
  $("word").onkeyup = function( ) {
    clearTimeout(submitTimer); // Clears any previously scheduled submission
  }
}
```

Reload the application and you should see the delay between typing the word and seeing the results appear. We've now capped the number of browser-server calls to one per second, which is one style of *Submission Throttling*. It works using timers; as explained in the *Scheduling* (Chapter 7) pattern, JavaScript lets us set a one-off event in the future and cancel it too. The above code ensures that each keystroke schedules a call in one second and cancels any pending call.

Step 4: Refactoring to an External Library

*Go to the working directory (/*tutorial/ajaxagram/*; this is the same for all the steps). Note that you'll find completed code within the installation package under directory* /tutorial/ajaxagram/ajaxified/ richer/performant/library/, *and on online demo for this step at* http://ajaxify.com/tutorial/ ajaxagram/ajaxified/richer/performant/library/.

The final refactoring isn't actually related to a particular pattern, but is a reminder of the importance of libraries and frameworks throughout the patterns. While most patterns cover low-level JavaScript concepts that are worth knowing, that doesn't mean you have to hand-code everything yourself. There's an ever-growing list of production-ready components available, as documented in Appendix A. The demo here shows how we can achieve the same functionality by reusing a library.

A prime candidate is the remoting performed by Ajaxagram. There's very little reason to directly use XMLHttpRequest nowadays, so we'll refactor to one of the many libraries that wraps it in a clean API. We'll use ajaxCaller (*http://www.ajaxify.com/run/testAjaxCaller/*), a small component developed specifically for the demos in this book.

Add a new <script> tag to *index.html* to include the library:

```
<head>
<title>AjaxPatterns.org - Ajaxagram ()</title>
```

```
        <script type="text/javascript" src="ajaxagram.js"></script>
        <script type="text/javascript" src="http://ajaxify.com/tutorial/resources/
            ajaxCaller.js"></script>
        <link rel="stylesheet" type="text/css" href="ajaxagram.css" />
    </head>
```

The above line will pull the script down from my ajaxify.com server; as with the progress indicator earlier, you're welcome to leave it like that.* Alternatively, you can download the script (or copy it from the code package *tutorial/resources*)/ to the current directory and change the URL accordingly (use src="ajaxCaller.js").

submitWord( ) now becomes almost trivial:

```
    function submitWord( ) {

        // Show progress indicator and clear existing results
        $("progress").className = "waiting";
        $("results").innerHTML = "";

        var word = $("word").value;
        ajaxCaller.getPlainText("anagrams.phtml?word="+word,updateAnagramsDisplay);
    }
```

In addition, you can remove the generic createXMLHttpRequest( ) function. That's a lot of code we no longer need thanks to the external library.

Refactoring Exercises

The final Ajaxagram makes a simple platform on which to play around with further patterns. Here are a few exercises you can try out. Let me know how it goes (contact me at *michael@mahemoff.com*). I'd be pleased to link to any examples from the tutorial's homepage.

Foundational technology patterns

On-Demand JavaScript (Chapter 6)

Instead of downloading all of *ajaxagram.js* at the start, simply download the bootstrapping code and have it fetch the rest of the script on demand.

Programming patterns

Web Services (Chapter 9) patterns

Experiment with the response emerging from the anagrams.phtml web service. Try returning an *HTML Message* (Chapter 9) or an *XML Message* (Chapter 9) instead.

Call Tracking (Chapter 10)

As the first step mentioned, the anagrams list sometimes contains results for several queries at once. The refactoring to the *Submission Throttling* (Chapter 10) pattern basically fixed this by enforcing a gap between submissions. However, you don't always

---

* As explained in the *On-Demand JavaScript* (Chapter 6) pattern, it's perfectly feasible to reference an external JavaScript file. However, beware that there's always some risk involved as you're executing code from a server you have no control over.

want to use Submission Throttling; even if you do, there's no guarantee it will solve this problem. Introduce Call Tracking for a more direct attack.

Submission Throttling (Chapter 10)

We applied one kind of Submission Throttling, but try for the kind discussed in the Code Example section of Chapter 10.

Cross-Domain Proxy (Chapter 10)

Instead of calling your own server for the anagrams, relay the call to my server at *ajaxify.com/tutorial/ajaxagram/ajaxified/anagrams.phtml*.

Browser-Side XSLT (Chapter 11)

Transmit the anagrams in XML format and convert them with XSLT for display.

Browser-Side Templating (Chapter 11)

Show the results using a template framework.

Browser-Side Cache (Chapter 13)

Cache previous anagram lists.

Predictive Fetch (Chapter 13)

For the basic version, which uses a button for submission, make a pre-emptive call in anticipation of a button press.

Fat Client (Chapter 13)

Forget the server altogether and compute the anagrams in the browser.

Functionality and Usability patterns

Data Grid (Chapter 14)

Show the list of anagrams in a Data Grid, allowing for search, filtering, and so on.

Suggestion (Chapter 14)

Suggest words from a dictionary as the user types.

On-Demand JavaScript (Chapter 6)

Instead of downloading all of *ajaxagram.js* at the start, simply download the bootstrapping code and have it fetch the rest of the script on demand.

Popup (Chapter 15)

Produce the results in a Popup.

Portlet (Chapter 15)

Encapsulate the search as a Portlet and slap it on a web site you maintain.

Virtual Workspace (Chapter 15)

The demo produces many, many results for long queries, which is why the input field is limited to five letters. Allow more letters and show the results as a Virtual Workspace. You'll probably want to make the algorithm itself more flexible.

Unique URLs (Chapter 17)

Make sure each query corresponds to a unique URL.

Development patterns

Diagnosis (Chapter 18) patterns

Apply the various tools mentioned in this chapter.

Service Test (Chapter 19)

Create a standalone HTTP client to test *anagrams.phtml*. Note that `AnagramTest` already tests the backend logic, so the most important thing is simply to check the service interface works.

System Test (Chapter 19)

Apply the various tools mentioned in System Test.

Projects and Katas

Now it's over to you. Here are some suggestions for projects you can work on. You might like to approach these as "Katas" (*http://blogs.pragprog.com/cgi-bin/pragdave.cgi/Practices/Kata/*), short exercises that you can keep returning to. Alternatively, add all the bells and whistles and make them full-blown projects. Check *http://ajaxpatterns.org/Katas* for the latest list, and please add links to any of your online efforts.

Two-Person chat

Allow two people to chat in real-time via the browser.

Filesystem navigator

Navigate a server-side filesystem. Bonus points for sanely displaying file contents.

Search portlet

Build a portlet to access your favorite web service, using a *Cross-Domain Proxy* (Chapter 10) pattern or an *On-Demand JavaScript* (Chapter 6) pattern if the web service happens to offer a compatible service (such as Yahoo's JSON API). Results should be displayed inside the portlet, without any page refresh.

Drag-And-Drop cart

Create a shopping cart that allows items to be dragged in and out and uploads details to the server. Note that several libraries support drag-and-drop.

Am I Ajax Or Not

Create a clone of AmIHotOrNot.com. Show two random images (or even just random numbers), let the user click on their favorite, and ensure the server records their choice. For bonus points, show scores in the browser; e.g., offer a popup showing the number of "wins" for the two items being displayed.

Whack-A-Mole game

"Moles" appear at random places on the page and the user must quickly eradicate them by clicking on them. Provide a timer and report the user's score.

Image slideshow

Present a sequence of images using Ajax for navigation. You might also include some visual effects.

Web Site Tuning bookmarklet

Build a bookmarklet that allows the user to tweak the page's style settings; pop up a dialog with fields such as background color and font size.Bookmarklets (*http://en. wikipedia.org/wiki/Bookmarklet*) aren't regular Ajax applications, but they are still a great way to play with Ajax technologies.

Conclusions

The first part of this chapter showed you how to create a basic Ajax application. After performing that section, you should be comfortable about the basics of Display Manipulation (Chapter 5), Web Remoting (Chapter 6), and Dynamic Behavior (Chapter 7). The second part of this chapter introduced a number of the Ajax Patterns—the point is not to understand those patterns in detail, but to get a feel for the sort of thing the patterns do. That is, to see how they build on top of the basic technologies to improve usability, maintainability, and so on. The final part of this chapter suggested several exercises—I recommend you try one or two if you're still coming to grips with Ajax.

It should be clear by now that although Ajax is a great leap forward for the Web, it's no magic bullet. Developers need to tread carefully in order to ensure their Ajax apps are easy to maintain and easy to use. The next chapter summarizes several key principles for Ajax system design and introduces the Ajax Patterns, which offer practical advice on applying those design principles.

CHAPTER THREE

Ajax Design: Principles and Patterns

AJAX DOES A LOT FOR WEB USABILITY, HAS ALREADY DELIVERED SOME STUNNING APPLICATIONS, AND IS clearly the "in" thing at this time. But it's no magic bullet. Careful design is always required, and it must be tailored to the technology at hand. By monitoring the state of Ajax applications, we continue to learn about what works and what doesn't, and about how developers are succeeding in their design trade-offs. This chapter explains these lessons at a high level and introduces the patterns, which discuss them in depth.

Desirable Attributes of Ajax Applications

Ajax is about improving user experience and delivering value to the organizations that own and use web applications. Here, we'll look at the key attributes of an ideal Ajax application. Reality dictates that you'll never get the best of all worlds, so you'll have to make trade-offs based on how important you consider each attribute. The Ajax Patterns are intended to help you deal with these trade-offs.

Usability

Ajax applications should be as intuitive, productive, and fun to use as possible.

Developer productivity

Development should be as efficient as possible, with a clean, maintainable code base.

Efficiency

Ajax applications should consume minimal bandwidth and server resources.

Reliability

Ajax applications should provide accurate information and preserve the integrity of data.

Privacy

While user-generated data can and should be used to improve the user experience, users' privacy should also be respected, and users should be aware of when and how their data is used.

Accessibility

Ajax applications should work for users with particular disabilities and of different ages and cultural backgrounds.

Compatibility

As an extension to accessibility, Ajax applications should work on a wide range of browser applications, hardware devices, and operating systems.

Designing for Ajax

By studying existing Ajax applications, as well as any relevant precursors, it's been possible to distill a number of important design principles for Ajax, which are shown in this section. The thinking behind the principles was a big influence on the pattern discovery process, and knowing them will help to apply the patterns.

We'll begin by looking at principles of user-centered design, followed by those of software design. Of course, you can never fully separate those concerns, and they're often in conflict with each other. Dealing with those conflicts is really a key concern of the patterns. Incidentally, it's worth checking out a good online resource that takes the opposite perspective: Ajax Mistakes (*http://swik.net/Ajax/Ajax+Mistakes*) is a long list of Ajax mistakes and gotchas, as well as anti-patterns originally authored by Alex Bosworth and now maintained on a wiki.

Usability Principles

Follow web standards

Try hard enough, and you can do some very confusing things with Ajax, even more so as rich graphics become commonplace. Rather than reinventing the Web as we know it, use Ajax to build a "better Web," an enhanced layer over what's already there. Respect the conventions that users are already familiar with.

The browser is not a desktop

Further to the previous principle, Ajax is a richer brand of the traditional web site rather than a webified brand of the traditional desktop. True, desktop widgets like sliders are migrating towards Ajax, but only when they make sense in a web context and often in a modified form. We're also seeing application categories like word processors head online as well, but again, the best products will be those that fit in with the Web rather than blindly replicating the desktop experience.

If it's different, make it really different

Subtle differences confuse people. If you've decided it makes sense to diverge from a standard or a common idiom, ensure your design is distinct enough to avoid confusion.

Provide affordances

Affordances (*http://en.wikipedia.org/wiki/Affordance*) are as important as ever in Ajax. You may have a fancy new drag-and-drop technique for updating a form, but will the user even know it's possible? Visual design, dynamic icons, and status areas all help here.

Smooth, continuous interaction

Avoid the start-stop rhythm of conventional web apps. Full page refreshes are a distraction and a time-waster. If used at all, they should be reserved for significant, infrequent activities such as navigating to a conceptually new place or submitting a large form.

Customization

Application preferences haven't been very important on the Web. Why bother personalizing background colors for a shopping site you use once a month, especially if it means sitting through a tedious sequence of form submissions? But for some web applications, the user might be spending eight hours a day working with them, and customization suddenly feels a whole lot more useful. With Ajax driving the customization process, it's a lot easier too.

Make it fun

Ajax makes the Web a lot more fun than it used to be. Techniques like visual effects, drag-and-drop, and periodic updates are sometimes labelled "gimmicks" or "eye candy," as if users don't actually enjoy those things. Applied with care and ideally, user testing, they can definitely add real value, even in "serious" applications.

Software Design Principles

Embrace JavaScript

Thanks mostly to the interest in Ajax, JavaScript (*http://www.crockford.com/javascript/ javascript.html*) is no longer seen as a basketcase language to be avoided at all costs. It can actually be surprisingly powerful (cut the sniggering already!), provided that developers are willing to study the idioms, patterns, and idiosyncrasies.

Accept workarounds where necessary

Because Ajax is firmly based on standard browser facilities, there's simply no getting around the many constraints imposed by modern browsers. If you seek the benefits of a rich web application that will run immediately on any modern browser, and you consider usability to be critical, then you can only use whatever hacks are necessary. You might well lament that Ajax development is inherently troublesome and pine for a cleaner way to get the job done (I know I do). But the point is that you don't get a lot of say in what the vast majority of the world is already using, and will continue to use in the next few years. Maybe web development *will* be neater one day, but here in the present, the land of reality, it's advisable to deal with the technology at hand and work around—or exploit—whatever cheap tricks are available if they ultimately enable useful functionality that would otherwise be unachievable.

Tame asynchrony

The browser-server communication of an Ajax App is asynchronous by nature. This leads to several risks: users might not be told that a call has failed or timed out; calls might be processed in a nonatomic manner; or the browser might forget why a call was made by the time its response has arrived. As explained in several patterns, there are techniques available to monitor and control calls so that these situations don't arise.

Develop for compatibility

Where JavaScript programming still has issues is in portability. At a syntax level, Java-Script is reasonably consistent across browsers, as the ECMA standardization process (an effort to define JavaScript standards; see *http://en.wikipedia.org/wiki/ECMAScript*) has generally been respected by all the major browser makers. However, it's still a moving target, so older browsers of any variety simply won't support some features. Moreover, the DOM remains a serious portability concern. Despite gradual improvements over the years, there remain many subtle differences, and we're set for more divergence in the future. Developing for compatibility means being explicit about which versions are targeted, using portable libraries where available, and architecting so that portability concerns are isolated from core logic.

Reduce bandwidth

If there's frequent network activity, you'll want to think carefully about the size of the messages being passed back and forth.

Deal with latency

When people talk about "how fast" their connection is, they're usually discussing throughput rate; e.g., "a 4 megabit connection." That's great for downloading large content, but what about interactivity? Latency—basically the time for a bit to travel between browser and server—is usually more important than throughput rate (*http:// richui.blogspot.com/2005/09/ajax-reducing-latency-with-cdn.html*). In web apps where the server may be halfway across the world, you can't reasonably respond to each keystroke or mouse movement due to latency overheads. The challenge is to make the application feel responsive while reducing the frequency of interactions. Techniques like *Submission Throttling* and *Predictive Fetch* make the trade-off by decreasing frequency but increasing the amount of data sent each time.

Partition into multiple tiers

As in any web architecture, Ajax applications should use multiple tiers to help separate concerns. This advice is commonly misinterpreted as implying "keep the presentation simple," a mistake that unfortunately leads to pathetically barren user interfaces. Don't be afraid to create rich, intelligent user interfaces with JavaScript; just be sure to develop for compatibility and ensure your business logic is separate from your presentation logic. In addition, practice "unobtrusive JavaScript" and "unobtrusive CSS." That is, keep your initial HTML page clean by referencing external JavaScript and CSS files; no embedded JavaScript or CSS. JavaScript and CSS should be kept apart too; where possible, the script should change an element's display by switching its CSS class rather than micromanaging style information directly.

Go easy on the browser

Unfortunately, your Ajax App will probably end up being one of many things running in the client machine. This is exacerbated by the fact that JavaScript is pretty slow anyway, meaning that you have to exercise restraint in how much happens in the browser.

Practice graceful degradation

Where a browser doesn't support advanced features, Ajax applications should gracefully fall back to use whatever *is* possible. In an ideal world, the same functionality would still be available, albeit with less bells and whistles. But even if you need to sacrifice functionality—and you often will—it should be done in a graceful manner. (Think "polite error messages" and not "complicated stacktraces.")

Ajax Patterns Overview

The Ajax Patterns show how people have used the design principles effectively in real-world Ajax applications. It might seem funny that we can have so many patterns about Ajax, a term that was coined only a few months before work on these patterns began. However, the ideas are not new; there were many Ajax features on the Web before the term came about to describe them. The healthy Net economy has helped a lot too, with hundreds of new sites now using Ajax, along with powerful tools (RSS, Technorati, Google, and wikis) to locate them as soon as they're available.

With over 60 patterns, it's useful to classify the patterns hierarchically. At a high level, the book is divided into four parts, each corresponding to a different focus area—Foundational Technology, Programming, Functionality and Usability, and Development. Beyond that, each part is divided into several chapters, where each chapter includes related patterns. For instance, Foundational Technology Patterns (Part II), includes Web Remoting (Chapter 6), which includes several patterns for web remoting. Here's a summary of each part:

Foundational Technology patterns (11 patterns)

The foundational technologies are the building blocks that differentiate Ajax from conventional approaches, and this section explains typical usage.

Programming patterns (23 patterns)

These are the features of architecture and code that serve the software design principles listed previously. These include, among other things, design of web services; managing information flow between browser and server; populating the DOM when a response arrives; and optimizing performance.

Functionality and Usability patterns (28 patterns)

These are the things that matter to users, including widgets and interaction techniques; structuring and maintaining what's on the page; visual effects; and functionality that Ajax makes possible.

Development patterns (8 patterns)

These are process patterns advising on best practices for development, as opposed to all the previous patterns, which are "things" that live inside an Ajax application. The practices are about diagnosing problems and running tests.

Figure 3-1 shows where the four parts sit in the context of an Ajax application. Most patterns—those in the first three parts—are about *the product*, while the remaining part, Development patterns, is about *the process*. Of the product-oriented patterns, the Foundational Technologies explain how to use the crude web technologies such as XMLHttpRequest and the DOM. At a medium level are the Programming patterns, guiding on strategies to use these technologies. At a high level are the Functionality and Usability patterns. Overall, the Foundational Technology patterns are at the core of the Ajax Patterns language; the remaining three parts all build on these, and are fairly independent from one other.

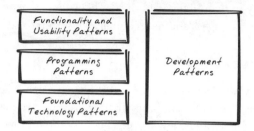

FIGURE 3-1. Ajax Patterns: four parts

On the inside covers of this book, you'll find an alphabetically ordered reference of all the patterns, providing summaries and page numbers. The introduction to each part of the book and to each chapter also contains some summary information.

In addition, the following pages contain pattern maps for each of the four high-level groups—Foundational Technologies, Programming, Functionality and Usability, and Development. The diagrams in Figures 3-2 through 3-5 follow these conventions.

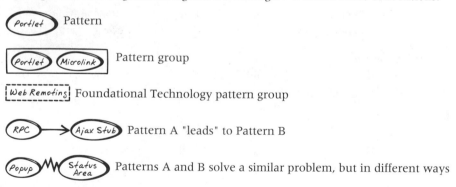

Anatomy of a Pattern

All of the patterns follow the same basic format, though certain fields are left out where appropriate. This section explains the meaning of each section.

Evidence

How much real-world evidence exists for the pattern, on a 3-point scale and presented graphically? It's a rather subjective estimate, but use the following icons as a guide:

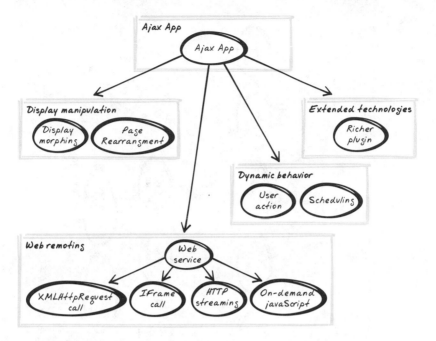

FIGURE 3-2. Foundational Technology patterns

○○○
    Suggests the idea is purely speculative

◉○○
    Suggests there's at least a proof-of-concept or an early usage

◉◉○
    Suggests there's a few established examples

◉◉◉
    Suggests the pattern is in widespread usage

Tags

    Tags—or keywords—help people locate the pattern and get a sense of its focus.

In a Blink

    This is a sketch to set the scene for the pattern.

Goal Story, Developer Story

    A story is a typical scenario to explain how the pattern is used or what the benefit will be to end users. This pattern has been implemented. Each story is based on a "persona"—a fictitious person (*http://www.evolt.org/article/Practical_Persona_Creation/4090/ 56111/*)—to make the story more realistic. (And quite frankly, talking about specific people lets me say "he" and "she" instead of obfuscating the text with gender-neutral language!)

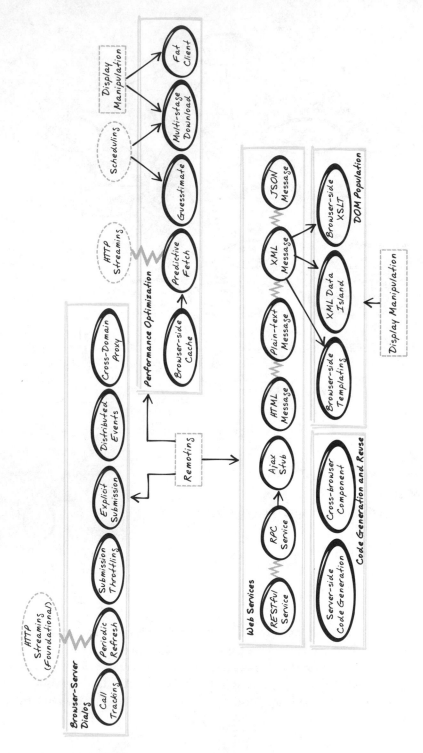

FIGURE 3-3. Programming patterns

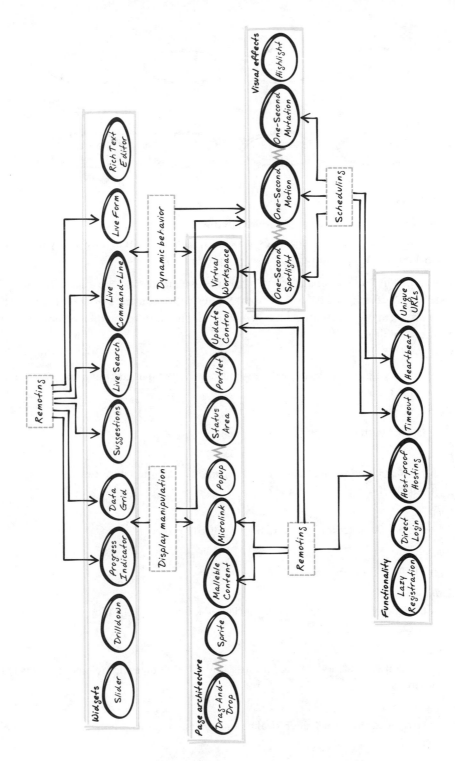

FIGURE 3-4. Functionality and Usability patterns

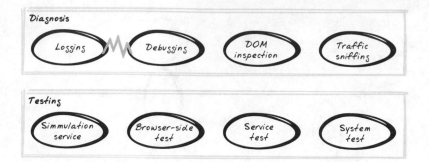

FIGURE 3-5. Development patterns

A small cast of personae is used throughout the patterns. Their names are mnemonic in that they reflect the personae's roles. It's cheesy, but it will hopefully help you remember what these people do without having to refer back here.

The stories in Foundational Technology Patterns (Part II) and Functionality and Usability Patterns (Part IV) are all "Goal Stories"; they illustrate how users interact with a system once the pattern has been implemented. Here are the personae used in all the Goal Stories:

Bill
> A Bill-paying citizen with a wife, 2.4 kids, and a dog named after a contemporary sitcom character.

Doc
> A Doctor with geeky tendencies.

Frank
> A Factory Floor Manager, often stressing about machine safety and worker productivity.

Pam
> A Project Manager for a perpetually overdue IT project.

Reta
> A Retailer of high-class fashions.

Sasha
> A Socialite with plenty of time for social bookmarking, social blogging, and social tagging.

Stuart
> A Student with plenty of time for music and other hobbies not related in any way to his studies.

Tracy
> A fast-paced financial Trader, dealing in any asset type where there's a buck to be made.

Then there are the stories in Development Patterns (Part V), which show how a Developer uses a particular pattern. These are present in all the "Programming" and "Development" patterns, reflecting the nature of those sections. There are two aptly named developers who appear throughout these stories:

Dave
A senior Developer, skilled in the various Ajax-related technologies.

Devi
A senior Developer, also skilled in the various Ajax-related technologies.

Problem
The problem that is being addressed.

Forces
The forces that arise in addressing the problem.

Solution
A brief solution statement (the first sentence of the section), followed by an elaboration of the technique.

Decisions
Each decision is posed as a question. The decisions are *not* a FAQ section to help clarify the solution—such material would belong in the solution itself. Instead, they are "reusable decisions"—that is, decisions that will often arise once you decide to incorporate this pattern. There is no precise answer given, because each decision must be made pragmatically. The description can only guide you in making the decision, first and foremost by flagging that the decision is there to be made. And beyond that, by alerting you to the variables involved and the consequences of going in one direction or the other.

Real-World Examples
Real-world examples of the pattern at work. Where real-world evidence is lacking, proof-of-concepts and libraries are used instead. Some examples may not be strictly Ajaxian but are included to illustrate a particular point.

Code Example: Refactoring Illustration
A code example and walkthrough.

Where the system is an Ajax Patterns demo rather than an external application, it's usually a "Refactoring Illustration" because an earlier version is being refactored according to the given pattern. This is explained further at the end of this chapter. Note that Martin Fowler originally defined "refactoring" as a code change without any user-observable behavior change. I am using the broader definition, now in common industry parlance, of a small, incremental improvement, which may well be externally visible.

Alternatives
Other patterns that solve the same problem in a different way. These are often, but not always, Ajax Patterns documented elsewhere in this book.

Related Patterns

Other Ajax Patterns that are somehow related to this pattern, other than the alternative patterns that would have appeared in the previous section. Usually, this means the Related Pattern is a possible follow-up pattern. It may also mean the patterns are somehow similar; e.g., they rely on the same technology.

Metaphor

A metaphor to help remember the pattern. Some people will find this annoying (and should therefore skip over) and others might find it a helpful way to firm up their understanding of the pattern and help remember it later on.

Want to Know More?

Links to any original references and other useful material.

Acknowledgments

Most patterns in the collection were not just speculations, but were discovered from what others were actually doing. As well as the examples above and the initial Acknowledgments section, this section is a place where people can be acknowledged for their contributions.

Ajax Patterns Demos

The Ajax Patterns Demos appear in many patterns as Refactoring Illustrations and also in the Solution section. They're all online at *http://ajaxify.com/run/*, and it would be worth trying them out. In addition, the full code base can be downloaded from that location; its installation is explained in the Appendix B. It includes the demos as well as completed code for Chapter 2. Note the demos have been tested on Firefox 1.5 and IE6, though most of them work on comparable browsers as well.

The server-side code is all PHP, but most of it is fairly trivial, so it should be fairly easy for all programmers to comprehend. PHP was chosen as it's quite easy for anyone to set up, on any platform. Also, the language itself is fairly "generic" in that anyone with web development experience should have no difficulty following the code.

The demos are organized around a refactoring theme. For most of the examples, there is an initial, "embryonic," Ajaxian application. Then, several parallel refactorings are applied to the same demo, each in a separate subdirectory. And each of these refactorings may have a further refactoring applied, contained in a deeper subdirectory. A tree structure emerges on the site, with each application having evolved in different ways.

For example, look at the evolution of Finite Cache Sum Demo (*http://www.ajaxify.com/run/ sum/xml/cached/expiry/*), which has the path */sum/xml/cached/expiry/*.

/sum/

First, there is the basic demo at */sum/*. Enter some numbers and the server responds with a sum. As a basic Ajaxian application—with no form submission involved—there are some foundational technologies illustrated here, but that's about it.

/sum/xml/

Next, the sum is refactored to receive results in XML form, as a demo is done for the *XML Message* pattern. The "xml" prefix on the URL tells you its lineage.

/sum/xml/cache

One benefit of the new XML form is its convenience for caching, so a further evolution is a basic cache. This is a refactoring illustration for the *Browser-Side Cache* pattern.

/sum/xml/cache/expiry

Finally, the cache undergoes further improvement. This time, a concession to the laws of physics is made, and the cache is now of finite size. Unused elements expire. So here's a further refactoring illustration for *Browser-Side Cache*.

Conclusions

This chapter has covered how people are designing for Ajax and introduced the Ajax Patterns. The pattern language (just like Ajax itself) isn't a magic bullet, but a tool intended to improve your mastery of Ajax web development. You can use it as a reference for "quick-fix" problem solving, but you probably gain more if you also treat it as an educational resource to learn more about the recurring problems and solutions in Ajax. The remainder of this book constitutes the patterns themselves, divided into four parts according to their area of concern—Foundational Technologies, Programming, Functionality and Usability, and Development.

PART TWO

Foundational Technology Patterns

THE FOUNDATIONAL TECHNOLOGY PATTERNS OUTLINE THE "BUILDING BLOCKS" AT THE HEART OF ANY Ajax application. The patterns are considered atomic within the pattern language, in the sense that all later patterns build on these basic techniques. To keep the Ajax Patterns concise, you will only encounter technologies that add something to conventional web development; there's no "Form Submission" pattern, for instance.

Ajax itself is a pattern, hence the first pattern Ajax App (Chapter 4), which acts as the root for all the Ajax patterns. The next few chapters look at the three core technologies involved in creating an Ajax App. Display Manipulation (Chapter 5) patterns are about repainting the user interface. Web Remoting (Chapter 6) patterns document several alternatives for communicating with the server. The Dynamic Behavior (Chapter 7) patterns are about events—those derived by users and those based on timing. Finally, Extended Technologies (Chapter 8) explains how you can extend an Ajax App with nonstandard technologies.

Not all of these are patterns in a conventional sense—some might argue that a pattern like *XMLHttpRequest Call* is simply an overview of a technology. Personally, I do see them as patterns insofar as they are good, proven ways to solve recurring problems—it's just that the problems arise in different contexts and might be applied by different people (such as someone sketching out a potential project or setting up its overall architecture). So while the patterns here do have a different quality, I find the pattern form is a suitable way to document these things, and I find that these foundational technologies—whether you prefer to call them patterns or not—fit nicely into the overall pattern language.

CHAPTER FOUR

Ajax App

THIS CHAPTER CONTAINS JUST A SINGLE PATTERN, THE ROOT FOR THE ENTIRE PATTERN LANGUAGE:
Ajax App.

Ajax App

Ajax, Balanced, Client-SOA, DHTML, Fast, Fat, Interactive, Platform, RichInternetApplication, Rich, Thick, Web2.0, and WebApp

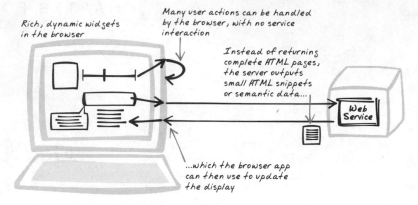

Rich, dynamic widgets in the browser

Many user actions can be handled by the browser, with no service interaction

Instead of returning complete HTML pages, the server outputs small HTML snippets or semantic data...

Web Service

...which the browser app can then use to update the display

FIGURE 4-1. Ajax App

Goal Story

Pam's begun entering staff appraisals into a new Ajax App. She's pleased to see the data entry is much faster: fields are validated as soon as they're filled out, searches are integrated into the form rather than in annoying popups, and the remaining form fields keep mutating to reflect what she's entered so far.

Problem

How can you create a rich application?

Forces

See Chapter 1 for more details on the forces driving Ajax, which are summarized here.

- Users like working and playing in the browser and are now more willing to keep their data online, but are nonetheless frustrated with conventional "click 'n' wait" interfaces.

- Companies like web apps running on their Intranets because it makes deployment much easier, but they continue to be burned by unusable web apps that don't deliver the same value as a comparable desktop app.

- Developers are now well-versed in the basic patterns of web architecture and ready to take on new challenges.

- Technology has opened up new opportunities for the Web: broadband and beyond is becoming ubiquitous in many countries; servers can process huge quantities of requests per second; and storage is growing to the point where it's feasible for individuals to host most of their personal data online.

Solution

Produce an Ajax App—a rich application capable of running inside any modern web browser. The user fires up an Ajax App by typing in a URL, clicking a link, or activating a bookmark. The Ajax App is then downloaded into the browser and the user can begin working with it immediately.

Ajax is fundamentally a user-centered pattern. As mentioned in the first chapter, the major force driving Ajax is the needs of users and their organizations to get more out of the Web. For too long, people have endured pages that take forever to load, widgets that make no sense, and forms that conveniently "forget" their data when they take too long to fill out. There are good reasons for people to continue using a browser, as noted in Chapter 1, but it's in the interests of web site owners and employers to do a better job at making that interaction productive and enjoyable.

Ajax aims to improve user experience within the constraint of respecting browser standards. Standard-based design obviously has the benefit of portability, but also has a usability component in itself; users interact with hundreds of web sites and appreciate consistency, a quality that quickly erodes when you rely on plugins, browser-specific features, and "creative" design ideas. Sure, incorporate a novel widget or a funky layout when it works, but for most things, the standard way works best.

Non-standard technologies also break consistency; one reason Flickr (*http://flickr.com*) began migrating from Flash to Ajax was because users want to right-click to save images, a standard broken by Flash (*http://www.ajaxian.com/archives/2005/05/ajax_summit_eri.htm*). Again, don't be afraid to use a technology like Flash to achieve something standard browsers won't do—that's the whole idea behind the *Richer Plugin* (Chapter 8) pattern. Some people will say it's not an Ajax App if it uses Flash, but the definition here would include a mostly Ajax App that delegates to Flash (or other plugins) to fulfill some specialized task. In any event, the definition really isn't worth arguing about (after all, you can define "Ajax" however you like); the important thing is to ask what helps users—sometimes, it's better to incorporate some Flash or Java; other times, a desktop solution really is the best approach.

The standard technologies are discussed in Chapter 1. They include several well-established technologies: HTML, CSS, HTTP, CGI, and form submission, and server-side scripting. In addition, there are several more technologies that are only now becoming seriously popular and standardized in the browser: JavaScript, the Document Object Model (DOM), the Event Model (DHTML), and Web Remoting.

Decisions

Will your application be "Ajax Deluxe" or "Ajax Lite"?

There are two archetypal architectures for Ajax, and all applications lie somewhere along the spectrum between these extremities.[*]

---

[*] Harry Fuecks explains essentially the same distinction as "Client/SOA" versus "HTTP++" (*http://www.sitepoint.com/blogs/2006/02/15/two-kinds-of-ajax-html-vs-client-soa/*) Likewise, Craig Shoemaker contrasts "Ajax Applications" with "Ajax Websites."

Ajax Deluxe

Ajax Deluxe uses Ajax to the max: applications feel similar to a desktop in that the browser is driving the interaction—it mediates all interaction between the user and server, so there are no—or few—direct page refreshes. Similarly, there's no need for session tracking in the server, because in the absence of page refreshes, all relevant state can be retained inside the browser script. The server need not know about HTML at all, and might just offer generic *Web Services*. An example is the Ajax calendar, Kiko (*http://kiko.com*).

Ajax Lite

An Ajax Lite App feels more like a conventional web app overall, but one that's been sprinkled with Ajax here and there. For instance, Ajax might be used to validate a form before it's submitted using standard form submission, or it might be used to reveal some instructions on the page when a user requests help. An example is Delicious (*http://del. icio.us*), which works fine on legacy browsers, but offers the Ajax *Suggestions* (Chapter 14) pattern for the many browsers that support it.

Which will you use? The Deluxe approach suits a development team with more advanced web programming knowledge and access to relevant tools and cross-browser libraries, and generally leads to a nicer, more effective user interface. It also facilitates a well-partitioned architecture, since the presentation logic can be completely isolated inside the browser, and the business logic completely isolated in the server. However, Deluxe applications may place a strain on the browser and network capabilities, and might not even be possible if the browser is outdated. Ajax Lite is a better answer for older browsers, since the Ajax features can usually be "turned off" to support graceful degradation.

What browser requirements will there be to run your Ajax App?

One of the reasons why Ajax has taken off now, in spite of people having tried similar things earlier on, is that browsers are now more consistent. For an Ajax App, you'll need to decide which browsers you're targeting and which browsers just aren't worth the effort. XMLHttpRequest is the main constraint, because it usually appears later in a browser's feature set than other foundational technologies. Roughly, we're looking at browsers from around 2001 onwards. A typical guideline is: Internet Explorer 5+ for Windows, Firefox 1+, Mozilla 1+, Safari 1.2+, or Opera 7.6+ (*http://en.wikipedia.org/wiki/ Ajax_%28programming%2*). Other browsers such as Netscape and Konqueror might be considered too. Whether you'll support all these browsers, or just a subset, depends on how important the diversity is, how much expertise or library support you have, and how much time you can devote to testing.

How will you treat browsers with insufficient technologies for Ajax?

Building on the previous point, what happens when your application requires features not provided by the browser being used. As explained in *Cross-Browser Component* (Chapter 12), you can either check for specific features or you can check browser versions. If you do the former, you have the opportunity for graceful degradation—to cut out one specific feature or provide a simpler alternative. It's more work, but lets you support more users. The alternative is to give up and suggest the user upgrade browser, sometimes the only thing you can reasonably do.

How much processing power will be required of the browser?

A few early Ajax Apps have already been bitten by assuming too much of the client-side environment. Unfortunately, JavaScript doesn't execute too quickly, especially when the user has lots of browser windows open, as well as a music player, mail client, and the usual array of resident background apps. There are no well-established guidelines here, so the main thing to do is simulate the kind of environments your app will run in, and test, test, test.

How much networking capacity will be required?

With Ajax Apps, there are two networking factors to consider:

Throughput (bandwidth)
  How much data can be transferred per second?

Latency
  How much time between a packet leaving the browser and arriving at the server (or vice versa)?

In some cases, Ajax actually reduces throughput requirements by avoiding full page refresh. Yet, it's important to consider, because there can still be a strain caused by patterns like *Periodic Refresh* (Chapter 10), which continuously pulls down new data. When you consider that some Ajax features (e.g., *Live Search* [Chapter 14]) require round trips to the server on just about every keystroke, you can see why latency is becoming a growing theme in web design. For smaller packets, which are common in Ajax Apps, latency is actually a much greater source of delay than throughput, especially across long distances (*http://richui.blogspot.com/2005/09/ajax-reducing-latency-with-cdn.html*). Again, it comes down to benchmarking and deciding what's feasible. If a round trip takes several hundred milliseconds, responding to each keystroke will probably cause more frustration than joy.

Real-World Examples

Please refer to the examples in Chapter 1.

Code Example

Please refer to the code examples in Chapter 2.

Alternatives

Conventional web app

Ajax represents an evolution from the conventional web app, where interactivity was limited to form-based interaction with a little JavaScript enhancement, such as client-side validation. Over conventional web apps, Ajax has the following advantages:

- Less waiting time, which makes users more productive and less frustrated.
- The browser can be kept up-to-date without the user having to keep hitting refresh.
- Superior widgets make input more expressive.
- Visual effects and dynamic browser activity make the application feel more alive and give users a better feeling of control.

Conventional web apps do have some advantages:

- Users are more familiar with conventional apps.
- Developers don't need to learn new techniques.
- They are compatible with older and non-standard browsers.

Flash app

As pointed out earlier in the "Solution," a standard web app that uses some Flash here and there can still be considered an Ajax App. Here, though, we're comparing Ajax to full-blown Flash, which creates the kind of applications that won't do anything unless Flash is enabled.

Flash and Ajax are actually a close match. Google Maps (*http://maps.google.com*) caused surprise when it came out, as many assumed that only Flash could produce something as rich inside the browser. Yahoo! then turned it full circle by producing a similar product, Yahoo! Maps (*http://maps.yahoo.com/*), in Flash. Despite the similarities, significant differences do remain. Compared to Flash, Ajax has the following benefits:

- Ajax is more portable as it runs on any standard browser, although Flash support is still quite widespread.
- Ajax Apps will often be more consistent, using standard web conventions familiar to most users. Flash has less established conventions, so using an App is somewhat less predictable.
- Ajax works better with nonbrowser clients such as search engine robots.
- Ajax plays nicer with browser settings such as color preferences, and also with browser-specific features; e.g., skins, autocompletion, and Greasemonkey-style enhancements.
- Ajax is safer long-term as there's no lock-in to a proprietary plugin.
- Due to its open nature, the community of Ajax developers is growing rapidly, so that libraries, techniques, and (cough) patterns are evolving rapidly.

Following are the benefits of Flash over Ajax. Whether these are compelling enough to write a pure Flash app depends on the circumstances; keep in mind that the most appropriate solution is often a combination of Flash and Ajax when it's not possible to stick with pure Ajax.

- Flash offers richer graphics and video.

- Flash allows for sound effects and playback of sound files, as well as audio input.

- Rich graphical programming may be easier in Flash because, unlike Ajax, it's designed with those kind of applications in mind.

- Flash allows for local storage.

Java applets

For some Java developers, Ajax is déja vù. In the mid-to-late '90s, Java applets were destined to take over the browser and turn the desktop into a trivial sideshow. It didn't happen for various reasons, and Java applets are now rarely seen on the Web. Still, they persist in the enterprise, and as with Flash, it's possible to combine the technologies. Some have speculated that all the interest in Ajax might breathe some life into the world of applets; it doesn't seem to be the case so far, but it's too early to be sure.

Ajax has several advantages over Java applets:

- Ajax Apps load in a matter of seconds, where Java applets take longer because they tend to use larger libraries and have to load them all to get started.

- Ajax Apps look and feel like standard web apps, while Java applets feel more like desktop apps and somewhat out of place in the browser.

- Ajax features can grow organically from a conventional web app, whereas Java uses a completely different programming style that has to be written from scratch.

- Java versions have changed over the years, and there are often incompatibilities between an applet and the Java environment used by the browser. Furthermore, you usually have to lag a few years behind the most recent version of Java.

Java applets have several advantages over Ajax:

- Java is often used on the server side, so there are synergies in a 100 percent Java solution, such as shared code and the ease with which developers can transcend tiers.

- Many people know Java already, and an applet architecture means they virtually don't have to know anything at all about web technologies.

- There is good support for desktop-like user interfaces, if that's what is desired.

Sun has more recently introduced Java Web Start as a cross between the desktop and the browser. Web Start apps run off the desktop, but can be launched by activating a URL in the browser. The huge waiting times of applets are avoided because libraries can be held locally and shared across applications. It's a useful alternative to applets and more geared toward the enterprise, though it also hasn't taken off in a big way.

Desktop app

There has always been a decision to make between the desktop and the Web. Ajax ramps up the web argument, with even mainstays of the desktop, like word processors and spreadsheets, becoming commonplace in the browser. Microsoft's "Live" strategy, which involves Ajaxified versions of its Office apps, is a major case in point. Still, other applications like games and multimedia tools won't be budging from the desktop for a long time to come.

Ajax offers the following advantages over the desktop:

- An Ajax App doesn't need to be installed; it's available on any computer with a browser. Thus, it suits people who use multiple computers and people who use computers that they can't control.

- Ajax data is hosted on the network, so users can access it from anywhere, and it can be backed up automatically. While this is feasible with desktop apps too, it doesn't tend to happen that way for several reasons; e.g., data migration would be difficult because there are so many different desktop versions running at the same time.

- Most users are comfortable with web interaction mechanisms, and well-designed Ajax Apps exploit that familiarity.

- Ajax works well with the Web. Users can bookmark a "position" within an Ajax App, click on a hyperlink within the Ajax App, and so on.

- Ajax Apps are upgraded with no user intervention.

- Developers can choose the server-side programming and runtime environment according to their own needs, whereas desktop apps impose many constraints.

Ajax has bridged the gap, but desktop apps can still do many things that are beyond the realm of standard web browsers (see also *Richer Plugin* [Chapter 8]):

- Provide local file access.

- Use sound, taking full advantage of modern sound cards.

- Use rich graphics, taking full advantage of modern video cards.

- Use keyboard shortcuts, where support is varied in the browser.

- Provide hardware access.

- Provide communication to machines other than the base server, and in protocols other than HTTP.

- Provide OS-specific interaction, such as popping up alerts.

- Offer faster processing, since JavaScript running in a browser is much, much slower. than executable machine code running on standalone.

Mobile app

With mobile apps growing in parallel with Ajax, it's worth considering them as an alternative, albeit a less direct one. As it happens, Ajax itself may actually become a good platform for mobile apps, with Opera now providing Ajax support on its mobile platform (*http://www.opera.com/products/mobile/platform/*).

Related Patterns

All of the patterns in this language relate in some way to Ajax App. In particular, the earlier "Solution" points to the Foundational Technology patterns that really define what Ajax is all about.

CHAPTER FIVE

Display Manipulation

FOR AN END USER, THE MOST OBVIOUS THING ABOUT AJAX IS ITS VISUAL APPEARANCE. AJAX APPS TEND
to look richer, and the interface tends to update smoothly, more like a desktop app than a
conventional web app. This chapter describes the two main technologies for updating the
user interface. *Display Morphing* focuses on changes to a single element, while *Page Rearrangement* involves changes to the page structure. Along the way, we'll look at the Document Object Model (DOM). DOM manipulation is key to many of the Ajax Patterns.

Display Morphing

Display, DOM, Graphics, GUI, Morph, Page, Paint, Reference, Rich

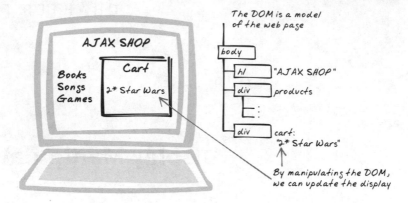

FIGURE 5-1. Display Morphing

Goal Story

Stuart is answering a question in an online quiz, with a countdown box showing how much time remains. The countdown label changes each second, and the color gradually shifts from green to red as the countdown proceeds.

Problem

How can you dynamically update display elements?

Forces

- As the user's task and context changes, applications need to present different types of information.

- As information the user is working on changes, information being displayed becomes stale.

- Stale information is a big problem in conventional web apps. Because the information cannot change until it's out of date, you sometimes see disclaimers such as "May Be Out of Date" or instructions like "Click to Refresh."

- Submitting and redrawing the entire page interrupts the user's flow.

Solution

Morph page elements by altering styles and values in the Document Object Model (DOM), such as text and color properties. The DOM represents the state of the web page at any time. When JavaScript manipulates the DOM, the browser notices the changes and immediately reflects them in the user interface. To morph a page element's display, you get a reference to it and change its properties. This allows you to change the display of any element on the page—headings, div elements, images, and even the document object itself. Note: an online demo (*http://ajaxify.com/run/display*) illustrates the code concepts throughout this Solution and the code snippets loosely follow from the demo.

To further illustrate the DOM, consider the following piece of HTML:

```
<div id="display">
  <img id="photo" src="photo.jpg"/>
  <div id="dimensions">
    <input id="width" name="width" type="text" size="20"/>
    <input id="height" name="height" type="text" size="20"/>
  </div>
</div>
```

Figure 5-2 shows the structure that arises when the browser transforms the HTML string into a DOM model. Since each node has attributes, we can represent the model in more detail, as shown in Figure 5-3. To learn more about the DOM, experiment with the tools mentioned in *DOM Inspection* (Chapter 18). You can point them at a web page to view the corresponding DOM model.

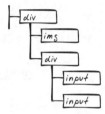

FIGURE 5-2. *DOM structure*

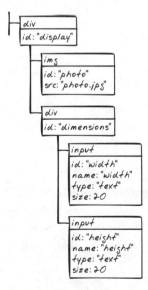

FIGURE 5-3. *DOM structure with attributes*

Each node has a number of standard attributes and operations. Those below let you inspect surrounding DOM context:

parentNode

The element's parent node.

```
childNodes[]
```
An array of all immediate child nodes.

```
getElementsByTagName("tagName")
```
An array of all child nodes of type tagName (e.g., h1 for all level-1 headings).

The structure can be manipulated as well as inspected. Following are the key manipulation methods available on all nodes (discussed further in *Page Rearrangement*):

```
appendChild(newChild)
```
Appends newChild.

```
insertBefore(newChild, oldChild)
```
Inserts newChild just before oldChild.

```
removeChild(oldChild)
```
Removes oldChild.

You can also inspect the node itself; useful properties include:

```
id
```
The node's ID.

```
nodeType
```
Usually 1 to denote a standard element. 2 represents a tag attribute and 3 represents a text node (explained later in this section).

```
tagName
```
The name of the tag (e.g., "h1").

For a more complete set of properties and operations, a good source is available at HowTo-Create.co.uk (*http://www.howtocreate.co.uk/tutorials/index.php?tut=0&part=28*).

Before using any of these properties, the first thing you need to do is get hold of a node somewhere in the DOM. Here's how to grab a reference to an image node with an ID of "logo" buried anywhere inside the DOM:

```
var logo = document.getElementById("logo");
```

getElementById( ) will recurse through the whole document to find the element with a given ID property. Since calls like this are extremely commonplace, a convenience function is used throughout the demos. The function name is just one character, $, which leads to a neater syntax like this (as explained in Chapter 2):

```
var logo = $("logo");
```

Now that we have a reference to the image node, we can play around with its properties. To start with, we can change its src property, which will cause it to load a new image:

```
logo.src = "Images/web.png";
```

We can also set the image's alt text, which will show up on text browsers, and as a tooltip on some browsers):

```
logo.alt = "The World Wide Web"
```

So far, we've altered a couple of image-specific properties. Each HTML element has its own set of properties that can be manipulated via DOM manipulation. There are references such as the w3schools web site (*http://www.w3schools.com/htmldom/dom_reference.asp*) that list the properties for each element.

Another common task is manipulating text, which in the DOM is actually represented by special text nodes. This is a little confusing as there's no corresponding HTML tag. Look at the following text, which seems to have some text freely roaming inside a <p> tag:

```
<p>Oh no! It's <strong>Mr. T</strong>!</p>
```

Text always resides inside. This is also a little confusing as there's no corresponding HTML tag; the text nodes are implicit. In the example above, what the DOM holds is actually a paragraph node <p> with three children: a text node, a strong node with a text node inside it, and another text node. It's represented in the DOM as follows:

```
<p>
    <textnode>Oh no! It's </textnode>
    <strong><textnode>Mr. T</textnode></strong>
    <textnode>!</textnode>
</p>
```

Although the initial HTML is trivial, building up a message like this with DOM manipulation is somewhat complex:

```
message.appendChild(document.createTextNode("Oh no! It's "));

var strong = document.createElement("strong");
strong.appendChild(document.createTextNode("Mr. T"));
message.appendChild(strong);

message.appendChild(document.createTextNode("!"));
```

Even when text nodes aren't involved, directly manipulating the DOM can get quite ugly. A popular alternative is to use innerHTML, which lets you specify an HTML snippet. Thus, we can rewrite the code above by simply setting the innerHTML property:

```
message.innerHTML = "Oh no! It's <strong>Mr. T</strong>!";
```

By setting the element's innerHTML property, we've effectively delegated the DOM manipulation to the web browser. It's much simpler and easier to understand than direct DOM manipulation and is supported by all modern browsers. However, use it with caution, because if you give it an invalid HTML string, you might end up with a subtle bug related to an unexpected DOM state. Also, there are some subtle portability issues, which mean that a particular HTML segment won't always produce quite the same DOM model. For instance, certain kinds of whitespace will be captured as a text node by Firefox, but are then ignored by IE (*http://www.agavegroup.com/?p=32*). So if you use `innerHTML`, be careful about subsequent DOM manipulations on and around that content.

On the whole, direct DOM manipulation is often more appropriate for complex operations. IE also offers an `outerHTML`, less commonly used, which will not only set the element's contents, but also overwrite the element itself. With `outerHTML`, it's as if the element is replaced by the contents of its `outerHTML` property.

If we're looking at changing the display, a particularly important aspect to consider is CSS style. CSS styles and classes are just regular properties and can be manipulated just like the others. Assume the stylesheet defines a CSS class called `inYourFace`. When we change the message's `className` property to `inYourFace`, its display will automatically update to reflect the `inYourFace` definition.

```
[CSS]
.inYourFace {
    padding: 10px;
    background-color: #ff4444;
    font-size: 250%;
}

[Javascript]
message.className = "inYourFace";
```

As explained the next section, changing appearance by switching classes is a good practice, but there are also times when the JavaScript needs to manipulate style directly via the style property present on all elements. style itself has a number of properties, as you would see in a stylesheet, but with JavaScript-ish camelCase (`backgroundColor`) like that shown below, as opposed to the CSS hyphenated style (`background-color`):

```
message.style.padding= "10px";
message.style.backgroundColor = "#ff4444";
message.style.fontSize = "250%";
```

Decisions

Will you alter the display via classname or style?

For those morphings related to CSS properties, you have a choice between manipulation via style and `className`. As a general rule of thumb, use `className` when you can and use style for special situations. Using `className` follows the principle of unobtrusive JavaScript, because it clears away any mention of fonts, colors, and layout from the code. Thus, the code logic is clearer and the presentation details are encapsulated better inside the stylesheet.

So what are those special cases where style *should* be altered? Here are a few situations:

Style depends on some variable
For example, an HTML histogram, where the height of each element is calculated according to the value it represents.

Animation

Animations are a special case of the previous point, where styles usually vary according to elapsed time.

Multiple variables

Sometimes each style property is to be tied to a particular variable; e.g., font reflects age, color reflects keyboard focus, and so on. There would be too many combinations to hold each as a separate style. You could, however, hold each as a separate class, since an element can have more than one class (its class property can be a whitespace-separated list of class names).

Prototyping

When in creative-coding mode, setting the style directly is sometimes easier than messing around with a separate stylesheet. But don't forget to refactor later on!

What sort of properties will be used?

In modern browsers, the DOM is very powerful, so you can change just about anything you can see. The following are some of the properties that can be typically altered. Note that, as just mentioned, many of the CSS styles will usually be altered indirectly, via className.

Color—style.backgroundColor, style.fontColor

- Change to a distinguishing color to highlight an entire image or control—for example, to draw the user's attention or indicate that an item has been selected.

- Change to a distinguishing color to highlight a range of text. This could be combined with a font color change to indicate that text has been selected.

- Change to a symbolic color to denote some status change; e.g., "red" for stopped, and "green" for running.

- Provide an animation effect by fading or brightening a control. This can draw attention more effectively than can a sudden change in the control itself.

- Change color according to a variable; e.g., the brightness of a blog posting's header varies according to the number of times it's been viewed.

Background Image—style.backgroundImage

- Change the image to indicate the status of an element; e.g., a control might be stopped or started, or source code might be OK, have warnings, or have errors.

Border Style—style.borderWidth, style.borderColor, style.borderColor

- Highlight/Select an element to draw attention to it.

- Indicate whether some text is editable or read-only.

Font Style—stylefontSize, style.fontWeight, style.fontStyle

- Change the size, weight, and/or slant of a font to highlight some text.

Inner/Outer HTML—style.innerHTML, style.outerHTML

- Change some text content.

- Change arbitrary HTML, possibly changing the nested HTML of an element as well.

Image Source—src

- Change an image object by modifying src to point to another image URL.

Real-World Examples

Ajax-S

Robert Nyman's Ajax-S (*http://www.robertnyman.com/ajax-s/*) is a slideshow manager—think "Powerpoint Lite"—that morphs the slide content as you flick through the presentation (Figure 5-4).

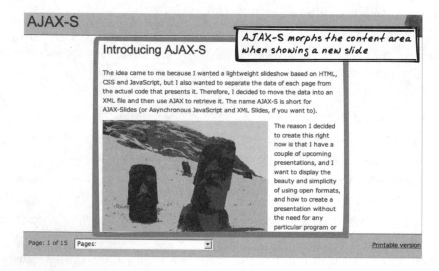

FIGURE 5-4. Ajax-S

Digg Spy

Digg Spy (*http://digg.com/spy*) shows new stories and events such as user moderation as they happen (Figure 5-5). What's interesting from a Display Morphing perspective is the fade effect used to highlight each item as it appears.

Ajax Spell Checker

The Ajax Spell Checker (*http://www.broken-notebook.com/spell_checker/index.php*) highlights any misspellings. It morphs the words into a red, underlined form that is familiar to any MS-Word user. A similar service is also offered by another Ajax App, Gmail (*http://gmail.com*).

FIGURE 5-5. Digg Spy

Code Example: AjaxPatterns Countdown Demo

The example is a simple countdown demo (*http://www.ajaxify.com/run/countdown/*). A number counts down with the background color indicating "heat level"—green at the start, and transitioning to red at the end.

The div that changes color is called timeout. Its initial declaration simply specifies its ID and class:

```
<div id="timeout" class="status"></div>
```

Using techniques covered in the *Scheduling* (Chapter 7) pattern, the startup sequence arranges for onTick( ) to be called every 100 milliseconds. At each interval, timeout is modified. innerHTML changes to alter the text and style.backgroundColor changes to alter the color:

```
$("timeout").innerHTML = Math.round(secsRemaining);
$("timeout").style.backgroundColor = calculatePresentColor( );
```

The background color is determined by a function that manages the transition from green to red according to secsRemaining. Colors are usually represented with hex RGB values—e.g., you can set style.backgroundColor to the string, #00ff00, to make it green. However, there's a more convenient notation for this, based on percentages, so an equivalent representation is rgb(0%,100%,0%). The algorithm here gradually increases the red component from 0 percent to 100 percent and decreases the green component from 100 percent to 0 percent. Blue is fixed at 0 percent. At each moment, the red component is assigned to the percentage of time remaining and the green component to the percentage covered so far.

```
function calculatePresentColor( ) {
  var secsSoFar = TOTAL_SECS - secsRemaining;
  var percentSoFar = Math.round((secsSoFar / TOTAL_SECS) * 100);
  var percentRemaining = Math.round((secsRemaining / TOTAL_SECS) * 100);
  return "rgb(" + percentSoFar + "%, " + percentRemaining + "%, 0%)";
}
```

Related Patterns

Page Rearrangement

Page Rearrangement looks at manipulating the overall structure of the page, whereas this pattern looks at the appearance of individual elements. Together, the two patterns cover all aspects of display manipulation.

Metaphor

Display Morphing is like using a magic paintbrush to change the appearance of anything on the page.

Want To Know More?

- InnerHTML versus DOM Discussion between Alex Russell and Tim Scarfe (*http://www. developer-x.com/content/innerhtml/default.html*)

Page Rearrangement

Add, Adjust, Change, Delete, DOM, Move, Overlay, Rearrange, Restructure, Remove

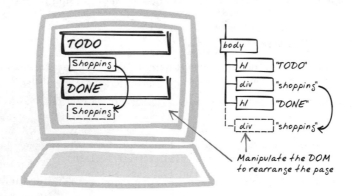

FIGURE 5-6. Page Rearrangement

Goal Story

Doc is looking at a X-ray image in an online diagnostics system. When the mouse rolls over the body, an "advice box" appears at the bottom of the page with stats to help interpret the image. In case the box gets in the way, he's able to drag it around the page.

Problem

How can you dynamically restructure the page?

Forces

- As the user's task and context changes, Ajax Apps need to present different information.

- Changes to page structure should be as smooth as possible.

- Refreshing the page breaks continuity and also clears JavaScript state.

- Refreshing the page only allows for a discrete transition from one appearance to another—it's not possible to gradually fade or move an item.

Solution

Add, remove, move, and overlay elements by manipulating the DOM. The DOM is a hierarchical structure that defines how elements relate to one another. By adjusting the DOM structure, you can adjust where elements appear on the page. There are also critical CSS styles that affect page structure—you can change these by manipulating DOM elements' style attributes. Note: an online demo (*http://ajaxify.com/run/page*) illustrates the code concepts throughout this Solution and the code snippets loosely follow from the demo.

Adding is normally achieved by introducing a new element as a child of an existing *container* element, such as body or div. For example, you can create a new div element and add it to a parent div:

```
var message = document.createElement("span");
$("container").appendChild(message);
```

Another way to insert an element is to append to the innerHTML property of the container element:

```
$("container").innerHTML += "<span></span>";
```

The opposite action is *removing*. By removing an element from the DOM, you take it off the display:

```
$("container").removeChild($("message"));
```

As a variant of adding and removing, you can keep an element on the page but toggle its visibility using CSS. There are two alternative style properties you can use: the visibility style and the display style. The former will always preserve layout while the latter will cause the element to squeeze in and out when it's shown or hidden. So with no visibility, it's like the element's still there but wearing a coat of invisible paint. This makes layout easy, because everything stays where it is, but it can be ugly to have a big patch of whitespace on the page. With the display style, it's more like the element's really disappeared, so the other elements squeeze in to take the place it had occupied. This makes layout a bit more complex, but is usually better visually. The visibility property alternates between visible and hidden:

```
$("message").style.visibility = "visible"; // Now you see me
$("message").style.visibility = "hidden";  // Now you don't ("Invisible paint")
```

display is actually used for more than just showing and hiding an element—it also defines how an element appears when it *is* visible. Briefly, the main options are block (the default for div elements), inline (the default for span elements), and none (when it's not to be shown).

```
$("message").style.display = "block";  // Now you see me, with block layout
$("message").style.display = "inline"; // Now you see me, with inline layout
$("message").style.display = "none";   // Now you don't ("Gone away")
```

You can *move* an element around in a couple of ways. First, you can remove it from one place in the DOM and add it to another:

```
container.removeChild(message);
extraContainer.appendChild(message);
```

Second, you can adjust CSS properties. The most direct styles are left, right, top, and bottom, which define the coordinates of the element in question:

```
message.style.top = "150px";
message.style.left = "50px";
```

But what is the (0,0) point these coordinates are relative to? The precise meaning of these properties is modulated by the positioning element.

- If static, the coordinates have no effect—the element is positioned according to standard CSS layout rules.

- If relative, the coordinates are relative to the position it would normally be positioned under standard CSS layout rules—they suggest how far its displaced.

- If absolute, the coordinates are relative to the top-left of the entire document.

- If fixed, the coordinates are relative to the top-left of the browser viewport (the portion of the browser window that shows the page). Even if you scroll the document, the element will stick right on the same point on the screen as before.

Positioning is set with standard CSS styles:

```
message.style.left = "150px";
```

Finally, you can also *overlay* elements. An HTML document has "2.5" dimensions, which is to say that it has a limited notion of depth in which elements are able to overlap each other. The critical CSS style here is zIndex, which signifies an element's depth. When two elements occupy the same portion of the page, the element that will appear in front is the one with the higher zIndex. The zIndex is not a real depth, because all that matters is the *relative* ordering of zIndex values. Against a zIndex of zero, it makes no difference whether an element's zIndex is 1, 10, or 100. The default value is 0, and a zIndex can take on any positive or negative value.

```
message.style.zIndex = -100; // Behind of all elements with default zIndex
message.style.zIndex = 100;  // In front of all elements with default zIndex
```

Decisions

Which positioning style to use?

A single application can combine different types of positioning. In most cases, static—the default positioning—suffices. Nonstatic positioning is most commonly used with more free-floating elements, such as *Sprites* (Chapter 15) or elements suitable for *Drag-And-Drop* (Chapter 15). For nonstatic positioning, relative positioning tends to be the most useful, because it allows you to move the element around within a defined container.

How will you protect against memory leaks?

Continuously adding and removing elements leads to the risk of memory leaks. JavaScript is supposed to perform garbage collection, automatically removing variables that are no longer referenced. However, it's sometimes buggy (notoriously in IE) and, in any event, you have to be sure that elements are really dereferenced when they're no longer used. Some general guidelines are as follows:

Avoid global variables where possible
Local variables go out of scope, so if a local variable points to a deleted element, the element will disappear. But if a global variable points to such an element, it will stick around.

Explicitly nullify references
If you're sure a variable will no longer need to use the value it references, set the variable to null.

Avoid or destroy circular references
You can sometimes end up with a cyclic structure that no one's using anymore, but that sticks in memory because garbage collection isn't smart enough to remove it (it concludes each object is still relevant because at least one reference exists). This can happen, for instance, when an object's event handler refers back to the object itself (see "Javascript Closures" [*http://jibbering.com/faq/faq_notes/closures.html#clMem*] for more details).

Test, test, test.
It may not be fun, but you need to stress test your application under different browser environments, monitoring memory usage to ensure it's stable. (See *System Test* [Chapter 19]).

Real-World Examples

TadaList

TadaList (*http://tadalist.com*; a screencast is available at *http://www.tadalist.com/theater*) allows users to manage TODO items (Figure 5-7). Each TODO item is a phrase, like "Finish homework," and the user can add, remove, and rearrange items.

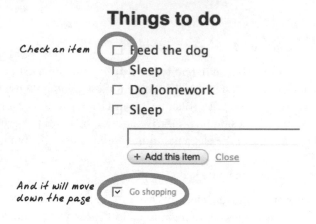

Things to do

Check an item ☐ Feed the dog
                  ☐ Sleep
                  ☐ Do homework
                  ☐ Sleep

(+ Add this item) Close

And it will move ☑ Go shopping
down the page

FIGURE 5-7. TadaList

Super Maryo World

Super Maryo World (*http://www.janis.or.jp/users/segabito/JavaScriptMaryo.html*) is an out-right Ajaxian video game, a clone of the classic Super Mario Bros game implemented with standard Ajax technologies (Figure 5-8). The manipulation of game characters and fixtures illustrates how elements can rapidly be added, removed, and moved around. It's Page Rearrangement, real-time!

Page elements constantly move around in an Ajax video game

FIGURE 5-8. Super Maryo World

Kiko

Kiko (*http://kiko.com*) is a direct-manipulation Ajax calendar application. You can add and remove appointments, drag them around to change the time, and stretch them out to increase duration.

Code Example: AjaxPatterns Basic Wiki

The Basic Wiki Demo (*http://ajaxify.com/run*) periodically polls for a fresh list of messages to display. Each time the list is retrieved, it removes all existing messages and adds the new list. The containing element is called messages, and removing all messages involves running a loop across each of its children:

```
while ($("messages").hasChildNodes()) {
  $("messages").removeChild($("messages").firstChild);
}
```

Each message is used to create a new textarea element (among other things), which is then added to a new div, which in turn is added to the messages container:

```
for (var i=0; i<wikiMessages.length; i++) {
  var messageArea = document.createElement("textarea");
  ...
  messageDiv = document.createElement("div");
  ...
  messageDiv.appendChild(messageArea);
  ...
  $("messages").appendChild(messageDiv);
  ...
}
```

Related Patterns

Display Morphing

The *Display Morphing* pattern (see earlier in this chapter) addresses an element's appearance; this pattern talks about elements' location, visibility, and "height above the page" (zIndex). Together, the two patterns cover all aspects of display manipulation.

Metaphor

Page Rearrangement is like adding, removing, and rearranging Post-It notes on a whiteboard.

CHAPTER SIX

Web Remoting

NOW THAT WE'VE SEEN HOW AJAX APPS CAN MANIPULATE THE DISPLAY, IT WOULD BE USEFUL IF THEY could use that capability to show data arriving from the server. We'd also like to accept input and upload it to the server. The Web Remoting patterns let JavaScript directly issue calls to the server. The point is to let the browser make a query or upload some data, without actually refreshing the page.

The first pattern is *Web Service*, which explains how the server side exposes functionality to be accessed by the browser.

The remaining patterns are the most useful and most common mechanisms for web remoting.* *XMLHttpRequest Call* is a clean way for the browser script to invoke and catch responses from the server. *IFrame Call* provides a similar use by exploiting IFrame functionality. *HTTP Streaming*, also known as "Push" (or "Comet"), allows the server to continue streaming new data down the pipe, without the browser having to issue new

---

* Other techniques do exist, and are mentioned in "Alternatives" in *XMLHttpRequest Call* later in this chapter.

requests. *On-Demand JavaScript* is a fairly broad-scoped pattern and is included in this section because one style, `Script Tag Generation`, is a distinctive technology that's becoming a popular way to directly access external domains.

Of the four techniques, *XMLHttpRequest Call* is the cleanest, because `XMLHttpRequest` is specifically designed for web remoting. Nevertheless, all of the techniques are effective, and each has a certain set of situations where it's the superior choice. See the "Alternatives" section for *XMLHttpRequest Call* for a comparison of the various techniques.

Web Service

API, HTTP, Microcontent, REST, RPC, Share, SOAP, Platform

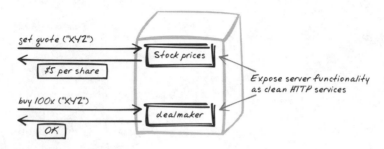

FIGURE 6-1. Web Service

Goal Story

In a financial forecasting app, Tracy runs an algorithm to forecast the next four interest rates. The browser script uploads the parameters to an "Interest Rate Forcaster" web service, which eventually outputs a concise list of future rates, free of any HTML markup: 4.5, 3.4, 4.0, 4.1.

Problem

What will Ajax Apps call on the server?

Forces

- Ajax Apps can access the server directly and require well-scoped services instead of the conventional-style scripts that output an entire HTML page.

- Many organizations like to expose their functionality and data for third parties to access. The API needs to be clean and easy to use.

Solution

Expose server-side functionality as fine-grained, easy-to-use Web Services. "Web Service" is an overloaded term, and the Ajax Patterns use a fairly broad definition:

- A Web Service is a standard HTTP service.

- A Web Service has a well-defined, consistent interface—input and output assumptions, message formats, and exception handling are all clearly understood by its developers and ideally documented in some manner.

- A Web Service accepts fine-grained input parameters and outputs fine-grained responses, such as an XML document, a simple string, or a snippet of HTML. If it outputs an entire HTML document, it's probably not a Web Service.

Under this definition, there is considerable flexibility involved in creating a Web Service:

- A Web Service might be open to the public, might be protected by a secure authentication mechanism, or might be hidden from the public by a firewall.

- A Web Service might be built by a tool or handwritten.

- A Web Service might use messages according to any protocol, such as SOAP, or might use custom messages.

Deciding on all these things is the main task involved in creating a Web Service.

Web services are the latest in a long tradition of distributed computing, with technologies like SunRPC, CORBA, and EJB along the way. They've arisen quite separately from Ajax, as a general-purpose way to expose services to interested clients. These clients are usually standalone processes with no user interface as well as desktop clients and web server scripts. Until recently, they were irrelevant to anything inside a web browser, which could only communicate with services capable of returning an entire HTML page. But thanks to remoting technologies, JavaScript can now make use of such services. Indeed, a clean Web Service is actually the best thing for remoting technologies to call—it makes the call easier, and having a fine-grained response is good for the response handler. Thus, there's a strong synergy between Ajax and web services.

Here's the PHP code for a one-liner web service to perform a sum (imaginative, I know):

```
<?
  echo $_GET["figure1"] + $_GET["figure2"];
?>
```

You can try the service by entering *http://ajaxify.com/run/xmlHttpRequestCall/sumGet.phtml?figure1=5&figure2=10* in your browser's address bar. The entire response will be "15." As the example shows, a web service's response can be as simple as a single value. Other times, it might be some HTML, but even then, it will usually only be a snippet rather than an entire page. For example, the above service could be refactored to show the result as a heading:

```
<?
  echo "<h1>" . ($_GET["figure1"] + $_GET["figure2"]) . "</h1>";
?>
```

A collection of related services like these forms an HTTP-based API that exposes server functionality. Most Ajax Apps will access the API from the browser via the *XMLHttpRequest Call* and alternative remoting techniques. In addition, third parties can access Web Services and use them for their own applications, web or not.

This section introduces only the concept of web services. There are a number of decisions you need to make when designing such services for your own application. Will the service output XML to be processed in the browser, HTML to be displayed directly, or some other format? How will the URLs look? What sort of input will it take? All these issues are discussed in Chapter 9.

Decisions

How will the web service be used?

The single most important decision about a web service, as with any form of API, is to know how it will be used. In particular, will it be available for third-parties as a generic interface to your system, or are you developing it purely for an Ajax browser app to access? If the latter, then you might want to practice feature-driven development and let the browser app drive web service design—see *Simulation Service* (Chapter 19).

If there *are* third parties involved, it becomes a balancing act between their needs and the needs of your browser app. Since they will probably be accessing your server from more powerful environments than the average web browser, you might need to add some redundancy to support each type of client. The API for third parties might be more general, whereas the browser sometimes needs an API that knows something about the application. In an extreme case, it tracks application state and outputs the actual HTML to be shown to the user.

How will you prevent third-party usage?

Web services are seen as having a kind of synergy with Ajax, as Ajax Apps can talk to the same interface already being offered to third-party clients. However, sometimes you want the web service to be closed to third parties. That's going to be difficult on the public Web, since pretty much anything a browser can access will also be available to third-party clients. So, you might have spent ages designing a nice, clean web service to make browser scripting as painless as possible, only to discover that third parties are reaping the benefits. There's no magic bullet, but here are a few suggestions:

- Require users to be logged in, with an authenticated email address, in order for the application to make use of web services. You can then use cookies or upload unique session IDs to authenticate the user.

- Consider using a system like Captcha (*http://www.captcha.net/*), where the user is forced to perform a challenge that should be about impossible for an automated script to do. You might require a challenge be solved once an hour, say.

- Use standard filtering techniques, like blocking certain IP addresses and refusing requests if they arrive too frequently.

- Use obfuscation and encryption. This idea is based on a tricky little anti-spam plugin for Wordpress, *HashCash* (*http://wp-plugins.net/plugin/wp-hashcash/*). By outputting a customized piece of obfuscated JavaScript that's used to decrypt web service content, you force any client programmer to do two things: first, hook into a JavaScript engine in order to execute the code; second, consume resources performing the decryption. Neither is impossible, but they do make the task less appealing. Unfortunately, they also break the clean nature of web services, though you should be able to abstract the messy details with a suitable JavaScript API.

Real-World Examples

Just about any Ajax App has some kind of web service. In these examples, we'll look at a public API designed for third-party usage, then at a couple of services accessed only from a corresponding Ajax browser script.

Technorati API

Technorati (*http://technorati.com*) exposes its search capability for third-party use. To perform a query, run an HTTP GET on the following URL: *http://api.technorati.com/ search?key=1234&query=serendipity*, where "1234" is your personal technorati key and "serendipity" is the search query. You'll get an XML document that lists the results.

NetVibes

NetVibes (*http://netvibes.com*) is an Ajax portal that gets it content from several web services. To get weather data, the browser invokes a service like this:

```
http://netvibes.com/xmlProxy.php?url=http%3A//xoap.weather.com/weather/local/
    USNY0996%3Fcc%3D*%26unit%3Dd%26dayf%3D4
```

The service is actually a proxy because it passes through to a real weather service at weather.com. As the URL shows, you can specify parameters such as location (USDNYC0996), units (d), and number of days ahead (4). The output is an XML document without any HTML markup:

```
<weather ver="2.0">
  <head>
    <locale>en_US</locale>
    <form>MEDIUM</form>
    ...
  </head>
  <dayf>
    ...
    <hi>N/A</hi>
    <low>46</low>
    <sunr>7:18 AM</sunr>
```

```
        <suns>4:34 PM</suns>
        ...
    </dayf>
    ...
</weather>
```

Wish-O-Matic

Alexander Kirk's Wish-O-Matic (*http://wish-o-matic.com*) provides Amazon recommendations. The browser posts the following information to a service at *http://alexander.kirk.at/*
wish-o-matic/search=grand&catalog=Books&page=1&locale=US&_=. The service then responds
with a list of books. Unlike the previous service, the data is pure HTML, ready for immediate display in the browser.

```
search=grand&catalog=Books&page=1&locale=US&_=

<table><tr><td style="width: 500px">
    <b>Author:</b> Kevin Roderick<br/><b>Title:</b> Wilshire Boulevard:

    The Grand Concourse of Los Angeles<br/><b>ISBN:</b> 1883318556<br/><a
    href="javascript:void(add_item('1883318556', 'Wilshire Boulevard: The Grand
        Concourse of Los Angeles',
    'http://images.amazon.com/images/P/1883318556.01._SCTHUMBZZZ_.jpg'))">My
    friend likes this item!</a></td>
    ...
    </td></tr>
    </table>
    <br/>
    <a href="javascript:void(prev_page())">&lt; prev</a> |
    <a href="javascript:void(next_page())">next &gt;</a>
```

Code Example: AjaxPatterns testAjaxCaller

AjaxCaller is a JavaScript HTTP client used in examples throughout this book (explained
later in this chapter in "Code Example: AjaxPatterns TestAjaxCaller" for *XMLHttpRequest*
Call). Here, we'll look at a web service used in the testAjaxCaller application (*http://*
ajaxlocal/run/testAjaxCaller/), a very simple service that just echoes its input.

httpLogger begins by outputting a request method (e.g., "GET" or "POST"), its own request
URL, and CGI variables present in the URL and body:

```
echo "<p>Request Method: $requestMethod</p>";
echo "<p>Request URL: ".$_SERVER['REQUEST_URI']."</p>";
echo "<p>Vars in URL: ".print_r($_GET, TRUE)."</p>";
echo "<p>Vars in Body: ".print_r($_POST, TRUE)."</p>";
```

A separate function is used to read the body, which can also be outputted with a regular
print or echo statement:

```
function readBody( ) {
  $body="";
  $putdata = fopen("php://input", "r");
  while ($block = fread($putdata, 1024)) {
    $body = $body.$block;
  }
  fclose($putdata);
  return $body;
}
```

Related Patterns

Web Services patterns

All the patterns in Web Services (Chapter 9) explain various strategies for designing Web Services with clean, maintainable interfaces.

Web Remoting patterns

The remaining Web Remoting patterns explain how the browser invokes a server-side Web Service.

Cross-Domain Proxy

The main point of this pattern is to guide on designing your own Web Services pattern. However, there are times when your server script will need to call on an external web service, as explained in *Cross-Domain Proxy* (Chapter 10).

Simulation Service

A *Simulation Service* (Chapter 19) is a "dummy" service that produces canned responses, a useful device while developing the browser-side of an Ajax App.

Service Test

The nice thing about web services, compared to most aspects of web development, is that it's easy to write automated tests, as described in *Service Test* (Chapter 19).

XMLHttpRequest Call

Call, Callback, Download, Grab, Live, Query, Remoting, RemoteScripting, Synchronise, Synchronize, Upload, XMLHttpRequest

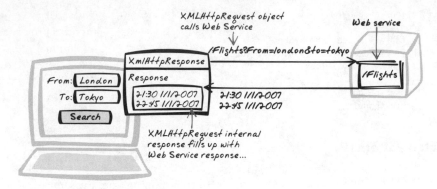

FIGURE 6-2. XMLHttpRequest Call

Goal Story

Reta's purchasing some items from a wholesaler's web site. Each time she adds an item to the shopping cart, the web site issues an XMLHttpRequest to save the latest cart contents. There's no form submission, so the item is added instantaneously, which saves Reta time as well as helping her understand what's going on.

Problem

How can the browser communicate with the server?

Forces

- Ajax Apps require browser-server communication. User-generated information must be uploaded and new server information must be downloaded.

- Because Ajax Apps should have a smooth and continuous feel, browser-server communication must be unobtrusive.

- Ajax Apps should be highly responsive, so calls should involve minimal data transfer.

- As the network is often unreliable and performance is inconsistent, calls should be asynchronous, allowing the user to keep working while network calls are in progress.

Solution

Use XMLHttpRequest objects for browser-server communication. JavaScript lacks a portable mechanism for general network communication, a restriction that's always been in place for security reasons and will probably remain. But thanks to the XMLHttpRequest object—now available in all major browsers—JavaScript code *can* make HTTP calls back to its originating server and get hold of the results. Doing so enables you to make fine-grained server calls and deal with responses as you wish, unlike conventional form submissions, which cause a complete page refresh. Note: an online demo (*http://ajaxify.com/ run/xmlHttpRequestCall*) illustrates the code concepts throughout this Solution and the code snippets loosely follow from the demo.

This pattern uses the sum web service described earlier in *Web Service*, with a URL like *http://ajaxify.com/run/xmlHttpRequestCall/sumGet.phtml?figure1=5&figure2=10*. It returns just the sum, "15" in this case. You can test that by typing the full URL in the browser, but here we want to call it from JavaScript and catch the result. Here's a very basic example:

```
var xhReq = new XMLHttpRequest();
xhReq.open("GET", "sumGet.phtml?figure1=5&figure2=10", false);
xhReq.send(null);
var serverResponse = xhReq.responseText;
alert(serverResponse); // Shows "15"
```

The sequence begins by creating a new instance of XMLHttpRequest. xhReq.open() then prepares a call on the test service, sumGet.phtml (the code's running from the same path, so the domain and path need not be qualified). The GET signifies the request method to be used. The false argument says the call is synchronous, meaning that the code will block until a response comes back. The send command completes the request. Because the call is synchronous, the result is ready as soon as the next line is executed. The XMLHttpRequest object has saved the response from the server, and you can access it with the responseText field.

The above example shows that the fundamental technology is pretty simple. However, be aware that it's a very basic usage that's not yet fit for production. Fundamental questions remain, which are answered throughout this Solution:

- How do you get hold of an XMLHttpRequest?
- How do *asynchronous* calls work?
- How do you handle errors?
- What if the service requires a POST or PUT request rather than a GET?
- What constraints apply to external domains?
- How can you deal with XML responses?
- What's the API?

As you read all this, be aware that many, many libraries are available to handle remoting (see Appendix A). **Most developers shouldn't need to touch** XMLHttpRequest **directly.** Having said that, it's good to be aware of the capabilities and limitations of XMLHttpRequest Calls, along with the other web-remoting techniques. This knowledge will help you select the most appropriate library and help with any bugs you might encounter.

Creating XMLHttpRequest objects

In most browsers, XMLHttpRequest is a standard JavaScript class, so you just create a new instance of XMLHttpRequest. However, Microsoft is the inventor of XMLHttpRequest, and until IE7, IE offered it only as an ActiveX object. To make things even more fun, there are different versions of that object. The following code shows a factory function that works on all browsers that support XMLHttpRequest:

```
function createXMLHttpRequest() {
    try { return new ActiveXObject("Msxml2.XMLHTTP"); } catch (e) {}
```

```
        try { return new ActiveXObject("Microsoft.XMLHTTP"); } catch (e) {}
        try { return new XMLHttpRequest(); } catch(e) {}
        alert("XMLHttpRequest not supported");
        return null;
    }
    ...
    var xhReq = createXMLHttpRequest();
```

You really need to use a function like this for maximum portability. Once you have the object, its basic functionality and API are pretty consistent across browsers, but be sure to test carefully as there are a few subtle implementation differences in some browsers. (If you're curious, the "Solution" in *HTTP Streaming* [later in this chapter] highlights one such inconsistency.)

You can also reuse an XMLHttpRequest; it's worthwhile doing so in order to prevent memory leaks. To be safe, start a new call only when there's not one already in progress. As explained below, it's possible to inspect the status of a call, and you should only start a call if the status is 0 or 4. So if it's anything else, first call the abort() method to reset status.

Asynchronous calls

I previously mentioned in the "Solution" that under synchronous mode, "the code will block until a response comes back." Some hardened readers probably writhed uncomfortably at the thought. We all know that some requests take a long time to process, and some don't come back at all. Pity the user when a server script is buried in an infinite loop.

In practice, XMLHttpRequest Calls should almost always be asynchronous. That means the browser and the user can continue working on other things while waiting for a response to come back. How will you know when the response is ready? The XMLHttpRequest's readyState always reflects the current point in the call's lifecycle. When the object is born, it's at 0. After open() has been called, it's 1. The progression continues until the response is back, at which point the value is 4.

So, to catch the response, you need to watch for a readyState of 4. That's easy enough, because XMLHttpRequest fires readystatechange events. You can declare a callback function using the onreadystatechange field. The callback will then receive all state changes. The states below 4 aren't especially useful and are somewhat inconsistent across browser types anyway (*http://www.quirksmode.org/blog/archives/2005/09/xmlhttp_notes_r_2.html*). So most of the time, all we're interested in is, "Are you in state 4 (i.e., complete) or not?"

Based on all that, here's an asynchronous version of the code shown earlier:

```
    var xhReq = createXMLHttpRequest();
    xhReq.open("GET", "sumGet.phtml?figure1=5&figure2=10", true);
    xhReq.onreadystatechange = onSumResponse;
    xhReq.send(null);
    ...
    function onSumResponse() {
      if (xhReq.readyState != 4)  { return; }
      var serverResponse = xhReq.responseText;
      ...
    }
```

As shown, you declare the callback method in XMLHttpRequest's onreadystatechange property. In addition, the third argument of open( ) is now true. This argument is actually called the "asynchronous flag," which explains why we're now setting it to true. The callback function, onSumResponse, is registered using onreadystatechange and contains a guard clause to ensure the readyState is 4 before any processing can occur. At that point, we have the full response in responseText.

JavaScript also supports "closures"—a form of anonymous function—which suggests a more concise boilerplate structure for asynchronous calls:

```
var xhReq = createXMLHttpRequest( );
xhReq.open("get", "sumget.phtml?figure1=10&figure2=20", true);
xhReq.onreadystatechange = function( ) {
  if (xhReq.readyState != 4)  { return; }
      var serverResponse = xhReq.responseText;
      ...
};
xhReq.send(null);
```

Use closures sparingly, because you're defining a new function each time. It's slower than referring to an existing one and might also lead to memory leaks.

Asynchronous calls are essential, but also more error-prone. If you look at the callback mechanism, you might notice the potential for a subtle, but serious, bug. The problem arises when the same instance of XMLHttpRequest is simultaneously used for different calls. If Call 2 is issued while the object is still waiting for the response of Call 1, what will the callback function receive? In fact, it's even possible the callback function itself is changed before the first call returns. There are ways to deal with this problem, and they're the topic of the *Call Tracking* (Chapter 10) pattern.

Detecting errors

Sometimes, a request doesn't come back as you expected it, or maybe not at all. You scripted the call wrong, or there's a bug in the server, or some part of the infrastructure just screwed up. Thinking asynchronously is the first step to dealing with these problems, because at least your application isn't blocked. But you need to do more than that.

To detect a server error, you can check the response status using XMLHttpRequest's status flag. This is just a standard HTTP code. For example, if the resource is missing, XMLHttpRequest.status will take on the famous "404" value. In most cases, you can assume anything other than 200 is an error situation. This suggests adding a new check to the callback function of the previous section:

```
xhReq.onreadystatechange = function( ) {
   if (xhReq.readyState != 4)  { return; }
   if (xhReq.status != 200)  {
   var serverResponse = xhReq.responseText;
   ...
};
```

That's great if the browser knows a problem occurred, but sometimes the request will be lost forever. Thus, you usually want some kind of timeout mechanism (*http://ajaxblog.com/ archives/2005/06/01/async-requests-over-an-unreliable-network*) as well. Establish a *Scheduling* timer to track the session. If the request takes too long, the timer will kick in and you can then handle the error. XMLHttpRequest has an abort( ) function that you should also invoke in a timeout situation. Here's a code sample:

```
var xhReq = createXMLHttpRequest( );
xhReq.open("get", "infiniteLoop.phtml", true); // Server stuck in a loop.
var requestTimer = setTimeout(function( ) {
xhReq.onreadystatechange = function( ) {
  if (xhReq.readyState != 4)  { return; }
  clearTimeout(requestTimeout);
  if (xhReq.status != 200)  {
    // Handle error, e.g. Display error message on page
    return;
  }
  var serverResponse = xhReq.responseText;
  ...
};
```

Compared to the previous example, a timer has been introduced. The onreadystatechange( ) callback function will clear the timer once it receives the full response (even if that response happens to be erroneous). In the absence of this clearance, the timer will fire, and in this case, the setTimeout sequence stipulates that abort( ) will be called and some recovery action can then take place.

Handling POSTs and other request types

Up to this point, requests have been simple GET queries—pass in a URL and grab the response. As discussed in the *RESTful Service* (Chapter 9), real-world projects need to work with other request types as well. POST, for example, is suited to calls that affect server state or upload substantial quantities of data. To illustrate, let's now create a new service, sumPostGeneric.phtml, that does the same thing as postGet.phtml but with a POST message. It's called "generic" because it reads the full message body text, as opposed to a CGI-style form submission. In this case, it expects a body such as "Calculate this sum: 5+6" and returns the sum value:

```
<?
  $body = readBody( );
  ereg("Calculate this sum: ([0-9]+)\+([0-9]+)", $body, $groups);
  echo $groups[1] + $groups[2];

  // A PHP method to read arbitrary POST body content.
  function readBody( ) {
    $body="";
    $putData = fopen("php://input", "r");
    while ($block = fread($putData, 1024)) {
      $body = $body.$block;
    }
    fclose($putData);
```

```
      return $body;
  }
?>
```

To POST an arbitrary body, we give XMLHttpRequest a request type of POST and pass the body in as an argument to send( ). (Note that with GET queries, the send( ) argument is null as there's no body content).

```
var xhreq = createxmlhttprequest();
xhreq.open("post", "sumPostGeneric.phtml", true);
xhreq.onreadystatechange = function() {
  if (xhreq.readystate != 4) { return; }
  var serverResponse = xhreq.responsetext;
  ...
};
xhreq.send("calculate this sum: 5+6");
```

Quite often, though, you'll be posting key-value pairs, so you want the message to look as if it were submitted from a POST-based form. You'd do that because it's more standard, and server-side libraries make it easy to write web services that accept standard form data. The service shown in the code example following the next one, sumPostForm.php, shows how PHP makes light work of such submissions, and the same is true for most languages:

```
<?
  echo $_POST["figure1"] + $_POST["figure2"];
?>
```

For the browser script to make a CGI-style upload, two additional steps are required. First, declare the style in a "Content-Type" header; as the example below shows, XMLHttpRequest lets you directly set request headers. The second step is to make the body a set of name-value pairs:

```
var xhreq = createxmlhttprequest();
xhreq.open("post", "sumPostForm.phtml", true);
xhReq.setRequestHeader('Content-Type', 'application/x-www-form-urlencoded');
xhreq.onreadystatechange = function() {
  if (xhreq.readystate != 4) { return; }
  var serverresponse = xhreq.responsetext;
  ...
};
xhreq.send("calculate this sum: 5+6");
```

GET and POST are virtually ubiquitous, but *RESTful Service* points out there's a time and place for other request methods too, such as PUT and DELETE. You don't have to do anything special with those other methods; just set the request type in the open( ) call and send( ) an appropriate body (the item you're putting in the case of PUT; a null argument in the case of DELETE).

Constraints on external domains

On discovering XMLHttpRequest, a common reaction is to start dreaming up an interface that pulls in content from popular web sites and mashes it altogether to into one big Web 2.0

soufflé. Unfortunately, it's not so simple because of a key security rule imposed by all major browsers: XMLHttpRequest can only access content from the originating server. If your application lives at *http://ajax.shop/admin*, then your XMLHttpRequest objects can happily reach *http://ajax.shop/admin/products.html* and *http://ajax.shop/products/contents.html*, shouldn't be able to reach *http://books.ajax.shop/contents.html*, and definitely won't have access to *http://google.com*.

This "same-origin policy" (or "same-domain policy") (*http://www.mozilla.org/projects/security/components/same-origin.html*) will be familiar to developers of Java applets and Flash, where the policy has always been in place. It's there to prevent all kinds of abuse, such as a malicious script grabbing confidential content from one server and uploading it to another server under their own control. Some have suggested it's possibly overkill, that most of the risks it tries to prevent are already possible by other means (*http://spaces.msn.com/members/siteexperts/Blog/cns!1pNcL8JwTfkkjv4gg6LkVCpw!2085.entry*). However, restrictions like this won't be lifted lightly; the rule's likely to be around for the long term, so we had better learn to work with it.

Given same-origin restrictions, then, how do all those Ajax mashup sites work (*http://housingmaps.com*)? The answer is that the cross-domain transfers usually run through the originating server, which acts as a kind of proxy—or tunnel—allowing XMLHttpRequests to communicate with external domains. *Cross-Domain Proxy* (Chapter 10) elaborates on the pattern, and its "Alternatives" section lists some clever workarounds that do allow the originating server to be bypassed.

XML responses

The discussion here has swiftly ignored the big elephant in the room: XML. XMLHttpRequest, as its name suggests, was originally designed with, yes, XML in mind. As we've already seen, it will actually accept any kind of response, so what's special about XML? With XMLHttpRequest, any responses can be read via the responseText field, but there's also an alternative accessor: responseXML. If the response header indicates the content is XML, and the response text is a valid XML string, then responseXML will be the DOM object that results from parsing the XML.

The Display Maniputlation (Chapter 5) patterns have already illustrated how JavaScript supports manipulation of DOM objects. In those patterns, we were only interested in one particular DOM object, the HTML (or XHTML) document representing the current web page. But you can manipulate any other DOM object just as easily. Thus, it's sometimes convenient to have a web service output XML content and manipulate the corresponding DOM object.

The prerequisite here is a *Web Service* (see earlier in this chapter) that outputs valid XML. There are many libraries and frameworks around for automatically generating XML from databases, code objects, files, or elsewhere. But don't think you have to start learning some fancy XML library in order to create XML web services, because it's fairly easy to hand code them too, at least for simple data. The service just needs to output an XML

Content-type header followed by the entire XML document. Here's an XML version of the sum service shown earlier—it outputs an XML document containing the input figures as well as the sum result:

```
<?
  header("Content-Type: text/xml");
  $sum = $_GET["figure1"] + $_GET["figure2"];
  echo <<< END_OF_FILE
<sum>
  <inputs>
    <figure id="1">{$_GET["figure1"]}</figure>
    <figure id="2">{$_GET["figure2"]}</figure>
  </inputs>
  <outputs>$sum</outputs>
</sum>
END_OF_FILE
?>
```

The call sequence is the same as before, but the callback function now extracts the result using responseXML. It then has a first-class DOM object and can interrogate it using the standard DOM API:

```
var xhReq = createXMLHttpRequest();
xhReq.open("GET", "sumXML.phtml?figure1-10&figure2=20", true);
xhReq.onreadystatechange = function() {
  if (xhReq.readyState != 4) { return; }
  xml = xhReq.responseXML;
  var figure1 - xml.getElementsByTagName("figure")[0].firstChild.nodeValue;
  var figure2 = xml.getElementsByTagName("figure")[1].firstChild.nodeValue;
  var sum = xml.getElementsByTagName("outputs")[0].firstChild.nodeValue;
  ...
};
xhReq.send(null);
});
```

The name "XMLHttpRequest" relates to its two primary functions: handling HTTP requests and converting XML responses. The former function is critical and the latter is best considered a bonus. There are certainly good applications for XML responses—see *XML Message* (Chapter 9), and *XML Data Island* and *Browser-Side XSLT* (Chapter 11)—but keep in mind that XML is not a requirement of Ajax systems.

You can also upload XML from browser to server. In this case, XMLHttpRequest doesn't offer any special XML functionality; you just send the XML message as you would any other message, and with an appropriate request type (e.g., POST or PUT). To support the receiving web service, the JavaScript should generally declare the XML content type in a request header:

```
xhReq.setRequestHeader('Content-Type', "text/xml");
```

The XMLHttpRequest API: a summary

We've looked at how to achieve typical tasks with XMLHttpRequest, and now here's a quick summary of its properties and methods based on an Apple Developer Connection article (*http://developer.apple.com/internet/webcontent/xmlhttpreq.html*). The API is supported by IE5+, the Mozilla family (including all Firefox releases), and Safari 1.2+.

XMLHttpRequest has the following properties:

onreadystatechange
> The callback function that's notified of state changes. 0=UNINITIALIZED, 1=LOADING, 2=LOADED, 3=INTERACTIVE, and 4=COMPLETE. (As explained earlier in "Asynchronous calls," states 1–3 are ambiguous and interpretations vary across browsers.)

readyState
> The state within the request cycle.

responseText
> The response from the server, as a String.

responseXML
> The response from the server, as a Document Object Model, provided that the response "Content-Type" header is "text/html," and the responseText is a valid XML string.

status
> HTTP response code (*http://www.w3.org/Protocols/rfc2616/rfc2616-sec10.html*) received from the server. This should normally be 200; most values indicate an error.

statusText
> The HTTP response code description received from the server; e.g., "Not Found."

And these are XMLHttpRequest's methods:

abort( )
> Stops the request and resets its readyState back to zero. (See "Detecting errors," earlier in this chapter.)

getAllResponseHeaders( )
> Returns a string of all response headers, separated by a newline as in the original message.

getResponseHeader(headerField)
> Returns the value for a particular header field.

open(requestMethod, url, asynchronousFlag, username, password)
> Prepares XMLHttpRequest (See the "Solution," earlier.). Only the first two parameters are optional. username and password can be used for authentication.

send(bodyContent)
> Sends the message along with specified body content (null if no body content is to be sent; e.g., for GET requests). (See the "Solution," earlier.)

setRequestHeader(headerField, headerValue)
> Sets a request header. (See "Handling POSTs and other request types," earlier.)

Decisions

What kind of content will web services provide?

As mentioned in the solution, XML is not the only kind of content that XMLHttpRequest can deal with. As long as you can parse the message in JavaScript, there are various response types possible. The patterns on web services highlight a number of response types, including HTML, XML, JSON, and plain-text.

How will caching be controlled?

It's possible that an XMLHttpRequest response will be cached by the browser. Sometimes, that's what you want and sometimes it's not, so you need to exert some control over caching.

With cache control, we're talking about GET-based requests. Use GET for read-only queries and other request types for operations that affect server state. If you use POST to get information, that information usually won't be cached. Likewise, if you use GET to *change* state, you run the risk that the call won't always reach the server, because the browser will cache the call locally. There are other reasons to follow these this advice too; see *RESTful Service* (Chapter 9).

Often, you want to suppress caching in order to get the latest server information, in which case, a few techniques are relevant. Since browsers and servers vary, the standard advice is spread the net as wide as possible by combining some of these techniques:

- You can make the URL unique by appending a timestamp (*http://www.howtoadvice.com/ StopCaching*) (a random string, or a string from an incrementing sequence, is sometimes used too). It's a cheap trick, but surprisingly robust and portable:

    ```
    var url = "sum.phtml?figure1=5&figure2=1&timestamp=" + new Date().getTime();
    ```
- You can add a header to the request:

    ```
    xhReq.setRequestHeader("If-Modified-Since", "Sat, 1 Jan 2005 00:00:00 GMT");
    ```
- In the *Web Service* set response headers to suppress caching (*http://www.stridebird.com/ articles/?showarticle=1&id=33*). In PHP, for example:

    ```
    header("Expires: Sat, 1 Jan 2005 00:00:00 GMT");
    header("Last-Modified: ".gmdate( "D, d M Y H:i:s")."GMT");
    header("Cache-Control: no-cache, must-revalidate");
    header("Pragma: no-cache");
    ```
- Use POST instead of GET. Requests that are of POST type will sometimes cause caching to be suppressed. However, this particular technique is not recommended because, as explained in *RESTful Service*, GET and POST have particular connotations and shouldn't be treated as interchangeable. In any event, it won't always work, because it's possible some resources will actually cache POST responses.

On the other hand, caching is a good thing when the service is time-consuming and unlikely to have changed recently. To encourage caching, you can reverse the above advice; e.g., set the Expires headers to a suitable time in the future. In addition, a good approach for smaller data is to cache it in the program itself, using a JavaScript data structure. *Browser-Side Cache* (Chapter 13) explains how.

How will you deal with errors?

The section on error detection left open the question of what to do once we discover a server timeout or nonstandard error code. There are three possible actions:

Try again
Retry a few times before giving up.

Inform the user
Tell the user what's gone wrong and what the consequences are. For instance, inform him that his data hasn't been submitted and he should try again in a few minutes.

Do nothing
Sometimes, you have the luxury of ignoring the response (or lack thereof). That might be because you're issuing low-importance Fire-and-Forget calls (*http://www.ajaxian. com/archives/2005/09/ajaxian_fire_an.html*), where you're uploading some data without waiting for any response.

Real-World Examples

Lace Chat

Brett Stimmerman's Lace Chat (*http://www.socket7.net/lace/*) is an Ajax chat application that uses XMLHttpRequest in two ways: to upload messages you type and to download all the latest messages from the server (Figure 6-3).

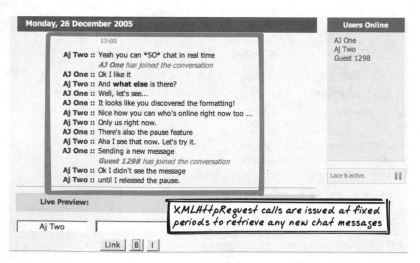

FIGURE 6-3. Lace Chat

Backbase

Backbase's Demo RSS Reader (*http://www.backbase.com/demos/RSS*) uses XMLHttpRequest to pull down titles of recent articles (Figure 6-4). When you click on one of those titles, a new XMLHttpRequest will pull down the entire content.

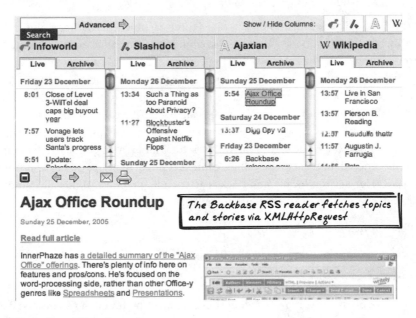

FIGURE 6-4. Backbase RSS Reader

Anyterm

Phil Endecott's Anyterm (*http://anyterm.org/demos.html*) is an Ajax terminal emulator allowing you to run telnet or SSH within the browser. It uses XMLHttpRequest Calls to upload keystrokes and download the latest screen state.

Mint

Mint (*http://haveamint.com/*) is a web site statistics package. Site owners include Mint Java-Script on each page, which quietly inspects the user's browser settings and uploads them using an XMLHttpRequest.

Code Example: AjaxPatterns TestAjaxCaller

The example (*http://ajaxpatterns.org/xmlHttpRequestCall/*) referenced in the "Solution," earlier, covers most typical XMLHttpRequest usage. In practice, many people adopt Ajax frameworks and libraries rather than calling XMLHttpRequest directly. That's the approach taken with all of the Ajax Patterns demos, which use a library called *ajaxCaller.js* that was developed in parallel to the demos themselves. It's a fairly basic library, but offers a simple interface for the functionality that's typically required of XMLHttpRequest. In this section, I'll introduce the library by showing a few usages within the AjaxCaller Test Demo (*http://ajaxify.com/run/testAjaxCaller*).

The simplest call is getting some plain-text: just specify the URL and the callback function.

```
ajaxCaller.getPlainText(url, onResponse);
```

For all calls, the callback function always takes three arguments. The first argument is the result, either a string or a DOM object. The second is an associative array mapping header fields to header values. The third is a "calling context." Think of calling context as an optional value that travels alongside the request and the corresponding response, returned to the callback function in exactly the same form as you passed it in when the call was issued. Usually it holds information about the call; e.g., if the call was made to send off a purchase order, the calling context might contain the item that was ordered. Then, ajaxCaller will pass the context into the callback function, which can mark the item as successfully ordered. In reality, the calling context is not actually passed to and from the server; ajaxCaller keeps it locally and tracks each pending request. If this all sounds a bit complicated, check out *Call Tracking* (Chapter 10).

The callback function looks as follows:

```
function onResponse(text, headers, callingContext) {
  // Use text (a string), headers, and callingContext
}
```

And since it's only the text that's used most of the time, the function can also be declared in a simpler form.*

```
function onResponse(text) {
  // Use text (a String)
}
```

getPlainText( ) is one of four commonly used methods. The others are getXML( ), postForPlainText( ), and postForXML( ). Together, these four cover both common request types (GET and POST) and both response types (text and XML).

```
ajaxCaller.getXML(url, callbackFunction);
ajaxCaller.postForXML(url, vars, callbackFunction);
ajaxCaller.getPlainText(url, callbackFunction, callbackContext);
ajaxCaller.postForPlainText(url, callbackFunction, callbackContext);
```

There are also a number of more general methods—for example, get( ) provides more flexible GET requests. In addition to a URL and a callback function, get( ) lets you specify some variables to be appended to the URL, a flag to indicate whether the response is XML, and the callingContext as discussed above.

```
var vars = {
  flavour: "chocolate",
```

---

* Because of the way JavaScript handles function calls, the library call will still go to the function in this form, even though the call contains three arguments.

```
        topping: "nuts"
    };
    ajaxCaller.get("httpLogger.php", vars, onResponse, false, "iceCreamRequest");
```

There are general operations for other request types too. postVars( ) creates a CGI-style POST upload and postBody( ) creates an arbitrary-body POST upload. There are similar methods for other request types; e.g., PUT, TRACE, OPTIONS, DELETE, and HEAD.

Alternatives

This section lists all alternatives I'm aware of, some more limited than others. The more obscure techniques are included for the sake of completeness and also in the hope they might spark a few ideas.

Page refreshes

The conventional way to communicate with the server is for the browser to request an entirely new page, which is pretty extreme when you stop and think about it. It might be appropriate if the user's navigating to a completely different part of a web site, but it's overkill if you want to update a football score at the bottom of the page or upload some user input. The most familiar kind of full page refresh is the hyperlink, which causes the browser to issue a GET request, clear the current page, and output the response. The other kind of full page refresh is a form submission, which causes the browser to pass some parameters with the request—which will be GET, POST, or some other method—and, as with a hyperlink, replace the previous page with the new response. With web remoting, any user-interface changes are completely at the discretion of the script running inside the page. These conventional techniques are still available, but most server communication uses XMLHttpRequest Call and related technologies.

IFrame Call

IFrame Call (see later in this chapter) is the main alternative to XMLHttpRequest. Like XMLHttpRequest, it allows for remote calls using GET, POST, and other request types. But whereas XMLHttpRequest is designed specifically for web remoting, IFrame Call exploits the IFrame to do something it was never really intended to do, and the code shows it. Here's a summary of XMLHttpRequest's strengths over IFrame Calls:

* Being designed specifically for web remoting, the XMLHttpRequest API is easier to use, especially when it comes to non-GET request types. However, this is no great advantage as it's generally recommended that you use a wrapper library to avoid working with either API. (XMLHttpRequest's API may be better, but it's not great!)

* XMLHttpRequest offers functionality not available to *IFrame Call*, such as the ability to abort a call and track the call's state. This can have important performance implications (*http://www.ajaxian.com/archives/2005/09/ajaxian_fire_an.html*).

* XMLHttpRequest is typically faster, especially with shorter responses (*http://me.eae.net/ archive/2005/04/02/xml-http-performance-and-caching/*).

* XMLHttpRequest parses XML in a simple, portable, manner; IFrame is unrelated to XML.

- On those browsers that do support `XMLHttpRequest`, the API is more consistent than that of IFrame.

- `XMLHttpRequest` is rapidly gaining the virtue of widespread familiarity. This not only helps other developers understand your code, but also means you benefit from tools such as those which monitor `XMLHttpRequest` traffic (see *Traffic Sniffing* [Chapter 18]).

For all these reasons, `XMLHttpRequest` should be the default choice. However, there are some specialized situations where *IFrame Call* is superior:

- IFrame works on many older browsers that don't actually support `XMLHttpRequest`.

- IFrame happens to have some specialized properties (if only by complete fluke) for browser history and bookmarkability, at least for IE, as discussed in *Unique URLs* (Chapter 17).

- `XMLHttpRequest` on IE won't work if security measures disable ActiveX, a policy sometimes enforced in the enterprise (*http://verens.com/archives/2005/08/12/ajax-in-ie-without-activex/*).

- IFrame may offer a more portable solution for *HTTP Streaming* as discussed in that pattern.

HTTP Streaming

HTTP Streaming (see later in this chapter) also allows for web remoting, and unlike `XMLHttpRequest`, the connection remains open. Functionally, the key advantage over `XMLHttpRequest` is that the server can continuously push new information to the browser. From a resource perspective, streaming is good insofar as there's less starting and stopping of connections, but there are serious scaleability issues as it's rarely feasible to keep open a huge amounts of connections and maintain numerous server-side scripts.

Richer Plugin

The *Richer Plugin* (Chapter 8) pattern discusses Java, Flash, and other plugins and extensions. These components often have permission to call the server programmatically. and in some cases, can be used as proxies available to JavaScript code.

On-Demand JavaScript

On-Demand JavaScript (see later in this chapter) describes a couple of ways to download JavaScript on the fly. One involves `XMLHttpRequests` (and therefore isn't foundational in itself), but the other is an alternative transport mechanism, a different technique for web remoting. It works by adding a `script` element to the document body, which has the effect of automatically pulling down a named JavaScript file.

Image-Cookie Call

Brent Ashley's RSLite library (*http://www.ashleyit.com/rs/rslite/*) is an unusual alternative based on images and cookies. An image's source property is set to the service URL, which is simply a means of invoking the service. The service writes its response into one or more cookies, which will then be accessible from the JavaScript once the call has completed.

Stylesheet Call

Another way to get at server state is to dynamically change a CSS stylesheet. Just like setting a new JavaScript or image source, you set a stylesheet's href property to point to the web service. In Julien Lamarre's demo of this technique (*http://zingzoom.com/ajax/ajax_with_stylesheet.php*), the web service actually outputs a stylesheet, and the response is embedded in the URL of a background-image property!

204 Response

An old—and pretty much obsolete—trick is to have the server respond with a 204 "No Content" response code. Browsers won't refresh the page when they see this code, meaning that your script can quietly submit a form to such a service with no impact on the page. However, you can only use the 204 trick for "fire-and-forget" calls—while the response may contain information embedded in the headers, there's no way for a browser script to access it.

Import XML Document

There's a technique specifically for retrieving XML documents that uses similar technology to XMLHttpRequest. Peter-Paul Koch described the technique back in 2000 (*http://www.quirksmode.org/dom/importxml.html*), and recently suggested it can now be written off (*http://www.quirksmode.org/blog/archives/2005/01/with_httpmapsea.html*).

Metaphor

An XMLHttpRequest Call is like the browser having a side conversation with the server while carrying on the main conversation with the user.

IFrame Call

Call, Callback, Download, Frame, IFrame, Live, Query, Remoting, RemoteScripting, Upload

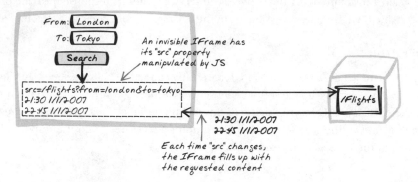

FIGURE 6-5. IFrame Call

Goal Story

Bill's ordering a car online and the price is always synchronized with his choice. This happens because of a hidden IFrame. Each time he changes something, the browser populates a form in the IFrame and submits it. The IFrame soon contains the new price, which the browser copies into the visible display. XMLHttpRequest could have accomplished the feat too, but it's not supported in Bill's outdated browser.

Problem

How can the browser communicate with the server?

Forces

Refer to the section "Forces" in *XMLHttpRequest Call*.

Solution

Use IFrames for browser-server communication. Much of the fuss in Ajax concerns the XMLHttpRequest object, but sometimes other remoting techniques are more appropriate, and IFrame Call is one of those (see the "Alternatives" section of *XMLHttpRequest Call*, earlier in this chapter, for a comparison). IFrames are page-like elements that can be embedded in other pages. They have their own source URL, distinct from their parent page, and the source URL can change dynamically. IFrame Calls work by making the IFrame point to a URL we're interested in, and then reading the IFrame's contents once the new content has loaded. Note: an online demo (*http://ajaxify.com/run/iframe*) illustrates most of the code concepts throughout this Solution and the code snippets loosely follow from the demo.

To begin with, you need an IFrame in the initial HTML, and an event handler registered to catch the onload event. (It would be less obtrusive to register the handler with JavaScript, but due to certain browser "features," that doesn't always work.)

```
<iframe id='iFrame' onload='onIFrameLoad();'></iframe>
```

We're using the IFrame as a data repository, not as a user interface, so some CSS is used to hide it. (The more natural choice would be display: none, but as an experimental demo shows [*http://ajaxlocal/run/iframe/displayNone/*], browser strangeness makes it infeasible.)

```
#iFrame {
  visibility: hidden;
  height: 1px;
}
```

On the server, we're initially going to use the web service discussed in *XMLHttpRequest Call*: sumGet.phtml. To call the service, we'll change the IFrame's source:

```
$("iFrame").src = "sumGet.phtml?figure1=5&figure2=1";
```

We already registered an onload handler in the initial HTML. The handler will be called when the new content has loaded, and at that stage, the IFrame's body will reflect the content we're after. The following code calls a function, extractIFrameBody( ), which extracts the body in a portable manner (based on *http://developer.apple.com/internet/webcontent/iframe.html*).

```
function onIFrameLoad( ) {
  var serverResponse = extractIFrameBody($("iFrame")).innerHTML;
  $("response").innerHTML = serverResponse;
}
```

That covers the GET call. To illustrate POSTing, we'll invoke the sumPost.phtml service, also discussed in *XMLHttpRequest Call*. POST calls are a bit more complicated because we can't just change the source. Instead, we dynamically inject a form into the IFrame and submit it. In this example, the arguments ('5' and '2') are hardcoded, but they could easily be scripted by manipulating the input elements.

```
var iFrameBody = extractIFrameBody($("iFrame"));
iFrameBody.innerHTML =
    "<form action='sumPostForm.phtml' method='POST'>" +
      "<input type='text' name='figure1' value='5'>" +
      "<input type='text' name='figure2' value='2'>" +
    "</form>";
var form = iFrameBody.firstChild;
form.submit( );
```

As with conventional form submission, the IFrame will be refreshed with the output of the form recipient. Thus, the previous onload handler will work fine. Figure 6-6 illustrates the overall process.

Another approach with IFrames is to have the server output some JavaScript that alters the parent or calls a function defined in the parent. The code will automatically be called when the page loads, so there's no need for an onload handler. Unfortunately, this

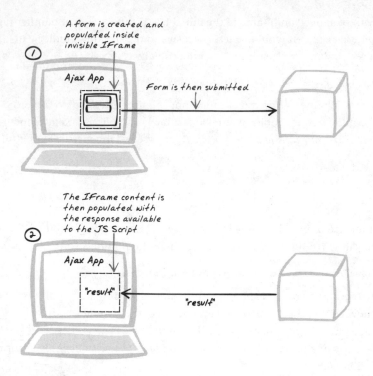

A form is created and populated inside invisible IFrame

① Ajax App

Form is then submitted

The IFrame content is then populated with the response available to the JS Script

② Ajax App

"result"

"result"

FIGURE 6-6. Posting a form via IFrame Call

approach creates substantial coupling between the server and browser. In contrast, note how the examples above used completely generic web services—the services only know how to add numbers together and nothing about the calling context. That's possible because all behavior was encapsulated in the onload( ) function.

As *Call Tracking* (Chapter 10) discusses, there are problems—and suitable workarounds— with simultaneous *XMLHttpRequest Calls*, and the same is true for IFrames. First, you need to create a separate IFrame for each parallel call—you don't want to change an IFrame's source while it's waiting for a response. Second, you need to investigate and test limitations, because the application can grind to a halt if too many calls are outstanding.

There's one last problem with IFrame Call: browser UIs aren't really built with this application in mind, so some things might seem funny to users. In particular, Alex Russell has pointed out two issues that arise with IFrame Calls under IE: the "phantom click" and the "throbber of doom" (*http://alex.dojotoolkit.org/?p=538*). The former repeats a clicking sound every time an IFrame request takes place, and the latter keeps animating the throbber icon while the IFrame is loading. These devices are great for a full page refresh, like when you click on a link, but they suck when a script is trying to quietly talk with the server behind the scenes. In Alex's article, he explains how he unearthed a fantastic hack inside Gmail's (*http://gmail.com*) chat application. The hack suppresses the annoying behavior by embedding the IFrame inside an obscure ActiveX component called "htmlfile," which is basically a separate web page. As the IFrame isn't directly on the web page anymore, IE no longer clicks and throbs. See Alex's blog post (*http://alex.dojotoolkit.org/?p=538*) for full details.

Make no mistake: IFrame Call is a pure hack. IFrames were never intended to facilitate browser-server communication. It's likely the technique will slowly fade away as XMLHttpRequest gains popularity and as legacy browsers are retired. Nevertheless, it does retain a few advantages over *XMLHttpRequest Call*, mentioned in the "Alternatives" section of that pattern.

Real-World Examples

Google Maps

Google Maps (*http://maps.google.com*), perhaps the most famous Ajax App, lets you navigate through a map of the world (Figure 6-7). Location and metadata is required from the server, and this content is retrieved using IFrames. Google also uses XMLHttpRequest for downloading XSLT stylesheets (a technique described in *Browser-Side XSLT* [Chapter 11]).

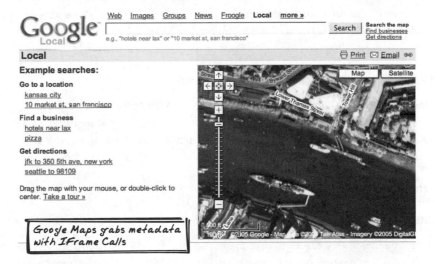

FIGURE 6-7. Google Maps

Scoop framework, Kuro5hin

Scoop (*http://scoop.kuro5hin.org*), an open source content management system, uses IFrames for discussion areas (Figure 6-8). Using the "dynamic comments" module, users can drill down a discussion thread without reloading the whole page. Scoop powers the popular Kuro5hin web site (*http://kuro5hin.org*) among others.

PXL8 Demo

Michele Tranquilli has an excellent tutorial on IFrames with embedded examples (*http://www.pxl8.com/iframes.html*).

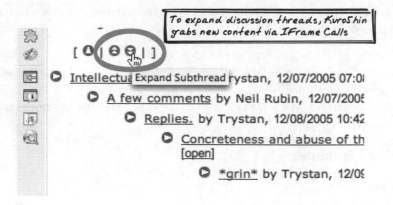

FIGURE 6-8. Kuro5hin

HTMLHttpRequest Library

Angus Turnbull's HTMLHttpRequest (*http://www.twinhelix.com/javascript/htmlhttprequest/*) is a portable web-remoting library that initially attempts to use XMLHttpRequest, and if that fails, falls back to IFrame. The tool is documented in the Code Examples section of *Cross-Browser Component* (Chapter 12).

Code Refactoring: AjaxPatterns Sum Demo

The Basic Sum Demo (*http://ajaxify.com/run/sum*) uses XMLHttpRequest, and there's a version available that's been refactored to use IFrame (*http://ajaxify.com/run/sum/iframe*). There's no walkthrough here, as it's very similar to the GET component of the demo discussed earlier in the "Solution."

Alternatives

XMLHttpRequest Call

XMLHttpRequest Call (see earlier in this chapter) is the natural alternative to IFrame Call. The "Alternatives" section of that pattern, earlier in this chapter, compares the two approaches.

Frame Call

Before IFrames, there were plain old frames. As a user-interface concept, they've had a few public relations problems over the years, but they do at least provide a means of remote scripting similar to IFrame Calls (even if it was accidental). Since IFrames are now widely supported, it's unlikely you'll ever need to use frames for remote scripting (or anything else, for that matter).

Metaphor

A hidden IFrame is an invisible friend you can delegate queries to.

HTTP Streaming

Connection, Duplex, Live, Persistent, Publish, Push, RealTime, Refresh, Remoting, RemoteScripting, Stateful, ReverseAjax, Stream, TwoWay, Update

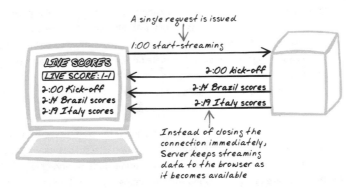

FIGURE 6-9. HTTP Streaming

Goal Story

Tracy's trading application contains a section showing the latest announcements. It's always up-to-date because the announcements are streamed directly from the server. Suddenly, an important announcement appears, which triggers her to issue a new trade. The trade occurs with a new XMLHttpRequest, so the announcement stream continues unaffected.

Problem

How can the server initiate communication with the browser?

Forces

- The state of many Ajax Apps is inherently volatile. Changes can come from other users, external news and data, completion of complex calculations, and triggers based on the current time and date.

- HTTP connections can only be created within the browser. When a state change occurs, there's no way for a server to create a physical connection to notify any interested client.

Solution

Stream server data in the response of a long-lived HTTP connection. Most web services do some processing, send back a response, and immediately exit. But in this pattern, they keep the connection open by running a long loop. The server script uses event registration or some other technique to detect any state changes. As soon as a state change occurs, it pushes new data to the outgoing stream and flushes it, but doesn't actually close it. Meanwhile, the browser must ensure the user interface reflects the new data. This pattern discusses a couple of techniques for Streaming HTTP, which I refer to as "page streaming" and "service streaming."

IS IT PRACTICAL?

Note that this pattern, though it's used in production systems, remains somewhat experimental, especially the *service-streaming* variant. There are issues of feasibility, scaleability, and browser portability. One particular gotcha is the effect of proxies. Sometimes, a proxy sitting somewhere between server and browser will buffer responses, an unfortunate optimization that prevents real-time data from flowing into the browser. Even worse, some proxies will, with the best of intentions, take it upon themselves to close the connection after an idle period. Another issue is server performance, given the number of persistent connections that must be handled.

HTTP Streaming works best when you can control factors such as the web server, the network, and even the browser where possible. Scaleability is often over-emphasized, so streaming might be practical on more systems than one might expect. Furthermore, some modern servers (e.g., Twisted, at *http://twistedmatrix.com/*) are being developed with streaming-style architecture in mind and are able to maintain many long-lived connections.

Page streaming involves streaming the original page response (Figure 6-10). Here, the server immediately outputs an initial page and flushes the stream, but keeps it open. It then proceeds to alter it over time by outputting embedded scripts that manipulate the DOM. The browser's still officially writing the initial page out, so when it encounters a complete <script> tag, it will execute the script immediately. A simple demo is available at *http://ajaxify.com/run/streaming/*.

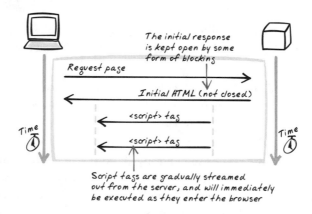

FIGURE 6-10. *Page streaming*

For example, the server can initially output a div that will always contain the latest news:

```
print ("<div id='news'></div>");
```

But instead of exiting, it starts a loop to update the item every 10 seconds (ideally, there would be an interrupt mechanism instead of having to manually pause):

```
<?
  while (true) {
?>
    <script type="text/javascript">
      $('news').innerHTML = '<?= getLatestNews() ?>';
    </script>
<?
    flush(); // Ensure the Javascript tag is written out immediately
    sleep(10);
  }
?>
```

DON'T FORGET TO FLUSH: A PHP TIP

Each language and environment will have its own idiosyncrasies in implementing this pattern. For PHP, there's fortunately some very useful advice in the flush( ): online comments (*http://php.net/ flush*). It turned out to be necessary to execute ob_end_flush( ); before flush( ) could be called. There's also a max_execution_time parameter you might need to increase, and the web server will have its own timeout-related parameters to tweak.

That illustrates the basic technique, and there are some refinements discussed next and in the "Decisions" section, later in this chapter. One burning question you might have is how the browser initiates communication, since the connection is in a perpetual response state. The answer is to use a "back channel"; i.e., a parallel HTTP connection. This can easily be accomplished with an *XMLHttpRequest Call* or an *IFrame Call*. The streaming service will be able to effect a subsequent change to the user interface, as long as it has some means of detecting the call—for example, a session object, a global application object (such as the applicationContext in a Java Servlet container), or the database.

Page streaming means the browser discovers server changes almost immediately. This opens up the possibility of real-time updates in the browser, and allows for bi-directional information flow. However, it's quite a departure from standard HTTP usage, which leads to several problems. First, there are unfortunate memory implications, because the Java-Script keeps accumulating and the browser must retain all of that in its page model. In a rich application with lots of updates, that model is going to grow quickly, and at some point a page refresh will be necessary in order to avoid hard drive swapping or worse. Second, long-lived connections will inevitably fail, so you have to prepare a recovery plan. Third, most servers can't deal with lots of simultaneous connections. Running multiple scripts is certainly going to hurt when each script runs in its own process, and even in more sophisticated multithreading environments, there will be limited resources.

Another problem is that JavaScript must be used, because it's the only way to alter page elements that have already been output. In its absence, the server could only communicate by appending to the page. Thus, browser and server are coupled closely, making it difficult to write a rich Ajaxy browser application.

Service streaming is a step towards solving these problems (Figure 6-11). The technique relies on *XMLHttpRequest Call* (or a similar remoting technology like *IFrame Call*). This time, it's an XMLHttpRequest connection that's long-lived, instead of the initial page load. There's more flexibility regarding length and frequency of connections. You could load the page normally, then start streaming for 30 seconds when the user clicks a button. Or you could start streaming once the page is loaded, and keep resetting the connection every 30 seconds. Flexibility is valuable, given that HTTP Streaming is constrained by the capabilities of the server, the browsers, and the network.

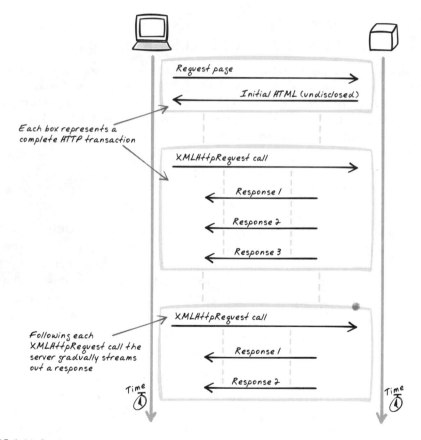

FIGURE 6-11. Service streaming

As for the mechanics of service streaming, the server uses the same trick of looping indefinitely to keep the connection open, and periodically flushing the stream. The output can no longer be HTML script tags, because the web browser wouldn't automatically execute them, so how does the browser deal with the stream? The answer is that it polls for the latest response and uses it accordingly.

The `responseText` property of `XMLHttpRequest` always contains the content that's been flushed out of the server, even when the connection's still open. So the browser can run a periodic check; e.g., to see if its length has changed. One problem, though, is that, once flushed, the service can't undo anything its output. For example, the `responseText` string arising from a timer service might look like this: "12:01:00 12:01:05 12:01:10," whereas it would ideally be just "12:01:00," then just "12:01:05," then just "12:01:10." The solution is to parse the response string and look only at the last value—to be more precise, the last *complete* value, since it's possible the text ends with a partial result. An example of this technique (*http://www.ajaxify.com/run/streaming/xmlHttpRequest/countdown/*) works in this way. To ease parsing, the service outputs each message delimited by a special token, `@END@` (an XML tag would be an alternative approach). Then, a regular expression can be run to grab the latest message, which must be followed by that token to ensure it's complete:

```
function periodicXHReqCheck( ) {
  var fullResponse = util.trim(xhReq.responseText);
  var responsePatt = /^(.*@END@)*(.*)@END@.*$/;
  if (fullResponse.match(responsePatt)) { // At least one full response so far
    var mostRecentDigit = fullResponse.replace(responsePatt, "$2");
    $("response").innerHTML = mostRecentDigit;
  }
}
```

That's great if you only care about the last message, but what if the browser needs to log all messages that came in? Or process them in some way? With a polling frequency of 10 seconds, the previous sequence would lead to values being skipped; the browser would skip from 12:01 to 12:01:10, ignoring the second value. If you want to catch *all* messages, you need to keep track of the position you've read up to. Doing so lets you determine what's new since the previous poll, a technique used in "Code Refactoring: AjaxPatterns Streaming Wiki," later in this chapter.

In summary, service streaming makes streaming more flexible, because you can stream arbitrary content rather than JavaScript commands, and because you can control the connection's lifecycle. However, it combines two concepts that aren't consistent across browsers—`XMLHttpRequest` and HTTP Streaming—with predictable portability issues. Experiments suggest that the *page-streaming* technique does work on both IE and Firefox (*http://ajaxify.com/run/streaming/*), but service streaming only works properly on Firefox, whether `XMLHTTPRequest` (*http://ajaxify.com/run/streaming/xmlHttpRequest/*) or IFrame (*http://ajaxify.com/run/streaming/xmlHttpRequest/iframe/*) is used. In both cases, IE suppresses the response until it's complete. You could claim that's either a bug or a feature; but either way, it works against HTTP Streaming. So for portable page updates, you have a few options:

- Use a hybrid (*http://ajaxlocal/run/streaming/xmlHttpRequest/iframe/scriptTags/*) of page streaming and IFrame-based service streaming, in which the IFrame response outputs script tags, which include code to communicate with the parent document (e.g., `window.parent.onNewData(data);`). As with standard page streaming, the scripts will be executed immediately. It's not elegant, because it couples the remote service to the browser script's structure, but it's a fairly portable and reliable way to achieve HTTP Streaming.

- Use a limited form of service streaming, where the server blocks until the first state change occurs. At that point, it outputs a message and exits. This is not ideal, but certainly feasible (see "Real-World Examples" later in this chapter).

- Use page streaming.

- Use *Periodic Refresh* (Chapter 10) instead of HTTP Streaming.

Decisions

How long will you keep the connection open?

It's impractical to keep a connection open forever. You need to decide on a reasonable period of time to keep the connection open, which will depend on:

- The resources involved: server, network, browsers, and supporting software along the way.

- How many clients will be connecting at any time. Not just averages, but peak periods.

- How the system will be used—how much data will be output, and how the activity will change over time.

- The consequences of too many connections at once. For example, will some users miss out on critical information? It's difficult to give exact figures, but it seems fair to assume a small intranet application could tolerate a connection of minutes or maybe hours, whereas a public dotcom might only be able to offer this service for quick, specialized situations, if at all.

How will you decide when to close the connection?

The web service has several ways to trigger the closing of a connection:

- A time limit is reached.

- The first message is output.

- A particular event occurs. For example, the stream might indicate the progress of a complex calculation (see *Progress Indicator* [Chapter 14]) and conclude with the result itself.

- Never. The client must terminate the connection.

How will the browser distinguish between messages?

As the "Solution" mentions, the service can't erase what it's already output, so it often needs to output a succession of distinct messages. You'll need some protocol to delineate the messages; e.g., the messages fit a standard pattern, the messages are separated by a special token string, or the messages are accompanied by some sort of metadata—for example, a header indicating message size.

Real-World Examples

LivePage

LivePage (*http://twisted.sourceforge.net/TwistedDocs-1.2.0/howto/livepage.html*) is part of Dono-van Preston's Nevow framework (*http://nevow.com*), a Python-based framework, built on the Twisted framework (*http://twistedmatrix.com/*). Events are pushed from the server using XMLHttpRequest-based service streaming. For compatibility reasons, Nevow uses the tech-nique mentioned in the "Solution" in which the connection closes after first output. Donovan explained the technique to me:

> When the main page loads, an XHR (XMLHttpRequest) makes an "output conduit" request. If the server has collected any events between the main page rendering and the output conduit request rendering, It sends them immediately. If it has not, it waits until an event arrives and sends it over the output conduit. Any event from the server to the client causes the server to close the output conduit request. Any time the server closes the output conduit request, the client immediately reopens a new one. If the server hasn't received an event for the client in 30 seconds, it sends a noop (the javascript "null") and closes the request.

Jotspot Live

Jotspot Live (*http://jotlive.com/*) is a live, multiuser wiki environment that uses HTTP Streaming to update message content (Figure 6-12). In an interview with Ajaxian.com (*http://www.ajaxian.com/archives/2005/09/jotspot_live_li.html*), developer Abe Fettig explained the design is based on LivePage (see the previous example).

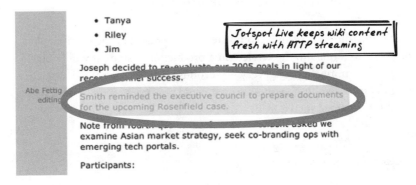

FIGURE 6-12. *JotSpot Live*

Realtime on Rails

Martin Scheffler's Realtime on Rails (*http://www.uni-weimar.de/~scheffl2/wordpress/?p=19*) is a real-time chat application that uses service streaming on Firefox and, because of the restrictions described in the earlier "Solution," *Periodic Refresh* on other browsers.

Lightstreamer engine

Lightstreamer (*http://www.lightstreamer.com/*) is a commercial "push engine" used by companies in finance and other sectors to perform large-scale HTTP Streaming. Because it works as a standalone server, there are many optimizations possible; the company states that 10,000 concurrent users can be supported on a standard 2.4GHz Pentium 4 (*http://www.softwareas.com/http-streaming-an-alternative-to-polling-the-server#comment-3078*).

Pushlets framework

Just van den Broecke's Pushlets framework (*http://www.pushlets.com/doc/whitepaper-s4.html*) is a Java servlet library based on HTTP Streaming that supports both page-streaming and service-streaming mechanisms.

Code Refactoring: AjaxPatterns Streaming Wiki

The Basic Wiki Demo (*http://ajaxify.com/run/wiki*) updates messages with *Periodic Refresh*, polling the server every five seconds. The present Demo (*http://ajaxify.com/run/wiki/streaming*) replaces that mechanism with service streaming. The AjaxCaller library continues to be used for uploading new messages, which effectively makes it a back-channel.

The *Web Service* remains generic, oblivious to the type of client that connects to it. All it has to do is output a new message each time it detects a change. Thus, it outputs a stream like this:

```
<message>content at time zero</message>
<message>more content a few seconds later</message>
<message>even more content some time after that </message>
... etc. ...
```

To illustrate how the server can be completely independent of the client application, it's up to the client to terminate the service (in a production system, it would be cleaner for the service to exit normally; e.g., every 60 seconds). The server detects data changes by comparing old messages to new messages (it could also use an update timestamp if the message table contained such a field):

```
while (true) {
  ...
  foreach ($allIds as $messageId) {
    ...
    if ($isNew || $isChanged) {
      print getMessageXML($newMessage); // prints "<message>...</message>"
      flush();
    }
  }
  sleep(1);
}
```

The browser sets up the request using the standard open( ) and send( ) methods. Interestingly, there's no onreadystatechange handler because we're going to use a timer to poll the text. (In Firefox, a handler might actually make sense, because onreadystatechange seems to be called whenever the response changes.)

```
xhReq.open("GET", "content.phtml", true);
xhReq.send(null);
// Don't bother with onreadystatechange - it shouldn't close
// and we're polling responsetext anyway
...
pollTimer = setInterval(pollLatestResponse, 2000);
```

pollLatestResponse( ) keeps reading the outputted text. It keeps track of the last complete message it detected using nextReadPos. For example, if it's processed two 500-character messages so far, nextReadPos will be 1001. That's where the search for a new message will begin. Each complete message after that point in the response will be processed sequentially. Think of the response as a work queue. Note that the algorithm doesn't assume the response ends with </message>; if a message is half-complete, it will simply be ignored.

```
function pollLatestResponse( ) {
  var allMessages = xhReq.responseText;
  ...
  do {
    var unprocessed = allMessages.substring(nextReadPos);
    var messageXMLEndIndex = unprocessed.indexOf("</message>");
    if (messageXMLEndIndex!=-1) {
      var endOfFirstMessageIndex = messageXMLEndIndex + "</message>".length;
      var anUpdate = unprocessed.substring(0, endOfFirstMessageIndex);
      renderMessage(anUpdate);
      nextReadPos += endOfFirstMessageIndex;
    }
  } while (messageXMLEndIndex != -1);
```

After some time, the browser will call xhReq.abort( ). In this case, it's the browser that stops the connection, but as mentioned earlier, it could just as easily be the server.

Finally, note that the uploading still uses the AjaxCaller library. So if the user uploads a new message, it will soon be streamed out from the server, which the browser will pick up and render.

Alternatives

Periodic Refresh

Periodic Refresh (Chapter 10) is the obvious alternative to HTTP Streaming. It fakes a long-lived connection by frequently polling the server. Generally, Periodic Refresh is more scalable and easier to implement in a portable, robust manner. However, consider HTTP Streaming for systems, such as intranets, where there are fewer simultaneous users, you have some control over the infrastructure, and each connection carries a relatively high value.

TCP connection

Using a *Richer Plugin* like Flash or Java, the browser can initiate a TCP connection. The major benefit is protocol flexibility—you can use a protocol that's suitable for long-lived connections, unlike HTTP, whose stateless nature means that servers don't handle long connections very well. One library that facilitates this pattern is Stream (*http://www. stormtide.ca/Stream/*), consisting of an invisible Flash component and a server, along with a JavaScript API to make use of them.

Related Patterns

Distributed Events

You can use *Distributed Events* (Chapter 10) to coordinate browser activity following a response.

Metaphor

Think of a "live blogger" at a conference, continuously restating what's happening each moment.

Want To Know More?

* Donovan Preston on his creation of LivePage (*http://ulaluma.com/pyx/archives/2005/05/ multiuser_progr.html*)

* Alex Russell on Comet (*http://alex.dojotoolkit.org/?p=545*)

Acknowledgments

Thanks to Donovan Preston and Kevin Arthur for helping to clarify the pattern and its relationship to their respective projects, LivePage and Stream.

On-Demand JavaScript

Behaviour, Bootstrap, CrossDomain, Dynamic, JavaScript, LazyLoading, OnDemand, ScriptTag

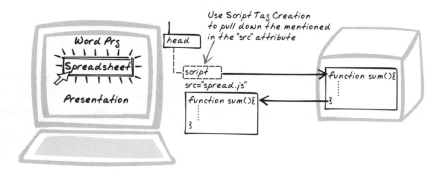

FIGURE 6-13. On-Demand JavaScript

Goal Story

Bill's logging into his bank web site. The login form comes up straight away, and as he types in his username and password, the browser is quietly downloading the JavaScript necessary for the rest of the application.

Problem

How can you deploy lots of JavaScript code?

Forces

- Ajax Apps make heavy use of JavaScript. Richer browser behavior means bulkier Java-Script to download.

- Downloading JavaScript has a performance impact. Interaction cannot fully begin until all initial JavaScript has been loaded.

- Bandwidth is also a concern with heavy JavaScript content. Often, not all JavaScript that's loaded is actually used, leading to a waste of bandwidth.

Solution

Download and run JavaScript snippets. The initial page load includes some Java-Script code, which—among other things—contains the bootstrapping code necessary to pull down further JavaScript. There are two techniques available: *Script Tag Creation* and *Service Eval*. Each will now be described, following by three main applications of the pattern.

With *Script Tag Creation*, use DOM manipulation to inject a new script element into the page. Perhaps surprisingly, the effect will be exactly the same as if the <script> tag had been encountered on startup: the referenced JavaScript will be downloaded and executed automatically. The tag can be attached to either the head or the body, though the former is more common as that's where you'd usually find script tags:

```
var head = document.getElementsByTagName("head")[0];
script = document.createElement('script');
script.id = 'importedScriptId';
script.type = 'text/javascript';
script.src = "http://path.to.javascript/file.js";
head.appendChild(script);
```

How will you know when the script has loaded? It seems browsers vary in their behavior here, with some loading the script synchronously and some not. In IE, you can be notified with a mechanism similar to XMLHttprequest's (*http://www.xml.com/lpt/a/2005/11/09/fixing-ajax-xmlhttprequest-considered-harmful.htmlonreadystatechange*). With other browsers, you might need to keep polling for some indication it's loaded (where the indication depends on what the script is meant to do). If you happen to control the server script, you could implement a notification mechanism; i.e., complete the script by calling back to a listener, if it exists. There's actually a promising proposal, JSONP (*http://bob.pythonmac.org/archives/2005/12/05/remote-json-jsonp/*), which aims to have a simple, flexible mechanism like this, standard across the entire industry.

Script Tag Creation doesn't let you retrieve any old text; it has to be valid JavaScript. And your script won't be able to read it directly because the browser will use it only for evaluation. So how can you get hold of some data from an external server? The most common way is for the remote JavaScript to assign a variable to the required data:

```
var characters = new Array("Mario", "Sonic", "Lara");
```

The content is usually a data structure, just like a standard *JSON Message*, but it requires an assignment as well, in order to be referenced in the code. It could also be a function that returns the desired value. Either way, the browser code has to use whatever name is mentioned in the script, which isn't ideal. Again, the idea of a flexible script mechanism like J is worth considering, as it would let the caller decide on the variable name.

Service Eval is the other technique for On-Demand JavaScript, though not as prominent as *Script Tag Creation* for reasons we'll discuss later. Under *Service Eval*, a *Web Service* is called with a standard *XMLHttpRequest Call*, it outputs some JavaScript as response content, and the JavaScript is then executed with an eval( ) call. We're just inspecting the *XMLHttpRequest Call's* responseText property, which we could manipulate before evaluating, so the body doesn't have to be a complete, valid piece of JavaScript (unlike with *Script Tag Creation*).

Any code not inside a function will be executed immediately. To add new functionality for later on, the JavaScript can add directly to the current window or to an object that's already known to exist. For example, the following can be sent:

```
self.changePassword = function(oldPassword, newpassword) {
  ...
}
```

The XMLHttpRequest callback function just needs to treat the response as plain-text and pass it to eval( ). A warning: here again, asynchronicity rears its ugly head. You can't assume the new code will be available immediately after requesting it, so don't do this:

```
if (!self.changePassword) {
  requestPasswordModuleFromServer( );
}
changePassword(old, new) // Won't work the first time because
                         // changePassword's not loaded yet.
```

Instead, you either need to make a synchronous call to the server, add a loop to keep checking for the new function, or explicitly make the call in the response handler.

On-Demand JavaScript has three distinct applications:

Lazy Loading
: Defer loading of bulky JavaScript code until later on. Works with either On-Demand JavaScript technique (*Service Eval* or *Script Tag Creation*).

Behavior Message

Have the server respond with a kind of "Behavior Message," which dictates the browser's next action. Works with either On-Demand JavaScript technique (*Service Eval* or *Script Tag Creation*).

Cross-Domain Scripting

Using *Script Tag Creation*, bypass the standard "same-origin" policy that normally necessitates a *Cross-Domain Proxy*. Works only with *Script Tag Creation*.

Let's look at Lazy Loading first. Conventionally, best practice has been to avoid including JavaScript unobtrusively—by including it in one or more script tags:

```
<html>
  <head>
    <script type="text/javascript" src="search.js"></script>
    <script type="text/javascript" src="validation.js"></script>
    <script type="text/javascript" src="visuals"></script>
  </head>
  ...
</html>
```

Lazy Loading builds on this approach to suggest just a minimal initialization module in the initial HTML:

```
<html>
  <head>
    <script type="text/javascript" src="init.js"></script>
  </head>
  ...
</html>
```

The initialization module declares whatever actions are required to start up the page and perhaps enough to cover typical usage. In addition, it must perform a bootstrapping function, pulling down new JavaScript on demand.

The second application, Behavior Message, is a variant of the *HTML Message* pattern. Whereas Lazy Loading sets up library code for ongoing use, Behavior Messages take some transient code and runs eval( ) on it immediately—the script is not wrapped inside a function (although it may define some functions that it calls). Effectively, the browser is asking the server what to do next.

Cross-Domain Scripting is the third application of this pattern. script tags have always been able to include source JavaScript from external domains. The rule not only applies to static <script> tags, but also to dynamically created script tags as in the *Script Tag Creation* technique. Thus, unlike with XMLHttpRequest and IFrame, your script can directly access external content this way. And because the src property can be any URL, you can pass in arguments as CGI variables. The idea is becoming rather popular, with companies such as Yahoo! offering JavaScript APIs specifically for this approach (see "Real-World Examples," later in this section).

Running a script from an external domain can be useful when you trust it, and ideally control it. Other times, it's a definite security risk. Douglas Crockford, creator of JSON warns of the havoc an external script can wreak (*http://www.mindsack.com/uxe/dynodes/*) (emphasis mine):

> That script can deliver the data, but it runs with the same authority as scripts on the base page, so it is able steal cookies or misuse the authorization of the user with the server. A rogue script can do destructive things to the relationship between the user and the base server.... **The unrestricted script tag hack is the last big security hole in browsers.** It cannot be easily fixed because the whole advertising infrastructure depends on the hole. Be very cautious.

Decisions

Will you use Service Eval or Script Tag Creation?

The choice is between *Service Eval* and *Script Tag Creation* depends on several factors. *Service Eval* has the following benefits over *Script Tag Creation*:

- Being based on XMLHttpRequest, there's a standard mechanism for being notified when the script is ready, so there's no risk of calling functions that don't yet exist.

- You get access to the raw script code.

- There's more flexibility on the message format: you can, for example, send several JavaScript snippets inside different XML nodes, and have the browser script extract them out.

And *Script Tag Creation* has a couple of benefits over *Service Eval*:

- You can load JavaScript from external domains. This is the only significant functional difference between the two styles.

- The JavaScript will automatically be evaluated in much the same way as the JavaScript linked in the static HTML is evaluated when the <script> tag is first encountered. Thus, you don't have to explicitly add variables and functions to the document in order to use them later; you just declare them normally.

With Lazy Loading, how will you break modules down?

You'll need to decide how to carve up your JavaScript. Standard principles of software development apply: a module should be well-focused, and intermodule dependencies should be avoided where possible. In addition, there are web-specific concerns:

- Ideally, any given module is either not used at all, or used in entirety. What you don't want is a 5000-line module that's downloaded to retrieve a 3-line function. It's a waste of bandwidth that defeats the main purpose of On-Demand JavaScript.

- You need one or more modules present on startup. At least one is required to kick off further downloads as required.

- Keep in mind that code will probably be cached locally. Alexander Kirk has done some experimentation with caching of On-Demand JavaScript (*http://alexander.kirk.at/2005/10/11/caching-of-downloaded-code-testing-results/*), and it turns out that all major browsers will cache code created with *Script Tag Generation*. You can usually ensure that responses from XMLHttpRequest are also cached.

With Lazy Loading, at what stage will the script download the JavaScript?

It's easiest to download the JavaScript just before it's required, but that's not always the best approach. There will be some delay in downloading the JavaScript, which means the user will be waiting around if you grab it at the last possible moment. When the user's actions or the system state suggest some JavaScript will soon be needed, consider downloading it immediately.

Predicting if JavaScript is needed is an example of *Predictive Fetch* (Chapter 13)—grabbing something on the hunch that it might be needed. You need to make a trade-off about the likelihood it's required against the hassle caused if you hold off until later. For example, imagine you have some JavaScript to validate a completed form. If you wait until the end, you'll definitely not be wasting bandwidth, but it's at the expense of the user's satisfaction. You could download it when there's one field to go, or two fields, or when the form's first loaded. Each option increases the chance of a wasted download, but increases the chance of a smoother validation procedure.

Real-World Examples

MapBuilder

MapBuilder (*http://mapbuilder.sourceforge.net*) is a framework for mapping web sites (Figure 6-14). It uses On-Demand JavaScript to reduce the amount of code being downloaded. The application is based on a Model-View-Controller paradigm. Model information is declared in an XML file, along with the JavaScript required to load corresponding widgets. When the page starts up, only the required JavaScript is downloaded, instead of the entire code base. This is therefore a partial implementation of this pattern; it does ensure that only the minimal subset of JavaScript is ever used, but it doesn't load pieces of the code in a lazy, on-demand style.

Delicious/Yahoo! APIs

Social bookmarking web site Delicious (*http://del.icio.us*), and its owner, Yahoo!, both offer JSON-based APIs, with appropriate hooks to allow direct access from the browser via *Script Tag Creation*. The Delicious API (*http://del.icio.us/help/json*) will create a new object with the result (or populate it if it's already present). The Yahoo! API (*http://developer.yahoo.net/common/json.html*) allows you to specify a callback function in your script that the JSON will be passed to.

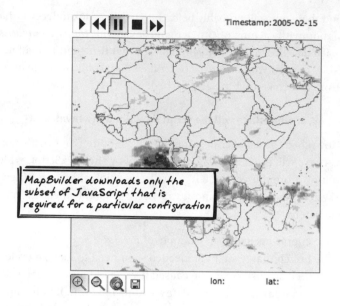

FIGURE 6-14. MapBuilder

Dojo packaging framework

Dojo (*http://dojotoolkit.org/download*) is a comprehensive framework aiming to simplify JavaScript development. As such, it provides a number of scripts, of which an individual project might only use a subset. To manage the scripts, there's a Java-like package system, which lets you pull in new JavaScript as required (*http://dojo.jot.com/WikiHome/Documents/ DojoPackageSystem*). You need only include a single JavaScript file directly:

```
<script type="text/javascript" src="/dojo/dojo.js"></script>
```

You then pull in packages on demand with the Dojo API:

```
dojo.hostenv.moduleLoaded("dojo.aDojoPackage.*");
```

Running the above command will cause Dojo to automatically download the modules under dojo.aDojoPackage.*

JSAN import system

The JavaScript Archive Network (JSAN) (*http://openjsan.org*) is an online repository of scripts. As well, it includes a library for importing JavaScript modules, also a convention similar to Java. The following call:

```
JSAN.use('Module.To.Include');
```

---

* It's possible not all modules will be downloaded, because the precise set can be defined by the package author and can be made dependent on the calling environment (whether browser or command line).

is mapped to *Module/To/Include.js*. `JSAN.includePath` defines all the possible top-level directories where this path can reside. If the includePath is `["/","/js"]`, JSAN will look for `/Module/To/Include` and `/js/Module/To/Include`.

Code Example, AjaxPatterns On-Demand JavaScript Wiki

Introducing On-Demand JavaScript to the Wiki Demo

In the Basic Wiki Demo (*http://ajaxify.com/run/wiki*), all JavaScript is downloaded at once. But many times, users will only *read* from the wiki—why download the code to *write* to it? So this demo refactors to On-Demand JavaScript in three stages:

1. The `uploadMessage` function is extracted to a second JavaScript file, *upload.js*. There's no On-Demand JavaScript yet because both files are included.

2. A further refactoring introduces On-Demand JavaScript by ensuring that *upload.js* file is only downloaded if and when an upload occurs. This version uses *Script Tag Creation*.

3. In yet another refactoring, the *Script Tag Creation* technique is replaced with *Service Eval*.

Separate JavaScript: Extracting upload.js

In the first refactoring (*http://ajaxlocal/run/wiki/separateJS/*), the upload function is simply moved to a separate JavaScript file. The initial HTML includes the new file:

```
<script type="text/javascript" src="wiki.js"></script>
<script type="text/javascript" src="upload.js">
```

The new *upload.js* now contains the `uploadMessage` function. Reflecting the separation, a couple of parameters are introduced to help decouple the function from the main wiki script:

```
function uploadMessages(pendingMessages, messageResponseHandler) {
    ...
}
```

The calling code is almost the same as before:

```
uploadMessages(pendingMessages, onMessagesLoaded);
```

We've thus far gained a bit of modularity, but don't have a boost to performance yet, since both files must be downloaded on startup.

Script Tag Creation On-Demand JavaScript

With On-Demand JavaScript, the *upload.js* is no longer required on startup, so its reference no longer appears in the initial HTML, leaving just the main module, *wiki.js*:

```
<script type="text/javascript" src="wiki.js"></script>
```

A new function has been added to download the script. To avoid downloading it multiple times, a guard clause checks if uploadMessages already exists, and if so, immediately returns. Following the *Script Tag Creation* technique, it adds a script element to the document's head, initialized with the *upload.js* URL and a standard JavaScript type attribute:

```
function ensureUploadScriptIsLoaded() {
  if (self.uploadMessages) { // Already exists
    return;
  }
  var head = document.getElementsByTagName("head")[0];
  script = document.createElement('script');
  script.id = 'uploadScript';
  script.type = 'text/javascript';
  script.src = "upload.js";
  head.appendChild(script);
}
```

The calling script just has to invoke this function. However, as mentioned earlier in the "Solution," it's possibly downloaded asynchronously, so a check must be made here too:

```
ensureUploadScriptIsLoaded();
if (self.uploadMessages) { // If not loaded yet, wait for next sync
  uploadMessages(pendingMessages, onMessagesLoaded);
  ....
```

If scripts are loaded asynchronously by the browser, the test will actually fail the first time, because the download function will return before the script's been downloaded. But in this particular application, that doesn't actually matter much—the whole synchronization sequence is run every five seconds anyway. If the upload function isn't there yet, it should be there in five seconds, and that's fine for our purposes.

Service Eval On-Demand JavaScript

The *Script Tag Creation* code is refactored here to use an *Service Eval* instead, where an *XMLHttpRequest Call* retrieves *upload.js* and evals it. The initial script—*wiki.js* differs only in its implementation of the JavaScript retrieval. The text response is simply passed to eval:

```
function ensureUploadScriptIsLoaded() {
  if (self.uploadMessages) { // Already exists
    return;
  }
  ajaxCaller.getPlainText("upload.js", function(jsText) { eval(jsText); });
}
```

The JavaScript response must also change. If it simply defined a global function like before; i.e.:

```
function uploadMessages(pendingMessages, messageResponseHandler) {
  ...
}
```

then the function would die when the evaluation completes. Instead, we can achieve the same effect by declaring the function as follows (this will attach the function to the current window, so it will live on after the script is evaluated).

```
uploadMessages = function(pendingMessages, messageResponseHandler) {
  ...
}
```

Related Patterns

HTML Message

The Behavior Message usage of this pattern is a companion to *HTML Message* (Chapter 9) and follows a similar server-centric philosophy in which the server-side dynamically controls browser activity.

Predictive Fetch

Apply *Predictive Fetch* (Chapter 13) to On-Demand JavaScript by downloading JavaScript when you anticipate it will soon be required.

Multi-Stage Download

The Lazy Loading application of this pattern is a like *Multi-Stage Download*, which also defers downloading. The emphasis in Multi-Stage Download is downloading semantic and display content rather than downloading JavaScript. In addition, that pattern is more about downloading according to a prescheduled sequence rather than downloading on demand.

Want to Know More?

- Dynamic Data Using the DOM and Remote Scripting, A Tutorial by Thomas Brattli (*http://www.dhtmlcentral.com/tutorials/tutorials.asp?id=11*)

CHAPTER SEVEN

Dynamic Behavior

WITH THE TECHNOLOGIES COVERED SO FAR, WE CAN CHANGE THE DISPLAY AND TALK TO THE SERVER.
But what will trigger these actions? Ajax Apps are generally driven from within the
browser, so that's where the actions will be triggered. Broadly speaking, there are two
types of triggers, each covered here: *User Actions*, such as mouse clicks and keypresses,
and *Scheduling*, where actions are scheduled to be run at some point in the future.

User Action

Action, Change, Click, Control, DHTML, DOM, Events, Keyboard, Mouse, Move, Type, Widget

FIGURE 7-1. User Action

Goal Story

Pam is booking a trip on the corporate travel planner. She sees a form with the usual fields and clicks on location. Suddenly, a list of cities fades in beside the form, and Pam selects Paris. Beside the city list, a second list appears, this one showing approved hotels. Pam chooses the Hilton, and both lists disappear. Pam's pleased to proceed with the destination on the updated form, which now reads, "Paris Hilton."

Problem

How can the application respond to user activity?

Forces

- A rich application allows users to interact with it, frequently and in different ways.

- Responses must be as quick as possible, so as to streamline performance, keep user attention, and help the user understand the application's cause-effect model.

- Using form submissions as the only response to user activity is slow and limits interactivity.

Solution

Handle most User Actions within JavaScript, using event handlers. The essence of Ajax is rich browser-based interaction, and DOM events are the technology that make it happen. DOM objects can register event handlers, functions that are notified when events occur. This callback model should be familiar to anyone who's worked with desktop GUI frameworks.

Let's say you want to run the following function when the user clicks a shutdown button:

```
function shutdown( ) {
  if (confirm("Are you sure you want to shutdown?")) {
    postShutdownMessageToServer( );
  }
}
```

EVENT HANDLING, BEHIND THE SCENES

If you've not worked with a modern user interface framework such as Java's Swing, you might wonder how JavaScript events work. The answer is that, behind the scenes, the operating system tells the browser what the user's doing, and the browser then passes this information to the script. For instance, the operating system—monitoring keyboard and mouse input—might notice that the user hit "X" while the keyboard focus was on the browser window. It will then notify the browser, and the browser will decide which element within the current web page has keyboard focus. If that element happens to have an associated keypress event handler, the browser will arrange for it to be invoked. Just prior to invoking it, it will construct an event object indicating the key that was pressed ("X"), the object that had focus at the time, and auxiliary information like the current mouse location and the current time. The browser will derive some of this information from the previous operating system notification, so other information might be queried there and then. When the event handler is invoked, this event object will be passed in as an argument.

User Actions are events associated closely with the DOM and use the same callback handler mechanism as many other programming environments, described by Gamma et al.'s (1995) Observer pattern. You'll see callback handlers used in other situations too:

onload and onunload are technically the same type of event as the User Actions described in this pattern because they work on DOM elements and use the same syntax. They relate to element lifecycles as opposed to user activity, which is why this pattern doesn't include them in the definition of User Actions. In most scripts, only the window (or document) onload is used; as this pattern shows, it's a good place to register User Actions, among other things. onunload is sometimes used to save data or confirm the user wants to quit.

The *XMLHttpRequest Call* (Chapter 6) pattern shows how you can register a callback to be notified of network activity as a remote call proceeds.

The *Scheduling* pattern shows how you can register a function to be executed at a certain time, or at fixed periods. There's no argument passed in, but the mechanism is similar to a DOM object event callback.

The simplest way to set this up is to declare a button with an onclick event handler:

```
<button id="quitButton" onclick="shutdown();"/>Quit</button> <!-- Obtrusive -->
```

Now the web browser will arrange for shutdown( ) to be called whenever the button is clicked. However, we can improve on this, because the above declaration mixes JavaScript with HTML. It's cleaner to just declare the button and deal with an event handler in a separate JavaScript file. Since we always want this behavior, we should declare it as soon as the page loads. To run something when the page loads, we can use another event handler that is triggered by browser activity rather than a User Action: onload.

```
[HTML]
<button id="quitButton"/>Quit</button>

[Javascript]
window.onload = function() {
  quitButton.onclick = shutdown;
}
```

Note that we're declaring this inside `window.onload` instead of "out in the open"; if you do the latter, you might get an error because the script might be executed before the button is actually on the page. You'll see the `window.onload` idiom used in most JavaScript code, including all the Ajax Patterns demos.

Instead of referencing a callback function, it's sometimes convenient to define the callback as a closure (anonymous function), as in:

```
quitButton.onclick = function() {
  if (confirm("Are you sure you want to shutdown?")) {
    postShutdownMessageToServer();
    quitButton.onclick=null;
  }
}
```

Registering events with JavaScript, as opposed to in HTML tags, is an example of unobtrusive JavaScript because it separates JavaScript from HTML. And defining the event handler in JavaScript also has another benefit: you can dynamically redefine actions in response to system events. Our `shutdown()` method could also redefine the handler to avoid a double shutdown:

```
function shutdown() {
  if (confirm("Are you sure you want to shutdown?")) {
    postShutdownMessageToServer();
    quitButton.onclick=null; // Quit button no longer triggers an event.
  }
}
```

Notice the model here involves a single handler for any event type; the above commands *set* the handler, in a manner that will remove any existing handlers. In most cases, that's just fine, and it has the merit of being completely portable. In some situations, though, it's nice to *add* a handler instead as it makes the code more modular. Two separate library functions can then register for the same events, without having to be aware of each other. Likewise, a function for removing would also be nice:

```
addEvent(quitButton, "click", postShutdownMessageToServer);
...
removeEvent(quitButton, "click", postShutdownMessageToServer);
```

Browsers do offer support for this functionality, but it's unfortunately varied, and a portable solution has been notoriously difficult. So much so that a competition was recently held to find the best `addEvent()` and `removeEvent()` functions, and you can find the winner, a 15-line script online (*http://www.quirksmode.org/blog/archives/2005/10/how_do_i_create. html*). Dojo Toolkit (*http://dojotoolkit.org*) also supports this behavior as part of its sophisticated event library.

It's not always enough for the event handler to know *that* an event has occurred; it also needs to know *about* the event. For example, the same event handler might be used for three different buttons, in which case it will need to know which of the buttons was clicked. For this reason, the web browser creates an event object upon each user event, containing various bits of information. In Firefox, it's passed to the event handler, so you just ensure an event parameter exists:

```
function shutdown(ev) {
  ...
}
```

In previous examples, we omitted the event parameter, which is just fine since parameters are optional in JavaScript functions—omitting them just means you don't get an opportunity to use them.* As it happens, IE doesn't pass the value in anyway, and instead holds the event in a window attribute. Again, JavaScript's loose handling of parameters means you won't actually get an error by including the parameter in IE. However, the value will always be null, which isn't very useful. What all this leads to is the following boilerplate code, which you can use whenever you care about the event. An "equalizer" statement gets hold of the event whichever browser we're in:

```
function shutdown(ev) {
  event = event || window.event;
  ....
}
```

The event object contains various information, such as which element was clicked and where the mouse was. The various event types are covered next.

Decisions

What events will the script listen for?

Many events are made available to JavaScript code, and more come out with each new browser upgrade. Following are some frequently used and portable events, along with typical applications. Check the following out for more info on events: *http://www.quirksmode.org/js/events_compinfo.html*, and *http://www.gatescript.com/events.html*.

All handler functions accept a single parameter representing the event, and as discussed earlier in the "Solution," you have two options: ignore the parameter altogether (as in the initial shutdown( ) examples), or—if you care about the event details—include the parameter and equalize it (as in the shutdown(ev) examples above).

Key pressing—onkeypress, onkeydown, onkeyup

- onkeypress and onkeydown occur immediately after a key is pressed, and will also repeat if the key is held down. onkeyup is called just once, upon the key's release.

---

* Strictly speaking, you can still read all parameter values using the special arguments array.

- They can be used to enhance standard text editing. For instance, you can confine a phone number text field to contain only numbers, or you can show a word count while the user types.

- They're sometimes used to automatically leave a field once it's valid—e.g., to proceed to the next field after five digits have been added to a zip code field. However, doing so is often counter-productive, as users generally perform faster when behavior is consistent, even at the expense of minor technical shortcuts.

- They can be used to create keyboard shortcuts for custom controls. You can determine if the user's mouse is over the control with the onmouse* functions, and if so, respond to particular keypresses.

WHICH KEYS TO USE FOR SHORTCUTS?

Web browsers have their own keyboard events, such as Up and Down for scrolling and the popular Ctrl-D for bookmarking. It's best to avoid using these—they'll confuse users if the browser allows them or simply fail to work if the browser forbids them. In addition, keyboard shortcuts might also conflict with operating system shortcuts such as those for cut-and-paste. This effectively means avoiding all standard shortcuts on all major operating systems. For all these reasons, the most common shortcuts are plain old keys—letters, numbers, and symbols, with no modifiers. However, that won't work while the user's editing text, so if that happens a lot, you'll need to be inventive and perhaps offer some flexibility.

Keyboard focus—onblur, onfocus

- In the case of editable fields, onblur indicates keyboard focus has been lost, suggesting an update has probably occurred, so is often used to initiate a remote call or some validation technique.

- onfocus suggests the user has begun working on a particular object, so it can be used to show online help or change the display inside a *Status Area*.

Mouse button clicking—onmouseup, onmousedown, onclick, ondblclick

- onclick and ondblclick indicate a button has been clicked or double-clicked. onmousedown and onmouseup indicate a button has been depressed or released. These latter events are more fine-grained than clicking, which implies the sequence of mousedown followed by mouseup has completed, both on the same element (note that click won't fire if the user releases the mouse button over a different element). The button control is specifically geared for catching click events to let the user do something, and radiobuttons and checkboxes can also be associated with click listeners to indicate changes.

- onmousedown and onmouseup can be used for panning behavior and for custom drag-and-drop functionality.

Mouse movement—onmouseover, onmouseout

- onmouseover and onmouseout indicate the mouse has just moved over, or has just left, an element. It can be useful to keep a pointerElement variable to track which element is currently selected.

- They can be used to change an element's style when the mouse rolls over it. This shows it's active and can convey that this is the element that will be affected if the user clicks the mouse button right now, or perhaps hits a certain key.

- They can also be used to provide help or further information in a *Status Area* or a *Popup*.

Selection—onselect

- onselect indicates when the user has selected some text.

- By tracking the selection, the application can provide information based on what the user's selected. For example, you could let the user search on a term by selecting it, and then morph the Search Results element.

- By tracking the selection, the application can also allow transformations to occur. For example, the textarea in many modern content management applications, such as mediawiki, allows the user to select some text and then change it, just like in a word processor. To italicize text on Wikipedia, select the text and click the <i> icon, which then wraps mediawiki markup (' ') around the selected text.

Value change—onchange

- onchange indicates a value has changed, so it's often used to initiate a remote call or some validation technique. This is an alternative to onblur. Unlike onblur, it is only called if the value is actually altered.

What attributes of the event will be inspected?

The event object contains several useful pieces of information about the event and what was going on at the time. Note that some of these attributes are set even for events you may not expect. For example, the ctrlKey modifier will be set even for a mouse-click event. This would allow you to detect a Ctrl-mouse press action. However, not all attributes are always set, so you need to be careful in testing for portability.

Following are some of the portable and more frequently used attributes of the event object:

Element—target (Firefox), srcElement (IE)

- target and srcElement indicate which element the event occurred on. To equalize across browsers:

      el = ev.target || ev.srcElement

  This is useful if you have a single function listening to lot of elements—for instance, an e-commerce itemClickListener monitoring all items for a click event. Inspecting this property will tell it which particular item was clicked.

Event Type—type

- type indicates which event type took place; e.g., click.

- This is a potential code issue, because it suggests the same function has been configured to handle multiple events. If it then needs to distinguish among the different types of events, it might be worth breaking it out into a handler function for each event type, with any common routines placed elsewhere.

Key code—which (Firefox), keyCode (IE)

- which and keyCode indicate the Unicode value of the key that was pressed.* This isn't completely consistent across browsers but is easy enough to equalize. Since you can't directly register a function against a specific key, this property is the only way to decide if a certain key was pressed.

Key modifiers—altKey, ctrlKey, shiftKey

- The altKey, ctrlKey, and shiftKey are modifiers indicating if the special keys Alt, Ctrl, and Shift were being held down while a key event occurred. You can use the modifiers to introduce keyboard shortcuts to the application. Since many single-modifier shortcuts are already used by one browser or another, portable applications often need to use double-modifiers. Thus, the key-handling function will need to perform a check like:

```
if (ev.ctrlKey && ev.shiftKey) {
    ... // perform ctl-shift shortcut
}
```

- There is also a meta-key modifier, which is generally not advisable as it's not supported by IE, and in any event, available only on certain keyboards.

Mouse buttons—button

- This indicates which mouse buttons were being associated with the event. In IE, 1 is left, 2 is right, and middle is 4. The value represents the sum of all buttons being pressed, allowing you to catch "chords"—multiple keys held down at once. In Firefox, 0 is left, 1 is middle, and 2 is right.

- This is a painful area due to serious incompatibility issues (*http://www.quirksmode.org/js/events_compinfo.html*). As well as the differences above, beware of incompatibilities when one button is being depressed while another is already depressed, and also incompatibilities in which events provide this property (sometimes only mouse clicks; sometimes others).

Mouse position—clientX, clientY

- These indicates the position of the mouse pointer when the event took place, relative to the browser window.

- This is useful for image-based applications, such as maps and simulators. It's often not practical to register event handlers here, so JavaScript code—with possible help of

---

* Find character codes with the Unicode chart at *http://www.macchiato.com/unicode/charts.html*.

web remoting—can determine exactly what the user clicked on by examining the coordinates.

Will event handlers be registered after the page has loaded?

Using JavaScript and the DOM, redefining event handlers is easy enough to do, but should you do it? Redefining the effect of user events must be done with caution, as there is great potential to confuse users. Sometimes, event redefinition occurs simply because the programmer can't be bothered adding a new control, or the UI is so small that designers want to reuse an existing control. So before deciding to redefine an event, ask yourself if there are alternatives. For example, could you add a second button instead of redefining the first button's action?

A few examples where event redefinition might be worthwhile:

- For state transitions. The JavaScript may have separate start( ) and stop( ) methods, and you need a toggle button to flip the state, since that is clearer and less error-prone than separate "on" and "off" buttons.

- For enabling and disabling. There is already disabled a available for standard controls (*http://www.quirksmode.org/js/disabled.html*), but for custom controls that you may have created, you might use event redefinition to cancel or re-enable the effects of interacting with the control.

- For actions that depend on dynamic information, such as which field has input focus.

However, in all of these cases, it's usually simpler to have a single method, always registered in the same way, and to allow that method's JavaScript to decide where to route the event.

Real-World Examples

Google Reader

Google Reader (*http://google.com/reader*) is a web-based RSS aggregator (Figure 7-2). You can change the current article by mouse-clicking on article titles. An interesting feature is keyboard shortcuts—when the page contains numerous articles, clicking "j" and "k" will scroll up and down to the previous or next story.

Google Maps

Google Maps (*http://maps.google.com*) uses a dragging action to pan the map within a *Virtual Workspace*, and the arrow keys can also be used.

Backpack

37Signals' Backpack (*http://www.backpackit.com/*) maintains items in a list and illustrates how you can use *Drag-And-Drop* in an Ajax App. *Drag-And-Drop* relies on monitoring the mouse button as well as position.

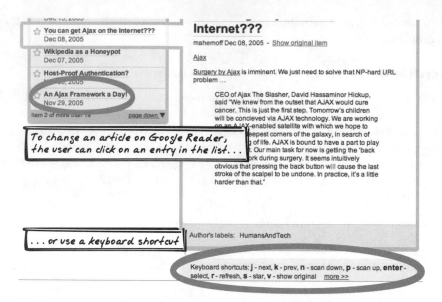

FIGURE 7-2. Google Reader

Code Example: Basic AjaxPatterns Demos

Here are a couple of basic examples from the Ajax demos. The Basic Time Demo (*http://ajaxify.com/run/time*) handles a button click like this:

```
$("defaultTime").onclick=requestDefaultTime;
```

The wiki tracks that focus and blur events in order to show the user which message is being edited and to upload any messages after a blur occurs. It also tracks mouse movement over each area, to provide an affordance indicating that the fields can be edited:

```
messageArea.onmouseout = onMessageMouseOut;
messageArea.onmouseover = onMessageMouseOver;
messageArea.onfocus = onMessageFocus;
messageArea.onblur = onMessageBlur;
```

Each of these passes to getMessage, which identifies the message element that was acted upon:

```
function getMessage(event) {
  event = event || window.event;
  return event.target || event.srcElement;
}
```

Alternatives

"Click 'n' Wait"

The conventional web app follows the "click 'n' wait" pattern, popular in 1970s mainframe-based client-server applications and revived in time for the late-1990s web generation, albeit in color. The only type of interactivity is the user submitting a static form to a server-side CGI script or clicking on a link. The script then reads some variables, does something, and outputs a whole new page of HTML. A full page refresh once in a while is OK, when a big context switch takes place, but basic updates are best controlled with JavaScript.

Richer forms

The "richer form" is richer than static HTML, but less so than Ajax. It involves enhancing a standard form with dynamic behavior, so as to make things clearer and help prevent the frustrating validation errors that often come back from the server. For instance, DHTML can be used to ensure a user enters only digits into a credit card field or to add some pop-up instructions for a form field.

Related Patterns

Display Morphing, Page Rearrangement

Display manipulation, as discussed in *Display Morphing* and *Page Rearrangement* (Chapter 5), is often triggered by User Events.

XMLHttpRequest Call, IFrame Call

Web remoting, as discussed in *XMLHttpRequest Call* and *IFrame Call* (Chapter 6), is often triggered by User Actions.

Scheduling

Cron, Event, Future, Loop, Periodic, Plan, Repeating, Schedule, Sequence, Timeout

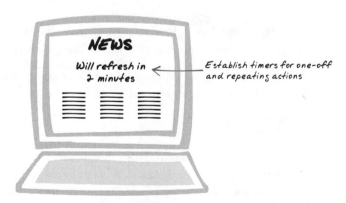

FIGURE 7-3. Scheduling

Goal Story

Frank's panning across a map of the factory. To ensure he monitors all regions, each is color-coded according to how recently it was investigated. It's implemented with Scheduling: after 5 idle minutes, the room turns orange; after 10 minutes, it turns red.

Problem

How can you run actions in the future, or repeatedly?

Forces

- Sometimes, an application needs to repeatedly run the same action; e.g., to extract new data from the server or to monitor application state.

- Sometimes, an application needs to run an action at some future time; e.g., to warn a user his session is about to time out.

- The server can't initiate a connection to the client, so there's no way to have the server "wake up" the client according to a schedule.

Solution

Use JavaScript timers to schedule actions. JavaScript's timer mechanism lets you schedule a one-off action or an action repeating at fixed intervals. In either case, what you specify is an action and a period of time in milliseconds. Note: an online demo (*http://ajaxify.com/run/scheduling*) illustrates the code concepts throughout this section and the code snippets loosely follow from the demo.

The naïve way to run an event in the future would be:

```
sleep(5000); // Nope, won't work.
expire();
```

That won't work because JavaScript doesn't have a sleep() capability—you can't just block in the middle of a script.* Instead, you need to schedule the execution.

The most basic usage is planning a one-off event in the future. For example, suppose an e-commerce application wants to expire a price offer after five seconds:

```
setTimeout(expire, 5000);
function expire() { $("price").innerHTML = "Expired"; }
```

What if something happens and you want to cancel the timer. For example, the user starts typing in a deal quantity, and the e-commerce application wants to hold off to give the user some more time. setTimeout actually returns a timer object, which allows for cancellation:

```
var expiryTimer;
...
expiryTimer = setTimeout(expire, 5000);
```

---

* There are some workarounds (*http://www.faqts.com/knowledge_base/view.phtml/aid/1602/fid/143*), though they're not really suitable for production.

```
$("dealQuantity").onkeypress = function( ) { // User typed something.
  clearTimeout(expiryTimer);
};
```

In this example, it might make more sense to *postpone*, rather than cancel, expiry alto-gether. You can achieve this by creating a new timer:

```
var expiryTimer;
...
expiryTimer = setTimeout(expire, 5000);
$("dealQuantity").onkeypress = function( ) { // User typed something.
  clearTimeout(expiryTimer);
  expiryTimer = setTimeout(expiryTimer, 2000); // 2 secs more after a keystroke.
};
```

So far, the future action has been a single function call (expire( )). Sometimes, it's more convenient to say what happens as part of the timeout, in which case you can wrap it all in a string. This prevents the need to create a function specifically to handle the timeout. The string will be evaluated upon timeout:

```
setTimeout("'$('price').innerHTML = 'Expired'", 5000); // Got rid of the function.
```

A string is also useful when you want to specify an argument, either fixed or dependent on some variable:

```
setTimeout("expireWithMessage('The deal is off!')", 5000);
setTimeout("expireWithMessage(name + ' deal is off!')", 5000);
```

You can pass a function instead of a string:

```
setTimeout(function( ) {
  expireWithMessage(name + ' deal is off!'); // Caution!
}, 5000);
```

That will work, but beware: the expression will evaluate at time of execution, not declara-tion. The name variable will resolve to the value of name when the timer fires, not when it's created. To make it more concrete, here's a script that issues two alerts. What do you think they say?

```
var name = "Ye Olde DotCom";
setTimeout("alert('Dealing with " + name + "')", 3000);
setTimeout(function( ) {
  alert(name + ' deal is off!'); // Caution!
}, 5000);
name = "New Formula 2.0";
```

If you run this script at *http://ajaxify.com/run/scheduling/name/*, you'll see two alerts:

```
Dealing with Ye Olde DotCom
New Formula 2.0 is off
```

What's going on? In the first case, name is packed into a new string object when the timer's created. That complete string will be used when the timer fires. In contrast, the second case involves a variable, name, which—being an ordinary JavaScript variable—is a pointer to some memory location. The value in the memory location will only be looked up when the timer fires.

How, then, do you pass an argument to the scheduled function so that it will evaluate when you set up the timer rather than when the timer actually fires? The easiest way is to build up a string, as shown above, but that's ugly for a long block of code. There's another technique based on closures, illustrated in a further refactoring (*http://ajaxify.com/run/scheduling/name/*). It's based on an idea by Scott Isaacs; see his explanation for more details (*http://spaces.msn.com/members/siteexperts/Blog/cns!1pNcL8JwTfkkjv4gg6LkVCpw!340.entry*).

The second type of Scheduling is repetition, and the mechanism is almost identical to one-off event handling. Instead of `setTimeout`, use `setInterval`. Again, the call will return a timer object, useful if you want the option of canceling the loop with `clearTimeout`. The second argument is again a period of time, but with `setInterval`, it represents the loop interval. The following code will call `refreshData` every five seconds:

```
setInterval(refreshData, 5000);
```

A common alternative is to loop with `setInterval`. Here, a new call to the same function is rescheduled, usually subject to some condition. Thus, the function call is repeated until some criterion has been reached.

The timing mechanism isn't super-precise, especially when the user's running lots of programs at the same time and the browser's managing several web pages at once. If timing is important, be sure to test on the targeted browser platforms and ensure your program compensates for any lag. For instance, you might need to cut off an animation effect if periodic timestamp queries suggest it's taking too long.

Real-World Examples

Claude Hussenet's Portal

Claude Hussenet's portal (*http://claudehussenet.com/*; see Figure 7-4) shows various news information, and uses a timer to keep it fresh, as discussed in *Periodic Refresh* (Chapter 10).

Google Suggest

Google Suggest (*http://www.google.com/webhp?complete=1&hl=en*) offers *Suggestions* from the server as you type a query (Figure 7-5). Instead of submitting the query string upon each keystroke, it uses a timer to limit how many queries are sent per second. The pattern's described in *Submission Throttling* (Chapter 10).

Apple iTunes counter

As iTunes Music Store neared its 500 millionth song download, Apple decorated its homepage (*http://apple.com*) with a counter that appeared to show the number of downloads in real-time. In reality, it was a *Guesstimate*. Every few minutes, it would grab the real sales data from the server and estimate how many songs are being sold per second. Between

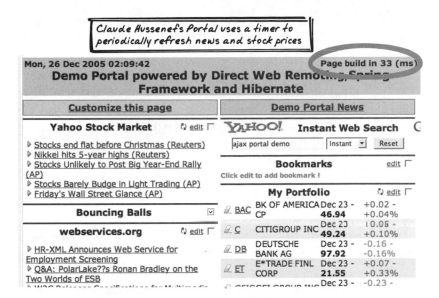

Claude Hussenet's Portal uses a timer to periodically refresh news and stock prices

FIGURE 7-4. Claude Hussenet's portal

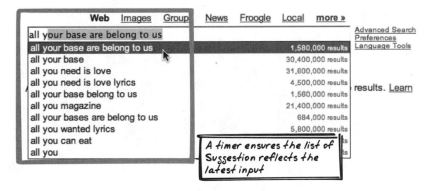

A timer ensures the list of Suggestion reflects the latest input

FIGURE 7-5. Google Suggest

those checkpoints, it would use a timer, combined with the estimated sales rate, to continuously update the counter display.

Backpack

37Signals' Backpack (*http://www.backpackit.com/*) maintains items in a list. When data changes, it uses a visual effect known as the "Yellow Fade Technique," where some text lights up and then fades away. As with most visual effects (see *One-Second Spotlight*, *One-Second Mutation*, and *One-Second Motion* [Chapter 16]), there's a reliance on timers to coordinate the display across time.

Code Example: AjaxPatterns Basic Wiki

The *Periodic Refresh* Basic Wiki Demo (*http://ajaxify.com/run/wiki*) involves a loop to synchronize with the server. The functions to start and stop the loop are encapsulated in their own functions, so as to hide timer details from the rest of the code:

```
function startPeriodicSync() {
  stopPeriodicSync();
  syncTimer = setInterval(synchronise, 5000);
}

function stopPeriodicSync() {
  clearInterval(syncTimer);
}
```

How are these used? Upon loading, an initial synchronization is performed, and startPeriodicSync() is called to synchronize thereafter. When the user starts typing inside a message, stopPeriodicSync is called, and the loop starts up again when the focus leaves the message area:

```
window.onload = function() {
  synchronise();
  startPeriodicSync();
}

function onMessageFocus(event) {
  ...
  stopPeriodicSync();
}

function onMessageBlur(event) {
  ...
  startPeriodicSync();
}
```

Alternatives

HTTP Meta Refresh

The HTTP Meta Refresh tag schedules the browser to load an entire page at some future time. It's used by conventional news portals, for example, to refresh all content every 15 minutes or so. However, it's very limited since it accepts no input from the browser and forces a complete page refresh, thus destroying all browser application states.

Metaphor

Alarm clocks perform an action at a specified time, and most also have a repetition capability allowing them to annoy their owners at the same time every day.

CHAPTER EIGHT

Extended Technologies

PARADOXICALLY, WE ROUND OUT THE FOUNDATIONAL AJAX TECHNOLOGIES WITH A PATTERN THAT'S all about "non-Ajax" technologies. The term "Ajax" usually relates to the technologies provided by standard web browsers—those covered in the previous chapters. However, it's pragmatic to bend that definition when there are useful "bonus" features that require extra capabilities; hence, the *Richer Plugin* pattern.

Richer Plugin

ActiveX, Applet, Extension, Flash, Greasemonkey, Hack, Java, Mashup, Plugin, Progressive-Enhancement, Remix

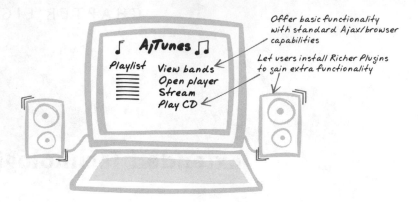

FIGURE 8-1. Richer Plugin

Goal Story

Sasha is using an online photo-sharing web site. Since she's become a big fan, she's taking the time to install some optional plugins from the site: an in-browser photo editor, a screen capture tool, and a browser toolbar.

Problem

How can you make an Ajax App even richer?

Forces

- Ajax makes web interaction much more like a desktop application, but there are limits. Many applications require functionality not available to Ajax Apps.

- If you develop a desktop application, even if it connects to the Internet, you forego many advantages of an Ajax App.

Solution

Make your application "more Ajax than Ajax" with a Richer Plugin. Ajax is certainly a step up in richness, but sometimes you need more than Ajax can offer. That's when you release a Richer Plugin that users install to get even more out of your application. The concept here is "progressive enhancement"—the application works fine in standard web browsers, but by installing the Richer Plugin, users can take the interaction to the next level.

What are the things that a Richer Plugin can achieve that an Ajax App can't? Here's a summary:

Browser morphing
    Adding buttons, toolbars, bookmarks, icons; changing browser behavior.

Local file access

Reading and writing files on the user's hard drive; unlike cookies, we sometimes want very large storage capacity and the ability to keep the data locally, without ever transferring to the server.

Sound

Playing music and sound effects.

Rich graphics

Providing rich graphics, changing dynamically; although this is changing with the gradual introduction of technologies like scalable vector graphics (SVG), even these can't come close to utilizing the power of a modern display.

Hardware access

Providing input from devices such as microphones, webcams, and gamepads; output to devices like printers and portable gadgets.

Extended communication

Providing communication from the client machine to locations beyond just the base server, and in protocols other than plain old HTTP.

Operating system interaction

Catching events such as shutdown initiation, changing preferences, popping up alerts, and reading hardware information.

Keyboard shortcuts

Providing a full range of keyboard shortcuts, including those that are platform-specific, while avoiding conflicts with the browser's own keyboard shortcuts.

The browser security model imposes these restrictions on web sites because it lets users freely surf the Web with no risk of being compromised (well, low risk). In its absence, users' systems would be in constant danger from malicious web site owners, complacent web site programmers, and devious users. By releasing a Richer Plugin, you allow users to say, "I trust this site to do certain things with my computer or browser," while keeping all other web sites tied down as before.

This pattern uses a loose definition of Richer Plugin to mean anything outside standard web technologies, which can take several forms:

- Hooking into an existing browser plugin framework, like Flash, Java, or Real. These are third-party plugins that are very common in many browsers. They're often packaged with the browser, and even if not, there's a good chance the user will have previously installed them for another application. Your application should work automatically as long as the plugin's installed.

- Building a browser-specific plugin. Users will then have to explicitly install it.

- Building a companion desktop application. This is not a replacement, because the user primarily interacts through the web site, but a means for better desktop integration, with features like pop-up alerts or quick entries. Many plugins of this nature integrate with frameworks such as Konfabulator (*http://konfabulator.com*) and Growl (*http://growl.info/*).

- Exploiting browser-specific functionality, such as the scalable vector graphics (SVG) capability introduced in Firefox 1.5 or IE's ActiveX components.

The main browsers all have a standard "plugin" mechanism, often used for standard third-party platforms like Java and Flash. There are simpler ways to extend behavior if you are building your own plugin. In IE, you can include ActiveX Controls, and Firefox has its own extension framework* (*http://developer.mozilla.org/en/docs/Extensions*).

A Richer Plugin should be implemented with caution. It breaks browser portability, one of the great advantages of Ajax Apps. It creates a layer of complexity to the web site, which must target users who do and don't have the plugin installed. It also demands a different skill set from standard web development. As a rule of thumb, use Richer Plugins only when there's no standard way to implement the same functionality.

Decisions

Will you reuse a third-party plugin or develop your own?

Having decided that you need extra functionality, the biggest decision is whether or not you'll to build a browser-specific plugin or to build on a standard plugin platform like Java or Flash.

A standard plugin platform has the following advantages:

- The plugin will likely save a lot of development if there's already a specialized API.

- The plugin is usually portable across browser versions. If you write a program in Java, for example, it should run the same no matter which browser and operating system it's used on.

- The plugin might already be installed on the user's browser. Often, browsers come with Java and other plugins preinstalled. And if not, there's a good chance the user's previously installed them.

- The user—or his employer—might trust it more than your own system. People generally trust brands like Flash and Java, so they might install those plugins and nothing else.

---

* This pattern doesn't discuss the Greasemonkey Firefox extension because, although a great tool, its primary purpose is to let users re-purpose an existing web site, and just about anything that can be performed with Greasemonkey could also be performed by the web site owner.

However, there are also advantages of writing your own plugin:

- You're not locked in to a relationship with the plugin provider. You're therefore in control of issues such as licensing and management of user data, and not at the mercy of another company's future plans for the plugin—or lack thereof.

- You can implement more functionality. Plugin platforms impose their own security model because it's expected different applications will run on them. So while Flash, for example, lets you extend the browser's multimedia capabilities, you can't use it to morph the Firefox toolbar.

- You can target browser versions not supported by a particular plugin platform.

- You can control the plugin installation process, as opposed to sending the user over to a third-party site.

What will happen if the plugin's not installed?

You'll need to consider the user experience when the plugin's not installed. How will you treat content—and links to content—that requires the plugin? For example, you could hide it altogether, explain what would be present if the plugin is installed, or perhaps provide an alternative representation. You also need to consider what to say if the plugin's not available on the user's platform.

In extreme cases, you could make the plugin mandatory. This might be plausible in an intranet setting and is really quite similar to a standard desktop application. However, it might be preferred to a desktop application if users are more comfortable in a web environment.

Real-World Examples

Amazon Mini Shop

Amazon Mini Shop (*http://extensionroom.mozdev.org/more-info/amazonsearch*) is a Firefox extension that lets users search within the sidebar and summarizes the results (Figure 8-2).

Google Toolbar and Google Suggest for Firefox

Google makes available a toolbar (*http://toolbar.google.com*) for both IE and Firefox. The toolbar augments standard browser behavior with a convenient search entry as well as several other features, including Google's page rank metric for the page. Google openly notes that they may collect information about web pages being viewed, data that many people assume is used to help fine-tune their search algorithms.

Google also offers a "Google Suggest for Firefox" extension (*http://toolbar.google.com/firefox/extensions/suggest/install.html*). This is a toolbar version of the Ajax Google Suggest web site (*http://www.google.com/webhp?complete=1&hl=en*).

The Amazon Mini Shop extension adds a sidebar to Firefox for specialized Amazon searches

FIGURE 8-2. Amazon Mini Shop

Odeo

Odeo (*http://odeo.com*) is a podcast manager (Figure 8-3). The main web site interaction—functionality like subscribing and tagging—uses standard web technologies, with many Ajax techniques. In addition, Odeo offers a number of Richer Plugins. Flash is used to play and record podcasts in the browser. For pulling down podcasts to a local machine, there's an Odeo "Syncr" desktop tool and also a more specialized Apple Dashboard widget.

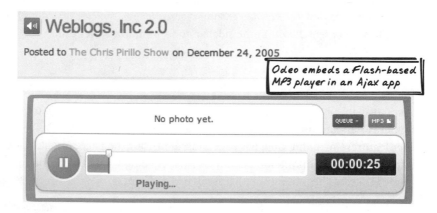

Odeo embeds a Flash-based MP3 player in an Ajax app

FIGURE 8-3. Odeo

TiddlyWiki

Jeremy Ruston's TiddlyWiki (*http://tiddlywiki.com*) is a SPA application (defined in the section "Alternatives," later in this chapter), an interesting variant of Richer Plugin. It's an entire wiki within a single HTML file, including the wiki script and the wiki content itself. Tiddlywiki is similar to Richer Plugin because it overcomes the local storage barrier by requiring users to save the wiki page locally and point the browser to that file.

Code Example: Amazon Mini Shop

It's beyond the scope of this book to cover plugins in detail, but this example gives an insight into the components of a Firefox extension, Paul Millar's Amazon Mini Shop Firefox extension (*http://extensionroom.mozdev.org/more-info/amazonsearch*). If you want to grab the code, visit the link with Firefox and install the extension. Then, look at *Extensions.rdf* in your firefox profile directory (e.g., under *~/.mozilla/firefox/* in Unix or under *c:\Windows\ Profiles\%USER%/Mozilla/Firefox*). Search for "amazoncomsearch" and you should see a nearby tag beginning with RDF:Description. Within that tag, the extension ID is in curly braces, and you need to go into a directory by that name, which is where the extension code is.

The extension contains several components. To start with, *chrome/amazoncomsearch.jar* is a jar file that can be opened with a standard unzipping utility. It contains the main resources for the extension. In Firefox, user-interfaces are set up with the XML User Language (XUL) (*http://xulplanet.com/tutorials/xultu/intro.html*), a format that looks similar to HTML. The sidebar UI is captured in one XUL file:

```
<?xml version="1.0"?>
<?xml-stylesheet href="chrome://global/skin/" type="text/css"?>

<page id="pageAmazonPanel" style="background-color: #ffffff;" title=
"Amazon Search"
        xmlns="http://www.mozilla.org/keymaster/gatekeeper/there.is.only.xul" xmlns:
html=
"http://www.w3.org/1999/xhtml" xmlns:rdf="http://www.w3.org/1999/02/22-rdf-syntax-ns#"
onload=
"disable();javascript:document.getElementById('txtAmazonSearch').focus()">

    <script type="application/x-javascript" src="chrome://amazoncomsearch/content/
amazonsearch.js"/>
    <hbox pack="center">
      <menulist flex="1" id="menuAmazonSearch" label="Search Category" onChange=
"change()">
        <menupopup id="popupAmazonSearch" onpopupshowing="popamazon()"/>
      </menulist>
    </hbox>
    ...
  </page>
```

There is also JavaScript code, which populates the UI and handles user-interface interaction similarly to a normal browser script. For example, an *XMLHttpRequest Call* is used to gather data from Amazon's web service:

```
aURL = "http://xml-"+value+".amznxslt.com/onca/xml?Service=AWSECommerceService&..."
...
httpReq.open("GET", aURL, true);
httpReq.send(null);
httpReq.onload = httpLoaded;
```

Among the remaining components, *chrome.manifest* is a meta-information file that points to the resources above. *install.rdf* provides meta-information about the application, such as its ID and creator. *install.js* is a script to handle initial installation of the extension. *defaults/preferences/ams.jar* provides defaults that are stored as standard Firefox preferences. In this case, there is only one preference: the Amazon site being searched (U.S., U.K., etc.). (You can see the settings in *prefs.js*.)

Alternatives

Desktop Client

The desktop client runs as a standard application in the user's operating system and connects to one or more servers using HTTP or any other protocol. It would make sense to use a *Desktop Client* if the required user interface is very different than a standard browser interface, or if it's difficult to extend the browser as desired. While the plugin frameworks provide more control than regular web applications have, the developer is still restricted relative to a standalone desktop client.

A variant is a "Richer Desktop Client." That is, an Ajax App to do most basic things, and a richer desktop client with extra features and improved usability. This is the strategy Microsoft might follow with Office Live.

Related Patterns

Fat Client

Fat Clients (Chapter 13) are sometimes replacements for desktop applications, used frequently and for long sessions. A Richer Plugin will enhance their experience, and the effort to set it up will eventually provide users with ample payback.

Single Page Application

Single Page Application (SPA) is a newer-than-Ajax term that describes an application whose entire logic and data are embedded in a single HTML file. Point the browser to the HTML file on a local drive; editing the data will update the file accordingly. In the extended case of Single Page Application and Development Environment (SPADE) (*http://trimpath.com/project/wiki/SinglePageApplicationAndDevelopmentEnvironment*), you can even update the code via the page itself! SPA is useful for certain specialized local applications where you want a web interface and local storage. A nice way to use it is to load it onto a

USB key along with a web browser, which allows you to maintain the content anywhere, even in the absence of a Net connection.

Bookmarklet

A bookmarklet (or "favelet") is a link that references JavaScript instead of a web location. For example, you can create a link like this: `<a href="javascript:alert('You are at' + document.location.href + '.');">Bookmark Me!</a>`. The user will be able to drag it to their toolbar, and when they click on it later on, it will run the script, which pops up the current location in this example. With a bookmarklet, you can build a custom Ajax App inside other web sites. Display Manipulation (Chapter 5) patterns and Dynamic Behavior (Chapter 7) patterns work as on a local site, so you can, for example, tweak any web site whenever the user clicks on the bookmarklet. One thing you can't do is issue *XMLHttpRequest Calls* (Chapter 6), due to the same-origin policy, but you can work around that with *On-Demand JavaScript* (Chapter 6). WizLite (*http://wizlite.com*), a collaborative annotation tool, is a great example of how powerful bookmarklets can be.

Browser-Side Cache

A Richer Plugin, with access to the local filesystem—or at least more sophisticated browser-based storage than normal cookies—can be a useful data repository for a *Browser-Side Cache* (Chapter 13).

Metaphor

Consider a regular web app as a black-and-white movie. Ajax adds color; Richer Plugin adds 3-D (or Smell-O-Rama if you wish).

Want to Know More?

- Firefox Extension Tutorial (*http://extensions.roachfiend.com/howto_bug.html*)
- Building ActiveX Controls for Internet Explorer (*http://msdn.microsoft.com/workshop/components/activex/buildax.asp*)
- Tutorial: Creating a Mozilla Extension (*http://www.mozilla.org/docs/tutorials/tinderstatus/*)

PART THREE

Programming Patterns

KNOWING THE FOUNDATIONAL TECHNOLOGIES IS ONE THING; APPLYING THEM IS ANOTHER. AJAX IS NOT rocket science, but there are still plenty of technical issues that will arise in building a serious Ajax App. The programming patterns focus on technical qualities of software—in particular:

Maintainability

Ensuring web services and browser code are easy to understand and work with

Robustness

Ensuring the application will prevent errors where possible and handle them gracefully when they do arise

Performance

Ensuring the application runs as quickly as possible and feels smooth and responsive from the user's perspective

The first chapter in this section, Web Services (Chapter 9), provides several alternative strategies for designing web services. Also related to Web Remoting, Browser-Server Dialogue (Chapter 10) looks at the flow of information between browser and server; e.g., synchronization techniques.

DOM Population (Chapter 11) covers several strategies for handling DOM population following a server response. Code Generation and Reuse (Chapter 12) contains a couple of general programming patterns for maintainability and portability. Finally, the Performance Optimization (Chapter 13) patterns are about improving not only speed of updates and communication, but also about optimizing the user experience in the face of inevitable delays.

CHAPTER NINE

Web Services

THE CONCEPT OF A WEB SERVICE HAS ALREADY BEEN INTRODUCED IN THE *WEB SERVICE* PATTERN, **BUT** the pattern leaves open many questions—for instance, what sort of messages will be sent to and from the service? How will the URLs look? How will the service relate to backend software? These are the kind of design and programming issues covered in this chapter.

RESTful Service is an overview of Representational State Transfer (REST), a popular set of patterns and idioms for consistent and intuitive web services. *RPC Service* has similar goals, but with a philosophy that leads to very different services. Neither REST nor Remote Procedural Call (RPC) are Ajax-specific, because they are general industry conventions for web services. However, the next pattern, *Ajax Stub, is* Ajax-specific, because it provides a convenient way to invoke RPC-style services from the browser.

The remaining patterns look at popular message formats used for communication between the browser and *Web Service*s. *HTML Message* is a message in HTML form, usually sent from the server to be morphed directly onto the page. In contrast, the remaining messages are raw responses that usually can't be displayed directly, and that may be transferred in both directions. They are *Plain-Text Message*, *XML Message*, and *JSON Message*.

RESTful Service

API, HTTP, REST, Standard, Universal, Web

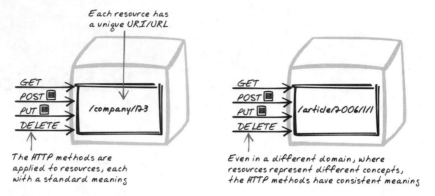

Each resource has a unique URI/URL

GET
POST
PUT
DELETE
/company/123

The HTTP methods are applied to resources, each with a standard meaning

GET
POST
PUT
DELETE
/article/2006/1/1

Even in a different domain, where resources represent different concepts, the HTTP methods have consistent meaning

FIGURE 9-1. RESTful Service

Developer Story

Devi's producing a public web site explaining pharmaceuticals to the public. The browser applications will pull down drug data from the server, and authorized users—such as drug manufacturers—will be allowed to upload new information. It's envisioned that third-party applications will also connect to the web server and provide their own user interfaces. For example, pharmacies will be able to use the information via their point-of-sale systems, and doctors will have access from their specialized consulting software. Devi opts to follow a RESTful architecture for all of the services exposed on the server. This makes it easy for the browser side of her own web app to access the data and exposes services in a standardized manner.

Problem

How do you expose services on the Web?

Forces

- The browser side of an Ajax App needs to call server-side services.

- There might be more than one browser-side application sharing the same server-side service.

- As well, it's often desirable for third-party applications to invoke the server-side service too.

- With numerous different applications—and a variety of developers—accessing the service, it ought to be easy to use.

- Taken as a whole, the server-based services in a single "application" form an Application Programming Interface (API). It's important that services work consistently within the API.

- The basic architecture of the Web does not force any type of service architecture—any given functionality could be exposed in a wide variety of styles.

Solution

Expose web services according to RESTful principles. Representational State Transfer (REST) is an architectural style—or "pattern"—guiding the architecture of web services. Like "Ajax" itself, "REST" is a broad term and can be broken down into many smaller patterns and idioms (enough to fill up an entire book!). The explanation here can't possibly do justice to the entire concept, but it's worthwhile being familiar with the general principles of REST. Because REST is such a large topic, be prepared for the reality that most real-world systems you'll encounter are only *somewhat* RESTful; they'll follow some principles and break others. Some people are now making the distinction between "High REST"—sticking closely to REST—and "Low REST"—following just a couple of core REST guidelines (*http://lesscode.org/2006/03/19/high-low-rest/*).

Motivating REST: many ways to skin a call

To motivate REST, let's consider a football service. Sufficiently authorized clients can read game records, upload new games, correct existing games, or delete games. We'll assume your backend's already written, but how would you offer it as a web service? How will client developers call it, and how will they learn about its interface?

To wit, following are a few random ways you might expose a game service—*note that these aren't necessarily RESTful!*

- GET call to a special newGame service, `http://example.com/newGame?id=995&bluebaggers=150&redlegs=60`

- POST or PUT call to a special newGame service, `http://example.com/newGame`, with an XML body like `<game id="995"><score team="bluebaggers">150</score><score team="redlegs">60</score></game>`

- POST or PUT call to a special newGame service, `http://example.com/newGame`, with a CGI-style body: `id=995&bluebaggers=150&redlegs=60`

- GET call to a multipurpose gameMaintenance service, `http://example.com/gameMaintenance/command=newGame&id=995&bluebaggers=150&redlegs=60`

- POST call to a multipurpose gameMaintenance service with a command-qualified URL, `http://example.com/gameMaintenance/command=newGame`, with an XML body like `<game id="995"><score team="bluebaggers">150</score><score team="redlegs">60</score></game>`

And we could go on. And then we could look at the other functions here. The point is this: as a service designer, you have many options for representing a single function. Is that, in itself, a problem? You might argue it's not a problem at all—just choose any old option, using some darts and a blindfold if need be. Then just create the service and document its usage—any competent developer will then be able to deal with it, right? That argument, however, is flawed on several counts:

- You might assume that the browser script for your web app, and perhaps some known external clients, are the only users of your service, making it relatively easy to create and document any service. In fact, your application resides within a larger Internet eco-system. Among the entities involved: the web browser (e.g., Firefox), which impacts issues like back-button handling and bookmarking; the web server (e.g., Apache), which impacts issues like caching and compilation; network routers and caches all along the way; robot applications such as those crawling the Web on behalf of search engines; and personal web agents that trawl through the Web on behalf of individuals. Your application will perform faster and more reliably if you follow certain conventions that are common among these entities.

- Ideally, a service should be intuitive and self-documenting: if a service is based on familiar conventions, you have only to specify the bare minimum for a developer to be able to use it. That's simply not possible if everyone chooses alternatives according to their own personal taste. The standards-based interface usually trumps the optimized interface that's technically superior but based on unfamiliar conventions. There are thousands of web services available on the Internet; developers should be able to assess them and put them into action with as little effort as possible.

- In the absence of any guiding principles, there's a disturbingly high likelihood you'll end up in tedious debates with colleagues over the most trivial issues, trying to arrive at an optimal API. (The blindfold and darts—or an impatient manager—would alleviate this kind of paralysis, but the other issues would still remain.)

So we've seen the argument for a convention-based approach to web services, but what's the convention? REST is one such convention, consisting of many different guidelines, that has broad industry support. Just about any functionality can be presented as a REST-ful API, and by doing so, it gains the advantage of a familiar, intuitive style. Many services on the Net already follow RESTful principles, to differing degrees. Also, many real-world entities such as browsers and caches tend to assume REST. These entities work better if REST is in place—a browser, for instance, might give better feedback; a cache will retain all the data that the programmer expected it to retain. And what will happen if REST is not in place? It's probably not the end of the world, but you'll find little things will go wrong and work in unexpected ways. For instance, hitting the browser's Reload button might cause a purchase order to be resubmitted. Or a cache might end up caching data it shouldn't, or it might not cache any data at all. Why these unfortunate events might occur will become clear as we learn about the RESTful principles.

Introduction to RESTful principles

So much for abstract motivation: what exactly are the RESTful principles (*http://www. xfront.com/REST-Web-Services.html*) all about? REST ultimately presents the server as a big blob of "resources" such as people, cars, or football games. Clients interact by inspecting and changing that state. Putting a purchase order on the server, for example, will trigger the server to affect the purchase described in the order. This contrasts with the Remote Procedural Call (RPC) approach, where the client would call a remote purchase( ) procedure. REST is based on data manipulation, RPC is based on procedural calls.

REST sees the universe as consisting of resources and operations performed on, and with, those resources. The resources and the operations can be represented as the HTTP concepts of URLs and call methods.

Resources as URLs

A resource is something like a "business entity" in modelling lingo. It's an entity you wish to expose as part of an API. Almost always, it's a noun; e.g., a person, a car, or a football game. Each resource is represented with a unique URL. So when you say a RESTful URL, it will be a thing rather than an action.

Operations as HTTP methods

REST leverages the existing HTTP methods, particularly GET, POST, PUT, and DELETE. Note that the XMLHttpRequest object, and some wrapper libraries such as ajaxCaller (*http://ajaxify.com/run/testAjaxCaller/*), support all these methods. If they're unfamiliar to you, consult the W3C HTTP 1.1 Specification (*http://www.w3.org/ Protocols/rfc2616/rfc2616-sec9.html*).

Another way to say it is in HTTP, any request a client can make involves a URL and an HTTP method. With REST, the URL is designed to represent a noun and the HTTP method always maps to one of several standard verbs, which will be performed against that noun.

How is the URL combined with the HTTP methods in practice? Returning to the example, a game is clearly an entity in this API. So REST says we create a scheme to expose each particular game as a unique URL—for example, *http://example.com/games/995*.

So far, this is all pretty unequivocal. Anyone familiar with REST will always be driven to create a unique URL for each game. There might be differences of opinion about the precise naming, but the basic concept will always be the same if you follow REST. Now that we have this unique URL, we can implement many functions around it, by leveraging the standard HTTP methods (*http://rest.blueoxen.net/cgi-bin/wiki.pl?RestFaq#nid1UP*).

- To get game results, the client simply issues a GET call on the URL. GET is the standard way to perform queries on the resource indicated by the URL. The response format is not dictated by REST, but XML is common due to it's self-describing and self-validating nature.

- To delete the game, the client issues a DELETE call on the URL. DELETE is the standard way to delete a resource.

- To update a game, the client builds a fresh game message and uploads it as the body of a PUT command. PUT is the standard way to update a resource's value.

- To create a new game, the correct action will depend on whether the client can guess what the game's URL will be. If the service just allocates the URL arbitrarily, perhaps

URLS OR URIS?

In strict HTTP parlance, there's a distinction to be made between Universal Resource Locators (URLs) and Universal Resource Identifier (URIs). URI is the more general term, as it describes a general resource. A URL is a particular type of URI that, in a somewhat vague sense, identifies a network location. You could define a protocol to represent books with URIs (e.g., isbn://12345), and those URIs wouldn't be URLs since they have no relationship with any network location; they are just a scheme for uniquely identifying objects. A string such as *http://ajaxpatterns.org/RESTful_Service* not only identifies an object (making it a URI), but also refers to a network location (making it a URL), one which will be used by various software to locate the resource.

Having done the Right Thing by pointing out the distinction, let me state why this pattern refers only to URLs. Most importantly, URLs are the language most developers are familiar with, even in contexts where URI is technically the appropriate term (which is arguably most of the time). Furthermore, there is confusion (*http://kyseo.blogspot.com/2005/12/uri-url-urns.html*) even among the RFCs that define these terms and the definitions have also shifted over time. The W3C states:

> People who are well-versed in URI matters tend to use "URL" and "URI" in ways that seem to be interchangable. Among these experts, this isn't a problem. But among the Internet community at large, it is. People are not convinced that URI and URL mean the same thing, in documents where they (apparently) do. When one sees an RFC that talks about URI schemes (e.g., [RFC 2396]), another that talks about URL schemes (e.g., [RFC 2717]), and yet another that talks of URN schemes ([RFC 2276]) it is natural to wonder what's the difference, and how they relate to one another. While RFC 2396 1.2 attempts to address the distinction between URIs, URLs and URNs, it has not been successful in clearing up the confusion.

Given the potential for confusion, and the fact that most developers exclusively use the term "URL," I've opted for the pragmatic approach: you'll only see "URL" used throughout this pattern, and indeed, throughout all others.

based on an auto-incrementing counter, then the client won't be able to guess it. When that happens, the new game is POSTed to a URL like *http://example.com/games,* and the server responds with the new game's URL (*http://example.com/games/995*). On the other hand, the client might be able to guess the URL, based on a naming convention. If the client guesses that the new game would have URL *http://example.com/games/2000/9/25,* then it can simply PUT the new game to that URL.

- To perform an arbitrary transaction, you'll also use one or more of these standard methods. So maybe the client wants a way to double the winner's score. In this case, there's probably no special service—the client just reads the old match, updates it, and

PUTs it back to the server. For more complicated transactions, you might design a new resource specifically to encapsulate the request (e.g., a "purchase order" resource), and the client will then be able to POST resources like this to the server. Many businesses work the same way—contracts/orders are passed around in order to request that things are done and to verify that they've been done. See the section "Handling arbitrary transactions" later in this chapter for more details.

In summary, each HTTP method will cause a well-defined action on the resource represented by the URL it operates on. The methods can be compared to SQL commands: GET is like "SELECT," DELETE is like "DELETE," POST is like "INSERT" with an auto-generated ID, and PUT is like "INSERT OR UPDATE IF EXISTS" with an ID specified.

Again, notice how most of this is unequivocal. True, you still have to decide on a precise URL convention and message formats, but that's fairly minimal. *Just by declaring "this is a REST interface," you're conveying many implicit rules to a REST-savvy developer.* Inform that developer of the URL and message conventions, and they'll be able to intuit most of the API. Compare that to an ad hoc, roll-your-own API, where each detail must be explained piecemeal. Considering that there are thousands of web services out there, it soon becomes clear why REST is an attractive option.

RESTful principles

Let's now look at the main REST principles in more detail.

URLs reflect resources

As explained in the previous section, each resource receives a unique URL. URLs generally look like nouns.

REST doesn't tell you what names to call your resources—there are infinite possibilities and the choice is up to you. They'll often reflect your conceptual model of the system and look similar to your database table names.

HTTP methods reflect actions

With REST, each HTTP method indicates the kind of action to be performed. Moreover, the REST API designer doesn't have to decide what each method means, because there are only a handful of methods, and REST standardizes the meaning of each—GETs for queries, POSTs for inserts, and so on, as explained above. Notice how resource names are *not* standardized in the same way. Businesses have different models, so you can't standardize on those things. But REST is saying that you can indeed model the resources so that the set of required actions is standard, thus ensuring APIs are consistent with one another.

Fortunately, the standard HTTP methods—when combined with a well-designed URL and resource scheme—are enough to let a client express just about anything it needs to. It's true that in an ideal world, there would be a few extra actions to make life a bit easier. For example, it would be convenient if there was a standard *LOCK* action to let a client deal exclusively with a particular resource.* However, you can still work around this by introducing a lock resource and letting clients lock things by manipulating those resources with the standard HTTP methods.

GET for queries, and only for queries

Refining the previous point, GET calls must be read-only. When you perform a read-only query of any kind, always use GET. Conversely, when your call will affect any data on the server, use one of the other methods: PUT, POST, and DELETE all change state. There are some caveats here—for example, if issuing a query ends up leaving a log message somewhere, does that constitute a change? Technically, yes; but common sense says no, it's not a significant change to the underlying resource, so it's acceptable to log the message in response to a GET request. Just be aware that the log might not read as intended; for instance, some clients will get the content from a cache, which means no log message will occur.

The reverse problem can happen too. GET requests are often cached, but the other types of requests are not. When you perform a query with POST, you deny the possibility of caching in the browser, within the client's network, or on your own server.

If you learn nothing else about REST, be sure to learn this guideline; of all the REST conventions, this is the best known and widely applied across the net (see the sidebar "The Backpack-Accelerator Incident" in this chapter).

Services should be stateless

In stateful interaction, the server remembers stuff from the past. For example, you could do this:

> Greg's Browser: Give me the next game to work on.
> Server: Work on game 995.
> ...
> Greg's Browser: Here's the result: bluebaggers 150, redlegs 60.
> Server: Thanks.
> (Server stores "bluebaggers 150, redlegs 60" for game 995.)

The server here has an implicit conversational state; it remembers the game Greg's working on. That makes testing harder, because you have to set the whole history up to test any particular interaction. Another problem is the fragile nature of the transaction; what if Greg's browser fails and ends up requesting two different games? When Greg uploads the score, the server could easily misinterpret which game he's talking about. Also, you can't cache effectively because a query result might depend on something that happened earlier.

---

* The WebDav protocol does just that. It adds several methods to HTTP, to support locking, property inspection, and moving resources around. These make REST easier to implement, but unfortunately, most Internet entities won't understand them, so it defeats one of the main purposes of REST on the open Internet.

THE BACKPACK-ACCELERATOR INCIDENT

An incident in mid-2005 highlights the importance of following "GET for queries, and only for queries" (*http://radar.oreilly.com/archives/2005/05/google_web_acce_1.html*). It involved the newly released Google Accelerator interacting with non-RESTful services. The accelerator is a proxy that jumps ahead of the user and prefetches each link in case the user should click on it (a non-Ajax example of *Predictive Fetch* [Chapter 13]). As with many other entities on the Net, it assumes services follow "GET for queries, and only for queries." The practical implication is that it indiscriminately clicks on any links.

The problem came when users logged into non-RESTful applications like Backpack (*http://backpackit.com/*). Because Backpack deletes items using GET calls, the accelerator—in its eagerness to run each GET query—ended up deleting personal data. This could happen with regular search engine crawlers too, though the issue doesn't tend to come up because they don't usually have access to personal accounts.

Some people argued Google went too far with the REST assumption (*http://www.loudthinking.com/arc/000454.html*); it's one thing to assume REST for caching a prior response, but another to proactively visit links that otherwise wouldn't have not been touched, especially when those are only visible to a logged-in user. The argument has some merit, but either way, many components will continue to make the same assumption as the Google Accelerator did, making it prudent to practice "GET for queries, and only for queries."

Furthermore, an objective of REST is to be able to switch clients at any time and receive the same result. If you switch "Greg's Browser" to "Marcia's Browser," the server will respond differently to the game result above, because it will assume Marcia's Browser is working on a different game number. While users are unlikely to switch browsers mid-conversation, other clients like caches and robots may well switch. Substitutability makes networks more scalable.

The upshot is that everything should be passed in at once. It's okay for the client to remember details about the conversation—REST says nothing about the client's activity—but the server must not. The server responses should be based on the server's global state and not on the state of the conversation; i.e.:

Greg's Browser: Give me the next game to work on.
Server: Work on game 995.

...

Greg's Browser: Here's the result **for Game 995**: bluebaggers 150, redlegs 60.
Server: Thanks, I'll store "bluebaggers 150, redlegs 60" for Game 995.

So are cookies used at all? Yes, cookies *can* be used, but mainly for authentication. They should only determine *whether or not* the server will accept a call, by not in any way *how* the server will respond. If authentication fails, an appropriate response, such as a 401 (Forbidden) header, will result. If authentication succeeds, the same call will always have the same effect, independent of the client who made the call. So if Greg's Browser says "Get All Games," Greg will see exactly the same thing as if the all-powerful administrator asked for the same thing, as long as Greg's allowed to see them. If the security policy forbids Greg from seeing all games, Greg's query will be denied. What *won't* happen is for Greg to receive just a minimal list of his own games—if that happened, the server would be using the cookie to determine the browser's response. To get a minimal list, the query must be explicit—"Get All of Greg's Games"—and of course, it must be Greg or the administrator that issues this request. If Marcia made that request, she'd get an authentication error.

An alternative to cookies is to use HTTP Basic Authentication, but this doesn't work too well in an Ajax context, because you don't have any control over the UI. The browser will typically pop up a dialog box, whereas you probably want to integrate any authentication directly into the interface, especially if using a pattern like *Lazy Registration*. HTTP Digest Authentication does allow more flexibility, but browser and server support is limited. Thus, while HTTP authentication is seen as "more pure," cookies are a reasonable workaround, provided you use them only for authentication.

Services should be idempotent

"Idempotent" means that once you pass a message to service, there's no additional effect of passing the same message again. Consider the deletion message, "Delete Game 995." You can send it once, or you can send it 10 times in succession, and the world will be the same either way. Likewise, a RESTful GET is always idempotent, because it never affects state. The basic conventions on GET/DELETE/PUT/POST, described earlier, are intended to support idempotency.

Services use hyperlinks

In resource representations returned by GET queries, use hyperlinks liberally to refer to related resources. With judicious use of hyperlinks, you can and should break information down. Instead of providing one massive response, include a modicum of information and point to further information using resource identifiers.

Services documents themselves

RESTful services can and should document themselves. The exact mechanism is not well-defined. But a couple of examples include:

- Base URLs can explain how the service works. For example, in the earlier example, *http://example.com/game/995* represents a particular game, but *http://example.com/game* represents no real entity, so its result could be an instructive document, in human-friendly language, with appropriate hyperlinks.

- Error responses should also be in human-friendly language and with examples and hyperlinks.

Services constrain data formats

As an extension to the previous point, RESTful services rely on standards such as Document Type Definitions (DTDs) and XML Schema to verify data formats as well as to document what's acceptable.

Handling arbitrary transactions

The REST definition is especially geared for creating—such as Amazon—reading, updating, and deleting (CRUD) operations. How about transactions and arbitrary actions, such as "Pause the printer" or "Email the catalogue to this user"? By definition, application-specific actions don't fit neatly with the standard REST actions. There will always be some pragmatic judgment required as to a suitably RESTful interface. A few possibilities have been mooted, with viewpoints varying (*http://rest.blueoxen.net/cgi-bin/wiki.pl?VerbsCanAlsoBeNouns*):

- If it makes sense to do so, reformulate the action as a standard persistence operation. For updates that are complex or entail business logic, you can provide a read-only service—accessed with GET queries—to help the client compute the new state.

- You can POST a message to the resource in question—for example, POST a "pause" message to a URL representing the printer.

- The server can expose a stateless "processor" resource to perform the action—e.g., a printer controller—and have clients POST command-like messages there, with URLs referencing the resources to be acted upon.

Weighing Up REST

Being a broad architectural style, REST will always have different interpretations. The ambiguity is exacerbated by the fact that there aren't nearly enough standard HTTP methods to support common operations. The most typical example is the lack of a search method, meaning that different people will design search in different ways. Given that REST aims to unify service architecture, any ambiguity must be seen as weakening the argument for REST.

Another issue is portability—while GET and POST are standard, you may encounter browsers and servers that don't deal consistently with DELETE, PUT, and other methods.

The main alternative to REST is RPC (see *RPC Service*, later). It's equally broad in definition, but the essential idea is that services are exposed at procedures. You end up POSTing into verb-like URLs such as */game/createGame?gameId=995* instead of RESTful, noun-like URLs such as */game/995*. In fact, the distinction is significant enough that some service providers, such as Amazon, actually provide separate APIs for each. As a general rule, any set of services could be exposed as either REST or RPC; it's just a question of API clarity and ease of implementation. Note also there is some overlap; as discussed in the *RPC Service* solution, RPC can still follow certain RESTful principles.

From an implementation perspective, REST and RPC differ in that REST requires some explicit design, whereas RPC tends to follow directly from the backend software model. In the example, it's likely there will be a `Game` class with a `createGame( )` method—that's just how most server-side software gets done. So it's a no-brainer to tack on a `/game/createGame` web service that mediates between the client and the backend method. In fact, there are many frameworks that will completely automate the process for you.

With REST, there's no direct mapping between web service and backend implementation—an impedance mismatch. You need to take a step back and explicitly design your API to be RESTful. If you're following feature-driven design, the API is the first thing you'll produce anyway, since the design will be "pulled" by the needs of clients, rather than "pushed" from the available technology. Once you've designed the API, the web service implementation will effectively be a kind of middleware Adaptor (see Gamma et al., 1995) to the backend services.

To summarize crudely:

- Any web service functionality can be exposed as either REST or RPC. There's a good argument that REST APIs are somewhat clearer, though that view is far from universal.

- REST APIs may be clearer, but they do require more design and maintenance because they tend to diverge from the backend technology. However, adaptor-style implementations of this nature are quite easy, so the overhead is not substantial and often justified in the effort to provide a clean interface, unaffected by the incidentals of the backend implementation.

Real-World Examples

I'm not aware of any Ajax Apps that access a truly RESTful interface on the server side. Consequently, the example here is a public API that conforms closely to REST. Note that several prominent industry interfaces are not covered here, because though they promote themselves as RESTful, they tend to break quite a few basic principles—for example, Amazon's REST API (*http://rest.blueoxen.net/cgi-bin/wiki.pl?HowAmazonsRESTComparesWithREST*). In industry parlance, REST is sometimes synonymous with "not SOAP," and it's incorrectly assumed that an interface is RESTful as long as it uses GET for reads and POST for writes.

Blogger API

Atom is a feed protocol built around RESTful principles. Blogger offers a good description on its use of Atom in its public API (*http://code.blogger.com/archives/atom-docs.html*). The API lets third-party applications read and change Blogger blogs. Blogger themselves could theoretically build an Ajax App that directly calls on the API.

A blog entry is one important resource in Blogger's API. For example, entry ID 1000 for user 555 "lives at" *http://blogger.com/atom/555/1000*. So to read that entry, just issue a GET on that URL. To change the entry there, just PUT an XML document to the same URL. To add a new entry, you don't yet know its ID, so you POST to a URL containing only the user ID—for example, *http://blogger.com/atom/555*. Note that each of these operations uses HTTP Basic Authentication and runs over HTTPS.

Code Example: AjaxPatterns RESTful Shop Demo

The Basic Shop Demo (*http://ajaxify.com/run/shop/*) employs an ad hoc web service to expose and manipulate store items and user shopping carts. In this demo, the cart service is refactored to become more RESTful. You can contrast this to the Refactoring Illustration in *RPC Service*. Note that some constraints make the RESTful service less than ideal here:

- URLs would ideally be prefixed with *http://ajaxshop.com*, but because it's running within the Ajax Demo framework, the prefix is longer: *http://ajaxify.com/run/shop/rest*.

- URLs would ideally avoid CGI-style variables and look like "/content/Movies" instead of /content?category=music. That's not possible here because there's no use URL-rewriting (to make the demos easy to install).

There are three resources: categories, items, and carts. GET is used to read each of these. Only carts can be modified, either by adding an item or clearing the cart. Both of these are handled by POST rather than PUT, since they are changes rather than replacements. Let's look at each service in more detail.

Reading categories list

An XML list of categories is exposed by GETting *http://ajaxify.com/run/shop/categories.phtml*. Here, categories is the resource and the HTTP method is GET since we're reading the resource. To avoid listing all category information here, there's a link to each specific category resource:

```
<categories>
    <category xlink="http://ajaxify.com/run/shop/rest/category.phtml?name=Books">
Books</category>
    <category xlink="http://ajaxify.com/run/shop/rest/category.phtml?name=Songs">
Songs</category>
    <category xlink="http://ajaxify.com/run/shop/rest/category.phtml?name=Movies">
Movies</category>
    </categories>
```

Reading an individual category

To drill down to an individual category, say "Movies," you GET `http://ajaxify.com/run/shop/category.phtml?name=Movies`, which provides the name and items. Since an item is defined solely by its name, and we can't perform operations on items themselves, there's no need to give it a URL.

```
<category>
  <name>Movies</name>
  <item>Contact</item>
  <item>Gatica</item>
  <item>Solaris</item>
</category>
```

As the system scales up, the list of all items gets excessive for someone who just wants to know the category name. So the next service provides just the items. If we want, we could then remove the list of items in the category name.

Reading cart contents

Being RESTful, we can't just access the shopping cart out using the current session—each operation must specify the cart's owner. The session is used here, but only for authentication.

To read the shopping cart of user 5000, we GET http://ajaxify.com/run/shop/rest/cart. phtml?userId=5000:

```
<cart userId="5000">
  <item>
    <name>Hackers and Painters</name>
    <amount>2</amount>
  </item>
  <item>
    <name>Accidental Empires</name>
    <amount>4</amount>
  </item>
</cart>
```

To test the authentication, visit the web app http://ajaxify.com/run/shop/rest and add a few items. Cut and paste your assigned user ID over the "5000" in the above URL. You'll be able to see your cart. Then try a different user ID, say 6000, and you'll be greeted with the following message along with a 401 (Forbidden) header:

```
You don't have access to Cart for user 6000.
```

Changing cart contents

Being RESTful, the cart URL remains the same whether we're manipulating or reading it. So when we make changes to user 5000's cart, we use the same URL as for reading it, *http://ajaxify.com/run/shop/rest/cart.phtml?userId=5000* (which would instead end with the cleaner */cart/5000* if we could use URL-rewriting).

To update the cart, we simply PUT a new cart specification to the cart's URL. If the user's just cleared the cart, the following will be uploaded:

```
<cart>
</cart>
```

If the user's added an item, the browser still does the same thing: just upload the whole cart; e.g.:

```
<cart userId="65590">
  <item>
    <name>Hackers and Painters</name>
    <amount>2</amount>
  </item>
  <item>
    <name>Accidental Empires</name>
    <amount>5</amount>
  </item>
</cart>
```

Note that working with PUT is quite similar to working with POST. As explained in *XMLHttpRequest Call* (Chapter 6), `XMLHttpRequest` has a `requestType` parameter. In the example here, the details are in any event abstracted by the AjaxCaller wrapper library:

```
ajaxCaller.putBody("cart.phtml?userId-"+userId, null, onCartResponse, true,
    null, "text/xml", cartXML);
```

How to mail the cart contents is more subjective, as discussed in the "Arbitrary Actions" section in the Solution. The approach here is to post an email address to the cart URL, e.g.:

```
<email-address>
  ajaxmail@example.com
</email-address>
```

SUPPORT FOR PUT AND DELETE

Supporting PUT and DELETE in the server depends on the programming environment. In Java, for example, it's trivial because servlets contain the methods doPut( ) and doDelete( ) alongside doPost( ) and doGet( ) methods. PHP, on the other hand, gives special treatment to GET and POST. Not only are variables exposed with the $_GET and $_POST arrays, but the POST body is accessible with $HTTP_RAW_POST_DATA. To read the body of a PUT call, the service here has to read from the input stream, *php://input (http://php.net/wrappers.php)*:

```
function readBody( ) {
    $body="";
    $putdata = fopen("php://input", "r");
    while ($block = fread($putdata, 1024)) {
      $body = $body.$block;
    }
    fclose($putdata);
    return $body;
}
```

It's partly inconveniences like this that drive some developers to compromise and use POST as a substitute for PUT and DELETION.

Alternatives

RPC Service

RPC Service (see later in this chapter) is an alternative to RESTful Service, as highlighted earlier in the "Solution."

Related Patterns

XML Message

*XML Message*s (see later in this chapter) are often used as the format of a REST service's response, and sometimes its input as well. XML fits well here because it's standards-based, broadly supported and understood, self-documenting, and capable of self-verifying when used with DTDs and XML Schemas. XML Messages tend to appear as the body of PUT and POST calls as well as in responses.

XML Data Island

A RESTful transaction often involves passing a resource back and forth, with each side augmenting its state. For instance, a server can deliver an initially empty shopping cart, the client can add an item to it, the server can set the total price, and so on. Instead of transforming to and from a custom data structure, it sometimes makes sense for the browser to retain the incoming *XML Messages* in an *XML Data Island* (Chapter 11) and transform it according to the interaction.

Unique URLs

Unique URLs (Chapter 17) also relates to URL design, though they differ in scope. Unique URLs relates to the URLs of the Ajax App itself, while RESTful Service involves the URLs of web services it uses. It's sometimes said that "Ajax breaks REST" because many Ajax Apps have a single URL regardless of state. Ironically, though, Ajax actually facilitates REST by encouraging a clean API to service the browser application. As for the browser application, Unique URLs do help make an Ajax App a bit more RESTful, though that's somewhat beside the point since it's the web services that a client would want to use.

Metaphor

REST is often likened to Unix—with its consistent usage of pipes and filters—and to SQL—with its standard persistence and querying commands—but can also be compared to Windows-based GUI platforms. There are standard actions like "Cut," "Paste," and "Popup Context Menu." Each object (e.g., documents, icons, and folders) accepts such actions and interprets them in a manner consistent with the action's meaning.

Want To Know More?

- Roy Fielding's Dissertation that introduced the REST Concept (*http://www.ics.uci.edu/ ~fielding/pubs/dissertation/top.htm*)
- REST Wiki (*http://rest.blueoxen.net/cgi-bin/wiki.pl*)

- Jeff Bone's breakdown of REST vs. RPC (*http://www.xent.com/pipermail/fork/2001-August/002801.html*)

- Roger Costello's "Building Web Services the REST Way" (*http://www.xfront.com/REST-Web-Services.html*)

- PUT versus POST discussion (*http://www.megginson.com/blogs/quoderat/archives/2005/04/03/post-in-rest-create-update-or-action/*)

Acknowledgments

Thanks to Tony Hill from the Thomson Corporation for reviewing this pattern and providing some great insights into REST.

RPC Service

Delegate, Facade, Procedure, Proxy, Remote, Remoting, RPC, SOAP, WSDL

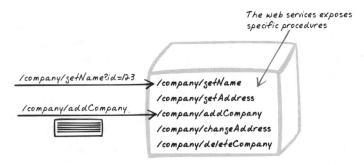

FIGURE 9-2. RPC Service

Developer Story

Dave's finished coding the backend services for some blogging software. There's an `ArticleRepository` object, for example, with functions to create, remove, update, and delete articles. Using a new product, he's able to effortlessly expose `ArticleRepository` as a web service API, with a different URL for each operation. Now he can code up the browser script for his own application to talk to the API, and there's a ready-made API available to third parties too.

Problem

How do you expose services on the Web?

Forces

Refer to the section "Forces" in *RESTful Service*.

Solution

Expose web services as Remote Procedure Calls (RPCs). Like REST, RPC is a broad term. It's somewhat ambiguous too, meaning different things to different people. This pattern uses a fairly general definition—a Remote Procedure Call (RPC) is a form of communication where the client invokes a remote procedure on the server. The definition implies:

- RPCs are generally characterized as actions. The URL is usually verb-like; e.g., */game/createGame?gameId=995* or */game/updater?command=createGame&gameId=995*.

- Typically, though not necessarily, the remoting is designed to be relatively transparent. The server's backend is developed, and a remoting framework acts as a bridge between client and server, allowing the client to directly invoke backend operations. Often, the remoting framework is distributed across both tiers, wrapping and unwrapping messages at each end.

Here are some concrete forms of RPC:

Procedure-style API

In the simplest case, it's just a matter of the URL style: the server exposes URLs that look like verbs and invite action, though they don't necessarily have any direct relationship to the backend technology.

XML-RPC

XML-RPC is a simple protocol for RPCs, using tags like `<methodCall>`, `<methodName>`, and `<params>`. An XML document is uploaded to make the call, and another document is returned with the response. There are many frameworks available to automatically expose backend services as XML-RPC and to invoke such services, so the remoting is fairly transparent from the developer's perspective.

SOAP

SOAP is based on exposing selected backend operations as HTTP-based services that can be accessed by certain clients. It's similar to XML-RPC, but offers a whole slew of additional functionality, such as custom data types and asynchronous messaging. The protocol is intended to automatic translation of SOAP calls to and from calls in the native languages being used. For instance, Enterprise Java Beans can automatically be exposed as web services using fancy code generators or mediating proxies. Unfortunately, the complexity of SOAP comes at a cost, and using it can sometimes feel like driving in a nail with a two-ton sledgehammer; some jaded developers have wondered whether SOAP is more about selling consulting services and toolkits than actually making life any easier.

Ajax Stub frameworks

These frameworks are an all-in-one package. XML-RPC and SOAP might automatically generate a web service for you, but you still have to invoke it yourself from an Ajax App. In contrast, *Ajax Stub* (see later in this chapter) frameworks such as SAJAX (*http://modernmethod.com/sajax*) create JavaScript wrappers for server-side operations as well as exposing them in the first place. The JavaScript code doesn't have to issue *XMLHttpRequest Calls* directly or even with an `XMLHttpRequest` wrapper. It instead calls a generic remoting function, capable of invoking operations on the backend. See the Refactoring Illustration in the section *Ajax Stub*, later in this chapter, for an example. The downside is that *Ajax Stubs* tend not to be fussed about exposing a clean API, because it's assumed the programmer will never need to look at how the server's invoked. Consequently, if a third party needs to use it, the API will quite possibly be uglier than an auto-generated XML-RPC or SOAP API.

Can RPC be RESTful? Some argue it can. *RESTful Service* is one of the largest patterns in this language, precisely because REST is a broad idea consisting of many principles and conventions. Given that RPC URLs represent actions rather than resources, it's a little over the top to say that RPC can be made truly RESTful. However, many of the REST principles do make sense in an RPC context, and it's advisable to follow them. Remember that many entities on the Internet, such as caches, are based on certain RESTful assumptions, and you'll be affected by those no matter how you design your interface. A few guidelines:

- Read-only queries should be made as GET requests, meaning that you shouldn't pass a query in the body.

- Anything that changes server state should be made with POST, including the command and arguments in the body. The command will already indicate the type of action that's occurring, so there's probably no need to use other HTTP methods such as PUT or DELETE.

- Stateful conversation is best avoided. Calls should pass in all the information they need explicitly. Session and cookies should not determine how the server responds to queries; if used at all, they should only be used for authentication.

Real-World Examples

Kiko

Kiko (*http://kiko.com*) is an online calendar application with a slew of Ajax features. The browser communicates to an interface using RPC-style URLs. For example, the following call retrieves my contacts:

```
http://www.kiko.com/kiko/kikoservlet?function=SelectContactsByUser , false ,
undefined , undefined)
```

A change is made in the same way. Here's what the browser called when I added an appointment:

```
http://www.kiko.com/kiko/kikoservlet?function=CreateAppt&starttime=2005-9-12 18:0:
00&endtime=2005-9-12 s18:30:00 , false , undefined , undefined)
```

Kiko invokes these URLs using POSTs, where the body is just an authentication key. Note that the service could be more REST-like, while retaining the RPC-style URLs, if Kiko wants to open the API to the public and ensure scaleability. To make it more REST-like, queries like SelectContactsByUser would be issued as GETs, with cookies used for authentication in place of the authentication key in the body. This would not only improve consistency across APIs, but also have the direct practical benefit of supporting caching, since GET responses can easily be cached. Also, POSTs could include all arguments inside the body, while retaining RPC-style URLs like */?function=CreateAppt*.

Flickr API

The Flickr API (*http://www.flickr.com/services/api/*), available to external developers, is a good example of an API with RPC-style URLs that also respects the basic REST conventions of GET strictly for reads and POST strictly for writes. Most calls include an API key, which the developer must apply for. A query for photo details such as owner and description is a GET call to a URL like this:

```
http://www.flickr.com/services/rest/?method=flickr.photos.getInfo&api_
    key=ap1000&photo_id=2000
```

You can also effect changes with the API. For example, you can tag an element by POSTing to a URL like this:

```
http://www.flickr.com/services/rest/?method=flickr.photos.addTags
```

containing a body like this:

```
api_key=ap1000&photo_id=2000&tags=Screenshot
```

Code Example: AjaxPatterns RPC Shop Demo

The Basic Ajax Shop Demo (*http://ajaxify.com/run/shop*) provides a web service to expose and manipulate store items and user shopping carts. In this demo, the cart and product services are refactored to provide a cohesive RPC service. You can contrast this to the Refactoring Illustration in *RESTful Service*.

A single service acts as a Facade (Gamma et al., 1995) to all server-side functionality. It accepts command-like URLs and routes them to the appropriate function. Read-only queries are of the following form, with the argument being optional:

```
services.phtml?command=queryType&someArg=someValue
```

State-affecting commands instead require all arguments, including the command, to be posted to a simple URL:

```
services.phtml
```

Because the URL is generic, the command must qualify what object it applies to; e.g., addToCart as opposed to add.

Reading the Categories list

To read the Categories, you GET *http://ajaxify.com/shop/rpc/services.phtml?command=get-Categories.*

Reading an individual category

To drill down to an individual category, say "Movies," you GET *http://ajaxify.com/shop/rpc/services.phtml?categoryName=Movies.*

Reading cart contents

To read cart contents, you GET *http://ajaxify.com/shop/rpc/services.phtml?command=getCart.* Note that cart access is based on the session, as with the Basic Shop Demo (and unlike the *RESTful Service* demo). It doesn't have to be like this, but doing so allowed for a minimal change.

Changing cart contents

To clear the cart, we POST a body of `command=clearCart` to `services.phtml`. To add an item, we POST the command and item in the body, such as `command=addToCart&item=Accidental Empires` to `services.phtml`.

Alternatives

RESTful Service

RESTful Service (see earlier in this chapter) is an alternative to RPC Service, but many tenets of REST can, and should, still be followed in RPC. See the RESTful Service "Solution" for a comparison.

Related Patterns

Ajax Stub

Ajax Stub (see later in this chapter) automates the production of RPC Services.

Plain-Text Message, XML Message

RPC is often used to design an application-independent web service API, or at least one that doesn't know anything about the user interface. That being the case, responses tend to be of a raw, semantic nature such as a *Plain-Text Message* (see later in this chapter) or an *XML Message* (see later).

Metaphor

Task-oriented user interfaces, such as simple menu systems and the new MS Office Task Ribbon idea, are similar to RPC. They explicitly offer the typical tasks you wish to achieve.

Ajax Stub

Delegate, Facade, Procedure, Proxy, Remote, Remoting, RPC

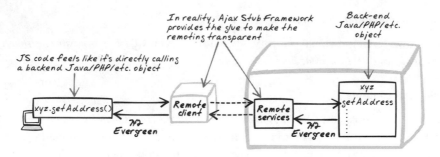

FIGURE 9-3. Ajax Stub

Developer Story

Devi begins working on the browser script for a trading application and soon decides she needs a way to execute a trade. There's already a method to do that on the backend TradeManager object, so after 15 seconds reconfiguring the Ajax Stub, the browser script is able to invoke the method.

Problem

How do you implement an *RPC Service* (see earlier in this chapter)?

Forces

- Some services have to reside on the server, for reasons of security, complexity, and performance. Thus, you need to expose web services to be accessed from the browser script.

- A web service should encapsulate only web-related logic and delegate any business and application logic to the backend.

- This creates a redundancy: the web service and the backend logic are tied together. When one changes, the other must change, leading to more work and the risk that you'll forget to change one or the other.

- The browser needs to access web services via XMLHttpRequest over HTTP, which is fundamentally different to the way both JavaScript and server-side scripts work. It's tedious to wrap and unwrap messages into a form suitable for transfer.

Solution

Use an *Ajax Stub* framework that allows browser scripts to directly invoke server-side operations, without having to worry about the details of XML-HttpRequest and HTTP transfer. The aim is to let the JavaScript call remote operations as if they were regular JavaScript functions, facilitating a more natural program style.

There are several frameworks to support stubbing of this nature. Typically, you declare which backend operations should be exposed, and the framework takes care of the remoting. It will provide a JavaScript stub object that will delegate the call over to the server side. For example, you might have a Java method like this:

```
public class Book {
  public String getEdition(int year) {...}
  ...
}
```

After configuring an Ajax Stub framework for handling remoting, it's light work to make call the class from within the browser:

```
editionLabel.innerHTML = book.getEdition();
```

Typical facilities include:

- Ability to convert JavaScript arguments and return values into server-side language constructs
- Sensible handling of server-side errors and exceptions
- Support for general XMLHttpRequest issues, such as timeouts

A stubbing framework usually consists of two components:

- A JavaScript component marshalls the call into an XMLHttpRequest, handles the call, and later unmarshalls the response.
- A server-side configuration component, with some configuration, that accepts the call, delegates to the backend operation, and marshalls the return value into a suitable response.

Decisions

How will you secure the server-side function?

With great power comes great responsibility. An Ajax Stub makes it easy, bordering on trivial, to directly expose business operations. That means it's also easy to let curious users do things they shouldn't. Since many Ajax Apps push the whole user interface out to the browser, the web tier is left publishing business methods. Harry Fuecks, author of the Ajax Stub toolkit JPSpan (*http://jpspan.sourceforge.net/*), gave this cautionary example on the Ajax Blog (*http://ajaxblog.com/archives/2005/05/25/a-grumpier-ajaxian*). A naïve export of a business operation could end up with a call like this:

```
var ccNum = AJAX.getCreditCardNumber(userId);
```

Anyone can edit the JavaScript and pass any argument to the credit card operation. Another stubbing framework, DWR (*http://getahead.ltd.uk/dwr/getstarted*), warns: "There is a danger that you could cause all sorts of security problems using this code. You need to think about security earlier rather than later."

Other approaches, such as *RESTful Service*, are also vulnerable to the same threat, but they tend to encourage more analysis, because you have to explicitly design the service interface. With Ajax Stub, you're effectively ticking a few boxes to say which backend operations can be executed.

A few guidelines:

- Even though you *can* publish an interface very quickly, that doesn't mean you should. Do take the time to consider the implications of making an operation available to the public (or whatever user base will be using your Ajax App), who will be able to call it with whatever arguments they please.

- The framework's module is exposed as a web service—your environment might be able to control access to particular services. For example, the DWR Framework for Java stubbing (*http://getahead.ltd.uk/dwr/security*) notes: "DWR allows you to grant access using two J2EE based mechanisms. Firstly you can define access to dwr based on J2EE roles. Secondly within DWR you can define access to methods on a role basis."

- Depending on the environment, the backend operation may need to use some form of authentication. In some cases, the operation will have direct access to request information such as the URL and cookies, which will facilitate authentication. The downside is that you've begun to incorporate web-related concepts into the business logic, which is what Ajax Stubs seek to avoid.

- Be wary of the framework as well. One Ajax Stub framework, CPAINT (*http://cpaint. sourceforge.net/*), caused some security alerts due to the possibility of malicious code being executed on the server (*http://secunia.com/advisories/16454/*). The team was quick to respond, and the Ajax Stub pattern is not inherently flawed, as some people had assumed. However, it's important to understand just what exactly the Ajax Stub framework is doing.

Real-World Examples

These examples cover available frameworks for creating Ajax Stubs.

SAJAX framework

SAJAX (*http://www.modernmethod.com/sajax/*) is an Ajax Stub framework that actually supports multiple backend languages. The browser side is the same for all, but there are different server-side proxy components depending on which language is used. Among the backend languages are ASP, ColdFusion, Perl, PHP, Python, and Ruby.

DWR framework

DWR (*http://getahead.ltd.uk/dwr/overview/dwr*) is an open source framework for Ajax Stubs to Java classes. On the server side, you run a DWR servlet and configure it with a separate XML file. In the browser, just include a JavaScript file. Java and JavaScript may not have much in common, but calls do at least look the same. A DWR JavaScript-to-Java call looks just like a Java-to-Java call.

CL-AJAX framework

Richard Newman's open source CL-AJAX (*http://www.cliki.net/cl-ajax*) supports stubbing of Common Lisp functions.

Code Refactoring: AjaxPatterns SAJAX Sum

In this refactoring illustration, the Basic Sum Demo (*http://ajaxify.com/run/sum*) is refactored to use an Ajax Stub (*http://ajaxify.com/run/sum/stub*), based on SAJAX (*http://www. modernmethod.com/sajax/*). To begin with, we do away with the old Sum service (sum.phtml) and create a standalone, backend, calculator module. Now that we're using an RPC approach, we'll call the operation add instead of sum, to make it distinctly a verb. So calculator.phtml looks like this:

```
<?
  function add($figure1, $figure2, $figure3) {
    echo $figure1 + $figure2 + $figure3;
  }
?>
```

With the stub, we can allow the browser-side script to directly invoke that function. The JavaScript call looks like this:

```
function submitSum( ) {
  x_add($("figure1").value,$("figure2").value,$("figure3").value,onSumResponse);
}
```

Here's how you set up the SAJAX glue between the JavaScript x_add and the PHP add. In PHP, we tell SAJAX which functions are exported:

```
<? require_once("Sajax.php"); ?>
  ...
  sajax_init( );
  sajax_export("add");
  sajax_handle_client_request( );
```

And in outputting the script, some PHP code generates the required JavaScript—in this case, the x_add( ) function, which will forward on to SAJAX on the server side and eventually interpret its response:

```
<script>
  <?
    sajax_show_javascript( );
  ?>
</script>
```

Alternatives

XMLHttpRequest Call

Ajax Stubs are built on top of *XMLHttpRequest Calls* (Chapter 6) and represent a different approach to the usual Ajax remoting. XMLHttpRequest Calls leave the user to deal directly with HTTP concepts and packing and unpacking of messages, tasks that Ajax Stubs take care of. The benefit of direct XMLHttpRequest Calls is that the server-side service interface is independent of the underlying implementation.

XML-RPC and SOAP

XML-RPC and SOAP are more generic (non-Ajax-specific) ways to develop *RPC Services* (see earlier in this chapter). Since Ajax Stubs tend to produce Ajax-specific services, XML-RPC or SOAP might be more appropriate if you're opening up to external clients.

Related Patterns

RPC Service

An Ajax Stub is one way to implement an *RPC Service*.

JSON Message

*JSON Message*s (see later in this chapter) are being used by several Ajax Stub frameworks because Ajax Stubs need to share data between browser and server; i.e., inbound arguments and outbound return values. These objects should be standard JavaScript objects in the browser and standard Java or PHP or whatever-your-language-choice objects on the server. In between, it's most convenient to transfer them as strings. JSON defines a standard way to convert objects in many languages to and from a string representation.

An even more ambitious standard is JSON-RPC (*http://json-rpc.org/*), a protocol for remoting that's touted as a lightweight alternative to XML-RPC. There's an Ajax Stub framework based on JSON-RPC, the aptly named JSON-RPC-Java (*http://oss.metaparadigm.com/jsonrpc/*).

HTML Message

AHAH, Direct, Display, HTML, InnerHTML, Message, Precise, ServerSide, Visual

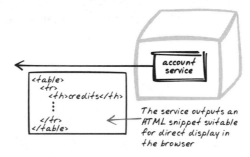

FIGURE 9-4. HTML Message

Developer Story

Dave's identified the need for a credit history service, providing a list of transactions. Java-Script resources are limited, so the entire HTML is created server side, and the browser application has only to morph a DOM element with the entire HTML response.

Problem

What format should be used for server responses?

Forces

- The browser display needs to be dynamic in Ajax Apps.

- The display changes by altering the DOM, and HTML is often used to specify the new value.

- The nature of the change is often complex and needs to be determined server side.

- Not all developers know JavaScript, and many feel its usage is best minimized.

Solution

Have the server generate HTML snippets to be displayed in the browser. In this approach to browser-server dialogue, the server-side service outputs some HTML, which is picked up by the XMLHttpRequest callback function and an element then morphed by setting its innerHTML property to the response HTML. In general, the server side is application-specific because the HTML response is closely tied to the application's display style.

The XMLHttpRequest allows callers to retrieve responses as either XML or plain-text. With HTML, it's usually easiest to retrieve it as a plain-text string. If the HTML is a pure XHTML document, XML is also an option, but usually that's not the case because there's no need for a header section. The entire response can be as simple as "You Win!". That's not an XHTML document because there's no <xml> tag, nor are there HTML header and body sections.

HTML Messages should be used with caution because they couple server-side services with browser display. That means it's difficult to develop the tiers in parallel. In mainte-nance, if you change the display by altering its initial HTML or any JavaScript manipula-tion, you often need to change the HTML-generating service too. There's also a risk on the server side that you might be coupling business logic with HTML generation. So when might an HTML Message be appropriate?

Performance
> Since browser-side parsing and rendering can be expensive, HTML Messages can make an application more responsive, especially if the HTML is cached on the server or the browser.

Server-Side Code Generation
> One case where HTML Messages make some sense is with *Server-Side Code Generation* (Chapter 12), where the server builds all the browser-side code for you. There are

strengths and weaknesses of such frameworks, and if you decide to use one, then browser-server coupling is not really an issue because all maintained code is server side anyway.

Legacy Code

Most legacy applications will use the conventional approach of publishing pages from the server. They therefore already have all the HTML generation present in the server-side environment, so if you're Ajaxifying a legacy application, a quick migration path is to retain the server-side HTML generation where possible.

Complex HTML

In the rare case that your HTML or JavaScript is particularly complex, you might prefer to generate it all on the server side, where development and debugging is sometimes easier.

Graceful Degradation

When there's a chance users won't have a recent browsers, HTML Messages allow you to encapsulate more logic in the server. Of course, if JavaScript is not enabled at all, the "messages" will have to be full pages.

Server-Centric Attitude

If you're concerned about keeping as much logic as possible in the one language and environment, or you'd prefer not to work much with JavaScript, HTML Messages are more appropriate.

Typically, HTML Messages rely on a block-level element existing in the DOM, often a div or form. The HTML Message will contain a specification for the entire contents of the element. Some of the XMLHttpRequest wrapper libraries, such as JAH/AHAH (*http://microformats.org/wiki/rest/ahah*) and Sack (*http://twilightuniverse.com/2005/05/sack-of-ajax/*), support HTML Messages by letting the caller directly state a DOM element as the callback destination instead of the usual callback function. When the response returns, the DOM element is automatically morphed with the service's response.

A variant of this pattern is Behavior Message; see *On-Demand JavaScript* (Chapter 6). Also, note that HTML Messages almost flow from server to browser; you'd rarely need to upload an HTML Message back to the server.

Decisions

At what level of granularity will the HTML apply?

In the extreme, the service could generate HTML for the entire document, making it similar to a conventional page refresh. In practice, you'll usually want to limit the HTML's level of granularity to well-defined, distinct page elements. For example:

- An account status
- A form
- A menu

How much style will be contained in the message?

You'll need to decide how much style is contained in the message. An HTML Message already ties the server to the browser somewhat, but style directives will tie it further to the server. In general, it's good practice to just include class names and element IDs so that the browser application can influence the style, usually with a standard CSS stylesheet. If you do this, you'll need to ensure the names are unique, and you'll need to decide on exactly which elements need to be given ID and class declarations.

Real-World Examples

Digg Spy

Digg Spy (*http://digg.com/spy*) shows new stories and events such as user moderation as they happen (see Figure 5-5). The *XMLHttpRequest Call* (Chapter 6) accesses a static URL (*http://digg.com/last10*) containing the last 10 submissions and integrates them into the page. The HTML looks like this:

```
<div class="news-body" id="main64115">
  <h3 id="title">
    <a href="http://digg.com/movies/How_LEGOs_Are_Made_"> How LEGOs Are Made! </a>
  </h3>
  <p class="news-submitted">
    <a href="/users/Akshun"><img src="/img/user-small/user-default.png" alt=
"Akshun" height="16" width="16"> </a>
    submitted by <a href="/users/Akshun"> Akshun </a> 14 hours 22 minutes ago
    (<a href="http://www.popandco.com/archive/moab/" class="simple tight" title=
"How LEGOs Are Made!"> ... </a>) </p>
  <p> </p>
  </div>
  <div class="news-body" id="main64550">
  ...
```

Rapha

Rapha (*http://www.rapha.cc*) is an e-commerce web site for cycling gear (Figure 9-5). The shopping cart is Ajaxian, requiring no page refresh to update. Each time an item is purchased, the HTML for the shopping cart is retrieved. For example:

```
<div id="basket">
  <h3>Your basket:</h3>
  <ul>
    <li>Small Softshell Jacket x 2</li>
  </ul>
  <p><a href="/basket/">Edit selection</a> | <a href=
"/checkout/">Go to checkout</a></p>
  </div>
```

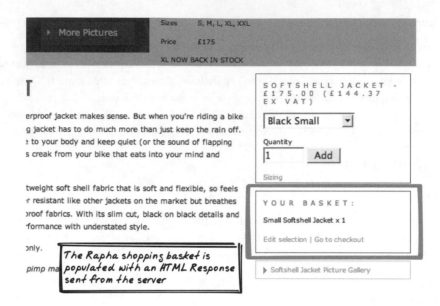

The Rapha shopping basket is populated with an HTML Response sent from the server

FIGURE 9-5. Rapha

Amazon Zuggest

Francis Shanahan's Amazon Zuggest (*http://www.francisshanahan.com/zuggest.aspx*) provides a *Live Search*: results are shown as you type. The server responds by providing the entire HTML for each result—for example:

```
<table>
    <tr><td valign=top width='20%'><b>Vempire Or Dark Faerytales in Phallustei</b><br>
    <a href='http://www.amazon.com/exec/obidos/redirect?tag=francshanacom-20%26link_
code=sp1%26camp=2025%26creative=165953%26path=http://www.amazon.com/gp/redirect.
html%253fASIN=B0000525ZY%2526tag=francshanacom-
20%2526lcode=sp1%2526cID=2025%2526ccmID=165953%2526location=/o/ASIN/
B0000525ZY%25253FSubscriptionId=16KBBOXN5XP4WSNNVKG2'
target=_blank>Click to View</a><br>
    [Music]<br>List Price<span class='lp'>$23.99</span><br>
    <span class='lnp'>1 NEW from $14.99[$13.50 used]</span>
    ...
    </td></tr><table>
```

TalkDigger

TalkDigger (*http://talkdigger.com*) is a webfeed meta-search. Enter a query, and it fires off parallel queries to different search engines (an example of *Multi-Stage Download*). Each result is returned as an HTML table to be added to the page.

Code Example: Digg Spy

Digg Spy (*http://digg.com/spy*) responds with the full HTML to be displayed as well as some meta-content at the end. The results are fetched periodically—filldigs( ) is triggered by the recurring lastdigs( ). filldigs( ) executes an *XMLHttpRequest Call*, extracts the HTML from the full response, and morphs the results panel using its innerHTML property:

```
function startlastdigs( ) {
  window.setInterval("lastdigs( )",15000);
}
function filldigs( ) {
  ...
  s.open("GET",url2,true);
  s.onreadystatechange=function( ) {
    if (s.readyState == 4) {
      ...
      b = responsestring2.split(split);
      ...
      document.getElementById('diggspy').innerHTML = b[0];
      ...
    }
  }
  ...
}
```

Alternatives

Plain-Text Message, XML Message, JSON Message

Plain-Text Message, XML Message, and *JSON Message* (see more on these later in this chapter) all involve sending raw data as opposed to concrete display detail. When the browser receives such responses, it can render it or use it in some other way, such as retaining some information. In contrast, HTML Messages are likely to be display directly and are not retained. A further difference is that HTML Messages tend to be responses only, whereas these other formats are often used for uploading data as well.

Related Patterns

On-Demand JavaScript

Where HTML Message provides snippets of HTML to be fused on to the page, *On-Demand JavaScript* (Chapter 6) can provide snippets of JavaScript to be executed immediately. The idea is introduced in that pattern as "Behavior Message."

Metaphor

Sending an HTML Message is like sending a photograph—there's a lot of visual detail, but any metadata, such as location and subjects, can only be inferred.

Plain-Text Message

●●○

Acknowlegement, Custom, PlainText, Semantic, String

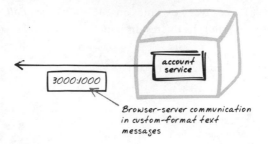

Browser-server communication in custom-format text messages

FIGURE 9-6. Plain-Text Message

Developer Story

Devi's working on an auto-completion form field. Every few seconds, the server needs to respond with a list of suggestions. Devi codes the server side to output the suggestions as a comma-separated list, as it's convenient to output on the server and easy to parse in the browser.

Problem

How can you transfer data between server and browser?

Forces

- Ajax Apps require messages to be transmitted back and forth.

- Both browser and the server must be able to access the message. That usually means the format must be easily accessed in JavaScript as well as in whichever server-side language is used.

Solution

Pass simple messages between server and browser in plain-text format. This is a broad pattern, because "plain-text" is an ambiguous term. The emphasis here is on keeping things simple—XML or JSON are often more appropriate for complex data structures, but can also add unnecessary complexity.

Despite the name, XMLHttpRequest is perfectly capable of working with plain-text responses. As discussed in *XMLHttpRequest Call* (Chapter 6) and *XML Message* (later), the browser script can decide how to interpret the response in XMLHttpRequest by switching between the responseText and responseXML properties.

Plain-text formats include:

Response Code
Sometimes, all that's required is a simple response code, such as a numeric ID or a text message such as "OK" or "Failed." Note that, in this case, an appropriate HTTP Response Code codes may be more standards-based and in line with *RESTful Service* conventions.

A simple text string

For example, a user's name.

A list

For example, a comma-separated list of search results.

A custom data format

For example, a list of strings, where each string is a comma-separated list of object attributes.

While browser support for XML is reasonably good, especially with third-party libraries, it's also quite easy to manipulate arbitrary text formats. JavaScript provides a standard string manipulation library, including the particularly helpful regular expression and grouping facilities.

The case for plain-text is particularly compelling in the following situations:

Simpler messages

The simpler the message, the more compelling the argument for plain-text messages. Once the string starts to get more complex, there's a better argument for relying on XML support from the browser and third-party libraries.

External clients

XML is often a better choice when it's not just the web app that's using the service. That's partly for reasons of convention—XML is simply a standard transfer format on the Internet. But there's also a more technical reason: using DTDs or XML Schemas, you can specify the format in an unambiguous manner that can be enforced whenever a document is encountered.

Skill base

XML may be a standard, but that's useful only if people know the standard. The better developers are with XML technologies in both the browser and the server, the more compelling the argument for XML.

Real-World Examples

Lace Chat

Brett Stimmerman's Lace Chat (*http://www.socket7.net/lace/*) is an Ajax chat app (Figure 9-7). When the page is initially shown, all user messages are downloaded as a single, long string. Within the string, each user message is captured as a set of attributes, separated by pipe characters:

```
1135646360:749||||date-1135646204||*Monday, 26 December
2005||||hour-17||*17:00||||1135646204||Posted about 3 minutes ago at
17:16||Aj Two||Yeah you can *SO* chat in real time||||1135646212||Posted
about 2 minutes, 52 seconds ago at 17:16||*Lace||AJ One
has joined the conversation||||1135646212||
```

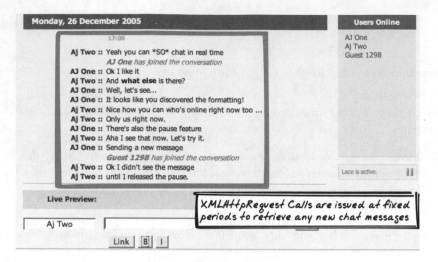

FIGURE 9-7. Lace Chat

Magnetic Poetry

In Magnetic Poetry (*http://www.broken-notebook.com/magnetic/*), you drag tiles around a workspace. When the browser receives an updated position, the message looks like a structured command statement:

```
Update magnetic_poetry set top_value=291, left_value=119 WHERE id=81
```

HousingMaps

HousingMaps (*http://housingmaps.com*) is a mashup between Google Maps and Craigslist (*http://craigslist.com*), a community-oriented classified advertising web site. The Housing-Maps portion is downloaded with an *XMLHttpRequest Call* that retrieves the 15 or so results matching a query. Each result represents a single home and is broken into a sequence of attributes, one line at a time, and prefixed with an identifier:

```
PA:34.0917
PN:-118.28
IC:p
DS:One Bath With Small Loft Duplex Near Sunset Junction
AD:Hyperion Ave &&& Sunset Blvd</line><line>Los Angeles</line><line>CA
...
I4:a.im.craigslist.org/rR/iv/X1dT18TzVO7cfjuQzouhKQ5EETuK.jpg
LC:1071999
PA:34.0763
PN:-118.294
IC:p
DS:1930&&#39;s Restored Spanish Beauty- 1St Month Free
AD:Berendo &&& Beverly</line><line>Los Angeles</line><line>CA
...
```

```
I4:a.im.craigslist.org/n0/Xm/SS3hSoIWLOsc8wOjaiLGQK5HFbzl.jpg
LC:1072004
...
```

Code Example: Lace Chat

The response in Lace Chat is a list of attributes, separated by pipe characters. Each complete record is separated by ||||, and each attribute within a record is separated by a smaller string, ||. The handling code first splits the string into an array of records, then splits out the attributes within each record:

```
// Records are separated by four pipes ||||
var results = this.httpGetObj.responseText.split('||||');
...
for (var i = 1; i < results.length; i++) {
  var first;
  // Fields are separated by two pipes ||
  var fields = results[i].split('||');
  ...
  var timeStr = fields[1];
  var textStr = fields[3];
  ...
  p.setAttribute('id', 'msg_' + fields[0]);
  ...
}
```

Alternatives

XML Message

As discussed in the "Solution," an *XML Message* may be a better alternative for more complex data.

XML Message

Document, Format, Hierarchical, PlainOldXML, POX, Semantic, Structured, XML

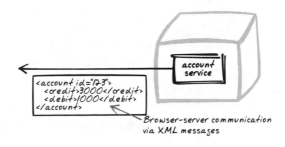

FIGURE 9-8. XML Message

Devloper Story

Dave is creating an Ajax search engine. The results are offered as a *RESTful Service*, so that external developers can create their own interface. The results are presented as XML, and Dave's own search interface pulls it down with an `XMLHttpRequest` call, then transforms the result to HTML.

Problem

How can you transfer data between server and browser?

Forces

- Ajax Apps require messages to be transmitted back and forth.

- Both browser and the server must be able to access the message. That usually means the format must be easily accessed in JavaScript as well as whichever server-side language is used.

Solution

Pass messages between server and browser in Extensible Markup Language (XML) format. It's feasible to pass XML in both directions. On the server side, it's a common way to expose structured data as text, and browser-side applications can download XML with an *XMLHttpRequest Call* and parse it in different ways. Where the browser needs to upload some complex data, it's fairly easy to serialize the data as XML and upload it in the body of an XMLHttpRequest Call.

XML is the definitive standard for data transfer across the industry, so just about any server-side development language has comprehensive support. The great advantage of XML over custom formats is the massive base of supporting frameworks, libraries, editors, and general tools. How you deal with XML on the server is language-specific, and a few choices are outlined in "Decisions," next. However you do it, make sure the server presents XML content with the appropriate header to ensure its handled correctly by XMLHttpRequest:

```
Content-type: text/xml
```

As the name implies, `XMLHttpRequest` was developed with XML transfer in mind. To retrieve an object with an `XMLHttpRequest`, first point it to a URL known to serve XML:

```
xReq.open("GET","http://ajaxify.com/run/portal/drilldown/drilldown.phtml
                ?categoryName=Overviews",true);
```

When `XMLHttpRequest` delivers a response, the response can either be interpreted as a DOM object or plain-text:

```
var domObject = xReq.responseXML
alert(domObject) // Outputs "[Object]" (IE)
                 // or "[object XML Document]" (Firefox)
```

```
var xmlString = xReq.responsetText
alert(domObject) // Outputs the whole string
                 // i.e. "<category ...> ... </category>"
```

In most cases, you want to use `responseXML` because it gives you a well-structured DOM object: a hierarchical structure that can be navigated using industry-standard conventions. With recent browsers, you can rely on some basic parsing functionality to interrogate DOM objects. HowToCreate has a good list of DOM traversal functions (*http://www. howtocreate.co.uk/tutorials/texterise.php?dom=1*) and many of the Ajax Patterns demos perform such parsing (e.g., the Basic Wiki Demo; see *http://ajaxify.com/run/wiki*).

If you're parsing XML, consider delegating to a cross-browser library. Sarissa (*http://sarissa. sourceforge.net*), for example, has a variety of cross-browser XML manipulation routines. Another library, Interactive Website Framework (IWF) (*http://sourceforge.net/projects/iwf/*), simplifies XML expressions. Instead of the following standard DOM query:

```
var node = doc.documentElement.firstChild.firstChild.getAttribute("size");
```

you can write this:

```
var node = doc.groceries.frozen[0].pizza[0].size;
```

With a DOM object representing server data, the receiver can do one or more things:

- Transform the XML into some HTML. (See "Decisions," next.)

- Interrogate it to decide what to do next.

- Store it for later use in an *XML Data Island*.

- Modify it based on client state and upload it again.

This discussion has mostly focused on downloading XML from server to browser. That's the most common direction, but XML can also flow upwards too. It's sometimes easier to upload complex data as an XML document than as a set of CGI-style variables. To do this with `XMLHttpRequest`, you simply pass in the whole XML string as the argument to `send( )`. You'll also need to ensure the transport type is suitable—typically, POST (or PUT).

```
xReq.send(xmlString);
```

The XML string being sent usually represents browser state or user input. Most often, it's simply built up with some manual coding, appending strings together and including variables where appropriate. However, you can also use a library like Sarissa or Anders Noras's XmlSerializer (*http://dotnetjunkies.com/WebLog/user/Profile.aspx?UserID=1095*) to convert from a DOM object—or some other object—into an XML string.

Finally, a note of caution. "XML" is the X in "AJAX," so it's sometimes considered a core Ajax technology. And its association with `XMLHttpRequest` also strengthens the argument for XML Messages. However, don't let all this make you feel obligated to use XML Messages. `XMLHttpRequest` supports transfers in any plain-text format, and it's fine to use *Plain-Text Messages* in many situations. XML is relatively simple, and there's good browser support, but sometimes it just doesn't fit the bill. The "Solution" for Plain-Text Message compares the two approaches in more detail.

Decisions

How will the server generate XML?

There are many ways the server might generate XML messages:

- By using custom code that hand-creates the XML string.

- By building up a DOM object and serializing it.

- By using a generic framework to convert standard data structures into XML.

- By retrieving existing XML documents from the filesystem or external sources.

Will you specify a DTD or Schema?

When you pass XML Messages back and forth, each end must assume the same document format. That's a standard requirement with XML, and you can define the format precisely using a separate document: either a Document Type Definition or a stricter XML Schema document.

When the browser needs to render the message, how it will transform the XML?

The browser doesn't always need to render incoming XML messages—sometimes it just uses the data. But, for situations when it does render the XML, there are a few options. In all cases, the script is building up some HTML, which will then be injected onto a DOM element by setting its innerHMTL property to the HTML string.

Manual JavaScript Conversion
   For simple messages, you might find it easier to just perform a little parsing and manually create an HTML string.

XSLT
   If you have the skill base and a suitable framework for the browsers you're targeting, *Browser-Side XSLT* allows for powerful conversion of XML.

Templating
   Sometimes, *Browser-Side Templating* is a happy medium between the above two approaches. You still have to parse the XML document somehow, but the HTML generation is more straightforward.

Real-World Examples

Netflix Top 100

When you roll over a movie title in the Netflix Top 100 (*http://www.netflix.com/Top100#*), a balloon soon appears with summary details (Figure 9-9). After the rollover, an *XMLHttpRequest Call* occurs, which receives movie details like this:

```
<MOVIES>
<MOVIE ID="60031236" POS="17" DS="0">
  <TITLE>Kill Bill: Vol. 2</TITLE>
  <SYNOPSIS>In this film noir tale written ... </SYNOPSIS>
  <DETAILS RATED="R" RELYEAR="2003" GENREID="296" GENRENAME="Action &&& Adventure"/>
  <STARRING>
    <PERSON ID="92495" NAME="Uma Thurman"/>
    <PERSON ID="20008295" NAME="Lucy Liu"/>
  </STARRING>
  <DIRECTOR>
    <PERSON ID="20001496" NAME="Quentin Tarantino"/>
  </DIRECTOR>
</MOVIE>
</MOVIES>
```

Movie details are downloaded as XML, then converted to HTML

FIGURE 9-9. Netflix

Protopage

Protopage (*http://protopage.com*) is a portal-style application with excellent personalization capabilities. Each time you change something on the page, a command is uploaded to the server via an *XMLHttpRequest Call*. For example, here's what the browser sent when I moved a *Portlet* around:

```
<command accountId="25570" protopageId="25568" protopagePath="mahemoff" name=
"save-panel-geometry">
  <param name="id">129644</param>
  <param name="left">216</param>
  <param name="top">476</param>
  <param name="width">423</param>
  <param name="height">71</param>
```

```
<param name="collapsed">false</param>
<param name="zIndex">33</param>
<param name="verticalScrollProportion">0</param>
</command>
```

Google Maps

Google Maps is perhaps the most famous usage of XML Messages. Meta-information is downloaded as XML and rendered with *Browser-Side XSLT*.

Code Refactoring: AjaxPatterns XML Sum

The Basic Sum Demo (*http://ajaxify.com/run/sum*) uses a *Plain-Text Message* to transfer the sum result from server to browser. So if the browser sends a GET query requesting the sum of 4 and 8, the entire response is "12." That works fine, but sometimes we'd like a response to contain the original query too—it's convenient for caching, for instance (see *Browser-Side Cache* [Chapter 13]). If we're going to provide the original figures of the sum, the data's becoming a bit more complex—we now have a list as well as different types of data. To keep the format self-describing, let's refactor to XML.

The XML Sum Demo (*http://ajaxify.com/run/sum/xml*) behaves the same as the original version, but the server side returns results like this (*http://ajaxify.com/run/sum/xml/sumXML. php?figure1=4&figure2=8&figure3=*):

```
<sum>
  <inputs>
    <figure id="1">4</figure>
    <figure id="2">8</figure>
    <figure id="3"></figure>
  </inputs>
  <outputs>12</outputs>
</sum>
```

To avoid confusion, the server-side service is now called sumXML.php, and reflecting the new location is the only change required to the browser call. The server-side service has been altered to output the full XML. Note the XML content-type declaration in the header, which is necessary for the *XMLHttpRequest Call*.

```
<?

  header("Content-Type: text/xml");

  $sum = $_GET["figure1"] + $_GET["figure2"] + $_GET["figure3"];

  echo <<< END_OF_FILE
<sum>
  <inputs>
    <figure id="1">{$_GET["figure1"]}</figure>
    <figure id="2">{$_GET["figure2"]}</figure>
    <figure id="3">{$_GET["figure3"]}</figure>
  </inputs>
  <outputs>$sum</outputs>
</sum>
```

```
    END_OF_FILE

    ?>
```

In this refactoring, the figures aren't used, but the sum is still required. The callback function therefore navigates through the response XML Message to obtain the sum figure.

```
function onSumResponse(xml, headers, callingContext) {
  var sum = xml.getElementsByTagName("outputs")[0].firstChild.nodeValue;
  self.$("sum").innerHTML = sum;
}
```

Alternatives

Plain-Text Message

As mentioned earlier in the "Solution," XML can often be overkill for simple messages, and *Plain-Text Messages* (see earlier in this chapter) are worth considering as an alternative.

JSON Message

Just like XML Message, *JSON Message* is a suitable representation for data of various complexities. The "Alternatives" section of JSON Message compares the two formats.

JSON Message

JSON, Marshal, Semantic, Serialize, YAML

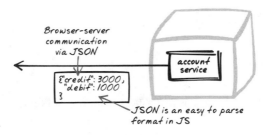

FIGURE 9-10. JSON Message

Developer Story

Devi is creating an Ajax calendar. The browser periodically polls for new appointments, which the server is sending as JSON messages. Since JSON messages are just JavaScript code for object creation, Devi's browser script needs only to run eval against each message in order to reconstruct the appointment.

Problem

How can you transfer data between server and browser?

Forces

- Ajax Apps require messages to be transmitted back and forth.

- Both browser and the server must be able to access the message. That usually means the format must be easily accessed in JavaScript as well as whichever server-side language is used.

Solution

Pass messages between server and browser in JavaScript Object Notation (JSON) format. JSON is a standard serialization format, created in 2002 as a cleaner and lighter alternative to XML. As with XML, the object can range in complexity from a simple string to a deep hierarchical structure. Also like XML, JSON is language-neutral, meaning that you could marshall a C++ object into JSON notation and unmarshall it to form an object in Perl. But in practice, JSON is particularly suited to browser-server communication because it's a format based on JavaScript.

In fact, a JSON Message *is* JavaScript. This is a valid JSON Message:

```
"Homer J."
```

You can test browser-based JSON conversion on the Basic JSON Demo (*http://ajaxify.com/run/json/*). As you'll see there, the JSON Message "Homer J." maps to the JavaScript string, Homer J..

Here's a more complex example (as on the demo, reformatted):

```
{"houseNumber":"742",
  "street":"Evergreen Terrace",
  "city":"Springfield",
  "postcode":"49007",
  "country":"USA",
  "comments": ["Deliveries accepted.","Familiar address, huh?",""]
}
```

As you can see, this JSON message is just a JavaScript object literal. You convert it like this:

```
var name = eval("(" + nameJSON + ")");
```

Or like this (*http://jibbering.com/2002/4/httprequest.html*) if it takes your fancy:

```
var name=new Function("return " + nameJSON)();
```

Note that you don't even need a JSON library in the browser. The browser can pick up a JSON string using an *XMLHttpRequest Call* and simply run the standard eval function.

However, there is actually a JavaScript JSON library (*http://www.crockford.com/JSON/js. html*), which adds two important capabilities: parse( ) for safer string-to-object conversion, and stringify( ) for object-to-string conversion. The former is an alternative to manual JavaScript evaluation, because evaling arbitrary messages puts your app at risk of running malicious JavaScript code. Thus, the string-to-object conversion should be executed if you don't trust the message. To parse a string, use the following codee:

```
var name = JSON.parse(nameJSON);
```

If you need to upload something to the server, you'll need to convert a JavaScript object to JSON with stringify( ). The Basic JSON Demo (*http://ajaxlocal/run/json/*) shows this conversion process too. The call looks like this:

```
var nameJSON = JSON.stringify(name);
```

So far, the examples have considered only JavaScript conversion. But JSON wouldn't be very useful if you could only convert to and from JavaScript objects—you need to convert at the other end too, and your server side is probably not written in JavaScript. That's why there are JSON processors for many languages. Using these processors, you can easily share an object between JavaScript and your favorite server-side language.

A remoting modification (*http://ajaxify.com/run/json/remoting*) of the Basic JSON Demo (*http://ajaxify.com/run/json/*) sends JSON to the server, using *XMLHttpRequest Calls*. There, it's converted to standard PHP objects using Michael Migurski's JSON-PHP library (*http://mike.teczno.com/json.html*). The library works similarly to JSON libraries for Java, .Net, and other languages. The following code converts JSON to a standard object:

```
$json = new JSON( );
$newObject = $json->decode($jsonString);
```

while the following code performs the reverse operation:

```
$json = new JSON( );
$json = $json->encode($object);
```

Real-World Examples

Many web sites use JSON as their data transfer format for shuttling data between browser and server.

Kiko

Kiko (*http://kiko.com*) is an online calendar application with a slew of Ajax features (Figure 9-11). As you'd expect, the server holds a model of the calendar, and the browser keeps uploading changes using *XMLHttpRequest Calls*. JSON is the message format used for server responses—each response is a list of objects.

Delicious JSON Feed

Delicious (*http://del.icio.us/doc/feeds/json/*), a social bookmarking tool, provides a *Web Service* that exposes a user's recent bookmarks in the form of a JSON Message. For reasons discussed in *On-Demand JavaScript* (Chapter 6), this means a browser script can conveniently grab the data without the need for a *Cross-Domain Proxy*.

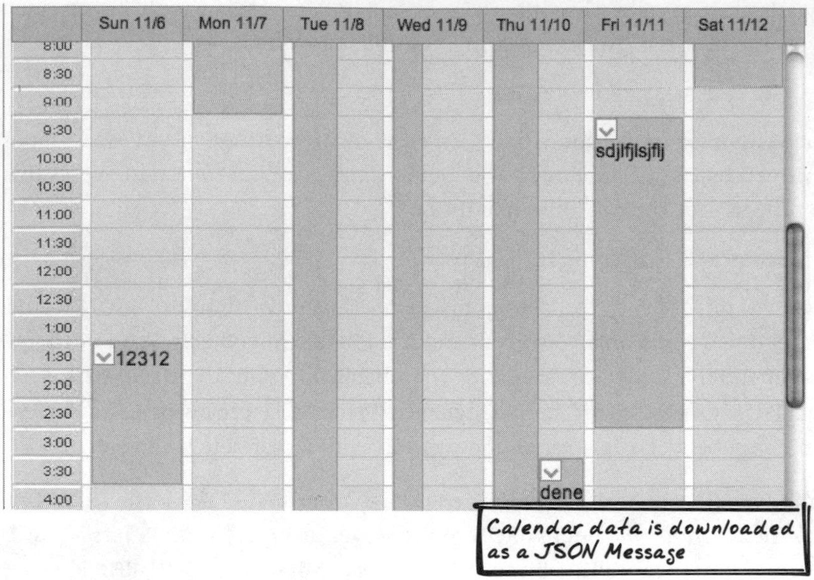

Calendar data is downloaded as a JSON Message

FIGURE 9-11. Kiko

Route Planning

Jim Ley's Route Planning application (*http://jibbering.com/routeplanner/*) shows you all the routes for a given airport (Figure 9-12), and, as his long-running XMLHttpRequest Tutorial (*http://jibbering.com/2002/4/httprequest.html*) explains, it uses JSON. For example, a JSON Message for the LAX airport is available at *http://jibbering.com/routeplanner/route. 1?LAX*. What the browser receives from the following JSON Message is an *XMLHttpRequest Call* (. . . has been substituted for multiple data items):

```
{from:'LAX',airports:[{id:"AMS",country:"NL",lat:"52.316666666667",lon:"4.
7833333333333",tz:"Europe/Amsterdam",name:"Amsterdam",shortname:"Schiphol"},...,{id:
"IAD",country:"US",lat:"38.95",lon:"-77.45",tz:"America/New_York",name:"Washington,
DC",shortname:"Washington Dulles International"}],routes:[{carrier:"star",toAirport:
"AMS",miles:5570},...,{carrier:"oneworld",toAirport:"DCA",miles:2304}]}
```

Ajax.Net framework

Ajax.Net (*http://ajax.schwarz-interactive.de/*) is one of several *Ajax Stub* frameworks that uses JSON Messages to transfer data, which can easily be converted to and from native objects at either end. For more details, see "JSON Message" in the "Related Patterns" section of *Ajax Stub*.

Code Example: Kiko

Kiko (*http://kiko.com*) responds to *XMLHttpRequest Call* with JSON Messages. When you log in, it downloads a list of appointments like this:

Route planning content is downloaded as a JSON message

FIGURE 9-12. Jibbering Route Planner

```
[
    {"title":"text","isevent":"bool",   "picture":"text","starttime":
"timestamp","endtime":"timestamp","recurs":"int2", "recurend":"timestamp","insystem":
"timestamp","recurstart":"timestamp",   "recurweek":"int2","description":
"text","defaultfree":"bool","location":"text","apptid":"int8"},{"title":"Roundup
meeting","isevent":"L","picture":"","starttime":"2005-09-16 19:00:00","endtime":"2005-
09-16 19:30:00","recurs":"1","recurend":"","insystem":"2005-09-12 14:52:10.
965713","recurstart":"2005-09-16 04:00:00","recurweek":"16","description":"Hopefully
just a quick roundup","defaultfree":"f","location":"Cyberspace","apptid":"9222"},
{"title":"Go Home!","isevent":"t","picture":"","starttime":"2005-09-15 21:00:
00","endtime":"2005-09-15 21:30:00","recurs":"0","recurend":"","insystem":"2005-09-12
15:00:33.659793","recurstart":"","recurweek":"","description":"","defaultfree":
"f","location":"Office, Bar, Home","apptid":"9288"}
    ]
```

Note that the message format here is a little unusual: everything is Strings, whereas JSON can store booleans and numbers directly. Consequently, the first element of the array includes some metadata to facilitate conversion, and the JavaScript includes a generic function to create native JavaScript objects from JSON messages like this.

Kiko's browser script also includes some conversion to JSON, as shown below (though I was unable to exercise this code). Typically, requests in Kiko are made as POSTs with CGI-style parameters, and only the responses are JSON.

```
var obj=json.stringify({'type':'newuser','email':email})
```

Alternatives

XML Message

JSON defines itself as a "fat-free alternative to XML." Before considering the differences between the formats, let's first look at what they have in common.

- Both are formats that depict an object as a plain-text string.

- Being plain-text string formats, both are suitable for transfer across HTTP. This means that both are suitable as inputs and outputs for a *Web Service*.

- Each format is supported by libraries in numerous languages, including JavaScript. There are libraries to convert from native objects to either format and back again to native objects.

JSON Message has several advantages over *XML Message* (see earlier in this chapter):

- JSON is more compact, and the lack of tags sometimes leads to a better visual representation of the underlying data.

- It's often claimed that JSON is faster for browsers to parse, though a recent investigation (*http://blogs.ebusiness-apps.com/dave/?p=45*) suggests XML parsing does scale better.

- JSON is a concrete data format. XML, in contrast, is really a meta-format, and a developer has many choices to make about the precise XML dialect to use. Each mapping strategy has its own conventions—for example, developers need to decide on tag names and between tag attributes or nested tags. Consequently, a server-side XML-object mapping framework may not be message-compatible with a JavaScript counterpart. Also, don't underestimate the amount of meetings and emails that will be necessary to resolve a seemingly trivial argument over data formats. In that sense, JSON is closer to a defined XML dialect than to XML itself.

- Within the browser, JSON has the edge in terms of support and consistency, since it's based on standard JavaScript.

- JSON happens to be quite compatible with YAML ("YAML Ain't Markup Language"; see *http://www.yaml.org/about.html*), a similar lightweight alternative to XML that's gaining traction in the dynamic scripting community.

XML Message (see earlier in this chapter) has several advantages over JSON Message:

- XML is vastly more familiar to the IT community than JSON.

- XML is more self-documenting. The header identifies which XML format is being used, and there's often a schema or DTD that defines the format precisely.

- XML has much more support in terms of libraries and tool support. JSON libraries tend to be simply about conversion, which its advocates would probably argue is all that's required. XML, on the other hand, has support in terms of DTD and Schema validators, XPath tools to interrogate the data, XSLT processors to perform translations, and so on. Furthermore, many IDEs, editors, and debugging environments make XML easy to work with.

- For any given task, developers usually have the luxury of choosing between several competing implementations.

Related Patterns

Ajax Stub

Being a portable object format, JSON is a useful way to facilitate calls from browser to server using an *Ajax Stub* (see earlier in this chapter) framework.

On-Demand JavaScript

Since a JSON Message is an ordinary JavaScript expression, it can be pulled in using *On-Demand JavaScript*. Data from external domains can be accessed this way, as explained in On-Demand JavaScript (Chapter 6).

Browser-Server Dialogue

W E'VE LOOKED AT THE BASIC TECHNOLOGIES FOR WEB REMOTING, WHICH LEADS TO QUESTIONS ABOUT browser-server information flow. How will you deal with multiple calls? How will you keep the browser and the server synchronized? How will you access external domains?

Call Tracking is about tracking calls and dealing with the asynchronous nature of Ajax. The next three patterns concern synchronization. With *Periodic Refresh*, the browser keeps requesting fresh information from the server. The opposite is *Submission Throttling*, where the browser keeps uploading new information *to* the server. An alternative to Submission Throttling, *Explicit Submission* involves uploading only when the user performs some action.

All of those patterns help manage bandwidth, but keeping things in sync can still be quite complex when there are lots of entities in the server and a rich interface in the browser. *Distributed Events* help manage the complexity.

Finally, *Cross-Domain Proxy* is a technique for mediating the dialogue between the browser and external servers.

Call Tracking

Asynchronous, Follow, Monitor, Parallel, Tracking, XMLHttpRequest

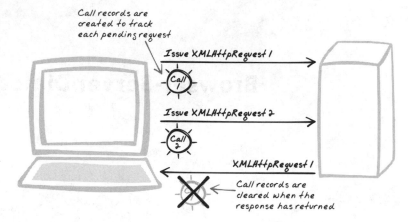

FIGURE 10-1. Call Tracking

Developer Story

Dave is writing an Ajax chat client, and he's concerned the more vocal users will hog server resources, so he decides to enforce a policy of no more than three pending server calls at any time. Thus, the browser script pushes messages into a queue and tracks the progress of each *XMLHttpRequest Call* (Chapter 6) containing those commands. He can enforce his maximum call count policy by tracking the state of each call.

Problem

How can you control parallel *XMLHttpRequest Calls* (Chapter 6)?

Forces

- Fast users and busy applications often stretch networks and servers to their limits.

- Asynchronous interaction is the only practical approach for Ajax applications. You don't want to block all interaction just because the network happens to be slow.

- The number of simultaneous requests must be controlled, because browsers can only handle a few at a time, and also to reduce the overall load.

Solution

Track XMLHttpRequest calls as they proceed from browser to server and back again. XMLHttpRequest is a fairly basic component that needs to be augmented or wrapped for better control over asynchronous dialogue. Furthermore, it is useful to keep all these wrappers in a collection. Note that this pattern is fairly low level, and the details should generally be encapsulated in a wrapper library.

The standard mechanism for Call Tracking requires an XMLHttpRequest wrapper. Consider the implementation of the Ajax Client Engine (ACE) library (*http://www.lishen.name/*). A Requester abstraction creates an XMLHttpRequest object upon construction:

```
function Requester( )
{
  var requester;
  if (window.XMLHttpRequest)
    {
      requester = new window.XMLHttpRequest( );
      ...
    }
  ...
}
```

Requester's response handler doesn't go directly back to the caller's registered event handler, but instead to a method of Requester. This internal callback can then perform logging and other tasks before passing control back to the caller's handler. There's also a caching mechanism, so the Requester will add and remove itself from the cache as the call progresses.

The most important reason to track calls is to tame the asynchronous nature of XMLHttpRequest. There's a potential bug in which the programmer treats XMLHttpRequest as a Singleton (Gamma et al., 1995). That is, there's only a single, global, XMLHttpRequest instance, but parallel calls are made (*http://smokey.rhs.com/web/blog/PowerOfTheSchwartz.nsf/d6plinks/RSCZ-6CDPEX*). An initial call will be pending, when suddenly a new call steps in. What happens here is unclear, as it's the sort of unanticipated behavior that will vary across browser implementations, but it certainly won't be a happy result. The first call will possibly be cancelled, and it's unlikely its event handler will be notified. The simplest way to resolve this problem is to create a new XMLHttpRequest instance each time, then use a closure; i.e.:

```
xhReq.onreadystatechange = function( ) {
    if (xhReq.readyState != 4) { return; }
    var serverResponse = xhReq.responseText;
    ...
};
```

We can consider this a limited form of Call Tracking, since we've at least ensured each pending call will have its own associated XMLHttpRequest. Still, we can achieve a lot more by wrapping requests and placing the wrappers in a collection, as demonstrated by ACE and other libraries:

Pooling
A collection of wrappers can be used as a cache. When each object has delivered its response, it's returned to the available pool (and its state reset in case of an error). This reduces object creation and destruction.

Limiting

Using a fixed-size pool (see the previous point), you have the option of limiting the number of simultaneous requests to reduce network load and prevent problems in the browser; most browsers will only allow a handful of pending requests at any time.

Detecting timeouts

As explained in *XMLHttpRequest Call* (Chapter 6), the framework can start a timer when the request is issued and notify the caller if a timeout occurs.

Sequencing

With all requests coordinated by a central piece of logic, it's possible to influence the sequence of calls going in and out of the server. While it's best to design for calls to be completely parallel, sometimes you might have constraints; e.g., you might want the server to process calls in the same order as the user initiates them; i.e., fire a request only when the previous response has been received.

Atomic Processing

Related to the previous point, you often need to ensure the browser will handle one response completely before moving onto the next. One scenario is appending a bunch of response information—if the responses are dealt with in parallel, you'll end up with interleaved messages. One style of Call Tracking is to create JavaScript Command (Gamma et al.) objects from each response, push them onto a queue, and have a separate thread execute them one at a time.

Passing in Call Context

Sometimes, a service's response is minimal and doesn't include any detail about the original call—for example, `false` as opposed to `<spellcheck term="misspeld">false </spellcheck>`. Indeed, sometimes there's no response at all, and the framework will need to inform the response handler of a timeout. In these cases, it's useful to provide some context about the original call. By tracking the call, a framework can remember a "call context" that the caller sets when the request is issued. When the framework eventually transmits the response to the caller's response handler, it also passes in the call context. See "Code Refactoring: AjaxPatterns Predictive Fetch Sum" in *Predictive Fetch* (Chapter 13) to see how a calling context can be used.

Logging

A wrapper can register itself as the wrapped object's response handler, and then log any changes. It can also poll for any new content (since there's no guarantee the event handler will be called when new content is added).

Real-World Examples

Ajax Client Engine (ACE) library

Li Shen's Ajax Client Engine (ACE) (*http://www.lishen.name/*) uses Call Tracking to ease development and harden the application in production. Among its many features are several related to Call Tracking:

- Long calls are timed out.

- Changes to `XMLHttpRequest`'s response state are logged.

- A service can be periodically polled.

- The caller can declare exactly when the callback method should be invoked.

AjaxCaller library

The AjaxCaller library (*http://ajaxify.com/run/Lib/js/ajaxCaller.js*), used throughout the AjaxPatterns demos for Web Remoting, uses Call Tracking to pool `Calls`, which wrap `XMLHttpRequest` objects.

libXmlRequest library

libXmlRequest (*http://www.whitefrost.com/reference/2005/09/09/libXmlRequest.html*) is another `XMLHttpRequest` wrapper. It keeps `XMLHttpRequest` objects in a pool so they can be reused, and tracks the response status in order to manage the pool.

Code Example: Ajax Client Engine (ACE)

In this example, we'll look at ACE's internal handling of call timeouts. The library consists of `Requester` objects, which wrap `XMLHttpRequest` objects. As explained earlier in the Solution, the wrapped `XMLHttpRequest` objects are created upon construction. When the wrapper is invoked to make a call, it creates a timer to cancel the request if it takes too long. The timer ID is held as an attribute of the wrapper.

```
timeoutId = window.setTimeout(endRequest, request.callbackTimeout * 1000);
```

To track the call, the wrapper registers itself as a request handler:

```
function beginRequest()
{
    ...
  requester.onreadystatechange = readystatechangeHandler;
    ...
}
```

Its handler is therefore called upon each change, and in the case of a complete call, cancels the timer:

```
function readystatechangeHandler()
    ...
  if (requester.readyState == Ace.ReadyState.Complete)
  {
      ...
    if (requester.status == Ace.Status.OK)
    {
```

```
      ...
      if (timeoutId)
      {
        window.clearTimeout(timeoutId);
        timeoutId = undefined;
      }
      ...
    }
    ...
  }
```

Alternatives

Fire-and-forget

Some calls need no tracking because they are low-priority uploads of information to the server. For example, a chat app might reasonably ignore the results of uploading the user's messages because a separate thread is continuously polling for *all* recent messages. Another example would be uploading information to support *Predictive Fetch* (Chapter 13), where the worst case is simply the lost opportunity of a performance optimization. Ajaxian.com featured an interesting article on optimizing for this kind of request (*http://www. ajaxian.com/archives/2005/09/ajaxian_fire_an.html*).

Global XMLHttpRequest

You may be able to get away with a single, global XMLHttpRequest under certain conditions and with care. For example, you can use a lock to ensure there's only one pending call at each time (which is really a special case of Call Tracking). However, you risk forcing the user to endure long waiting periods.

Metaphor

Call Tracking is like tagging self-addressed envelopes before you send them away, so you can track them as they return.

Acknowledgments

This pattern was originally inspired by Richard Schwartz's caution against the familiar anti-pattern of working with a global XMLHttpRequest (*http://smokey.rhs.com/web/blog/ PowerOfTheSchwartz.nsf/d6plinks/RSCZ-6CDPEX*).

Periodic Refresh

Auto-Update, Polling, Sync, Synchronise, Sychronize, Real-Time

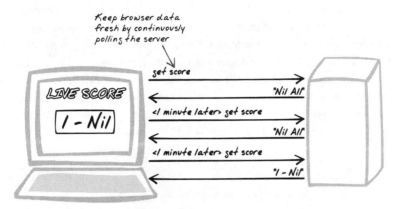

FIGURE 10-2. Periodic Refresh

Developer Story

Devi's coding up a ticket sales web site. For each event, she wants to keep the browser updated with the number of tickets remaining. Thus, she introduces a timer so that every 30 seconds, it calls a web service to pull down the latest sales stats.

Problem

How can the application keep users informed of changes occurring on the server?

Forces

- The state of many web apps is inherently volatile. Changes can come from numerous sources, such as other users, external news and data, results of complex calculations, and triggers based on the current time and date.

- HTTP requests can only emerge from the client. When a state change occurs, there's no way for a server to open connections to interested clients.

- One way to keep the browser updated is *HTTP Streaming* (Chapter 6), but, as the "Alternatives" section for that pattern explains, it's not always ideal. In particular, it's not very scalable.

Solution

The browser periodically issues an XMLHttpRequest Call to gain new information; e.g., one call every five seconds. The solution makes use of the browser's *Scheduling* (Chapter 7) capabilities to provide a means of keeping the user informed of latest changes.

In its simplest form, a loop can be established to run the refresh indefinitely, by continuously issuing *XMLHttpRequest Calls* (Chapter 6):

```
setInterval(callServer, REFRESH_PERIOD_MILLIS);
```

Here, the callServer function will invoke the server, having registered a callback function to get the new information. That callback function will be responsible for updating the DOM according to the server's latest report. Conventional web apps, even most of those using *XMLHttpRequest Calls*, operate under a paradigm of one-way communication: the client can initiate communication with the server, but not vice versa. Periodic Refresh fakes a back-channel: it approximates a situation where the server pushes data to the client, so the server can effectively receive new information from the browser. Indeed, as some of the examples show, the server can also mediate between users in almost real-time. So Periodic Refresh can be used for peer-to-peer communication too.

But before we get too carried away with Periodic Refresh, it's important to note that it's a serious compromise, for two key reasons:

- The period between refreshes would ideally be zero, meaning instant updates. But that's not realistic and the browser will always lag behind. Latency is particularly problematic when the user is interacting with a representation of volatile server-side data. For instance, a user might be editing an object without knowing that another user has already deleted it.

- There is a significant cost attached to Periodic Refresh. Each request, no matter how tiny, demands resources at both ends, all the way down to operating-system level. Traffic-wise, each request also entails some bandwidth cost, which can add up if refreshes are occurring once every few seconds.

So a key design objective must be to increase the average refresh period and reduce the content per refresh, while maintaining a happy user experience. One optimization is a timeout: the refreshes cease when the system detects the user is no longer active, according to a *Timeout* (Chapter 17) mechanism. You also want to make sure each refresh counts; it's wasteful to demand lots of updates if the network isn't capable of delivering them. Thus, the browser script can do some monitoring and dynamically adjust the period so it's at least long enough to cope with all incoming updates. Many of the Performance Optimization patterns can also be applied to Periodic Refresh—see the next section.

Decisions

How long will the refresh period be?

The refresh period can differ widely, depending on usage context. Broadly speaking, we can identify three categories of activity level:

Real-Time interaction (milliseconds)
    The user is actively interacting with the system, and his input relies on the server's output—for example, a chat user needs to see what others are saying, a trader needs to see

current prices, or a game player needs to see the state of the game. Here, the interval could be as low as a millisecond on a local machine or local network, or perhaps be 20–100 milliseconds on a global network.

Active monitoring (seconds)
The user relies on the server state for work outside the system—for example, a security officer watches sensor displays for suspicious activity, or a manager occasionally watches the fluctuation of sales figures during a particular window of time. In some cases, timeliness may be critical, making subsecond responses desirable. In other cases, a few seconds is sufficient feedback.

Casual monitoring (minutes)
Some applications are designed for the user to leave in a window or separate browser tab and view throughout the day. The information does not change often, and it's no drama if the user finds out a little later. Prime candidates here are portals and RSS aggregators. Refresh periods of 10 minutes or more are often acceptable for such content. A manual "Refresh Now" mechanism is worth including where the refresh period is longer than a few seconds. It can relate to the entire application or to specific components.

Sometimes, the best solution uses multiple Periodic Refresh cycles in parallel, each with a frequency reflecting the user's needs. An interactive wiki, for example, might update news headlines every 10 minutes, online statuses of other users every minute, and content being edited every second.

Real-World Examples

Lace Chat

Instant messaging (or "online chat") applications pre-date the Web, and, unlike email and other services, web interfaces have never quite worked out, partly due to the fact that people don't enjoy frequent full-page refreshes. Ajax makes it possible to avoid a complete refresh by pulling down messages with an *XMLHttpRequest Call* (Chapter 6). Only the new messages need to be sent in each periodic response. In fact, there are several applications under development. Lace Chat (*http://socket7.net/lace/*), for example, is only a proof-of-concept, but provides good evidence that web-based chat is feasible. Every few seconds the messages update to show any new messages other users may have entered. When you post a message, it's also handled as an XMLHttpRequest Call.

Magnetic Poetry

Like a wiki, Magnetic Poetry (*http://www.broken-notebook.com/magnetic/*) involves a shared workspace (Figure 10-3). In this case, users move tiles through the space, and the application updates once a second to reflect the new space. As of version 1.7, the entire tile set is sent each time, but there's the potential to compress the information by sending only recent tile positions. This enables two users to work on the area simultaneously, and one can even see a tile being dragged by a different user, like a low-frequency animation.

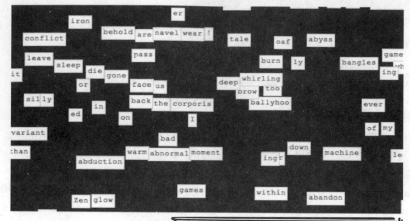

Magnetic Poetry updates once a second to show any rearrangement made by other users

FIGURE 10-3. *Magnetic Poetry*

Claude Hussenet's portal

Portals, by definition, display various kinds of information. And often that information is of a dynamic nature, requiring periodic updates. Claude Hussenet's portal (*http://www.claudehussenet.com/portal/Welcome.do*) contains several portlets:

- World news headlines (taken from Moreover—see *http://moreover.com*—and Yahoo! News—see *http://news.yahoo.com*). The server appears to generate these from an RSS feed.

- New online articles appearing on TheServerSide.com and DevX.com. Again, these are taken from RSS feeds.

- Customized stock portal. The server appears to maintain a record of all current stock prices and is capable of delivering those requested by the browser.

In each case, the information is volatile and needs to be periodically updated, as is typical for many portlets. Also characteristic of portal applications is the relatively long refresh period, 15 minutes in this case. Each portlet contains a manual refresh too, for immediate results.

Code Examples

Lace

Lace Chat (*http://socket7.net/lace/*) handles Periodic Refreshes to show all users' chat messages.

The timer is set on startup to periodically call the get( ) function, which initiates the *XMLHttpRequest Call* (Chapter 6) for new messages:

```
this.timerID = setInterval(function () { thisObj.get(true); }, interval);
```

get( ) performs a straightforward query of the server:

```
this.httpGetObj.open('POST', this.url, true);
this.httpGetObj.setRequestHeader('Content-Type','application/x-www-form-urlencoded;
charset=UTF-8');

var thisObj = this;
this.httpGetObj.onreadystatechange = function () { thisObj.handleGet(system); };
this.httpGetObj.send(param);
```

If the server has changed at all, the entire contents are returned. How does Lace know if the server has changed? Each time the server responds, it generates a hash for the contents. And when the browser next calls for a refresh, it includes the last hash as a parameter to the call. The server sends a full response only if the current hash differs from that specified by the browser:

```
[lib_lace.php]
function getMessageHash( ) {
  ...
  return md5(implode(file(LACE_FILE)));
}

[lace.php]
$_hash = getMessageHash( ); if ($_hash == $hash) exit; // no change exit($_hash.
'||||'.getFileContentsRaw( ));
```

Code Refactoring: AjaxPatterns Periodic Time

The Basic Time Demo (*http://ajaxify.com/run/time*) requires the user to manually update the time display by clicking a button. We'll perform a quick refactoring to re-fetch the time from the server every five seconds (*http://ajaxify.com/run/time/periodicRefresh*).

First, we'll create the function that initiates the server calls. Here, we already have two functions like that, one for each display. So, let's ensure we call both of those periodically:

```
function requestBothTimes() { requestDefaultTime(); requestCustomTime(); }
```

Then, the Periodic Refresh is simply a matter of running the request every five seconds:

```
function onLoad( ) { ...  setInterval(requestBothTimes, 5000); ...  }
```

One more nicety: the function in setTimeout begins to run only after the initial delay period. So we're left with empty time displays for five seconds. To rectify that, requestBothTimes is also called on startup:

```
function onLoad( ) { ...  requestBothTimes( );
                          setInterval(requestBothTimes, 5000); ...  }
```

Now, the user sees the time almost as soon as the page is loaded.

Alternatives

HTTP Streaming

One of the forces for this pattern is that HTTP connections tend to be short-lived. That's a tendency, not a requirement. As *HTTP Streaming* (Chapter 6) explains, there are some circumstances where it's actually feasible to leave the connection open. Streaming allows for a sequence of messages to be downloaded into the browser without the need for explicit polling. (Low-level polling still happens at the operating system and network levels, but that doesn't have to be handled by the web developer, and there's no overhead of starting and stopping an HTTP connection for each refresh, nor of starting and stopping the web service.)

Related Patterns

Distributed Events

You can use *Distributed Events* (see later in this chapter) to coordinate browser activity following a response.

Fat Client, Browser-Side Cache, Guesstimate

A little work on performance issues can help make the system feel more responsive. Some of the performance optimization patterns help:

Fat Client (Chapter 13)
   Reduces the need for server processing by pushing functionality into the browser.

Browser-Side Cache (Chapter 13)
   Reduces queries by retaining query data locally.

Guesstimate (Chapter 13)
   Gives the user a sense of what's happening without actually performing any query.

Submission Throttling

Submission Throttling (see the next pattern) also involves a periodic call to the server. The emphasis there is on uploading browser-side changes, whereas the present pattern focuses on downloading server-side changes. The two may be combined to form a general-purpose "synchronize" operation, as long as the update frequency is sufficient in both directions. This would improve performance by reducing the amount of overall traffic. The Wiki Demo (*http://ajaxify.com/run/wiki*) takes this approach.

Heartbeat

It's inevitable that users will leave their browser pointing at web sites they're not actually using. The rising popularity of tabbed browsing—now supported by all the major browsers—only exacerbates the problem. You don't want to keep refreshing the page for idle users, so use *Heartbeat* (Chapter 17) to detect whether the user is still paying attention.

Metaphor

A movie is refreshed at subsecond intervals to provide the illusion of real-time activity.

Submission Throttling

Buffer, Queue, Performance, Throttle

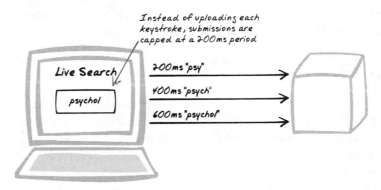

FIGURE 10-4. *Submission Throttling*

Developer Story

Devi's producing an Ajax chat web site and wants to transmit text as the user types. However, she knows some users will type faster than the system can cope with so she introduces a throttling mechanism that ensures no more than one message is uploaded every 200 milliseconds.

Problem

How can information be submitted to the server?

Forces

- Information is often uploaded in bursts; e.g., a chat tool incurs many hits when a user becomes passionate about the topic, or a data entry tool incurs many hits when the user responds to some new information.

- It's difficult for the server to cope with lots of messages at once.

- Browsers can only handle a limited number of pending *XMLHttpRequest Calls* at any moment.

- Each message has overheads, such as packet headers and requires some processing at each stage of the browser/server round-trip.

Solution

Instead of submitting upon each JavaScript event, retain data in a browser-based buffer and automatically upload it at fixed intervals. As with many applications of buffering and throttling, the purpose is to strike a balance between responsiveness and resources. In most cases, it would be ideal to respond to every keystroke and mouse movement—so, for example, like a desktop application, tooltips could come directly from the server as the user mouses around. But that's not practical due to bandwidth considerations, and possibly server constraints too. So to ease bandwidth—and to lessen server processing, call detail is accumulated and periodically uploaded.

Exactly what the buffer holds is application-specific, but there are two general styles: data buffers and command queues.

In the first buffer style, the buffer holds some data to be uploaded. Consider implementing a *Suggestion* (Chapter 14) interface like Google Suggest (*http://www.google.com/webhp?complete=1&hl=en*), which keeps showing information based on what's been typed. The simplest thing would be to add an "onchange" listener to the text field and upload the buffer when each change occurs. However, what if you get a fast typist, one of those folks who revels in their "words per minute" metric? Banging out 100 words per minute means perhaps 10 characters per second, or a call every 100 milliseconds—feasible with a local-host web server, maybe workable on an intranet, but not scalable for most public Internet applications. So *Suggestion* systems, and more generally *Live Command-Lines* (Chapter 14), run a fixed-period timer. Every 500 milliseconds, say, the browser checks if there was a change since the last call, and if so, uploads to get some information and remembers what was uploaded to avoid doing so again. Effectively, the result for the current text field is cached, and the cache can only change on fixed periods.

A similar pattern might be used on a *Live Form* (Chapter 14), where the entire form is periodically uploaded to the server, even though some fields are blank, along with an indication of the user's progress. The server can then use some intelligence to critique the form data, so as to provide live feedback.

The other style of buffer is a command queue. Here, Commands (see Gamma et al., 1995) are held in a queue, and the whole queue periodically uploaded to the server before being cleared. Some kind of serialization must take place, so the Commands must be represented as Strings and the Queue must ensure they can be pulled apart by the server; e.g., by separating them with a delimiter character. It's up to the developers to agree on a protocol for defining how Commands are represented as Strings. For example, a wiki might use the string "Del Issues" to delete the Issues page. Another technique would be to store the commands as custom JavaScript objects and serialize them into *JSON Messages* (Chapter 9).

Submission Throttling might appear to optimize technical resources at the expense of usability, but can actually be a boon for users too. There's a reason why the Windows and Apple operating systems don't show copious logging details when booting. Technical users may appreciate the comprehensive output of a Linux boot sequence, but most users consider it overload—much more information than they actually care about. Throttling is a good way to prevent information overload in the browser, especially error messages that might come back because the user is only halfway through an edit.

Decisions

How will the server deal with incoming commands? Will all commands still be valid?

Submission Throttling is vulnerable to integrity issues, because synchronization is being deliberately downgraded. The universe will have moved on since the user submitted the original commands—the time will be different, new information may be available, existing information may have changed or been deleted, and other users may have executed commands in the meantime. All of these scenarios are unavoidable manifestations of the asynchronous nature of Ajax, and the design must take them into account.

The server needs to decide whether to process each incoming command as it's quite possible some are no longer valid. For example, a stock purchase order might be refused on the basis that the price has just risen or because the server has since expired an initial quote it made to the client. Some of these decisions can be made by standard techniques such as atomic database transactions, but others might require some custom business logic. Furthermore, some business logic will be required to decide what to do with the rest of the Commands in a queue, should one Command in the middle fail. Sometimes, it's okay to keep processing the rest and sometimes not.

How will buffer uploads be triggered?

The most obvious algorithm for upload sequencing is a timer. Every minute (say), the browser polls the buffer and makes the corresponding call sequence. Or, if nothing has changed, it might do nothing for another minute. If a timer is used, a decision must be made as to when it will trigger. First, the period is usually fixed, but does not have to be. It might be increased during times of known server activity, or even altered to respond to those constraints dynamically. Furthermore, it might be based on the user in question: service level can be tweaked by giving premium users shorter throttle periods.

A variant, usually more useful, is to cap the rate but immediately send the first command after a long wait. This helps a user who changes information only occasionally. Let's say the throttle period is 30 seconds. With a standard, fixed-interval, algorithm, the following sequence occurs:

1. 00 secs: system polls, no activity so no upload
2. 30 secs: system polls, no activity so no upload
3. 60 secs: system polls, no activity so no upload
4. 65 secs: infrequent user does something; no upload yet

5. 75 secs: infrequent user does something; still no upload

6. 90 secs: system polls and uploads both pending commands

We can still cap the rate at 30 seconds, but upload a command immediately if there's been no activity for the past 30 seconds:

1. 00 secs: system polls, no activity so no upload

2. 30 secs: system polls, no activity so no upload

3. 60 secs: system polls, no activity so no upload

4. 65 secs: infrequent user does something

5. 65 secs: system notices and uploads command immediately

6. 75 secs: infrequent user does something; this time, the command must wait since there was a recent call

7. 95 secs: system polls, uploads if there was any further activity after 65 secs

Prioritization is another technique. A timer might be used for regular events, but with priority given to any critical commands. A *Live Form* (Chapter 14) might periodically upload the progress of an individual field, so the server can provide suggestions, for example. But as soon as the user proceeds to the next field, a call takes place immediately.

A further consideration is the user's activity during upload. It's wise to avoid uploading something the user is currently working on, especially if other users will see it and if they probably won't be working on it much longer. So, one policy might involve uploading only after a period of idle activity.

How many buffers per browser application?

There's no reason to have just one buffer for all commands. It's possible to have several buffers running in parallel, providing you have considered the consequences of commands arriving in a different order to the user requesting them. Prioritization was already mentioned above, which would be one reason to have several buffers—higher-priority buffers being processed with greater frequency.

Here's how a blog reader might use three buffers in parallel:

- A low priority queue uploads comments submitted by the user. *Throttle period: 15 seconds*.

- A medium priority queue pulls down requested feeds from the server. *Throttle period: 3 seconds*.

- A high priority text buffer lets the user tag articles with a *Suggestion* mechanism. While it's not necessary to upload upon each keystroke, any new information must be transferred quite rapidly. *Throttle period: 0.2 seconds*.

This example illustrates that it's quite easy to run several buffers without threat to data integrity and without user confusion.

How long should the throttle period be?

Deciding on the throttle period requires some analysis of user needs. As the previous blog reader example demonstrates, there is a range of periods that might be required:

- For background synchronization, the period can be a few minutes if resource constraints apply, although it should ideally be in the order of 10 seconds. If it is several minutes, users should be kept informed with appropriate *Progress Indicators* (Chapter 14), lest they quit and lose work before the upload kicks in. Ideally, there should be an *Explicit Submission* (later in this chapter) mechanism as well, to allow immediate saving.

- At the other end of the spectrum, for low-level interaction while the user types and mouses around, the period must be in the order of 100 milliseconds.

Real-World Examples

Google Suggest

Google Suggest (*http://www.google.com/webhp?complete=1*) features *Suggestions*, so when you type "A," the browser pops up a list of popular searches beginning with "A." To prevent against excessive queries, Google Suggest (*http://serversideguy.blogspot.com/2004/12/google-suggest-dissected.html*) uses Submission Throttling.

Zuggest

Zuggest (*http://www.francisshanahan.com/zuggest.aspx*) is a *Live Search* (Chapter 14) showing Amazon results as you type (Figure 10-5). So type "Ab" and you'll get results like "Basic Ab Workout for Dummies" and "Absolutely Fabulous." The results are images as well as text, so it would be expensive to search for something you weren't interested in. So, if you're searching for "Absolutely," it's best to avoid searching for "Ab" and "Abso" and "Absolut" along the way, which is the kind of thing the Google Suggest algorithm would do.

To ensure searches are relevant, Zuggest applies a delay while typing. The assumption is that you'll be typing at a rate of at least one character per second. Any time you hit a key, you'll see a "Waiting until you're done ..." message, and you'll have a second to hit another key. If no key is pressed, the application assumes you were looking for the current term, and performs a remote call.

As explained in the *Fat Client* pattern, the wiki demo (*http://ajaxify.com/run/wiki*) throttles in a similar manner.

Gmail

Gmail (*http://gmail.com/*) has an auto-save feature that periodically uploads a message being composed.

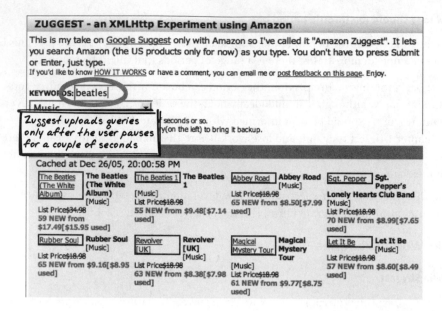

ZUGGEST - an XMLHttp Experiment using Amazon

This is my take on Google Suggest only with Amazon so I've called it "Amazon Zuggest". It lets you search Amazon (the US products only for now) as you type. You don't have to press Submit or Enter, just type.

If you'd like to know HOW IT WORKS or have a comment, you can email me or post feedback on this page. Enjoy.

KEYWORDS: beatles

Music

Zuggest uploads queries only after the user pauses for a couple of seconds   seconds or so.
    y(on the left) to bring it backup.

Cached at Dec 26/05, 20:00:58 PM

| The Beatles (The White Album) [Music] List Price$34.98 59 NEW from $17.49[$15.95 used] | The Beatles (The White Album) [Music] List Price$18.98 55 NEW from $9.48[$7.14 used] | The Beatles 1 [Music] | The Beatles 1 | Abbey Road | Abbey Road [Music] List Price$18.98 65 NEW from $8.50[$7.99 used] | Sgt. Pepper | Sgt. Pepper's Lonely Hearts Club Band [Music] List Price$18.98 70 NEW from $8.99[$7.65 used] |

| Rubber Soul List Price$18.98 65 NEW from $9.16[$8.95 used] | Rubber Soul [Music] | Revolver [UK] List Price$18.98 63 NEW from $8.38[$7.98 used] | Revolver [UK] [Music] | Magical Mystery Tour | Magical Mystery Tour [Music] List Price$18.98 61 NEW from $9.77[$8.75 used] | Let It Be List Price$18.98 57 NEW from $8.60[$8.49 used] | Let It Be [Music] |

FIGURE 10-5. Zuggest

Prototype framework

Prototype (*http://prototype.conio.net/*) offers a reusable component, `TimedObserver`, which performs Submission Throttling. ListSomething (*http://listsomething.com/*), a search engine for classified ads, utilizes `TimedObserver` for its *Live Search*.

Code Example: AjaxPatterns Assistive Search

The Assistive Search demo (*http://ajaxify.com/run/assistiveSearch*) throttles in a similar manner to Google Suggest and other Ajax search apps.

`requestValidCategoriesLoop` runs repeatedly; the precise interval (in milliseconds) is determined by the `THROTTLE_PERIOD` constant (about 100 milliseconds). The last server query is always stored, and there's nothing to do if the current query remains the same as the previous query. If there has been a change, the new query is submitted to the server:

```
function requestValidCategoriesLoop() {
  if (query()!=latestServerQuery) {
    vars = {
      queryType: "getValidCategories",
      queryText: escape(query())
    }
    ajaxCaller.get("categories.php", vars, onValidCategoriesResponse,
                   false, null);
    latestServerQuery = query();
  }
  setTimeout('requestValidCategoriesLoop();', THROTTLE_PERIOD);
}
```

Related Patterns

Periodic Refresh

Periodic Refresh (see earlier) is somewhat the reverse of Submission Throttling: instead of periodically uploading user input, Periodic Refresh periodically downloads server state.

Progress Indicator

A common trend while performing a periodic update is to include a small *Progress Indicator* (Chapter 14), often as a *Popup* with a message such as a "Saving."

Metaphor

Science-fiction writers have speculated that interstellar communication would work like this. Because the trip is so great, each imperial command must contain a big load of information—the inter-galactic emperor can't just tell the colonials to "go fetch a kettle" ... (20 light-years later)..."now add some water"....

Explicit Submission

Submit, Packet, Performance

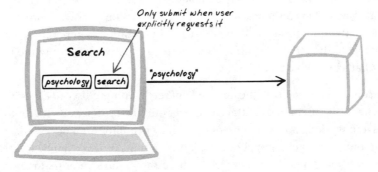

FIGURE 10-6. Explicit Submission

Developer Story

Devi's producing an Ajax chat web site. She decides text will only be transmitted after the user explicitly clicks a "Done" button.

Problem

How can information be submitted to the server?

Forces

- It's difficult for the server to cope with lots of messages at once.

- Each message has overheads, such as packet headers, and requires some processing at each stage of the browser-server round-trip.

- Users often need to manipulate a small work unit privately, and then upload it as a whole atomic unit to the server.

Solution

Instead of automatically submitting upon each browser event, require the user to explicitly request it; e.g., submit upon a button click. Typically, the user performs some work for a few seconds or minutes, and then clicks a button to tell the server. It's a familiar pattern on the Web as it feels similar to standard form submission.

The most common example is a text field, which may be an input or textarea control. While it would be possible to transmit keystrokes as they happen, that's often not desirable. In a wiki, for instance, imagine what would happen if a user deleted a paragraph in order to replace it. Any other user viewing the wiki would see the paragraph disappear! Furthermore, the history would reflect that transition state.

Where there's only one input field, it sometimes makes sense to rely on onchange or onblur events to detect that the change has been made. But how about when there are several closely related fields? Even then, some automatic submission is okay, to provide some validation information, for instance. However, if the information is important enough to cause a change to the server, Explicit Submission is a good way to ensure the user intended what's been uploaded.

As well as some inconvenience, the downside of relying on the user to explicitly submit data is…what if the user doesn't? Have you ever quit the browser and forgot to submit a form you were working on? The consequences may be minor for a query-and-report application, but for data entry applications, large amounts of work can be lost when the user forgets to submit it or doesn't realize it's necessary to do so. For that reason, Explicit Submission can sometimes be complemented by automated *Submission Throttling*. For instance, Gmail (*http://gmail.com*) will only send mail upon an Explicit Send command, but nonetheless has an Autosave feature that will periodically upload an in-progress message as a draft.

Decisions

How will the user request the submission?

The submission mechanism should ideally be similar to those in similar non-Ajax systems.

Buttons are one common idiom, with a generic label like Submit, Done, or Go!. More meaningful names are usually clearer, being specific to the task being conducted—for instance, "Buy," "Search," or "Delete." Buttons have the benefit of making the Explicit Submission mechanism stupidly obvious: "I click the button, the info's submitted; I don't click it, it's not submitted."

Relying on a significant keystroke, usually Enter, can also work in the right context, and, by using the keyboard, it supports power users.

Listening for the onblur is another explicit technique, albeit with a submission mechanism that is not apparent from the UI. The nice thing about onblur is that the application can continue submitting without interrupting the usual flow of events. On a *Live Form*, for instance, users can force a submission with Tab or Shift-Tab, which they would have hit anyway to move out of the tab. It also means the user can click somewhere else on the mouse to force a submission. The downside is the risk of accidental submission. There's also the question of what the user can do to prevent a submission occurring, having already begun typing something? Perhaps they can blank the field, but clearly, communi cating this to the user is not easy.

How will you deal with frequent submissions?

Explicit Submission leaves open the possibility of too many submissions at once. This might happen because the user is working too fast, or simply because he has grown impatient and begun banging on the mouse button or the Enter key. A few coping strategies are as follows:

- Limit frequency of submissions with *Submission Throttling* (earlier in this chapter). While that pattern emphasizes automated submissions, it's still possible to throttle Explicit Submissions.

- After a user has made a submission, use *Page Rearrangement* (Chapter 5) to remove the submission button.

- Soothe impatient users with *Progress Indicators* (Chapter 14) and *Guesstimates* (Chapter 13).

- Prevent excessive delays with Performance Optimizations like *Predictive Fetch* (Chapter 13).

- Show the initial Submission control in a *Popup* (Chapter 15), and then close it upon submission. This is sometimes used for login forms.

No matter how you prevent multiple submissions, be sure to design the server so it can cope with them. *RESTful Service* (Chapter 9) helps here because it can handle such situations gracefully; e.g., by rejecting any invalid queries.

Real-World Examples

Lace Chat

Brett Stimmerman's Lace Chat (*http://www.socket7.net/lace/*) is an Ajax chat application. Lace users type the entire message and then explicitly submit with a Say button. You can also hit Enter after typing the message. Most chat applications work this way. It's a little more efficient, but the main benefit is actually for the user. It might be confusing to other users to see a partially constructed message, so the composer of that message should rectify any errors before posting the message.

The Fonz

"The Fonz" text adventure (*http://www.mrspeaker.webeisteddfod.com/2005/04/17/the-fonz-and-ajax/*) is a command-line game (Figure 10-7). In typical command-line fashion, you type something and submit the whole command at once. Interestingly, command lines don't have to work that way—it's feasible to provide hints or some validation support as the user types. The Assistive Search Demo (*http://ajaxify.com/run/assistiveSearch/*) illustrates this point.

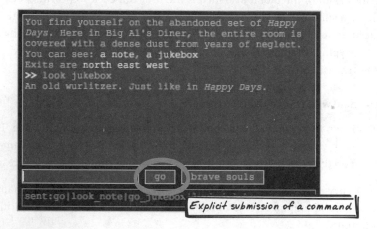

FIGURE 10-7. The Fonz

A9

A9 (*http://a9.com*), as with many search engines, requires Explicit Submission before it searches for the user's query (Figure 10-8).

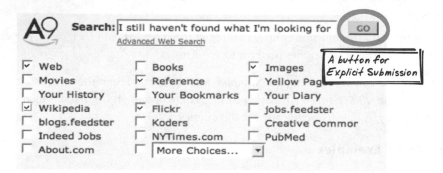

FIGURE 10-8. A9 search

Code Refactoring: AjaxPatterns Form-Based Sum

The Basic Sum Demo (*http://ajaxify.com/run/sum*) illustrates Explicit Submission. In the basic case, there are some input fields and a button, just sitting in a div:

```
<div>

  <div id="figure">
    <input type="text" class="figure" id="figure1"
           name="figure1" size="3" value="4"/><br/>
    <input type="text" class="figure" id="figure2"
           name="figure2" size="3" value="6"/><br/>
    <input type="text" class="figure" id="figure3"
           name="figure3" size="3" value="" /><br/>
  </div>

  <input type="button" id="addButton" value="Add" />

</div>
```

The button is configured to submit the form when it is clicked, an example of Explicit Submission:

```
$("addButton").onclick = function( ) {
  submitSum( );
}
```

We now refactor to an alternative form of Explicit Submission, in which a standard form (*http://ajaxify.com/run/sum/form*) makes the submission. It's still an "Ajax submission" involving no page refresh, but it leverages the standard form mechanism. There are two reasons you might do this in real life: it's a step towards graceful degradation, since non-JavaScript browsers will require the data to be held in a standard form; it will "feel" more like a form to the user—e.g., the Enter key will automatically submit, and any CSS styling for forms will apply to it.

The initial HTML has been wrapped by a form tag. With standard JavaScript enabled, the action URL makes no difference because it will never be accessed, but if we want, we could point it to a conventional server-side script that would process the form in the event that JavaScript is turned off. The regular button control has been replaced by a submit button:

```
<form action="http://ajaxify.com/run/sum/form/">

  <div id="figure">
    <input type="text" class="figure" id="figure1"
           name="figure1" size="3" value="4"/><br/>
    <input type="text" class="figure" id="figure2"
           name="figure2" size="3" value="6"/><br/>
    <input type="text" class="figure" id="figure3"
           name="figure3" size="3" value="" /><br/>
  </div>

  <input type="submit" id="addButton" value="Add" />

</form>
```

The script hooks into onsubmit, which will be called when the new submit button is clicked. It arranges for an XMLHttpRequest submission via submitSum( ), then returns false to prevent a conventional form submission and page refresh.

```
$("sumForm").onsubmit = function() {
    submitSum();
    return false;
}
```

Alternatives

Submission Throttling

Submission Throttling (see earlier) talks about automated, periodic submissions, where the present pattern is about the user forcing submissions to take place. The patterns can certainly be combined. Consider text editors that often harden their explicit Save mechanisms with automated backup. An Ajax App can use automated submissions, but allow for manual intervention when the submission must take place NOW.

Related Patterns

Live Form

Live Forms (Chapter 14) often use onblur and onfocus events, a subtle type of Explicit Submission.

Progress Indicator

Follow up submissions with a *Progress Indicator* (Chapter 14) to give some feedback.

Metaphor

An author drafts each chapter of a book in entirety before submitting it for editorial review.

Distributed Events

Events, Feed, Listener, Messaging, MVC, Notification, Observer, PublishSubscribe, RSS, Refresh, Semantic, Synchronise, Synchronize, Update, WebFeed

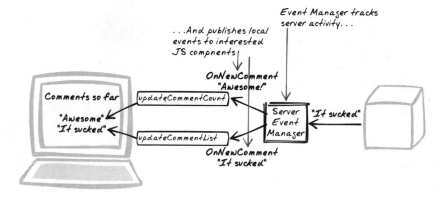

FIGURE 10-9. Distributed Events

Developer Story

Devi's producing a web app for auditors at a financial institution, aiming to highlight substantial transactions. Relevant transactions are already published on the enterprise messaging system, and Devi transforms it into an RSS feed on the web server. The browser script then checks the feed every few seconds, and updates the view whenever it detects a substantial transaction occurred.

Problem

How do you decouple code in a complex application?

Forces

- Ajax Apps involve at least two tiers: a browser tier and a web server tier. In practice, the web server tier is often dependent on further tiers and external systems.

- Each tier can be quite complicated, containing many stateful entities (objects, HTML controls, or regular variables).

- The state of all these entities must often be synchronized, in order to keep users and external systems up-to-date. The synchronization needs to occur within a tier as well as across tiers—for example, an HTML table needs to change whenever browser-side user preferences change, but also whenever the server-side database changes.

- Keeping all these objects synchronized can become complex—there are about n^2 possible message paths from one object to another.

Solution

Keep objects synchronized with an event mechanism. This is a classic software pattern applied to Ajax, related to the Observer (Gamma et al., 1995) and "Publisher-Subscribe" (Buschmann et al., 1995) patterns, and also a key feature in the classic "Model-View-Controller" architecture. The DOM already provides an mechanism for low-level events, but the events discussed here are more semantic in nature; i.e., related to business and application concepts such as "account deleted." Note that the term "event" is used in a broad manner to mean any subscription-based approach that alleviates the need for direct calls from source to destination. Any publish-subscribe messaging mechanism falls under this definition.

Here's a scenario to motivate the concept of events. Say you have 10 objects with interdependent states. That is, when one object changes, any number of the other nine must change accordingly. The naive implementation would endow each object with an understanding of the other nine objects. Each time it's changed, an object would then tell each other object how to update. Each object now knows the other nine intimately. When one changes, the other nine must be updated—a major blow to encapsulation.

As with many programming problems, you can create a better solution by adding another layer of indirection—in this case, an event mechanism. Let each object broadcast changes instead of directly telling others how to respond. The changes should generally occur in semantic terms—rather than saying "someone's clicked me," an object should say "counting module has begin," or, "transaction has successfully completed." And let any object register to be notified whenever a message like this occurs. For larger systems, thinking in terms of events is easier as it breaks down the synchronization logic. You have one simple task to make objects broadcast events whenever they occur. And you have a separate task to decide how objects should actually respond to events, if they care about them at all.

On the Web, this pattern can be applied in different ways:

Server-to-browser
>   Page elements can be kept in sync with server objects.

Browser-to-browser
>   Page elements can be kept in sync with each other.

Browser-to-server
>   Server objects can be kept in sync with each other.

Server-to-server
>   Server objects can be kept in sync with each other.

Browser-to-server and server-to-server are both feasible, but beyond the scope of the Ajax Patterns because they are more about server-side architecture.

As we saw in Chapter 7, JavaScript offers some event-handling support, but there's no generic event API. To use distributed events then, you'll need to roll your own event system, which is easier than it sounds. Server-to-Browser propagation works something like this. There's a Server Event Manager, with two responsibilities. First, it runs a *Periodic Refresh* (see earlier in this chapter) or participates in *HTTP Streaming* (Chapter 6) to check if any server activity has occurred. Second, it offers an event propagation facility so that interested browser entities can register to discover any changes. When a server change occurs, the Server Event Manager constructs an event object based on the server's output and passes it any interested listener. To do this, the manager must retain a collection of listeners and the event types they are listening to. The minimal set of services would then be:

- `addListener (eventType, listener)`
- `removeListener (eventType, listener)`

These listeners can be callback functions, like the callback function used by `XMLHttpRequest`. Or, they can be objects that contain a function with a standard callback name for the event type being registered, such as `onUpdate( )`.

With Browser-to-Browser propagation, you can also have a Central Server Manager to accept events and notifications. Alternatively, each object can be responsible for creating and propagating events specific to itself. That is, each object capable of generating events needs to allow other objects to register themselves for the events.

Observer is a special case of this pattern that arises frequently. The events are not user actions but change notifications. Event listeners are *observing* an object and responding to its state. Often, it's used to keep state in sync. An HTML table, for example, can render the latest state of a timetable object on the server side.

Finally, note that this pattern is somewhat speculative and open-ended, but the main purpose should be clear: to add a layer of intermediation so that objects can encapsulate their own responses to system activity, rather than being told what to do by other objects.

Decisions about Distributed Events

Will you publish a history or just the current state?

Given the nature of HTTP, server data must be retrieved periodically—the server can't directly call the browser when something happens. If the server exposes only the current state, there are two problems.

Change detection
The browser can only infer a change has occurred by comparing the previous value, or perhaps by using a version ID or timestamp.

Intermediate states
The browser will miss values that occurred between updates.

Neither of these are showstoppers, so exposing only the current state may well be feasible. The alternative is to publish a history of states along with timestamps. That's more work to output and parse, and it also requires some form of storage on the server. If you are following that option, it's worth formatting the changes using a standard feed-based approach such as RSS or Atom. You'll benefit from the abundance of libraries for both browser and server. As a bonus, the service will be generic enough to be used by external clients, if that's a requirement.

For observer-style events, will you propagate the details of what's changed, or just point to the object that's changed?

Often, events concern an object that's changed state. Sometimes, you only need to propagate a pointer to the object; the recipient will then interrogate the object as required. Other times, you need to send the change itself. The latter approach is useful for functionality that requires not just the object's current state, but the nature of the change. For example, imagine you have an auditing function that logs whenever a budget balance has been increased. It will be much easier if the change event indicates that an increase has occurred. Otherwise, it will have to manually compare the budget against its previous state. For server-to-browser events, indicating the change may be better for performance since it may alleviate a follow-up call to the server.

What information will accompany the event notification?

When an event occurs, there's usually several pieces of information to pass to listeners—for example, a source object (an object that's just changed), the nature of the change or action that's occurred, and meta-information such as event time and unique ID. You can pass this information in different ways:

String message
    Pass the information as a single string.

Single event object
    Pass in a single event object containing attributes for each piece of information.

Parameter list
    Pass the information as separate parameters.

Each style has its strengths. A string message is the most flexible approach and has the benefit of being a portable format that will work on the server as well. Unfortunately, a string message must often be parsed and formatted to convert to and from useful JavaScript values. A single event object is easier to manipulate and, like a string message, can usually be extended without breaking existing code—the callback function still takes a single value. You can create a factory function to create the event and expose properties, so its interface can be made explicit if you so desire. Finally, a parameter list makes for a cleaner callback function implementation, since you don't have to extract variables from a wrapper object. However, a long list of parameters is cumbersome and difficult to maintain.

Will events be processed synchronously or asynchronously?

The simplest way to handle events is synchronously. As soon as something happens, the event manager immediately notifies all interested parties. All this happens in the same thread of execution, so each event handler becomes a bottleneck—the main program flow that triggered the event won't be able to proceed until each event handler has executed.

If some event handlers are slow, you can get more stable performance by handling events asynchronously. Here, the manager maintains a collection of pending events. Each time a new event arises, it simply adds it to the collection and returns—a very quick operation. Using a repeating timer (see *Scheduling* [Chapter 7]), the manager periodically pulls off pending events and notifies listeners.

There are various decisions involved in asynchronous event handling. First, what sort of collection do you use? A queue is most common, to ensure that events are handled in the order they arise. But sometimes a stack is more appropriate, so that if the manager falls behind, at least the most recent events will have been handled. Another decision is scheduling of the event handler, the object that picks events off the collection. The simplest style is a pure repeating timer, but if the handling takes too long (longer than the timer interval), you'll end up with multiple processes picking off events. One way to prevent this situation is to have the event handler monitor its own progress and cease activity after a certain time has elapsed.

Real-World Examples

ActiveMQ Servlet Adaptor

ActiveMQ (*http://activemq.codehaus.org/*) is an open source implementation of Java Messaging Service (JMS) (*http://java.sun.com/products/jms/*), an official Sun standard for enterprise messaging. As such, it provides a way to pass Java objects and strings between different processes, and includes a publish-subscribe mechanism allowing a process to subscribe for all messages in a particular "topic."

Normally, the processes run server side, but using a servlet adaptor, ActiveMQ effectively gives the web app, through JavaScript, full ability to send and receive messages.

MapBuilder

MapBuilder (*http://mapbuilder.sourceforge.net*) is a framework for mapping web sites, heavily influenced by MVC. The model holds application data such as current maps, positions, and dimensions. The configuration process wires each model to a number of interested widgets, all of which receive notifications when the model has changed.

Dojo Events Library

Dojo (*http://dojotoolkit.org/download*) is a comprehensive framework aiming to simplify JavaScript development. One thing it does is enhance JavaScript's standard event management. This includes publish-subscribe functionality. You register one or more functions as *publishers* and one or more functions as *subscribers*. When a publisher function is called, all of the subscriber functions will also be called.

LivePage Library

LivePage (*http://twisted.sourceforge.net/TwistedDocs-1.2.0/howto/livepage.html*), mentioned in *HTTP Streaming* (Chapter 6) examples, is a framework based around Distributed Events.

Code Refactoring: AjaxPatterns Distributed Events Wiki Demo

The Basic Wiki Demo (*http://ajaxify.com/run/wiki*) has a single callback function that serves two purposes: to parse the incoming message and to display it to the user. That's okay for a simple application, but what if we want to scale up the display operation by displaying different messages in different ways or performing some action when a single message has changed? It won't be a great surprise that Distributed Events are one way to make the browser script more modular, and this refactoring shows how.

Refactoring to an event mechanism

The first refactoring lays the groundwork for a richer message handling by introducing an event mechanism. There are some minor user-interface differences, for coding convenience. For example, instead of a single "synchronize" point, downloading and uploading are split into independent timing mechanisms; there's no more background color change while waiting for a message to upload; and a *One-Second Spotlight* (Chapter 16) effect now occurs when a message has updated, to compensate for the loss of color change. Also, note that a different version of ajaxCaller is used, which allows a callback object to be specified in addition to a callback function.

A model object has been introduced to track the state of each message and to play the role of an event manager, notifying listeners of changes. One type of listener receives notification of any new messages. The other type receives notification of updates to a specific message. New message listeners are held in a single array. Update listeners are held in an array of arrays, with all subscribers to a particular message held in an array that's keyed on the message ID:

```
newMessageListeners: new Array( ),
messageUpdateListenersById: new Array( ),

addNewMessageListener: function(listener) {
  this.newMessageListeners.push(listener);
},
addMessageUpdateListener: function(messageId, listener) {
  var listeners = this.messageUpdateListenersById[messageId];
  listeners.push(listener);
},
```

Notification then works by iterating through the collection of relevant listeners:

```
notifyNewMessageListeners: function(newMessage) {
    for (i=0; i<this.newMessageListeners.length; i++) {
      this.newMessageListeners[i](newMessage);
    }
},
notifyMessageUpdateListeners: function(updatedMessage) {
    var listenersToThisMessage =
      this.messageUpdateListenersById[updatedMessage.id];
    for (i=0; i<listenersToThisMessage.length; i++) {
      listenersToThisMessage[i](updatedMessage);
    }
}
```

How do these events arise? The model object must be started manually and will then periodically poll the server:

```
start: function( ) {
  this.requestMessages( );
  setInterval(this.requestMessages, DOWNLOAD_INTERVAL);
}
...
requestMessages: function( ) {
  ajaxCaller.getXML("content.php?messages", messageModel.onMessagesLoaded);
},
```

As before, the server provides an *XML Message* (Chapter 9) describing all messages. The model steps through each message in the XML, constructing an equivalent JavaScript object. If the message ID is unknown, the new message listeners are notified, and an array of update listeners is also created for this new message. If the message differs from the current message with the same ID, it's changed, so all the update listeners are notified. Recall that the message update notification is fine-grained: only listeners to a particular message ID are notified; hence the extraction of a message-specific list of listeners.

```javascript
onMessagesLoaded: function(xml, callingContext) {
  var incomingMessages = xml.getElementsByTagName("message");
  for (var messageCount=0; messageCount<incomingMessages.length;
      messageCount++) {
    var messageNode = incomingMessages[messageCount];
    var content = this.getChildValue(messageNode, "content");
    content = (content==null ? "" : unescape(content));
    var incomingMessage = {
      id: this.getChildValue(messageNode, "id"),
      lastAuthor: this.getChildValue(messageNode, "lastAuthor"),
      ranking: this.getChildValue(messageNode, "ranking"),
      content: content
    };
    var currentMessage = this.messagesById[incomingMessage.id];
    if (!currentMessage) {
      this.messageUpdateListenersById[incomingMessage.id]=new Array();
      this.notifyNewMessageListeners(incomingMessage);
    } else if (!this.messagesEqual(incomingMessage, currentMessage)) {
      this.notifyMessageUpdateListeners(incomingMessage);
    }
    this.messagesById[incomingMessage.id] = incomingMessage;
  }
},
getChildValue: function(parentNode, childName) {
  var childNode = parentNode.getElementsByTagName(childName)[0];
  return childNode.firstChild == null ? null : childNode.firstChild.nodeValue;
},
messagesEqual: function(message1, message2) {
  return    message1.lastAuthor == message2.lastAuthor
         && message1.ranking == message2.ranking
         && message1.content == message2.content;
}
```

A new `messagesDiv` object has also been created to encapsulate the message-handling logic. On startup, it subscribes for notification of new messages. For each message, it performs a similar function to what was previously done on each update: it creates all the message information and appends to the page, along with a newly introduced visual effect (courtesy of Scriptaculous; see *http://script.aculo.us*).

```javascript
start: function( ) {
  messageModel.addNewMessageListener(this.onNewMessage);
},
...
onNewMessage: function(message) {
  var messageArea = document.createElement("textarea");
  messageArea.className = "messageArea";
  messageArea.id = message.id;
  messageArea.serverMessage = message;
  ...
  messageDiv.appendChild(lastAuthor);
  messageDiv.appendChild(messageArea);
```

```
        ...
    $("messages").appendChild(messageDiv);
    Effect.Appear(messageDiv);
        ...
    }
```

The `messageDiv` has another responsibility: it must update the display when a message has updated. Thus, it registers itself as a listener on each message. The easiest way to do this is upon adding each new message:

```
onNewMessage: function(message) {
    ...
    messageModel.addMessageUpdateListener(message.id, function(message) {
      var messageDiv = $("messageDiv" + message.id);
      var lastAuthor = messageDiv.childNodes[0];
      var messageArea = messageDiv.childNodes[1];
      if (messageArea.hasFocus) {
        return;
      }
      lastAuthor.innerHTML = message.id + "."
        + "<em>" + message.lastAuthor + "</em>"+"."
        + message.ranking;
      messageArea.value = message.content;
      Effect.Appear(messageDiv);
    });
  },
```

Compared to the previous version, we're now only redrawing a message when it's actually changed. Using an event mechanism has helped to separate the logic out. Now, it's the `messageDiv` itself that decides how it will look after a message comes in, which is much more sane than the message-receiving callback making that decision.

Introducing a watchlist

The refactoring above wouldn't be very useful if we stopped with an event mechanism. Good for your work experience perhaps, but we haven't yet added any functionality to justify the effort; it's basically the same application as before. Not to worry Watchlist Wiki Demo (*http://ajaxify.com/run/wiki/events/watchlist*) to the rescue! A new watchlist monitors interesting messages, so that when a message you're watching is updated (by you or someone else), the watchlist will add a summary line.

To start with, the HTML now includes a watchlist table:

```
<div id="summary">
  <table id="watchlist">
    <tr>
      <th>Author</th>
      <th>Message</th>
    </tr>
    <tbody id="watchlistBody"></tbody>
  </table>
</div>
```

Which messages are in your watchlist? That's determined by a new checkbox control, one per message:

```
onNewMessage: function(message) {
  ...
  var watching = document.createElement("input");
  watching.type = "checkbox";
  watching.messageId = message.id;
  watching.onclick = onWatchingToggled;
  ...
}
```

When the user wants to watch a message, she selects its checkbox. A single function updates the watchlist for all chosen messages. Remember that message update events are fine-grained, so we need to ensure this callback is registered to receive notifications for all the chosen messages and nothing else. So when a user deselects a message, we'll unregister the function as a listener on that message. Note that this functionality necessitated the creation of an function to unregister listeners, which was never required in the previous version.

```
function onWatchingToggled(event) {
  event = event || window.event;
  var checkbox = event.target || event.srcElement;
  if (checkbox.checked) {
    messageModel.addMessageUpdateListener(checkbox.messageId, onWatchedMessageUpdate);
  } else {
    messageModel.removeMessageUpdateListener(checkbox.messageId,
        onWatchedMessageUpdate);
  }
}
```

onWatchedMessageUpdate will now receive notification of any new messages that are being watched. It simply adds a summary row to the table and runs a visual effect:

```
function onWatchedMessageUpdate(message) {

  var summary = message.content;
  if (summary.length > 35) {
    summary =   summary.substring(0, 15) + "..."
              + summary.substring(summary.length - 15);
  }

  var row = document.createElement("tr");

  var authorCol = document.createElement("td");
  authorCol.className = "authorSummary";
  authorCol.innerHTML = message.author;
  row.appendChild(authorCol);

  var contentCol = document.createElement("td");
  contentCol.className = "contentSummary";
```

```
    contentCol.innerHTML = summary;
    row.appendChild(contentCol);

    if ($("watchlistBody").childNodes.length > 0) {
      $("watchlistBody").insertBefore(row, $("watchlistBody").childNodes[0]);
    } else {
      $("watchlistBody").appendChild(row);
    }
    Effect.Appear(row);

}
```

We now have two independent functions that receive notifications of new messages arriving from the server. Each can use the information however it pleases. This is a much more scalable approach than having the server message recipient dictate how the browser should respond.

Related Patterns

Periodic Refresh, HTTP Streaming

For server-to-browser propagation, *Periodic Refresh* (see earlier) or *HTTP Streaming* (Chapter 6) is required.

RESTful Service

Distributed Events usually involve a browser element observing a server-side entity. REST is ideal for this purpose as it provides a simple, standard way to exposes server state.

XML Data Island

If the server responds with XML and you need to retain state locally—e.g., to track differences—an *XML Data Island* (Chapter 11) would be useful. Under some technologies illustrated in that pattern, XML Data Islands allow for automated updates—when the data island changes, then a control is updated, and vice versa.

Metaphor

The old newspaper analogy still works. People can subscribe to any number of newspapers, and each newspaper can have any number of subscribers. The algorithm does not explicitly mention any particular subscriber; rather, when a newspaper comes out, it simply loops through each subscriber and sends a copy to each of them.

Cross-Domain Proxy

Aggregator, Fusion, Mash-Up, Mashup, Mediator, Mix, Proxy, Tunnel

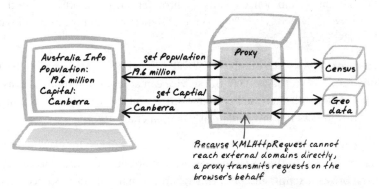

FIGURE 10-10. Cross-Domain Proxy

Developer Story

Dave's working on a job-hunting web site and wants to "mash up" content from various other sites. Each job ad is accompanied by a review from a corporate forum web site, recent company news, and a stock ticker. To get these details into the browser, the server queries several sites and exposes their content as a web service that the browser can query.

Problem

How can you augment your application with services available elsewhere on the Web?

Forces

- There's a lot of data and useful services on the Web. Much of it is freely available. It's usually more effective to leverage that content than to replicate it yourself.

- The "same-origin policy" constrains most Web Remoting (Chapter 6) techniques, meaning that the browser script can only talk to the server from whence it came, and not to anyone else.

- External servers often use protocols and message formats that would be difficult for browser-side scripts to process. They may also require authentication, and such details should not be exposed in the browser.

- To comply with service agreements, web site owners often have to control and monitor all traffic to and from their web service, which is impossible if their server is being bypassed.

Solution

Create proxying and mediating web services to facilitate communication between the browser and external domains. As explained in *XMLHttpRequest Call* (Chapter 6), the same-origin policy means the browser script can only talk to the server from whence it came, which is the "base server." Hence, any communication with external domains must go via the base server.

The simplest form of proxy is a dumb *Web Service* (Chapter 6) that simply routes traffic between browser and external server. The service can accept the remote URL as a parameter. That URL will then be accessed synchronously, and the service will output its response. All this follows the Proxy pattern (Gamma et al., 1995).

A cleaner type of Cross-Domain Proxy is more closely based on the Facade or Adaptor pattern (Gamma et al.). In this case, the base server presents the interface that's most suitable to the browser script, and performs whatever manipulation is necessary to interact with the external script. For example, the external server might present a complex, over-engineered, SOAP-based *RPC Service*, but you want the browser to deal in simple *Plain-Text Messages* (Chapter 9). The likely solution is to present the plain-text *Web Service*, dress up requests into SOAP messages, and undress responses into Plain-Text Messages.

The Facade/Adaptor approach is generally better for two reasons. First, it keeps the client simple, protecting it from dealing with the details of the protocol used to communicate with the external server. Second, it's more secure: the first approach will allow any client to call out to any server they feel like, whereas the second approach will allow you to exert much more control over what kind of communication takes place.

A Cross-Domain Proxy is implemented using some form of HTTP client library to access the remote server. Generally, the connection should be quite straightforward—specify the URL and grab the response as a string. However, it might get more complex if the remote web service relies on cookies and authentication, parameters that the proxy might have to pass on from the Ajax request that initiated the call.

Decisions

What external content will be accessed?

In theory, anything you can do with a browser can theoretically be accomplished by an automated HTTP client. However, there are likely to be legal constraints, and technical challenges too if there is serious usage of JavaScript or browser plugins. Furthermore, your script will be vulnerable to changes in the site layout, and many content providers have deliberately performed subtle changes to prevent automated access. Thus, relying on the ever-increasing collection of public APIs and structured data would make a better choice.

You can find a collection of public APIs at *http://wsfinder.com*. Some popular APIs include Amazon, Delicious, EvDB, Flickr, Google Maps, Google Search, Technorati, and Yahoo Maps.

How will you connect to the external server?

If you're scraping content directly from a public web site, you'll need to use the underlying web protocol, HTTP. And even if you're talking to an API, you'll probably be communicating with HTTP anyway. In some cases, API publishers will provide code to access the content, rather than just publishing the specification. Also, with more complex web services protocols like SOAP, you don't have to write a lot of low-level code yourself. In many cases, though, the easiest thing to do is talk HTTP and manually format and parse messages yourself.

Many scripting languages feature built-in libraries to communicate in HTTP and are often well-equipped for Cross-Domain Proxy implementations due to strong support for regular expression manipulation. A PHP example is featured in the code example that follows shortly.

In the Java world, for instance, the standard API provides some relatively low-level support for HTTP clients, but you can use some of the web site testing libraries to quickly extract content from external sites. HttpUnit is a good example, and it also has some support for JavaScript manipulation. To grab some content:

```
import com.meterware.httpunit.WebConversation;
import com.meterware.httpunit.GetMethodWebRequest;
import com.meterware.httpunit.WebRequest;

public class PatternSorter {

  public String getContent(String url) {
    try {
      WebConversation wc = new WebConversation();
      WebRequest request = new GetMethodWebRequest(url);
      String response = wc.getResponse(request).getText();
    } catch(Exception ex) {
      throw new RuntimeException("Could not get content from " + url, ex);
    }
  }

  public static void main(String[] args) {
      System.out.println("http://ajaxpatterns.org");
  }

}
```

How will you deal with errors and delays in accessing the service?

At times, there will be errors accessing an external web service. Think twice before attributing blame because the problem might be at your end, or somewhere along the network. This has implications for any error messages you might show users. Ideally, you should be able to detect that an error has occurred, and then log the details for immediate attention. In responding to the user, you have several options:

- Ensure you have a good server-side framework in place to detect errors, so they're not directly—ignorantly—passed on to users. In addition, be sure to detect timeouts and handle them proactively; e.g., respond with an appropriate error message.

- In some cases, you will simply have to admit failure and show an error message to users. If possible, suggest an alternative or tell them when they should try again.

- Provide reduced functionality.

- Switch to a prearranged substitute web service.

- Rely on cached results, if they're still relevant.

Under what licensing terms will you access the remote service?

The legals of invoking *Web Services* (Chapter 6) are tricky, vaguely-defined, and always evolving. Some services are open for public use, others require you hold an API key, and others are critical enough to warrant authentication via digital signatures. In each case, there are usage terms involved, even if they're not explicit, and you will need to investigate issues such as the authentication mechanism, the number of queries per day, how the data will be used, server uptime, and support level.

Real-World Examples

WPLicense

The WPLicense Wordpress plugin (*http://yergler.net/projects/wplicense*) presents the blogger with some forms to specify their preferred license statement, based on the Creative Commons model. The server is acting as a middleman between the browser and the Creative Commons API (*http://api.creativecommons.org/rest/1.0/*).

Housing Maps (Craigslist and Google Maps)

Housing Maps (*http://housingmaps.com*) is a mashup between Google Maps (*http://maps.google.com*) and Craigslist (*http://craigslist.com*), a community-oriented classifieds advertising web site. What does that mean? It means you get to see a list of advertised homes on one side and view a map of those homes one the other side, using the familiar Google Maps thumbtacks to pinpoint the locations of the advertised homes. (See Figure 10-11.)

A few features:

- Click on a thumbtack and you'll see a *Popup* (Chapter 15) balloon appear, showing a summary of the classified ad: price, terms, address, and photos. The balloon contains a hyperlink to the ad at Craigslist

- Change a category (e.g., price) and you'll see both the thumbtacks and home lists update. Change the city and you'll see the map change as well.

- You can pan and zoom as on Google Maps.

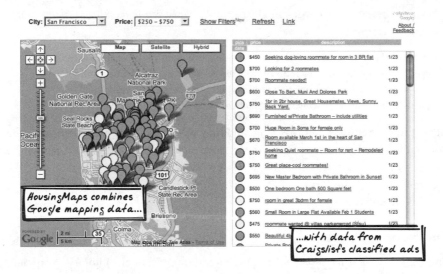

FIGURE 10-11. Housing Maps

Cross-Domain Proxy is used to grab housing data from Craigslist, while the map images are fetched directly from Google's server into the browser.

Bill Gates Wealth Clock

This was not Ajaxian, but noteworthy as the first prominent mashup application and a precursor to the Ajaxian Cross-Domain Proxy pattern. Web guru Philip Greenspun mixed data from several sources to produce a "wealth clock" showing Bill Gates' worth at any time (*http://groups-beta.google.com/group/nf.general/browse_thread/thread/bc7fc7bfab19937f/ 88fa32f2cf6dd6bb*). This is no longer working, unfortunately (*http://rhea.redhat.com/bboard-archive/webdb/0006ad.html*), but the code is still available (*http://philip.greenspun.com/seia/ examples-basics/wealth-clock.tcl.txt*). See Figure 10-12.

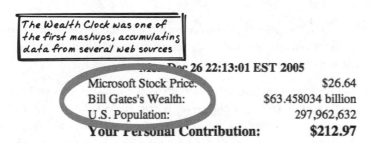

FIGURE 10-12. Bill Gates Wealth Clock

The price per stock was extracted from Yahoo! Finance. The number of stocks in Gates' portfolio came from Microsoft reports (it was not automatically extracted). And the U.S. population came from the U.S. Census Bureau.

Here's what Greenspun said back in 2001 (*http://philip.greenspun.com/teaching/teaching-software-engineering*):

> (M)any of the most interesting and challenging problems of the coming decades will center around the Internet and Web as a distributed computing environment. An "island" site such as amazon.com or photo.net is probably less representative of the future than *http://www.webho.com/WealthClock* (Bill Gates Personal Wealth Clock).

Another prominent usage of Cross-Domain Proxying in "Web 1.0" was meta-searching, as performed by crawlers such as MetaCrawler.com (*http://metacrawler.com*). Again, all the work was done in the server, and the browser response was usually opened while the results came back to the server, so at least some information could be shown while requests were still out.

CPaint library

CPaint (*http://cpaint.sourceforge.net/:*) is a Web Remoting (Chapter 6) library. A special "proxy" URL can be established (*http://cpaint.sourceforge.net/doc/frontend.class.cpaint.set_proxy_url.html*), pointing to a proxy on the originating server, so that remoting to external domains has virtually the same API as to the originating server.

Code Example: WPLicense

See the Code Example in *Live Form* (Chapter 14) for a full background on the WPLicense's license selection process, but here's a quick summary:

- A field lets the user select a license type (e.g., Creative Commons versus Public Domain versus Sampling).

- Once the license type is chosen, it's immediately sent to the server, and the server responds with a form consisting of questions relevant to this particular type. If the license is Creative Commons, for example, one of the questions is "Allow commercial uses of this work?"

- Each time the user changes one of the license options, the server updates some hidden fields. These fields will be uploaded to the server, to be persisted when the user eventually submits the form.

What all this glosses over is the Cross-Domain Proxy pattern that goes on behind the scenes. At each of these three stages, the server is actually interacting with CreativeCommons.org via its public API (*http://api.creativecommons.org/rest/1.0/*), which you can read about at *http://api.creativecommons.org*. The plugin provides a clean separation between web server logic and cross-domain mediation: a separate PHP file (`ccwsclient.php`) hosts several API facade operations, accepting and returning data structures in standard PHP style. This client in turn delegates all the XML infrastructure stuff to a third-party library MiniXML, at *http://minixml.psychogenic.com*.

Let's now zoom in on the three steps.

1. Retrieving license types

The server doesn't have the license types hardcoded. Instead, it retrieves them via a web service. This is the core of the Cross-Domain Proxy functionality—the PHP function fs will retrieve content from the specified URL:

```
$WS_ROOT = "http://api.creativecommons.org/rest/1.0/";
...
$xml = file_get_contents($WS_ROOT);
```

In fact, you can see exactly what's pumped into $xml by visiting *http://api.creativecommons.org/rest/1.0/*, and then choose View Page Source. Alternatively, use a command-like application such as curl (curl http://api.creativecommons.org/rest/1.0/), which yields the following XML (reformatted):

```
<licenses>
  <license id="standard">Creative Commons</license>
  <license id="publicdomain">Public Domain</license>
  <license id="recombo">Sampling</license>
</licenses>
```

Once we know what license types are available, it's a matter of transforming the XML into an HTML selector. XSLT could be used here, but it's just as easy to do it manually:

```
foreach($license_classes as $key => $l_id) {
  echo '<option value="' . $key . '" >' . $l_id . '</option>';
};
```

2. Retrieving license questions

Presenting the questions gets interesting, because the server must now present questions and accept answers without the programmer knowing in advance what those questions will be.

Browser requests for license questions invoke a URL that depends on the user's chosen license type. If the license type is Creative Commons, which has the ID "standard," the URL is *http://api.creativecommons.org/rest/1.0/license/standard/*. Visit that URL, and you'll see the questions and possible answers. For example:

```
<field id="derivatives">
  <label xml:lang="en">Allows modifications of your work?</label>
  <description xml:lang="en">The licensor permits others to copy, distribute and
      perform only

unaltered copies of the work, not derivative works based on it.</description>
  <type>enum</type>
  <enum id="y">
    <label xml:lang="en">Yes</label>
  </enum>
  <enum id="sa">
    <label xml:lang="en">ShareAlike</label>
  </enum>
```

```
    <enum id="n">
      <label xml:lang="en">No</label>
    </enum>
  </field>
```

Equipped with all that information about each question, the server must now transform it into an HTML selector. Ultimately, a loop is used to traverse the entire data structure and generate a selector for each field:

```
foreach ($fields as $f_id=>$f_data) {
  $result .= '<tr><th><nobr>' . $f_data['label'] . '</nobr></th><td>';
  // generate the appropriate widget
  if ($f_data['type'] == 'enum') {
    $result .= '<select class="lic_q" id="'.$f_id.'" lic_q="true" size="1">';
    foreach ($f_data['options'] as $enum_id=>$enum_val) {
      $result .= '<option value="'. $enum_id . '">' . $enum_val . '</option>';
    } // for each option
    ...
```

As explained in the *Live Form* (Chapter 14) discussion, this new form HTML is directly placed onto a div.

3. Handling user answers

The Creative Commons' issueLicense web service accepts XML input of all the license criteria, and then outputs a document containing a URL for the license criteria, along with some other, related information. In a similar manner to the previous code, all of this information is transformed into HTML. This time, it's used to populate several fields, rather than generate any new input fields.

Alternatives

On-Demand JavaScript

A fairly old cross-domain technique is to use *On-Demand JavaScript*; see the discussion of *Cross-Domain Loading* for that pattern in Chapter 6. The main benefit over Cross-Domain Proxy is reduced resources—the base server is bypassed, so there's no bandwidth or processing costs involved. However, there's a major constraint: the server must expose a suitable script to fetch, because it's not possible to just extract arbitrary information from a server. Additional problems include lack of server-side logging, inability to reach services that require authentication, and the security concerns described in On-Demand JavaScript.

Shared document.domain

When we speak of the "same-origin" policy, we're not necessarily referring to the true domain a document is served from; each document has a mutable domain property (for example, document.domain) that turns out to be the critical factor in cross-domain calls. If two documents declare the same domain property, regardless of their true origin, they should be able to communicate with each other using XMLHttpRequest. Jotspot developer Abe Fettig has explained how to exploit this knowledge for making cross-domain communication practical (*http://fettig.net/weblog/2005/11/28/how-to-make-xmlhttprequest-connections-to-another-server-in-your-domain/XMLHttpRequest Call*). The trick relies on embedding the external document and having that document—as well as your own document—define the same document.domain property. Thus, as with the *On-Demand JavaScript* alternative, it does have one key constraint: the external server must explicitly cooperate. In addition, you can't just declare an arbitrary domain; it has to be a "parent" of the true domain (*http://www.mozilla.org/projects/security/components/same-origin.html*; i.e., "shop.example.com" can declare "example.com" but not "anyoldmegacorp.com". Due to these constraints, it's best suited to a situation where there's a direct relationship between the respective site owners.

Images

Images have always worked across domains, with various benefits (syndication) and more than a few problems ("bandwidth theft") along the way. As noted in the "Alternatives" section of *XMLHttpRequest Call* (Chapter 6), images can be used for general-purpose remoting, usually with 1-pixel images that will never be rendered. While that's a hack you'll likely not need these days, transfer of legitimate images remains a useful capability. When you run the Google Maps API (*http://www.google.com/apis/maps/*) in your web page, for example, it pulls down map images directly from Google's own servers.

Related Patterns

Performance Optimization patterns

Since external calls can be expensive, the Performance Optimization patterns apply. They may be applied at the level of the browser, or the server, or both. For example, caching can take place in the browser, the server, or both.

Want to Know More?

See WSFinder: a wiki of public web services (*http://www.wsfinder.com/*).

CHAPTER ELEVEN

DOM Population

WHAT DOES THE BROWSER DO ONCE IT RECEIVES A RESPONSE FROM THE SERVER? SEVERAL OPTIONS ARE covered in this chapter. *XML Data Island* explains how you can store an XML document within the web page's DOM instead of converting it into a custom data structure. It also touches on some browser-specific features that let you tie the document's value to the display. XML responses are also the primary concern of *Browser-Side XSLT*, explaining how an XML document can be converted to XHTML for inclusion on the page, or modified for uploading back to the server. *Browser-Side Templating* is not XML-specific; it brings to JavaScript the embedded scripting template concept popular in many server environments, such as JSPs and PHP scripts.

XML Data Island

Data, DOM, Storage, XBL, XML

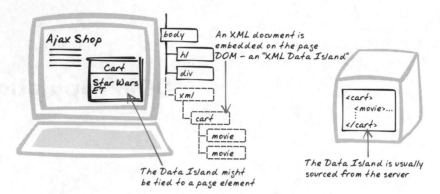

The Data Island might be tied to a page element

An XML document is embedded on the page DOM – an "XML Data Island"

The Data Island is usually sourced from the server

FIGURE 11-1. XML Data Island

Developer Story

Dave's demographics viewer stores each table of statistics as an XML document. A big cache of XML documents is held within the page, one for each table. The user can rearrange the tables and switch them between visible and hidden, but all the XML metadata remains on the page. To render the tables, Dave exploits the browser's ability to translate XML into HTML tables.

Problem

How can you render incoming XML and retain the data?

Forces

- Many Ajax Apps receive *XML Message*s and must convert them into HTML.

- The incoming data often has to be retained as well.

Solution

Retain XML responses as XML Data Islands—nodes within the HTML DOM.
Strictly speaking, an XML Data Island is an XML document embedded in a standard XHTML document, usually within an <xml> tag. Say the initial page looks like this:

```
<html>
  <head>
    ...
  </head>
  <body>
    <h1>Top Score</h1>
    <p>Here's the ... </p>
    ...
```

```
        <xml id="scoreData"></xml>
    </body>
</html>
```

After an *XMLHttpRequest Call* (Chapter 6) brings the browser an *XML Message* (Chapter 9), the message is retained in the tag, using techniques described in a moment. The result is a web page DOM like this:

```
<html>
    <head>
        ...
    </head>
    <body>
        <h1>Top Scores</h1>
        <p>Here's the ...  </p>
        ...
        <xml id="scoreData">
            <score>
                <title>Galaga"</title>
                <player>AAA</player>
                <score>999610</score>
            <score>
        </xml>
    </body>
</html>
```

How do you do something like that in JavaScript? You might assume it's pretty trivial, given that HTML itself is XML (or close enough to it). But unfortunately, it's not as easy as you'd expect and also is browser-dependent. If you have the XML string, you can set scoreData element's innerHTML as the string value. If you have only a DOM node, you can convert it to an XML string by inspecting its innerHTML property. However, this won't work on all browsers and might lead to portability problems as browsers interpret the string in different ways. An alternative is to avoid string manipulation and directly graft one DOM node onto another. The document object has two useful methods here: cloneNode( ) and importNode( ). Again, there are plenty of portability issues to consider—see Peter-Paul Koch's discussion (*http://www.quirksmode.org/blog/archives/2005/12/xmlhttp_notes_c.html*). In most cases, the easiest, most portable, solution will be to use a library like Sarissa (*http://sarissa.sourceforge.net*).

In a more general sense, this pattern involves retaining *XML Message*s regardless of how you store them. While the DOM is a convenient place for storage and has some value-added features described below, you could also save the XML in a normal JavaScript variable. The key characteristic of the pattern is that you're retaining the *XML Message* and using it as a data structure, rather than transforming it into a custom JavaScript object.

It's easy enough to do this, but what's the point? Here are three applications:

Transforming XML Data Islands to and from HTML

XML Data Islands are traditionally an IE-specific capability. From IE5, you can tie HTML controls to an embedded XML document. When the XML data changes, the HTML is also updated. And when the HTML changes—if the control is mutable—the

XML is updated. In IE, to tie an HTML element to a data island, you indicate the XML data island, preceded by a # and the field within that island. So to create an `input` field based on the player field above:

```
<input type="text" datasrc="#scoreData" datafld="player">
```

Now, this is an IE-specific function, but Firefox has its own alternative: eXtensible Binding Language (XBL) (*http://www.zdnetasia.com/techguide/webdev/0,39044903,39236695,00. htm*). The idea is similar, but the updating behavior isn't automatic. With Mozilla, you have to create an XBL document that explicitly states how HTML controls relate to the XML.

Even without these browser-specific capabilities, it's still fairly straightforward to make the transformation using a technology like *Browser-Side XSLT* (see later in this chapter).

Retaining XML for later use

Sometimes it's useful to retain the response for later use. For example, you can keep it to build up a *Browser-Side Cache* (Chapter 13). Another application is for validation—the browser might receive a raw XML document containing some form fields, then augment it with user responses before uploading it back to the server.

To store a response for later use, you could wrap it into a custom data structure. But that requires some coding effort and also complicates things a bit by adding a new data structure. When the response is an *XML Message*, you have an alternative: just keep the XML. While it may not be the optimal format, it's still a structured format that you can query quite easily.

Including an XML document on initial page load

The initial page load sequence sometimes requires an XML document. For example, the XML document might describe the initial data to be viewed or it might be a stylesheet for *Browser-Side XSLT*. You could go through the motions of extracting it with a further *XMLHttpRequest Call*, but it would be faster to load the XML as part of the initial page load. An XML Data Island is an easy way to do this. Just output the XML content wrapped inside an `<xml>` tag. Alternatively, IE lets you specify a URL in the `src` attribute.

Real-World Examples

PerfectXML Demo

Darshan Singh's IE demo (*http://www.perfectxml.com/articles/xml/islandex.htm*) is explained in the corresponding PerfectXML article (*http://www.perfectxml.com/articles/xml/msxml30.asp*). It's a straightforward table, populated by an *XML Data Island* embedded in the corresponding HTML. The demo works in IE only.

Mozilla.org demo

Thad Hoffman's Mozilla demo (*http://www.mozilla.org/xmlextras/xmldataislands/example1.html*) is explained in a corresponding mozilla.org article (*http://www.mozilla.org/xmlextras/ xmldataislands/*): corresponding mozilla.org article. It simulates IE's behavior, using standard

XML parsing in JavaScript, to convert XML to HTML. The demo works only in Mozilla or Firefox.

TechRepublic demo

Philip Perkin's example explains how to use Mozilla's answer to XML Data Islands, eXtensible Binding Language (XBL); see Figure 11-2 (*http://techrepublic.com.com/5100-3513_11-5810495.html*). The code's online and there's a demo available (*http://www.phillipweb.com/mozilla/mozilla_xbl.htm*).

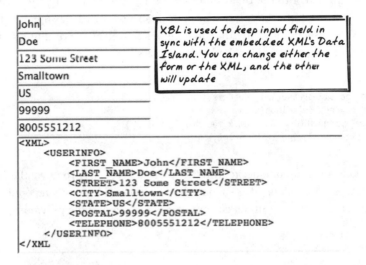

FIGURE 11-2. XBL demo

Code Refactoring: AjaxPatterns XML Data Island Sum

This example adds a very simple caching mechanism to the Basic Sum Demo (*http://ajaxify.com/run/sum*). The most recent XML response is retained as an XML Data Island, so if the user tries to resubmit the query, no server call occurs. In the absence of an XML Data Island, the script would need to retain the call and response in a custom data format. But retaining it as XML means no data format has to be created. Instead of manually navigating the document with the standard DOM API, the Interactive Website Framework (IWF) library (*http://iwf.sourceforge.net*) is used. IWF lets you treat the DOM object more like a custom data structure—as the following code shows, it lets you drill down using tag names rather than generic XML names.

Some minor changes are made to the XML format for easier parsing, leading to the following data format (*http://ajaxify.com/run/sum/xml/dataIsland/sumXML.php?figure1=4&figure2=6*):

```
<sum>
  <inputs>
    <figure1>4</figure1>
    <figure2>6</figure2>
    <figure3></figure3>
  </inputs>
```

```
<outputs>10</outputs>
</sum>
```

To the initial HTML, a placeholder has been introduced to retain the most recent XML response—the XML Data Island:

```
<xml id="sumResponse"></xml>
```

The XML is retrieved as a plain-text document and IWF is used to transform it into a special DOM-like format for convenient parsing. The IWF document is interrogated to get the sum, which is injected onto the DOM status element as before. Finally, the XML Data Island is populated with the XML response in its plain-text format (as opposed to a DOM object). The XML response includes the input figures as well as the resulting sum, so we'll be able to use it later on to decide whether the figures have changed since the last response.

```
function onSumResponse(xml, headers, callingContext) {
  var doc = new iwfXmlDoc(xml);
  $("sum").innerHTML = doc.sum.outputs[0].getText()
  $("sumResponse").innerHTML = xml;
}
```

The XML Data Island is used to decide whether a call is necessary. To make the effect more visible, the status area is blanked as soon as the user clicks submit. It's repopulated with the retained value if it turns out the current data is the same as the previous query:

```
function submitSum() {
  $("sum").innerHTML = "---";
  var figures = {
    figure1: $("figure1").value,
    figure2: $("figure2").value,
    figure3: $("figure3").value
  }
  var sumResponseXML = $("sumResponse").innerHTML;
  if (sumResponseXML!="") {
    doc = new iwfXmlDoc(sumResponseXML);
    var alreadyStoredInDOM = (
          figures.figure1 == doc.sum.inputs[0].figure1[0].getText()
      && figures.figure2 == doc.sum.inputs[0].figure2[0].getText()
      && figures.figure3 == doc.sum.inputs[0].figure3[0].getText()
    );
    if (alreadyStoredInDOM) {
      // No need to fetch - just retrieve the sum from the DOM
      $("sum").innerHTML = doc.sum.outputs[0].getText();
      return;
    }
  }
  ajaxCaller.get("sumXML.phtml", figures, onSumResponse, false, null);
}
```

Alternatives

Browser-Side XSLT

Browser-Side XSLT (see the next pattern) is a more general way to transform XML into HTML. In addition, the patterns are related insofar as Browser-Side XSLT can use an XML Data Island to store stylesheets.

Browser-Side Templating

Browser-Side Templating (see later) is a general technique for converting XML or other data formats into HTML.

Browser-Side Cache

XML Data Island can be used to store a *Browser-Side Cache* (Chapter 13).

Metaphor

The name itself is the metaphor: an island of data amid a pool of HTML content.

Browser-Side XSLT

Presentation, Render, Style, Stylesheet, Transform, View, XML, XPath, XSLT

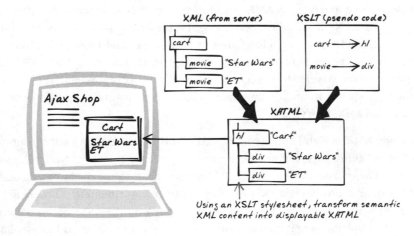

FIGURE 11-3. Browser-Side XSLT

Developer Story

Dave has just received a request to change the weather portlet on the homepage. The image must now be on the bottom, not the top, and the wording should be more precise. The browser receives periodic weather updates in the form of an XML specification, and it uses Browser-Side XSLT to get HTML for the portlet. The stylesheet is embedded inside the static homepage HTML file. So Dave just has to tweak the XSLT to get all the browsers rendering the new design.

Problem

How can you render incoming XML?

Forces

- Many *Web Services* (Chapter 6) output *XML Messages* (Chapter 9), and Ajax clients have to convert them into HTML.

- While modern browsers provide good support for XML parsing via the JavaScript's DOM support, the direct interface is lengthy and tedious to use.

- Code gets complex and error-prone when you mix HTML generation with application logic. JavaScript is not well-suited to programmatically building up HTML strings from input XML.

Solution

Apply XSLT to convert XML Messages into XHTML. XSLT—Extensible Stylesheet Language Transformations (*http://www.w3.org/TR/xslt*)—is a language for transforming XML documents into other forms. Here, XML is transformed to XHTML, a type of HTML that conforms to the XML standard. (You could get away with converting to plain-old HTML, but things works better if you stick to XHTML.) XSLT is fairly well-supported in modern browsers and, although browser APIs vary, there are good cross-browser toolkits available.

XSLT is well-suited to rendering XML. An XML document is designed to encapsulate a data object, and an XSLT stylesheet is a strategy for presenting such objects. Previously, XSLT has been used as a server-side technology—the server grabs some XML from a repository or another process and creates a web page by transforming it into XHTML. All that happens on the server. More recently, browsers have incorporated XSLT functionality, so the browser can automatically create an HTML page by marrying together an XML document with an XSLT stylesheet.

Browser-Side XSLT is slightly different. Here, the XML document does not constitute the contents of the entire page, but it does constitute a response from an *XMLHttpRequest Call* (Chapter 6). The transformation to XHTML can take advantage of the browser's built-in XSLT support, or alternatively an XSLT processor can be implemented in JavaScript, building on the browser's more primitive XML features. However the XSLT occurs, you're unlikely to be implementing it yourself. There are a couple of good cross-browser libraries available, discussed in later in this chapter in "Real-World Examples."

It's beyond the scope of this pattern to explain XSLT in any detail; however, here's a quick overview:

- An *XSLT stylesheet* is itself an XML document.

- An *XSLT processor* transforms an XML document into another form, by parsing the original document and using the stylesheet as the transformation strategy.

- XSLT expressions are specified in another language, XPath. Among its capabilities, XPath provides a powerful mechanism for expressing a position within an XML document. For example, the XPath expression /category/items/category will match twice when the following document is processed:

```
<category>
  <items>
    <category name="popular">
      <!-- XPath expression matches this category node -->
      ...
    </category>
    <category name="extras">
      <!-- XPath expression matches this category node -->
      ...
    </category>
  </items>
</category>
```

- A stylesheet is composed of rules. Each rule has a pattern that defines when it applies, and a template that dictates what will be output each time the pattern is encountered. Continuing with the example, here's a full rule:

```
<xsl:template match="/category/items/category">
    <div class="category"
         onclick="retrieveCategory('{@name}')">
         <xsl:value-of select="@name"/>
    </div>
</xsl:template>
```

When each node is reached, the template is outputted. @name refers to the name attribute on the category tag. So when the processing engine reaches the following XML segment:

```
<category name="extras">
```

the following XHTML will be output:

```
<div class="category"
     onclick="retrieveCategory('{extras}')">
     <xsl:value-of select="extras"/>
</div>
```

This discussion has focused on the most obvious application of Browser-Side XSLT: conversion to HTML for display to the user. You can also convert the XML to JavaScript too, and then execute it with the eval( ) method. For example, it would be possible to build a native JavaScript object by converting some XML into some code that creates the object.

Decisions

How will you obtain the XSLT stylesheet?

Any Browser-Side XSLT processor requires two things:

- An XML document
- An XSLT stylesheet

Both are usually passed in to the XSLT processor as plain strings representing the entire document (as opposed to URLs, say). The XML document usually comes from an *XMLHttpRequest Call* (Chapter 6), but where does the XSLT stylesheet come from? You have a few options.

Store the stylesheet server side

You can hold the file server side, and then use an independent *XMLHttpRequest Call* (Chapter 6) to retrieve it. In this case, you'll probably want to keep the copy in a *Browser-Side Cache* for later use. Also, if you use an asynchronous call, which is advisable, there's a potential race condition: you need to ensure the stylesheet is retrieved before any transformation takes place, possibly with a loop that keeps checking for it. The later section "Code Refactoring: AjaxPatterns XSLT Drilldown Demo" demonstrates this approach.

Handcode the stylesheet as a JavaScript string

You can build up a string in JavaScript, though this leads to messy code that blurs the distinction between logic and presentation. There is one benefit of this approach: the stylesheet is dynamic, so could potentially vary according to the current context.

Store it inside the initial HTML document

You can tuck the stylesheet somewhere inside the initial HTML document where it won't be seen by the user. Techniques include:

- Make it the content of an invisible textarea.
- Store it in an *XML Data Island* the within document.

Real-World Examples

Google Maps

Google Maps (*http://maps.google.com*) is the most famous application of Browser-Side XSLT, where the technology is used to transform data such as addresses and coordinates into HTML. Based on this work, the Googlers have also released Google AJAXSLT (*http://goog-ajaxslt.sourceforge.net*), an open source framework for cross-browser XSLT and XPath.

Kupu

Kupu (*http://kupu.oscom.org/demo/*) is an online word processor (Figure 11-4) that stores content in XML and renders it with Browser-Side XSLT, using the Sarissa framework described shortly (Figure 11-4).

AJAX-S

Robert Nyman's AJAX-S (*http://www.robertnyman.com/ajax-s/*) is a slideshow manager, where raw content is maintained in XML, and transformed to slides using Browser-Side XSLT.

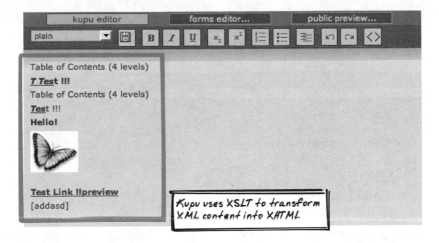

FIGURE 11-4. Kupu Word Processor

Sarissa framework

Sarissa (*http://sarissa.sourceforge.net/doc/*) is an open source, cross-browser framework for all things XML. XSLT is supported as well as XML parsing, XPath queries, and `XMLHttpRequest` invocation.

Code Refactoring: AjaxPatterns XSLT Drilldown Demo

This refactoring is similar to that performed in *Browser-Side Templating* but uses XSLT instead of templating. The starting point, the Basic Drilldown Demo (*http://ajaxify.com/run/ portal/drilldown*), converts XML to HTML using a series of JavaScript string concatenations. The callback function, which receives the XML, therefore performs lots of string concatenations as follows:

```
html+="<div id='categoryName'>" + categoryName + "</div>";
```

In this refactoring, all that string handling is replaced by an XSLT transformation using the Sarissa library (*http://sarissa.sourceforge.net/doc/*). One slight complication is the stylesheet—how does the script access it? The solution here is to keep it as a separate file on the server and pull it down on page load:

```
var xsltDoc;
window.onload = function( ) {
  ...
  ajaxCaller.getXML("./drilldown.xsl",function(response) {xsltDoc = response;});
  ...
}
```

As was mentioned earlier in "Decisions," there's a race condition here, because the XML response may come before the stylesheet. To deal with this, the drilldown callback function keeps looping until the stylesheet is defined:

```
function onDrilldownResponse(xml) {
  if (xsltDoc==null) {
```

```
            setTimeout(function( ) { onDrilldownResponse(xml); }, 1000);
            return;
        }
        ...
    }
```

Beyond that, the callback function is simply an invocation of Sarissa's XSLT processor:

```
function onDrilldownResponse(xml) {
    ...
    var xsltProc  = new XSLTProcessor( );
    xsltProc.importStylesheet(xsltDoc);
    var htmlDoc = xsltProc.transformToDocument(xml);
    var htmlString = Sarissa.serialize(htmlDoc);
    $("drilldown").innerHTML = htmlString;
}
```

The only thing left is the stylesheet itself, shown below. I'll spare a walkthrough. The output here is the same as that in the Basic Drilldown Demo (*http://ajaxify.com/run/portal/ drilldown*), which generates the HTML using manual JavaScript processing.

```
<?xml version="1.0"?>
<xsl:stylesheet version="1.0"
                xmlns:xsl="http://www.w3.org/1999/XSL/Transform">

  <xsl:template match="/">
    <html>
      <body>
        <xsl:apply-templates/>
      </body>
    </html>
  </xsl:template>

  <xsl:template match="/category">
    <div id='categoryName'><xsl:value-of select="@name" /></div>
    <xsl:if test="@parent!=''">
      <div id='parent' onclick='retrieveCategory("{@parent}")'>
        Back to <xsl:value-of select="@parent" />
      </div>
    </xsl:if>
    <xsl:apply-templates/>
  </xsl:template>

  <xsl:template match="/category/items/link">
    <div class="link"><a href="{url}"><xsl:value-of select=
"name"/></a></div>
  </xsl:template>

  <xsl:template match="/category/items/category">
    <div class="category"
         onclick="retrieveCategory('{@name}')">
         <xsl:value-of select="@name"/>
    </div>
  </xsl:template>

</xsl:stylesheet>
```

Alternatives

Browser-Side Templating

Browser-Side Templating (see the next pattern) is a solution for rendering content in any format—plain-text, XML, and so on. You could extract key variables from an *XML Message* and render them with a templating engine. Browser-Side Templating is a simpler approach as it builds on existing JavaScript knowledge, while Browser-Side XSLT allows for more powerful transformations and avoids the cumbersome querying of XML in JavaScript.

Related Patterns

XML Message

Browser-Side XSLT is driven by the need to deal with incoming *XML Messages* (Chapter 9).

XML Data Island

Browser-Side XSLT can be used to render an element contained in an *XML Data Island* (see earlier). Also, XML Data Island is a good place to stick an XSLT stylesheet.

Metaphor

Browser-Side XSLT is a strategy for presenting abstract data in a human-readable form. People do this all the time with diagrams. For instance, a family tree is one way to render the abstract set of relationships in a family. A UML diagram is a visual representation of some (real or imagined) code.

Browser-Side Templating

Pages, Presentation, Render, Template, Transform, View

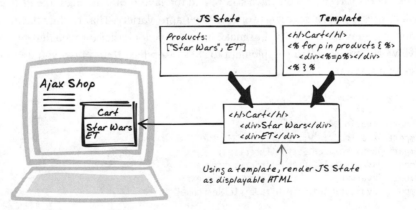

FIGURE 11-5. Browser-Side Templating

Developer Story

Devi has just been assigned to make the user profile more verbose. The original version takes an XML document about the user and renders it all with a jungle of JavaScript code that accumulates a big HTML string amid if-then conditions and loops. Devi decides the first step is to refactor all that into a Browser-Side Template, isolating the HTML generation. As a result, introducing the new content becomes trivial.

Problem

How can you separate presentation from logic?

Forces

* Generating HTML in the browser is a good way to isolate all presentation logic in one tier.

* To render context-specific information within the browser, you need to rely on a dynamic mechanism. It's not feasible to just set an element's innerHTML property to point to a static HTML page.

* Code gets complex and error-prone when you mix HTML generation with application logic. JavaScript is not well-suited to programmatically building up HTML strings.

Solution

Produce templates with embedded JavaScript and call on a browser-side framework to render them as HTML. The template contains standard HTML and allows context variables to be substituted in at rendering time, which gives it more flexibility than a static HTML page. In addition, you can also intersperse JavaScript code. For instance, generate an HTML table by running a loop—one iteration for each row.

The templating idea has been used for a long time on the Web, which is evident in frameworks like Perl's HTML::Mason, Java's JSPs, and the layout of languages like PHP and ASP. All of these are syntactic sugar of the "killer app" variety. That is, they technically don't add any new functionality, but make life a whole lot easier for web developers. In the Java world, the standard complement to JSPs is servlets. Here's how you'd write a message in a servlet:

```
package com.example.hello;

import java.io.IOException;
import java.io.PrintWriter;
import javax.servlet.ServletException;
import javax.servlet.http.HttpServlet;
import javax.servlet.http.HttpServletRequest;
import javax.servlet.http.HttpServletResponse;

public class HelloServlet extends HttpServlet {
```

```
     protected void doGet(HttpServletRequest request,
                          HttpServletResponse response)
            throws ServletException, IOException {
        response.setContentType("text/html");
        PrintWriter out = response.getWriter( );
        out.println("<html>");
        out.println("<head><title>Hi Everyboddeee!</title></head>");
        out.println("<body>");
        out.println("  Your name is <%context.name %>\"" + request.getAttribute("name") +
            "\".");
        out.println("</body></html>");
        out.close( );
     }
}
```

Not pretty. There are printing commands all over the place, escaped special characters, quote marks, and error handling. What happened to the simplicity of HTML? Code like this is best avoided because it mixes presentation with logic. The following JSP, using the standard JSTL library, achieves the same thing in a more lucid, maintainable style:

```
<%@ taglib prefix="c" uri="http://java.sun.com/jstl/core" %>
<html>
<head><title>Hi Everyboddeee!</title></head>
<body>
  Your name is <c:out value="$name" />.
</body>
</html>
```

With many Ajax Apps, it's deja vu. Often, the browser receives a raw response such as a *Plain-Text Message* (Chapter 9) or an *XML Message* (Chapter 9) and must then render it as HTML, ruling out server-side templates. A common approach is to manually traverse the structure programmatically and create some HTML to be injected via some element's innerHTML property. The old "bucket of print statements" strikes again.

The solution here recapitulates in the browser what all those server-side templating frameworks offer. A templating framework, while not immensely difficult to implement, is probably not the sort of thing you'd want to write yourself. This pattern, then, is only made possible by the fact that frameworks already exist, and some are mentioned in the following examples. Here's a quick example of a template in Ajax Pages format (*http://ajax-pages.sourceforge.net/*):

```
<html>
<head><title>Hi Everyboddeee!</title></head>
<body>
  Your name is <%= name %>.
</body>
```

The JavaScript template is in similar format to the JSP above and follows standard conventions of templates. That is:

• Any code is contained inside <% and %> tags.

• Any expression to be substituted in the HTML is contained inside <%= and %> tags.

- To apply the template, create a processor and pass it a context. With Ajax Pages:

```
var ajp = new AjaxPages();
ajp.load("template.ajp");
var processor = ajp.getProcessor();
element.innerHTML = processor({name: username});
```

Decisions

How will you obtain the template?

You'll generally pass the template to the processor as a string, but where does that string come from? The options here are the same as with *Browser-Side XSLT* (see earlier in this chapter): store it server side; hardcode it as a JavaScript string; and store it inside the HTML document. See the "Decisions" section in Browser-Side XSLT for more details.

Will the template include any code? How much?

Code in templates is somewhat frowned upon because it defeats the purpose of templates as a place to isolate the presentation. Certainly, more complex calculation are best performed in plain JavaScript or on the server side, but if managing the display requires some logic, a template is a reasonable place to put it. Examples include:

Loops
A collection is passed in to the template. The template outputs the entire collection by looping over the collection. It's much better for the template to perform the looping, rather than calling JavaScript, because there is usually some HTML before and after the loop. If JavaScript outputted that HTML, there would be too much coupling between the JavaScript and the template.

Conditionals
if-then conditions and switch statements are sometimes better performed by the template too. However, if the body of each branch is long, you might prefer to include a different template for each.

How to prepare the template's context?

In the case of Ajax Pages (*http://ajax-pages.sourceforge.net/*), you're allowed to pass in a context variable at rendering time. That's usually a good thing, as it provides an alternative to the template using global variables. The most obvious thing to do is pass some existing objects to the template, but sometimes the calling code can prepare some extra information. The aim is to perform as much processing as possible in the JavaScript code, so as to avoid any complex logic being performed within the template. For example, sometimes the template contains a simple if-then condition like this:

```
<% if (context.credits == 0) { %>
  You need more credits!
<% } else { %>
  You have <%=context.credits%> credits!
<% } %>
```

The logic isn't especially complex, but scaling up with this approach can be problematic. As an alternative, let the JavaScript do some processing:

```
var creditsMessage = credits ?
  "You need more credits!" : "You have " + credits + " credits!";
```

The template then gives you a clear picture of the HTML it will generate:

```
<%= context.creditsMessage %>
```

Real-World Examples

Ajax Pages framework

Gustavo Ribeiro Amigo's Ajax Pages (*http://ajax-pages.sourceforge.net/*) is an open source templating framework. There's a basic blog demo (*http://ajax-pages.sourceforge.net/examples/blog/index.html*) on the project homepage (Figure 11-6).

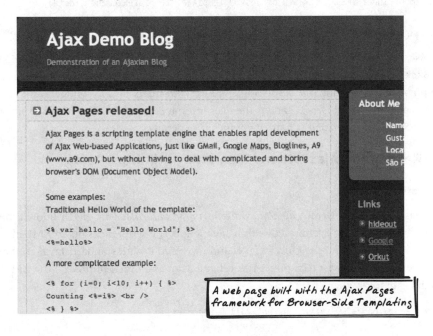

FIGURE 11-6. Ajax Pages demo

JavaScript Templates framework

JavaScript Templates (JST) (*http://trimpath.com/project/wiki/JavaScriptTemplates*) is an open source templating framework from TrimPath. JST offers a richer set of functionality at this time, including:

- Expression modifiers. The "capitalize" modifier, for instance, occurs in expressions like `${name|capitalize}`.

- A special syntax for loops and conditions.

- Macros.

These features may be useful if you're relying heavily on templating, but there's also an argument that JavaScript alone is sufficient, so there's no need to add the burden of learning a second set of similar syntax.

Here's how a JST template looks:

```
{for p in products}
  <tr>
     <td>${p.name|capitalize}</td><td>${p.desc}</td>
     <td>$$${p.price}</td>
     <td>${p.quantity} : ${p.alert|default:""|capitalize}</td>
  </tr>
{/for}
```

With the string in a DOM element on the web page, you can apply the template with a one-liner:

```
element.innerHTML = TrimPath.processDOMTemplate("templateElement", data);
```

Backbase framework

Backbase (*http://backbase.com/*) is a commercial framework that extends standard XHTML with Backbase-specific tags (BXML). It's a more over-arching framework, as the tags are more powerful than standard templating engines, with many tags for widgets and visual effects available; e.g., <b:panel> tag for the user interface. See the "Real-World Examples" in *Server-Side Code Generation* (Chapter 12) for more details.

Code Refactoring: AjaxPatterns Templating Drilldown Demo

Initial version

In the Basic Drilldown Demo (*http://ajaxify.com/run/portal/drilldown*), the Drilldown menu itself is a bunch of HTML generated within JavaScript. The script picks up an XML file containing a specification for the current level and traversed it with standard JavaScript and XML access. See *Drilldown* (Chapter 14) for details, but as a quick summary, the XML file looks like the following:

```
<category name="Overviews" parent="All Categories">
  <items>
    <link>
      <url>http://en.wikipedia.org/wiki/AJAX</url>
      <name>Wikipedia Article</name>
    </link>
    <link>
      <url>http://www.adaptivepath.com/publications/essays/archives/000385.php</url>
      <name>First Ajax</name>
  </link>
  <category name="Podcast Overviews" parent="Overviews" />
</items>
</category>
```

The manual HTML generation looks like this:

```
function onDrilldownResponse(xml) {

    var category = xml.getElementsByTagName("category")[0];
    var html="";

    var categoryName = category.getAttribute("name");
    html+="<div id='categoryName'>" + categoryName + "</div>";

    //(Much more appending to html)

    $("drilldown").innerHTML = html;

}
```

Refactored to render from a template

For all the reasons just described, the HTML generation in the initial version is messy. The refactoring in this section introduces a template for the drilldown menu (*http://ajaxify.com/run/portal/drilldown/template*). Instead of the lengthy HTML generation in onDrilldownResponse( ), the method becomes a simple application of an AjaxPages template:

```
function onDrilldownResponse(xml) {
    var ajp = new AjaxPages( );
    ajp.load("category.ajp");
    var processor = ajp.getProcessor( );
    $("drilldown").innerHTML = processor( {xml: xml} );
}
```

So we're passing the entire XML string into the template, and the template's converting it to HTML. Let's see how that template (category.ajp) looks. First, it performs a little preprocessing on the XML string:

```
<%
    var category = context.xml.getElementsByTagName("category")[0];
    var categoryName = category.getAttribute("name");
    var parent = category.getAttribute("parent");
    var items = category.getElementsByTagName("items")[0].childNodes;
%>
```

Then, it outputs the HTML. Note that looping and conditions are implemented with regular JavaScript, a fair reason to include JavaScript within a template.

```
<div id='categoryName'><%=categoryName%></div>

<%
    if (parent && parent.length > 0) {
%>
        <div id='parent' onclick="retrieveCategory('<%=parent%>')">Back to <br/>
        <%=parent%></div>
<% } %>
<%
    for (i=0; i<items.length; i++) {
```

```
        var item = items[i];
        if (item.nodeName=="link") {
          var name = item.getElementsByTagName("name")[0].firstChild.nodeValue;
          var url = item.getElementsByTagName("url")[0].firstChild.nodeValue;
%>
          <div class="link"><a href="<%=url%>"><%= name %></a></div>
<%
        } else if (item.nodeName=="category") {
          var name = item.getAttribute("name");
%>
          <div class='category'
                onclick="retrieveCategory('<%=name%>')"><%=name%></div>
<%
      }
    }
%>
```

We now have exactly the same external behavior as before, but the templating approach has helped separate presentation from logic.

Refactored to improve template context

In the previous version, the context consisted of only one thing: the entire XML string. As mentioned earlier in "Decisions," it's sometimes worthwhile doing some preparation before passing the context over to the template. In the preceding example, the template begins by extracting out a few convenience variables from the XML. That's arguably okay, because it means the XML format is coupled only to the template, and not to the Java-Script. However, there's also an argument that the JavaScript should simplify the template's work by passing in a richer context. This further refactoring explores that avenue (*http://ajaxify.com/run/portal/drilldown/template/prepareContext*).

The change is quite small. The XML callback function now passes in a more detailed context:

```
function onDrilldownResponse(xml) {
  var ajp = new AjaxPages();
  ajp.load("category.ajp");
  var processor = ajp.getProcessor();
  var category = xml.getElementsByTagName("category")[0];
  $("drilldown").innerHTML = processor({
    categoryName: category.getAttribute("name"),
    parent: category.getAttribute("parent"),
    items: category.getElementsByTagName("items")[0].childNodes
  });
}
```

The template no longer needs the convenience variables as it can now refer to properties of the context:

```
<div id='categoryName'><%=context.categoryName%></div>

<%
  if (context.parent && context.parent.length > 0) {
%>
```

```
<div id='parent' onclick="retrieveCategory('<%=context.parent%>')">Back to
  <br/>
  <%=context.parent%></div>
<%
  }
%>
...
<%
  for (i=0; i<context.items.length; i++) {
  ...
%>
```

Alternatives

Browser-Side XSLT

In many cases, the browser receives an XML response. Where the browser is converting XML to HTML, *Browser-Side XSLT* (see earlier) is a very direct alternative to this Browser-Side Templating. Templating simplifies presentation but still requires parsing of the XML, which can be cumbersome. XSLT simplifies the parsing as well, being designed specifically for the purpose of transforming XML.

Related Patterns

XML Message

Templating is well-suited to transforming an *XML Message* (Chapter 9) into HTML.

JSON Message

Templating is well-suited to transforming an object from a *JSON Message* (Chapter 9) into HTML.

Metaphor

Think of a physical template—a document with most content already present, with a few blanks to populate with current values.

CHAPTER TWELVE

Code Generation and Reuse

THERE ARE TWO GENERAL PROGRAMMING PATTERNS IN THIS CHAPTER. *SERVER-SIDE CODE GENERATION* IS one technique people are using to avoid working directly with HTML and JavaScript. *Cross-Browser Component* is a component that's been developed for portability across the major browsers.

Server-Side Code Generation

AutoGenerated, CodeGen, Framework, Library

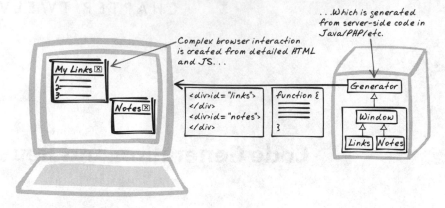

FIGURE 12-1. Server-Side Code Generation

Developer Story

Dave's creating a web app with a trendy new server-side framework, ZeroWeb. The framework lets him write everything in Java as if he's writing a standalone GUI application. It's capable of using that code to generate a conventional edition of the application, An Ajax edition, a desktop edition, and—for an extra $99.95—a smartphone app too.

Problem

How do you avoid using HTML and JavaScript?

Forces

- HTML and JavaScript are the only code recognized by standard browser—any Ajax App must be represented in a combination of these formats.

- Ajax is increasing the complexity of HTML and JavaScript. Whereas JavaScript was previously used for simple tasks like navigation support or form validation, it's now driving the interaction in many applications.

- Most Ajax Apps also have a substantial backend, which is rarely implemented in JavaScript.

- It's difficult to completely separate the roles of browser-side developer and server-side developer. In fact, it's often more desirable to have the same developer working on a vertical slice of functionality; i.e., contributing a little to all tiers in order to deliver a new requirement. Thus, the same developer is often expected to work across tiers, where the environment differs significantly.

- Server-side development has certain advantages over JavaScript development. In some cases, there's better support for code editing, refactoring, testing, and so on.

- Sometimes, you want different user interfaces for the same application—a non-Ajax version or a desktop version, for example.

Solution

Automatically generate HTML and JavaScript from server-side code. You write code in a standard server-side language like Java and it's converted to HTML and Java-Script. Depending on the framework, you might not need to code directly in HTML or JavaScript at all. Since you're unlikely to create such a framework yourself, this pattern relies on a certain category of publicly available Ajax framework (see Appendix A).

In the case of all code being auto-generated, the code is something like a conventional desktop application. Widgets and event handlers are defined, and the browser generates the appropriate HTML, along with *XMLHttpRequest Calls* (Chapter 6) and general Java-Script handling. As well, the framework will often generate *Ajax Stubs* to deal with incoming calls and pass them to appropriate application code.

In other frameworks, the approach is more mixed. The framework might let you create a *Slider* with just a single tag, for example. But in the tag, you'll specify a JavaScript function to be called whenever the slider value changes.

There are several arguments for Server-Side Code Generation:

* It may be more productive, as the server-side language and framework may be more expressive and also because the framework might remove redundancy across the tiers (such as a data structure having a JavaScript representation as well as a server-side representation).

* Developers don't have to know HTML and JavaScript; they can work in the server-side language and environment they're most familiar with.

* The framework can help with graceful degradation. In other words, it can free the developer of worrying about browser portability, JavaScript, or cookies being turned off, or *XMLHttpRequest Calls* timing out.

* The framework can, in theory, deliver multiple platforms simultaneously. A single code base can be used to generate a web application (Ajaxian or not), standalone desktop application, and maybe even a mobile application.

However, code generation does comes at a cost to usability. Look at it this way: anything you could generate from the server, a skilled developer could also hand code. The reverse is not true; given enough time and talent, it's always possible to build a custom solution that's superior in terms of usability. So, to be worthwhile, the framework must add enough value in terms of productivity and support for non-experts, to be compensated for the drop in usability. Whether this can be achieved really depends on two things: how much users will gain from a custom-built application, and how much of a boost the framework will give you. On the second point, consider a few counter-arguments to the benefits above:

* The first point, about developers not having to learn HTML and JavaScript, has traditionally held the most weight. Server-side developers in the past produced minimalist *satisficing* interfaces rather than *optimal* ones, allowing them to focus on the server side.

It's not uncommon to see advice against anything relatively complex being performed on the server side. But as Ajax becomes more prominent, this argument becomes less compelling. As discussed in *Fat Client* (Chapter 13), JavaScript is undergoing a renaissance—developers are learning more about it, tools and libraries are evolving, and patterns are emerging. All this reduces the argument for isolating developers from HTML and JavaScript.

- A server-side framework may well be able to handle graceful degradation and browser versions transparently. But to the extent that's possible in the server, a script can equally achieve the same effect in the browser, as discussed later in *Cross-Browser Component* (see later in this chapter). Portability is really a lame-duck argument for using server-side frameworks.

- The dream of transforming a single code base into a variety of different user-interface styles has been around for a while. Certainly, many modern UI toolkits are cross-platform, running on different operating systems from the same code base. However, can a single code base lead to both a web app and a desktop application? It's possible in theory and in proof-of-concept demos, but in practice, users expect applications to follow the conventions of the platform and that's difficult to achieve with a single generation.

An interesting variant of Server-Side Code Generation is "Browser-Side Code Generation"; the Backbase framework (*http://backbase.com*) is a case in point. With Backbase, the server outputs a specialized markup language, BXML, and the browser converts it into HTML, CSS, and JavaScript.

I expect the full-featured frameworks to become particularly prominent on intranet applications, where new functionality is often more critical than usability, and users can be trained to work around problems. Hand-coded HTML and JavaScript is more likely for public dot-coms where alternatives are abundant and the pressure of competition means it's critical to optimize the user interface. In those environments, there is still some role for Server-Side Code Generation, but mainly as a helper for very specific tasks and with some flexibility, rather than as the overarching architectural style.

Real-World Examples

These examples describe frameworks that support this pattern in different ways.

Echo2

Echo2 (*http://www.nextapp.com/products/echo2/*) is an open source framework by NextApp, which takes the "whole hog" approach and generates *all* HTML and JavaScript from Java source code. An online demo (*http://demo.nextapp.com/InteractiveTest/ia*) shows how Echo2's user-interface widget classes manifest themselves in the browser (Figure 12-2).

Ruby On Rails framework

Ruby On Rails (*http://rubyonrails.com*) is a web framework that embeds Ruby inside web pages. That in itself is not new, but Rails offers built-in helper classes to speed up page

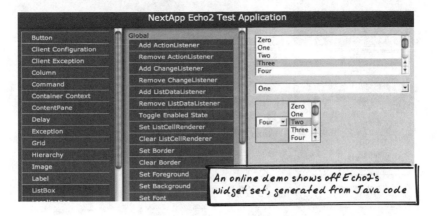

An online demo shows off Echo2's widget set, generated from Java code

FIGURE 12-2. Echo2 demo

construction. They often lead to the Scriptaculous library being invoked, but the programmer doesn't use it directly. For example, you can issue an *XMLHttpRequest Call* followed by *Display Morphing*, using the following embedded Ruby call (*http://www.onlamp.com/pub/a/onlamp/2005/06/09/rails_ajax.html*):

```
<%= link_to_remote( "click here",
              :update => "time_div",
              :url =>{ :action => :say_when }) %>
```

Backbase

Backbase (*http://backbase.com/*) is a commercial framework that extends standard XHTML with Backbase-specific tags (BXML). A Backbase client-side framework translates the BXML to HTML, CSS, and JavaScript, making it easy to implement many standard Ajax features. So there's a widget tag that looks like this:

```
<b:panel>
```

and another tag for various visual effects:

```
<s:fxstyle>
```

There are several innovative demos available from the Backbase homepage (*http://www.backbase.com/#home/pulldown/demos.xml[2]*) (Figure 12-3). On the server, Backbase offers programming interfaces for both .NET and JSF and offers visual development tools for Visual Studio .NET as well. As with the other tools here, the developer doesn't have to deal with HTML or JavaScript, but the framework also lets people customize the generation for specialized browser appearances and behavior. Note that, as mentioned earlier in the "Solution," Backbase is actually a kind of client-side, rather than server-side, code generation.

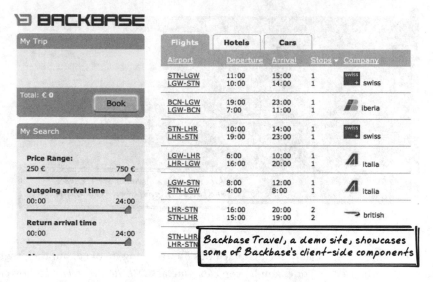

Flights | Hotels | Cars

Airport	Departure	Arrival	Stops ▾	Company
STN-LGW	11:00	15:00	1	swiss
LGW-STN	10:00	14:00	1	
BCN-LGW	19:00	23:00	1	iberia
LGW-BCN	7:00	11:00	1	
STN-LHR	10:00	14:00	1	swiss
LHR-STN	19:00	23:00	1	
LGW-LHR	6:00	10:00	1	italia
LHR-LGW	16:00	20:00	1	
LGW-STN	8:00	12:00	1	italia
STN-LGW	4:00	8:00	1	
LHR-STN	16:00	20:00	2	british
STN-LHR	15:00	19:00	2	

Backbase Travel, a demo site, showcases some of Backbase's client-side components

FIGURE 12-3. Backbase Travel demo

AjaxTags library

AjaxTags (*http://ajaxtags.sourceforge.net/*) is a collection of JSP tags to ease development of Ajax interaction. There's an `<autocomplete>` tag for *Suggestion* and an `<ajax:update>` field to perform a *Display Morphing* (Chapter 5) with the response of an *XMLHttpRequest Call* (Chapter 6).

Comfort.ASP library

Comfort.ASP (*http://www.daniel-zeiss.de/ComfortASP/*) takes an unusual approach by automatically adding Web Remoting (Chapter 6) to a conventional, non-Ajax application. By instrumenting the HTML, the framework can intercept standard form submissions and transform them into *XMLHttpRequest Calls*. By monitoring server output, Comfort's server-side script can respond to these calls by sending back only deltas—the difference between the current HTML and the desired HTML.

Code Example: Echo2 Number Guess

Echo2 (*http://www.nextapp.com/products/echo2/*) provides full source for a tutorial application, Number Guess (*http://www.nextapp.com/products/echo2/doc/tutorial/application.html*). The user guesses a number between 1 and 100, the application tells them if it's higher or lower, the user tries again, and so on. Note that the code is available, but there's no online demo at present.

An Echo2 application is run as a Java servlet extending Echo2's `WebContainerServlet`. The superclass takes care of most interaction; the concrete servlet must do just one thing: declare an `ApplicationInstance`. In Echo2, an `ApplicationInstance` object is the application state for a given user:

```
/**
 * Guess-a-number Tutorial Application Servlet Implementation.
 */
public class NumberGuessServlet extends WebContainerServlet {

    /**
     * @see nextapp.echo2.webcontainer.WebContainerServlet#newApplicationInstance( )
     */
    public ApplicationInstance newApplicationInstance( ) {
        return new NumberGuessApp( );
    }

}
```

The main application object initializes a new window and controls two top-level user-interface elements: a GamePane on startup, which is where the main action takes place, and a CongratulationsPane upon victory:*

```
public class NumberGuessApp extends ApplicationInstance {

    private Window mainWindow;

    public Window init( ) {
        mainWindow = new Window( );
        mainWindow.setTitle("Echo2 Guess-A-Number");
        startNewGame( );
        return mainWindow;
    }

    void startNewGame( ) {
        ...
        mainWindow.setContent(new GamePane( ));
    }
    void congratulate(int numberOfTries) {
        mainWindow.setContent(new CongratulationsPane(numberOfTries));
    }

}

class GamePane extends ContentPane implements ActionListener {
    ...
}

class CongratulationsPane extends ContentPane implements ActionListener {
    ...
}
```

The GamePane is built up by adding subelements and registering events. It acts as an ActionListener for the buttons it contains; hence, there's an actionPerformed event, which encapsulates the guess evaluation logic. The code illustrates that a framework like Echo2 paves the way for a style of web programming that's almost identical to traditional desktop coding.

* All comments are omitted in the code sample.

```
class GamePane extends ContentPane implements ActionListener {

    private int randomNumber = ((int) Math.floor(Math.random( ) * 100)) + 1;
    private int lowerBound = 1;
    private int upperBound = 100;
    private int numberOfTries = 0;
    private TextField guessEntryField;
    private Label statusLabel = new Label( );
    private Label countLabel = new Label("You have made no guesses.");
    private Label promptLabel= new Label("Guess a number between 1 and 100: ");
    private int guess;

    GamePane( ) {
        super( );

        Column layoutColumn = new Column( );
        layoutColumn.setCellSpacing(new Extent(10));
        add(layoutColumn);
        ...
        Button submitButton = new Button("Submit Your Guess");
        submitButton.setActionCommand("submit guess");
        submitButton.setForeground(Color.BLACK);
        submitButton.setBackground(Color.GREEN);
        submitButton.setWidth(new Extent(200));
        submitButton.addActionListener(this);
        layoutColumn.add(submitButton);
    }

    public void actionPerformed(ActionEvent e) {
        if (e.getActionCommand( ).equals("new game")) {
            ((NumberGuessApp) ApplicationInstance.getActive()).startNewGame( );
        } else if (e.getActionCommand( ).equals("submit guess")) {
            ++numberOfTries;
            ...
            if (guess == randomNumber) {
                ((NumberGuessApp) ApplicationInstance.getActive())
                    .congratulate(numberOfTries);
            } else if (guess < 1 || guess > 100) {
                statusLabel.setText("Your guess, " + guess  + " was not between
                    1 and 100.");
            } else if (guess < randomNumber) {
                ...
            }
            ...
        }
    }
}
```

Alternatives

Browser-Side Templating

Browser-Side Templating (Chapter 11) is a form of Client-Side Code Generation, an alternative to Server-Side Code Generation.

Related Patterns

HTML Message

Server-Side Code Generation produces HTML responses, so is technically one form of *HTML Message* (Chapter 9). It's also a form of JavaScript Response, the variant described in *On-Demand JavaScript* (Chapter 6). However, the emphasis in those patterns is on directly created HTML and JavaScript, rather than delegation to a generation framework.

Cross-Browser Component

Agnostic, Common, Component, CrossBrowser, Independent, Portable

Create a portable component that can be easily be used in all browsers

FIGURE 12-4. Cross-Browser Component

Developer Story

Dave has developed a cross-browser sprite engine, allowing users to easily drag a sprite around the screen. The library provides a browser-independent interface, taking into account browser incompatibilities regarding detection of mouse position and positioning of icons. When a new drag-and-drop requirement comes along, programmers can code to Dave's library in blissful ignorance of the underlying browser incompatibilities.

Problem

How can you manage cross-browser incompatibilities?

Forces

- A major selling point of Ajax is portability—the ability to run an application on any platform with a modern browser.

- There are numerous browsers on the market, and while IE still dominates, the market is becoming increasingly fragmented. IE currently has around 85–90 percent share on average web sites, but within certain user groups, Mozilla is actually far more popular. A recent survey of AjaxPatterns.org traffic showed 47.5 percent hits from Firefox, 30.1 percent from IE, and 2.7 percent from Safari.

- Browsers vary from each other in subtle and not-so-subtle ways. Sometimes, a browser simply doesn't support certain functionality. Other times, two browsers offer the same functionality, but it must be accessed in different ways. While the W3C (*http://www. w3c.org*) establishes standards for browsers, not all are followed.

- When creating a web program, you want to focus on business and application logic, without being distracted by idiosyncrasies of underlying browsers. Cross-browser compatibility is a cross-cutting concern, best dealt with as a separate task at a separate time.

Solution

Create Cross-Browser Components, allowing programmers to reuse them without regard for browser idiosyncrasies. A Cross-Browser Component abstracts away from underlying browser issues, offering a single API that can be used on any supported browser.

Following are a couple of examples of cross-browser incompatibilities. For simplicity, only the two most popular browsers are discussed: IE and Firefox. Other browsers are also important, and not surprisingly, introduce further incompatibility issues. The following are two examples:

XMLHttpRequest

> XMLHttpRequest, a critical Ajax component, is constructed in a browser-specific way, as established in *XMLHttpRequest Call* (Chapter 6). Most browsers include a specific XMLHttpRequest class, but with IE prior to version 7, it's created as an ActiveX component instead. Furthermore, there are some subtle behavior differences. For example, XMLHttpRequest on Opera lagged behind in terms of support for features like authentication (*http://www.scss.com.au/family/andrew/webdesign/xmlhttprequest/*). An even greater problem is that many older browsers simply don't support this object, even though similar functionality can nonetheless be achieved using IFrames.

opacity

> opacity—or transparency—is becoming important in Ajax applications, as discussed in *Popup* (Chapter 15) and in *One-Second Spotlight* (Chapter 16). However, portability is poor (*http://www.sitepoint.com/newsletter/viewissue.php?id=3&issue=102&format=html*). Recent versions of Firefox, Opera, and Safari allow for the CSS3 opacity style, older versions use their own different names, and IE uses a completely different approach based on a DirectX filter.

Any application using the features above must take into account cross-browser portability. Business and application logic is complex enough, without tangling it further with `if-then` portability statements. A better solution, and a common approach in the general area of portability, is to isolate cross-browser concerns.

Some browsers are available in multiple operating systems—Firefox, for example, runs in MS-Windows, Apple, Linux, and many other operating systems. It would be nice to assume a given browser was identical across all operating systems, but that's not the case. Some aspects of browsers rely on OS-specific features, which is where further incompatibilities arise. For example, IE's drag-and-drop capability not only depends on which version of IE is being used, but also on whether it's running on Apple or MS-Windows.

As a simple example, many libraries exist to make `XMLHttpRequest` calls portable. These libraries are examples of Cross-Browser Components, because the user doesn't have to worry about the browser being used. Most of these libraries internally use another form of Cross-Browser Component—a factory function that retrieves a suitable `XMLHttpRequest` object.

ajaxCaller (*http://ajaxify.com/run/testAjaxCaller/*), for example, contains the following factory function:

```
createXMLHttpRequest: function() {
    try { return new ActiveXObject("Msxml2.XMLHTTP"); } catch (e) {}
    try { return new ActiveXObject("Microsoft.XMLHTTP"); } catch (e) {}
    try { return new XMLHttpRequest(); } catch(e) {}
    alert("XMLHttpRequest not supported");
    return null;
}
```

The function allows any code to create a new `XMLHttpRequest` object without worrying about browser specifics. The returned object is a Cross-Browser Component.

Note that this pattern applies as much to server-side code as to browser-side JavaScript. Whatever HTML comes from the server also needs to be portable. For that reason, you can also create server-side components that will generate portable HTML. So if you create custom JSP tags for your project, the JSP coder should be able to use them without having to make any browser-specific checks.

Decisions

What browser-specific criteria is used to create the Cross-Browser Component?

What criteria do you use to decide on a creation strategy? There are, broadly speaking, two approaches:

Version-dependent
Behavior is based on the browser version.

Feature-dependent
Behavior is based on checking for the existence of specific features—specifically whether a property or method exists.

The `XMLHttpRequest` example in the earlier "Solution" is an example of *feature-driven* behavior. Before trying to create a new `window.XMLHttpRequest`, we check if `window.XMLHttpRequest` exists. An equivalent version-dependent check would do something like this:

```
/* Version-Dependent Check (Unadvisable!!!) */
return determineIfCurrentBrowserIsIE( ) ?
  new ActiveXObject('Microsoft.XMLHTTP') : new XMLHttpRequest( );
```

In the above example, a function determines if the current browser is IE. Based on that knowledge, the right mechanism can be used to create an `XMLHttpRequest` object. How might the version be determined? There are a few ways. First, the `navigator` object reports directly on this information. Useful properties include (*http://www.javascriptkit.com/jsref/navigator.shtml*):

`navigator.appName`
    Browser name; e.g. "Netscape"

`navigator.appVersion`
    Browser version; e.g., "5.0 (X11; en-US)"

`navigator.UserAgent`
    Detailed browser and platform details; e.g., "Mozilla/5.0 (X11; U; Linux i686; en-US; rv:1.7.9) Gecko/20050711 Firefox/1.0.5"

Ironically, the `navigator` object's behavior is itself somewhat inconsistent across versions, so you need to handle strings like the `userAgent` differently. If you go this route, consider a browser detection library like TechPatterns' JavaScript Browser & OS Detection (*http://techpatterns.com/downloads/javascript_browser_detection.php*) or Webreference's JavaScript Browser Sniffer (*http://webreference.com/tools/browser/javascript.html*). Portability aside, the problem with direct interrogation is that the browser sometimes tells fibs—Opera, for example, lets users manually choose which browser to self-identify as, because some sites refuse to support browsers reporting as Opera.

An alternative way to detect browser version is to rely on a distinctive feature. For example, many scripts use `document.all` as a simple check for Internet Explorer (*http://weblogs. asp.net/jgalloway/archive/2005/08/07/421798.aspx*):

```
    isIE=document.all;
```

Version-dependent behavior is feasible, quite common, and often recommended as the appropriate solution. One benefit over *feature-dependent* behavior is that you have only one or two variables to deal with; with feature-dependent behavior, you have to consider many combinations—what if the browser supports X but not Y?

However, there do remain some fundamental problems with any *feature-dependent behavior*. First, it's cumbersome to track all the browser versions that support a particular feature. In many cases, you risk ruling out other browsers that may well support the feature. Also, version checks are often used in a binary way: either your browser's supported and you can run the app, or it's not supported and you're out of luck. But if you focus on specific features, you can support *progressive degradation*: have a basic application that works for all browsers, with certain additional features available only to those browsers that support them.

What if a feature isn't supported by the current browser?

Sometimes, a browser simply doesn't support a feature. What does a cross-browser API do when asked for functionality the browser doesn't provide? There are a couple of options:

Do nothing
> Throw an exception or return null to indicate the object couldn't be created.

Provide a custom version
> The browser may not support an object natively, but you might be able to create a custom version from other supported objects.

Real-World Examples

This section contains one example that showcases a particularly interesting type of cross-browser compatibility. For more examples of Cross-Browser Components, refer to Appendix A. Many of the JavaScript libraries mentioned there, like Dojo and Scriptaculous, aim to provide components that work on all major browsers.

HTMLHttpRequest library

Angus Turnbull's HTMLHttpRequest (*http://www.twinhelix.com/javascript/htmlhttprequest/*) is a cross-browser library for Web Remoting (Chapter 6). Unlike many of the recent Ajax libraries, it's able to gracefully degrade to IFrame usage when executed on older browsers. The API's still the same, so a programmer can access web remoting in the same way, regardless of the browser in question.

Code Example: HTMLHttpRequest Library

HTMLHttpRequest (*http://www.twinhelix.com/javascript/htmlhttprequest/*) is a cross-browser remoting component. It works by wrapping around a real, concrete remoting object—either an XMLHttpRequest object or an IFrame, only one of which will be set. The construction code below makes extensive use of feature-dependent behavior to decide, at each stage, whether to proceed with a particular strategy. There is also some use of feature-dependent behavior to ensure that Opera and IE5 don't follow a particular path.

```
function HTMLHttpRequest(myName,callback){
  this.myName=myName;
  this.callback=callback;
  this.xmlhttp=null;
  this.iframe=null;
  ...
  if(window.XMLHttpRequest){
    xmlhttp=new XMLHttpRequest();
    if(xmlhttp.overrideMimeType)
      xmlhttp.overrideMimeType('text/xml')
  }
  if(!xmlhttp) {
```

```
        if(   document.createElement && document.documentElement
            && (window.opera||navigator.userAgent.indexOf('MSIE 5.0')===-1)) {
            ...
        } else if (document.body && document.body.insertAdjacentHTML) {
            ...
        }
        ...
    }
    return this;
}
```

Related Patterns

Server-Side Code Generation

Server-Side Code Generation (see earlier) is often a convenient way to generate Cross-Browser Components, allowing you to perform all the abstraction logic server side.

On-Demand JavaScript

If you design carefully, you can separate out the implementations for each platform. Use the *Lazy Loading* technique of *On-Demand JavaScript* (Chapter 6) to ensure that only code required for the user's own platform is downloaded.

Metaphor

Using a Cross-Browser Component is like working with a certified professional. The professional may have gained their certification in different ways and might offer different services, but there remains a basic set of services that you can expect to be carried out adequately.

Want to Know More?

- Good discussion on cross-browser issues and specifically enhancing IE applications to support Mozilla by Doron Rosenberg (*http://www-128.ibm.com/developerworks/web/library/wa-ie2mozgd/*)

- Quirksmode, by Peter-Paul Koch, is a web site providing comprehensive compatibility resources (*http://quirksmode.com*)

CHAPTER THIRTEEN

Performance Optimization

THE **P**ERFORMANCE **O**PTIMIZATION PATTERNS IMPROVE THROUGHPUT AS WELL AS APPLY SOME USER-centered techniques to ease the pain of waiting for the server. *Browser-Side Cache* talks about implementing a custom cache within the application and explains why it's sometimes more suitable than the standard web browser cache. *Predictive Fetch* extends the cache concept by proposing that likely actions be anticipated, so that required data is already sitting in the browser by the time it's required. Another very different way to achieve zero network delay is to simply take a stab at the required value, the idea behind *Guesstimate*.

Multi-Stage Download proposes parallel or scheduled downloads so as to reduce bottlenecks and grab the most critical details as early as possible.

Fat Client is one of several possible Ajax architectural styles that helps optimize performance by pushing as much logic as possible—and potentially storage—over to the browser side.

Browser-Side Cache

Auto-Update, Memoise, Memoize, Sync, Synchronise, Sychronize, Real-Time

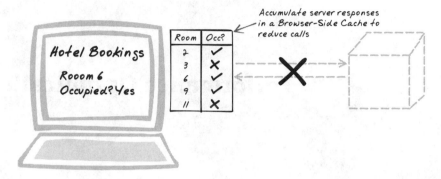

FIGURE 13-1. Browser-Side Cache

Developer Story

Devi's produced a physics simulation and, though it's functional, she's disappointed that it keeps pausing to request calculations from the server. To speed it up, she sets up a cache that will retain the calculations locally.

Problem

How can you make the system respond quickly to user activity?

Forces

• The application should respond to user actions quickly—ideally, instantaneously.

• Many user actions require a response from the server.

• Responses from the server can be noticeably latent due to data transfer and server processing overheads.

Solution

Retain server results in a Browser-Side Cache. The cache is a JavaScript map-style object that holds query-result pairs; the queries are cache keys and the server results are server results. So whenever the browser needs to query the server, first check the cache. If the query is held as a key in the cache, the corresponding value is used as the result, and there's no need to access the server. Caching like this is performed in many systems, but there are some interesting Ajax-specific issues, such as the relationship with the browser's built-in cache and the asynchronous nature of calls.

XMLHttpRequest Call (Chapter 6) explains that call results can already be cached by the browser, so you might wonder why this pattern exists. After all, the browser not only handles caching for you, but can cache huge quantities of data using the filesystem, and, unlike a Browser-Side Cache, this data will usually live beyond the current session. The reason you'd use a Browser-Side Cache is to exert more control over caching. You get to choose how much data is cached and how long it lasts, whereas those things are set by the user in a web browser cache. Moreover, you bypass the notorious portability issues associated with cache control, choosing exactly what will be and what will not be cached. Another advantage of a Browser-Side Cache over the web browser's cache is that you can save JavaScript objects you've built up, thus saving the effort of reconstructing them later on (a process known as "memoisation").

What exactly is the format of the key and value? In the simplest case, the query would just be the URL, and the result would be the response body. However, that's not so useful because if you make calls correctly, as discussed in *XMLHttpRequest Call* (Chapter 6) and *RESTful Service* (Chapter 9), the browser will handle caching on your behalf, and as it's backed by the filesystem, it can cache much greater quantities of data. However, more useful are caches that hold high-level semantic content—typically the results of processing server responses.

A cache data structure requires some way to access the key-value pairs "randomly"—that is, directly, without having to traverse the entire data structure until the desired key-value pair is found. In JavaScript, a cache can be created using an associative array (in JavaScript, this is the same as an object). So an empty array is created at startup and gradually accumulates server results. Of course, an Ajax App lives indefinitely, so the array could continue growing if not controlled. There are a few ways to handle this, as discussed later in "Decisions."

It's common in many systems to treat the cache as a Proxy, as shown in Figure 13-2 (see Gamma et al.'s [1995] Proxy pattern). That is, clients retrieve results from an object called something like "ResultFetcher," which encapsulates anything to do with fetching of results. From their perspective, the ResultFetcher just provides results. It doesn't matter to the client whether all results are directly pulled from the server or whether some of them are cached inside ResultFetcher.

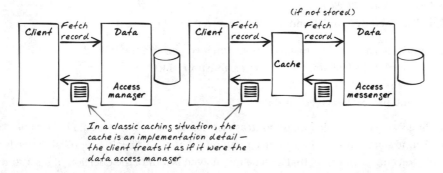

In a classic caching situation, the cache is an implementation detail — the client treats it as if it were the data access manager

FIGURE 13-2. *Standard synchronous caching setup*

Here's where the asynchronous nature of XMLHttpRequest adds a slight complication. Under normal circumstances, a caching ResultFetcher always returns the desired value synchronously, whether the result was in the cache or not. But with Ajax, it can only do this if the result was indeed found in the cache. Otherwise, the server response will come back some time later, after the fetching function has already returned. To deal with this, you might consider having the requester pass a callback function to the fetching procedure. So the fetching procedure never returns anything directly, but instead ensures the callback function is eventually called with the desired value. If it knows the value immediately, the callback function will be called straightaway, and if not, it will be called later on. In other words, the ResultFetcher has roughly the same interface and external behavior as XMLHttpRequest (or a suitable wrapper).

Decisions

What will be stored as keys? For values?

The solution mentioned a couple of possibilities for keys and values. In the first instance, they might simply be URLs and response bodies. Using the entire URL and response body does come at a cost, however. Both contain a lot of useless information, which limits how many items can be stored in the cache. An alternative is to use semantically related values. For example, the key might be customer names, and the values might be customer objects. Semantic values also lets you incorporate other data, such as results from calculations.

How will cache size be kept under control?

You typically keep the cache size under control by deciding on its capacity and on some way to remove elements when that size has been reached. Each new element usually results in an older element being discarded. For efficiency, you might discard a large batch at once, and then let the cache gradually build up again.

Two common algorithms are (*http://en.wikipedia.org/wiki/Cache_algorithms*):

Least Recently Used (LRU)
   The discarded item is the one with the longest time since it was last retrieved.

Least Frequently Used (LFU)
   The discarded item is the one that has been retrieved the least.

Both algorithms are feasible in JavaScript, provided you use the right data structure. "Code Example: Cached Sum Demo," later, illustrates LRU.

How will you protect against stale data?

Regarding stale data, the first question to ask is, "How recent does the data have to be?" If it's real-time stats being used by a nurse to monitor a patient's health, it probably needs to be pretty recent. So much so, that a cache might even be out of the question. If it's a student perusing a 50-year old article on ancient Athenian literature, a 12-hour cache will do fine.

There are several ways to enforce this decision:

- Attach a timestamp to each item that goes into the cache. Whenever you retrieve an item, inspect the timestamp to determine if the result is recent enough.

- As a variant on the above, schedule a periodic loop to actively delete stale items.

- Implement a browser-server protocol that allows the browser to determine if items are stale. So the browser might keep a timestamp for each item, and the server exposes a service to accept a timestamp. The server only needs to send the whole response if the value has changed since that time. An alternative to timestamps would be a hash function—a function that the browser runs against the cached value that can then be compared by the server against the item's most recent hash value, to see if a change has occurred.

- Implement a service on the server that announces changes that have occurred. Use *Periodic Refresh* (Chapter 10) to actively listen for such changes and to delete from the cache any items that have changed.

Real-World Examples

This section contains a *XMLHttpRequest Call* library with caching support. "Real-World Examples" in *Predictive Fetch* includes several other systems with Browser-Side Caches.

libXmlRequest library

Stephen W. Cote's libXmlRequest (*http://www.whitefrost.com/servlet/connector?file=reference/2003/06/17/libXmlRequest.html*) was one of the earlier wrappers of the XMLHttpRequest object. A typical asynchronous request looks like this:

```
getXml(path, callbackFunction, 1, requestId);
```

To make the request cached, simply add an extra argument at the end:

```
getXml(path, callbackFunction, 1, requestId, 1);
```

The approach shows how cache functionality can be made orthogonal to core application functionality.

Code Example: Cached Sum Demo

The Basic Sum Demo (*http://ajaxify.com/run/sum/*) has to resort to the server each time the cache is reached. This refactoring adds caching functionality to reduce server calls and is implemented in three stages.

Including the query in the response

The asynchronous nature of *XMLHttpRequest Call* separates the initial query from the response, so it's not always clear when a request comes in what the corresponding request was. One way to achieve this is to include the original query as part of the response. That's the first refactoring here. The refactoring is detailed in *XML Message* (Chapter 9), and the net effect is a response like the one that is shown next (*http://ajaxify.com/run/sum/xml/sumXML.php?figure1=4&figure2=8&figure3=*).

```
<sum>
  <inputs>
    <figure id="1">4</figure>
    <figure id="2">8</figure>
    <figure id="3"></figure>
  </inputs>
  <outputs>12</outputs>
</sum>
```

Previously, the response was just 12. The resulting value is extracted from the XML in a slightly different way, but the inputs are not used until the next iteration.

An infinite cache

The next refactoring creates a very basic cache—one that has no regard for the laws of physics—it just keeps growing indefinitely. That's a bad thing, but a useful stepping stone to the final iteration. The cache holds the sum against a figuresString, simply a comma-separated list of the three figures.

First, the cache is created by a global variable and initialized from the onload method:

```
var sumByFigures;
...
function restartCache(html) {
  sumByFigures = new Array();
  ...
}
```

Each time a sum is submitted, figuresString is calculated to form a key for the cache. The cache is then interrogated to see if it already contains that sum. If not, an asynchronous call is set up. Either way, the ultimate consequence is that repaintSum() will eventually be called with the new sum. If the result is already cached, it will be called straightaway. If not, it will be called after the server has returned.

```
function submitSum() {
  ...
  var figuresString =
    figures.figure1 + "," + figures.figure2 + "," + figures.figure3;
  var cachedSum = sumByFigures[figuresString];
  if (cachedSum) {
    repaintSum(cachedSum);
  } else {
    repaintSum("---");
    ajaxCaller.get("sumXML.php", figures, onSumResponse, true, null);
  }
}
```

onSumResponse not only calls repaintSum() with the value in the response, but also pushes the result onto the cache:

```
function onSumResponse(xml, headers, callingContext) {
  var sum = xml.getElementsByTagName("output")[0].firstChild.nodeValue;
  repaintSum(sum);

  var figures = xml.getElementsByTagName("figure");
```

```
    var figuresString =   figures[0].firstChild.nodeValue + ","
                        + figures[1].firstChild.nodeValue + ","
                        + figures[2].firstChild.nodeValue;
    sumByFigures[figuresString] = sum;
}
```

Finally, repaintSum is the function that detects a change—either way—and simply morphs the display:

```
function repaintSum(html) {
    self.$("sum").innerHTML = html;
}
```

A finite cache

The final cache (*http://www.ajaxify.com/run/sum/xml/cached/expiry/*) enhances the previous version by introducing a least-recently used disposal algorithm. Each time a new item is added to the cache, the least recently used item is discarded from the cache. It would be inefficient to trawl through the entire cache each time that happens, comparing usage times. So, in addition to the associative array, a parallel data structure is composed. It's a queue, where each new item is pushed to the tail of the queue and gradually approaches the head as further items are pushed on. When the queue is full and an item is pushed on to the tail, each item moves down one, and the head item "falls off" the queue, so it is deleted from both the queue and the associative array. Whenever an item is retrieved, it's sent back to the tail of the queue. That's what ensures the least recently used item is always at the head.

The queue itself is a class with the following functions: enqueue( ), dequeue( ), and sendToTail( ). It works by tracking the head, the tail, and the size, and by keeping the items in a doubly linked list. For example, enqueue( ) is defined like this:

```
Queue.prototype.enqueue = function(obj) {
    newEntry = {
        value: obj,
        next: this.tail
    }
    if (this.tail) {
        this.tail.prev = newEntry;
    } else { // Empty queue
        this.head = newEntry;
    }
    this.tail = newEntry;
    this.size++;
}
```

Back to the sum application, which now declares a queue as well as the associative array:

```
var figuresQueue, sumByFigures;
```

Each time a new element arrives from the server, it's sent to encache( ). encache will lop the least recently used item off both data structures if the queue is full. Then it will add the new item to both.

```
function encache(figuresString, sum) {
  // Add to both cache and queue.
  // Before adding to queue, take out queue head and
  // also remove it from the cache.
  if (figuresQueue.size == cacheSize) {
    removedFigures = figuresQueue.dequeue(figuresString);
    delete figuresString[removedFigures];
  }
  figuresQueue.enqueue(figuresString);
  sumByFigures[figuresString] = sum;
  $("queueSummary").innerHTML = figuresQueue.describe();
}
```

Whenever the cache is queried, the queried value is not only returned, but is also sent back to the tail of the queue to mark it as having been recently used:

```
function queryCache(figuresString) {
  // Recently used, so move corresponding entry back to tail of queue
  // if it exists.
  figuresQueue.sendToTail(figuresString);
  $("queueSummary").innerHTML = figuresQueue.describe();
  return sumByFigures[figuresString];
}
```

With these abstractions in place, there is not much change to the core part of the sum script. submitSum( ) queries the cache and calls the server if the result is not found. And the server response handler ensures new results are added to the cache:

```
function submitSum( ) {
  ...
  var cachedSum = queryCache(figuresString);
  if (cachedSum) {
    repaintSum(cachedSum);
  } else {
    repaintSum("---");
    ajaxCaller.get("sumXML.php", figures, onSumResponse, true, null);
  }
}
...
function onSumResponse(xml, headers, callingContext) {
  ...
  encache(figuresString, sum);
}
```

Alternatives

Built-in browser cache

As explained in the solution, the built-in browser cache is an alternative form of cache. It's better suited for larger data HTML, but is more difficult to control than a Browser-Side Cache.

Server-side cache

Caching data on the server cuts down on processing, especially when the data is shared by multiple users. However, that's mainly a benefit if the server processing is the bottleneck. Bandwidth is more often the chief constraint, and the server-side cache won't reduce browser-server traffic. The best option is often a combination of browser-side and server-side caching.

Related Patterns

Submission Throttling

Browser-Side Cache focuses on "read caching," in which responses from the server are held in the cache. Another flavor of caching is "write caching," where output is held in a buffer to defer outputting to its true destination. *Submission Throttling* (Chapter 10) is a form of write-caching.

Predictive Fetch

Anticipate, Fetch, Guess, Prefetch, Preload, Prepare, Ready

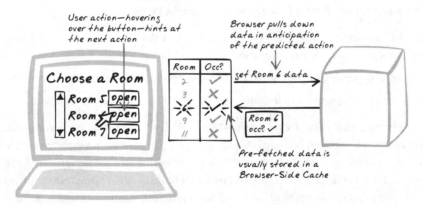

FIGURE 13-3. Predictive Fetch

Developer Story

Dave's tuning a music web site and the logs tell him that users who listen to a song for more than a minute are quite likely to click the Purchase button. So he introduces a new timer—at the one-minute mark of each song, the browser will quietly download pricing data just in case the user wants to buy it later on.

Problem

How can you make the system respond quickly to user activity?

Forces

- The application should respond to user actions quickly; ideally, it should feel instantaneous.

- Many user actions require a response from the server.

- Responses from the server can be noticeably latent due to data transfer and server processing overheads.

Solution

Pre-fetch content in anticipation of likely user actions. Pre-fetching attempts to remove the delay altogether for certain user actions.

The obvious motivation for instantaneous feedback is efficiency: the things can happen faster because the user's not sitting around waiting for results. In reality, though, the proportion of overall time waiting might actually be quite small. The more severe problem is distraction, because delays will break the user's concentration, along with the sense of frustration at not being in control. The other problem is that for real-time applications, the user is slower to respond to state conveyed by the server. A chat session will be more strained, and a remote device under browser control will be more erratic.

Here are some occasions when Predictive Fetch might be used:

- The user's navigating a *Virtual Workspace* (Chapter 15) such as a large table. Pre-fetch the results of moving in each direction.

- The user's converting between two currencies. Pre-fetch the major currency rates.

- The user's reading some articles. Pre-fetch all stories in her favorite category.

Predictive Fetch usually requires a *Browser-Side Cache* (earlier in this chapter) in order to accumulate the pre-fetched content. In addition, you can exploit the web browser's built-in cache in a couple of ways—see *Browser-Side Cache*, earlier, for a comparison of these techniques. To get something in the web browser's built-in cache, one technique is to issue *XMLHttpRequest Calls* for content you'll need later on, using the techniques mentioned in that pattern to encourage the content to be cached. The response handler does nothing here—the point is simply to bring the content into the browser, where it will be cached for later on. The other technique is for images: create a dummy image (`document.createElement("img")`) object and set its `src` property to whatever image URL you want to preload. Again, we're only doing this to ensure the image goes in the cache, so the image isn't actually attached to the page.

It's rarely possible to pre-fetch for *all* actions, so the designer has to be smart about anticipating which actions are most likely. Higher priority will be given to content that is more important or more likely to be used.

One problem with pre-fetching is the application will be a bit erratic. The user might be surprised that some commands respond instantaneously, while similar commands take a long time. While some variation is always expected on the Web, the main problem comes when the data arrives immediately. The user will reasonably question whether the app was really taking their action into account (*http://www.baekdal.com/articles/Usability/usable-XMLHttpRequest/*). For that reason, a useful but counter-intuitive trick is to actually fake a small delay and use a visual effect like *One-Second Spotlight* (Chapter 16) to hint that the server really was involved.

Decisions

How much information will be pre-fetched?

Pre-fetching comes at a cost. Anticipating the user's actions is a guessing game, and for each guess that goes wrong, some resources have been wasted. Designers must make a trade-off involving the likelihood that pre-fetched data will be used, the user benefit if it is used, and the overhead if it's not used. This could involve some fairly heavy user analysis combined with statistical methods.

In practice, it's feasible to use some initial rules of thumb and proceed on a more empirical basis. With the right design, it should be easy enough to discriminately turn pre-fetching on and off. Thus, by studying logs and comparing the effects of pre-fetching different aspects, it's possible to evolve the algorithms being used.

Will it be the server or the browser that anticipates user actions?

The request for information will always come from the browser, but it's feasible for either the server or the browser to anticipate what the user will need next. If the browser is to decide, it can simply issue a request for that information. If the server is to decide, the browser can, for example, issue a periodic request for general information—perhaps with some indication of current state—and the server can then push down whatever information it decides might come in handy for the browser.

What information can be used to anticipate user actions?

It's likely you'll use some information about the present and the past to help predict the future. There's a lot of data you could potentially use to help decide what the user will do next:

User's profile
    The user's profile and history should provide strong cues. If the user always visits the Books area as soon as they log on, then the homepage should pull down Books content.

User's current activity
    It's often possible to predict what the user will do next from their current activity. If a user has just added an item to his shopping cart, he will likely be conducting a purchase in the not-too-distant future; consider downloading his most recent delivery address.

Activity of other users
    Sometimes, a rush of users will do the same thing at once. If the user has just logged into a news portal while a major news event is in progress, system-wide statistics will inform the server that this user is probably about to click on a particular article.

Collaborative filtering

As an extension of the previous point, a more sophisticated technique is to correlate users based on information such as their profile and history. People are likely to behave similarly to those whose details are highly correlated. So if a user tends to look at "Sport" followed by "Weather," then the system should start pre-fetching "Weather" while the user's looking at "Sport."

Real-World Examples

Google Maps

Some experimentation with Google Maps (*http://maps.google.com*) suggests Predictive Fetch is used while navigating the map (Figure 13-4). The evidence is that you can slowly move along the map in any direction, and you won't see any part of the page going blank and refreshing itself. If you move quickly, you'll see the refresh behavior. Based on that observation, the map is apparently fetching content beyond the viewable area, in anticipation of further navigation.

When you scroll too quickly with Google Maps, you'll notice some incomplete image tiles

FIGURE 13-4. Google Maps loading

map.search.ch

map.search.ch (*http://map.search.ch*) includes familiar buttons for zooming and panning. The difference is that at as soon as a mouse pointer hovers over a button, a call is made to anticipate the user clicking on it. This is a good compromise between downloading in every possible direction and zoom level or doing nothing at all.

Firefox "Prefetch"

This is not entirely an Ajax example, but it's worthwhile noting a particular Firefox (and Mozilla) feature called "prefetching." The HTTP protocol allows for new link types to be defined, and Firefox happens to define a "Prefetch" link type (*http://www.mozilla.org/ projects/netlib/Link_Prefetching_FAQ.html#What_is_link_prefetching*). A "prefetch" link looks like this:

```
<link rel="prefetch" href="/images/big.jpeg">
```

When Firefox sees such a link appear, it will generally fetch the associated content, which is ready to be shown immediately. An application can exploit that feature by including links to content that is likely soon to be requested.

Google Search, for example, slaps a prefetch directive around the first search result, but states that this occurs for "some searches" only. I am guessing, based on some experimentation, that this means searches where Google is highly confident the top search will be chosen. So a search for the highly ambiguous term "anything," results in no prefetch directive. Meanwhile, a search for IBM, where it's obvious what most users seek, will direct Firefox to prefetch the first result:

```
<link rel="prefetch" href="http://www.ibm.com/">
```

International Herald Tribune

Another example is The *International Herald Tribune* (*http://www.iht.com/*), which caches entire articles to provide instant gratification when you click on Next Page.*

Code Refactoring: AjaxPatterns Predictive Fetch Sum

The Basic Sum Demo (*http://ajaxify.com/run/sum/*) allows the user to enter a set of figures, but he must wait for the server in order to see the sum. The Cached Sum Demo (*http://ajaxify. com/run/sum/xml/cached/*) improves on the situation a bit, by ensuring recent sums do not need to be re-fetched. However, there is still no anticipation of user behavior. In this refactoring (*http://ajaxify.com/run/sum/predictive/*), a new sum is fetched each time the user types something. By the time he has pressed the Add button, the browser should hopefully have the result waiting in the cache, ready to be displayed immediately. Each time a new sum is anticipated, the browser fetches the result, and a callback pushes it into the cache.

The code change is actually fairly straightforward. As before, clicking on the Add button causes a server sum request. This time, though, a flag is set to indicate its a real user submission as opposed to a pre-fetch. The call will "remember" the flag; i.e., using ajaxCaller's callingContext, the flag will be passed to the callback function when the response is issued:

```
$("addButton").onclick = function() {
  submitSum(true);
}
```

For Predictive Fetch, each release of a key triggers a sum submission, with the callback false to indicate this was *not* a user submission.

---

* This example is taken from an O'Reilly Network article (*http://www.oreillynet.com/pub/wlg/6782*).

```
$("figure1").onkeyup = function() { submitSum(false); }
$("figure2").onkeyup = function() { submitSum(false); }
$("figure3").onkeyup = function() { submitSum(false); }
```

submitSum( ) will perform the same request as before, but this time passes in the flag as a calling context:

```
ajaxCaller.get("sumXML.php", figures, onSumResponse, true, isUserSubmitted);
```

The isUserSubmitted flag is then retrieved by the callback function, which will only change the display if the corresponding query was user-submitted. Either way, the result is then pushed into the cache for later retrieval:

```
function onSumResponse(xml, headers, callingContext) {
  var isUserSubmitted = callingContext;
  ...
  if (isUserSubmitted) {
    repaintSum(sum);
  }
  ...
}
```

Alternatives

Fat Client

Sometimes, the server is invoked to perform some logical processing, rather than to access server-side data. If that's the case, it may be possible to process in JavaScript instead, as suggested by *Fat Client* (see later).

Server priming

In some cases, the reverse may be more appropriate: it might make sense for the browser to hint to the server what the user is working on, without the server actually responding. How is this useful? It allows the server to get started on processing, so that the required information can be cached server side but not actually pushed into the browser's own cache.

Related Patterns

Guesstimate

Guesstimate (see the next pattern) is another performance optimization based on probabilistic assumptions. A Guesstimate involves the browser guessing the current server state, whereas a Predictive Fetch involves guessing what the user will do next.

Browser-Side Cache

Browser-Side Cache (see earlier) is a prerequisite to Predictive Fetch—the predictively fetched data has to be stored in some form of cache.

Metaphor

Time-shifted media—evident in Tivo, offline RSS readers, and podcatchers—is an example of Predictive Fetch.

Guesstimate

Approximate, Estimate, Extrapolate, Fuzzy, Guess, Guesstimate, Interpolate, Predict, Probabilistic, Sloppy, Trend

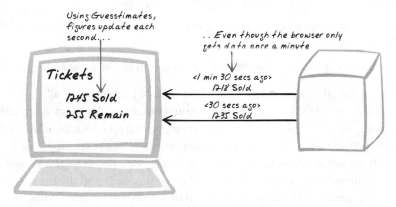

FIGURE 13-5. Guesstimate

Developer Story

Devi's producing a taxi tracker so the head office knows where its fleet is at any time. The taxis only transmit their location every 10 seconds, which would ordinarily lead to jerky movements on the map. However, Devi wants the motion to be smooth, so she uses interpolation to guess the taxi's location between updates.

Problem

How can you cut down on calls to the server?

Forces

- To comprehend system activity and predict what might happen next, it's useful to have frequent updates from the server.

- It's expensive to keep updating from the server.

Solution

Instead of requesting information from the server, make a reasonable guess.
There are times when it's better to provide a good guess than nothing at all. Typically, this pattern relates to dynamic situations where the browser periodically grabs new information, using *Periodic Refresh*. The aim is help the user spot general trends, which are often

more important than precise figures. It's a performance optimization because it allows you to give almost the same benefit as if the data was really arriving instantaneously, but without the bandwidth overhead. For this reason, it makes more sense when using *Periodic Refresh* than *HTTP Streaming*, because the latter doesn't incur as much overhead in sending frequent messages.

One type of Guesstimate is based on historical data. There are several ways the browser might have access to such data:

- The browser application can capture recent data by accumulating any significant observations into variables that last as long as the Ajax App is open.

- The browser application can capture long-term data in cookies, so it's available in subsequent sessions.

- The server can expose historical data for interrogation by the browser application.

Equipped with historical data, it's possible to extrapolate future events, albeit imprecisely. Imagine a collaborative environment where multiple users can drag-and-drop objects in a common space, something like the Magnetic Poetry Ajax App (*http://www.broken-notebook. com/magnetic/*). Using a *Periodic Refresh* of one second, users might see an erratic drag motion, with the object appearing to leap across space, then stay still for a second, then leap again. A Guesstimate would exploit the fact that the motion of the next second is probably in the same direction and speed as that of the previous section. Thus, the application can, for that second, animate the object *as if* it were being dragged in the same direction the whole time. Then, when the real position becomes apparent a second later, the object need not leap to that position, but a new estimate can be taken as to where the object's moving, and the object can instead move smoothly toward the predicted location. In other words, the object is always moving in the prediction of its current predicted location. Dragging motion is an example where users would likely favor a smooth flow at the expense of some accuracy, over an erratic display that is technically correct.

How about long-term historical data, stretching over weeks and months instead of seconds and minutes? Long-term data can also be used for a Guesstimate. Imagine showing weather on a world map. The technically correct approach would be not to show any weather initially, and then to gradually populate the map as weather data is received from the server. But the philosophy here would suggest relying on historical data for a first-cut map, at least for a few indicative icons. In the worst case, the Guesstimate could be based on the previous day's results. Or it might be based on a more sophisticated statistical model involving several data points.

Historical data is not the only basis for a Guesstimate. It's also conceivable the browser performs a crude emulation of business logic normally implemented server side. The server, for example, might take 10 seconds to perform a complex financial query. That's a problem for interactivity, where the user might like to rapidly tweak parameters. What if the browser could perform a simple approximation, perhaps based on a few assumptions and rule-of-thumb reasoning? Doing so might give the user a feel for the nature of the data, with the long server trip required only for detailed information.

There are a few gotchas with Guesstimate. For example, the Guesstimate might end up being an impossible result, like "-5 minutes remaining" or "12.8 users online"! If there's a risk that your algorithm will lead to such situations, you probably want to create a mapping back to reality; for instance, truncate or set limits. Another gotcha is an impossible change, such as the number of all-time web site visitors suddenly dropping. The iTunes example discussed later in this chapter provides one mitigation technique: always underestimate, which will ensure that the value goes up upon correction. With Guesstimate, you also have the risk that you won't get figures back from the server, leading to even greater deviation from reality than expected. At some point, you'll probably need to give up and be explicit about the problem.

Decisions

How often will real data be fetched? How often will Guesstimates be made?

Most Guesstimates are made between fetches of real data. The point of the Guesstimate is to reduce the frequency of real data, so you need to decide on a realistic frequency. If precision is valuable, real data will need to be accessed quite frequently. If server and bandwidth resources are restricted, there will be fewer accesses and a greater value placed on the Guesstimate algorithm.

Also, how often will a new Guesstimate be calculated? Guesstimates tend to be fairly mathematical in nature, and too many of them will impact on application performance. On the other hand, too few Guesstimates will defeat the purpose.

How will the Guesstimate be consolidated with real data?

Each time new data arrives, the Guesstimate somehow needs to be brought into line with the new data. In the simplest case, the Guesstimate is just discarded, and the fresh data is adopted until a new Guesstimate is required.

Sometimes, a more subtle transition is warranted. Imagine a Guesstimate that occurs once every second, with real data arriving on the minute. The 59-second estimate might be well off the estimate by 1 minute. If a smooth transition is important, and you want to avoid a sudden jump to the real value, then you can estimate the real value at two minutes, and spend the next minute making Guesstimates in that direction.

The iTunes demo in the "Real-World Examples" section, later in this chapter, includes another little trick. The algorithm concedes a jump will indeed occur, but the Guesstimate is deliberately underestimated. Thus, when the real value arrives, the jump is almost guaranteed to be upward as the user would expect. Here, there is a deliberate effort to make the Guesstimate less accurate than it could be, with the payoff being more realistic consolidation with real data.

Will users be aware a Guesstimate is taking place?

It's conceivable that users will notice some strange things happening with a Guesstimate. Perhaps they know what the real value should be, but the server shows something completely different. Or perhaps they notice a sudden jump as the application switches from a Guesstimate to a fresh value from the server. These experiences can erode trust in the application, especially as users may be missing the point that the Guesstimate is for improved usability. Trust is critical for public web sites, where many alternatives are often present, and it would be especially unfortunate to lose trust due to a feature that's primarily motivated by user experience concerns.

For entertainment-style demos, Guesstimates are unlikely to cause much problem. But what about using a Guesstimate to populate a financial chart over time? The more important the data being estimated, and the less accurate the estimate, the more users need to be aware of what the system is doing. At the very least, consider a basic message or legal notice to that effect.

What support will the server provide?

In some cases, the server exposes information that the browser can use to make a Guesstimate. For example, historical information will allow the browser to extrapolate to the present. You need to consider what calculations are realistic for the browser to perform and ensure it will have access to the appropriate data. A *Web Service* exposing generic history details is not the only possibility. In some cases, it might be preferable for the server to provide a service related to the algorithm itself. In the Apple iTunes example shown later in the "Real-World Examples" section, recent real-world values are provided by the server, and the browser must analyze them to determine the rate per second. However, an alternative design would be for the server to calculate the rate per second, reducing the work performed by each browser.

Real-World Examples

Apple iTunes counter

As its iTunes Music Store neared its 500 millionth song download, Apple decorated its homepage (*http://apple.com*) with a rapid counter that appeared to show the number of downloads in real-time (Figure 13-6). The display made for an impressive testimony to iTunes' popularity and received plenty of attention. It only connected with the server once a minute, but courtesy of a Guesstimate algorithm described later in "Code Example: iTunes Counter," the display smoothly updated every 100 milliseconds.

Gmail Storage Space

The Gmail homepage (*http://gmail.com*) (Figure 13-7) shows a message like this to unregistered users:

> 2446.034075 megabytes (and counting) of free storage so you'll never need to delete another message.

But there's a twist: the storage capacity figure increases each second. Having just typed a couple of sentences, it's up to 2446.039313 megabytes. Gmail is providing a not-so-subtle message about its hosting credentials.

The Apple iTunes counter updates frequently, using a Guesstimate

FIGURE 13-6. iTunes counter

A Google approach to email.

Gmail is an experiment in a new kind of webmail, built on the idea that you should never have to delete mail and you should always be able to find the message you want. The key features are:

- **Search, don't sort.**
  Use Google search to **find the exact message** you want, no matter when it was sent or received.

- **Don't throw anything away.**
  Over 2678.980219 megabytes (and counting) of free storage so you'll never need to delete another message.

Gmail continuously updates the storage capacity, using Guesstimate

FIGURE 13-7. Gmail storage

Andrew Parker has provided some analysis of the homepage (*http://www.avparker.com/2005/07/10/itunes-gmail-dynamic-counters/*). The page is initially loaded with the storage capacity for the first day of the previous month and the current month (also the next month, though that's apparently not used). When the analysis occurred, 100 MB was added per month. Once you know that, you can calculate how many megabytes per second. So the algorithm determines how many seconds have passed since the current month began, and it can then infer how many megabytes have been added in that time. Add that to the amount at the start of the month, and you have the current storage capacity each second.

Code Example: iTunes Counter

The iTunes counter* relies on a server-based service that updates every five minutes. On each update, the service shows the current song tally and the tally five minutes prior. Knowing how many songs were sold in a five-minute period allows for a songs-per-second figure to be calculated. So the script knows the recent figure and, since it knows how many seconds have passed since then, it also has an estimate of how many songs were sold. The counter then shows the recent figure plus the estimate of songs sold since then.

There are two actions performed periodically:

- Once a minute, doCountdown( ) calls the server to get new song stats.

- Once every 100 milliseconds, runCountdown( ) uses a rate estimation to morph the counter display.

The key global variables are rate and curCount:

- rate is the number of songs purchased per millisecond, according to the stats in the XML that's downloaded each minute.

- curCount is the counter value.

So each time the server response comes in, rate is updated to reflect the most recent songs-per-millisecond figure. curCount is continuously incremented according to that figure, with the output shown on the page.

The stats change on the server every five minutes, though doCountdown( ) pulls down the recent stats once a minute to catch any changes a bit sooner:

```
//get most recent values from xml and process
ajaxRequest('http://www.apple.com/itunes/external_counter.xml',
            initializeProcessReqChange);
//on one minute loop
var refreshTimer = setTimeout(doCountdown,refresh);
```

It fetches is the counter XML:

```
<root>
  <count name="curCount" timestamp="Thu, 07 Jul 2005 14:16:00 GMT">
    484406324
  </count>
  <count name="preCount" timestamp="Thu, 07 Jul 2005 14:11:00 GMT">
    484402490
  </count>
</root>
```

setCounters( ) is the function that performs the *Guesstimate* calculation based on this information. It extracts the required parameters from XML into ordinary variables—for example:

---

* An expanded analysis of the iTunes counter can be found on my blog at *http://www.softwareas.com/ ajaxian-guesstimate-on-download-counter*. Some of the comments and spacing has been changed for this analysis.

```
preCount = parseInt(req.responseXML.getElementsByTagName
            ('count')[1].childNodes[0].nodeValue);
```

When a change is detected, it recalculates the current rate as *(number of new songs) / (time elapsed)*. Note that no assumption is made about the five-minute duration; hence, the time elapsed (dataDiff) is always deduced from the XML.

```
//calculate difference in values
countDiff = initCount-preCount;
//calculate difference in time of values
dateDiff = parseInt(initDate.valueOf()-preDate.valueOf());
//calculate rate of increase
// i.e. ((songs downloaded in previous time)/time)*incr
rate = countDiff/dateDiff;
```

This is the most accurate rate estimate possible, but next, the script reduces it by 20 percent. Why would the developers want to deliberately underestimate the rate? Presumably because they have accepted that the rate will always be off, with each browser-server sync causing the counter to adjust itself in one direction or another, and they want to ensure that direction is always upwards. Making the estimate lower than expected just about guarantees the counter will increase—rather than decrease—on every synchronization point. True, there will still be a jump, and it will actually be bigger on average because of the adjustment, but it's better than having the counter occasionally drop in value, which would break the illusion.

```
rate = rate*0.8;
```

As well as the once-a-minute server call, there's the once-every-100-milliseconds counter repaint. runCountdown( ) handles this. With the rate variable re-Guesstimated once a minute, it's easy enough to determine the counter value each second. incr is the pause between redisplays (in this case, 100 ms). So every 100 ms, it will simply calculate the new Guesstimated song quantity by adding the expected increment in that time. Note that the Gmail counter example just discussed calculates the total figure each time, whereas the present algorithm gradually increments it. The present algorithm is therefore a little more efficient, although more vulnerable to rounding errors.

```
//multiply rate by increment
addCount = rate*incr;
//add this number to counter
curCount += addCount;
```

And finally, the counter display is morphed to show the new Guesstimate. The show was all over when the tally reached 500 million songs, so the counter will never show more than 500 million.

```
c.innerHTML = (curCount<500000000) ?
            intComma(Math.floor(curCount)) : "500,000,000+";
```

Related Patterns

Periodic Refresh

A Guesstimate can often be used to compensate for gaps between *Periodic Refresh* (Chapter 10).

Predictive Fetch

Predictive Fetch (see earlier) is another performance optimization based on probabilistic assumptions. Predictive Fetch guesses what the user will do next, whereas Guesstimate involves guessing the current server state. In general, Guesstimate decreases the number of server calls, whereas Predictive Fetch actually increases the number of calls.

Fat Client

Guesstimates require some business and application logic to be calculated in the browser, a characteristic of *Fat Client*s (see later).

Metaphor

If you know what time it was when you started reading this pattern, you can Guesstimate the current time by adding an estimate of your reading duration.

Multi-Stage Download

Download, Incremental, Multi-Stage, Parallel

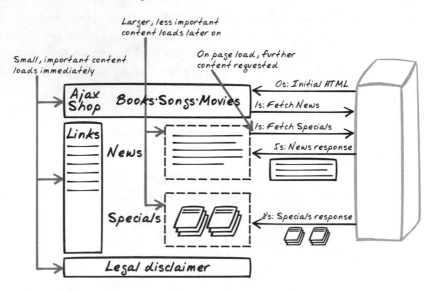

FIGURE 13-8. Multi-Stage Download

Developer Story

Dave's been informed an e-commerce homepage is turning many users away with its absurdly slow initial download. He refactors it so the initial download is nothing more than a banner and the key navigation links. News and featured items are still on the page, but they're pulled down separately, after the initial page has loaded.

Problem

How can you optimize downloading performance?

Forces

- Content can be time-consuming to load, especially when it contains rich images.

- Users rarely need to read all the content on the page.

- Users often have to click through several times to locate a particular item.

- Users sometimes browse around by exploring links between pages.

Solution

Break content download into multiple stages, so that faster and more important content will arrive first. Typically, the page is divided into placeholders (e.g., div elements) with the content for each placeholder downloaded independently. *XMLHttpRequest Calls* can be issued simultaneously or in a serial sequence, and the page will gradually be populated as the calls return.

The pattern applies when an application needs to download a lot of content from the server. Typically, this occurs on startup and also when a major context switch occurs. By breaking up the call, you can deliver faster and more important data earlier on. You avoid bottlenecks that occur when a single piece of content blocks everything else from returning.

The initial download of a page might be very small, containing just a skeleton along with navigation links and enough context to help the user decide if it's worth sticking around. That's the critical content for a fresh visitor, and there's no need to make him wait for the rest of the page to load. The browser can request the main page content as a separate call.

This pattern is in some respects an Ajaxian upgrade of the old technique of filling up a page gradually, where the server continues flushing the buffer and the user can see the page as it loads. Ajax makes the whole thing more powerful, because the latter downloads can attach to any existing part of the page.

One resource risk is having too many requests at once. Thus, consider a (purely speculative) Multiplex Call variant. Establish a browser/server protocol that lets the browser wrap multiple requests and the server wrap multiple responses. Then, issue only a single call with all required data inside. The immediate response might return a few results only, so the browser waits a bit, and then makes a further request for outstanding data. The whole process repeats until the browser has all the data.

Decisions

How will the page be divided into blocks?

The trickiest decision is how to divide the page into blocks, each of which will be downloaded individually. Since the blocks are downloaded in parallel, the main advice is to create small blocks of initial content to ensure the initial download is quick, and to group together content that's likely to be ready at the same time. Also, too many blocks will give the initial load an ugly appearance and may have the undesirable effect of causing already displayed elements to move around. For a fresh visitor, one example would be to create blocks as follows:

- A block of general information about the web site; e.g., name, summary, and a small icon.

- A navigation block showing links within the site.

- A block of general information about the current page, such as a heading and summary text. In a web app, this may be dynamic information based on what processing is being performed.

- One or more blocks of main page content.

- One or more blocks of auxiliary information; e.g., cross-site promotions, advertising, and legal notices.

Some of these may be combined too, as it's important to avoid too many blocks. So you might have a single request to retrieve both navigation and general information, which is then split and painted onto separate blocks.

Note that this doesn't have to apply to a homepage—if you are offering *Unique URLs*, visitors can jump into an Ajax App at different points, so the main page content might actually be quite "deep" into the application.

How will the page be structured?

Ideally, this pattern should not affect the page appearance, but will require some thinking about the underlying HTML. In particular:

- As new information loads, it's possible the browser application will automatically rearrange the page in order to accommodate new information. This can lead to the user clicking on the wrong thing, or typing into the wrong area, as items suddenly jump around the page. Ideally, information will not move around once it has been presented to the page. At least for images, it's worthwhile defining the width and height in advance, as CSS properties.

- CSS-based layout is likely to play a big part in any solution, as it provides the ability to exercise control over layout without knowing exact details.

What happens to the blocks while their content is being downloaded?

The entire DOM itself can be established on the initial load, so that divs and other structures are used as placeholders for incoming content. If that's the case, most of those elements can be left alone, but if the user is waiting for something specific that may take some time, it would be worth placing a *Progress Indicator* on the block where the output will eventually appear.

It's also possible to construct the DOM dynamically, so that new elements are added as new content arrives. This approach may be more work, but it may help to decouple the browser and the server. With the right framework in place, it means that the browser does not have to know exactly which items will be downloaded. The browser might ask the server to send all adverts, and the sender simply responds by sending down an XML file with three separate entries, which the browser then renders by adding three new divs.

Will the calls be issued simultaneously?

Let's say you're at a point where you suddenly need a whole lot of content. Should you issue several requests at once? Not necessarily. Keep in mind there are limits on how many outgoing requests the browser can handle at one time and consider what's best for the user. If there's a bunch of content that might not be used, consider deferring it for a bit with a JavaScript setTimeout call. That way, you can help ensure the user's bandwidth is dedicated to pulling down the important stuff first.

Real-World Examples

Kayak

Kayak (*http://kayak.com*) is a travel search engine. You tell it where you're going, and it then searches through many online travel sites to build up a set of options for you.

While waiting for a search query, the results page initially shows just the site banner, the search you entered, and a *Progress Indicator* (Figure 13-9). As the results for each external site arrives, Kayak adds the site name and whatever flights it found there. The flights aren't just appended, but kept in sorted order. You also have the option to finish the search by clicking an Enough Results button.

NetVibes

NetVibes (*http://netvibes.com*) is an Ajax portal that launches parallel *XMLHttpRequest Calls* on startup, one for each *Portlet*. Many portals follow this pattern.

TalkDigger

TalkDigger (*http://talkdigger.com*) is an Ajaxian meta-search for web feeds. Traditional meta-searches usually output results to the browser as they're received from individual engines, so the results page isn't well-ordered. With TalkDigger, each individual search engine gets its own div on the page. As the results come in, they're placed on the right spot.

FIGURE 13-9. Kayak Progress Indicator

Code Example: AjaxPatterns Portal

The code example is a portal demo (*http://ajaxify.com/run/portal*) that downloads content in various stages (Figure 13-10):

1. The page banner and key links are downloaded immediately, as part of the initial HTML.

2. On page load, a place is set aside for side links, which are then requested and injected into the placeholder.

3. Likewise, the main content is also requested on page load.

4. Finally, an ad is requested after a short delay. This ensures the main content arrives first, so the ad doesn't affect the overall flow. (If you're feeling entrepreneurial, you can refactor it to reverse the order.)

The initial HTML contains the header and placeholders for the content that will be injected. There's an initial Loading message for each of these:

```
<h1>ajax patterns Portal demo</h1>

<a href="http://ajaxpatterns.org">Ajax Patterns Wiki</a> |
<a href="http://ajaxify.com">Ajax Demos</a> |
<a href="http://ajaxpatterns.org/Ajax_Examples">Ajax Examples</a>

<div class="spacer"> </div>

<div id="leftLinks">
  <div id="siteLinks">Loading ...</div>
  <div class="spacer"> </div>
  <div id="ad">Loading ...</div>
</div>
<div id="allPatterns">Loading ...</div>
```

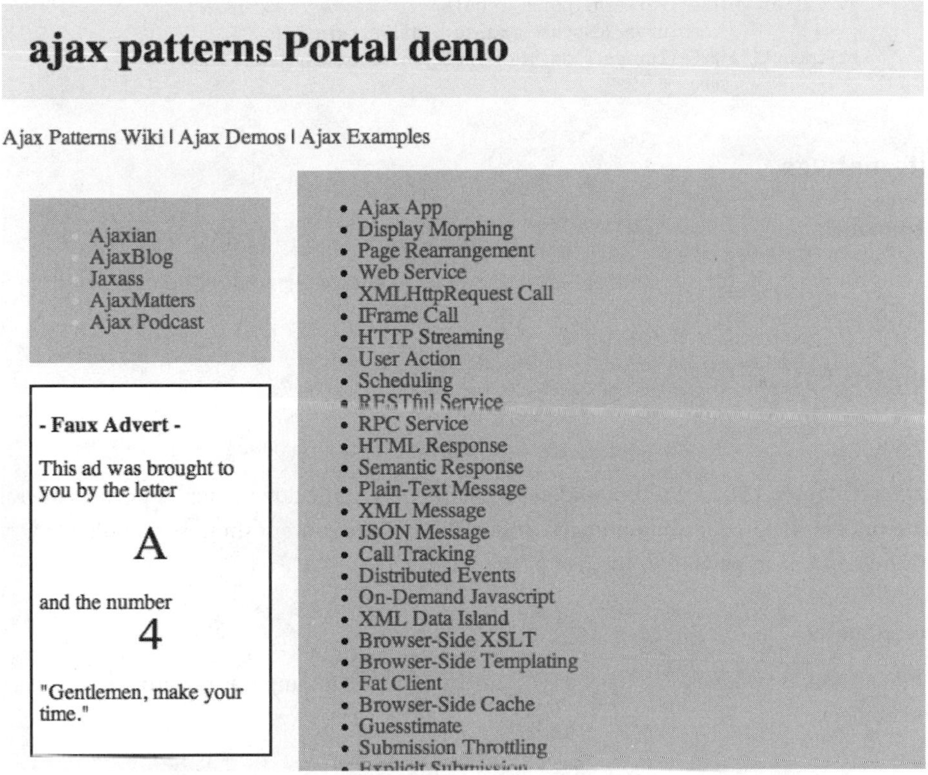

ajax patterns Portal demo

Ajax Patterns Wiki I Ajax Demos I Ajax Examples

Ajaxian
AjaxBlog
Jaxass
AjaxMatters
Ajax Podcast

- Faux Advert -

This ad was brought to
you by the letter

A

and the number

4

"Gentlemen, make your
time."

- Ajax App
- Display Morphing
- Page Rearrangement
- Web Service
- XMLHttpRequest Call
- IFrame Call
- HTTP Streaming
- User Action
- Scheduling
- RESTful Service
- RPC Service
- HTML Response
- Semantic Response
- Plain-Text Message
- XML Message
- JSON Message
- Call Tracking
- Distributed Events
- On-Demand Javascript
- XML Data Island
- Browser-Side XSLT
- Browser-Side Templating
- Fat Client
- Browser-Side Cache
- Guesstimate
- Submission Throttling
- Explicit Submission

FIGURE 13-10. Multi-Stage Download Portal demo

The side links and main content are loaded immediately on page load, and sent to a callback function that morphs the corresponding div:

```
window.onload = function( ) {
  ajaxCaller.get("sideLinks.html", null,
                 onServerResponse, false, "siteLinks");
  ajaxCaller.get("allPatterns.phtml", null,
                 onServerResponse, false, "allPatterns");
  ...
}

function onServerResponse(html, headers, elementId) {
  $(elementId).innerHTML = html;
}
```

A few seconds later—probably after all the content has been loaded—the ad content is
requested:

```
window.onload = function( ) {
  ajaxCaller.get("sideLinks.html", null,
                 onServerResponse, false, "siteLinks");
```

```
ajaxCaller.get("allPatterns.phtml", null,
               onServerResponse, false, "allPatterns");
setTimeout("ajaxCaller.get('ad.html',null,onServerResponse,false,'ad')",
           5000
}
```

Alternatives

All-In-One

As was mentioned, the alternative—and the de facto choice—is to download everything in one go.

Related Patterns

Portlet

Portlets (Chapter 15) are good candidates for content-specific downloads. A portal's overall structure can be downloaded initially, and each Portlet's content then be downloaded (and refreshed) in parallel to the rest of the page.

Guesstimate

While a block is waiting to be loaded, you might populate it temporarily with a *Guesstimate* (see earlier).

Progress Indicator

While a block is waiting to be loaded, you might populate it temporarily with a *Progress Indicator* (Chapter 14).

On-Demand JavaScript

Like Multi-Stage Download, *On-Demand JavaScript* (Chapter 6) involves an initial download followed by further downloads later on. That pattern focuses specifically on JavaScript content rather than display and semantic content. It's also about downloading only when needed. The emphasis here is on downloading according to an initial schedule. Other patterns, such as *Microlink* and *Live Search*, cover on-demand downloading of display and semantic content.

Metaphor

Multi-Stage Download mirrors agile project management. If you can deliver some really useful things early on, why hold off until everything else is ready?

Fat Client

BrowserSide, Decoupled, DHTML, Fast, Responsive, Rich, Thick

A faster feedback loop...

...because more work is done in the browser...

...and less work on the server

FIGURE 13-11. Fat Client

Developer Story

Dave's new mortgage application is very quick as it avoids server calls wherever possible. After some benchmarking, he discovered that optimized JavaScript is actually fast enough to run the financial algorithms in the browser, so that users now receive almost immediate feedback as they tweak parameters.

Problem

How can you architect the system to feel truly rich and interactive?

Forces

- The application should respond to user actions quickly—ideally, instantaneously.

- Responses from the server can be noticeably latent due to data transfer and server processing overheads.

Solution

Create a responsive Ajax App by performing remote calls only when there is no way to achieve the same effect in the browser. Whereas the server is traditionally the realm of more complex processing, this pattern suggests harnessing the browser for all it's worth. In the extreme case, it means running just about everything inside the browser, but that's not the main message here. The main message is to reconsider the traditional server-centric view of web architecture; for developers to be more conscious about decisions on matters regarding where the various components live. Placing more logic inside the browser gives you the opportunity to make the application more responsive.

Web apps usually have several layers:

- User interface
- Application logic
- Business logic
- Data access
- External system communication

The user interface is what the user sees and interacts with. The application logic concerns the dialogue between the user and the computer, the flow of information back and forth—for example, given a particular user action, what should the computer do next? The business logic concerns knowledge about the domain and the web site owner's practices and policies. The data access layer concerns reading and writing data to a persistent store. External system communication is also necessary in many enterprise systems, where outside systems play the role of information sources and sinks.

Conventional web apps concentrate UI code in the browser, using a mix of HTML and CSS, with some JavaScript used to perform a few basic UI tricks like placing keyboard focus or showing some animation or offering a dynamic menu. Everything else is usually managed on the server. This pattern reconsiders the balance by suggesting that some applications are better served pushing application and business logic into the browser (Figure 13-12).

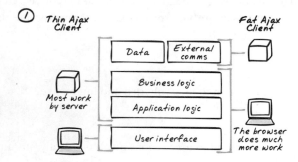

FIGURE 13-12. Responsibilities of a Fat Client

With application logic in the browser, an inversion of control occurs in which the browser now controls the flow of activity. When the user performs some action, it is the browser that decides how to respond, and it calls the server only if necessary, and for very specific services.

The advice to hold business logic in the browser is anathema to most literature on serious web site development and should not be taken lightly. Business logic in the browser has numerous problems:

- Programming in JavaScript can be difficult because many features familiar to mainstream developers are unavailable. The standard API is minimal and object-oriented facilities are based on prototypes rather than classes. Indeed, the usage of dynamic typing is also uncomfortable for many developers in the Java and C# camps.

- Portability is a further complication due to the number of platforms that must be supported, and their subtly inconsistent behaviors.

- Development is also a challenge. Coding, refactoring, debugging, automated testing, and monitoring, are standard in modern IDEs like IntelliJ Idea, but support at this level is minimal for JavaScript.

- Security is another constraint that forces logic server side. Savvy users can peruse code and data in the browser and can even tamper with what's sent back to the server. Obfuscation—making the code difficult to read—is a very weak defense.

- Business and application logic should be held on the server, where they can be reused by other clients.

- Web data generally can't be saved on the local machine.

Are any of these showstoppers? Let's look at how we can cope with each of these problems:

- JavaScript may be different from server-side languages, but many programmers are discovering it's a lot more powerful than previously assumed (*http://www.crockford.com/javascript/javascript.html*). Until recently, the main resources on JavaScript were "cut-and-paste this code" web sites, but there are an increasing number of books and resources that take the language seriously. The language has undergone a renaissance in parallel with Ajax. New idioms and patterns are emerging, along with a pile of cross-browser frameworks to augment the relatively bare native API. The recent introduction of JSAN (*http://openjsan.org*)—a repository of JavaScript libraries like Perl's CPAN—will only further reuse. Object-oriented concepts, including inheritance and aggregation, are indeed possible, if not in a manner familiar to all server-side developers. Dynamic versus static typing is a matter of taste that shouldn't affect a language's credibility; the dynamic approach of JavaScript may not be everyone's preference, but JavaScript is hardly an outsider here.

- Browsers are more standard nowadays, and many of the new libraries abstract away browser dependencies (see *Cross-Browser Component* [Chapter 12]). For example, over a dozen libraries offer a browser-independent factory method to retrieve XMLHttpRequest.

- Recent tools are making life a lot easier; some are discussed in Development Patterns (Part V).

- Security remains an issue, but it's possible to deploy the application so that security-critical functionality can be exposed server side in well-defined services, with the bulk of the application logic held locally and calling on those services as required. There might be duplication because browser-side validation is also important for quick feedback, using JavaScript to create a screening test before passing a request to the server.

However, there are ways to deal with such duplication if it's a serious issue. For instance, with server-side JavaScript, you can have the same script running in the browser and the server, or you can use some custom, declarative notation to capture business rules and have processors for it on both sides.

- It's true that certain business logic needs to be made available to multiple clients and therefore needs to exposed as *Web Services*, in which case there's a good argument for keeping it inside the server. (It could also be executed in the server as well as the browser, though that's a fairly unusual practice.) Often, though, business logic is application-specific, and that's even more the case for application logic (notwithstanding grandiose plans for running the same app on mobile phones and desktops).

- Browsers cannot normally persist data locally, but a background thread can be used to periodically synchronize with the server. In the 1990s, many desktop applications forced users to explicitly save their work, whereas today, many desktop applications now save periodically and upon the user quitting. In the same way, it's now feasible for web apps to persist data transparently, without affecting workflow. If local persistence is critical enough to break away from "pure Ajax," some easily deployed Flash libraries are available (e.g., Brad Neuberg's AMASS; see *http://codinginparadise.org/projects/storage/README.html*).

None of this says that programming in JavaScript is more productive than programming in Java or C# or Ruby. In most cases, it isn't and never will be. Serious JavaScript programming is nonetheless a very real proposition. Professional software development involves choosing the language that fits the task at hand. Given the many benefits of browser-side coding, there are at least some circumstances that make JavaScript the language of choice for implementation of business and application logic.

Decisions

How will business and application logic be implemented in the browser?

Conventional applications use JavaScript for a little decoration. Even when a lot of JavaScript is used, it's often packed into tightly scoped library routines, to perform little tricks like validating a form's fields match regular expressions or popping up a calendar. These are just little detours on the well-travelled road between browser and server. In contrast, a Fat Client responds to many events itself, delegating to the server only if and when it deems necessary.

All this implies a very different usage of JavaScript, and there are some techniques that can help. It's beyond the scope of this chapter to cover them in detail, but here are a few pointers:

- It's easy to fall into the trap of "paving the cow paths"* by applying design styles from other languages to JavaScript. It's usually more productive to embrace JavaScript as a unique language with its own idiosyncratic features and usage patterns, and to be wary of applying architectural concepts from your favorite server-side language if they don't seem to fit in.

- JavaScript uses a prototype-based paradigm, which is worth learning about. Object-oriented concepts like inheritance are certainly possible, but it's important to appreciate how they fit in to the prototype model.

- Development and deployment practices apply as much to a rich browser application, and are as important as testing the server code, as discussed in Development Patterns (Part V).

- JavaScript runs slower than equivalent desktop applications, so optimization is important. Also, consider issues memory usage and be aware of browser-specific bugs that might lead to memory leaks.

- Break complex applications into multiple JavaScript files and consider managing them with *On-Demand JavaScript*.

- Reuse, Reuse, Reuse. As Appendix A shows, there's a proliferation of JavaScript frameworks and libraries becoming available.

Real-World Examples

NumSum

NumSum (*http://numsum.com*) is an Ajax spreadsheet that provides all the basic spreadsheet functionality in JavaScript: insertion and deletion of rows and columns; various formulas; the ability of a user to enter values into any cell; text-formatting (bold, italic, or underlining); text-justification; and embedded links and images.

The basic spreadsheet is implemented as a `table`. Table cells aren't actually editable, so the script needs to simulate an editable table. An event handler ensures that a cell becomes active when the user clicks on it, and that cell is then morphed to reflect subsequent user input.

Gmail

Gmail (*http://gmail.com*), like several of its competitors, presents a rich, Ajax interface to a mail system. Conventional web mail offerings rely heavily on form submissions and page reloads—a new page must be opened each time the user wants to start composing an email, finish composing an email, or open up an email message. With Gmail, the list of emails is always present and regularly refreshed. Partial edits are periodically saved as well. All of these activities are handled within the browser using a combination of Display Manipulation (Chapter 5) and Web Remoting (Chapter 6).

---

* "Paving the cow paths" refers to the way cows mindlessly follow an old path, continuing to walk around trees that aren't actually there anymore.

DHTML Lemmings

DHTML Lemmings (*http://www.oldgames.dk/freeflashgames/arcadegames/playlemmings.php*) shows how much can be achieved with some clever JavaScript hacking (Figure 13-13). It's a full-featured implementation of the Lemmings PC game utilizing a *Richer Plugin* only for sound—the entire game runs on DHTML, DOM, and CSS. The gameplay consists of a static image for the current level, with *Sprites* used to render the lemmings and other objects in the game. There is a periodic timer continuously checking the current state of each object, and DOM manipulation of the objects' properties is used to render their states at any time.

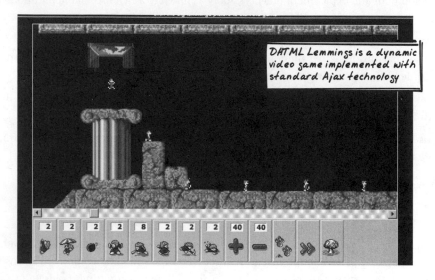

FIGURE 13-13. DHTML Lemmings

JS/UIX shell

JS/UIX shell (*http://www.masswerk.at/jsuix/*) is a demo of an in-browser Unix shell (Figure 13-14). In its current form, it's a demo only. But it's capable of all the basic operating systems commands and even includes a vi editor! The approach stands in contrast to browser-side terminal emulators, which are thin applications that pass characters back and forth. With appropriate server-side integration, the application could be made into a functional multiuser application. Command line remains the mode of choice for many power users, and this demo shows how an Ajax Fat Client can achieve it.

Code Example: AjaxPatterns Basic Wiki

The Wiki Demo (*http://ajaxify.com/run/wiki*) is based on Fat Client principles, though its functionality is fairly limited. All of the interaction and rendering occurs locally. The only interaction with the server is a periodic synchronization event, when the following occurs:

- Pending messages are uploaded, an example of *Submission Throttling* (Chapter 10).

- All current messages are retrieved from the server, so that messages from other users are shown. This is an example of *Periodic Refresh* (Chapter 10).

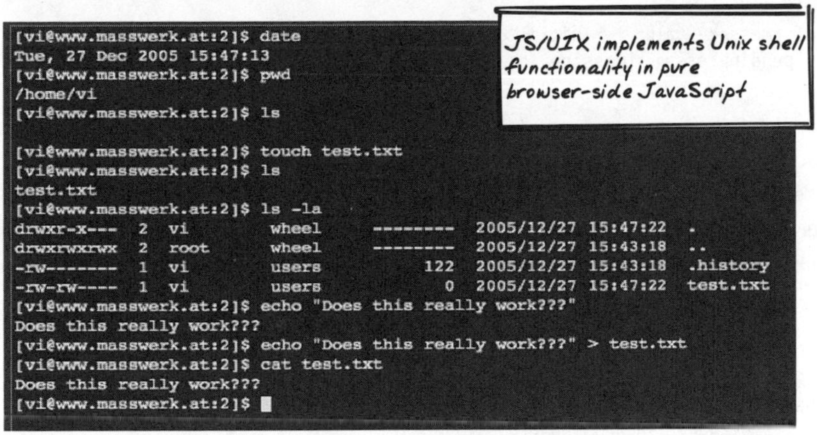

```
[vi@www.masswerk.at:2]$ date
Tue, 27 Dec 2005 15:47:13
[vi@www.masswerk.at:2]$ pwd
/home/vi
[vi@www.masswerk.at:2]$ ls

[vi@www.masswerk.at:2]$ touch test.txt
[vi@www.masswerk.at:2]$ ls
test.txt
[vi@www.masswerk.at:2]$ ls -la
drwxr-x---  2  vi      wheel    --------     2005/12/27 15:47:22  .
drwxrwxrwx  2  root    wheel    --------     2005/12/27 15:43:18  ..
-rw-------  1  vi      users        122      2005/12/27 15:43:18  .history
-rw-rw----  1  vi      users          0      2005/12/27 15:47:22  test.txt
[vi@www.masswerk.at:2]$ echo "Does this really work???"
Does this really work???
[vi@www.masswerk.at:2]$ echo "Does this really work???" > test.txt
[vi@www.masswerk.at:2]$ cat test.txt
Does this really work???
[vi@www.masswerk.at:2]$ █
```

JS/UIX implements Unix shell functionality in pure browser-side JavaScript

FIGURE 13-14. JS/UIX shell

There's a timer to ensure synchronization occurs after five seconds of inactivity:

```
var syncTimer = null;

function startPeriodicSync() {
  stopPeriodicSync();
  syncTimer = setInterval(synchronise, 5000);
}

function stopPeriodicSync() {
  clearInterval(syncTimer);
}
```

The timer starts on page load and is suspended each time the user begins to modify some text:

```
window.onload = function() {
  synchronise();
  startPeriodicSync();
}

function onMessageFocus(event) {
  ...
  stopPeriodicSync();
}

function onMessageBlur(event) {
  ...
  startPeriodicSync();
}
```

The script also contains a variable to accumulate pending messages whenever the user changes something:

```
var pendingMessages = new Array();
...
function onMessageBlur(event) {
```

```
...
if (message.value != initialMessageContent) {
  pendingMessages[message.id] = true;
...
}
```

The synchronization event builds up some XML to post to the server, based on the pendingMessages array that has been accumulated. If no changes are pending, it simply requests the current server state. If there are changes pending, it posts those changes as an XML message. Either way, the server will respond with an XML specification of its current state.

```
function synchronise( ) {

  var messageTags = "";
  for (messageId in pendingMessages) {
    var initialServerMessage = $(messageId).serverMessage;
    messageTags += "<message>";
    messageTags += "<id>" + messageId + "</id>";
    messageTags += "<lastAuthor>" + $("authorIdSpec").value + "</lastAuthor>";
    messageTags += "<ranking>" + initialServerMessage.ranking + "</ranking>";
    messageTags += "<content>" + escape($(messageId).value) + "</content>";
    messageTags += "</message>";

    $(messageId).style.backgroundColor = "#cccccc";
  }

  var changesOccurred = (messageTags!="");
  if (!changesOccurred) {
    ajaxCaller.getXML("content.php?messages", onMessagesLoaded);
    return;
  }

  var changeSpec = "<messages>" + messageTags + "</messages>";
  ajaxCaller.postBody
    ("content.php", null, onMessagesLoaded, true, null, "text/xml", changeSpec);
  pendingMessages = new Array( );
}
```

The main application logic is virtually orthogonal to server synchronization. The only concession is the accumulation of pending messages, to save uploading the entire browser state each time. The timer and the synchronization process know about the core wiki logic, but the core wiki knows nothing about them and can therefore be developed independently. It's easy to imagine how the wiki could evolve into something with much richer browser-side features, like formatted text and draggable messages and so on.

Alternatives

Thin client

A thin client contains only basic JavaScript and frequently refers back to the server for user interaction. This is likely to remain the dominant style for Ajax Apps and is useful in the following circumstances:

- It's important to support legacy browsers. Graceful degradation is still possible with Fat Clients, but requires more work, and there's the potential for a lot of redundancy.

- Business logic requires sophisticated programming techniques and libraries that can only be implemented server side.

- Business logic involves substantial number crunching or other processing that can only be performed server side.

- Due to bandwidth and memory constraints, the application cannot be held locally.

- There is complex dialogue required with external services, and due to cross-domain security policies, those services cannot be accessed from the browser.

Desktop client

A desktop client runs as a standard application in the user's operating system, and connects to one or more servers using HTTP or any other protocol. Compared to a Fat Client, a desktop client can be richer and faster. However, the benefits of a web-enabled application are lost as a result. You can compensate for some of these benefits:

- Portability can be achieved with a platform-neutral programming platform.

- Centralized data can be achieved by ensuring all data is retained server side.

- Familiar user interfaces can be achieved by tailoring to each individual platform's look-and-feel.

In some contexts, a desktop client represents the best of both worlds: a rich client backed by a powerful server. In other situations, a Fat Client based on Ajax principles is a more appropriate sweet spot: a powerful server, a rich-enough client, and easy access through any modern web browser.

Related Patterns

Periodic Refresh

Periodic Refresh (Chapter 10) is a relatively unobtrusive way for the client state to be enriched with any new server-side information.

Submission Throttling

Submission Throttling (Chapter 10) is a relatively unobtrusive way for the server to be notified of any significant changes that have occurred in the browser.

Widgets

If the user is going to spend a long time in the browser, the various widgets (Chapter 14) should be adopted to improve the experience.

On-Demand JavaScript

Since Fat Clients tend to contain bulkier scripts, *On-Demand JavaScript* (Chapter 6) is useful for managing them.

Drag-And-Drop

Drag-And-Drop (Chapter 15) is familiar to many desktop users and helps to make a large application feel more natural. Whereas more conventional web clients rely on form-style interaction, Fat Clients can feel more rich if they support Drag-And-Drop.

Host-Proof Hosting

Where a Fat Client is seen as a replacement for a desktop equivalent, *Host-Proof Hosting* (Chapter 17) might be considered to avoid compromising on the superior security a localized solution sometimes offers.

Metaphor

Agile development methodologies such as Scrum aim for an "inversion-of-control." Workers (like the Fat Client) are empowered to plan their own activities, and management's role (the Server) is to offer whatever services workers request in order to conduct those activities.

Want to Know More?

- Google Groups Discussion: "Applications in the Browser or the Server?" (*http://groups-beta.google.com/group/ajax-web-technology/browse_thread/thread/e40317a830ad841d/06483bf77587a62c#06483bf77587a62c*)

- "JavaScript: The World's Most Misunderstood Programming Language" by Douglas Crockford (*http://www.crockford.com/javascript/javascript.html*)

- "JavaScript is not the devil's plaything" by Cameron Adams (*http://www.themaninblue.com/writing/perspective/2005/04/12/*)

PART FOUR

Functionality and Usability Patterns

AJAX IS FUNDAMENTALLY ABOUT DELIVERING VALUE TO USERS AND THEIR ORGANIZATIONS. **T**HE PREVIOUS parts have mostly covered technical issues that support developers, and now it's time to consider the user experience: how Ajax user interfaces will look, and what users will be able to do with them.

Many of the patterns combine display manipulation with the web remoting capability of Ajax. Others, such as *Slider* and *Rich Text Editor*, can be used in the absence of remoting, and still make an important contribution to the richness of Ajax interfaces. Most of the patterns here have been seen before in a desktop context and even on the Web in Flash or Java form; the point of documenting them here is to explore what works with standard browser technology and explain how these ideas can be implemented the Ajax way.

The first three chapters are all about user interface. Widgets (Chapter 14) introduces a number of widgets that are being woven into many Ajax interfaces. A higher-level perspective is taken by Page Architecture (Chapter 15), where the focus is on page layout, content breakdown, and techniques for exposing server-side content. With the popularity of Ajax, the Web is undergoing a rise in visual effects somewhat unprecedented on conventional desktop systems; the most common effects are described in Visual Effects (Chapter 16).

The stack of Ajax technologies opens up several possibilities that haven't been fully explored in a web context. The patterns in Functionality (Chapter 17) are a little more speculative than those in other sections, but more and more real-world usages for them are emerging. They are worth looking at as they might let you build things in a way you hadn't considered before.

CHAPTER FOURTEEN

Widgets

THE WIDGETS PROVIDED BY STANDARD **HTML**—TEXT INPUTS, RADIOBUTTONS, AND SO ON—HAVEN'T changed much for ten years and are getting a little tired. So many people have been building their own widgets on top of the standard HTML offerings, and a few patterns have emerged. It's unlikely you'll need to build these widgets yourself, because library implementations are available for almost all of them. Nevertheless, it's worth it to consider when to use them and how to configure them.

The chapter starts with smaller, isolated widgets and builds up to more complex components. *Slider* is "the widget HTML forgot"—a typical slider widget so useful it's surprising it hasn't yet become standard HTML. *Progress Indicator* is a simple message or animation shown while waiting for a web remoting call. *Drilldown* is a control for selecting an element within a hierarchy.

Traditional HTML widgets are turbo-charged in the next couple of patterns. *Data Grid* is a "table on steroids," with tools for querying and restructuring that will be familiar to users of spreadsheets and database report tools. And *Rich Text Editor* is a "textarea on steroids," with options such as font size and color similar to those of a modern word processor.

Suggestion is similar to the traditional combo-box, a mixture between browsing and searching that relies on web remoting to locate a set of options against a partial text input. *Live Search* works similarly but shows search results rather than helping to complete a text field. It also works with nontext controls.

Finally, *Live Command-Line* and *Live Form* are higher-level patterns that tie together various widgets and patterns. The former is largely speculative and explores techniques to help people learn and use command-line interfaces within the Web. The latter is a more proven Ajax Pattern—a form that keeps changing in response to user input.

Slider

Continuous, Lever, Multiple, Range, Slider

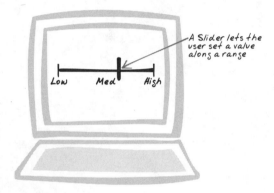

FIGURE 14-1. Slider

Goal Story

Stuart is rating his lecturer online. Each answer lies somewhere between "Strongly Disagree" and "Strongly Agree." Unlike conventional surveys, the scale is continuous, because Stuart uses a Slider to set a precise value along the spectrum.

Problem

How can users specify a value within a range?

Forces

- Most data is constrained to reside within a range.
- Prevention is better than cure; the user interface should be designed such that the user is forced to choose a value within the range instead of the interface checking and providing an error message later on.

Solution

Provide a Slider to let the user choose a value within a range. The user drags a handle along one dimension to set the value. As a variant, two handles on the same Slider can allow the user to choose a range instead of a single value.

Standard HTML contains two related input controls: radiobuttons and selectors. Each of these lets you specify a value from a fixed list of choices. The biggest advantage of a Slider is that the data range can be continuous as well as discrete. Of course, "continuous" is an approximation, since you can only have as many choices as there are pixels in the Slider range. But with most Sliders, that means you have hundreds of unique values, which is continuous for most intents and purposes.

A Slider can also show discrete data by identifying several points along the range. When the user releases the handle, the Slider jumps to the nearest point. Why use a Slider when radio buttons and selectors already support discrete data? A Slider provides a better visual indication that the data resides in a spectrum. Also, it's often faster because the user can click anywhere in the region as opposed to aiming precisely at a radiobutton or opening up a dialog box.

A further benefit of Sliders is their excellent support for comparing similar data. When several Sliders share the same range, they can be placed in parallel to show how the variables differ. For example, a product survey could ask questions such as "Were you happy with the price?" and "How easy was it to start using?" The answers lie on a different scale but ultimately map to the same range from "Unhappy" to "Happy." Placing these horizontal rows in parallel helps the user stick to the same scale and compare each factor to the others.

Because Sliders aren't standard controls, you'll need to either use a library or roll your own. Typical control mechanisms include the following:

- Dragging the handle moves it directly.

- Clicking on either side of the handle moves it a little in that direction.

- While the Slider has keyboard focus, pressing left and right arrows move it in either direction. It's sometimes useful to offer an accelerator key such as Shift, which, held down at the same time as the arrow, speeds up the handle movement. Keyboard controls are particularly important when the control is part of a form.

- Receiving notifications from external sources. The Slider is sometimes synchronized with another object, so if that object changes, the Slider must update too.

A typical implementation separates the scale from the handle. The scale consists of a line, possibly with some notches and labels. The handle is usually an image, with the zIndex property set to place it "in front of" the main Slider. There are several event handlers required to support all of the mechanisms above, and the Slider handle itself is manipulated using techniques discussed in *Drag-And-Drop* (Chapter 15). In addition, movements will often trigger other activity, such as an *XMLHttpRequest Call* or a change to another page element.

Decisions

How will you orient the Slider?

There are two options for orientation: horizontal or vertical. Following are a few considerations:

Data type
Sometimes the nature of the data dictates which option is more logical. For instance, Google Maps uses a vertical Slider for zoom, which corresponds to a feeling of flying toward and away from the map as you zoom in and out.

Layout
Aesthetic appearance and space conservation are important. Many forms will feature horizontal Sliders because they fit well underneath questions. Vertical Sliders would lead to a lot of whitespace.

Proximity
Where the Slider controls something else on the page, you'll probably want to place them near each other, which might dictate orientation.

Comparison
As mentioned earlier in the "Solution," Sliders work well when placed in parallel, which means a common orientation.

What scale will you use?

There are quite a few ways to present a variable, and the choice will depend on the nature of the data and what users are comfortable with. Examples include:

- Qualitative descriptions ("Low", "High"). This might seem suited only to discrete ranges, but the labels can also be used as markers within a continuous range.

- Absolute values.

- Percentages (typically ranging from 0 to 100).

How will you present the scale?

There are various strategies for presenting the scale:

- Provide no labels; rely on context and conventions. For instance, users—at least in western countries—usually assume Sliders increase in value to the right.

- Provide just a label at either end.

- Provide labels at several points along the range.

The labels are usually shown alongside the Slider, but to conserve space, you can sometimes show them inside it.

Real-World Examples

Yahoo! Mindset

A product of Yahoo Labs, Yahoo! Mindset (*http://mindset.research.yahoo.com/*) lets you tweak search results with an unusual type of Slider that ranges from "shopping" on one end to "researching" on the other (Figure 14-2). Pull the "Ajax" results towards "shopping" and you'll see links to cleaning products and football. Pull it to the right and you'll see some information about web design (and, it must be said, more football). Also of note: the Slider is "Live"—each time you change it, the results are automatically updated via an *XMLHttpRequest Call*.

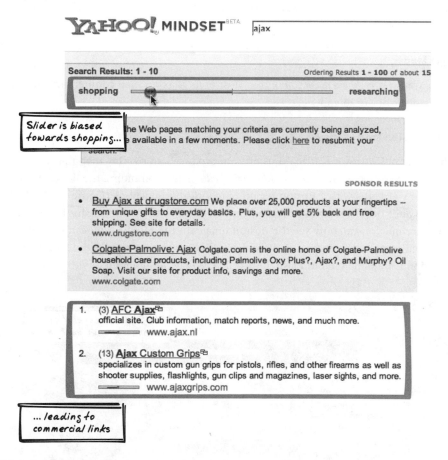

FIGURE 14-2. Yahoo! Mindset

Amazon Diamond Search

Amazon Diamond Search (*http://www.amazon.com/gp/gsl/search/finder/002-1527640-2908837?%5Fencoding=UTF8&productGroupID=loose%5Fdiamonds*) presents several elaborate Sliders (see Figure 14-5). Each lets you specify a range, which acts as a filter for the diamond search. There are several innovative aspects of the presentation, discussed next.

- The labels are dynamic. As you drag the handles, the labels show exactly the value that's been specified.

- There's a graphic inside the Slider, which represents the variable in each case. Price, for example, is shown as an increasing histogram, and Cut shows several diamonds of decreasing cut quality.

- The Slider graphic is faded outside the selection region.

- Each Slider has a *Microlink* (Chapter 15) that opens up an explanation about that variable.

- The Sliders are horizontal and parallel to each other. Unfortunately, the directions aren't aligned—price and carat increase from left to right, but cut quality increases from right to left.

Google Maps

Google Maps (*http://maps.google.com*), like most of its Ajaxian map counterparts, uses a Slider to control the zoom level.

Katrina-Boston map overlay

In the wake of hurricane Katrina, Boston.com produced an overlay map (*http://www. boston.com/news/weather/hurricanes/multimedia/globe_map/*) combining the flood-affected area of New Orleans with a Boston region of identical proportions (Figure 14-3). A Slider is used to alter opacity: at one extreme, you can only see the New Orleans image; at the other extreme, you can only see the Boston image. In the middle, you can see both images, with one or the other dominant depending on the position of the Slider. The application is implemented in Flash, but could easily be implemented with standard Ajax technology.

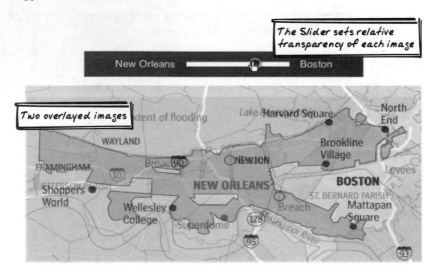

FIGURE 14-3. Katrina-Boston overlay map

WebFX Slider Demo

The WebFX Slider Demo (*http://webfx.eae.net/dhtml/slider/slider.html*) shows a few different Sliders, in both horizontal and vertical orientations. You can set the Slider directly and also update it with some text inputs.

Code Example: Yahoo! Mindset

The Yahoo! Mindset Slider (*http://mindset.research.yahoo.com/*) is created with several images. There are images for the vertical lines at the center and extremes. The main horizontal bar is created with a single vertical line; it's 1 pixel wide, but the image width is set to 150 pixels, thus creating a horizontal bar. There's a handler registered for the click event (which pulls the handle in that direction):

```
<img id="slidergrayrightimg"  src="images/gray_bar.gif"
  height="36" width="150" unselectable="on"
  onClick="setup('1505998205%3Ac26b16%3A105900dfd3e%3Aff4', 'ajax');
  endDrag(event); return false;">
```

The Slider handle, called `sliderball`, is also an image:

```
<img id="sliderball" src="images/aqua_ball_trans.gif"
  onMouseDown="dragStart(event, '1505998205%3Ac26b16%3A105900dfd3e%3Aff4',
    'ajax'); return false;" unselectable="on"
  style="position: relative; z-index: 1; top: 0px; left: -136px;"
  height="36" width="18">
```

A drag function is registered to handle moving the mouse after the handle has been selected. Based on the current mouse position, it calculates where the Slider should be and calls a function to move it:

```
function dragStart(e, sID, q) {
  ...
  document.onmousemove = function(e) { drag(e); };
  document.onmouseup = function(e) { endDrag(e); };
  ...
}

function drag(e) {
  ...
  var relativePos = e.clientX - sliderOffset;
  ...
  moveSlider(relativePos);
}
```

The `moveSlider` function redraws the handle based on its relative position (positive or negative offset from the center):

```
function moveSlider (relativePos) {

  var centerPoint = (maxRight - minLeft) / 2;
  var centerBuffer = 5;

  //the ball position is relative
  var ballPos = (-(maxRight - minLeft)) + (relativePos-(ballWidth/2));
  document.getElementById('sliderball').style.left = ballPos+'px';
```

```
    ...
  }
```

Finally, when the Slider is released, the handle's position is finalized and an *XMLHttp-Request Call* is issued to bring the results in line with the new value:

```
function endDrag(e) {
  ...
  var relativePos = e.clientX - sliderOffset;
  drag(e);
  ...
  var sliderURI = "/searchify/slider?UserSession="+sessionID+
                  "&SliderValue="+threshold+"&query="+query;
  (Sends XMLHttpRequest to SliderURI)
}
```

Alternatives

Conventional controls: radiobuttons and selector field

As mentioned in the solution, a Slider performs similar functionality to radiobuttons and selectors.

Related Patterns

Drag-And-Drop

The Slider handle is usually manipulated with a *Drag-And-Drop* (Chapter 15) action.

Metaphor

Sliders are a UI metaphor based on physical sliders in control devices such as audio-visual consoles.

Progress Indicator

Activity, Feedback, Hourglass, Meter, Progress, Waiting

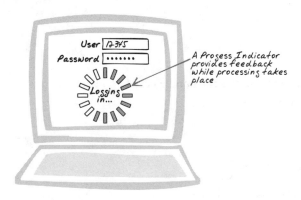

FIGURE 14-4. Progress Indicator

Goal Story

Reta has made a sale and is typing in the details. She completes the credit card details and proceeds down the page to delivery dates. Meanwhile, the status area has appeared beside the credit card details. While she completes the rest of the form, the status area continues to update with the current verification stage—initially "submitted," then "responding," then "verified."

Problem

How can you provide feedback while waiting for server responses?

Forces

- Ajax Apps often make *XMLHttpRequest Calls* (Chapter 6) to query and update the server.

- To provide good feedback, you should provide an idea of which page elements are affected by any update.

- Users like to feel in control, and that control is taken away when the user is waiting for a response. It's not just the delay that should be minimized, but the *perceived* delay.

Solution

Indicate the progress of server calls. You can't always reduce delay, but you can include a Progress Indicator to ease the pain. A Progress Indicator helps maintain the user's attention, improves the user's understanding of how the system works, and also communicates that the system is still alive even if a response hasn't yet occurred.

The Progress Indicator is typically introduced to the DOM once an *XMLHttpRequest Call* begins and removed when the call has returned. The easiest way to detect whether the call has returned is using the XMLHttpRequest callback function. An indicator need not relate to a single call—it can show progress for a sequence of related calls.

Sometimes it's a *Popup* (Chapter 15) element instead of a new element directly on the page. A popular idiom is a small opaque Popup on the corner of the page showing just a word or two (i.e., "Saving…", "Loading…").

For shorter delays, typical Progress Indicators include:

- A small message like "Updating document"
- An animated icon (there's now a library of open source Progress Indicator icons available at *http://mentalized.net/activity-indicators/*)

For longer delays, the following can be used:

- A meter showing how much progress has been made
- An estimate of time remaining

- A sequence of messages indicating what's happening at present

- Content that's engaging but not directly related to the progress, such as "Tip of the Day" or a canned graphical depiction of system activity

Of course, you can combine these approaches. Generally speaking, some form of unobtrusive animation is worthwhile in any Progress Indicator, because it at least tells the user that something's happening, even if progress is temporarily stuck. In addition, longer delays should usually be completed with a visual effect such as *One-Second Spotlight* (Chapter 16), since the user's focus has probably moved elsewhere by that stage.

Note that one form of indicator to *avoid* is changing the cursor. Many traditional GUIs switch over to a "rotating hourglass" or related icon during delays. That's probably inappropriate for Ajax because it's something the actual browser software will do too—e.g., while loading a new page—so it's likely to create confusion.

Decisions

What sort of Progress Indicator will you use?

A well known set of guidelines is summarized in Jakob Nielsen's Usability Engineering (*http://www.useit.com/papers/responsetime.html*). Following is a quick summary:

- If the delay is less than 0.1 second, the user will feel it's instantaneous. No feedback necessary.

- If the delay is between 0.1 second and 1 second, the user will notice it but it won't break their flow of thought. No feedback necessary.

- If the delay is between 1 and 10 seconds, the user's flow of thought is interrupted as he awaits the response. Basic feedback necessary; i.e., an indication *that* a delay is occurring. Ajax examples include animated icons and simple text messages.

- If the delay is greater than 10 seconds, the user will want to proceed to other tasks. Detailed feedback necessary. Ajax examples include progress meters and messages showing current state.

The precise figures may require some adjustment and I suspect a web context requires them to be dropped a bit. For example, users will probably want some feedback for a delay of 0.5 second rather than 1 second, and more detailed information is probably appropriate after 2–3 seconds rather than 10 seconds.

Bruce Tognazzini also offers some useful guidelines (*http://www.asktog.com/basics/ firstPrinciples.html#latencyReduction*).

How will you provide feedback during longer delays?

For longer delays, you need to help the user track how much progress has been made, typically using a progress meter that shows percent complete. Sometimes, a long delay can come from a single *XMLHttpRequest Call*, because although the network transfer may be quick, the backend processing might not be. For example, the call might trigger a major database operation.

You probably won't get any useful information about its progress by monitoring the responseText component of XMLHttpRequest. The responseText tends not to populate in a linear fashion, for two reasons. First, there are usually backend calculations involved, during which no output can occur. Thus, output tends to happen either in bursts or all at the end. Second, the output is often compressed using the standard HTTP content encoding facility, and the compression algorithm will force data to be outputted in bursts. The XMLHttpRequest's readyState won't tell you very much either. For reasons described in *XMLHttpRequest Call* and *HTTP Streaming* (Chapter 6), tracking support is inconsistent across browsers.

So if you can't monitor the progress of an XMLHttpRequest Call, how can you help the user understand how much progress has been made? One thing you can do is *Guesstimate*: predict the total time, and start running a timer to monitor how long it has been since the call began. The prediction of total duration need not be hardcoded every time; you could have the application track download times and reflect them in future estimates. This sort of thing is quite common; e.g., in the download-time estimates given by a web browser.

If you want more accuracy, introduce a second monitoring channel. While the primary request takes place, a sequence of monitoring requests are issued to ask the server for a progress estimates. For example, the server might be looping through 1,000 records, running a transformation on each and saving it to the database. The loop variable can be exposed in a second *Web Service* so that the browser monitoring can inform the user.

Not all Progress Indicators concern a single XMLHttpRequest Call. Indeed, those requiring a progress meter are longer processes, likely incorporating several XMLHttpRequest Calls. With those, you have much better opportunity for real-time progress monitoring; each time a call returns, further progress has occurred. In a simple model, you can show that progress is 50 percent complete when two of four calls have returned.

Real-World Examples

Amazon Diamond Search

Amazon Diamond Search (*http://www.amazon.com/gp/gsl/search/finder/002-1527640-2908837?%5Fencoding=UTF8&productGroupID=loose%5Fdiamonds*) is a *Live Search* that shows a Progress Indicator while updating the number of results (Figure 14-5). The indicator is a simple animation depicting a block moving back and forth with a "LOADING RESULTS" message. One nice design feature is the placement of the Progress Indicator on the result status. It replaces the results once searching has begun and remains until the new results are shown. Thus, it serves to invalidate the previous results at the start and focuses the user's attention on the new results at the end.

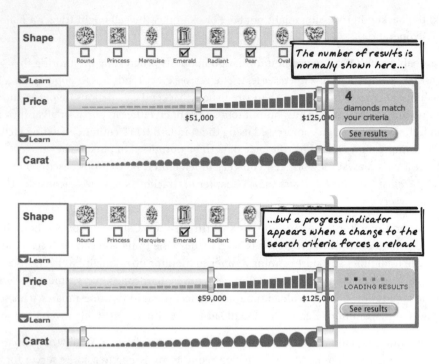

FIGURE 14-5. Amazon Diamond Search

Amazon Zuggest

Like Amazon Diamond Search, Francis Shanahan's Amazon Zuggest (*http://www.francisshanahan.com/zuggest.aspx*) is a *Live Search* that shows a Progress Indicator while searching is underway. In this case, the indicator is a text message such as "Searching... beat." It occupies its own fixed area, and when searching is complete, morphs into another message: "Done!"

Protopage

Protopage *(http://www.protopage.com/)* is an Ajax portal. Each time you make a change, such as dragging a *Portlet* (Chapter 15), an opaque "Saving…" message appears in the bottom-right corner. This is a good model for a *Fat Client* application, in which server synchronization should be unobtrusive.

TalkDigger

TalkDigger (*http://talkdigger.com*) simultaneously calls several search engines, showing a Progress Indicator on each result panel. It's interesting because it shows how to use Progress Indicators in a *Multi-Stage Download* (Chapter 13) situation.

Kayak

Kayak *(http://kayak.com)* illustrates how to handle a longer delay. When you search for a trip, it creates a result page with several forms of progress feedback:

- The number of search results so far.

- A progress meter that fills up from left to right.

- A sampling of web sites that are being searched.

- A nice graphic depicting a retro, pre-electronic airport display board. Initially, each character is random. As the search of a particular web site proceeds, the random characters are replaced with the correct character for that web site. Meanwhile, the characters that remain unpopulated continue to flicker from one random character to another. Once all characters have been corrected and the web site name displays correctly, the display becomes random again and starts revealing another web site. All this is an excellent example of a graphic that is engaging and at the same time indicative of the processing that's occurring.

The Pick'em Game

The Pick'em Game *(http://www.pickemgame.com/welcome/picksheet)* is an office pool game allowing you to predict this week's football winners. It provides a form where you declare a prediction and confidence level for each game. Above the form is a small instruction message, and when data is being saved, it morphs into a Progress Indicator. The indicator is a spinning disk and an "Updating Pick Sheet" message. (The demo page doesn't perform a real remote call.)

Code Refactoring: AjaxPatterns Progress Indicator Demo

This demo *(http://ajaxify.com/run/sum/progress)* introduces a progress display to the Basic Sum Demo *(http://ajaxify.com/run/sum/progress)*. It's a simple animated GIF that shows up while waiting for the sum to return.

An Img tag for the animation is present in the initial HTML:

```
<img id="progress" class="notWaiting" src="progress.gif">
```

The script will toggle the image's CSS class depending on whether you're in waiting mode or not. The stylesheet ensures that it's visible when waiting and invisible when not:

```
.waiting {
  visibility: visible;
}

.notWaiting {
  visibility: hidden;
}
```

With the styles defined, the script just has to flick the CSS class back and forth as the waiting status changes:

```
function submitSum( ) {
  $("progress").className = "waiting";
  ...
}

function onSumResponse(text, headers, callingContext) {
  $("progress").className = "notWaiting";
  ...
}
```

Related Patterns

Status Area

A Progress Indicator is usually presented as a *Status Area* (Chapter 15).

Popup

The Progress Indicator can sometimes reside in a *Popup* (Chapter 15).

One-Second Spotlight

Once a long process has completed, use a *One-Second Spotlight* (Chapter 16) to point this out to the user.

Guesstimate

Sometimes you don't know how long a task will take or how much progress has been made so far. A sloppy guess is better than nothing at all, so make a *Guesstimate* (Chapter 13) of the progress.

Distributed Events

When a call comes in, you need to close off the Progress Indicator. There's a risk here that you'll end up with a single function that mixes Progress Indicator stuff with the logic of processing the response. Separate that logic using *Distributed Events* (Chapter 10).

Metaphor

Banks and post offices often use ticket-based queueing systems, showing the number that's currently being served.

Want to Know More?

- Gnome Guidelines, Chapter 7: Feedback (*http://developer.gnome.org/projects/gup/hig/1.0/feedback.html*)

- AskTog.com First Principles of Interaction Design, Latency Reduction (*http://www.asktog.com/basics/firstPrinciples.html*)

Drilldown

Drilldown, Menu, Progressive

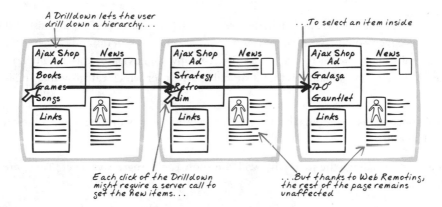

FIGURE 14-6. Drilldown

Goal Story

Pam is booking a trip on the corporate travel planner. She sees a form with the usual fields and clicks on location. Suddenly, a list of cities fades in beside the form, and Pam selects Paris. Beside the city list, a third list appears, this one showing approved hotels. Pam chooses the Hilton, and both lists disappear. The location field now contains "Paris Hilton" as Pam had intended.

Problem

How can the user select an item in a hierarchical structure?

Forces

- Applications and web sites are often arranged in hierarchies. To navigate, users need to choose a page from within the hierarchy.

- Hierarchy navigation should be fast.

Solution

To let the user locate an item within a hierarchy, provide a dynamic Drilldown.
The Drilldown allows for navigation through a hierarchy and ultimately for an item to be chosen. At each level, there are several types of elements in the Drilldown:

Current category
    A read-only name for the present level.

Individual items
    Items the user can choose in order to end the interaction.

Child categories

Deeper levels the user can drill down to.

Ancestor categories

Parent category and above that let the user "drill up."

In some hierarchies, items and categories are mutually exclusive: items only exist at the edges—or leaves—of the hierarchy. Even when that's the case, items and categories should be distinguished for the sake of clarity. The upward navigator goes by different names, but a general guideline is that it should tell the user which category that she is going back to.

Typical applications include navigating and filling out a field by drilling down a hierarchy of candidate items.

As the user drills down the hierarchy, will you show each progressive level? There are three main options (Figure 14-7):

- Keep the Drilldown in a fixed area. Each time the user clicks on a category, the Drilldown morphs to show only that category. This has the benefit of preventing page rearrangement.

- Show all levels at once. Each time the user clicks on a category, expand out the Drilldown region to add a new list for each category.

- As a variant on the second approach, all levels are shown, but the submenus are rendered in front of the rest of the document, so the menu is effectively modal: nothing else can be done from the time the menu is opened to the time the selection is made. This approach is similar to choosing an application from the Windows Start menu.

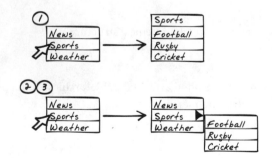

FIGURE 14-7. Drilldown styles

The first two options are modeless; the third is modal. Modeless interaction works well with Ajax, where it's possible to dynamically update, without page refresh, the menu as well as any surrounding content related to the user's selection. Specifically:

- Each navigation through the Drilldown can result in a server call to fill the next level with the latest content or even auto-generate new content.

- The display throughout the application can change to reflect the state of the Drilldown, giving the user a "tour" through the hierarchy. As a user drills down from the top level to a deep category, the application is always synchronized with the current level, so the display reflects the medium-depth categories along the way. Because the interaction is modeless, the user is then free to stay on those categories.

- The user can iterate between drilling down and performing other tasks. Imagine the user is a human resources clerk who needs to use a Drilldown to select an "employee of the month." She's already decided on the region and drills down to show all of the employees there. Now that she can see each candidate, she can go perform some research in another region of the page, or on another web site. When she returns, the Drilldown is still there, waiting to be completed.

Decisions

Will you call on the server each time the user navigates through the Drilldown?

Sometimes the entire hierarchy is loaded as a one-off event. Other times, categories can be pulled down as required using an *XMLHttpRequest Call* (Chapter 6). The choice is governed by two things:

- How big is the hierarchy? The more items, and the more information per item, the less desirable it is to transfer and cache the data.

- Is the hierarchy subject to change? In this case, you'll need to retrieve fresh data from the server at the time a category is opened up. In a more extreme case, the server might even generate the hierarchy data on demand. For instance, an RSS feed aggregator might present a Drilldown with categories such as "sports feeds" or "politics feeds." The contents of these will be generated at the time the user drills down to a particular feed.

Real-World Examples

Betfair

Betfair *(http://betfair.com)* uses a Drilldown to locate an event you wish to bet on (Figure 14-8). At the top level, the "All Markets" Drilldown contains various categories in alphabetical order, from "American Football" to "Special Bets" to "Volleyball." Clicking on "Special Bets" yields several countries, along with a "General" category, and you can continue to drill down to the list of bets. Clicking on one of those bets sets the main page content.

"All Markets" is one of two Drilldowns. The other is "My Markets," a personalized Drilldown available to registered users.

Backbase portal

The Backbase portal demo *(http://projects.backbase.com/RUI/portal.html)* contains several independent *Portlets*. Of interest here is the "local directory" Portlet, which is actually a

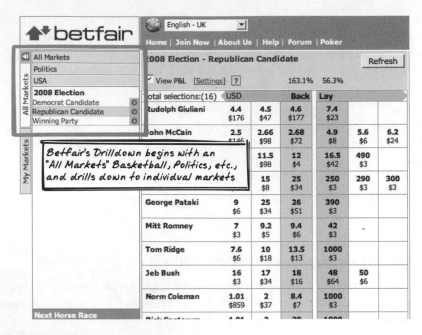

FIGURE 14-8. Betfair

Drilldown with top-level categories such as "education" and "health" drilling down to relevant links.

OpenRico accordian widget

The OpenRico framework (*http://openrico.org/rico/demos.page?demo=ricoAccordion.html*) includes an accordian widget. Clicking on a category bar reveals the content. Because it lacks a deep hierarchy of categories, it's technically not a Drilldown, but it's a good solution when you do have a flat set of categories.

Code Refactoring: AjaxPatterns Drilldown Portal

Overview

The basic Portal Demo (*http://ajaxify.com/run/portal*) illustrates *Multi-Stage Download* (Chapter 13), showing how different content blocks can be downloaded in parallel. One of those is a block of links to Ajax resources. To keep the block small, only a few links are present. But is there any way we could keep the link block physically small while offering a large number of links? Of course there is…a Drilldown will occupy roughly the same space, yet with a little interaction, the user will be able to navigate through a large collection of links.

The Drilldown Portal Demo (*http://ajaxify.com/run/portal/drilldown*) introduces a Drilldown. A Category can contain any combination of Categories and Links (Figure 14-9). For instance: The top-level category, "All Categories," contains only Categories, the "Websites" category contains just links, and the "Overviews" category contains some overviews as well as a subcategory, "Podcast Overviews" (Figure 14-10). Categories and links are rendered similarly, but not identically. Each category menu includes a link to the previous category level.

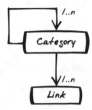

FIGURE 14-9. Categories and Links: the Composite Pattern

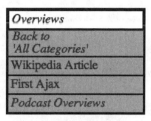

FIGURE 14-10. Drilldown with Categories (Italicized) and Links

The basic interaction sequence works like this:

1. User clicks on a category.

2. A callback function detects the click and issues an XMLHttpRequest query on the desired category.

3. Server responds with the new category name, its parent (null in the case of the top-level category), and each category and link in the Drilldown. All of this is in XML format.

4. Browser replaces existing Drilldown with a Drilldown based on the new category information.

On page load, the Drilldown is blank, and the browser requests information for the top-level category. The server response triggers the creation of a new Drilldown.

Browser-side implementation

The initial HTML just shows a blank div. The width is constrained because the Drilldown's parent container has a fixed width:

```
<div id="drilldown">Loading ...</div>
```

On page load, the top-level category is requested:

```
retrieveCategory("All Categories");
```

Then begins the standard process of requesting a category with XMLHttpRequest, then rendering the menu accordingly. This occurs not only on page load, but every time the user clicks on a category within the drop-down.

The server returns an XML file with category data.* The specification contains the name, the parent name, and a list of items. Each item is either a category or a link. Note that only the information for this level of the Drilldown is provided.

```
<category name="Overviews" parent="All Categories">
  <items>
    <link>
      <url>http://en.wikipedia.org/wiki/AJAX</url>
      <name>Wikipedia Article</name>
    </link>
    <link>
      <url>http://www.adaptivepath.com/publications/essays/archives/000385.php</url>
      <name>First Ajax</name>
  </link>
  <category name="Podcast Overviews" parent="Overviews" />
</items>
</category>
```

The browser then parses this XML, using the standard DOM API, to produce HTML for the Drilldown. Links are shown as standard HTML anchor links; categories are Div elements. Event handlers ensure that when a category is clicked, including the "Back To (previous)" category, the browser will kick off another retrieve-and-render cycle:

```
function onDrilldownResponse(xml) {

  var category = xml.getElementsByTagName("category")[0];
  var html="";

  var categoryName = category.getAttribute("name");
  html+="<div id='categoryName'>" + categoryName + "</div>";

  var parent = category.getAttribute("parent");
  if (parent && parent.length > 0) {
    var parentName = category.getAttribute("parent");
    html+="<div id='parent' onclick=\"retrieveCategory('" + parent + "')\""
          + "'>Back to <br/>'" + parent + "'</div>";
  }

  var items = category.getElementsByTagName("items")[0].childNodes;
  for (i=0; i<items.length; i++) {
    var item = items[i];
    if (item.nodeName=="link") {
      var name = item.getElementsByTagName("name")[0].firstChild.nodeValue;
      var url = item.getElementsByTagName("url")[0].firstChild.nodeValue;
      html+="<div class='link'><a href='" + url + "'>" + name + "</a></div>";
    } else if (item.nodeName=="category") {
      var name = item.getAttribute("name");
      html+="<div class='category' "
              + "onclick='retrieveCategory(\""+name+"\")'>"+name+"</div>";
    }
```

---

* For example, you can see the data for the "Overviews" category at *http://ajaxify.com/run/portal/drilldown/drilldown.phtml?categoryName=Overviews.*

```
    }
    $("drilldown").innerHTML = html;
  }
```

Server-Side Implementation

The server-side implementation relies on the *Composite* pattern (see Gamma et al., 1995).
A Category consists of further Category objects and also of Link objects. We rely on Category
and Link having two common operations:

asXMLTag( )
> Renders the item as an XML tag. For categories, there is a special optional parameter
> that determines whether or not the tag will include all items.

findItems($name)
> Recursively finds an item—either a Category or a Link—having the specified name.

With these operations encapsulated in the Category and Link objects, the main script is
quite small:

```php
require_once("Link.php");
require_once("Category.php");
require_once("categoryData.php");

header("Content-type: text/xml");

$categoryName = $_GET['categoryName'];
$category = $topCategory->findItem($categoryName);
if ($category) {
  echo $category->asXMLTag(true);
} else {
  echo "No category called '$categoryName'";
}
```

Further refactoring: a Drilldown with dynamic content

In the refactoring above, the top-level category, and all of the data underneath it, is hardcoded in categoryData.php. In fact, the hierarchy data could easily be generated on demand
to create a Drilldown with dynamic content. In a further refactoring (*http://ajaxify.com/run/
portal/drilldown/syncLinks*), a *Cross-Domain Proxy* (Chapter 10) is introduced to grab the
actual results from the AjaxPatterns Wiki Links Page (*http://ajaxpatterns.org/Ajax_Links*). It's
not a true Cross-Domain Proxy because instead of grabbing the results in real-time, a process runs to pull them every sixty seconds and store them locally, where they can be
picked up by the Drilldown script.

Alternatives

Live Search

Drilldown lets the user locate an item by browsing through a hierarchy. *Live Search* (see
later) instead lets you locate an item by typing, and the data need not be hierarchical.

Tree

Like a Drilldown, a Tree widget lets the user navigate a hierarchy, just like the tree of files and folders in desktop file managers. Tree widgets, even if they expand and collapse, tend to take up more space than Drilldowns, but the more detailed view can be useful for longer, more complex, tasks.

Related Patterns

Microlink

Content blocks, produced when particular categories or items are selected can be associated with the Drilldown. Thus, the Drilldown contents are being used as *Microlinks* (Chapter 15).

Browser-Side Cache

If each navigation event leads to a query of the server, consider retaining results in a *Browser-Side Cache* (Chapter 13).

Portlet

A Drilldown is usually a form of *Portlet* (Chapter 15). It has its own state, and the user can usually conduct a conversation with the Drilldown in isolation.

Data Grid

Database, Query, Report, Summary, Table

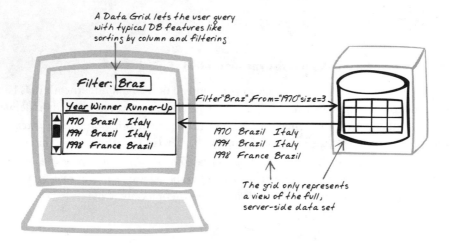

FIGURE 14-11. Data Grid

Goal Story

Reta is doing a little data mining on this season's sales figures. She's scrolling through a table showing a row for every transaction. Noticing that higher sales figures tend to come in the morning, she sorts the table by sales figure. There's too much data there, so she filters out any transactions below $1,000, then groups the transactions by time of day.

Problem

How can you help users explore data?

Forces

- Ajax Apps have their own databases, as well as access to external systems.

- Users need a way to explore all this data, in order to verify it, understand how it works, predict future trends, and so on.

- You can't anticipate what users will need to do with data.

Solution

Report on some data in a rich table and support common querying functions. A Data Grid has the familiar database client interface: a table with a row for each result and a column for each property. Think of it as a traditional table on steroids. Typical database client functionality is as follows (and it's feasible to achieve each of these in an Ajax interface):

Sorting

Each column can be usually be sorted by clicking on the header. To let the user sort by more than one category, use a sorting algorithm that preserves the order of equal values. Then, users can click on one header followed by the other.

Filtering

The user can *filter in* to retain data matching certain criteria, or *filter out* to exclude that data.

Grouping

Data can be grouped by similarity. A large table is essentially broken into smaller tables, in which each item in a smaller table is similar to the other items in that table.

Aggregate calculations

Calculations can be performed across the whole table—for example, a sum or average for a column, or a sum of the products of two columns in each row.

Editing

Some Data Grids allow fields to be edited.

With the magic of Web Remoting (Chapter 6), the grid can become a *Virtual Workspace* (Chapter 15), giving the illusion of holding a massive set of data. In reality, the data lives on the server, and each *User Action* leads to a new server call. Most queries lead to a structured response, such as an *XML Message* or a *JSON Message*, containing a list of results for JavaScript rendering, or alternatively an *HTML Message* with the specific view the user will see. The semantic style has the advantage of encouraging performance optimizations such as *Predictive Fetch*, which are essential if you want the grid to feel responsive.

Decisions

Will the Grid be Read-Only or Mutable?

Editing a table directly can be more productive for experts, though it's often more difficult for novices than editing a single record in a form, since a form usually has a more verbose interface. Grid mutability adds a couple of extra considerations:

- You need to validate the data. In a live context, this might mean showing a *Progress Indicator* during validation, then Highlighting invalid columns.

- Cells should ideally morph into input widgets when a user begins editing them. For instance, create a drop-down when the user begins to change a constrained field.

Real-World Examples

OpenRico Data Grid example

The OpenRico Data Grid example (*http://openrico.org/rico/livegrid.page*) shows a list of movies, each with several fields: ranking, title, genre, rating, votes, and year (Figure 14-12). You can scroll down the list and sort each column header. You can also bookmark a position in the table (an example of *Unique URLs*).

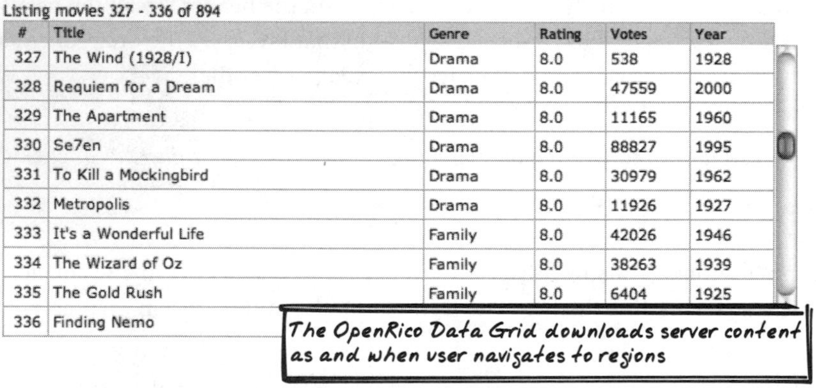

Listing movies 327 - 336 of 894

#	Title	Genre	Rating	Votes	Year
327	The Wind (1928/I)	Drama	8.0	538	1928
328	Requiem for a Dream	Drama	8.0	47559	2000
329	The Apartment	Drama	8.0	11165	1960
330	Se7en	Drama	8.0	88827	1995
331	To Kill a Mockingbird	Drama	8.0	30979	1962
332	Metropolis	Drama	8.0	11926	1927
333	It's a Wonderful Life	Family	8.0	42026	1946
334	The Wizard of Oz	Family	8.0	38263	1939
335	The Gold Rush	Family	8.0	6404	1925
336	Finding Nemo				

The OpenRico Data Grid downloads server content as and when user navigates to regions

FIGURE 14-12. OpenRico Grid Movie demo

NumSum

NumSum (*http://NumSum.com*) is a spreadsheet, and spreadsheets are a special, powerful case of Data Grids; they are to Data Grids what Data Grids are to conventional tables (Figure 14-13).

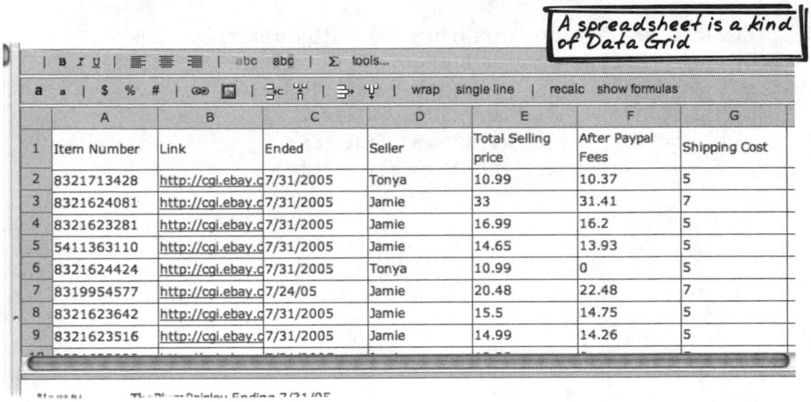

> A spreadsheet is a kind of Data Grid

FIGURE 14-13. NumSum

Oddpost

Oddpost (*http://oddpost.com/learnmore*) is an Ajax mail client with a very similar look and feel to desktop clients like Outlook. The subject headers table is a form of Query-Report Table. As with the OpenRico example, you can scroll through the table and sort by column.

Delta Vacations

Delta Vacations (*http://www.deltavacations.com/destination.aspx?code=MONTEGOBAY*) appears as a *Live Search* example, but it also serves as an example of filtering. Initially, all hotels in a destination are shown, and typing a search term retains only matching results.

Code Example: OpenRico Data Grid

The OpenRico Data Grid example (*http://openrico.org/rico/livegrid.page*) uses OpenRico's LiveGrid API. In the initial HTML, there are two tables: one for the column headers and one for the data. Note that the data table declares all the visible table rows, initialized with the values in the first few rows. This is an example of a *Virtual Workspace* (Chapter 15)— the rows will always stay fixed, but their data will change as scrolling occurs:

```
<table id="data_grid_header" class="fixedTable" cellspacing="0" cellpadding=
"0" style="width:560px">
  <tr>
    <th class="first tableCellHeader" style="width:30px;text-align:center">#</th>
    <th class="tableCellHeader" style="width:280px">Title</th>
    <th class="tableCellHeader" style="width:80px">Genre</th>
    <th class="tableCellHeader" style="width:50px">Rating</th>
    <th class="tableCellHeader" style="width:60px">Votes</th>
    <th class="tableCellHeader" style="width:60px">Year</th>
  </tr>
</table>

<table id="data_grid" class="fixedTable" cellspacing="0"
       cellpadding="0" style="width:560px; border-left:1px solid #ababab">
```

```
<tr>
  <td class="cell" style="width:30px;text-align:center">1</td>
  <td class="cell" style="width:280px"> Bend of the River</td>
  <td class="cell" style="width:80px">Western</td>
  <td class="cell" style="width:50px">7.3</td>
  <td class="cell" style="width:60px">664</td>
  <td class="cell" style="width:60px">1952</td>
</tr>
...
</table>
```

The grid is initialized on page load, with some configurable options passed in:

```
var opts = { prefetchBuffer: true, onscroll: updateHeader };
onloads.push( function() {
  tu = new Rico.LiveGrid(
          'data_grid', 10, 950, 'getMovieTableContent.do', opts )}
);
```

The grid will then handle all user events. Notice the getMovieTableContent.do argument in its construction. That's the URL that will feed the grid with further data. It must be capable of accepting in certain parameters, such as initial position and number of rows to retain. For example, to load the page initially and scroll all the way to the end (rows 940 and on), the *XMLHttpRequest Call* (Chapter 6) goes to the following URL: getMovieTableContent. do?id=data_grid&page_size=10&offset=940&_=. What's retrieved are 10 movies starting at 941 in an XHTML format, as shown in the following example. The grid component then updates itself with those rows.

```
<?xml version="1.0" encoding="ISO-8859-1"?>

<ajax-response>
  <response type="object" id='data_grid_updater'>
  <rows update_ui='null' >

  <tr>
    <td>941</td>
    <td convert_spaces="true"> El Dorado</td>
    <td> <span style="font-weight:bold"> Western </span> </td>
    <td>7.4</td>
    <td>2421</td>
    <td>1966</td>
  </tr>
  ...
</rows>
</response>
</ajax-response>
```

Related Patterns

Virtual Workspace

As explained earlier in the "Solution," Data Grids are usually *Virtual Workspaces* (Chapter 15).

Browser-Side Cache

To improve performance, retain data in a *Browser-Side Cache* (Chapter 13).

Predictive Fetch

To improve performance, consider *Predictive Fetches* (Chapter 13) that preload nearby results and aggregation functions.

Progress Indicator

Longer updates should be accompanied by a *Progress Indicator* (see earlier).

Metaphor

A Data Grid is the natural sequel to the traditional HTML table.

Acknowledgments

Christian Romney (*http://www.xml-blog.com/*) suggested the idea of a sort-and-filter pattern from which this pattern evolved, and also pointed out the Delta Vacations example.

Rich Text Editor

Editor, Formatting, Fonts, Rich, Text, Textarea, Toolbar, Write, WordProcessor, WYSIWYG

FIGURE 14-14. Rich Text Editor

Goal Story

Pam is working on a presentation for the steering committee; style will count here. From the toolbar, she sets the font to Arial, the size to 24 pt, and switches italics on. She then types out the heading, selects it, and moves to the toolbar again to set the color scheme.

Problem

How can users create and maintain rich content?

Forces

- Many Ajax Apps let users create and edit substantial chunks of content.

- Rich content for the Web needs to make the most of HTML and go well beyond a string of plain-text.

- Most users don't know HTML; even "easy" markup substitutes for HTML are complicated and inconsistent.

Solution

Incorporate a Rich Text Editor widget with easy formatting and WYSIWYG* display. Typically, the widget looks like a mini word processor: a toolbar on top with a rich editing area underneath. The editing area is usually a div rather than a textarea, meaning that any HTML content is possible.

Typical features include:

- Flexible font styles, sizes, boldfacing, etc.

- Flexible color schemes

- Embedded images

- Embedded tables

- Bullet-point and numeric lists

- Indenting and flexible text alignment

All of these features are usually accessible by the toolbar, as well as via keyboard shortcuts. It would also be possible to make them available from drop-down menus, though the main examples to date have avoided doing so. In addition, the toolbar sometimes offers other operations too:

- Undo, Redo

- Cut, Paste, Copy

- Save (*Explicit Submission* [Chapter 10])

- Spellcheck

Rich Text Editors are a great tool for nontechnical users, but as with GUI word processors, they can slow down power users. If power users are important to you, a few guidelines apply:

---

* "What You See Is What You Get" (WYSIWYG) interfaces are a staple of windows-based apps, where the editing interface is essentially the same as the output (i.e., a printout or a presentation).

- Offer an alternative "WYSIWYN" (What You See Is What You *Need*) interface, where the user can enter raw HTML and/or some other text-based markup such as Markdown (*http://daringfireball.net/projects/markdown/*).

- Offer keyboard shortcuts and advertise them well, e.g., as tooltip *Popups* (Chapter 15) on the corresponding toolbar icons.

- Offer personalized toolbars and keyboard bindings.

The major browsers do have some support for rich text editing. Firefox has Midas (*http:// kb.mozillazine.org/Firefox_:_Midas*), an embedded text editor, and IE (*http://msdn.microsoft. com/workshop/author/dhtml/reference/properties/contenteditable.asp*) has a similar editor available on items flagged as contentEditable. However, neither mechanism is portable, and with both versions, you're stuck with whatever version the user's browser has. For that reason, the best solution right now is probably the *Cross-Browser Component* (Chapter 12) libraries mentioned in the following "Real-World Examples."

Real-World Examples

FCKEditor library

Frederico Caldeira Knabben's FCKEditor (*http://www.fckeditor.net/*) is a feature-rich, open source *Cross-Browser Component* you can pull into your own projects (Figure 14-15). It also has some server-side integration and web remoting support.

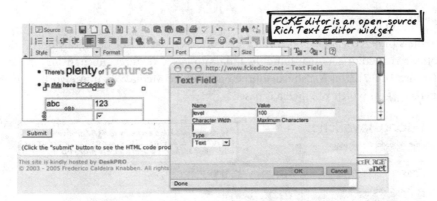

FIGURE 14-15. FCKEditor

Jotspot, Dojo Rich Text Editor

Jotspot is a wiki host that allows editing in three formats: WYSIWYG, markup, or XML (i.e., the underlying XHTML). The WYSIWYG supports all the Rich Text Editor capabilities mentioned in the previous Solution, and is based on the open source Dojo Rich Text Editor component (*http://dojotoolkit.org/docs/rich_text.html*). (See Figure 14-16.) In the simplest case, using the component is as simple as declaring a div with the right class.

```
<div class="dojo-Editor"> Initial
        content </div>
```

FIGURE 14-16. Jotspot Dojo Editor

Writely

Writely (*http://writely.com*) promotes itself as "The Web Word Processor." It edits content using a mechanism similar to that used by Jotspot. One nice feature is a spell-check.

Wikipedia

Wikipedia's (*http://Wikipedia.org*) editing interface is characteristic of slightly older editors that offer a rich editing toolbar but only a markup-based textarea mechanism for the content (Figure 14-17). This is also true of the open source MediaWiki framework (*http://mediawiki.org*) on which Wikipedia is based.

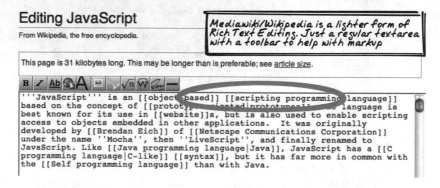

FIGURE 14-17. Wikipedia editor

Rich Text Editor

Kevin Roth's Rich Text Editor (*http://www.kevinroth.com/rte/demo.htm*) is a good demo of the native browser support mentioned in the preceding "Solution" because it provides an editor built on top of whichever browser it's running in.

Code Example: FCKEditor

This example introduces the FCKEditor API and looks at some of the internals. To use FCKEditor in your own project, first create a regular textarea:

```
<textarea id="comments"></textarea>
```

FCKEditor can then replace the text editor with a rich editor:

```
var commentsEditor = new FCKeditor("comments");
commentsEditor.ReplaceTextarea();
```

To track usage, register an initialization handler for the global FCKEditor module, which applies to all editor instances. Here you probably want to set up an event handler that will fire when a user changes an individual editor. See the API documentation (*http://wiki.fckeditor.net/*) for more details and options.

```
function FCKeditor_OnComplete(editor) {
  editor.Events.AttachEvent('OnSelectionChange', onEditorChange);
}
function onEditorChange(editor) {
  // Respond to change.
  // You can get the editor contents with editor.GetXHTML();
}
```

Now the internals. `ReplaceTextarea` will locate the textarea object, hide it, then insert the Rich Text Editor content just above it.

```
FCKeditor.prototype.ReplaceTextarea = function()
   ...
   var oTextarea = document.getElementById( this.InstanceName ) ;
   oTextarea.style.display = 'none' ;
   ...
   this._InsertHtmlBefore( this._GetIFrameHtml(), oTextarea ) ;
```

`_GetIFrameHtml()` outputs the HTML for the editor IFrame, and its source is `fckeditor.html`. The editor is structured as a three-row table. The top row is the toolbar (and some other controls for expanding and collapsing it); the second row is the WYWIWYG editing area, backed by an `IFrame`; the third row shows the HTML source, which is usually invisible.

```
<table height="100%" width="100%" cellpadding="0" cellspacing="0"
      border="0" style="TABLE-LAYOUT: fixed">
  <tr>
    ...
    <td id="eToolbar" class="TB_ToolbarSet" unselectable="on"></td>
    ...
  </tr>
  <tr id="eWysiwyg">
    <td id="eWysiwygCell" height="100%" valign="top">
```

```
            <iframe id="eEditorArea" name="eEditorArea" height="100%" width="100%"
                    frameborder="no" src="fckblank.html"></iframe>
        </td>
    </tr>
    <tr id="eSource" style="DISPLAY: none">
      <td class="Source" height="100%" valign="top">
        <textarea id="eSourceField" dir="ltr" style="WIDTH: 100%; HEIGHT: 100%">
            </textarea>
      </td>
    </tr>
  </table>
```

The toolbar consists of toolbar buttons linked to commands. The commands follow the
Command pattern (Gamma et al., 1995)—they are objects encapsulating a command and
can be launched from the toolbar or with a keyboard shortcut. The command is identified
in each toolbar button declaration as well as several display properties.

```
var FCKToolbarButton = function (commandName,

  label, tooltip, style, sourceView, contextSensitive)
```

For example, here's the toolbar button to paste plain-text:

```
oItem = new FCKToolbarButton('PasteText',

  FCKLang.PasteText, null, null, false, true);
```

The PasteText command in the preceding example is ultimately tied to a Command object that
will launch a Paste Text dialog.

```
FCK.PasteAsPlainText=function( ) {
    FCKDialog.OpenDialog('FCKDialog_Paste',FCKLang.PasteAsText,
    'dialog/fck_paste.html',400,330,'PlainText'); }
```

Manipulations of the WYSIWYG editor content involve getting hold of the content element and simply altering its HTML. In the case of the Paste operation, it appends the new
HTML, sHtml, at the right place.

```
var oEditor = window.parent.InnerDialogLoaded( ) ;
...
oEditor.FCK.InsertHtml(sHtml) ;
```

Related Patterns

Virtual Workspace

For editing large chunks of text, you might want to experiment with a *Virtual Workspace*
(Chapter 15).

Progress Indicator

Provide a *Progress Indicator* (see earlier) while saving text. Indeed, many text editors take a
while to start up as well, partly due to scripting overhead and partly due to toolbar images.
Thus, a Progress Indicator might help during loading as well.

Status Area

Create a *Status Area* (Chapter 15) to help the user monitor details such as word count and cursor position, if these aren't already provided by the Rich Text Editor widget. You'll need to hook into the widget's event model to keep the status up-to-date.

Metaphor

A Rich Text Editor is like an embedded GUI word processor.

Suggestion

Auto-Complete, Fill, Intelligent, Populate, Predict, Suggest, Wizard

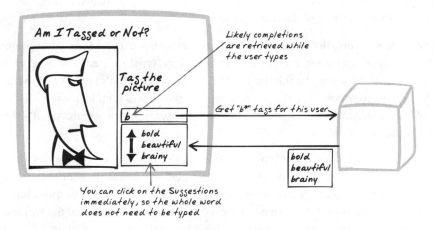

FIGURE 14-18. Suggestion

Goal Story

Doc is typing out an electronic prescription. He intends to prescribe "Vancomycin 65 mg," but as soon as he types in "V", the system has already detected a handful of likely choices, based on the patient's history and Doc's prescription style. Doc selects "Vancomycin 65 mg" from the list and proceeds to the next field.

Problem

How can you improve throughput?

Forces

- Free text remains the most powerful way for humans to communicate with computers. The trend seems to be toward more typing than ever before due to instant messaging, blogging, and email. Even search engines are undergoing a transformation to become general-purpose, as described in *Live Command-Line* later in this chapter.

- When presented with a free text area, people don't always know what they're meant to type in.

- Though many users are now quick on the keyboard, there are still many users for whom the Web is a click-mostly experience.

- Typing speed remains a bottleneck even for fast typists, most of whom think faster than they can type.

- People make mistakes when they type.

Solution

Suggest words or phrases that are likely to complete what the user is typing. The user can then select the Suggestion and avoid typing it in full. The results usually come from an *XMLHttpRequest Call* (Chapter 6)—the partial input is uploaded and the server responds with a collection of likely matches.

Suggestion has its roots in "combo boxes"—fields on traditional GUI forms that combine a text input with a drop-down list. The elements are kept synchronized. The user is free to type any text, and the current selection in the list will track what's been typed so far. The user is also free to choose an element from the list, which will then be posted back to the text field. In some cases, the list constrains what the user types; in other cases, it's there to provide Suggestions only.

It's the latter style that has become popular in recent years—free text entry, with some Suggestions for completion at any time. Auto-completion became popular with Internet Explorer 5, which auto-completed fields based on user history. Most users are comfortable with the approach, as all the modern browsers offer a similar feature, and the technique is also popular in mobile phone text messaging and East Asian text entry.

In an Ajaxian context, Google set the standard with its introduction of Google Suggest (*http://www.google.com/webhp?complete=1*), which suggests the most popular terms to complete the user's search query. Its release surprised many, as Google had managed to completely replicate conventional combo-box behavior, but this time, the terms were dynamically fetched from the server instead of being present when the form was created.

The mechanics of a Suggestion usually work like this:

- A standard `input` field is used. At the same time, an initially invisible `div` element is created to contain the Suggestions as they appear. The `input` field needs an event handler to monitor the text it contains so as to ensure that the list always highlights whichever Suggestion matches.

- Instead of requesting a Suggestion upon each keypress, *Submission Throttling* is usually adopted. Thus, every 100 milliseconds or so, the browser checks whether anything has changed since the last request. If so, the server is passed the partial query as a GET-based *XMLHttpRequest Call*.

- The server then uses some algorithm to produce an ordered list of Suggestions.

- Back in the browser, the callback function picks up the Suggestions and does some *Display Morphing* (Chapter 5) to show them to the user in a format that allows them to be selected. Each entry will have an event handler, so that if the entry is clicked, the input field will be altered.

A combo-box is not the only way to render results, but it has the dual virtues of efficiency and familiarity. "Code Example: Kayak," later in this section, covers Kayak's implementation.

You might think the main benefit of a Suggestion is to cut down on typing, but that's not the case. If anything, it's often slower to enter a single word using Suggestion, as it's a distraction and probably requires some mousing. The main benefit is to offer a constrained set of choices—when there are more choices than would fit in a standard option list, but still a fixed set. For Google Suggest, it's a list of choices that are considered probable based on search history. In tagging web sites, it's a list of tag names that have been used in the past. In travel web sites, it's a list of airports you can include on your ticket.

Decisions

What algorithm will be used to produce the Suggestions?

Ultimately, the Suggestion algorithm needs to find the most likely completions.

A few rules of thumb:

- In general, historical data is the best predictor. Log what users commonly search for and use that as a basis for Suggestions. So when the user types "A," suggest the most frequent responses beginning with "A."

- Personalize. Instead of completing "A" with the most common "A"-query *all* users have entered, return the most common "A"-queries for *this* user. The only problem here is lack of data, so consider a collaborative filtering algorithm to provide Suggestions based on similar users.

- Recent history is a more pertinent guide, whether you're personalizing the results or not. In some cases, it makes sense to provide only recent queries. In other cases, consider weighting recent results more heavily, but taking into account older queries as well.

- In some cases, it might make more sense for the browser to provide *Guesstimates* (Chapter 13) rather than real results from the server in real-time. This information might be based on what's in a *Browser-Side Cache* (Chapter 13) and, potentially, on a few algorithms to help the browser decide what's relevant.

How will the Suggestions be ordered?

Typical ordering algorithms include:

- Estimated likelihood, e.g., historical frequency.

- How recently the query was last used.

- Alphabetical or numerical order.

- Application-specific ordering. A currency list often begins with the U.S. Dollar, for instance.

However you order your Suggestions, the first item is particularly important because it can be designed to enable the user to select the first element without explicitly choosing it from the list. For example, Google's combo-box implementation automatically inserts the first element in the text field, though with a text selection over the completion text so the user can easily override it.

How many Suggestions will be shown?

Deciding how many Suggestions to show is a balancing act. You want to show enough Suggestions to be useful, but not so many that the good ones get lost in the crowd. Space is limited as well, even if you use a pop-up list.

It's generally useful if your Suggestion algorithm not only ranks Suggestions, but also makes a relevance estimate. Then, you can ensure Suggestions are shown only if they are particularly useful. Sometimes it isn't really worth it to show any Suggestions.

What auxiliary information will be present with each Suggestion?

The core part of the Suggestion is always a word or phrase that completes what the user is typing. You can augment each Suggestion with supportive information. Google Suggest, for example, shows how many results each completion has. It would even be possible to present the Suggestions in a table, with several columns of background information per completion. Taken to an extreme, the Suggestion resembles a *Live Search* (see later in this chapter).

Real-World Examples

Kayak

Kayak (*http://kayak.com*) is a travel search engine that suggests airports as you type in a location (Figure 14-19). The Suggestions appear in a combo-box format similar to Google Suggest.

Google Suggest

Google Suggest (*http://www.google.com/webhp?complete=1*) was probably the first public usage of Suggestion and remains an excellent example. Results are shown in a combo-box style. The combo-box appearance is achieved with a custom control. A div is placed just

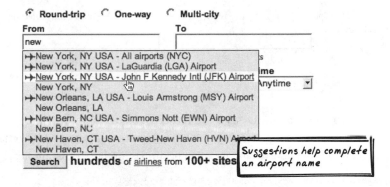

Search with us, book with them.™

Flights | Hotels | Cars | Deals | Buzz

FIGURE 14-19. Kayak airport Suggestions

under the text input, with a Suggestion on each row, and the zIndex property is used to make the div appear "in front of" the usual page content.

Delicious, Amazon

Delicious (*http://del.icio.us*) and Amazon (*http://amazon.com*) both offer Suggestions to help complete tags (Figure 14-20). As you type a tag, several Suggestions appear immediately and are populated below the field. You can click on a Suggestion to complete the term.

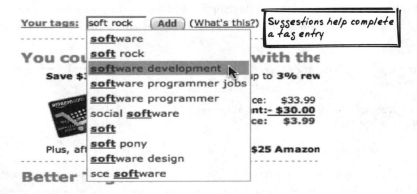

FIGURE 14-20. Amazon tag Suggestions

Code Example: Kayak

Kayak *(http://kayak.com)* is a slick, Ajaxian interface with a handy Suggestion feature for source and destination airports. The list of Suggestions appears below the input field, is referred to in the code as a smartBox, and exists as long as the input field has focus.

Whenever a key is pressed, the smartBox is aborted—which stops any pending request—and a new request is initiated. A check is made to ensure that the text entry actually contains something, otherwise the smartBox is closed:

```
function _typer(input)
   {
        if ((_input != null ) && _input.value.length > 0) {abortSmartBox();_
runSearch(input);


   }
        else {_setValue(-1);closeSmartBox();}
      }
```

_runSearch() kicks off a call to the server to receive the Suggestion list. The query goes to *http://www.kayak.com/m/smarty.jsp?where=LOCATION*. The result is some XML containing the airport names and codes and what appears to be an ID number, for example:

```
<i>28501</i><m>L</m><d>London, United Kingdom</d><a>LON</a>
```

The callback function accumulates an HTML string to be inserted into the smartbox. A loop runs over each result, appending a div element to the HTML:

```
var html = ""; var list = "";
for (var j = 0; j < ii.length; j++) {
    var id=client.getTagText(results[0], "i", j);
    var str=client.getTagText(results[0], "d", j);
    var match=client.getTagText(results[0], "m", j);
    ...
    list += _divB + _spanB + icon + str + _spanE + _divE;cnt++;
}
```

Also of interest is the optional icon, which appears beside the airport name, as shown in the preceding code. Depending on the resulting XML, the icon is chosen from one of two images:

```
var _iconAir = "<img style='vertical-align: middle' src='/images/airport_icon.gif'
border=
'0'>";
var _iconLoc = "<img style='vertical-align: middle; visibility: hidden' src=
'/images/place_icon.gif' border='0'>";
...
icon = (match == "L") ? _iconLoc : _iconAir;
```

An event handler monitors key presses. As the user moves up and down, the airport text is changed according to the selection, and the selection is incremented or decremented:

```
case UP:
    _cursel--;if (_cursel<0){_cursel=0;}selChoice(_cursel);
...
case DOWN:
    _cursel++;if (_cursel>=_ids.length){_cursel=_ids.length-1;}selChoice(_cursel);
```

Finally, the value is set when the user clicks tab or enter. In the former case, focus will also proceed to the next field:

```
        case ENTER:
            if (_ids.length>0){
                _setValue(_cursel);
                closeSmartBox( );
            }
        ...
        case TAB:
            if (_cursel>=0&&_cursel<_ids.length){_setValue(_cursel);}
```

Alternatives

Selector

In some cases, a plain old HTML selection input will suffice. Most modern browsers support navigation through the drop-down with a keyboard, so it's an easy, viable alternative if the range of inputs is constrained.

Related Patterns

Browser-Side Cache

A *Browser-Side Cache* (Chapter 13) is a practical way to speed up the search.

Guesstimate

Sometimes the browser may be smart enough to derive Suggestions without resorting to the server. This is an application of *Guesstimate* (Chapter 13).

Predictive Fetch

Suggestion is similar to *Predictive Fetch* (Chapter 13). Predictive Fetch queries the server in anticipation of a future user action, whereas Suggestion queries the server to help the user complete the current action. In theory, you could actually combine the two patterns—perform a Predictive Fetch to pull down some Suggestions that might be needed in the future. On an intranet, for instance, it might be practical to continuously make 26 parallel queries in anticipation of the user, who might type any letter of the alphabet.

Submission Throttling

To cut down on queries, don't issue an *XMLHttpRequest Call* upon every keypress. Instead, apply *Submission Throttling* (Chapter 10) to cap calls to a maximum frequency.

Highlight

When one of the Suggestions in the list matches the free text input, it's usually a good idea to *Highlight* (Chapter 16) it.

Lazy Registration

Lazy Registration (Chapter 17) involves the accumulation of profile information, and profiles can be used to generate personalized Suggestions. You can also retain user preferences regarding the appearance and timing of Suggestion lists.

Live Search

When full result details are provided, Suggestion resembles a *Live Search* (see the next pattern). However, the design goals are different and this should usually be reflected in the user interface. A Suggestion is intended to complete a word or phrase; a Live Search is intended to locate or report on an item being searched.

Want to Know More?

- "How Search Engines Rank Web Pages" by Danny Sullivan (*http://searchenginewatch. com/webmasters/article.php/2167961*)

- "Google Suggest Dissected" by Chris Justus (*http://serversideguy.blogspot.com/2004/12/ google-suggest-dissected.html*)

Acknowledgments

Chris Justus's thorough analysis of Google Suggest (*http://serversideguy.blogspot.com/2004/ 12/google-suggest-dissected.html*) was very helpful in explaining the magic behind Google's Suggestion implementation.

Live Search

Feedback, Immediate, Live, Real-Time, Search

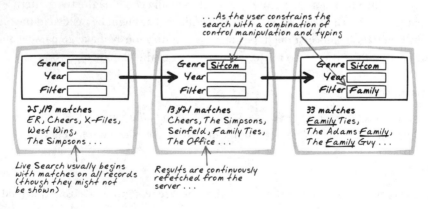

FIGURE 14-21. Live Search

Goal Story

Browsing a trade magazine, Reta has just spotted the "Curiously Costly" line of shoes and declared them a "must-have" for the upcoming season. She heads over to her favorite wholesaler's web site and sees an empty search form with an assortment of products underneath it and the message, "50,000+ items." First, she selects "shoes" from a drop-down and watches as the products below morph into a collection of shoes; the message is now "8,000+ shoes." Then, she begins typing. As she types "C," she now sees all 500 shoes beginning with "C." This continues until the search field contains "Curio," at which point only three items remain. One of those is "Curiously Costly," which is what Reta clicks on to successfully conclude the search.

Problem

How can users quickly search for an item?

Forces

- Ajax Apps often require a search capability. Users search for business objects, other users, web sites, and more.

- Sometimes the user is searching for a needle in a very large haystack. In the case of search engines, a haystack of over a billion items.

- To help deal with the complexity, users should be free to experiment.

Solution

As the user constructs and refines his search query, continuously show all valid results. The search query is a combination of controls that lets the user narrow down the collection of items. It may be a straightforward text field, or a complex arrangement of *Sliders* (see earlier in this chapter), radiobuttons, and other controls. The results appear in a separate region and are continuously synchronized with the query that's been specified. The search concludes when a result is chosen.

There are several benefits to using Live Search instead of the conventional style:

- Browsing and searching can be combined.

- Searching proceeds more quickly because no explicit submission is required. The results are ready almost immediately, so the user can experiment more easily.

- There's no page reload, so the interaction feels smoother; results are updated, but the input query is completely unaffected.

The most common form of Live Search right now closely mirrors traditional searching. The user types into a free-text search field, and results are frequently updated as the user types. So, searching for "cataclysmic," the user will see results for "c," "ca," and so on. (With *Submission Throttling* (Chapter 10) in place, the sequence might skip a bit, so a fast typist would see results "c," "cata," etc.)

Search and browse have often been considered mutually exclusive on the Web, which is unfortunate because both have their benefits. Search is good for finding something you already know about, while browse is good for exploring all of the items and stumbling across things you didn't know about. Live Search provides a way to combine the two. Some controls—such as selectors, radiobuttons, and *Sliders*—let the user choose an item from a small collection. If the search form can change dynamically (see *Live Form* later in this chapter), you can support browsing through a hierarchical structure.

Imagine how a web site search engine might achieve this. The initial control is just an empty text box and a selector with ten categories—Arts, Tech, News, and so on (Figure 14-22). The user chooses News on the selector and a new selector appears— World, Business, Science, etc. At any point, the user can change any selector. All the while, the results below are updating to show a sampling of results in the most specific category that's been specified. Furthermore, the text input is there all along, acting as an additional filter. So if you search at the top level, the interface degenerates into a standard live text search. But if you search while the selectors are set to a category, only the matching results from that category will be shown.

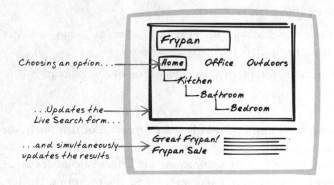

FIGURE 14-22. Live Search with Live Form

Live Search makes use of event handlers on the input controls, which listen for user activity and update the results. A typical sequence works like this:

1. The user changes a control; e.g., types a new character or clicks a radio button.

2. The entire input query—all of the input fields' settings—is transmitted to the server in an *XMLHttpRequest Call*.

3. The server decides which—if any—results should be shown and returns the list.

4. The browser replaces the list of results with this new list.

In the preceding scenario, the *XMLHttpRequest Call* need not occur in direct response to the user input. Often, *Submission Throttling* is used to delay the response.

A weaker form of Live Search doesn't show the actual results, but hints at them, e.g., indicating how many results and what type of results. The benefits to this are that there are less processing, improved caching opportunities (because there's much less to store), and no space required for results while the search is occurring.

Live Search is not always desirable. Showing intermediate results, which happens when the search involves typing, can be distracting (*http://looksgoodworkswell.blogspot.com/2005/12/distracting-or-narrowing-looking.html*) and is not very useful anyway. If the user is searching for "cataclysmic," does she really care about the results for "cat"? An alternative might be to require an *Explicit Submission* (Chapter 10) but apply *Predictive Fetch* (Chapter 13) to keep pulling down results according to the user's current input. That way, the results will be ready as soon as the user clicks on the search button.

Decisions

How will you interpret incomplete text?

The user begins searching for "cataclysmic." Having typed as far as "cat," what will you show?

- Matches for "cat," "catalogue," "cataclysmic," and anything else *beginning* with "cat"?
- Matches for "tomcat," "delicate," scatter," and anything else *containing* cat.
- Just matches for "cat".
- A combination, with a few of each.

In the first two preceding options, "cat" is implicitly transformed to "cat*" and "*cat*", where "*" represents any character. For most searches, the "cat*" style is preferable because the user knows what she is looking for—a user searching for "cataclysmic" has no need to search for "*aclys*"—so inserting a wildcard at both ends merely clutters the interface and increases search cost.

Whether to use a wildcard at all is another matter. That is, should "cat" match just "cat," or also "cataclysmic"? There are benefits on both sides, which is why combining them is worth considering. It also comes down to how many results you generally expect. If there's only one or two results for "cat," then you might want to anticipate further typing. If there's a heap of results for "cat" alone, then there are probably enough to show that you don't need to anticipate any further characters.

How verbose will the results be?

As with regular search, you need to decide how much each candidate result will show. Because the results are sent frequently, you might need to limit results to just a basic summary. An interesting variation on this would be to use *Multi-Stage Download*—get a quick summary immediately, then a few seconds later, if the user is inactive, refine the results with a second query.

What will happen when there are too many results?

You can usually show only a fraction of the results at once—typically, up to 50 or 100 results and probably much less than that if bandwidth and server processing are critical constraints. However, there could be thousands of results. In the worst case, before the user has specified anything, there are no constraints and every item is a candidate. So you'll need to decide what happens when there are too many results to show.

One option is not to show any results at all, on the basis that the user should refine his search. This is not always the best idea, because you will have missed an opportunity to provide a little feedback and help the user explore. So you often want a way to provide a reduced list of matches. The search algorithm might have a way to prioritize results, perhaps based on popularity or the user's personal history.

You could also consider using a *Virtual Workspace* (Chapter 15) to give the appearance of having loaded all results and thus allow the user to navigate through them. The OpenRico Yahoo! Search Demo (*http://openrico.org/yahooSearch.page*) provides search results in this way. It's not a Live Search, but you could easily incorporate a Live Search into the approach.

A further possibility would be to place the results "on rotation"—that is, run a *Periodic Refresh* (Chapter 10) to show an ever-changing collection of results. I haven't seen this in an Ajax Live Search, but a slideshow-type navigation—rapidly rotating images—has been used in other domains to reduce information overload (for example, some TVs support channel surfing with a collage of rapidly changing channels).

Real-World Examples

Delta Vacations

Delta Vacations has a hotel booking facility. After identifying a destination on the destination page (*http://www.deltavacations.com/destinations.aspx*), you can perform a Live Search for a hotel. For example, if you type "dis" in the Los Angeles page (*http://www.deltavacations.com/destination.aspx?code=LOSANGELES*), you'll promptly see all of the Disney hotels appear (Figure 14-23). You can also change the sort order dynamically.

ListSomething.com

ListSomething.com offers Live Search for classified ads (Figure 14-24).

Amazon Diamond Search

Amazon's Diamond Search (*http://www.amazon.com/gp/gsl/search/finder/102-1689279-4344148?productGroupID=loose%5fdiamonds*) is a unique search interface, incorporating several *Sliders* (see earlier in this chapter) to set such variables as shape, price, and number of carats (see Figure 14-5). Each time you alter a Slider, a message appears beside it showing the total number of results for the current search. Unfortunately, this is a weak variant of Live Search in which the results themselves are not shown until an *Explicit Submission* (Chapter 10) takes place.

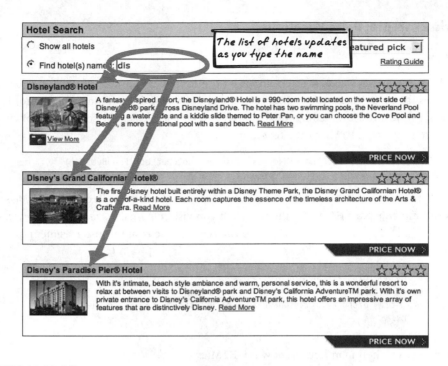

FIGURE 14-23. Delta

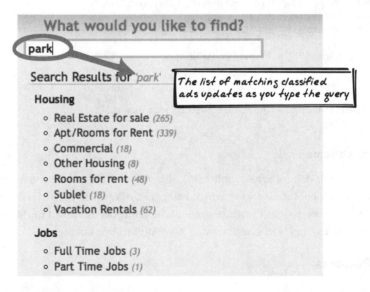

FIGURE 14-24. ListSomething.com

Skype

Skype's Skype-In service (*http://skype.com*) lets you choose a real-world phone number that will redirect to your Skype account. As you type some digits, you'll see Skype's available numbers.

Code Example: Delta Vacations

Delta Vacations

The Delta Vacations search registers an updateHotelList event handler on each control that manages the Live Search: the text input, a radiobutton pair determining whether to show all hotels or just those matching the text input, and a selector for the sort order. For example, here's the static HTML or the text input:

```
<input type="text" id="HotelNameBox" onfocus="setChecked('FindByName')"
onkeyup="updateHotelList('hdnDestCode', 'HotelNameBox', 'SortOptions');" />
```

updateHotelList( ) will then call the server. In this case, the server offers an *HTML Message* that outputs the exact HTML for the results. If you visit *http://www.deltavacations.com/ajax. aspx?d=LOSANGELES&n=dis&s=rating*, you can see that the result is just a segment of HTML:

```
<div id="H0" class="StandardHotel">
  <h2 class="FourStar">
    <a href="property.aspx?code=LAX0001&&dest=LOSANGELES">Disneyland Hotel</a>
    </h2>
    ...
```

The results are then morphed to show the HTML:

```
var container = document.getElementById('HotelListView');
if (null == container) return;
if (http.responseText)
{
  container.innerHTML = http.responseText;
}
else
{
  container.innerHTML = "No hotels matched your search.";
}
```

Assistive Search demo

The Assistive Search demo (*http://ajaxify.com/run/assistiveSearch*) can be considered a weak form of Live Search because it shows which categories of results will be retrieved but not the results themselves. It does illustrate some of the concepts discussed in this section and is analyzed in the examples in *Live Command-Line*, later in this chapter.

Related Patterns

Progress Indicator

While waiting for results to load after a user inputs data, you might choose to show a *Progress Indicator* (see earlier). Keep it fairly subtle, though, as it will appear and disappear frequently.

Data Grid

Live Search results can be shown in a *Data Grid* (see earlier).

Virtual Workspace

Early in the Live Search, there are often more results than you can show at once. Consider presenting them in a *Virtual Workspace* (Chapter 15) to let the user explore all the results.

One-Second Spotlight

One-Second Spotlight (Chapter 16) can be used to transition from older to newer results.

Submission Throttling

Instead of submitting upon each keypress, Live Searches often submit the input query at intervals—a form of *Submission Throttling* (Chapter 10) . In many cases, it makes sense to submit only after an idle period so that the search term is exactly what the user is looking for rather than an incomplete version.

Unique URLs

Different search queries should generally have *Unique URLs* (Chapter 17) associated with them.

Predictive Fetch

You can look at Live Search as a kind of *Predictive Fetch* (Chapter 13) in which the prefetched results are made visible.

Suggestion

Suggestion is similar to Live Search in that both involve performing a search to synchronize the display against an incomplete input. However, they differ in the following ways:

- Suggestion is not just about search—you can use it to complete words as a user types. The backend algorithm involves search but searching isn't the user's goal.

- Even in the context of search, Suggestion aims to complete the query, whereas Live Search aims to fill the results. If the search says "ab," a Suggestion will give you potentially useful terms—e.g., "abdominals," "absolutely"—while a Live Search will give you all items matching "ab" or "ab…."

Live Command-Line

Assistive, CLI, Command-Line, Grammar, Supportive

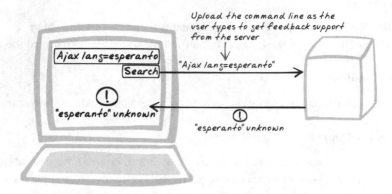

FIGURE 14-25. Live Command-Line

Goal Story

Frank is using an advanced query tool to run a report on current output. He begins entering an SQL-like query: "list all." At this point, a suggestion list appears with all the things that can be listed, and he chooses "products." Continuing on, the query now reads "list all products where" and a new list appears: "creationTime," "quality," and so on. He chooses "creationTime," and. then enters the rest manually, preferring to ignore further suggestions. The query ends up as "list all products where creationTime is today and quality is faulty." There's a tick mark next to the query to indicate that it's valid.

Problem

How can a command-line interface be supported?

Forces

- Users can only say so much with point-and-click interfaces. The command line is more expressive and remains the tool of choice for expert users.

- URLs and search fields are becoming general-purpose command-lines (*http://www. codinghorror.com/blog/archives/000296.html*).

Solution

In command-line interfaces, monitor the command being composed and dynamically modify the interface to support the interaction. The interface changes according to data, business logic, and application logic. When the command line is to be executed on the server, as is often the case, the browser usually delegates to the server the task of evaluating the partial command.

The command line is the quintessential expert interface and it's worth bearing in mind that most users are "perpetual intermediates" (*http://www.codinghorror.com/blog/archives/ 000098.html*). That is, they learn enough to get by and generally learn new things only as and when required. So, while a powerful command line may be a superior choice in the long run, most users simply don't have the time to spend learning it in advance.

Traditional command lines present a problem because they offer the user a blank slate. Everything the user types must be based on prior, upfront, learning, and the only feedback occurs after the command line has been executed. That's not only inefficient for learning, but downright dangerous for sufficiently powerful commands. The model is: human enters command, computer executes command.

The solution is to be more interactive: with a smarter, more proactive command line, the construction of a command—its quick evolution from nothingness to an executable string—becomes something of a human/computer collaboration. For example, you can:

- Indicate whether the command is valid before submitting it. If it's not valid, prevent it from executing and inform the user what's wrong and how it can be rectified.

- Offer to fix invalid commands.

- Offer *Suggestions* to help complete part of the command.

- Help the user predict what will happen when the command is executed. For a query, this means hinting at the result—e.g., estimating number of matches (see *Guesstimate* [Chapter 13]).

- Provide graphical widgets to help the user construct the command. For example, build up a mathematical expression using a calculator-like interface to introduce numbers and functions. The query is still represented as plain-text, but the text doesn't need to be entered by hand.

- Provide graphical widgets to help the user refactor the command. For example, you could provide a "delete this" button next to each condition in a query.

- Provide visualization tools to render the query in other formats. For example, certain numerical queries might be visualized graphically.

The benefits apply to novices and experts alike. In supporting novices, the technique has sometimes been referred to as a "training wheels" approach. Like training wheels on a bike, you get a feel for the more powerful interface while still being productive.

Often, the command goes to the server, so it usually makes sense for the server to advise the use regarding partial commands. Basically, the procedure goes like this:

1. *Submission Throttling* (Chapter 10) periodically uploads the partial command string as an *XMLHttpRequest Call.*

2. The server then processes the command and returns supporting information.

3. The browser updates the user interface accordingly.

As an Ajax feature, this pattern is largely speculative: I'm not aware of any production-level Ajax Apps, but the command-line interface is growing at the same time as Ajax; it's inevitable that these things will collide, and as the discussion here suggests, there are plenty of synergies. One source of inspiration here is the evolution of IDEs over the past five years, particularly in the Java space. Environments like Eclipse (*http://eclipse.org*) and IntelliJ Idea (*http://www.jetbrains.com/idea/*) internally represent source files as data structures, leading to features such as ongoing error detection, offers to fix errors, suggestions, powerful refactorings, and alternative displays. All of this happens without the user ever having to compile the source code. As another source of inspiration, there was a recent experiment on training wheels for the command line (*http://www.cs.utep.edu/nigel/papers/HCII2005.pdf*). Students learned about the Unix command line from either a book or a GUI "training wheels" interface, similar to a Live Command-Line. The training wheels interface was found to be more productive and a more pleasant experience, too.

Decisions

Where will the partial command be analyzed—browser or server?

It's possible to perform some kinds of analysis in the browser—for example, the browser can check the query against a constant regular expression. So should you try to support analysis in the browser or delegate it to the server?

There are several advantages to analyzing the command server side:

- The analysis can take into account server-side data, external services, and server-side hardware resources.

- In most cases, the command will ultimately be processed by the server, so this allows related logic to be kept in the same place.

- Since the command is just a text string, it's in a convenient form for uploading and server-side processing. Also, it's easier to keep earlier results in a *Browser-Side Cache* because the command constitutes a key for the cache.

The downsides are:

- There is an extra load on the server.

- Extra bandwidth is required to download richer responses.

- There is extra lag time between the user's input typing and the browser's response.

How much information will the server provide?

Producing more information for partial commands will consume more server resources. The information will also take a bit longer to download. You'll need to trade off resources in favor of supportive information. For example:

- In supporting validation, you can often rule out many errors with a simple regular expression. But more complex errors relating to the existence of business objects, for example, will get past that filter. Should you try to catch those too? Doing so would improve usability at the expense of resources.

- In hinting at the command's result, there's a spectrum of precision. For a query, you can say "there might be results," "there are results," or "there are 4123 results." In an extreme case, you can offer a *Live Search* (earlier in this chapter) and actually show the results.

Real-World Examples

I'm not aware of an all-encompassing Live Command-Line demo. However, the examples in *Live Search* and *Suggestion* (earlier in this chapter) are special cases of Live Command-Lines. There are also some JavaScript terminal emulators around, though they don't provide Live Command-Lines—see Web Shell (*http://a-i-studio.com/cmd/*) and JS/UNIX Unix Shell (*http://www.masswerk.at/jsuix/jsuix_support/*). Also, see the Try Ruby! tutorial (*http://tryruby.hobix.com/*) for an impressive web interface to the interactive Ruby programming environment.

YubNub

YubNub (*http://yubnub.org*) isn't Ajaxian, but it is noteworthy as the first explicit exploration of the "search as command line" meme. Yubnub lets users submit commands, which arc then mapped into external queries. For example, if you type in "sum 10 20" (*http://yubnub.org/parser/parse?command=sum+10+20*), you get the sum of 10 and 20; if you type in "ajax form" (*http://yubnub.org/parser/parse?command=ajax+form*, you get search results from ajaxpatterns.org for "form."

Code Example: AjaxPatterns Assistive Search Demo

The Assistive Search Demo (*http://ajaxify.com/run/assistiveSearch*) was inspired by services such as Google Search, which are trending toward a general-purpose command line. It aims to illustrate the "training wheels" style of command-line support.

The Assitive Search Demo has a typical search engine form—a free-range text input with a Submit button—in addition to several images, one for each category that can be searched. Thus, the user is alerted to the capabilities of the search. As the user types, the categories highlight and unhighlight to help predict what kind of results will be returned (Figure 14-26). All of this information comes from the server side; the browser application doesn't know anything about the categories. It calls the server and startup to discover the categories and corresponding images. A timer monitors the command line, continually asking the server which categories it matches. The browser then highlights those categories.

The startup sequence loads the categories and kicks off the command-line monitoring loop. The server is required to have an image for each category. If it says that there's a "phone" category, then there will be a corresponding image at *Images/phone.gif*. The images are all downloaded and placed alongside each other:

```
window.onload = function() {
    initializeCategories();
    requestValidCategoriesLoop();
    ...
}
```

donut homer scandal | Search

Try: *"donut homer scandal"*, *"555-10*2"*

FIGURE 14-26. *Assistive Search Demo*

```
}

function initializeCategories() {
  ajaxCaller.getPlainText("categories.php?queryType=getAllCategoriesCSV",
                          onAllCategoriesResponse);
}

function onAllCategoriesResponse(text, callingContext) {
    allCategoryNames = text.split(",");
    var categoriesFragment = document.createDocumentFragment();
    for (i=0; i<allCategoryNames.length; i++) {
      var categoryName = allCategoryNames[i];
      var categoryImage = document.createElement("img");
      categoryImage.id = categoryName;
      categoryImage.src = "Images/"+categoryName+".gif";
      categoriesFragment.appendChild(categoryImage);
    }
    document.getElementById("categories").appendChild(categoriesFragment);
}
```

The key to the Live Command-Line is the monitoring loop. Whenever a change occurs, it asks the server to return a list of all matching categories:

```
function requestValidCategoriesLoop() {
    if (query()!=latestServerQuery) {
      var vars = {
        queryType: "getValidCategories",
        queryText: escape(query())
      }
      ajaxCaller.get("categories.php", vars, onValidCategoriesResponse,
                     false, null);
      latestServerQuery = query();
```

```
        }
        setTimeout('requestValidCategoriesLoop();', THROTTLE_PERIOD);
    }
```

The server uses a bunch of heuristics to calculate the valid categories for this query. For instance, it decides if something belongs to the "people" category by looking up a collection of pronouns in the dictionary. A controller will ultimately return the categories as a comma-separated list generated with the following PHP logic:

```
function getValidCategories($queryText) {
    logInfo("Queried for '$queryText'\n");

    $cats = array();
    eregi(".+", $queryText) && array_push($cats, 'web');
    eregi("^[0-9\+][A-Z0-9 \-]*$", $queryText) && array_push($cats, 'phone');
    eregi("^[0-9\.\+\/\* -]+$",$queryText) && array_push($cats, 'calculator');
    isInTheNews($queryText) && array_push($cats, 'news');
    isInWordList($queryText, "./pronouns") && array_push($cats, 'people');
    isInWordList($queryText, "./words") && array_push($cats, 'dictionary');

    return $cats;
}
```

The browser dynamically updates the category images using a CSS class indicating whether they are valid, which it determines by checking whether they were in the list. There's also an event handler to perform searches on specific categories, as long as those categories are valid:

```
function onValidCategoriesResponse(text) {

    var validCategoryNames = text.split(",");

    // Create a data structure to make it faster to determine if a named
    // category is valid. For each valid category, we add an associative array
    // key into the array, with the key being the category name itself.
    validCategoryHash = new Array();
    for (i=0; i<validCategoryNames.length; i++) {
        validCategoryHash[validCategoryNames[i]] = "exists";
    }

    // For all categories, show the category if it's in the valid category map
    for (i=0; i<allCategoryNames.length; i++) {
        var categoryName = allCategoryNames[i];
        var categoryImage = $(categoryName);
        if (validCategoryHash[categoryName]) {
            categoryImage.onclick = onCategoryClicked;
            categoryImage.className="valid";
            categoryImage.title =
                "Category '" + categoryName + "'" +" probably has results";
        } else {
            categoryImage.onclick = null;
            categoryImage.className="invalid";
            categoryImage.title =
                "Category '" + categoryName + "'" + " has no results";
```

```
            }
        }
    }
```

Alternatives

Point-and-click

The command line involves typing, while point-and-click is a simpler interface style that shows available options and lets the user click on one of them.

Drag-And-Drop

Another means of issuing commands is with *Drag-And-Drop* (Chapter 15)—dragging an item into a trash can to delete it.

Related Patterns

Submission Throttling

Instead of processing the command upon each keystroke, use *Submission Throttling* (Chapter 10) to analyze it at frequent intervals.

Status Area

Feedback such as input validation and result prediction is usually shown in a *Status Area* (Chapter 15).

Highlight

Some parts of the command can be highlighted to point out errors, incomplete text, and so on. Also, aspects of the *Status Area* can be highlighted to help with prediction.

Progress Indicator

If it takes more than one second to process the command line, consider showing a *Progress Indicator* (see earlier).

Browser-Side Cache

Introduce a *Browser-Side Cache* (Chapter 13) to retain the server's analysis of partial commands.

Fat Client

Consider creating a *Fat Client* (Chapter 13) that tries to handle as much of the analysis as possible, thus reducing server calls.

Live Search

Live Search (see earlier) is an extreme version of Live Command-Line applied to search, where the command is effectively executed while the user types.

Suggestion

Providing *Suggestions* (see earlier) is one characteristic of Live Command-Lines.

Want To Know More?

- Yubnub (*http://yubnub.org*) lets users search different sites based on a command line. Users are allowed to add new commands; is this "social command line sharing"?

- Russell Beattie: "Search as Practical Artificial Intelligence" *(http://www.russellbeattie.com/notebook/1008310.html)*.

- Jeff Attwood: "Google-Fu: (T)he browser address bar is the new command line" *(http://www.codinghorror.com/blog/archives/000296.html)*.

Live Form

Dynamic, Live, Real-Time, Validation

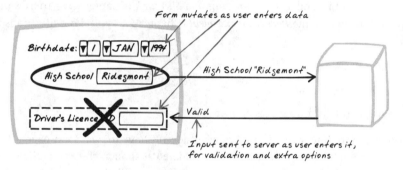

FIGURE 14-27. Live Form

Goal Story

Tracy is using a Live Form to apply for a new online brokerage account. Upon declaring her place of residence, some additional regulation-related questions specific to her region appear. Several asset classes can be traded. She clicks a box to indicate that she wants to trade in bonds, and further questions specifically for that asset class appear. She then clicks on another box, for options. A moment later, a warning appears that new users can trade in either options or bonds, but not both. After further refinement, she successfully submits the form and sees it fade into a welcome message.

Problem

How can the user submit data as quickly as possible?

Forces

- Most data submission tasks require some flexibility. A particular answer for one item may necessitate further questions. Often, this must occur server side, where business logic and data usually reside.

- Most data submission requires validation. This must occur server side to prevent browser-side manipulation of inputs.

- Users get frustrated waiting for data to be validated and continuously refining data upon each explicit submission.

Solution

Validate and modify a form throughout the entire interaction instead of waiting for an explicit submission. Each significant user event results in some browser-side processing, often leading to an *XMLHttpRequest Call*. The form may then be modified as a result.

Modifying the form is similar to responding to a *Microlink* (Chapter 15)—there's usually a server call followed by some *Page Rearrangement* (Chapter 5). Typical modifications include the following:

- New controls appear.

- Controls become disabled.

- Information and error messages appear.

The result is a more interactive form. The user doesn't have to wait for a page reload to find out if a form field is invalid, because it's validated as soon as she enters the value. Due to the asynchronous nature of *XMLHttpRequest Call*, the validation occurs as a background process while the user continues entering data. If there's an error, the user will find out about it while filling out a field further down on the form. As long as errors don't happen too often, this is no great inconvenience.

Validation doesn't always occur at field level though. Sometimes it's the combination of data that's a problem. This can be handled by checking validation rules only when the user has provided input for all related fields. A validation error can result in a general, form-level error message or a message next to one or more of the offending fields.

A Live Form usually ends with an *Explicit Submission* (Chapter 10), allowing the user to confirm that everything's valid. Note that unlike a conventional form, the Explicit Submission does not perform a standard HTTP form submission but posts the contents as an *XMLHttpRequest Call*.

Real-World Examples

WPLicense

WPLicense (*http://yergler.net/projects/wplicense*) is a plugin for the WordPress blogging framework, allowing users to specify a copyright license for their blog content

(Figure 14-28). Refer to *Cross-Domain Proxy* (Chapter 10) for details on the plugin and to the section "Code Example: WPLicense," later in this chapter, for a walkthrough of its *Live Search* implementation.

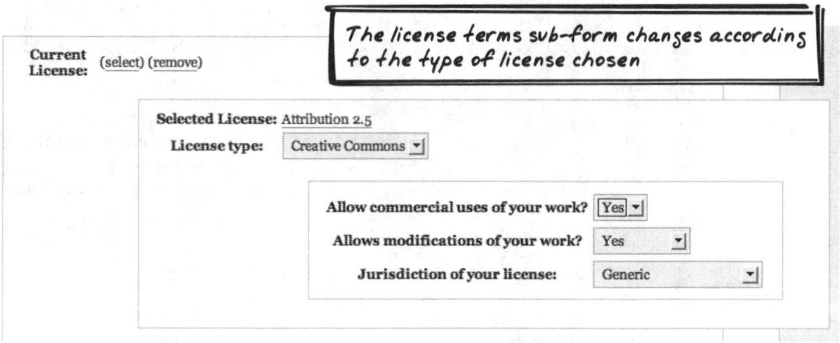

FIGURE 14-28. WPLicense

Betfair

Betfair (*http://betfair.com*) lets the user make a bet using a Live Form—one which changes but doesn't actually interact with the server (Figure 14-29). You can try this even as a nonregistered user by opening up a bet from the *Drilldown* (see earlier in this chapter) menu. There are three columns on the page: the left column shows the current bet topic within the Drilldown, the center column shows odds for all candidates, and the right column shows your stake in the bet. Click on a candidate to make it appear in your stake form, where you can then set the amount for the bet you're placing. As you change your stake, a *Status Area* shows your total liability. Another column shows your profit with respect to each potential outcome. There are also some "meta" controls—e.g., the "Back All" button, which creates an editable row for every candidate.

MoveableType Comment hack

Simian Design (*http://www.simiandesign.com/blog-fu/2005/07/ajax_comments_b.php#comments*) is a blog where you can add comments, Ajax style. As you type into the text box, a live preview appears beneath it and takes markup into account. If you click on Preview or Post, the text fades and an animated *Progress Indicator* (see earlier in this chapter) bar shows that the server is processing. *Page Rearrangement* then embeds the result in the page.

Code Example: WPLicense

WPLicense (*http://yergler.net/projects/wplicense*) is a form with a live component. Initially, the "License Type" field simply shows the current license, if any. But when the user clicks on the update link, a new block opens up and a conversation between the browser and server ensues to establish the precise details of the license. (More precisely, the conversation is between the browser and the Creative Commons web site; see the corresponding example in *Cross-Domain Proxy* (Chapter 10). Each license type has associated questions, so the license options are fetched according to the user's license type selection.

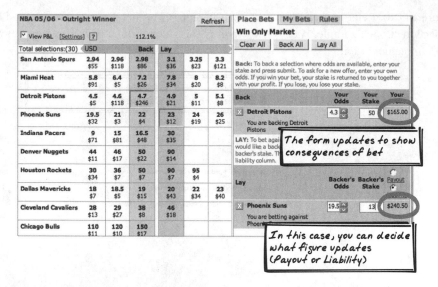

FIGURE 14-29. Betfair Live Form

When the user launches the plugin, a PHP function begins by drawing the Live Form. In this case, the form is ultimately submitted as a conventional POST upload, so the form has a conventional declaration:

```
<form name="license_options" method="post" action="' . $_SERVER[REQUEST_URI] . '">
  ...
  <input type="submit" value="save" />
  <input type="reset"  value="cancel" id="cancel" />
  ...
</form>
```

The current license is shown and loaded with initial values along with the link that triggers the cross-domain mediation to update the license setting:

```
<tr><th>Current License:</th><td>
  <a href="'.get_option('cc_content_license_uri').'">'.get_option('cc_content_license').'</a>

  ...
```

The form includes hidden input fields to capture information gleaned during the Ajax interaction. They will be populated by JavaScript event handlers:

```
<input name="license_name" type="hidden"
       value="'.get_option('cc_content_license').'" />
```

Also, an initially invisible div will be shown once the user decides to change the license. Don't confuse this with the hidden input fields—those will never be shown to the user, whereas this just happens to have a hidden style when the page initially loads. Most critically, the div contains a selection field:

```
<select id="licenseClass"> <option id="-">(none)</option>
  ...
```

```
      foreach($license_classes as $key => $l_id) {
        echo '<option value="' . $key . '" >' . $l_id . '</option>';
      }; // for each...
      ...
    </select>
```

Now for the live part. The `licenseClass` selector is associated with `retrieveQuestions`, a function that fetches the questions corresponding to the chosen license. The call is made courtesy of the Sack library (*http://twilightuniverse.com/2005/05/sack-of-ajax/*), which paints the server's HTML directly onto the `license_options``div`. When you switch to a new license class, the form automatically shows the questions associated with that class:

```
    el.onchange = function( ) {
      retrieveQuestions( );
    } // onchange

  function retrieveQuestions( ) {
    ajax = new sack(blog_url);
    ajax.element='license_options';
    ajax.setVar('func', 'questions');
    ajax.setVar('class', cmbLC.value); ''Current license passed to server''
    ajax.runAJAX( );
    ...
  }
```

The server determines the appropriate questions to ask and outputs them as *HTML Messages*. (See the section "Code Example: WPLicense" in *Cross-Domain Proxy* [Chapter 10] for details.)

Now how about those hidden fields? Well, not all the information related to the options is hidden: the license URL is shown to the user, so that also needs to be updated after an option is chosen. Each time the user changes the server-generated options, the server is called to get a bunch of information about the current selection. That information then comes back to the browser, and the callback function updates both the hidden fields and the URL accordingly:

```
    [Updating the hidden fields]

    document.license_options.license_name.value = licenseInfo['name'];
    document.license_options.license_uri.value  = licenseInfo['uri'];
    document.license_options.license_rdf.value  = licenseInfo['rdf'];
    document.license_options.license_html.value = licenseInfo['html'];

    [Updating the visible license URL]

    href_text = '<a href="' + licenseInfo['uri'] + '">' + licenseInfo['name'] + '</a>';
    document.getElementById("newlicense_name").innerHTML = href_text;
```

Now, what, so far, changed on a permanent basis? Well, nothing. Everything so far has served the purpose of setting up the form itself. But that's fine in this case, because the form is submitted in the conventional manner. So as soon as the user clicks on the Submit button, all of those hidden fields will be uploaded and processed as standard HTTP form data.

Related Patterns

Microlink

Like Live Form, *Microlink* (Chapter 15) opens up new content directly on the page. Indeed, a Microlink can be used on a Live Form to open up supporting information.

Live Search

Consider including a *Live Search* (see earlier) when users need to perform a search within the Live Form.

Suggestion

Consider offering *Suggestions* (see earlier) to help users complete fields within the Live Form.

Drilldown

Consider including a *Drilldown* (see earlier) when users need to identify an item within a hierarchy.

Progress Indicator

Use a *Progress Indicator* (see earlier) to show that the server is working to process a field with a Progress Indicator.

One-Second Spotlight

Since Live Forms are usually submitted with an *XMLHttpRequest Call*, a *One-Second Spotlight* (Chapter 16) effect, such as Fade Out, is a good way to convey that the form has been submitted.

Page Architecture

THE "**P**AGE **A**RCHITECTURE" PATTERNS ARE A VARIETY OF INTERACTION STYLES AND STRATEGIES FOR structuring content. In many cases, it is the possibility of web remoting that makes these patterns worth using.

Drag-And-Drop has been a fixture on the desktop for a couple of decades but is only now gaining currency in the browser. One situation in which it's used is with the *Sprite* pattern. A Sprite is a little icon that lives "in front of" the main document and can move around freely like a character in a video game. The next pattern, *Popup*, uses the same overlay technique, but for larger, dialog-style content.

Malleable Content is content that appears to be read-only but becomes editable upon a gesture such as a mouse rollover, a fairly new idiom because it relies on web remoting. Similarly, a *Microlink* is a link that uses remoting to conjure up content for insertion in the page.

A *Portlet* is a small component of the page that acts like a mini-application, capable of conducting a conversation with the server independent of the main page flow. A *Status Area* provides information about current and past activity and is relevant to Page Architecture because it helps reduce the space occupied by each individual element. *Update Control* allows the user to control information flow on the page. The final pattern, *Virtual Work-space*, lets the user explore a large server-side structure, yet it makes the remoting transparent, creating the illusion that everything's happening in the browser.

Drag-And-Drop

Drag, Move, Pull, Rearrange

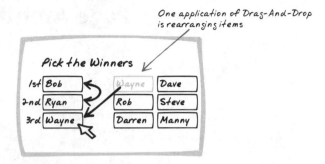

FIGURE 15-1. Drag-And-Drop

Goal Story

Stuart is purchasing books online. Each time he wants to buy one, he drags the book icon into a shopping cart.

Problem

How can users rearrange objects on the page?

Forces

- Object relationships are important and the user's task often involves changing those relationships.

- Ajax Apps often represent object relationships visually.

- Rearranging the visual structure from a separate form is messy—i.e., trying to map between the form and the visual structure is confusing and error-prone. It's easiest if users can directly manipulate the visual structure.

Solution

Provide a Drag-And-Drop mechanism to let users directly rearrange elements on the page. Drag-And-Drop has proven itself to be a powerful control mechanism in conventional desktop applications; it is certainly achievable using standard web technologies. The basics are straightforward: the user holds down the mouse button while the mouse hovers over a page element, then moves the mouse with the button still depressed. The element follows the mouse around until the user finally releases it.

Constraints are sometimes applied to the extent of movement. For example, an element may only be able to move in one direction, or within a bounding box. Also, the element might move permanently when the mouse is released, or flip back to its original position. Another variable is exactly which part of the element must be dragged. Sometimes it's better to define a "handle" region—a specified place where the element can be "picked up" for dragging. The main benefit to this is that it allows the user to click elsewhere in this region.

The following are among the applications:

Rearranging lists
> This simple task can be ridiculously tedious on the Web. Some web sites require an entire page reload each time you move an object up or down. Others have implemented the buttons in JavaScript, but you still have to click Up or Down repeatedly just to place a single item. Drag-And-Drop is a natural fit—just pick up the list items and drop them where you want them.

Rearranging items in a geometric space
> This is also a natural application: pick up the objects and drag them where you want them to go.

Operating on a geometric space
> This might include dragging a magnifying glass or an eraser through an image.

Building up a collection
> One example of collections building is dragging products into a shopping cart.

Expressing an action
> Perhaps the most famous use of Drag-And-Drop was Apple's original deletion mechanism, where you delete something by dragging it into the trash can. The basic idea is to represent a command visually as an icon and let the user drag items into it for processing.

There are a few ways to implement Drag-And-Drop:

- Reuse an existing library. Libraries are becoming increasingly powerful and portable, and it's likely that those available will do the job for you.

- Leverage built-in Drag-And-Drop. Unfortunately, this isn't much of an option because only Windows IE supports Drag-And-Drop explicitly.

- Roll your own Drag-And-Drop. This is not recommended due to portability issues.

Here are a few Drag-And-Drop libraries, all of which have good cross-browser support and online demos:

Scriptaculous (http://script.aculo.us)
> Provides, among other things, a general-purpose, portable Drag-And-Drop library

wzDragDrop (http://www.walterzorn.com/dragdrop/dragdrop_e.htm)
> A Drag-And-Drop library that also includes resize capability

DOM-Dra (http://www.youngpup.net/2001/domdrag/tutorial)
A lightweight Drag-And-Drop library

Tim Taylor's Drag-And-Drop Sortable Lists (http://tool-man.org/examples/sorting.html)
A library designed specifically for list manipulation, supporting Drag-And-Drop-based reordering

The basic approach used for Drag-And-Drop is as follows:

1. Event handlers inspect the incoming event to determine which element is being dragged.

2. An onmousedown handler saves the starting coordinates, sets the zIndex so that the element appears in front during the drag, and changes some other style settings to indicate a drag has begun.

3. A mousemove handler inspects the mouse's coordinates and moves the element accordingly using positioning style properties (usually left and top). Here's where cross-browser support gets nasty—mouse coordinates in the event object are seriously platform-specific.

4. An onmouseup handler restores normal style settings and performs any other cleaning up.

Decisions

What constraints will apply to the drag operation?

You will need to decide directions in which the element can move and how far it can move. Generally, this should be fairly obvious from the visual representation being manipulated; often, there is a container in which similar objects live. This should be the bounding box for dragging operations.

Real-World Examples

Magnetic Poetry

Magnetic Poetry (*http://www.broken-notebook.com/magnetic*) is a fun application that simulates dragging magnetic tiles around a fridge.

Backbase Portal

Backbase Portal (*http://projects.backbase.com/RUI/portal.html*) shows various *Portlets* in a three-column structure. Users can easily rearrange the *Portlets* to suit their own taste using a Drag-And-Drop mechanism. Google's portal (*http://www.google.com/ig*) and Microsoft's Start.com (*http://www.start.com/3/*) follow a similar approach.

A9 Maps

A9 Maps (*http://maps.a9.com*) offers photographs of map locations. A draggable magnifying glass appears on the map, and you can move it to different regions of the map to see what the area looks like in real life.

Code Example: Magnetic Poetry

Magnetic Poetry uses the DOM-Drag library (*http://www.youngpup.net/2001/domdrag/tutorial*) to support dragging. On initialization, each tile is passed successively to `Drag.init`. The tiles may only be dragged within the board region, so the container's dimensions are passed in during the initialization sequence:

```
for(i=1; i<=numWords; i++){
  var currentTile = document.getElementById("word_" + i);
  var x1 = parseInt(document.getElementById("board").style.left);
  var x2 =   parseInt(document.getElementById("board").style.width)
          - parseInt(currentTile.style.width) - 6;
  var y1 = parseInt(document.getElementById("board").style.top);
  var y2 =   parseInt(document.getElementById("board").style.height)
          - parseInt(currentTile.style.height) - 6;
  the last 4 args restrict the area that the tile can be dragged in
  Drag.init(currentTile, null, x1, x2, y1, y2);
}
```

The initialization is all you need to support dragging. With the preceding code, the tiles can now be happily moved around the board space. However, the application does a little more than that: it tracks the currently dragged tile, and it saves the position once dragging is finished using an *XMLHttpRequest Call*. To that end, onDragStart and onDragEnd handlers are registered on each of the tiles:*

```
echo 'document.getElementById("word_' . $i . '").onDragStart =
  function(x, y) { dragStart("word_' . $i . '", x, y); };';
echo 'document.getElementById("word_' . $i . '").onDragEnd =
  function(x, y) { dragEnd("word_' . $i . '", x, y); };';
```

Alternatives

Separate Editing Interface

The conventional solution has been to provide a visual representation in one region and controls in another. This is often cumbersome and error-prone.

Related Patterns

Sprite

Drag-And-Drop is often the mechanism used to move *Sprites* (see the next pattern) around.

---

* The JavaScript is outputted from a PHP script.

Portlet

A portal can be personalized by letting the user drag *Portlets* (see later) around.

Slider

A *Slider* (Chapter 14) is a special case of Drag-And-Drop, where the value indicator is dragged along the slider axis.

Sprite

Bitmap, Buffer, Character, Layer, Overlay, Shape, Sprite, Z-Index

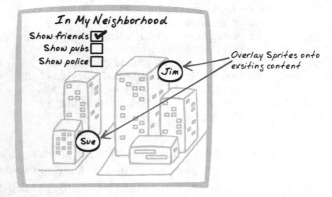

FIGURE 15-2. Sprite

Goal Story

Not for the first time, Pam is negotiating to eliminate a stack of requirements from the project goals. Having successfully convinced the client that "Security Features" was never really worthwhile, she drags a "Magic Eraser" Sprite from the Tool Palette to the "Security Features" requirement, jiggles the mouse a couple of times, and the eraser is animated for a second as the requirement fades away.

Problem

How can you ensure that visual content is flexible?

Forces

- Rich visual displays are often the most effective way to present information.

- Information frequently changes as the user interacts with and new data is received from the server; hence, the visual display needs to update frequently.

- It's expensive to continuously download new visual content.

Solution

Augment the display with Sprites—i.e., small, flexible, icon-like blocks of content. Typically, the Sprites are images, but they may also be div elements containing text or images or a combination of both. The name refers to the Sprites used in traditional graphics programming, particularly gamin—those little graphics representing players, enemies, and other objects capable of moving around a scene and animating themselves to reflect current activity. The entire scene does not need to be recomputed each time, only the Sprites. DOM elements are not (yet) capable of more advanced features such as arbitrary rotation, but many aspects of Sprites can actually be translated to a web context.

Google Maps is a case in point. If you search for "museum new york," a set of thumbtack Sprites will appear on the map, one for each museum. Then, if you click on a thumbtack, a new speech balloon Sprite will show up with the precise address. Using Sprites, Google spares itself the burden of preparing images for every possible configuration, and from generating images on the fly. All it needs to do is ensure that there's a basic display of the map in question, then overlay the thumbtacks and speech balloons.

Sprites are often implemented as div elements or simply as images. They usually appear "in front of" the rest of the document and are sometimes partially transparent. Following are the relevant CSS properties (also see *Page Rearrangement* [Chapter 5]):

zIndex
> Determines how elements are stacked. Sprites usually have a high value in order to appear in front of other elements.

left, right, top, *and* bottom
> Often used to position a Sprite. position can also be set to influence how the browser interprets these settings.

opacity
> Often used to make the Sprite partially transparent. (IE requires the alpha filter workaround; see *http://www.domedia.org/oveklykken/css-transparency.php*.)

backgroundImage
> Used to select a background image when the Sprite is a div. As long as there is no foreground content, the background image is shown. The image doesn't need to be rectangular because a transparent GIF file can be used to show any arbitrary shape.

You can also animate the Sprite by rapidly changing its appearance. Unfortunately, JavaScript cannot easily control animated GIFs, so that's not a viable option. However, animation is easy enough with some *Scheduling* (Chapter 7). One simple technique is to set up a recurring changeImage( ) action, in which the element's backgroundImage is continuously run through a cycle of different images. Ideally, you should preload the images to avoid a slow cycle the first time round. Several tricks are available for preloading, the most common being set an invisible image's source to point to the new image. An alternative animation technique is outlined in the section "Code Example: DHTML Lemmings," later in this chapter.

Decisions

What file format will the Sprite image be?

Sprites are usually images, but what file format should you use—JPEG, GIF, or PNG? There are several considerations:

- Portability
- Image quality
- File size
- Transparency

JPEG may be the most common format on the Web, but it is ruled out for most Sprites. It doesn't support transparent pixels, so the Sprite must be rectangular, and it is not actually very effective at storing the kinds of images typically used for Sprites: small, cartoonish line drawings. So JPEG is only a consideration in the rare case that you have a fairly large, rectangular, photo-like Sprite.

This leaves GIF and PNG as the most common choices. An intellectual property cloud used to hang over GIF, but the patent expired in 2003 (*http://en.wikipedia.org/wiki/Gif*), so it's no longer a valid reason to avoid GIF. PNG does have some technical advantages over GIF, particularly variable transparency, but unfortunately that has not been correctly implemented in IE6 and earlier. So to support older IE editions, you'll need to manipulate opacity if you want to achieve transparency, regardless of the format. Also, even older versions of IE don't support PNG at all (*http://www.libpng.org/pub/png/pngapbr.html*).

In summary, GIF should be the default choice; only use JPEG or PNG if there is a specific reason for doing so.

Will the Sprite be animated?

Ongoing animation can be distracting, but a quick animation is an effective way to convey what's happening. Consider how the "one-second" visual effects might be used:

- *One-Second Spotlight* (Chapter 16): You might *Materialise* a Sprite when it first appears or *Fade In* the Sprite when it's subject to an action.
- *One-Second Mutation* (Chapter 16): You might *Form* a Sprite when it first appears, or rapidly *Metamorphise* it in a cycle in order to provide the illusion of continuous change.

Real-World Examples

DHTML Lemmings

DHTML Lemmings (*http://www.oldgames.dk/freeflashgames/arcadegames/playlemmings.php*) by Tino Zijdel ("Crisp") is a game that uses Sprites in their traditional gaming sense. Lemmings are shown performing different actions, and the characters change shape as they move around the game space. The entire thing is orchestrated with DOM and CSS scripting.

Google Maps

As discussed earlier in the Solution, Google Maps (*http://maps.google.com*) overlays the basic map with thumbtacks to highlight certain locations. As an interesting variant, look at how thumbtacks are used by Housing Maps (*http://housingmaps.com/*), the Maps-Craigslist mashup overviewed in *Cross-Domain Proxy* (Chapter 10).

Quek

Quek (*http://www.quek.nl*) is a fun use of Sprites as chat avatars (Figure 15-3). The application is a "chat-and-surf" program, meaning that Quek users can chat about a web site they're visiting at the same time. Traditionally, such applications have involved *Richer Plugins* (Chapter 8), but Quek avoids any of that. It works by rendering the entire target web site, so you're always actually on a Quek page, but the page looks the same as the target site. Each user that logs into Quek is assigned a unique Sprite consisting of an image, a text ID underneath the image, and an input box (visible only on the user's own Sprite). Typing in the input box animates the Sprite image, and clicking Enter submits the message for all to see. Because the user is free to drag the Sprites around the page, the appearance is of several Sprites moving around and talking to each other, with the web page as a backdrop.

FIGURE 15-3. Quek

Code Example: DHTML Lemmings

DHTML Lemmings involves the most sophisticated use of Sprites I know of. The analysis here is only a rough summary of what's achieved. Note that the code uses some special handling for IE, which the author, Tino, explained to me is due to a bug where IE (at least some versions) bypasses the cache upon any background style change. To keep it simple, the following discussion skims overt IE-specific handling.

In DHTML Lemmings, each lemming is represented by a `Lemming` object, which is initialized with a number to identify the lemming and an initial position corresponding to the place where the lemming first appears on this particular level. Various other state information is also tracked:

```
function Lemming(i,top,left) {
  ...
  this.top = top;
  this.left = left;
  ...
  this.number = i;
  ...
}
```

Lemmings themselves are regular JavaScript objects and are not visible in the browser. To visually depict the lemming, a `div` element is created and made an attribute of the lemming, simply known as l. Thus, we might say the `Lemming` model "wraps" a Sprite as a means of separating semantic content from visual content. Each of these Sprites resides in the playground, an area representing the game space where the lemmings roam around. Both the playground and the Sprites are rendered with absolute positioning. Once the Sprite element has been created, event handlers are also added to support the gameplay:

```
function Lemming(i,top,left) {
  ...
  var l = document.createElement('div');
  l.number = i;
  l.className = 'lemming';
  l.style.top = top+'px';
  l.style.left = left+'px';
  ...
  l.onmouseover = lemming_target_on;
  l.onmouseout = lemming_target_off;
  l.onmousedown = lemming_target_sel;
  ..
}
```

At any moment, each lemming is performing a single action, such as walking or climbing, and the action is tracked by a property of `Lemming`, ani. When the game begins, the lemming falls from a trapdoor, so ani is always initialized to `fall`:

```
function Lemming(i,top,left) {
  this.ani = 'fall';
  ...
}
```

Each type of action requires unique animation and movement. A periodic timer ticks every 60 milliseconds and updates the game's state, including each lemming's appearance and positioning. Here's how the animation works. Each action is associated with a collection of 32×32-pixel icons. The icons are strung together horizontally and retained in a single image. The lemming's backgroundImage style is always set to the entire image associated with its current action (Figure 15-4). Because the lemming image is set to 32 pixels, with overflow hidden, you will only ever see one of the icons. To select the appropriate icon, the backgroundPosition property is set. Thus, the backgroundImage remains fixed while the lemming is performing an action, but the backgroundPosition flows rapidly through each of the icons, beginning at zero and decrementing by 32 pixels each time until it reaches the full width of the image (as a negative value), at which point it becomes zero again.

FIGURE 15-4. DHTML Lemmings—background image used in floating sequence

Whenever the action changes, the script sets the image and initializes the position. Then, for each "tick" of the timer, the icon is advanced by altering the position of the reference image:

```
Lemming.prototype.changeAnimation - function(ani) {
    ...
    this.pos.backgroundImage = lem[ani][this.dir];
    this.pos.backgroundPosition = '0px';
    ...
}

function lemming_animate(i) {
    if (l.curleft == l.maxleft) l.curleft = 0;
    else l.curleft -= 32;
    if (ie) l.imgpos.left = l.curleft+'px';
    else l.pos.backgroundPosition = l.curleft+'px';
}
```

Why is the appearance changed using backgroundPosition? Wouldn't it be simpler to just run through a sequence of separate image files and alter the backgroundImage instead? Tino explains that the reason is performance: The image is held in memory, whereas image-swapping would require images to be retrieved from the cache.

As for motion, each "tick" delegates to a Strategy function (Gamma et al., 1995) for the action taking place. The Strategy function then directly manipulates the Sprite's position. So to model a lemming falling vertically, the div's top increases with each tick:

```
function lemming_fall_ani(l) {
    ...
    l.top += 4;
    ...
}
```

Likewise, a walking action involves making a change to the `left` property:

```
function lemming_walk_ani(l) {
    l.left += l.dx;
}
```

Alternatives

Tiling

Tiling is a technique in which a big image is built up from small tiles. Google Maps works this way; each map image is actually a grid of smaller image files. The benefit is that the browser will cache each tile in memory. So if you pan a little in one direction, only the new tiles need to be downloaded. Like Sprites, tiling is a technique you can use to change visual content without extracting everything from the server. And Google Maps shows that the two techniques combine effectively.

Related Patterns

Popup

Popup (see the next pattern) is a close cousin of Sprite. Both share the appearance of being "in front of" the rest of the document (this is typically implemented with the `zIndex` style), but they differ semantically. The Sprite pattern is intended to cover small objects, which are often draggable, animated, and icon-like. Often, Sprites are a standard fixture of the application, have a sense of unique identity, and remain present throughout the application. Popup is more about a transient, informational block of content that appears in order to show something or accept some input, then vanishes again. Popups tend to be larger and more text-based and are often dynamic in content.

Drag-And-Drop

Sprites can often be dragged around a space.

Metaphor

Think of a 20th century cartoonist creating a sequence in which a mouse walks onto a series of transparent "cel" sheets that will eventually be overlayed on a background scene.

Want to Know More?

- PNG File Format (*http://www.libpng.org/pub/png/pngintro.html*)

Acknowledgments

Thanks go to Tino "Crisp" Zijdel, author of DHTML Lemmings, for clarifying the analysis in this pattern.

Popup

Balloon, Dialog, Hover, Popup, Transparent, Tooltip

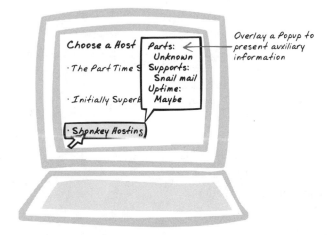

FIGURE 15-5. Popup

Goal Story

Frank is monitoring the factory equipment online and notices the T1000 machine is acting a little funny. He clicks on the icon, holds the mouse button down for a second, and up pops an information sheet about the T1000 model. The sheet is partially transparent and overlayed on top of a region of the plant diagram.

Problem

How can the user perform a quick task without distracting from the main flow?

Forces

- Users often need to make a quick change, which requires that they have some extra controls with which to interact.

- Users often need to perform a quick lookup, get further details about an object in the application, or just find some general information. This requires that extra information appear.

- Screen real estate is limited, and minor, quick changes don't warrant a major change to the user interface.

Solution

Support quick tasks and lookups with transient Popups, blocks of content that appear "in front of" the standard content. Usually, the content is partially transparent, is about the size of a standard dialog, and hovers above the page until the user explicitly closes it. A more subtle variant is the tooltip, a solid block usually containing content between one word and a paragraph in length. The tooltip itself has a trendy new variant, a cartoonish balloon. For *Progress Indicators* (Chapter 14), a popular idiom is to use a small label in the corner with a message like "Saving...." Figure 15-6 illustrates several popular styles.

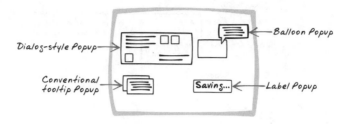

FIGURE 15-6. *Popup styles*

Popup is suitable for particular situations:

You expect the task to be quick
> The Popup is limited in space and its transparent appearance makes it difficult to work with for a long time.

You expect the user to perform the task immediately
> The rest of the document is partially blocked, making it difficult to work with while the Popup is around.

Often, a Popup has no permanent state; it becomes visible, and then is destroyed upon close. With many Popups, there can be only one of its kind at any given time.

Popups are usually divs. To ensure that only one Popup of a particular kind can appear, you can ensure that Popups are always created at the time they are required and deleted on close. On opening, you just need to check whether the Popup already exists on the page. Alternatively, you can simply create the Popup on startup and toggle between showing and hiding it—show it when the user needs a Popup and hide it afterwards. The only catch here is that the state won't be cleared, and often it's more effective to treat each Popup as a new entity.

The following CSS styles are often useful for creating a Popup.

opacity *(alpha filter in IE)*
> Used to produce a transparent feel.

zIndex
> Used to place a Popup "in front of" the rest of the document. A solid (opacity=1) element will completely occlude everything that its zIndex is higher than.

visibility
> Used to toggle whether the Popup is being shown.

Once the Popup is styled and is popping up at the right times, interaction proceeds as with any div element—the Popup just happens to look different that most content. Often, the interaction is similar to that of a *Portlet* (see later in this chapter)—i.e., each user action leads to an *XMLHttpRequest Call* (Chapter 6), with responses morphing the Popup.

Decisions

How will the Popup look?

The Popup's appearance is a compromise that allows you to present some different content without losing the original content. There's a tension between ease of Popup interaction and ease of comprehension and interaction with the rest of the page. Opacity and size will improve interaction with the Popup, but at the expense of the rest of the display. Different colors will also have an impact, and which color is the best depends on the content behind the Popup.

Here are some things to consider:

- Does the user need to see other page information while the Popup is present? If so, ensure that the Popup doesn't block it.

- How long will the Popup be present? If it will be a long time, consider making it less intrusive.

How will the user open and close the Popup?

There are two common approaches to opening the Popup:

- Clicking a button or an object related to the Popup content.

- Hovering over something for a while. Because this can happen quite often, it's more appropriate for a small, tooltip-style Popup.

There are several approaches to closing the Popup:

- Explicitly closing it with a button. Some Popups appear as desktop-like Popups, with an "X" on the top border of the window.

- Closing it when the interaction has come to a natural conclusion—e.g., a user submitting a form. In an Ajax App, the results of submitting it will soon be visible anyway, so there's still ample feedback.

- If the Popup was initiated with a hover event, closing it when the cursor hovers away from the underlying object.

- Closing it upon a timeout. This can be frustrating as it reduces user control. It also requires you to determine whether the user is in the middle of interacting with the Popup. If you use a timeout, consider providing a way to explicitly close it, too.

Real-World Examples

JSCalc

Cameron Adams' JSCalc (*http://www.themaninblue.com/experiment/JSCalc/*) provides a Popup calculator (Figure 15-7). You can use it while surfing on any site, because the calculator is actually a "bookmarklet"—a small JavaScript program which you add as a bookmark and then run by selecting it like a regular bookmark. The calculator appears as a grey, partially transparent display centered in front of the current page. You can type in equations, and when you eventually click on the rest of the page, the display fades away.

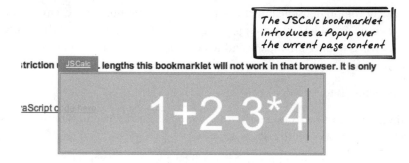

FIGURE 15-7. JSCalc

Flickr

Flickr (*http://flickr.com*) lets registered users add "notes" to anyone's photographs (Figure 15-8). A note initially appears as just a square outline over a region of the photo. When you hover over the note, its full text appears underneath. Creating a new note also uses a Popup effect to show a text field in which you can enter the note.

Netflix

The Netflix Top 100 (*http://www.netflix.com/Top100*) ranks films by all-time popularity (*Mystic River* is first right now, in case you're wondering). When you hover the mouse over a title, a speech balloon appears with a photo and summary. The effect is achieved with an *XMLHttpRequest Call* (Chapter 6). When you move the mouse away, the balloon disappears.

Hoversearch

HoverSearch (or "HoverSmack") (*http://www.forgetfoo.com/?blogid=3436*) is a Popup search. When you click on a hyperlink connected to an appropriate script, a transparent Popup appears and starts searching for a term. The results soon populate the Popup. The framework is capable of searching through different engines, including images, which are then shown in the Popup.

FIGURE 15-8. Flickr notes

Code Example: JSCalc

Being a bookmarklet, JSCalc is compressed into one line and has been reformatted in the following example. A div holds most of the calculator display and is appended to the page body. Since all pages have a body, the bookmarklet will work on any web page.

```
function JSC(){
  var d=document
  var b=d.getElementsByTagName('body')[0]
  var dv=d.createElement('div')
  ...
  b.appendChild(dv)
  ...
}
```

The calculator is positioned in the center of the document and has a slightly transparent opacity.

```
dvs.position='absolute'
dvs.top='50%'
dvs.left='50%'
dvs.width='300px'
dvs.height='60px'
...
dvs.opacity='0.95'
dvs.backgroundColor='#CCC'
```

Inside the div is a standard text input, also absolutely positioned on the page. It's given initial focus and registered with an onkeypress handler to track the calculation.

```
var inp=d.createElement('input')
...
inp.focus()
inp.onkeypress=function(e){
  ...
}
```

The Popup finishes when the user clicks anywhere outside of it. An onblur event is therefore registered. The Popup then fades out and is eventually destroyed in a *One-Second Spotlight*–style (Chapter 16) effect.

```
inp.onblur=function(e){ op(this.parentNode) }
function op(t){
  //(Fades out and removes the calculator elements)
}
```

Alternatives

Portlet

Portlet (see later) is another way to set up a parallel conversation. It differs from Popup in two ways: it's usually permanent or present for a long period of time, and it's usually not transparent. Because of their different characteristics, a Popup is more like a short detour, whereas a Portlet is like a completely parallel track.

Microlink

Microlink (see later) also opens up new content but mixes it directly on, as opposed to in front of, the existing content.

Related Patterns

Sprite

Sprite (see earlier) and Popup both appear "in front of" the rest of the document, but as the section "Related Patterns" in Sprite points out, their intent is different.

Drag-And-Drop

A *Drag-And-Drop* (see earlier) mechanism is a good thing for most Popups because it helps users reveal content that is underneath.

Slider

How transparent should the Popup be? The optimal value depends on the user's taste and the task he's working on. Thus, tie a Popup's opacity factor to a *Slider* (Chapter 14)—ranging from "invisible" to "solid"—for maximum flexibility.

Metaphor

Think of Terminator-style augmented reality, with a heads-up display helping you explore the world as you move through it.

Malleable Content

Affordance, Collaborate, Edit, Hint, Input, Microcontent, Mutable, Outline, P2P, Selection

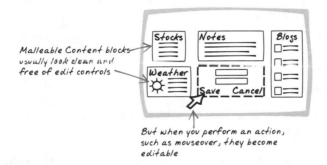

FIGURE 15-9. Malleable Content

Goal Story

Reta is logged in and is revamping the catalogue web site. It looks clean, a replica of the read-only page that public users will see. But as she runs the mouse down the screen, she sees that many regions can be edited.

Problem

How can you let users change content?

Forces

- The Web is not just about consuming information. Administrators, and increasingly everyday users, spend a lot of time adding and editing content.

- All users, no matter what their roles are, need to know what they're allowed to change.

- To encourage contributions and improve user experience, editing should be simple and free of barriers.

- Editable content pages are often ugly, with an overload of form controls, labels, and buttons. Worse, they create a divide between the contributors and the readers; while editing content, it's often difficult to imagine how a reader will see it.

Solution

Compose the page of Malleable Content blocks—small chunks of content that can be edited in page. The page is structured in chunks of small "microcontent," each editable in isolation. There might be a way to edit the whole page too, but the usual style of editing is to view the read-only display and carve up little pieces as you see fit.

The reload problem is one reason why conventional web sites must present large forms in which everything can be set at once. It's often the only practical way to edit content. However, users have difficulty relating the editing interface to the readable interface. Worse, it discourages editing; users are subjected to a sequence of at least two-page reloads in order to change a single character.

Ajax technologies lead to a smoother editing process. Display Manipulation (Chapter 5) and Dynamic Behavior (Chapter 7) help the user locate and open up editable Malleable Content. Display Manipulation also shows you how to conjure up a new editable area, or morph read-only Malleable Content into an editable form. Once the user has made the edit, you can seamlessly upload the response, as described in Web Remoting (Chapter 6), at which point the content can revert to read-only again.

In most cases, each block of Malleable Content is a div or textarea element. It can become editable in one of several ways:

- The display of the original element is adjusted and augmented with editing controls.
- A new div or textarea is created in its place.
- The original element becomes hidden and a hidden div or textarea is revealed.

Is that the sound of your inner usability critic banging his fists on the table and exclaiming "this defies everything that users have come to know about the Web"? Fair point. The forms are gone, so where's the affordance to let the user know what can be edited? Affordances can indeed be provided, as discussed in the following section.

Even if sufficient affordance can be provided, you might object that the whole thing is a complete departure from the usual forms-based approach. You've got me there. It certainly is a departure, but it's a departure from a ten-year-old approach that's remained frustrating since day one. Consistency is certainly an admirable goal—one that shouldn't be neglected because you have a few "one-percenter" improvements—but Ajax represents a new approach, and the benefits of in-page editing are just too big to ignore in the name of consistency. Better to adopt the approach and use sensible design to guide users through it. In any event, Malleable Content is likely to take off and will become familiar to users in the not-too-distant future.

Decisions

How will users locate Malleable Content and open it up for editing?

A read-only page will contain several editable Malleable Content blocks and various other regions that cannot be edited. Some of those regions are program-generated; others might be Malleable Content that this user is not permissioned to edit. So the user needs to know what can be edited. The static appearance should provide some cues, and events like mouse rollovers can refine that information.

The static appearance should make the location of the Malleable Content apparent. There are a few techniques to consider, some which are based on the Highlight pattern:

- When there are multiple Malleable Content blocks, increase spacing or alternate fonts between them to keep them distinct.

- Present the Malleable Content with a distinct background.

- Apply an explicit border around the Malleable Content.

- Expose the edit controls (e.g., Undo button), or the controls which initialize the edit (e.g., Edit button), but faded out.

- Add a label and auxiliary information beside each Malleable Content block. (See the following.)

These provide enough information for the user to detect that Malleable Content is present. However, too many of these cues will defeat the purpose of this pattern by making the whole thing hard to read. So you might use only a few subtle cues, or even none at all, and rely instead on dynamic behavior. Mouse movement is the most important activity to monitor; fields can be morphed to advertise their editability as the mouse rolls over them. Here, onmouseover sets up the cue and onmouseout takes it away. You can write a generic event handler and inspect the incoming event to see which piece of Malleable Content was altered. Then, apply (or unapply) the effect generically to that element.

All of the preceding static cues qualify as suitable dynamic cues, too. For example, change the background color as the mouse rolls over a particular block of Malleable Content, or make the label and edit controls visible only during that time. In addition, the cursor can also be varied using the cursor property. These dynamic cues, combined with just one or two static cues, are an effective way for users to pinpoint blocks of editable Malleable Content.

Will the Malleable Content be labelled? What auxiliary information will be included?

Many times, the Malleable Content has some form of identity, so you may wish to explicitly associate a name with it. The name might be shown above it as a heading or summary, on the side as an annotation, or as a tooltip.

The following auxiliary information, which can be automatically gathered by the server, might also be shown:

- The user who created the content

- The user who last edited the content

- The number of edits

- The creation date

- The last edit date

What content will be marked as Malleable Content? How big will the Malleable Content be?

Any editable information is a good candidate for inclusion as editable Malleable Content. One reason against making an item editable is that item's interaction with other data on the page. If there are certain combinations of data that are invalid, you may prefer to force the user to edit everything at once.

Malleable Content should be big enough to form a coherent unit of content, but small enough to be comfortably edited without scrolling and with enough room for some surrounding context. Of course, it's the users who will determine the exact size, and enforcing limits often achieves nothing but frustration. You can, however, influence the size of Malleable Content in several ways:

- Provide guidelines.
- Illustrate the guidelines and establish norms by restructuring existing content.
- Where the Malleable Content represents a data structure rather than just free text, ensure that the data structure is a suitable size. If it's too big, split it. If it's too small, aggregate it.

How will the user stop editing content?

Now you've decided how the user will open up content for editing, but how will she complete the edit? Here are the typical options:

- As soon as focus is blurred—e.g., when the user clicks on an external object—the content is saved and becomes read-only. This is good for power users who might wish to tab through content fields.
- Explicit controls, such as *Save* and *Cancel*, are added during editing. This may involve rearranging items on the page.

Is it okay to have several Malleable Content blocks open for editing at one time?

Because Malleable Content is an Ajax App, the user might not reload for a while, so he'll need to close each block manually in order to see the page become read-only again. You might enforce a rule that one field can be open at a time. This could be achieved by closing any existing block when a new one is opened, or by refusing to open a second block.

Real-World Examples

Flickr

When you manage one of your photos with Flickr (*http://flickr.com*), you'll see a title above the picture and a caption below it (Figure 15-10). Both are rendered in black-on-white and appear as ordinary read-only text, so there's actually no static cue. But it's easy enough to discover it, especially given that most users are aware that these items can be edited. Hover over these fields and the background will switch to a light tan color. Then, click the button, and the field becomes editable, as shown in Figure 15-10.

Several things happen here:

- A border appears, outlining the field and suggesting that it's editable.

- The entire text is initially selected, an additional cue that you're now editing the field and a useful time saver as typing a new entry automatically deletes the existing text.

- Save and Cancel buttons are inserted onto the page, slightly displacing the content below. Clicking on Save or Cancel reverts the content back to read-only; otherwise, the field remains open and multiple fields can be open at once

FIGURE 15-10. Flickr caption

Monket Calendar

The Monket Calendar (*http://www.monket.net/cal/*) lets you add events to a shared Ajax calendar (Figure 15-11). Each appointment is rendered as an orange-background rectangle with curves on either side. As the mouse hovers over a field, the field remains as is, but the cursor changes to a pointer style, suggesting that the field can be clicked. Once you click on the field, the rounded edges remain, but the central, horizontal component changes to white, the existing text is selected in full and becomes editable, and an "X" appears that lets you easily remove the appointment.

Tiddlywiki

With Tiddlywiki (*http://tiddlywiki.com*), controls appear as you roll the mouse over the Malleable Content (Figure 15-12). They are actually always present but are usually invisible, which means that surrounding fields don't move when you mouse around—the fields just toggle in their visibility status. One of these controls lets you edit: it switches the field into

FIGURE 15-11. Monket Calendar

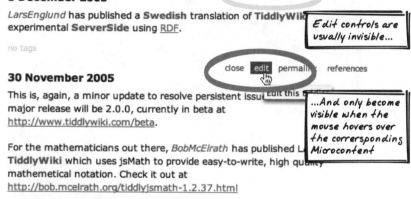

5 December 2005

LarsEnglund has published a **Swedish** translation of **TiddlyWiki** experimental **ServerSide** using RDF.

no tags

30 November 2005

This is, again, a minor update to resolve persistent issue major release will be 2.0.0, currently in beta at
http://www.tiddlywiki.com/beta.

For the mathematicians out there, *BobMcElrath* has published **TiddlyWiki** which uses jsMath to provide easy-to-write, high qu mathemetical notation. Check it out at
http://bob.mcelrath.org/tiddlyjsmath-1.2.37.html

There's also a new **Basque** translation of **TiddlyWiki** from *SéamusPálás* of the University of the Basque Country.

tags: news

10 November 2005

Revision 1.2.38 is a minor revision of **TiddlyWiki** that just addresses an issue with **Safari**. The next major release, *Revision 1.2.39*, has just entered beta at
http://www.tiddlywiki.com/beta/

FIGURE 15-12. Tiddlywiki

a textarea with an input field for the title. As you hover over the textarea, new controls appear, allowing you to save, cancel, or delete the item. It's possible to have more than one Malleable Content open at once.

Thomas Baekdal's Business Card Creator

Thomas Baekdal's Business Card Creator (*http://www.baekdal.com/articles/Usability/usable-XMLHttpRequest/*) contains a business card with mostly black content on a white background. As you hover over a field, the border changes, and when you edit, the background color also changes. This interaction style was the basis of the following wiki demo.

Code Example: AjaxPatterns Wiki

The Wiki Demo (*http://ajaxify.com/run/wiki*) breaks page content into a few Malleable Content blocks. A single div is declared in the initial HTML to hold these blocks:

```
<div id="messages"></div>
```

At periodic intervals, the incoming XML is parsed to extract each message into its own block of Malleable Content. Each message is actually a textarea but is rendered to appear read-only until it's edited. The CSS class, which initially corresponds to a grey background with no border, is set to show the text in read-only mode. Handlers are registered to provide dynamic cues that the Malleable Content can be edited and to handle the editing process:

```
function onMessagesLoaded(xml, callingContext) {

  for (var i=0; i<wikiMessages.length; i++) {
    ...
    var messageArea = document.createElement("textarea");
    messageArea.className = "messageArea";
    messageArea.id = serverMessage.id;
    messageArea.serverMessage = serverMessage;
    messageArea.rows = 3;
    messageArea.cols = 80;
    messageArea.value = serverMessage.content;
    messageArea.onmouseout = onMessageMouseOut;
    messageArea.onmouseover = onMessageMouseOver;
    messageArea.onfocus = onMessageFocus;
    messageArea.onblur = onMessageBlur;
    ...
    }
  ...
  }
```

We can examine each event handler to see how the editing cycle occurs. First, the user rolls over a message block. We'll outline the message with a dotted border to hint that it's in the twilight zone between read-only (no border) and editable (full border). We wouldn't want this to happen if the user was already editing the content, so we make an explicit check for that condition. Incidentally, you'll notice that the event handlers also manipulate colors here. That shouldn't be necessary; it is a workaround for the fact that some browsers unfortunately resize the border when it changes style. Without the workaround, the other content blocks would undergo slight movement each time one block changes.

```
function onMessageMouseOver(event) {
  var message = getMessage(event);
  if (!message.hasFocus) {
    message.style.borderStyle="dotted";
    message.style.borderColor="black";
  }
}
```

And when the user rolls off this message block, the appearance is reset:

```
function onMessageMouseOut(event) {
  var message = getMessage(event);
  if (!message.hasFocus) {
    message.style.borderStyle="solid";
    message.style.borderColor="white";
  }
}
```

Okay, our user has just rolled over a message block and now clicks on it to begin the edit. In the previous handler, we performed a check based on a hasFocus field to see whether the message was being edited. That's not built into the DOM, so we have to set it manually when the edit begins. During editing, the background is white and the border solid black. Finally, we ensure that no synchronization occurs while the user is editing (which is not always advisable):

```
function onMessageFocus(event) {
  var message = getMessage(event);
  message.hasFocus=true;
  message.style.borderStyle="solid";
  message.style.borderColor="black";
  message.style.backgroundColor="white";
  stopPeriodicSync();
}
```

The user signals end of edit by clicking elsewhere on the page, causing a blur event to occur. The message returns to its original read-only form. Or, if a change has occurred, the message is highlighted and will eventually be reset once the change has reached the server. Also, a resize function adjusts the height according to the new content. Finally, synchronization can begin again:

```
function onMessageBlur(event) {
  var message = getMessage(event);
  message.hasFocus=false;
  message.style.borderStyle="solid";
  message.style.borderColor="white";
  message.style.backgroundColor="#cccccc";
  resize(message);

  var initialMessageContent = message.serverMessage.content;

  if (message.value != initialMessageContent) {
    pendingMessages[message.id] = true;
```

```
      message.style.backgroundColor = "#ffcc33";
    }

    startPeriodicSync();

  }
```

Alternatives

Compound Edit

It's possible to edit the whole page content at once—the typical approach in conventional web apps. As explained earlier in this section, there are problems with the approach, but users may prefer it for long editing sessions. Ideally, both styles should be provided.

Related Patterns

Live Form

Upon becoming editable, a Malleable Content block might become a *Live Form* (Chapter 14).

Rich Text Editor

One way to edit Malleable Content is with a *Rich Text Editor* (Chapter 14).

Microlink

Malleable Content can be summoned onto the page using a *Microlink* (see the next pattern)—the approach used by TiddlyWiki (*http://tiddlywiki.com*).

One-Second Spotlight, One-Second Motion, and One-Second Mutation

The "One-Second" visual effects (Chapter 16) are a good way to support editing. It's becoming common to Fade In recently saved content as a means of hinting that it has been acknowledged. Mutations such as Blow Up and Disappear imply that Malleable Content is being deleted.

Highlight

Malleable Content is often highlighted to show that it's being edited and as a dynamic cue that it's available for editing.

Metaphor

Applications using Malleable Content are like a communal whiteboard.

Microlink

Appear, Conjure, Emerge, Hyperlink, Insert, Introduce, In-Page

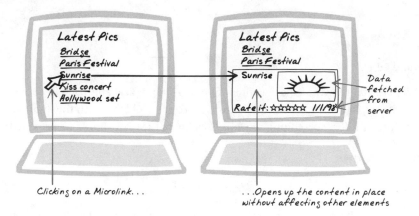

FIGURE 15-13. Microlink

Goal Story

Frustrated with a developer's productivity, Pam logs into the version control system and sees a "Project Committers" table. Each row includes a developer's name and photo, and Pam immediately clicks on one of the names. The row expands out to reveal a mini-summary of the developer's project activity, and a bunch of links to further content.

Problem

How can the user quickly navigate through content?

Forces

- Ajax Apps often respond to user requests by providing new content.

- To encourage interaction with the system, content should be shown quickly and without distraction.

- Page reloads slow down interaction, break concentration, and obscure the nature of whatever changes have occurred.

Solution

Provide Microlinks that open up new content on the existing page rather than loading a new page. Microlink is an Ajaxian upgrade of the traditional hyperlink. Most often, it entails fetching content from the server with an *XMLHttpRequest Call* and inserting it onto the page. The content is usually a tightly scoped block of Microcontent, though it need not be—a Microlink could be used to open a whole page of content, for example.

The term Microlink should not be taken here as a literal translation of textual hyperlinks. It's used to represent any form of content being inserted into the page. The trigger might be something as subtle as a form field focus event.

Microlinks can be used in many contexts:

- They can open a *Popup* (earlier in this chapter) to augment a particular word or phrase. Some conventional web sites provide glossary lookups in a pop-up window. A Microlink could instead be used to place a small explanation directly next to the term.

- They can be used to drill down by expanding out successively deeper levels of content. You could show all teams in a football league, each expanding to a list of players, in turn expanding to a list of games, and so on.

- They can let the user switch content around on the page, which is useful if the Microlinks are included in a *Drilldown* (Chapter 14).

The name "Microlink" refers to the subtle effect it has on interaction flow. Microlink carries several benefits over the full-blown page refresh caused by a standard hyperlink:

Content appears faster
There is much less to transfer because only the new content is loaded rather than the whole page. Also, the browser needs only to make a few changes to the DOM as opposed to rerendering the whole page.

Application flow is smoother
To the user, a page reload is distracting. Microlink avoids this distraction.

Changes are more salient
The user is able to watch as an element appears on the page. Visual effects can be used to further improve change detection.

Internal state is maintained
The browser-side application's state—as held in the DOM—is retained, whereas a page reload destroys it. This is a technical benefit.

Microlink usually involves an *XMLHttpRequest Call* (Chapter 6) followed by a *Page Rearrangement* (Chapter 5). Often, a new div is created and appended to a container element. As a variant, sometimes the Microlink refers to something already on the page, so the Microlink causes the script to make it visible or to scroll toward it (using document.scrollto).

Decisions

What will happen to other content?

A Microlink inserts new content into the existing page, and you obviously can't keep piling on content forever. Furthermore, you need to remove the clutter so that new content is more salient. At some point, you'll have to clean up existing content, and you'll need to decide how that should happen. Typical strategies include those described in the list that follows.

- The new content simply replaces the old content. The old content is overwritten, or the new content is added and the old content replaced.

- A fixed-capacity content queue is set up, such that newer content displaces older content, which eventually disappears.

- The user must explicitly close all content.

How will Microlink be presented visually?

Microlink presentation is tricky because you want to leverage existing knowledge about hyperlinks, but do it without causing confusion. Many interfaces will combine Microlinks and hyperlinks (e.g., links to company homepages or external web sites), and you don't want a situation where the user can't distinguish between them. Also keep in mind that Microlinks don't have to be words or phrases—they can, for example, be buttons or imagemaps.

You need to ensure that users know Microlinks are clickable. You also need to have some ability to predict what they'll see when that happens. To provide affordances that an element is clickable, consider doing the following:

- Change the cursor icon as the user hovers over the element; control this with the cursor style property.

- Leveraging the conventions of hyperlinks, namely blue text (color style) and underlining (textDecoration style), but be beware that this may cause confusion as well.

- Make the clickable region apparent visually using cues like borders and different background colors.

Real-World Examples

TiddlyWiki

TiddlyWiki (*http://tiddlywiki.com/*) is a wiki based on *Malleable Content* blocks. At any point in time, you're looking at a list of Malleable Content blocks. Each block contains text including hyperlinks to other Malleable Content as well as to external sites. The external links are distinguished using a bold font. When you click on a Microlink and the corresponding context doesn't yet exist, the context is inserted just below the block containing the Microlink. If it does exist, the window scrolls to show the content. For more on this, see the section "Real-World Examples" in Malleable Content earlier in this chapter, and the section *One-Second Mutation* (Chapter 16).

Tabtastic library

A great application for Microlinks is the tabbed content metaphor, in which different blocks of content are shown as tabs. The technique was popularized by Amazon in the late 1990s, and Ajax allows for the content in another tab to be downloaded without a page refresh. Tabtastic (*http://phrogz.net/JS/Tabtastic/index.html*) is a JavaScript toolkit you can use to incorporate tabs into your application—Microlink style. The web site demonstrates how it's done (Figure 15-14).

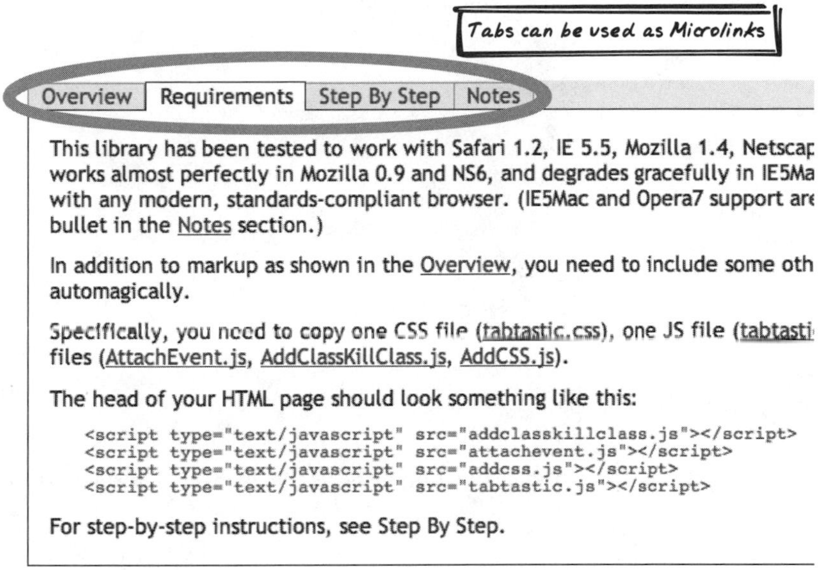

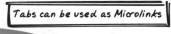

Figure content:

Overview | **Requirements** | Step By Step | Notes

This library has been tested to work with Safari 1.2, IE 5.5, Mozilla 1.4, Netscap works almost perfectly in Mozilla 0.9 and NS6, and degrades gracefully in IE5Ma with any modern, standards-compliant browser. (IE5Mac and Opera7 support are bullet in the Notes section.)

In addition to markup as shown in the Overview, you need to include some oth automagically.

Specifically, you need to copy one CSS file (tabtastic.css), one JS file (tabtasti files (AttachEvent.js, AddClassKillClass.js, AddCSS.js).

The head of your HTML page should look something like this:

```
<script type="text/javascript" src="addclasskillclass.js"></script>
<script type="text/javascript" src="attachevent.js"></script>
<script type="text/javascript" src="addcss.js"></script>
<script type="text/javascript" src="tabtastic.js"></script>
```

For step-by-step instructions, see Step By Step.

FIGURE 15-14. Tabtastic

Rpad

Rpad (*http://www.rpad.org/Rpad/*) provides an assortment of numerical analysis applications. Here, the linked content is not stored but dynamically generated. Click on Calculate within the General Demo (*http://www.rpad.org/Rpad/Example1.Rpad*) and you'll see several tables and graphs appear, freshly generated from the server.

Gmail

Gmail (*http://gmail.com/*) uses Microlinks to repeatedly switch main content around. There are *Microlinks* for all of your mailboxes, your contacts, for composing a new email, and so on.

The appearance is structured like most web sites—fixed-size blocks on the top and left containing links and search and the main content on the bottom right. However, most conventional web sites achieve this fixed structure by continuously reloading the entire structure, even if only the main content has changed. Gmail, however, is an Ajax App and only has to morph the main content area as each Microlink is clicked.

Code Example: TiddlyWiki

In TiddlyWiki, Microlinks are created as anchor elements with a custom CSS class, button. There's a general-purpose function used to create buttons, and the link creator delegates to it. It passes in display information as well as a function, onClickTiddlerLink, to handle what happens when the user clicks.

```
      var btn = createTiddlyButton(place,text,subTitle,onClickTiddlerLink,theClass);
```

Buttons are anchor elements rendered with a special CSS class, which provides a different appearance while being hovered over or activated:

```
.tiddler .button {
  padding: 0.2em 0.4em 0.2em 0.4em;
  color: #993300;
}

.tiddler .button:hover {
  text-decoration: none;
    color: #ccff66;
    background-color: #993300;
}

.tiddler .button:active {
  color: #ffffff;
  background-color: #cc9900;
}
```

When the link is clicked, the handler function inspects the event to determine the desired content:

```
function onClickTiddlerLink(e)
{
  if (!e) var e = window.event;
  var theTarget = resolveTarget(e);
  var theLink = theTarget;
  ...
}
```

The new *Malleable Content* can then be inserted. An algorithm determines where it will be placed and the createTiddler( ) function creates a new div to host the content. If animation is turned on, the new content block will appear to "leap out" from the hyperlink into its own region of the page, as detailed in *One-Second Motion* (Chapter 16). Otherwise, the window performs a straightforward scroll to show the new content:

```
function displayTiddler(src,title,state,highlightText,
    highlightCaseSensitive,animate,slowly) {
  var place = document.getElementById("tiddlerDisplay");
  var after = findContainingTiddler(src);
    // Which tiddler this one will be positioned after
  ...
  var theTiddler = createTiddler(place,before,title,state,highlightText,
                                 highlightCaseSensitive);
  if(src)
  {
    if(config.options.chkAnimate && (animate == undefined || animate == true))
    anim.startAnimating(new Zoomer(title,src,theTiddler,slowly),
                    new Scroller(theTiddler,slowly));
    else
      window.scrollTo(0,ensureVisible(theTiddler));
  }
}
```

Related Patterns

Malleable Content

Malleable Content (see earlier) is a companion pattern, because Microlinks are often used to conjure up Malleable Content blocks. however, a Microlink can also produce a more complex structure, too, such as the Gmail links that switch all of the main page content.

"One-Second" visual effects

The visual effects (*One-Second Spotlight*, *One-Second Mutation*, and *One-Second Motion*; see Chapter 16) help the user comprehend what's going on when a Microlink is clicked, as TiddlyWiki demonstrates.

Drilldown

The categories in a *Drilldown* (Chapter 14) are a kind of Microlink, as they cause the Drilldown content to change without a page reload.

Popup

A Microlink may be used to launch a *Popup* (see earlier).

Live Form

A *Live Form* (Chapter 14) can include Microlinks to more advanced controls and to content that supports the user's decision making.

Portlet

Block, Conversation, Dialogue, Gadget, Independent, Parallel, Portal, Portlet, Widget

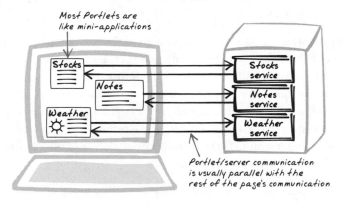

FIGURE 15-15. Portlet

Goal Story

The sidebar of Tracy's stock trading system contains a few independent blocks down the side: a currency Portlet, a calculator, and a miniature chart generator. Right now, she is checking on the USD/EUR exchange rate in one of those blocks. She types "USDEUR" into the text field, and the block updates a moment later to show the rate. Everything else on the page remains the same.

Problem

How can the user conduct rich conversations in parallel?

Forces

- A complex application contains a range of loosely related functionality. The user often needs to work on these things in parallel, gathering knowledge about one thing and using it to influence another.

- It isn't just different functionality, but different data that users need to work with in parallel.

- These conversations need to be "rich." They require conversational state to keep track of what's occurred so far and what can happen next, and they require interaction with the server.

- It's important to retain the state of each conversation between the user and the application. You don't want to invalidate one activity just because the user chose to initiate another.

Solution

Introduce Portlets—isolated blocks of content with independent conversational state. A Portlet is like a mini-application inside a regular application. It presents a little bit of information and usually some controls. The user can communicate via the controls, which causes the Portlet to update.

Usually, the Portlet state is completely independent of the rest of the application. For example, a travel web site can include a weather Portlet. Users are able to search for locations and drill down from a result to an extended forecast. The conversation can be as rich and stateful as the display allows. However, the conversation has no effect on the rest of the application. If the main site is in the middle of a booking transaction, it will stay that way while users spend a few minutes checking the weather. Browser/server communication will take place, but it won't affect the conversational state of the booking transaction, nor will it affect the state of any other Portlets.

In some cases though, actions on the Portlet can affect the general application state, and vice versa. A search Portlet can allow a user to locate content in the application. While locating the content, the user conducts a rich conversation alone with the Portlet, but once located, the user can click on the search result to open it up in the main content area.

If you aggregate Portlets together on the same page, you will end up with a Portals. A news Portal for example, contains a Portlet for each news category. But Portlets need not reside in Portals. A single Portlet can also be embedded in a regular web app (Figure 15-16), as the preceding example illustrates.

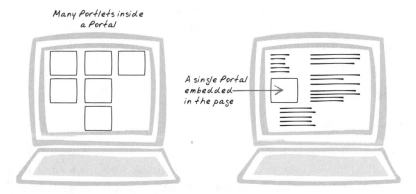

Many Portlets inside
a Portal

A single Portal
embedded
in the page

FIGURE 15-16. Portals and embedded Portlets

Portlets have been around for a long time, and Portals were once touted as the next big thing after search engines. However, they've never really taken off, and the interface is part of the problem. Chapter 1 explains in detail the problems with traditional portals and how much they gain from Ajax. The various Ajax Patterns help in different ways:

- *XMLHttpRequest Calls* alleviate the need to reload the entire page on each interaction. The response is minimal, and the state of everything else is effortlessly retained—a truly parallel conversation.

- *Display Morphing* lets you change the portal's appearance in response to user events and server responses.

- *Periodic Refresh* allows you to auto-update Portlets based on external changes and activity from other users.

- *Drag-And-Drop* lets you pick up Portlets and drag them around, a great improvement over the contrived page rearrangement interfaces used in the past.

An interesting variant is the "Cross-Domain Portlet," a mixture of *Cross-Domain Proxy* and *Portlet*. The idea is to let the user have a complete conversation with an external web site. Consider how this might impact Tim O'Reilly's proposal of "Advertising as Conversation" (*http://radar.oreilly.com/archives/2005/05/advertising_as.html*), where he suggested that web ads can work more as interactive conversations between user and advertiser rather than simply being mindless branding imagery. A Portlet can be used to mediate a complete conversation between advertiser and user. The preceding weather Portlet example could actually come from an external service provider. The travel site could even contain a booking Portlet. While viewing online discussions about a destination, a user can conduct a parallel conversation with an airline company to check flight availability.

Decisions

Will users be able to move Portlets around?

Drag-And-Drop provides a nice way to rearrange Portlets on the page, but do you really want to? Generally, Portal-style applications support this activity, but for regular applications with one or two Portlets, you need to decide if it's worthwhile. Often, you can support some constrained movement—for example, let the user move Portlets up and down a side column.

Real-World Examples

Claude Hussenet's Portal

Claude Hussenet's portal is a demo informational portal (*http://claudehussenet.com*). Information from different news sources, as well as customizable stock quotes and quick links (bookmarks), are available in independent Portals. Each can be refreshed independently, and all editing occurs in the Portlet and without reloading the entire page. A checkbox lets you show and hide each Portlet individually.

Google Homepage

Google Homepage (*http://www.google.com/ig*) is a portal with three columns of Portlets. Registered users can click on "Add content" to keep adding Portlets. Most of the Portlets, like news, RSS feeds, and Word of the Day, contain recent updates. There are also some more interactive Portlets: Search shows personal search history, Bookmarks lets you accumulate bookmarks in a Portlet, Gmail summarizes recent mail messages. All Portals' existing Portlets can be dragged around the page and edited. Editing morphs the Portal into a form. At present, unfortunately, the form is submitted as a regular form, causing a page refresh.

Backbase

The Backbase Portal Demo (*http://projects.backbase.com/RUI/portal.html*) contains several independent Portlets, each with its own state (Figure 15-17). This is only a demo, but it's a good demonstration of the independent nature of Portlets.

Dobrado

Dobrado (*http://dobrado.sourceforge.net*), an open source project, is different from the preceding information portals in a couple of ways. First, the *Portlet*s are free-flowing—they can be dragged anywhere on the page as opposed being restricted to the more common style of docking a Portlet into one of three columns. Second, Dobrado is not actually an information *Portal* per se, but rather a web site authoring application; for novices, it's easy to create a page by conjuring new Portlets, arranging them on the page, and typing in some content.

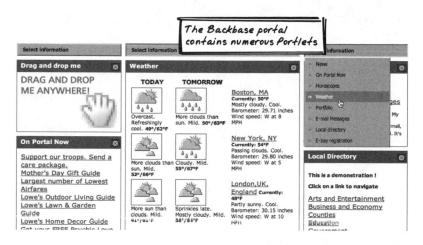

FIGURE 15-17. Backbase

Code Example: Claude Hussenet's Portal

Claude Hussenet's portal (*http://claudehussenet.com/*) delegates server calls to the Direct Web Remoting (DWR) framework (*http://www.getahead.ltd.uk/dwr/*). Let's focus on the "Quick Links" Portlet, which allows you to maintain a collection of bookmarks. (Some of the following code here has been reformatted.)

The initial HTML represents Quick Links as a table. There's a span for the links and another span for input:

```
<TABLE border="0" cellPadding="0" border="0" cellSpacing=0 width="100%" >
  <tr><td height="2" colspan="2" bgcolor=#FF6633><img height=
"1" src="/images/pixel.gif"></td></tr>
  <TR>
    <TD  valign="top" nowrap><B>Quick Links</B></TD>
    <TD width=1% align=right> <input type="checkbox"
id='buttonMinimizedPortletQuickLinks'

    value="Min" onclick="refreshPortletQuickLinks
    (document.getElementById('portletQuickLinks'));"></TD>
  </TR>
  <TR>
    <TD>
      <span id="portletQuickLinks" ><B>Loading Content</B></span>
    </TD>
  </TR>
  <TR>
  <TD>
      <span id="inputLinksPortletQuickLinks" ></span>
  </TD>
  </TR>
</TABLE>
```

A call is made on startup to get content from an *HTML Message* on the server. This delegates to a DWR function, and the server call finally morphs the links:

```
QUICKLinks.getContent(writePortletPortletQuickLinks,
   {timeout:3500,
     errorHandler:'sayHello2('+"'portletQuickLinks'"+')'});
...
function QUICKLinks() { }
   QUICKLinks.getContent = function(callback) {
       DWREngine._execute('/portal/dwr', 'QUICKLinks', 'getContent', callback);
   }
   ...
function writePortletPortletQuickLinks(data) {
   if (data!=null)document.getElementById("portletQuickLinks").innerHTML = data;
}
```

The input for new links has a Submit button, and when the user submits, a JavaScript function is invoked. It causes the new link details to be posted to the server. Because the server is keeping track of the session, it is able to send the HTML back for *all* links. The callback function is the same as before:

```
function addQuickLinksPortletQuickLinks(elem) {
   var name = document.getElementById("linkname").value;
   var link =document.getElementById("url").value;
   ...
   QUICKLinks.addLink(writePortletPortletQuickLinks,name,link);
}
```

Alternatives

Tabbed Browsing

Tabbed browsing is a workaround users resort to in order to conduct multiple conversations with the same web site.

Related Patterns

Periodic Refresh

Portlets often use *Periodic Refresh* (Chapter 10) to stay up to date.

Distributed Events

Using *Distributed Events* (Chapter 10) is a good way to keep the Portlet updated. This is particularly important when one Portlet is dependent on another: instead of tying them directly, use events to add a layer of indirection.

Drilldown

A dynamic *Drilldown* (Chapter 14) is an effective way to conserve space within a Portlet.

Live Form

Live Forms (Chapter 14) appear in many Portlets because they are a good way to conduct a rich conversation with the server in a manner that avoids any page refresh.

Cross-Domain Proxy

Portlest can be used to show a conversation to the user and to an external domain.

Metaphor

A portal full of Portlets is like having a 21st century dashboard as depicted in a 20th century sci-fi movie—a conversation with the president on one screen, a little navigation through the stars on another screen, and a looping fast-food ad in the middle.

Acknowledgments

Tony Hill of Thomson Consulting gave me the idea for the pattern diagram.

Status Area

Console, Log, Message, Status

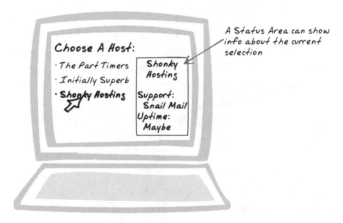

FIGURE 15-18. Status Area

Goal Story

Pam wants to revise the list of project issues. As she begins checking off those that are now resolved, she notices the Status Area below update, which is showing the number of issues resolved and the number still outstanding.

Problem

How can you show auxiliary information?

Forces

- The same data can be represented in different ways.
- Users often benefit from redundant summary information.

- Screen real estate is limited; you can't augment each field with its own summary information.

Solution

Include a read-only Status Area to report on current and past activity. The Status Area is usually auto-generated text based on some aspect of system state. The main purpose is to save space by occupying a region with information from different sources. This is done by dynamically altering the information according to current context.

Applications of the Status Area include the following:

- Summarizing information about elements the mouse is hovering over.

- Summarizing information about the element being edited.

- Summarizing information about the overall application state.

- Capturing past events in a log.

- Offering a preview.

Often, there's no server-side processing involved—the browser has enough information to maintain the Status content itself. For example, the browser can easily show a count of selected elements or a log of past data that's been retained. A Status Area can be particularly valuable for monitoring the state of dynamic objects. For example, an e-commerce system can use *Periodic Refresh* (Chapter 10) to continuously update the state of an order within a user's profile ("Submitted," "Credit Card Verified," "Stock Available," and so on).

The Status Area is usually a div element, with changes triggered by events such as mouse rollovers and form editing.

Note that this pattern is mostly speculative and is based on analogies from conventional desktop systems (where Status Areas are indeed commonplace).

Decisions

How will you size the Status Area? What if it overflows?

The Status Area is usually a relatively small element—sometimes just one row of text. You need to perform some analysis to determine the worst-case situation, i.e., what's the most content the Status Area can hold, and how will you deal with overflow. Strategies for dealing with this include:

- Compressing the text somehow—e.g., by trimming the message or extracting a summary.

- Introducing scrollbars. This is reasonable for a console-like Status Area that retains a history.

- Dynamically resizing the Status Area (which is not very common).

How will you structure the Status Area's content?

The Status Area need not be plain-text. It's often useful to keep a common structure in which each position always reflects the same variable. Consider which variables are being maintained and how they relate to each other.

Real-World Examples

BetFair

Betfair (*http://betfair.com*) includes a *Live Form* (Chapter 14) for creating new bets (see "Real-World Examples" in Live Form). A Status Area tracks your total liability, which is dynamically updated as you change the stake.

Lace Chat

Brett Stimmerman's Lace Chat (*http://www.socket7.net/lace/*) is an Ajax chat app. A Status Area contains a live preview of your message. As you type, a preview of the output, including any markup, is shown.

Code Refactoring: AjaxPatterns Status Wiki

The Basic Wiki Demo (*http://ajaxify.com/run/wiki/*) is refactored in the Status Wiki Demo to include a *Status Area* (*http://ajaxify.com/run/wiki/status*). While the focus is on a message, there's a Status Area below maintaining the word count, row count, and character count (Figure 15-19).

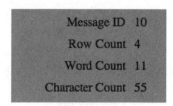

> Message ID 10
> Row Count 4
> Word Count 11
> Character Count 55

10.*Mike*.100.0

```
This is the first wiki entry!!!
Oh, one more thing ...|
```

FIGURE 15-19. *Showing the status of a wiki entry*

The static HTML has been refactored to include a Status Area with a table for all the values. This means the script need only set the actual count values rather than perform HTML manipulation:

```
<div id="status">
  <table id="statusTable">
    <tr>
```

```
                <td class="label">Message ID</td>
                <td class="value" id="messageId"></td>
        </tr>
        <tr>
                <td class="label">Row Count</td>
                <td class="value" id="rowCount"></td>
        </tr>
        <tr>
                <td class="label">Word Count</td>
                <td class="value" id="wordCount"></td>
        </tr>
        <tr>
                <td class="label">Character Count</td>
                <td class="value" id="characterCount"></td>
        </tr>
    </table>
</div>
```

The CSS stylesheet makes the status initially hidden:

```
#status {
  visibility: hidden;
  text-align: center;
}
```

When the message gains focus, it makes the status visible and calls showStatus() to set its values according to the message's initial state. The Status Area remains until the message is blurred. To update on each change, showStatus is called on keyup:

```
function onMessageFocus(event) {
  ...
  $("status").style.visibility = "visible";
  showStatus(message);
}

function onMessageBlur(event) {
  ...
  $("status").style.visibility = "hidden";
  ...
}

function onMessageKeyUp(event) {
  var message = getMessage(event);
  showStatus(message);
}
```

The showStatus message analyzes the message and posts its results to the status-table cells:

```
function showStatus(message) {
  $("messageId").innerHTML = message.id;
  $("characterCount").innerHTML = message.value.length;
  $("rowCount").innerHTML = message.value.split('\n').length + 1;
  var messageCopy = message.value.replace("\n", " ");
  messageCopy = message.value.replace(/^ */, "");
```

```
        messageCopy = messageCopy.replace(/ *$/, "");
        $("wordCount").innerHTML = messageCopy.match(/^ *$/) ? 0:messageCopy.split(/\s+/g).
    length;
      }
```

Alternatives

Popup

A *Popup* (see earlier) is another way to show auxiliary information without dedicating a permanent space on the page for it. A Status Area is less intrusive but at the expense of some screen real estate.

Browser Status Bar

Most browsers contain a status bar at the bottom, which you can access with the window. status object. That's an okay place to include status information, but it has drawbacks. First, it's a very rudimentary interface with no support for structured content, styling, and animation. Second, users expect URLs to appear there when they hover over hyperlinks, and you might be breaking that model. Finally, there are cross-browser issues. Firefox, for instance, disables scripting the status line by default due to security concerns (malicious web sites can fake the URL you're heading to).

Related Patterns

Periodic Refresh

Where the Status Area shows server-related status, use a *Periodic Refresh* (Chapter 10) to keep it up to date.

Metaphor

A Status Area is like a time-share property; both reduce real estate costs by letting multiple participants occupy the same area at different times.

Update Control

Backwards, FastForward, Forwards, Freeze, Pause, Push, Refresh, Rewind, Reverse, Speed, Sticky, Update

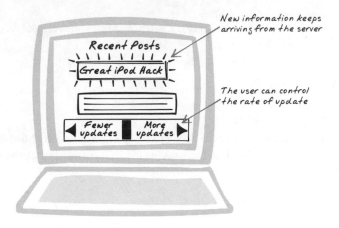

FIGURE 15-20. Update Control

Goal Story

Sasha is entranced by a world map that continuously updates with events from around the world. She plays around with the velocity controls, first speeding it up so there's a new event every second (no matter how trivial), then backtracking through previous events, and finally pausing on something that catches her eye.

Problem

How can the user deal with continuous information entering the browser and updating the page?

Forces

- Many Ajax Apps continuously grab data from the server and place it on the page.

- The web page has a limited area, so you'll need to remove or relegate older content.

- The optimum speed of updating depends on the user and his task. It should be fairly quick if the user is actively monitoring, for example, and probably quite slow if the content is a bit of eye candy at the edge of a page.

Solution

Let the user control the rate and criteria of updates. When using patterns such as *HTTP Streaming* (Chapter 6) and *Periodic Refresh* (Chapter 10), it's possible to keep grabbing fresh content from the server, so you can show news updates, system events, and more. The trend is increasing, with photo slideshows, news updates, and so on, and it can easily lead to information overload. This pattern is about giving the user control over the incoming stream of information. It takes several forms.

First, the user can control the rate of change, by pausing, rewinding, and fast-forwarding. Pausing is important for several reasons: it gives the user an ability to reflect on the content, it lets him keep the content open while perform work related to it, and it lets him interact with the content in the case that it contains links or other forms of control. This is a serious issue in interfaces like Digg Spy (*http://digg.com/spy*) that stream new links every second or so. Go to click a link and—BAM!—it's already been replaced by a new link by the time your mouse pointer gets there.

Rewinding is useful too, because it lets users see things they didn't catch the first time, or lets them revisit something in the light of new information.

Fast-forwarding is another form of Update Control. More generally, this relates to setting the speed of updates to be faster or slower than the application's default. With this tool, users can tailor update behavior to their own needs and the task they're performing. Different users will have different mental processing capabilities and preferences—some are hungry for a torrent of incoming data, whereas others prefer a more casual pace. Furthermore, consider how is the information being used. In one case, the user, perhaps a trader monitoring company news, might be actively watching the information. In another case, the user might be trying to find an interesting story to read while viewing a list of new RSS items. Instead of second-guessing how the user's using all of this content, the advice in this pattern is to set a suitable default rate and give her the power to change it.

In theory, you only need a single "speed control" to allow for Update Control. A negative speed corresponds to rewind, zero to pause, one to default speed, and a high number for fast-forward. This could be set with a *Slider* (Chapter 14) or an input field or both. However, you can probably do a better job than that. The media player metaphor is particularly compelling given how closely it relates to this problem as well as how universal the concepts are. You may also opt to control the speed by adapting to the user's behavior. If the mouse is hovering near some content, that's probably a good clue to pause it, especially if the content is interactive.

You can also let the user choose what kind of content will be shown, which is an indirect way of influencing the rate. For example, a user might select between "Critical", "Informational," and "All." Or the criteria may be more domain-specific, as with Digg Spy, which provides checkboxes for the kinds of things you want to monitor—new stories, new comments, and so on.

Real-World Examples

Digg Spy

Digg Spy (*http://digg.com/spy*) shows new stories and events such as user moderation as they happen (see Figure 5-5). The information can change so quickly that it's difficult to click on a link, but fortunately a pause button is present. In addition, you can indirectly control how fast the content appears by tweaking the filtering options, so, for example, you can ask Digg to show only you new story submissions.

Slide

Slide (*http://Slide.com*) shows a stream of visual content from Flickr, EBay, and elsewhere (Figure 15-21). A minus (-) button moves content to the left, a pause button pauses it, and a plus (+) button speeds it up. It will also pause when you hover the mouse over it. The rolling slideshow is implemented with Flash, but the idea is equally applicable to pure Ajax.

FIGURE 15-21. Slide

WBIR

WBIR (*http://wbir.com/*), a regional news provider, sometimes shows "slideshow images" (Figure 15-22). Like animated GIFs, these are a sequence of several images—shown one at a time—in the same container. But unlike animated GIFs, you can click to pause a single image.

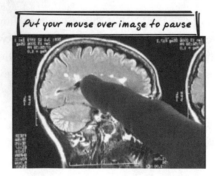

FIGURE 15-22. WBIR.com image

Code Example: Digg Spy

Digg Spy (*http://digg.com/spy*) includes a pause and a play button in the initial HTML. At any point in time, exactly one of these buttons is active and will respond to a click, which is registered to notify the togglePause( ) function. togglePause( ) doesn't actually check which button the event originated from, because it instead tracks the pause mode with an explicit pause variable. Thus, the first task of `togglePause( )` is to toggle the state of the `pause` variable.

```
function togglepause( ) {
  pause = !pause;
  ...
}
```

If we've just entered pause mode, `togglepause( )` cancels the timers used to make the updates. Otherwise, it does the exact opposite, i.e., schedules the updates, as well as making an initial update.

```
function togglepause( ) {
  ...
  if (pause == 1) {
    clearInterval(timer);
    clearTimeout(timer2);
    ...
  } else {
    update( );
    timer = setInterval('addaline(true)', scrollDelay);
    timer2 = setTimeout('update( )', updateDelay);
  }
  ...
}
```

The last thing `togglepause( )` does is call `write_pause`, which updates the container (play-pause-toggle) containing both buttons. The HTML is mostly the same in both cases, but the hyperlink to `togglepause( )` changes location according to which button should be active.

```
function write_pause( ) {
  if (pause == 0) {
    document.getElementById('pause-play-toggle').innerHTML = '<span class=
"spy-play"><strong>Play</strong></span><a href="#" onclick=
"togglepause( )" class="spy-pause">Pause</a></span>';
  } else {
    document.getElementById('pause-play-toggle').innerHTML = '<a href=
"#" class="spy-play" onclick="togglepause( )"><strong>Play</strong></a><span
class="spy-pause"><strong title="Pause the display of new items.">Pause</strong></span>
';
  }
}
```

Related Patterns

Periodic Refresh

Periodic Refresh (Chapter 10) is one means of keeping page content fresh—hence, a situation in which you might use Update Control.

HTTP Streaming

Like *Periodic Refresh* (Chapter 10), *HTTP Streaming* (Chapter 6) is a pattern that keeps page content fresh, the same situation in which Update Control applies.

Metaphor

Think of the navigation controls on a DVD player; conceptually, Update Control is very similar.

Acknowledgments

Thanks to Christopher Kruslicky for suggesting a pattern based around pausing, which ultimately led to this pattern.

Virtual Workspace

Camera, Desktop, Illusion, Infinite, InfiniteScrollbar, Lens, Move, Pan, Portal, Scroll, Solipsism, Viewport, Virtual, Visible, Window, Zoom

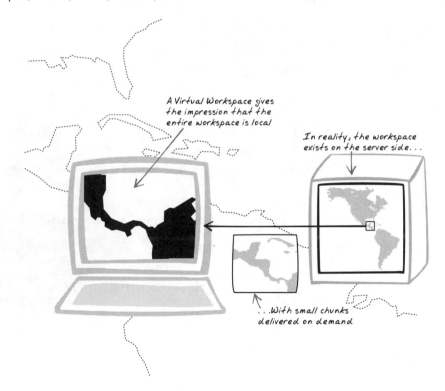

FIGURE 15-23. Virtual Workspace

Goal Story

Bill is using a meta-search engine to receive insurance quotes. The browser can't retrieve all 500 results at once, but Bill sees a table containing what looks like all the results. He can scroll up and down as if it were a regular table, and the newly appearing rows are populated on demand.

Problem

How can the user navigate through a large workspace?

Forces

- Ajax Apps often require data from the server.

- On the server side, data storage is virtually unlimited—search engines, for example, store billions of web pages. Even on corporate intranets, query results are often huge; try searching for every retail transaction on a given day.

- The application should respond to data requests as quickly as possible.

- Bandwidth constraints mean it's not feasible for an interactive application to download the entire search result. Yet users should be free to explore the whole thing.

Solution

Provide a browser-side view into a server-side workspace, allowing users to navigate the entire workspace as if it were held locally. The illusion is that the entire workspace is already in the browser, but the reality is that the server actually provides content on demand. At any time, the user is looking at an "opening" or "portal" into the entire workspace. He can pan across, jump to a different region, and zoom in and out. Each of these actions requires a view change, so the browser transparently fetches the data for the new portion of the workspace and renders it accordingly.

Here are some examples of navigable workspaces:

Lists
> These include search results and user preferences.

Tables
> These include *Data Grids* and spreadsheets.

Physical images
> These include diagrams, photos and maps.

Documents
> These include web content.

3D Models
> These include computer-rendered landscapes and visualizations of virtual models such as chemical molecules.

Time-dependent artifacts
> These include any artifact that changes with time—world population, for instance—and can be "navigated" by moving across time.

Users move through the space in different ways. Often they use a combination of the tools described next.

Scrollbars
> Users can make the content scroll incrementally or jump to a completely different region.

Dragging tool
> Gives the user the impression of dragging the document around while keeping the view fixed.

Keyboard shortcuts
> Users can scroll incrementally using directional keys. Page Up and Page Down are often used to completely replenish the current view with an adjacent region. Home and End are often used to jump to the start and end.

Direct command
> Users can use a separate control to specify an exact region—for example, typing in the dimensions they want to view. Or, for an image, placing a bounding box on a thumbnail view of the entire document.

There are also different zooming techniques:

Zoom slider
> This is an adjustable *Slider* that represents the current zoom level.

Keyboard shortcuts
> A common choice for zooming in and out is - and + (or =, since + usually requires pressing Shift-=).

Selecting a region
> This is used to zoom further into a region within the current view.

Depending on the mechanisms you're supporting, you'll need to add different types of event handlers. So, for keyboard shortcuts, watch for events like keydown; for dragging and selecting a region, watch for mousedown, mousemove, and mouseup. In some cases, you'll need a control separate from the view itself, as is the case with a zoom slider or a thumbnail sketch of the entire workspace.

Whatever the event mechanism, the upshot is that the browser script will sometimes receive notifications that there is a new desired region or zoom level, if that's applicable. At that point, a Web Remoting (Chapter 6) call must occur, passing the server the details of the new region. Upon reply, the old data is either replaced or shifted along and the new data is rendered.

This pattern is often very bandwidth-intensive, considering that the entire workspace can be massive and the interaction complex. For that reason, there are several important performance optimizations—for more details, see "Related Patterns" later in this chapter.

Decisions

How will you handle panning?

Panning, as opposed to jumping straight from one position to another, provides some unique design challenges. Unlike a complete jump, the user will expect a smooth transition from one position to another. Fortunately though, you already have most of the workspace loaded. Thus, a *Browser-Side Cache* (Chapter 13) is very important if you wish to achieve smooth scrolling. With this, you need only to load the new portion of the workspace instead of the whole thing. This leads to a few more specific questions:

- How much of the workspace will you cache? A standard caching trade-off between memory and speed.

- How will you track changes? Again, this should be the responsibility of the cache. At one level, the script will ask for the whole workspace, but the cache will decide which portion of that actually requires server content.

How will the view appear initially?

There has to be a default view position and zoom level within the overall workspace. A typical choice for the view is at the logical start or center. Zoom level should usually be quite high to let the user quickly drill down from the starting point.

What do you display while a region is being repopulated?

Most of the time, users are navigating to areas that are partly or completely unpopulated, requiring a result from the server to render them. What do you show in the interim? Here are a few options:

- Whatever was there previously, possibly with a change of appearance.

- Nothing—clear it while waiting.

- A *Progress Indicator* (Chapter 14).

- A *Popup* (see earlier in this chapter)—perhaps with just a single word—indicating what content will be placed there.

- A *Guesstimate* (Chapter 13) of the content, perhaps made by extrapolating neighboring data held in the cache.

How will you handle changes to the existing view?

Sometimes the workspace changes while the user is watching it. For example, a user might introduce a filter to a result set. A change to the workspace means the view must change too. The easiest approach is to abandon the previous view location and revert to the default. However, there is often a more logical solution. Following are some examples:

- You could keep the proportions the same as before—e.g., if the user was looking at rows one-third of the way down a table, then show the new rows that appear one-third of the way down the reduced table.

- You could fix on certain content—e.g., keep the top row in the same spot and show the remaining rows that are now directly below it. If the top row no longer exists, continue working downward until one of the rows does exist.

Real-World Examples

map.search.ch

http://map.search.ch is a Swiss Ajax map. Like Google Maps (*http://maps.google.com*) (which it predates) and similar products, the map constitutes a huge Virtual Workspace, and the user only views a tiny portion of it at any point in time. The map can be panned by dragging the workspace, clicking on arrow icons just outside its boundaries, and pressing the arrow keys. Zooming is controlled by clicking on a horizontal imagemap, clicking on Zoom In and Zoom Out buttons, or pressing Page Up and Page Down.

OpenRico Search Demo

The OpenRico Search Demo (*http://openrico.org/rico/yahooSearch.page*) is a *Cross-Domain Proxy* (Chapter 10) providing an Ajax interface to Yahoo! Search (Figure 15-24). Its philosophy was best summed up by OpenRico developer Bill Scott as "Death to Paging!" (*http://looksgoodworkswell.blogspot.com/2005/06/death-to-paging-rico-livegrid-released.html*). Instead of wading through a sequence of pages, you're presented with a single table containing all results. The results are a Virtual Workspace, and the table is a view into that space. Each time you navigate within the table, new results are pulled down from the server.

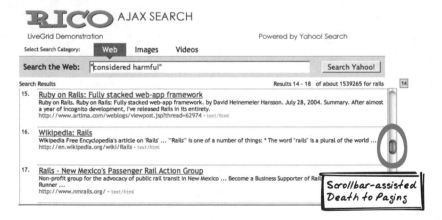

FIGURE 15-24. OpenRico Search Demo

Giant-Ass Image Viewer (GSV) library

Michael Magurski's GSV (*http://mike.teczno.com/giant/pan/*) is a library that lets web developers show an image of any size and allow the user to pan and zoom within it. The homepage contains a working demo.

Dunstan Orchard's blog

Dunstan Orchard's blog (*http://www.1976design.com/blog/colophon*) presents a slick panoramic, cartoonish view from his home. When the mouse rolls anywhere on the image, a couple of transparent *Popups* (see earlier in this chapter) appear on each side of the panorama. Rolling onto either of those and keeping the mouse there causes the banner to pan in that direction. Note that this is a different form of Virtual Workspace, since the whole workspace is local.

Code Refactoring: AjaxPatterns OpenRico Search

The OpenRico Search Demo is based on the OpenRico's LiveGrid API. In *Data Grid* (Chapter 14), the code example shows how to use the API. This example covers some of the API internals, specifically regarding the inclusion of a Virtual Workspace. Note that OpenRico uses Prototype (*http://prototype.conio.net/*) to allow for a more object-oriented coding style.

In OpenRico, the user's view is a GridViewPort object, which has a fixed row height and also tracks the view's starting position, i.e., the index that the top row of the GridViewPort corresponds to.

```
Rico.GridViewPort.prototype = {

  initialize: function(table, rowHeight, visibleRows, buffer, liveGrid) {
    ...
    this.rowHeight = rowHeight;
    this.div.style.height = this.rowHeight * visibleRows;
    ...
    this.startPos = 0;
  },
```

The results might include thousands of virtual rows, but the table itself is only about 20 rows (as determined by visibleRows). How, then, is the scrollbar created to make it appear as if there were thousands of rows? OpenRico creates a custom scrollbar. The trick is to create a 1-pixel-wide div whose height matches the height of the Virtual Workspace. The virtual height can be calculated since the scrollbar has access to the visible table height (visibleHeight), the number of virtual rows (metaData.getTotalRows()), and the number of rows in the view (metaData.getPageSize()). The scrollbar div's height is set to this virtual height, so the browser will render a scrollbar that appears to scroll across the entire virtual table:

```
createScrollBar: function() {
  var visibleHeight = this.liveGrid.viewPort.visibleHeight();
  // create the outer div...
  this.scrollerDiv  = document.createElement("div");
  ...
```

```
    // create the inner div...
    this.heightDiv = document.createElement("div");
    this.heightDiv.style.width  = "1px";
    this.heightDiv.style.height = parseInt(visibleHeight *
        this.metaData.getTotalRows()/this.metaData.getPageSize()) + "px" ;
    this.scrollerDiv.appendChild(this.heightDiv);
    this.scrollerDiv.onscroll = this.handleScroll.bindAsEventListener(this);

    var table = this.liveGrid.table;
    table.parentNode.parentNode.insertBefore(
      this.scrollerDiv, table.parentNode.nextSibling);
},
```

Events on the scrollbar are dispatched to handleScroll. After any scrolling behavior has occurred, this function calculates the portion of virtual space being viewed. The algorithm determines the new virtual row that should appear on top of the viewport. For instance, if the row height is 10 pixels, and the user has scrolled to 50 pixels from the top, then the virtual row is 5; the viewport will need to be refreshed such that the new top row is the fifth virtual row.

```
handleScroll: function( ) {
    ...
    var contentOffset = parseInt(this.scrollerDiv.scrollTop / this.viewPort.rowHeight);
    this.liveGrid.requestContentRefresh(contentOffset);
    this.viewPort.scrollTo(this.scrollerDiv.scrollTop);
    ...
},
```

requestContentRefresh fetches the required content into a *Browser-Side Cache* known as Buffer. With the buffer in place, you can smoothly scroll back to previously seen results without any call required:

```
fetchBuffer: function(offset) {
    ...
    var bufferStartPos = this.buffer.getFetchOffset(offset);
    this.processingRequest = new Rico.LiveGridRequest(offset);
    this.processingRequest.bufferOffset = bufferStartPos;
    ...
    callParms.push('id='        + this.tableId);
    callParms.push('page_size=' + fetchSize);
    callParms.push('offset='    + bufferStartPos);
    ...
    ajaxEngine.sendRequest.apply( ajaxEngine, callParms );
    ...
},
```

Eventually, the viewport table is populated with the new set of rows:

```
refreshContents: function(startPos) {
    ...
    for (var i=0; i < rows.length; i++) {//initialize what we have
      this.populateRow(this.table.rows[i + contentOffset], rows[i]);
    }
    ...
},
```

Alternatives

Virtual Magnifying Glass

Instead of showing a partial view, you could present the entire thing in low detail and offer a "Virtual Magnifying Glass" or "Virtual Fish-Eye Lens" to zoom in on the detail. This might sound like it could only be applied to an image, but it is also applicable to tables and other interfaces.

Related Patterns

Browser-Side Cache

Browser-Side Cache (Chapter 13) is very important with respect to the Virtual Workspace—if the user moves 1 percent down, you don't want to download the entire view again.

Predictive Fetch

It's useful to perform a *Predictive Fetch* (Chapter 13) on regions of the Virtual Workspace that the user is likely to navigate to next. Panning is a common task, so it's worthwhile caching the regions neighboring the current view. You might also cache at the next and previous zoom levels.

Guesstimate

Sometimes you might be able to quickly satisfy a navigation action with a *Guesstimate* (Chapter 13) while waiting for the real data to return.

Multi-Stage Download

If the response is large, break it into more than one part; download the most important information first, then follow up with more refined content.

Drag-And-Drop

Drag-And-Drop (see earlier) is often used to let the user pan by enabling her to drag the entire workspace across the view.

Slider

The zoom control is often a *Slider* (Chapter 14).

Unique URLs

Views need to be associated with *Unique URLs* (Chapter 17) so that the user can highlight a particular part of the workspace rather than the entire thing. That way, the user can easily bookmark the view or mail it to a friend.

Metaphor

Did you see *The Truman Show* (*http://www.imdb.com/title/tt0120382/*)? It's the story of a man who has no idea his whole world is fake, completely architected for the purposes of a reality TV show. As he walks around town, props are adjusted and the "townspeople" are directed a few seconds ahead of his arrival. There's a similar type of perception management going in Virtual Workspace; the illusion is that there's a whole world of content beyond the view, but the reality is that it's all constructed on demand.

Want to Know More?

Death to Paging—Bill Scott's LiveGrid Announcement (*http://looksgoodworkswell.blogspot. com/2005/06/death-to-paging-rico-livegrid-released.html*).

Acknowledgments

Thanks to Bill Scott for pointing out this example and keeping me updated on the progress of OpenRico and the LiveGrid functionality. Bill and fellow OpenRico developer Richard Cowin helped explain some of the implementation.

CHAPTER SIXTEEN

Visual Effects

A RICH INTERFACE IS MORE THAN STATIC WIDGETS; THERE'S A DYNAMIC COMPONENT THAT HAS A BIG impact on usability. Used carefully, visual effects can guide the user's attention and help him understand what the application is doing. And don't underestimate the aesthetic benefits. It might be eye candy, but *good* eye candy (not just "how good am I" hacks) makes passionate users.*

The "One-Second" effects are fleeting effects that sometimes convey a permanent transition from one state to another, and other times are used just to highlight something. *One-Second Spotlight* is a more general version of the popular "Yellow Fading Technique" and involves changes to brightness and color. In *One-Second Mutation*, the element changes shape, and in *One-Second Motion*, the element moves around.

---

* Donald Norman, traditional defender of "serious" usability principles, has more recently argued that emotions like fun and excitement do make a big impact and should be considered by designers (Norman, 2003). "Passionate Users" is a reference to the excellent Creating Passionate Users blog at *http://headrush.typepad.com/creating_passionate_users/*.

Highlight is a more permanent effect where one or more elements are highlighted, typically because the user has selected them.

One-Second Spotlight

●●●

Attention, Effect, EyeCandy, Fade, Fading, Graphics, Refresh, Update, YellowFadeTechnique

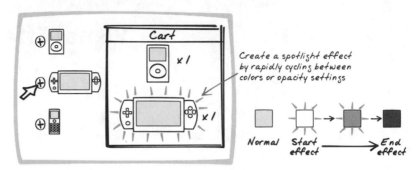

FIGURE 16-1. One-Second Spotlight

Goal Story

Tracy is checking out her portfolio, which shows each stock in its own row. Suddenly, "Neverland Mining Co." stock plummets, and its row lights up to reflect the change. Tracy's attention is drawn instantly to this visual effect, and she immediately begins to off-load her stake in the company.

Problem

How can you direct the user's attention to spots on the page?

Forces

- To ensure that the user is working with current data, the browser display must be frequently updated.

- With Ajax, it's possible to update only the portion of the screen that has changed, and if nothing has changed, the display will remain exactly as is.

- The screen can get cluttered with a lot of information, much of which might change at any time.

- While human vision is good at spotting changes, it's easy to miss a sudden change, especially if it's a subtle one.

Solution

When a display element undergoes a value change—or any other significant change—dynamically increase its brightness for about a second. As a device for communicating system activity, the One-Second Spotlight accomplishes several things:

- It highlights changes so the user doesn't have to actively monitor for changes and try to remember what—if anything—has changed.

- Because the spotlight lasts for a few seconds, the user has enough time to redirect attention to that item and study the details of the event—e.g., looking at an item's new value. In contrast, a standard transition would afford her no time whatsoever—if the user happened to blink, she could easily miss the change.

- When the animation technique follows certain conventions or mimics real-world phenomena, it can provide hints to the user about the nature of the event.

This pattern is a generalization of the technique 37signals introduced as the Yellow Fade Technique (*http://www.37signals.com/svn/archives/000558.php*). With that, an item lights up for a second after the user has edited it, and the lighting quickly fades away. Unlike a conventional application, in which a page refresh would occur, it's often unclear when an *XMLHttpRequest Call* has occurred. So a quick visual effect is almost essential for the user to understand what's happening.

From a technical perspective, the Yellow Fade Technique is usually achieved by suddenly switching the element's background-color style from white to yellow, then using *Scheduling* to run through a continuous spectrum of background colors, starting with yellow and ending with white.

In more general terms, One-Second Spotlight encompasses several types of animation. One or more of the following CSS styles are affected during the spotlight period:

color

Usually, the element's background changes, but font color is also a possibility. Though commonly assigned with Red-Green-Blue hex codes such as #ff00ff, animation algorithms can benefit from the percentage form, e.g., (100%, 0%, 100%). Often, the algorithm cycles through one or more of the Red, Green, and Blue components, e.g., gradually raising Red from 50 percent to 100 percent and lowering it back to 50 percent while holding blue and green constant. You might also prefer to represent the color as a combination of Hue-Saturation-Value (HSV) and cycle through one or more of those components. In this case, calculate the HSV values and convert them to RGB for display.

opacity

This style determines how transparent the element is; an opacity of zero means the item is solid, and an opacity of 50 percent means the browser background—or any items underneath the element—will be partially visible.

visibility

This style determines whether the element can be seen. Visibility does *not* affect page layout, so the element still occupies the same space on the page.

The possibilities are endless, but there are a few common effects. Firstly, there are straight-forward transitions from one style setting to another:

Fade Out

An element suddenly brightens and then fades back to its original appearance. This is useful for general highlighting and may also indicate that the element has been "sucked into" the server, i.e., the data is now safely stored server side. Since many pages use a white background, fading the background out to white is a natural choice for general attention grabbing.

Fade In

An element is suddenly dimmed and then brightens up to its original appearance. This is useful for general highlighting and may also indicate that the element has been "pushed out" of the server.

Fade Away

An element fades further and further out until it disappears altogether. If the element is already somewhat dim, it may be helpful to brighten it at the start of the animation. This effect often indicates that the element (or its value) has been suspended or destroyed.

Materialize

From nothing, an element fades into its regular appearance. If its regular appearance is somewhat dim, it may be helpful to fade it in to a higher level, then fade back out a bit. This can indicate that the element has been created or retrieved.

Switch

An element gradually switches its appearance from one setting to another. Instead of fading or brightening, though, an element might shift from red to blue. This effect is usually used to indicate a state change.

The other category of effects involves rapid oscillation and includes the following:

Total Flash

In rapid succession, an element completely disappears and then reappears. The transition to and from a state of disappearance can be achieved by continuous fading, or by simply toggling the `visibility` style. This effect is useful as a general attention grabber, although it brings back memories of the dreaded `<blink>` tag; be sparing in your use of flashing elements.

Shifting Flash

An element's appearance shifts several times from one setting to another. This can also be used as a general attention grabber if the element returns back to its original appearance. If the element permanently shifts from one setting to another, this effect will grab attention more effectively than *Switch*, which is a more subtle transition.

One typical implementation combines *Display Morphing* with *Scheduling*. To fade an item out, for instance, the following algorithm may be used:

1. Remember the element's current setting.

2. Set `element.style.color` to a bright setting.

3. Every 100 milliseconds:

   a. Fade the element a bit. More precisely, drop `color` by 10 percent (of the bright setting). This applies individually to each `color` component (R, G, B).

   b. Check if 1,000 milliseconds has already passed. If so, set the element back to its original setting (it should already be about that anyway).

The algorithm is based on interpolation. In moving from color A to color B, there are a number of discrete transitions that occur, say, once every 100 milliseconds. At each stage, the algorithm decides where on the spectrum from A to B the color should be. Since a color consists of three components—R, G, and B—the calculation occurs separately for each component.

So, let's say you're shifting from #ffffff to #000044. First, it's useful to represent these as decimal percentage settings: (100%, 100%, 100%) moving to (0%, 0%, 25%). And assume we're going to make 10 transitions. The red and green components will shift down 10 percent each step, and the blue component will shift down 7.5 percent each time. So it's just a matter of dropping the value for each color component at each transition, rounding off, and redisplaying the element.

If you want to make a transition to the background of the element, you can shift `opacity` instead of `color`. (Be aware that there are portability issues with `opacity` [*http://www.quirksmode.org/css/opacity.html*].)

The algorithm assumes a linear interpolation, where each transition drops by the same amount. You could also experiment with other transitions. An exponentially increasing interval, for example, would give an effect of an initially slow transition, leading to a quick burst at the end. A similar phenomenon is quite common with flash effects, where the flashing starts off slowly and speeds up at the end.

You probably won't have to hand code many of these effects because libraries like Scriptaculous (*http://script.aculo.us*; discussed below) are quite flexible and easy to incorporate.

Decisions

What events will trigger a spotlight?

An Ajax App undergoes multiple events; which warrant a spotlight? A spotlight can serve any of the following purposes:

- To draw the user's attention to a change
- To suggest that the user needs to do something
- To inform the user that a browser-server interaction has taken place
- To inform the user that another user has done something

Here are some examples:

- The user has just changed something. A *Fade Out* effect suggests that the change has been sent to the server.

- On the server, a new item has been created. A *Materialize* effect suggests that the item has just appeared.

- The user has forgotten to enter a form field. The field undergoes a *Shifting Flash* as its background shifts from white to red.

- An item has just changed value. A *Fade Out* effect suggests that the change was just picked up by the browser.

What color will be used?

Yellow, popularized by 37signals, is becoming something of a standard for fading effects. In general, though, the color has to take into consideration which element is affected, as well as surrounding elements and the page appearance in general.

Additionally, multiple colors can be used to good effect. For instance, each color can be used to represent a different type of event. In a multiuser context, JotSpot Live (*http:// jotlive.com*) illustrates how each user can be associated with a different color so that their recent edits appear as distinctly-colored fade effects.

How long should the spotlight last? How long will each transition be?

Asking how long the spotlight should last might seem a bit ridiculous for a pattern named "One-Second Spotlight." But the name, of course, only hints at one reasonable value. You'll have to decide on the precise duration of the overall effect and also on how many transitions will take place in that time.

Here are some considerations:

- A longer duration will have a greater window of time to be noticed.

- A longer duration will appear less dramatic, so it might be interpreted as a less critical event.

- A longer duration increases the likelihood of multiple spotlights occurring simultaneously, which might be confusing, especially if they are flash effects.

- A longer duration increases the likelihood of a second spotlight effect occurring on the *same* element while the first effect is in progress. That's not necessarily a problem in itself, but it does lead to an implementation issue; it's worth ensuring that an element is undergoing only one effect at a time to prevent any nasty issues, like flickering.

As far as transitions go, the trade-off is fairly clear: faster transitions look smoother but slow down the application. Is the user likely to leave your application in a background tab and only check it once an hour? If so, avoid slowing down the whole browser with high-granularity effects. Likewise if the application is already process-intensive.

This is an area where different browsers will act differently. For instance, what's the lowest possible transition time you can set? That will depend on the user's system and the browser in question. You can experiment with different parameters on the Time Spotlight Demo (*http://ajaxify.com/run/time/periodicRefresh/spotlightCustom/*).

Real-World Examples

37signals Backpack

37signals Backpack (*http://www.backpackit.com/*) maintains items in a list (Figure 16-2). When you click the Edit button, the read-only item morphs into a textarea. On saving, it becomes read-only again and is accompanied by a yellow *Fade Out* effect. All quite fitting for the company that coined the term, "Yellow Fade Technique."

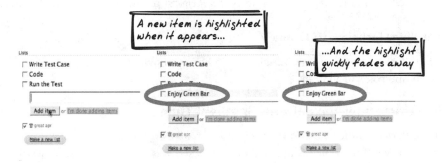

FIGURE 16-2. Backpack

chat.app

chat.app (*http://gamma.nic.fi/~jmp/chat/app.html*) shows text messages as you or others enter them. Each new message is highlighted with a yellow *Fade Out*.

Digg Spy

Digg Spy (*http://digg.com/spy*) shows new stories as they appear on the Web. Each time a block of new stories appears, it appears with a *Fade Out* effect—the background shifting from grey to white.

Coloir

Coloir (*http://www.couloir.org*) is a slideshow application. Each time you click next, an animated "loading" icon appears and a new photo fades in.

Odeo

Odeo (*http://odeo.com*) is a podcast subscription service. You can force Odeo to grab the latest feed for a podcast; during the delay, the entire document fades. An effect like this can be achieved with a partially transparent *Popup* element covering the whole document. It feels similar to the way Windows fades the entire screen when you're about to log out.

Scriptaculous library

Scriptaculous (*http://script.aculo.us*) is an excellent JavaScript library supporting many Ajax UI patterns. Its visual effects library is based on four fundamental effects:

- Altering opacity
- Altering scale
- Altering position
- "Parallel" effects—i.e., multiple effects at the same time

Combining these leads to any number of animation sequences, and many of the useful sequences are prepackaged.

The visual effects demo (*http://script.aculo.us/visual-effects*) provides many spotlight effects.

Fade Anything Technique (FAT) library

FAT (*http://www.axentric.com/posts/default/7*) is a library allowing easy scripting of a transition from one color to another.

Code Refactoring: AjaxPatterns Spotlight Time

The Time Periodic Refresh demo (*http://www.ajaxpatterns.org/run/time/periodicRefresh/*) shows the server time, which is updated every few seconds. It's not clear exactly when the time has changed, however, so this refactoring adds a spotlight effect each time a new result arrives from the server. There are actually a couple of refactorings here: one is hand-built and the other illustrates reuse of the Scriptaculous library.

Hand-built shift effect

The Time Spotlight Demo (*http://www.ajaxpatterns.org/run/time/periodicRefresh/ spotlightCustom*) lets the user set a few parameters and applies the corresponding effect (Figure 16-3). A fader object encapsulates the fading logic. The fade duration and transition interval are modifiable attributes:

```
fader.durationTime = parseInt($("fadeDuration").value);
fader.transitionInterval = parseInt($("transitionInterval").value);
```

The application asks fader to fade the div as soon as it's been modified:

```
function showCustomTime(text) {
  var customTimeLabel = $("customTimeLabel");
  customTimeLabel.innerHTML = text + "." + callingContext;
  fader.fade(customTimeLabel, $("startColor").value, $("endColor").value);
}
```

fader then kicks off the first transition, passing in a timeSoFar parameter of zero. The function is simpler using an array of percentage color values, but hex is more common, so a simple conversion takes place:

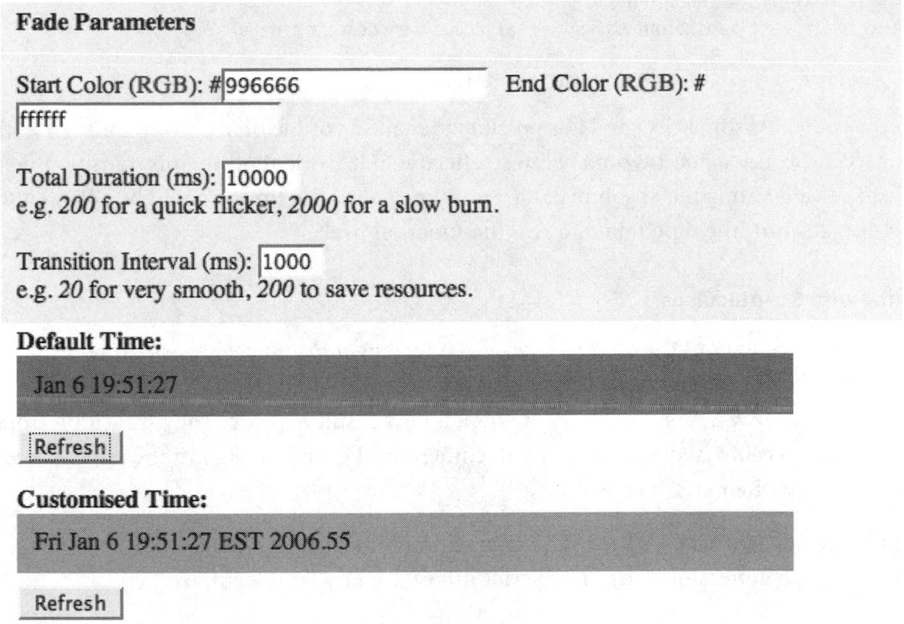

Fade Parameters

Start Color (RGB): #996666   End Color (RGB): #
ffffff

Total Duration (ms): 10000
e.g. *200* for a quick flicker, *2000* for a slow burn.

Transition Interval (ms): 1000
e.g. *20* for very smooth, *200* to save resources.

Default Time:

Jan 6 19:51:27

Refresh

Customised Time:

Fri Jan 6 19:51:27 EST 2006.55

Refresh

FIGURE 16-3. Time Spotlight Demo

```
fade: function(element, startRGB, endRGB) {
  this.nextTransition(
    element, this.rgbToPercents(startRGB), this.rgbToPercents(endRGB),0);
}
```

Each transition involves deciding how far along the fade it is and calculating the corresponding color style using a linear interpolation (as explained in the Solution for this pattern):

```
nextTransition: function(element, startColor, endColor, timeSoFar) {
  ...
  var currentColor = "rgb(";
  for (component=0; component<3; component++) {
    var currentComponent = Math.round(startColor[component] +
        proportionSoFar * (endColor[component] - startColor[component]));
    currentColor+=currentComponent + "%" + (component<2 ? "," : ")");
  }
  element.style.backgroundColor = currentColor;
  ...
}
```

Then it increments timeSoFar and finishes the fade if fade time has expired:

```
timeSoFar+=this.transitionInterval;
if (timeSoFar>=this.durationTime) {
  this.durationTime+ "\n";
  element.style.backgroundColor =
    "rgb("+endColor[0]+"%,"+endColor[1]+"%,"+endColor[2]+"%)";
  return;
}
```

```
var nextCall = function() {
  fader.nextTransition(element, startColor, endColor, timeSoFar);
}
setTimeout(nextCall, this.transitionInterval);
```

fader is coded for simplicity, and it is possible to make a couple of improvements. First, the repeated color calculation would be more effective if it worked on the pretransition delta instead of calculating the absolute color each time. Also, the timing could be adjusted to take into account the time taken to run the function itself.

Fading with Scriptaculous

The Time Scriptaculous Demo (*http://www.ajaxpatterns.org/run/time/periodicRefresh/ spotlightScriptaculous)* shows how easy it is to reuse an existing effects library. Here, the time displays show a `Materialize` effect when a new result appears. They transition from completely invisible (showing only the document background color) to the appearance determined by their class's style.

The refactoring is trivial. Include the Scriptaculous effects library, `effects.js`, and `prototype.js`, a general-purpose JavaScript utility used by Scriptaculous:

```
<script type="text/javascript" src="prototype.js"></script>
<script type="text/javascript" src="effects.js"></script>
```

Then, as with the hand-built `fader` presented earlier, invoking the effect is a one-liner:

```
new Effect.Appear("defaultTimeLabel");
```

Alternatives

One-Second Mutation and One-Second Motion

One-Second Mutation and *One-Second Motion* (see both later in this chapter) are also used to draw attention to a significant event. One-Second Spotlight can be used as both a general attention-getting device as well as to hint at a specific type of event, whereas those two patterns tend to be slightly more about depicting specific events. The effects can also be combined, e.g., shrinking an object as it fades away.

Related Patterns

Periodic Refresh

A change arising from a *Periodic Refresh* (Chapter 10) is often marked with aOne-Second Spotlight.

Timeout

A *Timeout* (Chapter 17) event, and any prior warnings, can be marked with a One-Second Spotlight. In community sites that show details about other users, the effect can also be used to mark changes to users' online status.

Metaphor

The pattern's name is the key here: a spotlight can be used to direct audience attention.

Acknowledgments

37signals introduced the Yellow Fade Technique into its products, and its Yellow Fade Technique article (*http://www.37signals.com/svn/archives/000558.php*) helped spread the meme.

One-Second Mutation

Auto-Update, Sync, Sychronize, Real-Time

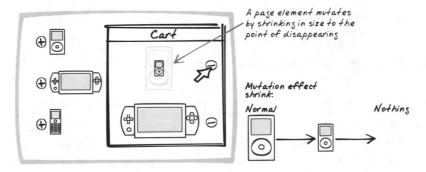

FIGURE 16-4. One-Second Mutation

Goal Story

Doc monitors a patient's condition, watching some histograms shrink and grow to reflect changes in the patient's body.

Problem

There's a lot of activity in an Ajax App; how can you help the user digest it all?

Forces

- To ensure that the user is working with current data, the browser display must be frequently updated.

- With Ajax, it's possible to update only the portion of the screen that has changed; if nothing has changed, the display remains exactly as is.

- The screen can get cluttered with a lot of information, much of which could change at any time.

- While human vision is good at spotting changes, it's easy to miss a sudden change, especially if the change is a subtle one.

- There are different types of changes, and those differences are important to users.

Solution

When a page element undergoes a value change or some other significant event, dynamically mutate its shape for about a second. In most cases, the mutation is used to reflect a permanent change. Instead of flipping from one form to another, the element gradually transitions into another form. The effect serves a few purposes:

- The mutation and the extended transition time make it likely that the user will notice that something has happened.

- The type of mutation hints at what sort of action has taken place.

- The gradual shift in appearance feels more natural than an instant transformation.

Mutation combines *Display Morphing* with *Scheduling*. A loop runs while the second of mutation progresses, with each transition occurring perhaps once every 50 milliseconds. Each transition will likely involve a change to at least one of the following CSS properties:

width
> An object can be thinned or fattened by changing its `width` value.

height
> An object can be heightened or shortened by changing its `height` property.

backgroundImage
> Instead of just resizing the element, it's possible to swap in a completely different image. Just like a movie, the DOM element quickly flips through various images to give the illusion of mutation. See the DHTML Lemmings walkthough in *Sprite* (Chapter 15) for more details.

position
> Manipulating position with `position`, `left`, `right`, `top`, and `bottom` is possible for certain mutation effects.

overflow
> Overflow can be set to `hidden` to enable the entire element to be present on the page while showing only a certain portion of it.

The first category of mutation involves making an object appear. The following are effective ways to communicate that the object has just been created or retrieved from the server.

Form
> An item "forms" from nothingness into its standard appearance—typically, by incremental, outward growth. It might grow from the center of the object, a corner, or some other position entirely. Typically, width and height increase at the same time.

Slide Out
> An item slides out. If the item slides in from the side, it appears to be pushed out like a sliding door. If the item comes in from the top, it appears like a garage door closing. If coming in from the bottom, the item appears to rise from the ground. Usually, either

width or height is fixed, while the other dimension gradually increases. The item's position changes simultaneously.

Reveal

An item is gradually revealed. It appears that the item has been there all along, and that a cover is gradually being lifted off. Here, one or both of width and height incrementally increases, while overflow is set to hidden so that part of the element is covered.

The next category of mutation involves some common disappearing acts—the opposite of the effects above—and a special effect for disappearing:

Disappear

An item changes from its standard appearance to nothingness.

Slide In

An item slides in from the top, side, or bottom.

Cover Up

An item is gradually covered up in one or both dimensions.

Blow Up

An item expands outward from its current side and simultaneously fades to nothingness.

There are also a few mutations that involve changing from one thing to another:

Grow

An item grows from one size to another. Height or width (or both) increases.

Shrink

An item shrinks from one size to another. Height or width (or both) decreases.

Metamorphise

An item shifts from one appearance to another. This is typically achieved with a change in background image. See *Sprite* (Chapter 15) for more details.

Most of these effects can be combined with *One-Second Spotlight* to give a 3-D effect. For example, an item can Materialize and Form at the same time. The human visual system uses both ambience and size as cues for distance, so the effect is that the item is reaching outward from behind the screen toward the user.

Note that you probably won't have to hand code effects, because libraries like Scriptaculous (discussed in the following "Real-World Examples") are quite flexible and are usually easy to incorporate into typical scripts.

Decisions

Most of the decisions in *One-Second Spotlight* are relevant here too. As with *One-Second Spotlight*, the "One-Second" part of the name is only a guideline.

Real-World Examples

TiddlyWiki

Jeremy Ruston's TiddlyWiki *(http://tiddlywiki.com)*, like many of its spin-offs, uses a Grow effect to introduce new content when you click on a *Microlink* (Chapter 15). The Microlink itself is the starting point. The new content block appears to leap out and, as it flows outward, grows into a full *Malleable Content* (Chapter 15) block (Figure 16-5). Actually, there are a few visual effects at work here:

- *One-Second Spotlight* (see earlier in this chapter) is used to fade in the *Malleable Content* being opened, in parallel to the element leaping out.

- One-Second Mutation is used to grow the transition element from its initial state as a small piece of link text into a full block of Malleable Content.

- *One-Second Motion* (see later in this chapter) is used to move the element from the *Microlink* position into the Malleable Content below.

There are a few possible variations depending on whether the content is already open and where it's placed.

Scriptaculous library

As mentioned in *One-Second Spotlight*, Scriptaculous is a general-purpose JavaScript library. Its visual effects demo *(http://script.aculo.us/visual-effects)* provides many of the mutation effects described here.

DHTML Lemmings

DHTML Lemmings is a full-featured implementation of the Lemmings PC game, which uses DOM manipulation to show the lemming creatures performing typical lemming-like activities, such as walking, digging, and clutching an umbrella to make a safe descent from the top of a cliff. As the characters move about, their appearance is animated using quick mutations. While the usage is somewhat different from the usual type of mutation, which tends to focus on highlighting particular pieces of information, it is still of particular interest because it involves manipulation of images instead of just CSS style. See the code walkthrough in *Sprite* (Chapter 15) for more details.

Code Example: TiddlyWiki

Let's look at how TiddlyWiki shows the Grow effect discussed earlier. In doing so, we'll see how its generic animation engine works.

TiddlyWiki delegates animation to an Animator, which is capable of animating according to a list of Strategy (Gamma et al., 1995) objects, or animations. Each encapsulates the strategy for a particular animation. At this time, there are just a couple of animation objects: a Zoomer and a Slider.

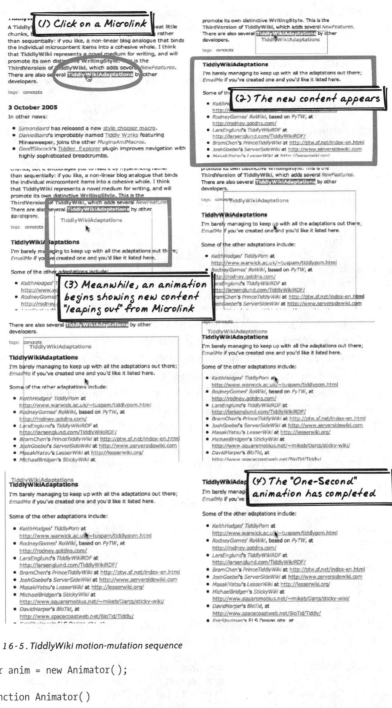

FIGURE 16-5. TiddlyWiki motion-mutation sequence

```
var anim = new Animator();

function Animator()
{
  ...
  this.animations = []; // List of animations in progress
  return this;
}
```

When a *Microlink* is clicked, the Animator is passed a Zoomer strategy, which is injected with the Microlink DOM object from which the content will leap out (src), a string title of the *Malleable Content* (title), the Malleable Content element in which the content will end up (theTiddler), and a flag indicating if the animation should be slow or not (I assume this is for debugging, and you can activate it by holding down Shift or Alt as you click on the link):

```
anim.startAnimating(new Zoomer(title,src,theTiddler,slowly));
```

startAnimating( ) pushes the new animation onto the list of running animations. If it's not already running, it sets up an animation loop:

```
Animator.prototype.startAnimating = function(animation)
{
  this.animations.push(animation);
  if(this.running++ == 0)
    {
    var me = this;
    this.timerID = window.setInterval(function( ) {me.doAnimate(me);},25);
    }
}
```

The loop runs every 25 milliseconds. It calls a tick( ) function on each running animation. By analyzing Zoomer's tick( ), you can see how the One-Second Mutation is achieved. Upon construction, Zoomer has already set up a bunch of variables to support this function, as well as an element (element) to be shown during the transition. The variables hold position information about the start and end elements. tick( ), then, is left with the task of interpolation: "if the item starts at point A and ends at point B, how should it look at a particular point in the journey?" The Animator provides a value f between 0 and 1 to define how far along the animation the object is, which makes things much easier. So, if the value is 0.5, the item's width will be halfway between the original width and the item's final width (Figure 16-6). The same idea applies for height and position:

```
this.element.style.left =
  this.startLeft + (this.targetLeft-this.startLeft) * f + "px";
this.element.style.top =
  this.startTop + (this.targetTop-this.startTop) * f + "px";
this.element.style.width =
  this.startWidth + (this.targetWidth-this.startWidth) * f + "px";
this.element.style.height =
  this.startHeight + (this.targetHeight-this.startHeight) * f + "px";
```

A *One-Second Spotlight* effect is also used here. The target object—the place the object is "leaping" toward—gradually fades in by way of the opacity property (and filter, for compatibility). Finally, the window is scrolled to show the target object:

```
this.targetElement.style.opacity = this.progress;
this.targetElement.style.filter = "alpha(opacity:" + this.progress * 100 + ")";
window.scrollTo(0,this.startScroll + (this.targetScroll-this.startScroll) * f);
```

The purpose of mutations is generally to provide a smooth transition from one state to another. Therefore, the final state should generally be reached simply by running the animation for the right period. No special handling needs to take place at the end, right?

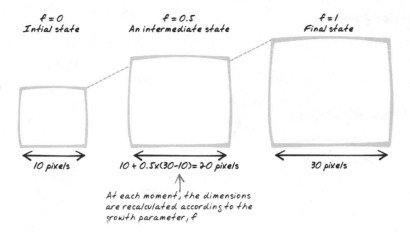

$f = 0$
Intial state

$f = 0.5$
An intermediate state

$f = 1$
Final state

10 pixels

$10 + 0.5 \times (30-10) = 20$ pixels

30 pixels

At each moment, the dimensions
are recalculated according to the
growth parameter, f

FIGURE 16-6. Growth factor

Well, in practice, there are rounding errors and approximations that make it good practice to explicitly set the final state. Thus, the Zoomer completes the animation by ensuring that the precise opacity is precisely 1 (in fact, the filter should ideally be set here too as a further security against rounding errors). The function also deletes the transient element it created to leap from source to target:

```
Zoomer.prototype.stop = function( )
{
  this.element.parentNode.removeChild(this.element);
  this.targetElement.style.opacity = 1;
  window.scrollTo(0,this.targetScroll);
}
```

Alternatives

One-Second Spotlight and One-Second Motion

One-Second Spotlight (see earlier) and *One-Second Motion* (see the next pattern) are also used to draw attention to a significant event. One-Second Mutation is particularly suited for indicating that certain types of changes, such as object creation and removal, have occurred. It is not as well suited for general-purpose attention grabbing.

Related Patterns

Sprite

Sprites (Chapter 15) are often changed in rapid succession to give the impression of a smooth transition.

Metaphor

Many of the individual effects have their own metaphors—that's why they're used! Slide Out looks like a physical object sliding outward, Grow looks like an object growing, and so on.

Acknowledgments

Many of the effects discussed in the preceding Solution are based on an analysis of the Scriptaculous implementation (*http://script.aculo.us*). Jeremy Ruston's TiddlyWiki code was also instructive, and Jeremy helped clarify part of the code.

One-Second Motion

Copy, Displace, Duplicate, Jump, Leap, Move, Movement, Motion, Rearrange, Transfer

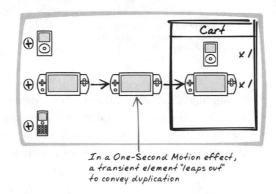

FIGURE 16-7. One Second Motion

Goal Story

Bill is adding a new monthly bank order. The existing orders are shown in the usual way—as a table with one row per order, sorted by cost. Once he is verified the new order form, it morphs to become a table row, then slowly drifts down the table. It soon reaches its rightful place in the sorted table, which is ordered by amount, and comes to rest after bouncing up and down a little due to reverberation.

Problem

How can you communicate that an element is shifting from one position to another?

Forces

- An element's location is important, as it can provide cues about its prominence and its relationship to other elements.

- An element sometimes needs to move from one place to another.

- Similarly, a new element sometimes needs to be created and then move from where it was created to another location.

- When an element changes position, the user often needs to know about it.

Solution

Incrementally move an element from one location to another, or temporarily move it, to communicate that an event has occurred. In most cases, the motion of the element involves a permanent change in its position. It can also be used to show a temporary displacement or gesture, such as a vibration effect.

There are several benefits of showing the motion explicitly:

- The motion and the extended transition time make it likely that the user will notice that something has happened.

- The motion will highlight the place where the element is moving to (it won't get lost on the page).

- The motion will feel more natural than an abrupt change.

The effect combines *Page Rearrangement* (Chapter 5) with *Scheduling* (Chapter 7). A loop runs for the duration of progresses, with each transition occurring perhaps once every 50 milliseconds. Each transition will likely involve a gradual change to the positioning style settings, usually to top and left. The position style can be set as absolute or relative, depending on the overall application design.

When an element has to move from point A to point B, in most cases it's logical for the trajectory to be the shortest distance from A to B, i.e., for the element to move as the crow flies. The algorithm in this case uses interpolation—for example, one-quarter of the time into the effect, an element will be one-quarter of the way between A and B—so, when moving from left to right, the left style of the element will be $(0.25*x(A) + 0.75*x(B))$, where x( ) represents the source and destinations' horizontal coordinate.

This assumes a linear interpolation. You can also experiment with other algorithms, e.g., you might like to accelerate the element as it proceeds, which is often a more realistic model.

Note that you probably won't have to hand code motion, because libraries like Scriptaculous (discussed in the "Real-World Examples") are quite flexible and usually easy to incorporate into typical scripts.

Decisions

What events will trigger a motion effect?

One-Second Motion is not very common (yet), but there are several potential applications. First, a permanent movement can show any of the following:

- A straightforward change from one place to another.

- One element being spawned from another, and then jumping out to a new location.

- An element being introduced into a space. Instead of making the element just appear, or fade in, you could make it arrive from a logical starting point. For example, a new data point in a chart can "fly in" from the corner.

A temporary movement has its own applications:

Attention-grabbing

> For general attention grabbing, motion is a killer app—humans are wired for sensitive motion detection as a means of survival. We've all seen enough annoying banner ads to know that. Extreme cases involve rapid vibration and rapid circuitous movement, such as tracing out a square 10 times a second. Of course, these extremes are rarely justified, and you can often use more subtle approaches to get the same effect (while causing a lot less annoyance).

Aesthetic effect

> People expect objects to move in certain ways based on their experiences in the physical world as well as learned expectations from conventions in movies, cartoons, and video games. For example, when a small object bumps into a big object, you expect the small object to fly off in the other direction and the big object to shake a little.

Gesture

> Some forms of motion rely on anthropomorphization—endowing the element with human-like characteristics—something users are surprisingly prone to do ("The computer doesn't like me today!"). In the Scriptaculous demo (discussed in this pattern's Code Example), the search form (*http://script.aculo.us/visual-effects*) shakes left and right when a validation error occurs, similar to a person shaking her head from side to side. Another effect would be to depict desire by showing an element temporarily "reaching" in a certain direction and pulling back again. This could be used as a hint to the novice user that he needs to drag the element in that direction.

Since motion can be distracting, you will likely want to limit its usage to the following situations:

- When the event is important enough that the user would probably appreciate having her attention diverted to it.

- When the user is likely to be focused on the motion already. Here, the motion is not used to attract attention, but rather to convey what's happening to the element.

- When visualization and motion are central to the application style; for example, if the application was tracking a car's movement every few seconds, it would probably be worthwhile to animate the move between sample points.

Also consider whether you should use motion at all. The conventional wisdom is that motion is more natural as a transition because it's based on the physical world. But how about the massive population that grew up with computers and might be perfectly comfortable with the sudden jumps that are only possible in a digital realm? Maybe not everyone will appreciate motion effects.

What will the element do when it reaches its destination?

In every example I've seen, the element stops suddenly at its destination. However, it might appear more natural if the element reverberates when stacked against another element.

Real-World Examples

Scriptaculous library

As mentioned in *One-Second Spotlight* (see earlier in this chapter), Scriptaculous is a general-purpose JavaScript library. The visual effects demo (*http://script.aculo.us/visual-effects*) supports motion-based effects.

TiddlyWiki

As detailed in *One-Second Mutation* (see earlier in this chapter), clicking on a TiddlyWiki *Microlink* (Chapter 15; see *http://tiddlywiki.com*) causes the entire content to "leap out" from the link and form in a new position.

Backbase Portal

The Backbase Portal Demo (*http://projects.backbase.com/RUI/portal.html*) contains a page full of *Portlets* (Chapter 15) arranged in three columns, each with its own menu. The menu contains all of the Portlets on the page, and choosing a Portlet causes it to move over to the top of the column. *One-Second Motion* is used to animate the Portlet's movement, allowing users to see that thePortlet has "flown in" to the top of a column from elsewhere on the page.

DHTML Lemmings

As detailed in *Sprite* (Chapter 15), DHTML Lemmings involves the movement of Lemming creatures through a game space. Each Lemming is represented as a DOM element.

MS-Windows

MS-Windows uses a form of One-Second Motion. When minimizing a window, the whole window appears to leap downward to its handle in the taskbar, like a large object being packed into a small container. The reverse process occurs upon activating the window. This is not an Ajax App, but is still significant, as it's frequently cited as a rationale for the kind of animation this pattern details.

Code Example: Scriptaculous Effects

Motion is one of the effects offered by the Scriptaculous effects library (*http://script.aculo.us/visual-effects*). Examining its implementation gives us an opportunity to look at the overall Scriptaculous effects engine, which also provides *One-Second Spotlight*– and *One-Second Mutation*–style effects.*

---

* Note that the engine code looks a little different to most JavaScript applications because it uses Prototype (*http://prototype.conio.net/*) to allow for a more object-oriented coding style.

The generic engine component controls the flow by continuously delegating to an individual effect object to perform an incremental animation. This is an example of the Strategy pattern (Gamma et al., 1995). The initialization sequence clears the frame count, computes the total effect time, and kicks off the loop:

```
start: function(options) {
  ...
  this.currentFrame = 0;
  this.startOn    = new Date().getTime();
  this.finishOn   = this.startOn + (this.options.duration*1000);
  ...
  if(!this.options.sync) this.loop();
}
```

The loop runs until the predicted finish time, at which point the animation cleans up and terminates. The most important thing here is the pos calculation, which determines how far along the animation is. The calculation is essentially timeSoFar/timeRemaining. So, one-quarter of the way through the animation, it will be 0.25. Next, a calculation takes place to support the fps option, which lets the caller state the maximum number of animation frames per second. If an animation is indeed required, the engine's render() function is called:

```
loop: function() {
  var timePos = new Date().getTime();
  if(timePos >= this.finishOn) {
    this.render(1.0);
    ...
    return;
  }
  var pos    = (timePos - this.startOn) / (this.finishOn - this.startOn);
  frame = Math.round(pos * this.options.fps * this.options.duration);
  if(frame > this.currentFrame) {
    this.render(pos);
    this.currentFrame = frame;
  }
  this.timeout = setTimeout(this.loop.bind(this), 10);
},
```

The main purpose of render() is to delegate to the effect strategy to perform the update. The strategy will receive a value between 0 and 1 to tell it how far the animation has proceeded.

The MoveBy effect takes a DOM element and tracks its start and end positions. The element's style is set to relative using a call to the effect engine's makePositioned() function. Because positioning is relative, you construct a MoveBy effect with relative arguments. To move an object 5 right and 10 down, you'd pass in 5 and 10 as parameters. The effect is to increase left by 5 and top by 10:

```
initialize: function(element, toTop, toLeft) {
  this.originalTop  = parseFloat(this.element.style.top || '0');
  this.originalLeft = parseFloat(this.element.style.left || '0');
  this.toTop        = toTop;
  this.toLeft       = toLeft;
```

```
    Element.makePositioned(this.element);
    ...
}
```

Remember that the effects engine delegates to `update()` for effect-specific behavior, passing in a progress ratio between 0 and 1. In the case of `MoveBy`, the algorithm performs the necessary interpolation calculation to see how far along the object should be (`topd` and `leftd`). Having made the calculation, all that remains is to update the DOM element's style:

```
update: function(position) {
  topd  = this.toTop  * position + this.originalTop;
  leftd = this.toLeft * position + this.originalLeft;
  this.setPosition(topd, leftd);
},
setPosition: function(topd, leftd) {
  this.element.style.top  = topd  + "px";
  this.element.style.left = leftd + "px";
}
```

The `MoveBy` effect in itself is useful for getting an object from A to B. But you can build on it to create effects such as motion displacements. One such effect, included in the Scriptaculous library, is `Shake()`, which swings an element left and right a few times. With the framework in place, the effect is easily defined as a sequence of moves:

```
Effect.Shake = function(element) {
  return new Effect.MoveBy(element, 0, 20,
    { duration: 0.05, afterFinish: function(effect) {
  new Effect.MoveBy(effect.element, 0, -40,
    { duration: 0.1, afterFinish: function(effect) {
  new Effect.MoveBy(effect.element, 0, 40,
    { duration: 0.1, afterFinish: function(effect) {
  ...
}
```

Alternatives

One-Second Spotlight and One-Second Mutation

One-Second Spotlight and *One-Second Mutation* (see both earlier in this chapter) are also used to draw attention to a significant event. One-Second Motion is suited for indicating that an object's state has changed in the case where there is some geometric mapping to each object's state. When used as a temporary displacement effect, One-Second Motion is sometimes an alternative to these other patterns.

Related Patterns

Sprite

A *Sprite* (Chapter 15) often undergoes motion similar to One-Second Motion and can make use of similar interpolation calculations.

Guesstimate

In some cases, the motion is a form of *Guesstimate* (Chapter 13). When an object is moving around according to state information, the motion effect is effectively an estimate of what's happening between positions.

Metaphor

Until "Beam Me Up" teleportation technology hits the markets, every visible movement in the physical world is an illustration of this pattern.

Highlight

Auto-Update, Sync, Sychronize, Real-Time

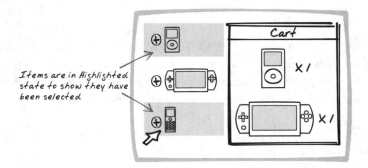

FIGURE 16-8.Metaphor

Goal Story

Sasha notices that a few spam comments have appeared on an old blog posting. When she clicks on the comments, they are successively Highlighted—the background color switches from white to yellow. Because she's already logged in, there's a Delete Spam button below the comments, which she clicks to send them where they belong.

Problem

How can you make elements stand out?

Forces

- An Ajax App can enable a lot of information to be shown at once—often information with many with different states.

- There is usually one element which the user is working on or about to activate.

- In addition, the user often needs to group several elements together to perform a common function. These elements must stand out from the crowd.

Solution

Highlight elements by rendering them in a consistent, attention-grabbing format. This pattern has been applied to dynamic web sites prior to Ajax but is particularly important in the context of rich displays and interaction.

Consistency is important here; when items are selected, they should look the same. One straightforward way to achieve this is with `selected` and `deselected` CSS classes. By dynamically switching the element's `className` property, you can easily Highlight and de-Highlight.

Highlighting is useful in the following ways:

- To show which particular element has input focus.
- To show which elements are selected.
- When the user rolls over an element, to indicate its boundaries and hint that some action will occur by clicking on it.
- To indicate that an element is particularly important.
- To indicate that an element is undergoing change.
- To prompt the user to perform some kind of work on the element.

Decisions

How will the Highlight look?

You want the Highlight to be noticeable but not distracting. Here are some guidelines for deciding how the Highlight should look:

- Tone down the Highlight if it's likely to occupy a large proportion of the page. This would happen if there are quite a few Highlighted elements or if each element is relatively large.
- Users often need to read and edit Highlighted elements, so ensure that the display is usable whether or not the element is Highlighted.
- Avoid Highlighting techniques that displace other elements on the page. For instance, increasing font size might increase the element's size, in turn pushing away other elements. The Highlight should ideally appear as an on-off toggle, only affecting the element in question.

How will the Highlight appear and disappear?

The most obvious thing to do is make Highlight state binary—an element is either Highlighted or it's not. But consider using visual effects to make the transition smoother and support visual pattern recognition (see the following "Teacher!" example).

Real-World Examples

Gmail

Gmail presents a list of mail messages one row at a time. You select messages by clicking on the checkbox, which causes the entire row to change to a light tan background color. The appearance of various tan-colored rows makes it easy to spot selected items, and the checkboxes also provide a clue.

A9

A9 provides search results in different "Columns." Visit the Preferences page, then request to add more Columns. If you have an account, you're allowed to choose multiple Columns at once. Each Column is shown as a horizontal block in the Preferences page, and when you click the Add button, the block Highlights to confirm your choice. The interface uses Highlighting effectively, but it would be even more helpful if *all* added elements remained Highlighted instead of just the most recent one.

Teacher!

Teacher! (*http://teacherly.com/*) shows a table of student grades and Highlights whichever row your mouse is hovering over. What's novel here is that when you move to another row, the Highlight doesn't just disappear, but slowly fades away (*One-Second Spotlight*). An AjaxPatterns demo replicates the effect (*http://ajaxify.com/run/time/periodicRefresh/ spotlightCustom/highlight/*).

Whitespace

Whitespace (*http9rules.com/whitespace/*) prominently Highlights links on the side menu as you roll the mouse over them. This is a common technique used on many web sites and can be achieved entirely by using CSS styling to modify the anchor tag, absent of any JavaScript.

Code Example: AjaxPatterns Wiki

The Wiki demo (*http://ajaxify.com/run/wiki*) uses Highlighting in a couple of ways:

- As the user rolls the mouse over a message and then clicks on it, the message is Highlighted to indicate its current status (Figure 16-9).

- When the message has changed and is being buffered for submission, the background color changes. Once it has been submitted, the color returns to normal.

The first example is detailed in *Malleable Content* (Chapter 15), in which I explain the buffering Highlight. When you click outside the message area, the application checks whether you changed any text from the version originally downloaded, and if so, that text is Highlighted and prepared for uploading:

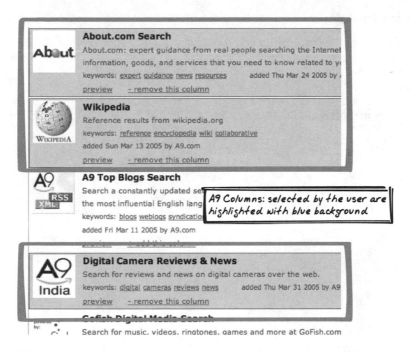

FIGURE 16-9. A9 columns

```
function onMessageBlur(event) {
  ...
  var initialMessageContent = message.serverMessage.content;
  if (message.value != initialMessageContent) {
    pendingMessages[message.id] = true;
    message.style.backgroundColor = "#ffcc33";
  }
  startPeriodicSync();
}
```

The sync is started again, so the item will soon be uploaded. If any further edits begin in the next few seconds, the upload will be placed on hold and the second message alteration will also be Highlighted. At any point in time, then, all of the buffered messages are Highlighted. When the messages are eventually uploaded, they revert to their normal, read-only color:

```
for (messageId in pendingMessages) {
  ...
  $(messageId).style.backgroundColor = "#cccccc";
}
```

Related Patterns

Status Area

The *Status Area* (Chapter 15) is a convenient place to explain why an element is Highlighted.

One-Second Spotlight

One-Second Spotlight (see earlier) is often convenient for transitioning into and out of longer-duration Highlight periods.

Metaphor

A fluorescent marker is used to highlight text.

CHAPTER SEVENTEEN

Functionality

THIS CHAPTER CONTAINS A NUMBER OF HIGHER-LEVEL PATTERNS THAT ARE MORE GEARED TOWARD offering new functionality than modifying the user interface. Technical barriers have prevented these from being used much on the Web, but Ajax technologies are helping to break down the barrier.

Lazy Registration addresses the issue of managing the lifecycle of a user profile. Instead of a binary "you're registered or you're not" perspective, Lazy Registration advocates a more gradual accumulation of user data and authentication credentials. A related pattern is *Direct Login*, which explains how to let the user securely log in without forcing a page refresh. It incorporates browser-side encryption, a theme at the heart of the next pattern, *Host-Proof Hosting*. The purpose of this pattern is to encrypt and decrypt data within the browser so that it can't be inspected by the hosting organization.

The next two patterns address monitoring the user's activity level. *Timeout* uses event-handling and scheduling to decide when the user is no longer active. *Heartbeat* is similar, but it brings the server into the equation; the browser keeps sending a heartbeat message to tell the server that the user is still active and that the application is still sitting in the browser.

Finally, *Unique URLs* restores some functionality that Ajax, to some degree, takes away. Bookmarkable URLs and browser history have always been an issue on the Web, but Ajax exacerbates the problem when developers choose not to use page refreshes. The *Unique URLs* pattern identifies a range of tricks to handle bookmarking, deep linking, the Back button, and related concerns.

Lazy Registration

Account, Authentication, Customisation, Customization, Incremental, Login, Password, Personalisation, Personalization, Profiling, Registration, User, Verification

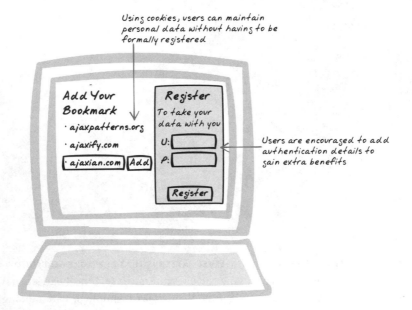

FIGURE 17-1. Lazy Registration

Goal Story

It's Saturday afternoon, and Stuart is busy planning the evening's activities. He visits a band listings web site, where he clicks on a map to zoom into his local area. Even though he has never visited the site before, a profile, which he can see on the top of the site is already being constructed. At this stage, the profile guesses at his location based on his actions so far. As he browses some of the jazz bands, the profile starts to show an increasing preference for jazz bands, and some of the ads reflect that. Since the jazz thing is a one-time idea, he goes into his profile and tweaks some of those genre preferences but leaves the location alone since the system's guess was correct. Finally, he decides to make a booking, at which point he establishes a password for future access to the same profile including his address, which is posted back to the profile.

Problem

How can the user customize the site while deferring formal registration?

Forces

- Public web sites thrive on registered users. Registered users receive personalized content, which means that the web site is able to deliver greater value per user. And registered users can also receive more focused advertising material.

- For nonpublic web sites, such as extranets used by external customers, registration may be a necessity.

- Most users don't like giving their personal information to a web server. They have concerns about their own privacy and the security of the information. Furthermore, the registration process is often time consuming.

- Many users spend time familiarizing themselves with a site before registering. In some cases, a user might interact with a site for years before formally establishing an account. There is a lot of valuable information that can be gained from this interaction that will benefit both the web site owner and the user.

Solution

Accumulate bits of information on the user as they interact while deferring formal registration. As soon as the user visits the web site, a user account with auto-generated ID is immediately created for her and set in a cookie that will remain in the browser. It doesn't matter if she never return; unused IDs can be cleared after a few months.

As the user interacts with the application, the account accumulates data. In many cases, the data is explicitly contributed by the user, and it's advisable to expose this kind of information so that the user can actually populate it. In this way, the initial profile may be seen as a structure with lots of holes. Some holes are eventually filled out automatically and others by the user himself. The user is also free to correct any of the filled-in data at any time (Figure 17-2).

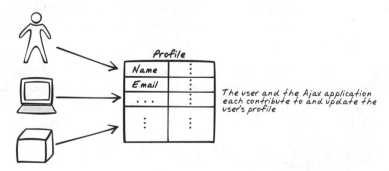

FIGURE 17-2. User Profile

Two particularly notable "holes" are a unique user identifier and a password. It is this combination of attributes that allows the user to access the profile from another machine or a different browser. They will also preserve the profile in the case that cookies are deleted from the user's browser. So, while this pattern is generally about gradual accumulation of profile data, there remains a significant milestone in the user/application relationship—the moment at which user ID and password are established.

Do the user ID and password have to be provided simultaneously? No. Even that can be incremental as long as you make the email address the unique identifier. In fact, this is pretty common nowadays. Email is usually required anyway, and it's unique, so why not make it the user ID? In the context of Lazy Registration, though, there's an additional benefit, as the email might be accumulated in the natural flow of events—the site might add the user to an announcements list, for example. In some cases, the email might even be verified during this process.

Sceptics may wonder why a user would want to actively work with her profile. The answer was formulated in a web usability pattern called "Carrot and a Stick" (*http://jerry.cs. uiuc.edu/~plop/plop99/proceedings/Kane/perzel_kane.pdf*):

> Determine what users consider to be a "valuable" carrot. Offer the end user a portion of that carrot before you request personal information. The content is withheld ("the stick") until the requested information is provided.

Thus, users will only enter information if there is a perceived benefit to them. There is plenty of evidence that this occurs—witness the social bookmarking phenomenon, where thousands of users make public their personal links. By exposing their profiles, many of those users are hoping the system will point them in the direction of related resources they have not yet heard of.

Some web sites have used this pattern for years, so what does it have to do with Ajax? *Lazy Registration* aims for a smooth approach in which the barrier is low for each new user contribution. For instance, you sign up for a web site's mailing list, and your email is automatically added to your profile and shown on the side of the page. With Ajax, there's no need to break the flow. No more "just go over there for a few minutes, then come back here, and if you're lucky, you might be looking at something similar to what you can see now." That's a big win for web sites aiming to drop the barrier of registration, and it's great for users, too.

It's standard practice for web sites to collect data about users. The aim of this pattern is to empower them to contribute to this. Instead of covertly building up a corpus of data on a user, you invite him to add value to his own experience by contributing and maintaining the data himself.*

---

* The Attention Trust (*http://www.attentiontrust.org/about*) is an organization which promotes this idea.

Several technologies are involved in Lazy Registration:

Database

You clearly need a persistent data store in order to retain user profiles.

XMLHttpRequest

Passing profile information back and forth with *XMLHttpRequest Calls* is the key to the smooth interaction mode you are seeking to achieve with this pattern.

Cookie manipulation and session tracking

A cookie, associated with your domain and identifying a unique session ID, must reside in the user's browser. The session ID can serve as a key on the server side to locate details about the user each time she accesses the web site. In conventional applications, the cookie is pushed from the browser to the server as a header in the response. That's fine for Ajaxian Lazy Registration when the user first accesses the system, though sometimes it may be convenient to use a more Ajax-oriented approach. The first such approach is to manipulate the cookie in JavaScript (*http://www.netspade.com/articles/javascript/cookies.xml*). The second is to set the cookie using the response from an *XMLHttpRequest Call*, which all browsers are apparently happy to deal with in the same way as they deal with cookies in regular page reloads. In practice, you're unlikely to be playing with cookies anyway. Most modern environments contain session-tracking frameworks that do the low-level cookie manipulation for you (also see *Direct Login*). They generally use either URL rewriting or cookie manipulation, and you need the latter to make this pattern work most effectively. Since responses from XMLHttpRequest set cookies in the same way as do entire page reloads, you should be able to change session data while servicing XMLHttpRequest Calls.

Decisions

What kind of data will the profile contain?

Usability and functionality concerns will drive decisions on what data is accumulated. By envisioning how users will interact with the web site, you can decide what kind of data must be there to support the interaction. For example:

- Do you want to provide localized ads? You'll need to know where the user lives.

- Do you want to use collaborative filtering? You'll need to capture the user's preferences.

In addition, consider that some users, such as employees working on an intranet web site, use certain Ajax Apps all day long. For that reason, the profile might also contain preferences similar to those on conventional desktop applications. Many options will be application-specific, but a few generic examples include:

- Enabling and disabling visual effects, such as *One-Second Spotlight* (Chapter 16).

- Setting *Heartbeat*-related (see earlier in this chapter) parameters, e.g., setting how long timeout will be and whether the system will prompt the user when it's coming up.

- Customizing *Status Area* (Chapter 15) display.

One issue that arises with Lazy Registration is the clearing of data. What if a user visits once and never comes back? You probably don't want to keep that data sitting there forever. Typically, you will probably have a script running daily to delete (or archive) the records of users whose last login was, say, three months ago.

How can the profile be accumulated?

You might know what data you need, but are users willing to give it to you? This comes back to the carrot-and-stick argument: you need to provide users a service that will make it worthwhile for them to provide that data. In addition, you need to communicate the benefit, and you must be able to assure them that the data will be safe and secure.

The least imaginative way to gain user data is to pay them for it, or, more deviously, pay others for it. Giving away a T-shirt in exchange for data was fine during the dot-com boom, but hopefully you can do better than that. Give the user a service they really need. For example:

- If you want the user to provide his email, offer to send email notifications.

- If you want the user to provide an ID and password, help him understand the benefits: he can log in from anywhere and the data will survive a hard-drive crash.

- If you want the user to provide his physical address, provide localized search features.

- If you want the user to rate your product, provide recommendations based on his ratings.

How much data should be stored in cookies?

How much you store in cookies depends on your general approach to the Ajax implementation: is the application browser-centric or server-centric? A browser-centric choice would be to pack as much as possible into the browser's local state so as to optimize performance, while running a full-fledged JavaScript application with a little server-side synchronization. A server-centric approach would rely only on data held server-side, with the browser accessing additional data on a need-to-know basis using *XMLHttpRequest Calls*.

One special concern is the security of cookies. If users access the application from a public PC, there's the risk of unauthorized access. In this case, it's especially advisable not to store sensitive information in the browser and to offer the possibility of cleaning cookies at the end of the session. (For instance, call the option "I'm on a public terminal.")

Real-World Examples

Memeflow

Steve Lacey's MemeFlow (*http://memeflow.com*) is a portal with RSS-backed *Portlets*. Its use of Lazy Registration is characteristic of several other portals (Figure 17-3). You can immediately build up a collection of your favorite feeds, and when you provide your username and password later on, those feeds will remain.

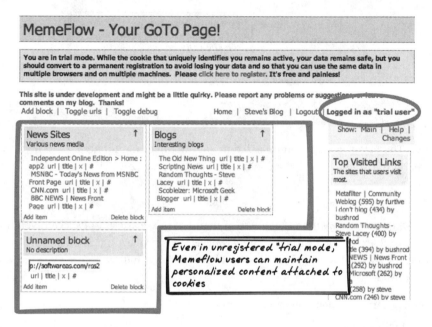

FIGURE 17-3. *Memeflow*

Blummy

Alexander Kirk's Blummy (*http://blummy.com*) is a bookmarklet manager (Figure 17-4). You can start adding bookmarklets to a personal "Blummy" container straightaway (this has a unique URL). When you register, you'll get a URL with your own name, but the old URL remains valid, so you can keep the bookmark you created before registering.

Kayak

Kayak (*http://kayak.com*) is a travel search engine that retains queries you've made. A query history is available for nonregistered users and becomes part of your profile once registered.

Palmsphere

Palmsphere (*http://palmsphere.com/store/home*) showcases Palm applications for download and purchase. Each item has a Favorite button—if checked, the item is one of your

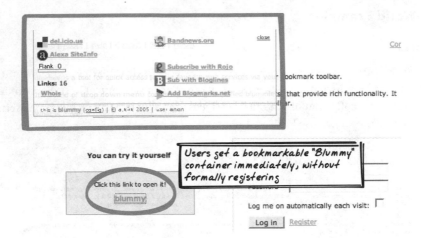

Users set a bookmarkable "Blummy" container immediately, without formally registering

FIGURE 17-4. Blummy

Favorites. The Favorites list is summarized in your Member Center area, even if you've never registered, and retained in a cookie for the next time you visit.

Amazon.com

Amazon (*http://amazon.com*) has begun incorporating Ajax features only recently, but it blazed the trail for Lazy Registration a long time ago. Visit Amazon (*http://amazon.com*) as a new user, browse for just a few seconds, and here's what you'll see before even beginning to register or log in:

• Shopping cart, to which you can add items

• Recently Viewed Items

• Page You Made—showing recent views and bookmarks related to those

• Ability to update your history by deleting items you viewed

• Ability to turn off Page You Made

• Ability to search for a friend's public wish list

Code Example: AjaxPatterns Shop Demo

The Ajax Shop Demo (*http://ajaxify.com/shop*) illustrates the kind of user interface described by this pattern (Figure 17-5).

When you run the demo, you'll notice a few things:

• You can add items to your cart right away.

• The application guesses your favorite category by watching what you're looking at. If you prefer, you can override the application's guess, and the application will no longer attempt to adjust it.

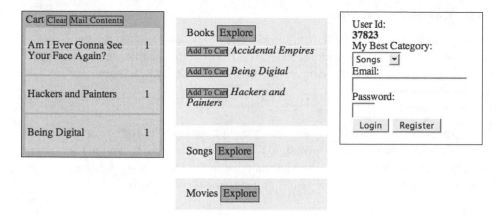

FIGURE 17-5. Ajax Shop Demo

- By offering you the ability to send the cart contents to your email address, the application provides you with an incentive to add your email to the profile without yet formally registering.

- The password and email verification process itself is unintrusive—the main flow of the site is uninterrupted. Even while you're waiting for verification mail, you can continue to play around with the main content. Figure 17-6 shows the application when the user has gone as far as entering an email address and password.

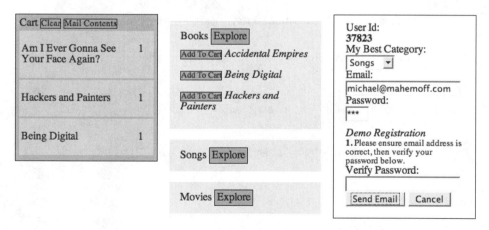

FIGURE 17-6. Ajax Shop Demo with email address and password entered

To keep things simple, it doesn't actually use a persistent data store; all information is held in the session. That's definitely not advisable for a real system, because you don't want to store passwords and other sensitive data there. Also, it means that the user, in theory, could bypass the email verification by inspecting the cookie. Nevertheless, the application demonstrates Lazy Registration from the user's perspective, and the underlying code provides some illustration of what's required to develop such an application.

Following are some of the features and how they were achieved.

Retrieval of categories and items

The application maintains the flow by avoiding any page reloads when categories and items are accessed. No information about categories or items is hardcoded; generic REST services are used to extract the data and are rendered locally in JavaScript.

Cart management

Again, the only real relevance of cart management is that page reloads are avoided. The cart contents are tracked in the session, so they should be present when the user resumes using the web site. When the user adds something to the cart, the JavaScript cart is *not* directly altered. Instead, the new item is posted to the server as XML:

```
function onAddItemClicked(item) {
  var vars = {
    command: 'add',
    item: item
  }
  ajaxCaller.postForXML("cart.phtml", vars, onCartResponse);
}
```

And likewise when the cart is cleared:

```
function onCartClearClicked( ) {
  var vars = {
    command: 'clear'
  }
  ajaxCaller.postForXML("cart.phtml", vars, onCartResponse);
}
```

For both operations, the server retrieves the session cart and alters its state:

```
$cart = $_SESSION['cart'];

if (isset($_POST["command"]) && $_POST["command"]=="add") {
  $item = $_POST["item"];
  $cart->add($item);
} else if (isset($_POST["command"]) && $_POST["command"]=="clear") {
  $cart->clear( );
}
```

Then, the server outputs the final state as an XML response:

```
header("Content-type: text/xml");
echo "<cart>";
$contents = $cart->getContents( );
foreach (array_keys($contents) as $itemName) {
  echo "<item>";
  echo "<name>$itemName</name>";
  echo "<amount>".$contents[$itemName]."</amount>";
  echo "</item>";
}
echo "</cart>";
```

In the browser, onCartResponse is registered to render the cart based on the resulting XML.

Mailing cart contents

The profile block contains, along with several other fields, the user's email. There's also a clickable Mail field on the cart:

```
<div>
  <div class="userLabel">Email:</div>
  <input type="text" id="email" name="email" />
</div>
...
<span id="cartMail">Mail Contents</span>
....
$("cartMail").onclick = onCartMailClicked;
```

When the user clicks on cartMail, the server checks that the email has been filled in and simply uploads a POST message for the mail to occur. In this case, there's no feedback to the web user, so the callback function is blank:

```
vars = {
  command: "mailCart",
  email: email
}
ajaxCaller.postForPlainText("cart.phtml", vars, function() {});
```

The server receives not only the command, but the email address itself, since this might not be in the user's profile yet. Just prior to sending the mail, the server retains the address as part of the user's session:*

```
function mailCart() {
  ...
  $email = $_POST["email"];
  // Add mail to the profile - it's part of the Lazy Registration.
  $_SESSION['email'] = $email;
  ...
}
```

Then, it's a simple matter of constructing a message from the server-side cart state and sending the email to the specified address using standard server-side libraries.

Tracking favorite categories

There's a fixed "favorite category" selector in the HTML. It begins empty and is populated when the categories are loaded:

```
<div id="favoriteCategoryInfo">
  My Best Category: <select id="favoriteCategory"></select>
</div>

function onAllCategoriesResponse(xml, ignoredHeaders, ignoredContext) {
  ...
  categoryExplores[category] = 0;
```

---

* Again, this is a simplification, because retaining the address would not be necessary—or desirable— if the user was already logged in.

```
        favoriteCategoryOption = document.createElement("option");
        ...
    }
```

There's also a mode variable to indicate whether the favorite category selection is automated. It begins in automated mode:

```
    var isFavoriteCategoryAutomated = true;
```

If in automated mode, the script watches each time the user explores an item. Each category is tracked according to how many times the item was explored, and the selector is altered if a new maximum is reached:

```
    var categoryExplores = new Array();
    ...

    function onExploreClicked(category) {
      ...
      if (isFavoriteCategoryAutomated) {
        categoryExplores[category]++;
        favoriteCategory = $("favoriteCategory").value;
        favoriteCategoryExplores = categoryExplores[favoriteCategory];
        if (categoryExplores[category] > favoriteCategoryExplores) {
          $("favoriteCategory").value = category;
        }
      }
    }
```

If the user decides to overwrite this *Guesstimate* by manually setting the preference, it will stay manual permanently:

```
    $("favoriteCategory").onclick = function() {
      isFavoriteCategoryAutomated = false;
    }
```

For the sake of simplicity, this field is not actually tracked in the server, though it could easily be incorporated into the user's profile.

Verifying password and email

Now for the most important part. The user is finally willing to verify her password and email. These could potentially be broken into two separate verification activities, but since they fit together as a formal registration step, they are combined in the demo.

The trick is to manage the process with a little state transition logic. The registration is broken into a few states with transitions between them. Each state requires you to handle events in a slightly different way. Each transition involves altering the UI a little to reflect what the user can do.

registerState holds the current state:

```
    /*
      "start": When page is loaded
      "mustSendMail": When instructions and verify password field shown
      "mustVerifySecretNumber": When email sent and user must enter secret
```

```
      number inside email
    "verified": When user is successfully logged in
*/

    var registerState = "start";
```

The HTML for this demo contains all the necessary fields and buttons. Their visibility is toggled based on the current state. For example, following are the password and password verification fields. The password field is always shown until the user is at the "verified" stage, whereas the "verify password" field is only shown after the user initiates the registration process:

```
<div id="passwordInfo">
  <div class="userLabel">Password:</div>
  <input type="password"ael id="password" name="password"/>
</div>

<div id="verifyPasswordInfo">
  <div id="regHeader">Demo Registration</div>
  <div class="regInstructions">
    <strong>1.</strong> Please ensure email address is correct and
    password is <strong>not</strong> confidential, then verify your
    password below.
  </div>
  <div class="userLabel">Verify Password:</div>
  <input id="verifyPassword" type="password" name="verifyPassword" />
</div>
```

All three buttons are declared and, again, their visibility will change depending on the current state:

```
<input type="button" id="login" value="Login"></button>
<input type="button" id="register" value="Register"></button>
<input type="button" id="cancel" value="Cancel"></button>
```

What's most important here is the Register button, which drives the process through each state. The Cancel button returns the state back to start, which causes the display to return to its initial state too. The purpose of the Login button is purely for demonstration. The Register button is present until the user is verified, and its label changes at each stage of the registration process. Its event handler remains the same throughout; the handler decides what to do based on the current state:

```
function onRegisterClicked() {
  if (registerState=="start") {
    registerState = "mustSendMail";
  } else if (registerState=="mustSendMail") {
    var submissionOK = sendMail();
    if (submissionOK) {
      registerState = "mustVerifySecretNumber";
    } else {
      return;
    }
```

```
        } else if (registerState=="mustVerifySecretNumber") {
          verifySecretNumber();
        }
        onRegistrationStateChanged();
    }
```

And onRegistrationStateChanged() exists purely to reveal and hide fields, and to change the button label based on the current state:

```
    function onRegistrationStateChanged() {

      if (registerState=="start") {
        $("userForm").reset();
        $("login").style.display = "inline";
        $("verifyPasswordInfo").style.display = "none";
        $("secretNumberInfo").style.display = "none";
        $("verifiedInfo").style.display="none";
        $("cancel").style.display = "none";
        $("register").value="Register";
      } else if (registerState=="mustSendMail") {
        ...
      } else if (registerState=="mustVerifySecretNumber") {
        ...
      } else if (registerState=="verified") {
        ...
      }
    }
```

Related Patterns

Direct Login

Direct Login (see the next pattern) is a companion pattern, since some dynamic behavior can allow for login and registration to appear on the same form.

Live Form

It's useful to maintain the profile details in a *Live Form* (Chapter 14) so that the user can easily add to them and the server can synchronize state and provide opportunities for further enhancement to the profile.

Timeout

When data is held in cookies, it's important to expire the cookies if there's a risk that others may gain access to the browser. *Timeout* (see later) helps the server decide whether the client is still active. If it's not, it may be wise to ensure that any sensitive data is wiped from the cookies held in the browser.

Guesstimate

Lazy Registration can sometimes involve inferring information about the user's profile by monitoring his behavior. Thus, it embraces the same nebulous principles as *Guesstimate* (Chapter 13), where a guess is acknowledged to be imprecise but better than no guess at all.

Metaphor

A good salesperson works the same way. While assumptions might be made based on a prospect's behavior, the salesperson is always listening; her assumptions are always open to challenge. (Malcolm Gladwell depicted this pattern of successful salespeople in *Blink* [Little, Brown, 2005]).

Want to Know More?

- OECD privacy guidelines (*http://www.oecd.org/document/18/0,2340,en_2649_201185_ 1815186_1_1_1_1,00.html*)

- Personalization versus Customization (*http://www.clickz.com/experts/archives/mkt/precis_ mkt/article.php/814811*)

Acknowledgments

The idea to handle Lazy Registration in this Ajaxian manner was originally proposed by Chris Were ("Tahpot")(*http://tahpot.blogspot.com/2005/06/lazy-registration-with-ajax.html*).

Direct Login

Access, Account, Authentication, Login

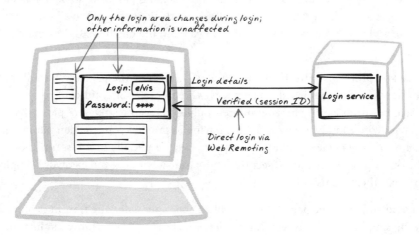

FIGURE 17-7. Direct Login

Goal Story

When Stuart logs in to perform an online exam, he is presented with a standard username-password form. He enters his username and password, but a few seconds later, the form becomes red and shows an error message underneath. He switches off Caps Lock and re-enters his credentials. This time, they're accepted. The form morphs to show his name and balance, and a new menu appears alongside it.

Problem

How can users present their credentials to the server?

Forces

- Login is a necessary evil—it should be as transparent as possible.

- Casual users may not bother to log in if the process interrupts their browsing experience.

- Login requires the browser to interact with the server in order to validate the username and password.

- The password should not travel in plain-text; it could be intercepted while traveling to the server.

Solution

Authenticate the user with an XMLHttpRequest Call instead of with a form-based submission, hashing in the browser for improved security. The essence of this pattern is a routine transformation from a submission-based approach to an Ajaxian, Web Remoting (Chapter 6) interaction style. But, in this pattern, I also discuss a very useful, though optional, technique that involves JavaScript-based hashing and is specific to the login process.

Conventional authentication usually requires the user and password to be uploaded as a standard form submission. The server usually converts the password to a hash (or "validator") value and checks it against a stored hash value in the database. If they match, the user is in.

There are two problems with this approach. Firstly, flushing the page can be a distraction. It might not take long, but it will usually leave the user in a different context, which will discourage her from logging in. Even more troublesome is the stream of pages that ensue when a password must be recovered (e.g., having to provide your maiden name, last purchase date, and the name of your favorite pet canary), especially in this security-conscious era. The other problem relates to security of the transmission; if the password is uploaded as plain-text, there's a risk of interception.

Direct Login addresses the page refresh problem and, optionally, the transmission problem too. In the simplest approach, you can implement *Direct Login* by simply sending the username and password in plain-text to the validation service using an XMLHttpRequest POST. Then, the server behaves similarly to a conventional server: it checks whether the password matches using a hash function and prepares for session management. XMLHttpRequest deals with cookies as it does regular form handling; this allows the session to be established in the same way as a conventional form submission. The only difference is the response content: instead of outputting a new HTML page, the server outputs an XML or plain-text acknowledgment, as well as any personalized content.

Passing the credentials over with XMLHttpRequest will improve usability, but as long as the password is being transferred in plain-text, there's still a security threat. Ensuring the whole transaction runs overs HTTPS is always the best measure, as this generally makes the transaction secure from interception. However, many web sites don't provide such a facility. Fortunately, there's a compromise that can prevent transmission of plain-text passwords. The technique, strictly speaking, is orthogonal to the Direct Login approach; you could apply it to conventional submission-based authentication as well. But since it makes heavy use of browser-side processing, it fits nicely with Direct Login.

The trick is to perform hashing in the browser. JavaScript is fast enough to transform the password into a hash value (not to mention that it's capable of doing it), and there are libraries available to implement popular algorithms.

The naïve way of hashing is to simply hash the password to match what should be in the database. But any interceptor would then be able to perform a *replay attack*—it could log in using the same details. So we need a more sophisticated approach, such as the following *double hashing* algorithm.

With double hashing, the server generates a one-time random seed (S). The browser then hashes twice: first, it hashes the password (P), hopefully to yield what is stored on the database (Ha; Hash attempt). But instead of sending that, the browser combines it with the one-time seed to form a new hash (Da; Double-hash attempt). This new hash is sent to the server. The server then pulls out the stored hash (H) from the database and combines it with the original one-time seed (S) to form a new hash, which must match the hash (Da) that was uploaded. This works because, in both cases, the initial password (P) has been passed through the same two hash functions. In the browser, the user's attempt is passed through a fixed hash function, and the result is immediately passed to a new hash function with one-time seed. In the server, the database already holds the result of hashing the real password using the fixed hash function. As long as the server uses the same seed and algorithm as the browser used to perform a second hashing, the two results should match. The server is also responsible for clearing the one-time seed after a successful login; otherwise, an interceptor could log in later on by uploading the same data. Here's a summary of the algorithm:

1. User visits web site

2. Server outputs initial page.

   a. Server generates one-time seed (S) and stores it.

   b. Server outputs page, including login form, with one-time seed embedded somewhere on the page (e.g., in a JavaScript variable).

   c. User enters username (U) and password (P)

3. Browser handles submission.

   a. Browser hashes password (P) using permanent hash function in order to arrive at the attempted hash value (Ha), which should be held in the database.

b. Browser combines attempted hash (Ha) with one-time seed (S) to create one-time, double-hashed value (Da).

c. Browser uploads username (U), double-hashed value (Da), and one-time seed (S).

4. Server authenticates

a. Verifies that one-time seed (S) is valid.

b. Server extracts stored hash for this user (H) and combines it with the seed (S) to get one-time, double-hashed value (D).

c. Server compares the double-hashed values (D and Da). If successful, it logs the user in (e.g., creates a new session and outputs a successful response code) and clears the one-time seed (S). If it is not successful, it either generates a new seed or decrements a usage counter on the existing seed.

Decisions

What hashing algorithm will be used?

You're going to be hashing in the browser as well as in the server, so you'll need a portable algorithm. Two popular standards are MD5 and SHA-1; both have implementations on JavaScript and on just about any server-side language you're likely to use.

How will you manage the one-time seed?

The double-hashing algorithm hinges on the one-time seed being used only once and on ensuring that the user authenticates with the seed that the server provided. You have to make a few decisions regarding this:

How does the seed expire?

In theory, the seed's lifetime shouldn't matter much since it will only be used once—there's no risk of someone intercepting a successful upload and reusing that data to authenticate. However, you'll probably want to clear any unused seeds periodically, e.g., once a day. More important than lifetime is number of validation attempts—perhaps you want to allow only three login attempts against the same seed. In this case, you'll need to associate a counter with the seed.

Is the seed uploaded back to the server?

The algorithm above requires that the seed be uploaded, but the server could instead track the session with a unique session ID and use that to look up the most recent seed it sent out. It's probably better to upload the seed in most cases, as it keeps the conversation as stateless as possible. With the seed having already been downloaded in plaintext, there's no significant threat posed by uploading it again.

Real-World Examples

NetVibes

The NetVibes (*http://netvibes.com*) portal handles the entire login process without any page refreshes.

Protopage

The Protopage (*http://protopage.com*) portal pops up a login box without opening a new page, though it sends you to a new page after the credentials are submitted.

Treehouse

Treehouse Magazine (*http://treehousemagazine.com/*), has a sidebar with a login *Microlink*. When clicked, it expands to form a login area, which can in turn morph into a registration area. It also degrades to use standard form submission if JavaScript is disabled.

Code Examples: Ajax Login Demo

James Dam's Ajax Login (*http://www.jamesdam.com/ajax_login/login.html*) presents a standard HTML form (Figure 17-8). Submission is disabled and handled instead by callback methods registered on initialization:

```
<form action="post" onsubmit="return false">
  <div id="login" class="login">
    <label for="username">Username: </label>
    <input name="username" id="username" size="20" type="text">
    <label for="password">Password: </label>
    <input name="password" id="password" size="20" type="password">
    <p id="message">Enter your username and password to log in.</p>
  </div>
  <label for="comments">Comments:</label>
  <textarea rows="6" cols="80" id="comments"></textarea>
</form>
```

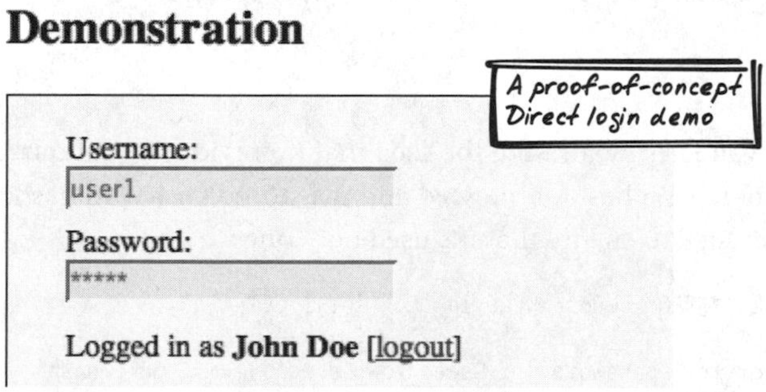

FIGURE 17-8. Direct login demo

As soon as the user signals his intent to authenticate, which is indicated by form field focus, a random, one-time seed is retrieved from the server if there isn't already one present. The response comes in two parts: an ID for the seed and the seed itself, both of which are saved as JavaScript variables. The server can later use the ID to retrieve the seed it sent:

```
function getSeed( ) {
    ...
    if (!loggedIn && !hasSeed) {
        http.open('GET', LOGIN_PREFIX + 'task=getseed', true);
        http.onreadystatechange = handleHttpGetSeed;
        http.send(null);
    }
    ...
}

function handleHttpGetSeed( ) {
    ...
    if (http.readyState == NORMAL_STATE) {
        results = http.responseText.split('|');
        // id is the first element
        seed_id = results[0];
        // seed is the second element
        seed = results[1];
    }
    ...
}
```

The seed is then used to hash the password upon submission. Notice that hex_md5( ), the double-hashing operation, is used twice.

```
// validateLogin method: validates a login request
function validateLogin( ) {
    ...
    // compute the hash of the password and the seed
    hash = hex_md5(hex_md5(password) + seed);

      // open the http connection
      http.open('GET',
        LOGIN_PREFIX +
        'task=checklogin&username='+username+'&id='+seed_id+'&hash=
 '+hash, true);
        ...
    }
```

The server then validates by locating the seed that it previously sent out, and checking if the hash value matches a hash of the seed and the stored password hash. If it does, the server deletes the seed to ensure that it's used only once:

```
sql = 'SELECT * FROM seeds WHERE id=' . (int)$_GET['id'];
...
if (md5($user_row['password'] . $seed_row['seed']) == $_GET['hash']) {
    echo('true|' .  $user_row['fullname'']);
    ...
    mysql_query('DELETE FROM s WHERE id=' . (int)$_GET['id']);
}
```

After calling for validation, the browser receives a response and the form is morphed to show whether login was successful.

Related Patterns

Lazy Registration

Lazy Registration (see earlier) is geared toward first-time registration as well as deferred login, and it makes use of Direct Login.

Host-Proof Hosting

Host-Proof Hosting (see the next pattern), like Direct Login, uses JavaScript to perform encryption-related functionality.

Timeout

Apply a *Timeout* (see later) to log users out.

Acknowledgments

- The idea for this pattern comes from James Dam's demo and write-up (*http://www.jamesdam.com/ajax_login/login.html*).

- Peter Curran of Close Consultants (*http://closeconsultants.com*) provided valuable feedback that helped me clarify my explanation of the algorithm.

Host-Proof Hosting

◯◯◯

ASP, DataCloud, Key, Secure, Untrusted

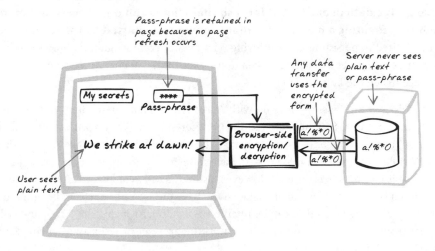

FIGURE 17-9. Host-Proof Hosting

Goal Story

Reta is dismayed to learn that a malicious hacker managed to download a chunk of the company's database containing personal details about all the customers in her store. Fortunately, she also learns that the pass-phrase she always entered was actually used to encrypt all that data, so the hacker won't be able to make sense of any of the contents.

Problem

How can you mitigate the effects of unauthorized access to your application data?

Forces

- Web apps require that some form of persistent data hold information about users, business state, past events, and so on.

- Security restrictions—using standard web technologies—prohibit users from storing web apps on the user's own hard drives. Even with *Richer Plugins* that allow it, many benefits of using a web app in the first place are lost. This means that persistent data is usually stored server side.

- Cookies allow some data storage within the browser, but cookie data is also transmitted to the server where it's vulnerable.

- Server-side storage is open to abuse: the administrators, along with anyone who is able to gain access to it, are able to extract sensitive information by reading the data, as well as effect malicious changes by tampering with it. The abuse can occur within an organization's own IT department or be inflicted by a third-party hosting company entrusted with the data.

Solution

Host sensitive data in encrypted form so that clients can only access and manipulate it by providing a pass-phrase that is never transmitted to the server. The server is limited to persisting and retrieving whatever encrypted data the browser sends it and never actually sees the sensitive data in its plain form. All encryption and decryption takes place inside the browser itself.

Just what does secure hosting have do with Ajax? The Ajaxian twist comes in the maintenance of the pass-phrase. You could use the browser-side encryption with a conventional application, but the pass-phrase would have to be entered upon each page refresh, since no JavaScript state survives a reload. With page refreshes occurring every few seconds, the pass-phrase is completely unusable. However, using Ajax to avoid page refresh means you can retain all session state in the browser, so the pass-phrase only needs to be entered at the start. After being entered, it can be retained as a standard JavaScript string and will disappear from the browser when the user quits the browser or visits another site. Suddenly, Host-Proof Hosting becomes usable.

Incidentally, don't take this pattern to be a new "Ajax-HTTPS" protocol. The issue here is how the data is actually stored, not how it's transmitted. In theory, the data itself need not travel over a secure connection because it's already encrypted. In practice, a secure connection might be worthwhile in order to reduce some of the vulnerabilities described later in this section.

Before you rush off to upload all your trade secrets to Shonky Hosting Inc., you should be aware that this idea isn't foolproof. On the one hand, the host is assumed to be inherently untrustworthy. But on the other hand, the script for the browser application is held right there on the server, and the browser runs whatever scripts come down from that URL. This leaves open the possibility that the host will tamper—to evil ends—with either the code itself or the outgoing HTML and JavaScript.

What if a rogue administrator from the hosting company decided to quietly add a small monitoring function to a JavaScript file and append its execution to a window.onload function. Then, the evil monitoring function could be made to run once a minute within the browser. It might, for instance, serialize the entire DOM and upload a summary back to the server with Web Remoting (Chapter 6), where more malicious code would log it somewhere convenient. A third-party hacker sitting between the browser and the server could also inject a script and could upload data to a remote site with one of several established techniques—for instance, by exporting browser data as CGI variables on the source URL of an external image under the hacker's control. In both scenarios, the application can continue as normal, and the poor user is none the wiser.

The threat of script injection certainly weakens the claim for this pattern, but it doesn't invalidate it altogether. While script injection is theoretically possible, it does require some skill on the host's part and is also detectable if you know what the code should and should not be doing. If you happened to discover that your application is uploading DOM details every sixty seconds (using a tool similar to those described in *Traffic Sniffing* [Chapter 18]), there's a good chance that something's blatantly wrong.

For practical purposes, also consider what happens if a hacker gains unauthorized access for a short time. She might well grab as much data as possible, but the data will be safely encrypted. In the unlikely event such a hacker was sophisticated enough to use script injection, she would only be able to gain pass-phrases of users who happen to be logged in during the time the server is under her control.

So pragmatic considerations suggest that the technique is safer than hosting the data in plain form, though it's by no means perfect. But is it so much safer as to warrant the extra performance overhead and coding effort and the constraint of zero page refreshes? That's a decision you'll need to make on a case-by-case basis, bearing in mind the critical nature of the data—the likelihood of the various types of attack.

In theory, there's an even stronger claim in favor of this approach. It might be possible to develop a general-purpose plugin to detect script injection. For a given application, such a plugin would have access to a certified copy of the source code. Then, it could monitor traffic and caution you about any unexpected activity. If such a plugin could be developed, the only way for script injection to succeed would be a conspiracy between the host, the code certifier, and the plugin manufacturer.

Decisions

What encryption algorithm and framework will be used?

You'll need an algorithm that's available in JavaScript as well as in your server-side environment. If the data is accessed by other clients, they obviously must have access to the algorithm too. A search reveals that several algorithm implementations are available, each with its own strengths and weaknesses. All of the following are open source.

- RC4, AES, Serpent, Twofish, Caesar and RSA are provided by Michiel Van Everdigen's open source package (*http://home.zonnet.nl/MAvanEverdingen/Code/*).

- TEA (Tiny Encryption Algorithm) is provided by Moveable Type UK (*http://www.movable-type.co.uk/scripts/TEAblock.html*).

- Blowfish is provided by farfarfar.com (*http://www.farfarfar.com/scripts/encrypt/encrypt.js*).

When will the pass-phrase be requested?

The browser will need to query for the pass-phrase as soon as encrypted data must be rendered. However, that might not be immediately. To make the encryption less intrusive, you might consider using something like the *Lazy Registration* pattern, where regular data is shown as soon as the user accesses the application, with encrypted data only accessible after the pass-phrase has been entered.

Real-World Examples

There are no public real-world examples to my knowledge. One precedent is Hushmail (*http://hushmail.com*), which uses a Java applet to allow access to email encrypted on the server.

Code Example: Host-Proof-Hosting Proof-Of-Concept

Richard Schwartz provides a proof-of-concept demo (*http://smokey.rhs.com/web/test/AjaxCryptoConceptProof.nsf/blowfish?OpenPage*) (Figure 17-10). For encryption, it delegates to a JavaScript Blowfish library. The application accepts a pass-phrase, a message key, and some message content. It then encrypts the message and uploads it. It also uploads the key, along with an encrypted version of the key, which can be used later to check that the user has the correct pass-phrase. The application then shows that the server is holding only the encrypted content and the key. You can then pull the encrypted content back down and decrypt it with the original pass-phrase.

The application itself is quite simple: it manipulates the "display" style settings of a series of forms in order to show or hide them. Thus, the user's pass-phrase remains in the pass-phrase input field at all times. This is the important thing about the demo; there's no form submission, so the pass-phrase needs to be entered only once.

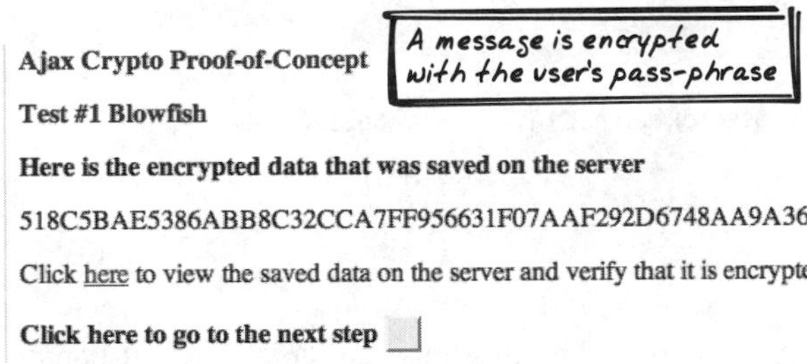

Ajax Crypto Proof-of-Concept

A message is encrypted with the user's pass-phrase

Test #1 Blowfish

Here is the encrypted data that was saved on the server

518C5BAE5386ABB8C32CCA7FF956631F07AAF292D6748AA9A3604A549FE633A0

Click here to view the saved data on the server and verify that it is encrypted. (Opens a new window.)

Click here to go to the next step

FIGURE 17-10. Host-Proof Hosting

When the application is ready to upload the encrypted data, it sets up the global variables required by the Blowfish library (ideally, the library would accept these as parameters). encodetext( ) is called (with "2" to specify the Blowfish algorithm), and it outputs the encrypted version in the form of a global variable:

```
saveCryptoText( ) {
    ...
    inpdata=window.document.inputForm.plaintextInput.value;
    passwd=window.document.inputForm.password.value;
    // invoke blowfish
    encodetext(2);
    data = data + "&check=" + outdata ;
    ...
}
```

The encrypted key is also attached:

```
inpdata=window.document.inputForm.check.value;
encodetext(2);
data = data + "&check=" + outdata ;
```

The data can now be sent to the server:*

```
url = "http://smokey.rhs.com/web/test/AjaxCryptoConceptProof.nsf/
SaveBlowfishDoc?OpenAgent" + data
    httpPost(url)
```

Later on, the application provides a list of message keys that have been sent to the server. When the user chooses one, the application requests an XML document from the server containing the message and key details (in practice, the message key could be verified before the body is downloaded). It first performs a check that the key is valid for this pass-phrase, then decrypts the message itself. Finally, a DOM object is morphed to display the decrypted text:

```
inpdata = "";
inpdata = getElementText(valuenode);
```

---

* RESTful principles suggest that, in practice, the data would be uploaded with a POST, because the data would affect the server state. Another reason to use POST is that it's not practical to encode an entire message in the URL. However, this application is a proof-of-concept, so GET is used here instead.

```
outdata = ""
decodetext(2);
...
window.document.all.decryptedText.innerHTML = stripNulls(outdata);
```

Alternatives

Richer Plugin

You might consider exploiting the increased permissions of a *Richer Plugin* (Chapter 8) to access a local data store. However, with this there is still a risk of malicious script injection from the server. Furthermore, you'll lose several key benefits of holding the data server side:

- Users will not be able to access the data from remote locations.

- Each local data store will need its own backup process. Uploading to a backup server will defeat the purpose of the local store.

- Each local data store must be protected against unauthorized access.

- The data stores will sometimes need to be migrated as the system changes.

Another application of *Richer Plugin* would be to hold the data server side but use the Richer Plugin in place of the JavaScript code to manage the local encryption and decryption. A plugin like this could also retain the pass-phrase.

Related Patterns

Direct Login

Direct Login, like Host-Proof Hosting, also involves using JavaScript for encryption-related activity.

Timeout

Apply a *Timeout* to clear the key from browser state after an idle period. This will help you prevent unauthorized users from accessing the encrypted data.

Metaphor

Caesar wonders whether he can entrust his aide with the top-secret recipe for victory wine. Fortunately, he's a pioneer of cryptography, so he just hands over the recipe in encrypted form.

Want to Know More?

Check out Richard Schwartz's blog entries:

- Overview of the idea and pertinent conversation in the comments section (*http://smokey.rhs.com/web/blog/PowerOfTheSchwartz.nsf/d6plinks/RSCZ-6C5G54*)

- Practical implementation issues (*http://smokey.rhs.com/web/blog/PowerOfTheSchwartz.nsf/plinks/RSCZ-6CCMCD*)

- Introducing the proof-of-concept application (*http://smokey.rhs.com/web/blog/PowerOfTheSchwartz.nsf/plinks/RSCZ-6CATX6*)

- A hypothetical scenario elaborating the idea (*http://smokey.rhs.com/web/blog/PowerOfTheSchwartz.nsf/plinks/RSCZ-6CHL5J*)

- My blog entry summarizing the idea (*http://www.softwareas.com/ajax-and-the-great-data-cloud-in-the-sky*)

- Chris Hammond-Thrasher comments on Ajax as a general solution to encryption issues, e.g., digital signatures and secure timestamps (*http://thrashor.blogspot.com/2005/05/more-on-ajax-and-secure-web.html*)

Acknowledgments

Richard Schwartz's blog entries provided the idea for this pattern, and its name is attributed to Richard Schwartz, Michael Griffes, and their colleagues at eVelocity. I am also grateful to others who have commented on the approach, notably Alex Russell, who has cautioned on the vulnerabilities of this approach, such as script injection.

Timeout

Logout, Screensaver, Session, Suspend, Timeout

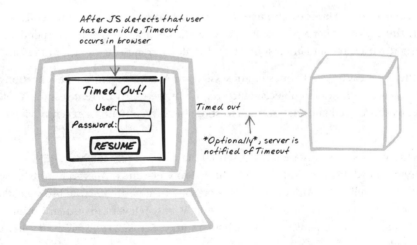

FIGURE 17-11. Timeout

Goal Story

Tracy was so keen on leaving the office Friday afternoon that she forgot to shut down the market news web site. Fortunately, the web site monitors mouse movements, meaning that if she doesn't interact with the page for an hour, it will suspend itself, saving a lot of wasted refreshes. On Monday morning, Tracy walks in and sees a screensaver-like animation in the browser, with a message indicating that updates have ceased. She clicks a mouse button and sees the screen update with the latest prices.

Problem

How can you tell whether the user is still working with the application?

Forces

- Users often leave an application in a browser window for hours or days without interacting with it. Many times, they abandon it altogether. The practice is becoming more prevalent as all major browsers now support multitab browsing.

- Ajax Apps often use *Periodic Refresh* or *HTTP Streaming* to keep informed about server state. The user may not care about the application anymore, but if it's still in the browser, a naïeve implementation will continue to poll the server indefinitely—a massive waste of bandwidth and resources.

- Ajax Apps often contain sensitive data which is at risk if the user forgets to log out when leaving a public terminal.

- Ajax Apps often involve collaboration and communication between users. To cultivate an awareness of other users and their activities, the server must track the state of individual browsers.

Solution

Have the browser Timeout the user after a period of inactivity and, optionally, inform the server. After a period of inactivity, the application is either suspended, requiring the user to manually resume it or shut down, requiring the user to restart.

This pattern raises the whole question of sessions in Ajax. Conventional applications usually have server-side session objects which represent the user's current session. Typically, this means short-lived information such as shopping cart contents or recently viewed items.

In Ajax, server-side sessions are not so useful. In fact, if you rely solely on *RESTful Services*, you may not need those session objects at all. In browser-centric Ajax Apps, the browser is a full-fledged application with all of the session state held within. So the browser state *is* the session. The server-side session, if used at all, is only relevant to authentication and has no impact on the response to any particular query. See *RESTful Service* (Chapter 9) for more details.

How is all of this relevant to Timeout? Well, consider this familiar nightmare scenario:

The user opens up a form, spends two hours populating it while researching the answers, and clicks submit. The browser then responds with "Your session has expired" and adds insult to injury by presenting a new blank form.

Stories like this are all too common because server-side session Timeouts ignore what's happening in the browser. If the user hasn't submitted a form in, say, 30 minutes, the session times out and all the data is lost. That's a problem if the user has been actively working on the browser side. With an Ajax App, the server has a better chance of staying in sync with the browser thanks to *XMLHttpRequest Calls* (Chapter 6) . In most environments, the server-side session will be automatically refreshed when an XMLHttpRequest Call comes in. However, this is not optimal either because the server still doesn't know why browser calls are occurring. For applications using *Periodic Refresh* (Chapter 10), for example, a server-side session will stay alive indefinitely even if the user has left the building.

By relying instead on browser-based Timeout detection, you can be more intelligent about how Timeouts will occur. Browser-based Timeout detection is based on *Scheduling* (Chapter 7). A timer is established to count down to Timeout state. Each significant activity cancels the timer and starts a new one in its place.

What activities are significant enough to restart the timer? Mouse movement is one candidate. You can monitor each mouse movement on the page; one of the following Code Refactoring illustrations below does exactly that. Mouse movements are a very broad indicator, and you might be concerned about "false positives": These may be suggestions that a user is still working with an application when they're in fact not, e.g., they just happened to move the mouse across the browser window while cycling through each open window. You'll also get some "false negatives": A user working only with the keyboard is liable to be timed out. If you'd prefer to keep the session going only if the user is actively changing data, you can instead catch events such as button clicks and keypresses within input fields.

Sudden Timeouts can be frustrating for users, so consider these feedback measures:

- Unobtrusively show Timeout status, e.g., number of minutes remaining. You might highlight the status as Timeout approaches, and also offer some background and instruction on avoiding the Timeout.
- When Timeout is approaching, offer a warning and an opportunity to explicitly restart the timer.

Once you've detected that the user is inactive, what do you do? Timeout can be used in several ways:

Stop Periodic Refresh
> Conventional applications tend to do nothing when the user is idle, but many Ajax Apps continuously poll the server. Thus, the Timeout should trigger cancellation of any *Periodic Refresh* timers.

Clear data

Sometimes an inactive application is a hint that the user may no longer be in control of a terminal. There's a risk that someone else could gain access to the user's data and permissions. After a Timeout, document.url can be pointed to the main application URL in order to refresh the page. In addition, you might decide to delete cookies holding sensitive data.

Save data

If you clear data, you might also consider first *saving* it on the server. There's nothing more annoying than arriving back from lunch and finding that a partly filled-out form has been cleared for security purposes. With an *XMLHttpRequest Call*, you have the option of saving the user's progress as a "draft."

Inform user

If you're performing Timeout activities, you'll need to provide some feedback to the user about what's happening and what he should do about it.

Inform server

Although the browser controls session Timeouts, the server can nevertheless be kept informed, and it can use server-side sessions for this purpose. There are quite a few applications of server-side session tracking:

Invalidating server-side session

The server can invalidate any server-side session data for security purposes.

Historical records

The server can retain Timeout data to help personalize the web site, to provide feedback to users, and also to inform you, the site operator.

Multiuser awareness

In multiuser systems and especially in any sites hoping to foster a community, users should be aware of each others' activities. Indeed, the "live web"—or, as Technorati puts it, "What's Happening on the Web Right Now?"—is becoming a key phenomenon on the Web. If the server is able to track what users are working on and how long they have been idle, this information (subject to privacy considerations) can be conveyed to other users. That's especially important when users are collaborating on the same workspace—for instance, in an Ajaxian wiki environment.

Pessimistic locking

Pessimistic locking is a technique used to prevent two users from working on the same thing at once. In a wiki, for example, a user can lock the article and thereby have sole access to it until it's saved or until the user is idle for a while. While this can be open to abuse on the public web, it would actually be quite a good model for many intranet applications. However, it hasn't been practical because of the risk that the user might walk away and leave the lock intact. Server-side session Timeouts don't help much because the user might be busily working in the browser but not be ready yet to submit content. But once the server is aware of what the user is doing in the browser, pessimistic locking starts to become practical. If the user hasn't done anything for the last 30 minutes, for example, she loses the lock. Again, Ajax helps with this, because with *Periodic Refresh* (Chapter 10), you can immediately inform the user that she has lost the lock.

Work scheduling

With this variant of *Predictive Fetch* (Chapter 13), it's possible for the server to proactively prepare for future actions. By tracking active users, the process becomes more focused. For example, a blog aggregator could run a periodic background process to build a list of unread articles for each active user should they decide to view the list.

So informing the server of a Timeout is a good thing. But there's still a small problem with this approach: What if the user quits the browser or moves away to another site? Then a Timeout will never occur and the server will blissfully continue assuming that the user is logged in for all eternity. To alleviate this problem, have the server refresh the user's record upon each incoming request that suggests user activity. The rest remains, however, of inadvertently timing out a user who is performing browser-only activity. So what we need is a way for the browser to keep telling the server that the user is still active, explicitly noting that a Timeout hasn't actually occurred. That's exactly what the *Heartbeat* pattern is about—see later in this chapter for more details.

Decisions

How long will the Timeout period be?

The Timeout period will depend on the purpose for having the Timeout period in the first place. For example, if the purpose is primarily to stop *Periodic Refresh* (Chapter 10), you need to weigh the benefits of reduced bandwidth and server costs against the frustration caused to users who will have to reactivate the page and wait a few seconds for the latest data. In practice, there are probably several reasons to use Timeout, and the needs in each situation must be taken into consideration.

How will Timeout affect the user interface?

A Timeout can impact the interface in different ways. You may choose to use any of the following:

- Wipe the entire display and show a message that the user was timed out or the session suspended. This is worthwhile if the data is sensitive.

- As a variant on the previous option, reload the entry point for the application (as if the user had typed in the main URL).

- Perform a *Page Rearrangement* to insert a message about the Timeout into the page.

In addition, if you want to be really sure that users know they've been timed out, you could produce an alert. Use Timeout alerts with caution: it's quite obtrusive, and you could probably make the Timeout equally obvious with a carefully considered page element. A *Popup* (Chapter 15) is a less obtrusive mechanism.

Real-World Examples

Many conventional web sites have a session Timeout feature, though it's implemented server side rather than the way I've described in this section.

Lace Chat

Brett Stimmerman's Lace Chat (*http://www.socket7.net/lace/*) is an Ajax chat app. As such, it requires a *Periodic Refresh* in order to keep showing new messages, a serious bandwidth concern if the user is no longer interested in the conversation. So after some idle time, a dialog box appears indicating that Lace has stopped; it includes a button allowing the user to resume (Figure 17-12). Lace also has a *Status Area* (Chapter 15) that always shows whether the application is running—i.e., whether the server is being polled. In fact, you can pause and resume it manually too. The Timeout mechanism hooks into this state by forcing the application to pause upon Timeout.

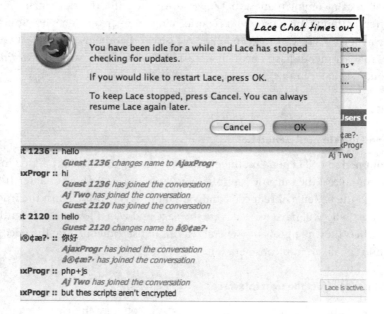

FIGURE 17-12. Lace Chat Timeout

Pandora

Pandora uses Flash to stream music into a browser. After a long idle period, it stops playing and produces a dialog to confirm that the user is still listening.

Session Warning Demo

Eric Pascarello has explained a demo system which has a standard server-side session Timeout but which also pops up a warning near Timeout allowing the user to renew the Timeout (*http://radio.javaranch.com/pascarello/2005/07/05/1120592884938.html*). There are implementations in both VB.net and JSP.

Operating system Timeouts

A precursor to Ajaxian Timeout is evident in operating systems, such as Apple OSX, that show a warning when they are about to enter standby mode. A pop-up dialog says something like "You haven't used the mouse or keyboard for 15 minutes. Standby mode will start in 30 seconds." The dialog will count down, and the user can prevent the Timeout with a keyboard or mouse action or by explicitly hitting a Cancel button. A similar precursor is present in remote terminal systems that output an idle warning to the console.

Code Refactoring: AjaxPatterns Timeout Wiki

Introducing Timeout to the wiki

Timeout is a very useful pattern for a wiki on several counts. Firstly, it cuts down on *Periodic Refresh* (Chapter 10) wastage. Secondly, it helps users understand what others are up to. Thirdly, it improves security if users are logged on. For all of these reasons, we will now add some Timeout functionality to the Basic Wiki Demo (*http://ajaxify.com/run/wiki*). (The Periodic Refresh Time Demo [*http://ajaxify.com/run/time/periodicRefresh*] also has a couple of similar Timeout refactorings under it.)

Initial refactoring: unconditional Timeout

This initial version, Timeout Wiki Demo (*http://ajaxify.com/run/wiki/timeout*), is merciless. Log into the wiki and, no matter what you do, you're timed out a few seconds later (Figure 17-13). The point, of course, is to introduce and prove the basic Timeout functionality, which can be built on later.

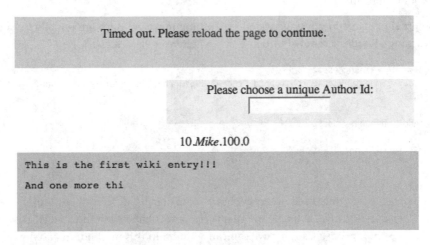

Timed out. Please reload the page to continue.

Please choose a unique Author Id:

10.*Mike*.100.0

This is the first wiki entry!!!

And one more thi

FIGURE 17-13. A timed-out wiki

A Timeout message that will initially be hidden is added to the initial HTML:

```
<div id="timeoutMessage">
  Timed out. Please <a href=".">reload the page</a> to continue.<br/>
</div>
```

The script begins by hiding the Timeout message and kicking off a Timeout timer:

```
window.onload = function() {
  ...
  $("timeoutMessage").style.display = "none";
  timeoutTimer = setTimeout(onTimeout, TIMEOUT_TIME);
}
```

When Timeout occurs, the Timeout message is made visible (with some fanfare, courtesy of a Scriptaculous effect [*http://script.aculo.us*]). Most importantly, the periodic sync stops, so the server is no longer polled. All the messages are removed from the page as well:

```
function onTimeout() {
  new Effect.BlindDown($("timeoutMessage"));
  stopPeriodicSync();
  removeMessages();
}
...
function removeMessages() {
  while ($("messages").hasChildNodes()) {
    $("messages").removeChild($("messages").firstChild);
  }
}
```

Warning that Timeout is pending

If only for the selfish reason that we want to avoid being flamed by the user, it would be nice to warn them that a Timeout is about to occur. And nicer still to let them prevent it from occurring. So this demo (*http://ajaxify.com/run/wiki/timeout/warning*) introduces a warning mechanism.

To the previous Timeout message we add a warning message. Both are initially invisible. The warning includes a renew button, which will invoke renewSession().

```
<div id="warningMessage">
  Near timeout. Please <button id="renew">Renew</button> your session now.
</div>

window.onload = function() {
  ...
  $("renew").onclick=renewSession;
  ...
}
```

renewSession() is not only used on renew but also on startup. It resets both the timeoutTimer and the warningTimer. Note that these timers have been introduced as variables in the script, precisely so that we can cancel them in this method. In addition, renewSession() kicks off the standard wiki sync timer and hides the warning and Timeout messages in the case that either is showing:

```
var timeoutTimer = null;
var warningTimer = null;
...
function renewSession() {
```

```
    $("warningMessage").style.display = "none";
    $("timeoutMessage").style.display = "none";
    clearInterval(warningTimer);
    clearInterval(timeoutTimer);
    warningTimer = setTimeout(onWarning, WARNING_TIME);
    timeoutTimer = setTimeout(onTimeout, TIMEOUT_TIME);
    startPeriodicSync();
}
```

So as long as the user clicks on the renew button while it's showing, he can force all timers to be restarted. But if he doesn't click on it, Timeout will proceed. We simply have to ensure that the warning message is shown before the Timeout message, i.e., WARNING_TIME must fall short of TIMEOUT_TIME. When Timeout occurs, we can assume that the warning is already being shown, so we replace it with the Timeout message. And as before, we stop synchronization and remove all messages:

```
function onTimeout() {
  new Effect.BlindUp($("warningMessage"));
  new Effect.Appear($("timeoutMessage"));
  stopPeriodicSync();
  removeMessages();
}
```

Monitoring mouse movements

A warning's better than nothing, but it does have the slight odor of techno-centeredness. From the user's perspective, why should she have to explicitly renew the session. What's this Timeout business anyway? For most users, it's better to handle Timeout on their behalf. This demo (*http://ajaxify.com/run/wiki/timeout/monitoring/*) builds on the initial Timeout demo to suspend activity when the user is idle.

Here, we'll make an assumption that the user is working with the mouse. That is, we can assume that the user is idle if (and only if) he hasn't used the mouse for a while. As before, we have only one Timeout message, which we've altered to help the user understand how to bring all of those messages back again:

```
<div id="timeoutMessage">
  Timed out. Please wiggle your mouse to continue.<br/>
</div>
```

The key to this pattern is watching for mouse movements on the page and renewing the session when one occurs. Actually, that's easy enough to achieve:

```
window.onload = function() {
  ...
  document.getElementsByTagName("body")[0].onmouseover = function(event) {
    renewSession();
  }
  ...
}
```

Calling a function on each mouse movement could get grossly inefficient. In real life, you might want to be just a little more intelligent about this. For example, use some sort of throttling algorithm to ensure that renewSession( ) isn't called more than once every few seconds.

renewSession( ) itself works similarly to the preceding warning demo: it hides the Timeout message and kicks off sync and Timeout timers.

```
function renewSession( ) {
  if ($("timeoutMessage").style.display!="none") {
    new Effect.BlindUp($("timeoutMessage"));
  }
  clearInterval(timeoutTimer);
  if (!syncTimer) {
    startPeriodicSync( );
  }
  timeoutTimer = setTimeout(onTimeout, TIMEOUT_TIME);
}
```

Related Patterns

Heartbeat

Heartbeat (see the next pattern) is a companion pattern that helps the server monitor whether the user is still working in the browser.

Periodic Refresh

For Ajax Apps, a big motivation for Timeout functionality is the prospect of reducing *Periodic Refreshes* (Chapter 10).

Progress Indicator

Progress Indicator (Chapter 14) is normally used for feedback during an *XMLHttpRequest Call*. However, another application of it would be to count down toward the Timeout. The display could be present as a permanent fixture, or, alternatively, you could introduce it near Timeout.

Direct Login

If your Timeout requires reauthentication for users to continue working with the system, you probably want to offer a *Direct Login* (see earlier).

Status Area

You can show Timeout-related messages and countdowns in a *Status Area* (Chapter 15).

Popup

You can show Timeout-related messages and countdowns in *Popups* (Chapter 15).

Metaphor

If a car engine remains idle long enough, you're probably going to assume that it's dead and give up trying to start it. To keep going would only be a waste of energy.

Heartbeat

ACK, Announcement, Flash, Heartbeat, Monitor, Signal

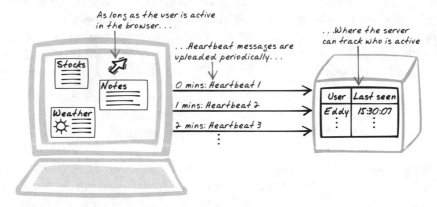

FIGURE 17-14. Heartbeat

Goal Story

For auditing purposes, Frank must run the factory decision support system all day long, so the server needs to ensure that it's always alive in the browser. But requests won't come in very often because it's a fat client, with the business logic in JavaScript. To ensure that the server keeps getting requests, the browser explicitly uploads a Heartbeat message every 10 minutes.

Problem

How do you know the user still has an application in the browser and is actively working with it?

Forces

- It's useful for the server to track whether the user is active, with several applications highlighted in the Solution of *Timeout*.

- Due to the stateless nature of HTTP, the server doesn't know when the user has quit the browser, experienced a browser crash, or surfed away to a different URL. Note that you could use the JavaScript onunload event to catch the last of these, but it won't work for the first two. In tracking the user's activity, the server may assume the user is still active when he has in fact abandoned the application.

- The user sometimes spends a long time working in the browser, but in a manner which yields no calls to the server—for example, filling out a long form or playing a game. The server has no way of knowing that the user's still around if no calls are made.

Solution

Have the browser periodically upload Heartbeat messages to indicate that the application is still loaded in the browser and the user is still active. The server keeps track of each user's "last Heartbeat." If the Heartbeat interval is 10 minutes and the user's last Heartbeat was longer than 10 minutes ago, the server knows that the user is no longer active. The objective is to help the server track which users are active. Session tracking isn't essential in Ajax Apps, where it's possible to hold all session data as JavaScript state, but, as described in the Solution of *Timeout*, there are still reasons to do it.

Heartbeat messages are uploaded to a special "Heartbeat service" using *XMLHttpRequest Calls*. Because they affect server state, they should be POSTed in. The Heartbeat service will update the user's last Heartbeat record, but how does it associate a Heartbeat message with a user? Heartbeat relies on some form of session management. One approach is to use cookies, either directly or via a cookie-based session framework. However, if you do that, the conversation will be stateful, thus violating a fundamental *RESTful Service* principle. A cleaner approach is to explicitly include the session ID in the Heartbeat body. Note that you shouldn't just upload the user ID, as others could easily fake the user ID.

Heartbeat is closely related to *Timeout*, but they work in different ways. You can use either independently, but Heartbeat works best as a supplement to *Timeout*. The point of Timeout is to stop the browser application after an idle period for security and bandwidth reduction. Notifying the server of Timeout events yields extra benefits, but it only works if the application is still sitting in the browser and working fine. That's why we use Heartbeat messages, which are, in a sense, the inverse of Timeouts, and therefore a good supplement. Whereas a Timeout message has the browser announce when a timeout has occurred (Figure 17-15), a Heartbeat message has it continuously announced that a Timeout *hasn't* occurred (Figure 17-16). As soon as the server detects a missed Heartbeat, it can assume the application is no longer running.

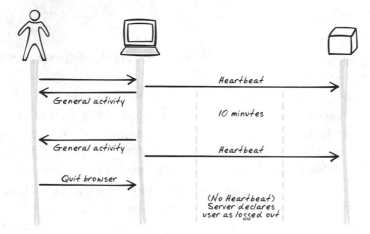

FIGURE 17-15. Heartbeat sequence

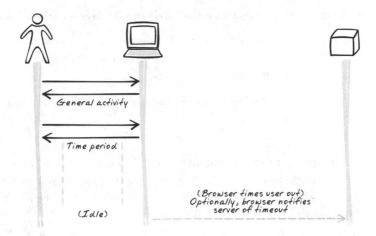

FIGURE 17-16. Timeout sequence

As an alternative to Heartbeat, you can maintain a "Last Seen" or "Last Request" field to track the last time the user issued a request. Thus, not only Heartbeat messages but any other messages will refresh the user's record. The Heartbeat is just a backup. Using these fields might paint a more meaningful picture if you're showing the timestamp to other users or feeding it into analysis.

This pattern is purely speculative in the context of Ajax applications. However, Heartbeats are commonplace in enterprise messaging systems, where they are used to monitor the status of components throughout a network.

Decisions

How will you maintain user records?

There are two main ways to maintain user records:

In memory
> The data is not persisted and will be lost once the user is timed out. In most environments, this will happen if you rely on standard session objects.

Directly in the database
> Within persistent user records. There's some extra storage and data maintenance involved, but the benefit is that you always know when the user was last seen.

What, if anything, will cause the browser application to stop sending Heartbeats?

One option is for the browser application to *always* send Heartbeats. This lets the server track whether the application is still sitting in the browser, which may be useful for analysis purposes. More likely, though, you probably want to send Heartbeats only if the user is actively working with the browser. Thus, as mentioned in the preceding Solution, the Heartbeat is effectively a message that says "the user has not yet timed out."

How much time between Heartbeats? How much delay until a user is declared inactive?

You need to decide on the time period between Heartbeats. If it's too long, the information will not be very useful. If it's too short, you'll be placing a strain on the network, as well as impacting browser and server performance.

The appropriate figure could vary from subseconds to up to 30 minutes or more depending on the following factors:

Application
 In some applications, up-to-the-second information is more critical. In a multiuser system, for example, users' work may be dictated by whoever else is present. If you wait 10 minutes to tell Alice that Bob has quit the chess game, she might be annoyed that she wasted the last 10 minutes thinking about her next move.

Available resources
 Ideally, the period should be as short as possible, though you can't always justify this. For an intranet application, you're likely to use a shorter period in recognition of better resources per user.

Real-World Examples

As this pattern is speculative, there are no real-world examples at this time.

Code Refactoring: AjaxPatterns Heartbeat Wiki

The *Timeout* pattern (see earlier in this chapter) refactored the wiki to produce the Timeout Wiki Demo (*http://ajaxify.com/run/wiki/timeout*), and two further refactorings from there. The present refactoring (*http://ajaxify.com/run/wiki/timeout/heartbeat*), as seen in Figure 17-17, creates a third version of the basic Timeout demo, introducing a Heartbeat. Note that Heartbeat can work independently of *Timeout* but works better in tandem, as this pattern demonstrates.

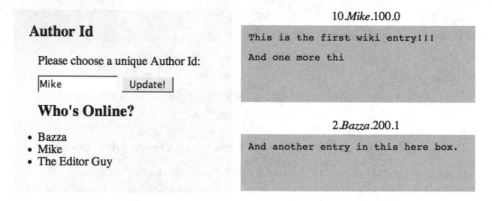

FIGURE 17-17. Showing user status via Heartbeat

To illustrate Heartbeat, I'll show one of its main applications—an application that lets users see who else is "currently online", i.e., who else has a recent Heartbeat registered.

Thus, each user is assigned a random ID, and a Heartbeat mechanism is used to maintain the "Currently Online" list.

But first, let's look at the Heartbeat mechanism. Server side, the Author class contains a lastRequest property:

```
class Author {
  private $id;
  ...
  private $lastRequest;
  ...
}
```

The Heartbeat service accepts a message with an author ID and updates the user's lastRequest. Note that a production system should accept a session ID rather than a user ID. The service extracts the author from the database and updates its lastRequest. If the author does not yet exist, a new record is created with lastRequest set to the present. Finally, the record is persisted:

```
if (isset($_POST['renew']) && $_POST['renew']=="true") {
  $authorId = $_POST['author'];
  $now = time();
  $author = $authorDAO->fetch($authorId);
  logInfo("Got author record for $authorId");
  if ($author) {
    logInfo("Updating timestamp for user $authorId");
    $author->setLastRequest($now);
  } else {
    logInfo("Adding author $authorId");
    $author = new Author($authorId, $now, $now);
  }
  $authorDAO->persist($author);
}
```

A periodic loop is set up to access the Heartbeat service. Because the Heartbeat call is "fire-and-forget," an empty callback function is used:

```
window.onload = function() {
  ...
  heartbeatTimer = setInterval(sendHeartbeat, HEARTBEAT_PERIOD);
  ...
}
function sendHeartbeat() {
  vars = {
    renew: true,
    author: authorId
  };
  ajaxCaller.postForPlainText("session.phtml", vars, function() {});
}
```

And that's the basic Heartbeat pattern. But there's a bit more to do because we're integrating it into *Timeout*. We want to stop sending Heartbeats when a timeout has occurred in the browser. In the preceding code, we created a variable, heartbeatTimer, to track the periodic Heartbeat calls. Since we have a handle on the periodic process, we are able to cancel it upon timeout:

```
function onTimeout( ) {
  ...
  clearInterval(heartbeatTimer);
  ...
}
```

The other feature here is the list of online users, which illustrates one way to use the Heartbeat data. session.phtml exposes an XML list of currently online users (*http://ajaxify.com/run/ wiki/timeout/heartbeat/session.phtml?current*). The fetchRecentlyActive method accepts a parameter indicating just *how* recently active the records should be. In this case, we ask for users with a request in the past 10 seconds:

```
if ($_GET="current") {
  header("Content-type: text/xml");
  echo "<authors>";
  foreach ($authorDAO->fetchRecentlyActive(10) as $author) {
    echo "<author>{$author->getId( )}</author>";
  }
  echo "</authors>";
```

In the browser, there's a div to contain the list:

```
<h1>Who's Online?</h1>
<div id="currentlyOnline"></div>
```

A timer is established to perform a *Periodic Refresh* on the current data. Every few seconds, the XML is requested and the callback function transforms it into HTML for display:

```
currentlyOnlineTimer = setInterval(updateCurrentlyOnline, CURRENTLY_ONLINE_PERIOD);

function updateCurrentlyOnline( ) {
  ajaxCaller.getXML("session.phtml?current", function(xml) {
    $("currentlyOnline").innerHTML = "<ul>";
    var authors = xml.getElementsByTagName("author");
    for (var i=0; i<authors.length; i++) {
      var authorName = authors[i].firstChild.nodeValue;
      $("currentlyOnline").innerHTML += "<li> " + authorName + "</li>";
    }
    $("currentlyOnline").innerHTML += "</ul>";
  });
}
```

As with the Heartbeat timer, the "currently online" timer is cancelled upon timeout, so no more *Periodic Refreshes* will occur:

```
function onTimeout( ) {
  ...
  clearInterval(currentlyOnlineTimer);
  ...
}
```

Related Patterns

Timeout

Timeout (see earlier) is a companion pattern, as discussed in the preceding "Solution."

Submission Throttling

Heartbeat resembles *Submission Throttling* and *Periodic Refresh* (Chapter 6) insofar as all have a continuous *XMLHttpRequest Call* cycle. However, Heartbeat has a more specific aim—namely, informing the server of browser state.

Metaphor

The name "Heartbeat" is, of course, taken from a metaphor with the biological heart.

Want to Know More?

Go to *http://www.mindspring.com/~mgrand/pattern_synopses3.htm#Heartbeat* for a brief summary of Enterprise Java Heartbeat pattern. See Mark Grand's "Java Enterprise Design Patterns" for the full pattern.

Unique URLs

Address, Bookmarks, Cut And Paste, Distinct, Favorites, Hyperlink, Location, Link, Mail, Share, Unique, URL

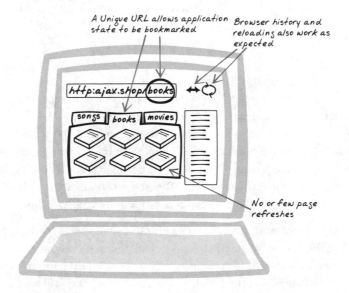

FIGURE 17-18. Unique URLs

Goal Story

Sasha is exploring a recent news event by browsing a map of the area. There's a Unique URL for each location, so she's able to link to it in her blog and add it to her social bookmarking account.

Problem

How can you assign distinct URLs to different parts of your application?

Forces

- Expressive URLs are vital. The ability to link from one site to another is arguably what made the Web successful. Furthermore, web surfers like to bookmark pages for later on. And these bookmarks are now a social phenomenon, with the advent of "link-blogs" and social bookmarking software like del.icio.us (*http://del.icio.us*).

- Browsers retain URLs in their histories, and the Back button will only work if URLs vary. The Back button is a big habit for many users. It can mean "Go back to where I was a minute ago." For many users, it can also mean "Undo my last action," and that mental model must be respected even though some experts deem it to be technically incorrect.

- A single address for your whole site is not enough; you need to support *deep linking* for links to be effective. That is, each distinct component of a web site should have its own URL.

- In conventional web sites, the URL changes when the page is refreshed—e.g., when the user submits a form or follows a link. But in Ajax Apps, the page never refreshes, so the browser won't change the URL.

Solution

Provide Unique URLs for significant application states. Each time a significant state change occurs—e.g., the user opens a new product in an e-commerce system—the application's URL changes accordingly. The objective is straightforward, but as discussed later in this section, the implementation requires a few unusual tricks. This Solution is fairly complex, because it delves into the details of building Unique URLs. Increasingly, though, reusable libraries will save you the effort, so be sure to check out what's available before directly applying any of the techniques here. The Real-World Examples identifies a couple of resources, and there will doubtless be others by the time you read this.

In Ajax, most server communication occurs with XMLHttpRequest. Since *XMLHttpRequest Calls* don't affect the page URL, the URL is, by default, permanently stuck on the same URL that was used to launch the Ajax App, no matter how many transfers occur. The only option you have to manipulate the URL is to use JavaScript. And, in fact, it's very easy to do that with the window.location.href property:

```
window.location.href = newURL; // Caution - Read on before using this.
```

Very easy, but there's one big problem: under normal circumstances, the browser will automatically clear the page and load the new URL, which sort of defeats the purpose of using Ajax in the first place. Fortunately, there's a cunning workaround you can use. It was originally conceived in the Flash world and has more recently been translated to an Ajax context. Mike Stenhouse's demo and article (*http://www.contentwithstyle.co.uk/Articles/38/fixing-the-back-button-and-enabling-bookmarking-for-ajax-apps*) provides a good summary of the approach, and the Solution here is based heavily on his work.

The cunning workaround relies on fragment identifiers—those optional components of URLs that follow the hash character (#). In *http://ajaxpatterns.org/Main_Page#Background*, for example, the fragment identifier is *Background*. The point of fragment identifiers has traditionally been to get browsers scrolling to different points on a page, which is why they are sometimes called "in-page links" or "named links." If you're looking at the Table of Contents on AjaxPatterns.org (*http://ajaxpatterns.org#toc*) and you click on the Background link—*http://ajaxpatterns.org/#Background*—the address bar will update and the browser will scroll to the Background section. Here's the point: no reload actually occurs. And yet, the browser behaves as if you clicked on a standard link: the URL in the address bar changes and the Back button sends you back from whence you came (at least for some browsers; more on portability later).

You can probably see where this is going. We want Ajax Apps to change the page URL without forcing a reload, and it turns out that changes to fragment identifiers do exactly that. The solution, then, is for our script to change only the fragment component. We could do this by munging the `window.location.href` property, but there's actually a more direct route: `window.location.hash`. So when a state change is significant enough, just adjust the URL property:

```
window.location.hash = summary;
```

Throughout this pattern, *summary* refers to a string representation of the current browser state—at least that portion of the state that's worth keeping. For example, imagine that you have an Ajax interface containing several tabs: Books, Songs, and Movies. You want to assign a Unique URL to each tab, so the summary will be the name of any of these tabs. If there were other significant variables, they would be integrated into the summary string. To keep the fragment synchronized with the current state, you need to identify when state changes occur and update the fragment accordingly. In the following tab example, you can do this by making the `onclick` handler set the `hash` property in addition to changing the actual content:

```
songTab.onclick = function( ) {
  window.location.hash = "songs".
  // ... now open up the tab
}
```

So now the URL changes from *http://ajax.shop/* to *http://ajax.shop/#songs*. That was easy enough, but what happens when you mail the URL to a friend? That friend's browser will open up *http://ajax.shop* and assume *songs* is an innocent, old-fashioned, in-page link. It will try to scroll to a *songs* element and won't find one, but it won't complain about it either; it will simply show the main page as before. We've made the URL change *after* a state change, but so far we haven't built in any logic to make the state change *after* a URL change.

State and URL need to be in sync. If one changes, the other must change as well. Effectively, there's a mini-protocol specific to your application that defines how state and URL map to each other. In the preceding example, the protocol says "The fragment always represents the currently open tab." Setting the fragment is one side of the protocol; the other side is reading it. After your friend opens *http://ajax.shop/#songs*, and after his browser unsuccessfully tries to scroll to the nonexistent *songs* element, we need to read the fragment and update the interface accordingly:

```
window.onload = function( ) {
  initializeStateFromURL( );
}

initializeStateFromURL( ) {
  var initialTab = window.location.hash;
  openTab(initialTab);
}
```

Good. Now you can mail the link, bookmark it, and link to it from another page. In some browsers at least, it will also go into your history, which means the Back button will work as expected. For a simple implementation, that's good enough.

However, the solution still isn't ideal, because what will happen if the application is already loaded? The most likely situations occur when clicking the Back button to revert to a previous state and when retrieving a bookmark while already on that application. In both cases, the URL will change in the address bar, but the application will do absolutely nothing!

Remember, we're making the application manipulate fragments precisely because the browser doesn't reload the page when they change. When it comes to Back buttons and bookmarks and the like, we're talking about changes that are initiated by the user, yet the browser treats these with exactly the same inaction as when our script initiates them. So our onload won't be called and the application won't be affected in anyway.

To make Unique URLs work properly, we have to resort to something of a cheap trick: continuously polling the fragment property. Whenever the fragment happens to change, the browser script will notice a short time later and update state accordingly. In this example, we could schedule a check every second using setInterval( ):

```
window.onload = function( ) {
  initializeStateFromURL( );
  setInterval(initializeStateFromURL, 1000);
}
```

In fact, we should only perform an action if the hash has recently changed, so we perform a check in initializeStateFromURL( ) to see if the hash has recently changed:

```
      var recentHash = "";
      function pollHash() {

        if (window.location.hash==recentHash) {
          return; // Nothing has changed since last polled.
        }
        recentHash = window.location.hash;

        // URL has changed. Update the UI accordingly.
        openTab(initialTab);

      }
```

The polling adds to performance overhead, but we now have a URL setup that feels like the real thing.

One last thing on this technique. I mentioned earlier that you can set `window.location.hash` manually after state changes. Now that we've considered the polling technique, you can see that it's also possible to do the reverse: change the URL in response to user events, then let the polling mechanism pick it up and change state accordingly. That adds a delay, but one big benefit is that you can easily add a hyperlink on the page to affect the system state.

Here's a quick summary of the technique just described, which I'll call the "page-URL" technique:

1. Ensure that `window.location.hash` always reflects application state.

2. Create a function, e.g., `initializeStateFromURL()`, to set application state from `window.location.hash`.

3. Run `initializeStateFromURL` on startup and at periodic intervals.

But wait, there's more! I mentioned earlier that each URL goes into history, but only "for some browsers." IE is one of the outliers here, so the above technique will fail IE's history mechanism, and the Back button won't work as expected. The good news is there's a workaround for it. The bad news is that it's a different technique and won't work properly on Firefox. So if you can live with everything working but IE history, go with the hash-rewrite technique. Otherwise, read on....

The IE-specific solution relies on IFrames and on their source URLs, so I'll call it the "IFrame-URL" technique. While IE won't consider a fragment change historically significant, it *will* recognize changes to the source URL of an embedded IFrame. Each time you change the source URL of an IFrame, the entire page will be added to the history. Think of each page in the history as not just the main URL but the combination of main URL and URLs of any IFrames. Its the combination that must vary in order to create a new history entry.

So to get IE history working, we can embed a dummy IFrame and keep changing its source URL to reflect the current state. When the user clicks Back, the source will change to its previous state. In theory, the browser could keep polling the IFrame's source URL to find out when it's updated, but, for some reason, reverted IFrames don't seem to provide the correct source URL. So a workaround is to make the actual IFrame body contain the summary of browser state, i.e., the string which was in the fragment identifier for the previous algorithm. Then, the polling mechanism looks at the IFrame body rather than its source URL.

For example, if the user clicks on the Songs tab, the IFrame source will change to `dummy.phtml?summary=Songs`. The body of `dummy.phtml` will be made (by the server) to contain this argument verbatim, i.e., the body of the IFrame will be "Songs." When the user later clicks somewhere else and then clicks the Back button, the browser will reset the IFrame's URL to *dummy.phtml?summary=Songs* and the body will once again be "Songs." The polling mechanism will soon detect the change and open the Songs tab.

Now we have history, but we haven't done anything about the URLs. So when the user clicks on the Songs tab, we not only change the IFrame source but also the main document URL using a fragment identifier like before. We also have to make sure that the polling mechanism looks at the URL as well as the IFrame source. If either has changed since last poll, the application state must be updated. In addition, the one that hasn't changed must also be updated, i.e., if the IFrame source has changed, the URL must be updated, and vice versa.

Here's a quick summary of the IFrame-URL technique:

- Embed an IFrame in your document.

- On each significant state change, update the IFrame's source URL using a query string (*dummy.phtml?summary=Songs*), and update the main page URL using a fragment identifier (*http://ajax.shop/#Songs*).

- Continuously poll the IFrame source URL and the main page URL. If either has changed, update the other one and update the application state according to the new value.

Note that this won't work on Firefox, because Firefox will include URL changes as well as IFrame changes in the history. Thus, each state change will actually add two entries to Firefox's history. As mentioned earlier, you'll probably need to implement both algorithms in order to fully support both browsers. A modified version of the second technique will do it as well. Also, be careful when using both approaches because there's a risk your polling mechanism will revert states too eagerly. If the user has begun changing a value and the polling mechanism kicks in, it's possible that the value will change back. If you separate input and output carefully enough, that can be avoided. A workaround is to suspend the polling mechanism at certain times. None of this is ideal, but a Unique URL mechanism is worth fighting for.

As a variant on changing the IFrame's source, Brad Neuberg—based on a hack by Danny Goodman—has pointed out that browsers will retain form field data (*http://codinginparadise.org/weblog/2005/08/ajax-tutorial-saving-session-across.html*). Instead of changing the IFrame source, you set the value of a hidden text field in the IFrame. That will solve the history problem, but you'll still need to do something about the main page URL to give the page a Unique URL.

To summarize all of this, here are all the things we'd want from Unique URLs and an explanation of how each can be achieved in Ajax.

Bookmarkable, linkable, and type-in-able

> `window.location.hash` makes the URL unique, so a user can bookmark it, link to it, and type it directly into her browser. `window.onload` ensures that the bookmark is used to set state. Polling or IFrame ensures that this will work even when the base URL (before the hash) is the same.

History and Back button

> `window.location.hash` will change, and polling ithis property will let you detect changes to the URL in most browers. A hidden IFrame is also required for portability; it can be polled too.

Back to Ajax App

> After leaving an Ajax App, the user should be able to click the Back button and return to the final state just prior to signing off. The techniques in *Heartbeat* will support this behavior.

URL handling is one of the greatest complaints about Ajax, with myths abounding about how "Ajax breaks the Back button" and how "You can't bookmark Ajax Apps." That an Ajax App can include full page refreshes is enough to debunk these myths. But this pattern shows that even without page refreshes, Unique URLs are still do-able, even if somewhat complicated. This pattern identifies some of the current thinking on Unique URLs, but the problem has not yet been solved in a satisfactory manner. The best advice is to watch for new ideas and delegate to a good library where applicable.

Decisions

How will you support search engine indexing?

Search engines point "robot" scripts to a web site and have them accumulate a collection of pages. The robot works by scooting through the web site, finding standard links to standard URLs, and following them. It won't click on buttons or type in values as a user would, and it probably won't distinguish among fragment identifiers, either. So if it sees links to *http://ajax.shop/#Songs* and *http://ajax.shop/#Movies*, it will follow one or the other, but not both. That's a big problem, because it means an entire Ajax App will only have one search link associated with it, and you'll miss out on a lot of potential visits.

The simplest approach is to live with a single page and do whatever you can with the initial HTML. Ensure that it contains all of the info required for indexing, focusing on meta tags, headings, and initial content.

A more sophisticated technique is to provide a Site Map page that is linked from the main page and that links to all URLs you want indexed with the link text containing suitable descriptions. There is one catch here: you can't link to URLs with fragment identifiers, so you'll need to come up with a way to present search engines with standard URLs even though your application would normally present these using fragment identifiers. For example, have the Site Map link to *http://ajax.shop/Movies* and configure your server to redirect to *http://ajax.shop/#Movies*. It's probably reasonable to explicitly check if a robot is performing the search, and if it is, to preserve the URL—i.e., when the robot requests *http://ajax.shop/Movies*, simply output the same contents as the user would see on *http://ajax.shop/#Movies*. Thus, the search engine will index *http://ajax.shop/Movies* with the correct content, and when the user clicks on a search result, the server will know (because the client is *not* a robot) to redirect to *http://ajax.shop/#Movies*.

Search engine strategies for Ajax Apps has been discussed in a *http://www.backbase.com/#dev/tech/001_designing_rias_for_sea.xml*: detailed paper by Jeremy Hartlet of Backbase. See that paper for more details, though note that some advice is Backbase-specific.

What will be the polling interval?

The solutions here involve polling either the main page URL, the IFrame URL, or both. What sort of polling interval is appropriate? Anything more than a few hundred milliseconds will cause a noticeable delay (though that's not a showstopper because users are used to delays in loading pages). From a responsiveness perspective, the delay should ideally be as short as possible, but there are two forces at work that will lengthen it:

Performance overhead
    Continuous polling will have an impact on overall application performance, so consider 10 milliseconds the bare minimum. Somewhere between 10 and 100 milliseconds is probably the best trade-off.

Overeager synchronization
    This is only a problem for the IFrame-URL approach and not the Page-URL approach. The IFrame-URL approach, as described in the Solution above, keeps Page URL, IFrame URL, and application state synchronized. Thus, there's the possibility that you will begin to change one of those things and it will "snap back" during a synchronization checkpoint. For example, you might begin changing application state and suddenly see it "snap back" because it's different than URL state. There are various pragmatic ways to avoid this sort of thing, but as long as you have to rely on polling, the problem might still arise for certain combinations of events. While far from ideal, a longer polling period will at least diminish the problem.

What state differences warrant Unique URLs?

In this pattern, I discuss "state changes" abstractly. When I say a "state change" should result in a new URL and a new entry in the browser's history, what kind of state change am I discussing? In an Ajax App, some changes will be significant enough to warrant a new URL, and some won't. Here are some guidelines:

- User preferences shouldn't change the URL—e.g., if a user opts for a yellow background, it shouldn't appear in the URL.

- When there's a particular thing the user is looking at—for example, a product in an e-commerce catalogue, or a general category—that thing is a logical candidate for a Unique URL.

- When it's possible to open several things at once, you'll probably need to capture the entire collection.

What will the URLs look like?

Unique URLs requires you to make like an information architect and do some URL design work. Possibly, you'll be controlling only the fragment identifier rather than the entire URL, but even the fragment identifier has usability implications. Here are some guidelines:

- Users sometimes hack URLs, which suggests that, in some cases, you might want to make the variable explicit. So instead of */#Movies*, consider *#category=Movies* if you want to make the URLs more hack-friendly. Also, this format is more like a CGI-style URL, which may be more familiar to users. The downside is that you'll need a little more coding to parse such URLs.

- As mentioned earlier, search engine indexing is also a consideration, and the fragment identifier will sometimes be mapped to a search engine–friendly URL. Therefore, ensure that the fragment identifier is as descriptive as possible in order to attract searchers. For example, favor a product name over a product ID, since the name is what users are likely to search for.

Real-World Examples

PairStairs

Nat Pryce's PairStairs (*http://nat.truemesh.com/stairmaster.html*) is an Extreme Programming tool that accepts a list of programmer initials and outputs a corresponding matrix (Figure 17-19). The URL stays synchronized with the initials that are being entered—e.g., if you enter "ap ek kc mm," the URL will update so that it ends with #ap_ek_kc_mm.

Dojo binding library

Dojo Toolkit's dojo.io.bind (*http://dojotoolkit.org/docs/intro_to_dojo_io.html*) lets you specify (or autogenerate) a fragment-based URL as part of a web remoting call. After the response arrives, the application's URL will change accordingly.

Really Simple History library

Really Simple History (*http://codinginparadise.org/weblog/2005_09_20_archive.html*) is a framework that lets you explicitly manage browser history (Figure 17-20). A call to dhtmlHistory.add(fragment, state) will set the URL's fragment identifier to fragment and set

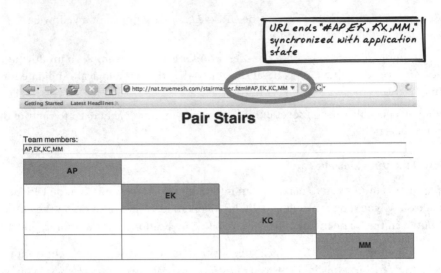

FIGURE 17-19. *PairStairs*

a state variable to state. A callback function can be registered to determine when the history has changed (e.g., the Back button was pressed), and it will receive the corresponding location and state. The library has recently been incorporated into the Dojo project.

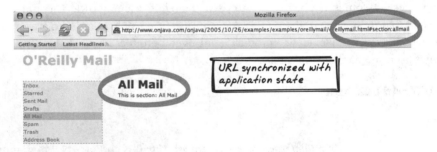

FIGURE 17-20. *Really simple history demo*

Code Refactoring: AjaxPatterns Unique URL Sum

This example refactors the Basic Sum Demo (*http://ajaxify.com/run/sum*) using both the Page-URL and IFrame-URL techniques. There are actually four implementations here:

- Unique URL Sum Demo (*http://ajaxify.com/run/sum/uniqueURL*) uses the Page-URL technique so that when state changes, the URL will change.

- Polling URL Sum Demo (*http://ajaxify.com/run/sum/uniqueURL/pollURL*) enhances the Unique URL Sum Demo by adding a polling mechanism, so that when the URL changes, the state will also change. Thus, the URL-state synchronization occurs in both directions.

- IFrame URL Sum Demo (*http://ajaxify.com/run/sum/uniqueURL/iFrame*) alters the Unique URL Sum Demo to use the IFrame-URL technique. In this version, the history will work correctly because the IFrame source is changed, but the main page URL is not actually updated.

- Full IFrame URL Sum Demo (*http://ajaxify.com/run/sum/uniqueURL/iFrame/updateURL/*) completes the IFrame-URL implementation by making the main page URL unique.

Unique URL Sum Demo

This first refactoring changes the fragment identifier (hash) when a sum is submitted. The fragment identifier always contains the main page state, which, in this case, is a comma-separated list of the three sum figures (e.g., #3,5,10):

```
function submitSum() {
  definedFigures = {
    figure1: $("figure1").value,
    figure2: $("figure2").value,
    figure3: $("figure3").value
  }
  hash =    "#" + definedFigures.figure1 + "," + definedFigures.figure2
          + "," +definedFigures.figure3;
  window.location.hash = hash;
  ajaxCaller.get("sum.phtml", definedFigures, onSumResponse, false, null);
}
```

This is only useful if the startup routine actually takes the fragment identifier into account. Thus, a new function, setInitialFigures(), is called on initialization. It inspects the fragment identifier, sets the parameters, and calls submitSum() to update the sum result:

```
function setInitialFigures() {
  figuresRE = /#([-]*[0-9]*),([-]*[0-9]*),([-]*[0-9]*)/;
  figuresSpec = window.location.hash;
  if (!figuresRE.test(figuresSpec)) {
    return; // ignore url if invalid
  }
  $("figure1").value = figuresSpec.replace(figuresRE, "$1");
  $("figure2").value = figuresSpec.replace(figuresRE, "$2");
  $("figure3").value = figuresSpec.replace(figuresRE, "$3");
  submitSum();
}
```

Polling URL Sum Demo

The previous version will update the URL upon state change, but not vice versa. This demo rectifies the problem by polling the URL and updating state if the URL changes. The functionality for updating state from URL is already present in the setInitialFigures() function of the previous version. We simply need to keep running it instead of just calling it on startup. So, setInitialFigures() has been renamed to pollHash() and is run periodically:

```
window.onload = function() {
  ...
  setInterval(pollHash, 1000);
}
```

The function is the same as before, but with just one change: a `recentHash` variable is maintained to ensure that we only change state if the hash has actually changed. We don't want to change state more times than are necessary:

```
var recentHash = "";

function pollHash() {
  if (window.location.hash==recentHash) {
    return; // Nothing has changed since last polled.
  }
  recentHash = window.location.hash;

  // ... Same code as in previous setInitialFigures() function ...
}
```

IFrame Sum Demo

The previous versions won't work on IE because a fragment identifier change is not significant enough to get into IE's history. So here, we'll introduce an IFrame and change its source URL whenever the document changes.

The initial HTML includes an IFrame. This is the IFrame whose source URL we'll manipulate in order to add entries to browser history. It's backed by a PHP file that simply mimics the summary argument; the body of the IFrame always matches the source URL, so we can find the summary by inspecting the body. In fact, we should be able to just inspect the source URL directly, but there seems to be some bug in IE that fails to update the source property when you go back to a previous IFrame (even though it actually fetches the content according to that URL). Incidentally, the IFrame would normally be hidden via CSS but is kept visible for demonstration purposes.

```
<iframe id='iFrame' name='iFrame' src='summary.phtml?summary='></iframe>
```

Each time a sum is submitted, the IFrame's source is updated:

```
function submitSum() {
  ...
  $("iFrame").src = "summary.phtml?summary=" + summary;
}
```

Instead of polling the URL, we're now polling the IFrame's body, which contains the state summary. Remember that in this version, the main page URL is fixed—we're only making IE history work, and not yet making the application bookmarkable. Whenever we notice that the IFrame source has been changed, we assume that it's because the Back button has been clicked. Thus, we pull out the summary from the IFrame body and adjust the application state accordingly:

```
window.onload = function() {
  ...
  setInterval(pollSummary, 1000);
}

function pollSummary() {
```

```
    summary = window["iFrame"].document.body.innerHTML;
    if (summary==recentSummary) {
      return; // Nothing has changed since last polled.
    }
    recentSummary = summary;

    // Set figures according to summary string and call submitSum( )
    // to set the result ...

}
```

The Back button will now work as expected on both Firefox and IE.

Full IFrame Sum Demo

This final version builds on the previous version by including Unique URLs for the main page so that you can bookmark a particular combination of figures. Note that this is an "IFrame URL" demo and won't work properly on Firefox for reasons explained in the preceding Solution.

The page contains an IFrame as before, and since we're now synchronizing the URL as well, there are actually three things to keep in sync:

- The application state, i.e., the three sum figures
- The page URL
- The IFrame URL

The algorithm is this: when one of these three changes, change the other two and update the sum result. To facilitate this, some convenience functions exist to read and write these properties:

```
function getURLSummary( ) {
  var url = window.location.href;
  return URL_RE.test(url) ? url.replace(/.*#(.*)/, "$1") : "";
}

function getIFrameSummary( ) {
  return util.trim(window["iFrame"].document.body.innerHTML);
}

function getInputsSummary( ) {
  return $("figure1").value +","+ $("figure2").value +","+ $("figure3").value;
}

function setURL(summaryString) {
  window.location.hash = "#" + summaryString;
  document.title = "Unique URL Sum: " + summaryString;
}

function setIFrame(summaryString) {
  $("iFrame").src = "summary.phtml?summary=" + summaryString;
}
```

The updateSumResult( ) is also straightforward:

```
function updateSumResult( ) {

    definedFigures = {
        figure1: $("figure1").value,
        figure2: $("figure2").value,
        figure3: $("figure3").value
    }
    ajaxCaller.get("sum.phtml", definedFigures, onSumResponse, false, null);

}

function onSumResponse(text, headers, callingContext) {
    self.$("sum").innerHTML = text;
}
```

Now for the actual synchronization logic. The first thing that might change is the application state itself. This occurs when the Submit button is clicked and will cause the IFrame and page URL to update:

```
window.onload = function( ) {
    self.$("addButton").onclick = function( ) {
        onSubmitted( );
    }
    ...
}

function onSubmitted( ) {
    var inputsSummary = getInputsSummary( );
    setIFrame(inputsSummary);
    setURL(inputsSummary);
    updateSumResult( );
}
```

The other two things that can change are the IFrame source (e.g., if the Back button is clicked) or the URL (e.g., if a bookmark is selected). There's no way to notice these directly, so, as before, we poll for them. A single polling function suffices for both:

```
window.onload = function( ) {
    ...
    pollTimer = setInterval(pollSummary, POLL_INTERVAL);
}

function pollSummary( ) {

    var iframeSummary = getIFrameSummary( );
    var urlSummary = getURLSummary( );
    var inputsSummary = getInputsSummary( );

    if (urlSummary != inputsSummary) { // URL changed, e.g., bookmark
        setInputs(urlSummary);
        setIFrame(urlSummary);
        updateSumResult( );
    } else if (iframeSummary != inputsSummary) { //IFrame changed,e.g., Back button
        setInputs(iframeSummary);
```

```
        setURL(iframeSummary);
        updateSumResult( );
      }

    }
```

One final point: The timer is suspended while the user edits a field in order to prevent the
URL or IFrame source from reverting the application state:*

```
window.onload = function( ) {
  ...
  // Prevent iframe from triggering URL change during editing. The URL
  // change would in turn trigger changing of the values currently under edit,
  // which is why it needs to be stopped.
  for (var i=1; i<=3; i++) {
    $("figure"+i).onfocus = function( ) {
      clearInterval(pollTimer);
    }
    $("figure"+i).onblur  = function( ) {
      pollTimer = setInterval(pollSummary, POLL_INTERVAL);
    }
  }
  ...
}
```

The application is now bookmarkable and has a working history. It's still not ideal,
because if you unfocus an edit field, the figures will revert to a previous state. Also, there
seems to be a browser issue (in both IE and Firefox), which means that the document URL
isn't updated after you manually edit it. Thus, you can change the URL using a bookmark,
but if you change it manually, it will not change again in response to an update of application state.

Alternatives

Occasional refresh

Some Ajax Apps perform page refreshes when a major state change occurs. For example,
A9 (*http://a9.com*) uses a lot of Display Morphing (Chapter 5) and Web Remoting
(Chapter 6) but nevertheless performs a standard submission for searches, leading to clean
URLs such as *http://a9.com/ajax*. Usually, that's enough granularity, so no special URL
manipulation needs to occur.

"Here" link

Some early Ajax offerings, like Google Maps and MSN Earth, keep the same URL throughout but offer a dynamic link within the page in case the user needs it. In some cases,
there's a standard link to "the current page"; in other cases, the link is generated on
demand. Various text is used, such as "Bookmark this Page" or "Link to this page." It's

---

* It's probably feasible to do something more sophisticated by tracking the history of URL, IFrame,
  and application state independently.

very easy to implement this but, unfortunately, it breaks the URL model that users are familiar with; thus users might not be able to use it. Time will tell whether users will adapt to this new style or whether it will fade away as Ajax developers learn how to deal with Unique URLs.

Want to Know More?

- "Uniform Resource Identifier (URI) Generic Syntax," by Tim Berners-Lee, Roy Fielding, and Larry Masinter for the Internet Engineering Task Force (*http://www.gbiv.com/protocols/uri/rfc/rfc3986.html*)

- "Designing RIAs For Search Engine Accessibility," by Jeremy Hartley of Backbase (*http://www.backbase.com/#dev/tech/001_designing_rias_for_sea.xml*)

- "Bookmarks and the Back Button in AJAX Applications," by Laurens Holst of Backbase (*http://www.backbase.com/#dev/tech/002_bookmarks.xml*)

- "Ajax History Libraries," by Brad Neuberg (*http://codinginparadise.org/weblog/2005_09_20_archive.html*)

- "Fixing the Back Button and Enabling Bookmarking for Ajax Apps," by Mike Stenhouse (*http://www.contentwithstyle.co.uk/Articles/38/fixing-the-back-button-and-enabling-bookmarking-for-ajax-apps*)

Acknowledgments

The Solution is based heavily on Mike Stenhouse's article (*http://www.contentwithstyle.co.uk/Articles/38/fixing-the-back-button-and-enabling-bookmarking-for-ajax-apps*).

PART FIVE

Development Patterns

THE PATTERNS IN THIS PART ARE NOT "THINGS" YOU'D SEE IN AN AJAX APP—AS IN THE PREVIOUS parts—but processes you can use to aid development.* Diagnosis (Chapter 18) patterns help with troubleshooting and monitoring the health of an Ajax App. Testing (Chapter 19) patterns help with testing at various levels and are based on the agile practice of testing as the application evolves.

---

* If the idea of process patterns seems odd, feel free to treat them as general guidelines instead. There's actually a relatively long history of patterns for software process and practice; for example, see Jim Coplien's "A Development Process Generative Pattern Language" (*http://users.rcn.com/ jcoplien/Patterns/Process/*).

CHAPTER EIGHTEEN

Diagnosis

IF THERE'S ONE CERTAINTY IN THE LIFE OF A DEVELOPER, IT'S BUGS. AJAX PROGRAMMING ISN'T ROCKET science, but you can still expect the odd moment of pain during development and maybe even in production. Fortunately, there are plenty of techniques, tools, and libraries available to help you isolate problems as they arise. This chapter breaks them into four categories.

Logging is just good old logging applied to the browser, where log messages can be shown in a popup, uploaded to the server, or shown in some browser-specific way. Likewise, *Debugging* is general-purpose debugging applied to JavaScript that is running within the browser.

The next two patterns are more Ajax-specific. *DOM Inspection* is about analyzing the dynamic state of the DOM. *Traffic Sniffing* is about watching traffic between browser and server.

Logging

Capture, Log, Message, Monitor, Record

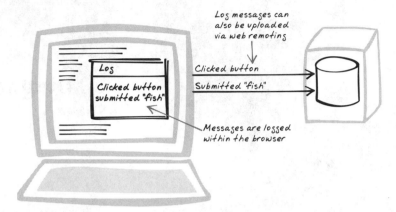

FIGURE 18-1. Logging

Developer Story

Dave's search engine keeps giving a blank result for certain queries. Fortunately, he previously added some Logging commands to see how the query is processed, so he makes the console visible and sets log level to verbose. After entering the query again, he now sees that one of the regular expressions is not matching the query as expected.

Problem

How can you track program process?

Solution

Instrument your JavaScript with log messages. Typically, the page contains a div element especially for Logging, and each significant action is appended there, e.g.:

```
$("log").innerHTML += "User searched for " + query + ".<br/>";
```

Even this simple implementation offers several benefits over the common alternative, debugging with an alertbox. Most importantly, the log element can be a *Popup* (Chapter 15): you can easily toggle visibility by dynamically switching CSS properties such as display, or even make it partly transparent. Further, Logging is unobtrusive—that is, there's no impact on application flow. Another benefit is that you have a history to consult if something goes wrong; there's no need to try replicating the problem.

Inspired by libraries such as Java's log4j (*http://logging.apache.org/log4j/docs/*), JavaScript Logging libraries usually provide some sort of filtering. Typically, a message is tagged with a priority level, e.g., "debug," or "info," or "error." You can then choose to only see messages above a certain level.

Logging impacts performance, not just in DOM manipulation but also in producing the messages themselves. You can end up with a memory problem as well unless some measure is taken to clear old messages, e.g., using a buffer to discard old messages.

Instead of Logging to a console on the page, some developers output messages to the browser status bar (using `window.status`), and Firefox developers also have the option of outputting to the browser console. However, this limits portability and requires some configuration (*http://www.make-believe.org/posts/05/10/24/0*).

Another approach that is gaining traction is to embrace Web Remoting (Chapter 6) and upload the data to a Logging web service.* This allows for permanent storage of the logs and can also be combined with server-side logs to paint a detailed picture of each interaction. Eric Pascarello, for example, has proposed the technique for usability testing (*http://radio.javaranch.com/pascarello/2005/11/01/1130878004388.html*). And log4js (*http://jroller.com/page/stritti?entry=logging_in_javascript_log4js*) supports an `XMLHttpRequest`-driven Logging strategy. The benefits of remote Logging must be balanced against concerns for users' privacy and consent.

Decisions

Will you log during production?

Most servers are configured to perform Logging during production as well as development, so should the browser log too? In the past, the answer was usually no. But Ajax makes the case for browser Logging more compelling for two reasons. Firstly, with more logic in the browser, there are more things that can go wrong and that need to be logged. Secondly, Web Remoting (Chapter 6) makes it possible to accumulate logs on the server in a completely unobtrusive manner. Still, remote Logging does consume application processing time as well as bandwidth, so you'll need to decide whether it's worth it, and if so, how much to log. In doing so, you'll also need to consider the user's privacy.

How will you change log settings between development and production?

In server-side *Logging* systems, log settings are usually altered by applying environment-specific filters. For example, in development, all messages are shown, whereas in production, only messages at information level and above are shown. But a familiar performance problem then arises: even though debug messages aren't being logged, the arguments must nevertheless be constructed, which takes time. A common solution is to include "if-then" statements—an unfortunate idiom that obscures the real point of code—to check the log level. Since JavaScript is generated by the server, you can do better than that: configure

---

* Ajax—more specifically, `XMLHttpRequest`—has been labelled a technique for "spying on users" (*http://www.devx.com/webdev/Article/28861*). However, techniques for remote *Logging* have been available for a long time. The main impact of Ajax is to increase rich activity in the browser, which might create further incentives to log user activity. See *http://www.softwareas.com/spying-on-users-with-xmlhttprequest*.

things so that log commands aren't even spit out in the first place. How you do this depends on the server-side environment. For example, a JSP developer could develop a JavaScript *Logging* tag whose implementation dynamically inspects the Logging configuration.

Tool Support

Lumberjack

Corey Johnson's Lumberjack (*http://gleepglop.com/javascripts/logger/*) is a JavaScript Logging framework that supports Logging at different levels. There's no setup required because it creates the Logging div itself, so you can immediately issue calls such as `Logger.info("User logged in.")`. The console is initially hidden, and you can toggle visibility with Alt-D.

fvLogger

David Miller's fvLogger (*http://www.fivevoltlogic.com/code/fvlogger/*) works similarly to Lumberjack. To use it, you just include a `div` with optional log level and make calls such as `error("No such record.");`.

log4js

log4js (*http://jroller.com/page/stritti?entry=logging_in_javascript_log4js*) is based more closely on log4j than other frameworks. In addition to various log levels, it supports pluggable Logging strategies. Logging strategies include: do nothing; log to pop-up window; and upload via *XMLHttpRequest Call*.

Mochikit

Bob Ippolito's Mochikit framework (*http://mochikit.com/doc/html/MochiKit/Logging.html*) has an API similar to those mentioned earlier and also adds features such as log listeners and a configurable message buffer. Interestingly, the standard way to launch the console is with a bookmarklet.

Code Example: Using Lumberjack

The Basic Ajax Pattern Reader (*http://ajaxify.com/run/reader/*) is refactored here to include Logging with Lumberjack (*http://gleepglop.com/javascripts/logger/*) (Figure 18-2). Lumberjack's *logger.js* is included, and the code is then instrumented to include log messages:

```
Logger.info("Received " + patternNames.length + " pattern names.");
...
Logger.debug("Received summary: " + summaryHTML.substring(0, 100) + "...");
...
Logger.info("Adding " + patternOption.value + " to playlist");
```

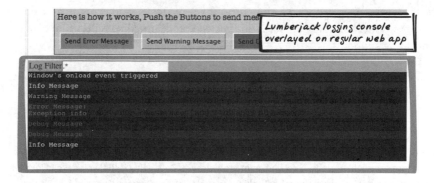

FIGURE 18-2. Lumberjack

Debugging

Break, Debug, Deduce, Fix, Inspect, Repair, Step, Test

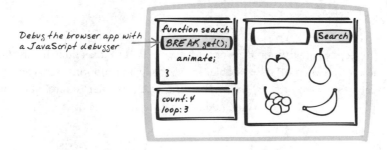

FIGURE 18-3. Debugging

Developer Story

Devi is scratching her head, wondering why a particular visual effect is so jerky; instead of growing gradually, the icon transitions from small to large in just a few, erratic, steps. Code analysis is getting her nowhere, so she fires up her JavaScript debugger, which allows her to step through the effect in her own time. After adding the box dimensions to a watchlist, she quickly diagnoses the cause as a number-rounding issue.

Problem

How can you diagnose errors and strange behavior?

Solution

Diagnose problems with a JavaScript debugger. JavaScript Debugging used to be as sophisticated as adding a few alert messages, but it has come a long way. A tool such as the Venkman debugger (*http://www.mozilla.org/projects/venkman/*), a popular Firefox extension, makes the point. Venkman has all the basic features you'd look for in a debugger of any language: breakpoints, call stacks, step in/out/over, watches, and error and exception triggers. Also, an interactive session lets you type code for immediate execution as well as basic profiling support.

TO DEBUG OR NOT TO DEBUG?

That is the question many developers have asked over the years, with many deciding that there are often more productive things to do. The main problem with Debugging is that you have to invest time setting up breaklists and watches and thinking up strategies for diagnosis, yet all of that is thrown away after the problem's solved. The same problem might arise later on, and you'll have to set it all up again. Even if you can save breakpoints and watches—as Venkman lets you do—they are often too fragile to be useful, whereas if you can create a unit test to check the same thing, or introduce a log message to monitor state, you'll have created a permanent asset for yourself and your team.

For basic error reporting without a custom debugger, use Firefox's built-in JavaScript Console, and on IE, switch off the "Disable Script Debugging" options. You can also define window.onerror to show any errors that arise, as the event handler is notified of the error message, URL, and line number. You could then perform *Logging* or create an alert, e.g.:

```
window.onerror = function(message, url, lineNum) {
  alert("Error: '" + message + "'. At " + url + ", Line " + lineNum);
}
```

Tool Support

Venkman

Venkman (*http://www.mozilla.org/projects/venkman/*) is an open source Firefox extension with quite sophisticated *Debugging* support, as discussed in the preceding Solution (Figure 18-4). When you open the debugger, it shows a list of JavaScript files, which you can then open to set breakpoints.

Microsoft Script Debugger

Microsoft makes Microsoft Script Debugger (*http://msdn.microsoft.com/library/default. asp?url=/library/en-us/sdbug/Html/sdbug_1.asp*) available for no cost. It offers basic Debugging functions, e.g., breakpoints, a basic call stack, step in/out/over, and error triggers (Figure 18-5). While not as feature-rich as Venkman, it's still useful for investigating IE-specific bugs. The IE Blog (*http://blogs.msdn.com/ie/archive/2004/10/26/247912.aspx*) lists several options for IE Debugging.

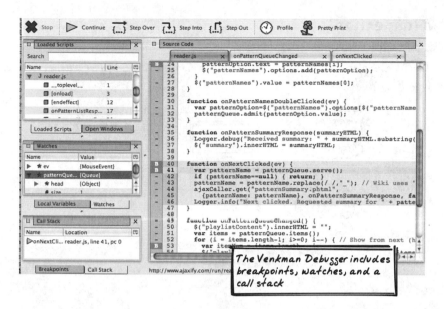

FIGURE 18-4. Venkman

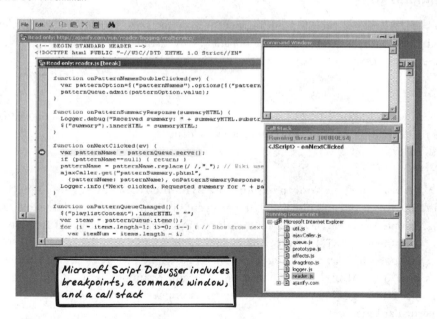

FIGURE 18-5. Microsoft Script Debugger

JavaScript HTML Debugger

JavaScript HTML Debugger (*http://www.htmldebugger.com/javascript_debugger/javascript_debugger.asp*) is a commercial tool from SplineTech. It's a standalone Windows application with functionality similar to Venkman but a greater emphasis on ease-of-learning.

DOM Inspection

DOM, Dynamic, Explore, Inspect, Interrogate, Investigate, Presentation, Render, Snapshot, State, View, Visualise, Visualize

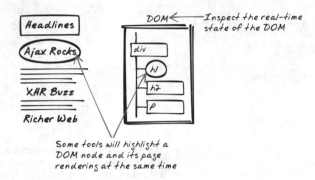

FIGURE 18-6. DOM Inspection

Developer Story

Devi keeps clicking on the Clear button, but the document text remains stubbornly unaffected. She fires up a DOM Inspection tool and discovers that the button's onclick event handler isn't present, which explains why nothing was happening.

Problem

How can you inspect the DOM's state at any time, taking into account DOM manipulations that may have occurred since the page was loaded?

Solution

Use a DOM Inspection Tool to explore the dynamic DOM state. The initial HTML for an Ajax App is often minimal and, in any event, likely to change over time due to DOM Manipulation. A DOM Inspection tool traverses the browser's current DOM model, rather than the initial HTML source, to build up a presentation of the current DOM. Many times, the tool is interactive, allowing you to drill down the hierarchy, search for keywords, and so on. All of this is very useful for checking assumptions and diagnosing problems, since many Ajax bugs arise because the programmer misunderstood the DOM state at a particular time.

Incidentally, DOM Inspection is useful beyond the fact that the DOM is dynamic. Even for static applications, an interactive exploration tool is often a good complement to the mound of text that makes up a complex HTML document.

Tool Support

Firefox DOM Inspector

Firefox ships with a DOM Inspector tool, accessible from the tools menu (Figure 18-7).*
The inspector is a popup window showing the DOM hierarchy on one side and facing a
summary of the selected node. The summary shows node attributes such as registered
event handlers, as well as CSS style information.

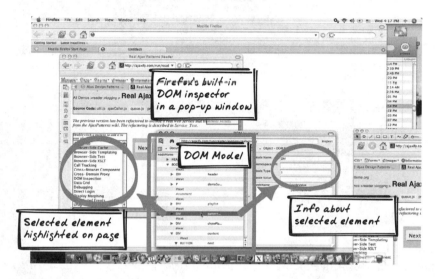

FIGURE 18-7. Firefox DOM Inspector

Firefox Web Developer Extension

Chris Pederick's Web Developer extension (*http://chrispederick.com/work/webdeveloper/*) is an
invaluable Firefox toolbar for web development (Figure 18-8). Among its vast feature set
are several commands especially relevant to DOM Inspection:

Display

These commands augment the page with DOM information, which makes a great alternative to exploring the DOM in a completely separate view. For example, *Display Topo-
graphic Information* alters the page to reveal the layout of DOM elements and *Display ID
and Class Details* augments each element with its id and class attributes.

Outline

There commands—for example, *Outline Block Level Elements* or *Outline Table Cells*—draw
outlines around elements of a particular type. In fact, you can define custom outlines to
outline any element you want.

---

* In Windows, you need to ensure that the Web Developer Tools option (*http://www.clagnut.com/blog/
340/*) is selected during installation.

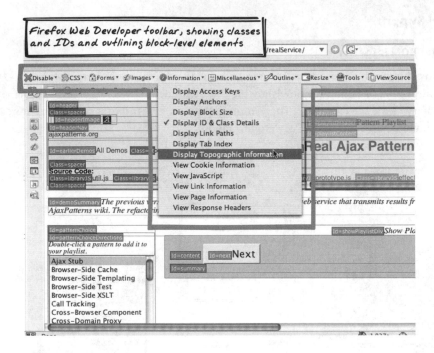

FIGURE 18-8. Web Developer toolbar

Form

These commands help expose form structure. *Display Form Details* augments the form with information about each control, while *View Form Information* opens up a summary page.

View Rendered Source

Jennifer Madden's View Rendered Source (*http://jennifermadden.com/scripts/View-RenderedSource.html*) is a Firefox extension that shows the entire DOM as an HTML document (Figure 18-9). Note that this is not the same thing as the good old View Source feature, because the rendered source reflects the DOM after any manipulation has taken place. The rendered source is shown in a pretty-formatted style, with colors and spacing to help convey the DOM structure. This is a free tool, and you can also purchase a slightly enhanced version for a small fee.

IE Developer Toolbar

Microsoft's free IE Developer Toolbar for IE6+ (*http://www.microsoft.com/downloads/details. aspx?FamilyID=e59c3964-672d-4511-bb3e-2d5e1db91038&displaylang=en*) has a number of DOM Inspection capabilities and is similar to the Firefox Web Developer Extension (Figure 18-10). It also includes a DOM Explorer similar to Firefox's DOM inspector (Figure 18-11).

You can find a list of IE DOM Inspectors at *http://blogs.msdn.com/ie/archive/2005/05/10/416156.aspx*.

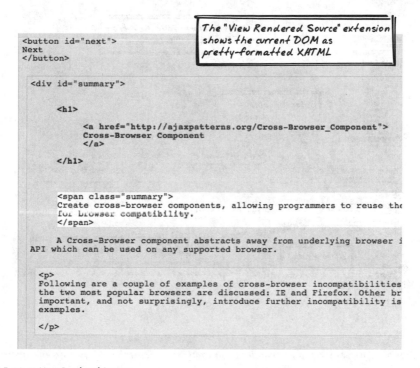

The "View Rendered Source" extension shows the current DOM as pretty-formatted XHTML

```
<button id="next">
Next
</button>
```

```
<div id="summary">

    <h1>

        <a href="http://ajaxpatterns.org/Cross-Browser_Component">
        Cross-Browser Component
        </a>

    </h1>


    <span class="summary">
    Create cross-browser components, allowing programmers to reuse the
    for browser compatibility.
    </span>

    A Cross-Browser component abstracts away from underlying browser i
API which can be used on any supported browser.

    <p>
    Following are a couple of examples of cross-browser incompatibilities
    the two most popular browsers are discussed: IE and Firefox. Other br
    important, and not surprisingly, introduce further incompatibility is
    examples.

    </p>
```

FIGURE 18-9. View Rendered Source

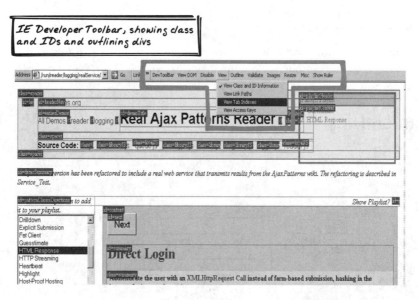

IE Developer Toolbar, showing class and IDs and outlining divs

FIGURE 18-10. IE Developer Toolbar

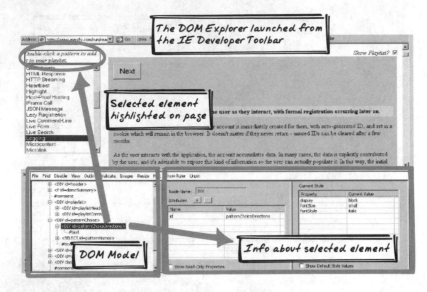

FIGURE 18-11. IE DOM Explorer

IEDocMon

Tim Tabor's IEDocMon (*http://www.cheztabor.com/IEDocMon/index.htm*) is an open source tool that extends IE to include an interactive view of the DOM.

Mouseover DOM Inspector

Steven Chipman's Mouseover DOM Inspector (*http://slayeroffice.com/tools/modi/v2.0/modi_help.html*) is a convenient bookmarklet that lets you explore the DOM by mousing over page elements. It works on all recent browsers except Safari.

Traffic Sniffing

Capture, Intercept, Log, Monitor, Network, Record, Sniff, Traffic

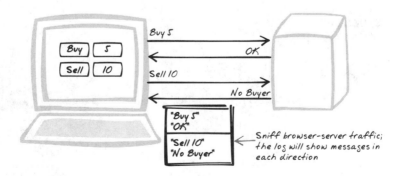

FIGURE 18-12. Traffic Sniffing

Developer Story

Dave hears a report that critical form data isn't being saved on the database. He turns a sniffer on and tries uploading the same data himself. The sniffer shows him an XML message being uploaded via `XMLHttpRequest`. When inspecting the message in an XML editor, he discovers that the JavaScript hasn't formatted it correctly.

Problem

How can you diagnose errors and strange behavior?

Solution

Diagnose problems by sniffing Web Remoting traffic. Many Ajax problems arise because Web Remoting (Chapter 6) messages are either wrong or are not sent at all. *Debugging* (see earlier in this chapter) and general *Logging* on either side of the network might help you infer what's being transmitted, but it's better to grab the traffic directly. There are various ways to do this:

- In the browser, use *XMLHttpRequest Calls* (Chapter 6) in a wrapper that logs the request and response (see *Logging* earlier in this chapter). This may be the most convenient technique, because the programmer is probably already looking at the browser. The downside is that you'll miss out on non–Web Remoting (Chapter 6) traffic, e.g., full page refreshes.

- Employ a generic network traffic monitor, filtering HTTP traffic to and from the server.

- Configure your browser to use a generic HTTP proxy and have the proxy log interesting traffic in either direction.

- In the server, intercept incoming and outgoing traffic for *Logging*. Server-side frameworks often have a common controller object which can be instrumented to capture information in either direction. In addition, interception facilities, such as Java's Servlet Filters, are often available.

Traffic Sniffing is a kind of *Logging* function. As such, you'll probably want similar filtering functionality, e.g., to see messages in only one direction, matching certain text, or to a particular URL.

Tool Support

XMLHttpRequest Tracing and XMLHttpRequest Debugging

Julien Couvreur has written two invaluable Firefox tools: XMLHttpRequest Tracing (*http://blog.monstuff.com/archives/000252.html*) unobtrusively logs traffic to the JavaScript console, while `XMLHttpRequest` *Debugging* (*http://blog.monstuff.com/archives/images/XMLHttpRequest-Debugging.v1.0.user.js*) is a much more powerful, interactive *Popup* tool that not only shows the messages but lets you set filters and configure the display (Figure 18-13). Both are Greasemonkey scripts (*http://greasemonkey.mozdev.org/*), so you'll need to install the Greasemonkey extension first.

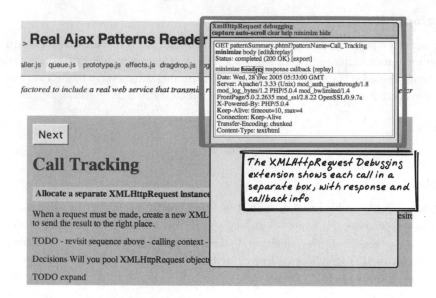

FIGURE 18-13. XMLHttpRequest Debugging

Fiddler

Fiddler (*http://www.fiddlertool.com/Fiddler/dev/*) is a Windows proxy specifically designed for analyzing and "fiddling" with browser-server traffic (Figure 18-14).

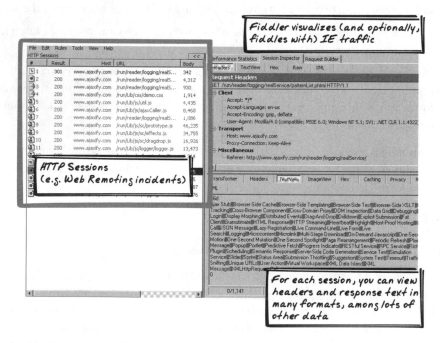

FIGURE 18-14. Fiddler

FlangeLib

Adam Vandenberg has noted that his personal *flangelib.js* library (*http://www.livejournal. com/users/piehead/tag/javascript*) contains an XMLHttpRequest wrapper to log traffic. While you're unlikely to use *flangelib*, it's mentioned here because some XMLHttpRequest wrapper libraries may eventually implement *Logging* functionality. The main barrier right now is the lack of an industry-standard Logging library.

Code Example: Using XMLHttpRequest Tracing

Following is the output from the XMLHttpRequest Tracing script during the initial load sequence for the Ajax Patterns Reader (*http://www.ajaxify.com/run/reader/logging/realService/*). First, the request is logged in the Firefox JavaScript console:

```
http://blog.monstuff.com/XmlHttpRequestTracing: [736] intercepted open (GET ,
patternList.phtml ,
true , undefined , undefined)
http://blog.monstuff.com/XmlHttpRequestTracing: [736] intercepted send (null)
```

Then, the result is displayed, showing response code (200) and content:

```
http://blog.monstuff.com/XmlHttpRequestTracing: [736] intercepted load: 200 Ajax
Stub|||Browser-Side
Cache|||Browser-Side Templating|||Browser-Side XSLT||| ....
```

Related Patterns

Logging

Traffic Sniffing in the browser is a form of *Logging* (see earlier).

CHAPTER NINETEEN

Testing

THANKS TO THE AGILE MOVEMENT, TESTING IS NO LONGER SEEN AS THE BIT AT THE END WHERE **QA** gives its stamp of approval. It's a core development technique, and if you're creating complex web apps, it's worth testing within and across all tiers.

Because of remoting, Ajax browser scripts usually rely on web services. But it's not much fun working on both sides at the same time, so *Simulation Service* explains how to create a "dummy" or "stub" web service to call from the browser. You can use it for tests or for prototyping. *Browser-Side Test* is simply a test of the JavaScript code sitting in the browser. The hardest thing is to exercise it in an automated fashion; the pattern also looks at that issue. *Service Test* involves no JavaScript, because it actually takes the place of the browser; an HTTP client is used to test the web service. *System Test* effectively simulates a user to exercise the application across all layers.

Simulation Service

Canned, Double, Dummy, Fake, Masquerade, Mock, Service, Shunt, Sim, Simulation, Stub

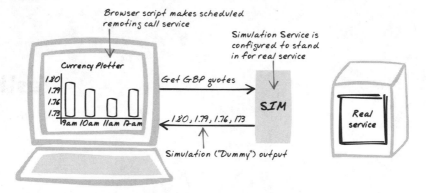

FIGURE 19-1. Simulation Service

Developer Story

Dave is beginning to work on a new email application. Eventually, the server will need to expose a mail API, so the browser can query for recent messages and upload new ones. However, that will require email expertise, and Dave wants to focus on the user interface in the browser for now. Thus, he hardcodes the responses he'd like in a "fake" server-side service. This allows him to proceed with user-interface development while his colleague takes care of the real server implementation.

Problem

How can you develop the browser script in parallel with the services it uses?

Solution

Develop the browser application against "fake" web services that simulate the actual services used in production. A Simulation Service is typically a hardcoded response that ignores any input parameters. So instead of:

```
$taxRate = calculateTaxRate($userId, $year);
print $taxRate;
```

a Simulation Service would just say:

```
print "0.1235";
```

It's also possible to do all this in a browser. If you use a library to perform Web Remoting (Chapter 6), you could make the implementation produce a hardcoded response, and ignore the server altogether.

In some cases, you might make the service more flexible; e.g., it can expose an operation to let the browser tell it what to output later on.

Simulation Service decouples the server and browser components of the application. Once the interface is defined, each can be developed in parallel. Moreover, this pattern paves the way for an agile process for building the application, based loosely on concepts such as Test-Driven Design (TDD) and lean manufacturing.

MOCKS, STUBS, SIMULATIONS

A Simulation Service is a kind of "stub." In software testing, simple stubs are created to provide isolated tests. Instead of working with real components, the tested component works with simple stubs. Because the stubs are simple and stable, any test failures can then be attributed to the tested component. Furthermore, stubs will always yield the same result, so it's easier to automate the test.

It's important to distinguish between "mocks" and stubs, because the terms are often used interchangeably (*http://www.softwareas.com/mocks-stubs-dependency-injection-and-xmlhttprequest*). Like a stub, a "mock" simulates a real component. But for a mock, the simulation is only a by-product of its true purpose: to verify that it's used correctly. Before a test, the mock is told what calls the component will make on it. As soon as that sequence is violated, the mock will complain and the test will fail. There are several potential applications for mocks in Ajax; one of those involves mock Services. The browser could start a test by telling a mock XMLHttpRequest wrapper what calls will soon be made. Then, the wrapper will throw an exception if that call isn't actually made. "Mock Service" is too immature a concept to form a pattern at this stage, but it's something that might emerge as Ajax developers focus on testing techniques.

Conventional web development is usually a bottom-up approach: first comes the database, then the data layer to access it, then the business components on top of that, and finally the user interface. This sequence might seem like the most logical thing to do, given the dependency relationships involved. But the problem is that the user interface is really the whole point of the application, so there's a good argument for starting there instead. For a given feature, flesh out the user interface and use that work to drive the service interface. So instead of designing the server side first and forcing the browser script to work with whatever interface arises, let the needs of the browser script drive the interface design. Consequently, the service will not only contain the precise functionality required by the browser, but also expose it with the most suitable interface.

Starting development in the browser sounds like a good idea until you realize the browser depends on the service, which doesn't yet exist! That's where a Simulation Service comes in: it lets you define *what* the service offers, not *how* the service achieves it. As you develop the browser script, you'll continue to come across refinements to the service—an extra operation here, a different response format there. In each case, changing the Simulation Service is usually as simple as editing the hardcoded response. Once you're confident with the requirements for the Service, you—or someone else—can go build the real thing.

Another application is in *Browser-Side Tests* (see later in this chapter). When testing a browser component, it's important to test only the component itself, and not the services it depends on. Imagine you're testing a browser component that renders news arriving from an RSS web service. An automated test could then interrogate the DOM and run a bunch of assertions to ensure it was formatted correctly. But if the component uses the real service, the resulting DOM will reflect the news of the hour. A human could manually verify it, but automation wouldn't be possible. A hardcoded response would eliminate that problem, allowing the assertions to be consistent with the simulated RSS. Furthermore, there's no dependence on the real implementation—no matter how complex the actual search algorithm, the rendering component will always be tested on its own merit.

Decisions

How will you switch between different services?

It's easy enough to create a Simulation Service, but how do you switch between the simulation and the real thing? And, how do you switch between different simulation services, since you might prefer one or the other for different tasks. Right now, there's no easy answer to that because there's no real support in the way of tools and libraries. Where the practice of Simulation Service is followed, most developers probably switch over to a real service in the most brute-force way possible: they edit the code. But doing so means there's a manual step involved in order to test or deploy. Here are a few ways to make the process more manageable:

- Keep the JavaScript pointing at the same service URL, but have your server-side build tool (e.g., ant) decide what implementation resides there.

- Build some configuration into the JavaScript to help it point to the correct service. This would be useful for an automated JavaScript-based test. You could even create a simple browser control to let the user choose which service is executed, which is helpful during development.

- Instead of hosting JavaScript in a static file, dynamically generate it from the server, so that variable URLs can be set on the fly.

Code Example: Simulation Service

The Ajax Pattern Reader (*http://ajaxify.com/run/reader/*) runs against a couple of *Cross-Domain Proxy* (Chapter 10) services. They fetch information from the AjaxPatterns.org web site and return them in a format easily parsed by the browser. For development purposes, the Basic version (*http://ajaxify.com/run/reader/*) uses Simulation Service.

The first service produces a *Plain-Text Message* (Chapter 9) containing the patterns in a pipe-separated list. A hand-created simulation (*http://ajaxify.com/run/reader/patternList. phtml*) is used instead of fetching the page from AjaxPatterns.org, parsing the HTML, and reformatting it.

```
Periodic Refresh|||One-Second Spotlight|||Slider
```

For comparison, the real service outputs a list that looks similar, but is much longer, and, of course, not hardcoded (*http://ajaxify.com/run/reader/logging/realService/patternList.phtml*).

```
Ajax Stub|||Browser-Side Cache|||Browser-Side Templating||| ... |||XML
    Message|||XMLHttpRequest Call
```

Similarly, there's a simulation of the summary service (*http://ajaxify.com/run/reader/ patternSummary.phtml?patternName=Slider*), whose job is to produce an *HTML Message* summarizing a given pattern. The simulation includes some rudimentary logic to make the response vary according to the input:

```php
<? $patternName = urlDecode($_GET["patternName"]); ?>
  <h1><?= $patternName ?></h1>
<? if ($patternName=="Periodic Refresh") { ?>
    With periodic refresh, it's all about the timer.
<? } else if ($patternName=="Slider") { ?>
    <p>The slider slides from left to right.</p>
    ...
<? } else {
    print ("Text goes here.");
  }

?>
```

The output from the real service is in the same format (*http://ajaxify.com/run/reader/logging/ realService/patternSummary.phtml?patternName=Slider*), but as with the list service, it's fetched from AjaxPatterns.org in real-time.

Related Patterns

Service Test

A Simulation Service is a good starting point for a real service. You might begin developing a *Service Test* (see later) against a Simulation Service, then evolve both into a real service and test.

Want to Know More?

- In Lean IT Processes terminology, the Simulation Service pattern facilitates a "Pull System," where design is driven by customer demands rather than technical capability (*http://abc.truemesh.com/archives/000093.html*).

- Categorization of Test Doubles, distinguishing between mocks, stubs, and so on. Under that categorization, the pattern here describes a "Fake" (*http://tap.testautomationpatterns. com:8080/Using%20Test%20Doubles.html*).

Browser-Side Test

Automated, IntegrationTest, JavaScript, Regression, UnitTest, TDD, Test

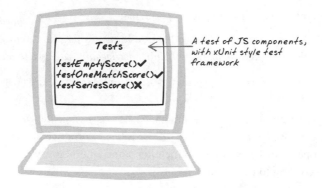

FIGURE 19-2. Browser-Side Test

Developer Story

Devi is about to embark on upgrading a blog reader and realizes she will be tinkering with the JavaScript RSS parser. The parser will need some refactoring, but fortunately there's already a JavaScript unit test for it. She proceeds to refactor the parser, ensuring the test still passes, and continues to enhance the test as she builds in further functionality.

Problem

How can you test JavaScript components?

Solution

Create automated tests of browser-side JavaScript components. This pattern is a mapping from automated testing in other languages, where frameworks like the xUnit series (*http://en.wikipedia.org/wiki/XUnit*—e.g., JUnit; see *http://junit.org*—are now popular. Several frameworks do the same for JavaScript. As with other languages, you can unit test an individual JavaScript component (e.g., a function) you've created, and also perform integration tests and system tests that work across several objects. And also like other languages, you can accumulate tests into a test suite object, so it's possible to run a full regression test.

The test is usually some JavaScript that performs some task and includes assertion to check the state is as expected. Usually, JavaScript frameworks include a Test Runner that will run a given set of tests, then morph the DOM to show results in a table. You usually build an HTML page, with test code embedded, and perhaps some inputs to control the test; e.g., Start and Stop buttons.

So the test is automated insofar as the programmer's not manually interacting with the application and verifying results. That's good enough while developing, but the demands of continuous integration suggest we need to go beyond that. How do you allow tools like Make, Ant, or Rake start and stop a JavaScript test?

One way to coordinate a Browser-Side Test is to simulate browser behavior. Using a JavaScript engine, you can programmatically execute some JavaScript code. For example, Java programmers have the Rhino library (a standard component of Java 6). If there's some DOM manipulation involved as well, an approach like *Browser Simulation*, discussed in *System Test* can be used. A second approach is to fire up a real browser using a shell command, specifying the test page as an argument. The test framework will then run in the browser, and the page must be configured to upload results to a service somewhere, which will expose them to the test process. The test process, upon detecting new results, shuts down the browser with an interprocess communication protocol or, failing that, kills the process.

Tool Support

Scriptaculous testing framework

The Scriptaculous framework (*http://script.aculo.us*) includes a unit-testing framework. It works in a similar manner as JsUnit frameworks (discussed next) and the nUnit frameworks they are modelled on. A Test Case is an object containing a sequence of methods beginning with "test"; e.g., testStringMatches( ), and optional setup( ) and teardown( ). The test is passed to a testrunner object. For each test method, the runner executes setup( ), then the test method, and then teardown( ). A library of assertions are available to verify state throughout the tests. As the tests proceed, the runner updates the UI to report on the results.

As with many Scriptaculous classes, the Runner object accepts an options argument. A particularly interesting option is resultsURL, which the runner will post results to. This is a facility that makes automated testing possible, as discussed earlier in the "Solution."

Scriptaculous also contains some functions that let you simulate mouse and keyboard; see *System Test*.

JsUnit framework (Hieatt)

Edward Hieatt's JsUnit (*http://www.edwardh.com/jsunit/*) is a testing framework that supports standard xUnit-like functionality. Each test is actually an HTML page containing the test in a script, and the HTML page is passed as an argument to a test runner page. There's a demo page available (*http://www.edwardh.com/jsunit/runner/testRunner.html?testpage=www.edwardh.com/jsunit/runner/tests/jsUnitTestSuite.html*).

JsUnit Framework (Schaible)

Jorg Schaible's JsUnit (*http://jsunit.berlios.de/index.html*) works in a similar manner as the preceding frameworks.

Code Example: Using Scriptaculous Unit-Testing

The Basic Ajax Pattern Reader (*http://ajaxify.com/run/reader/*) uses a queue abstraction to represent the playlist. The queue itself was developed with a Scriptaculous test case (*http://script.aculo.us*; see Figure 19-3). The setup method establishes a new queue:

```
setup: function() { with(this) {
  q = new Queue();
}},
```

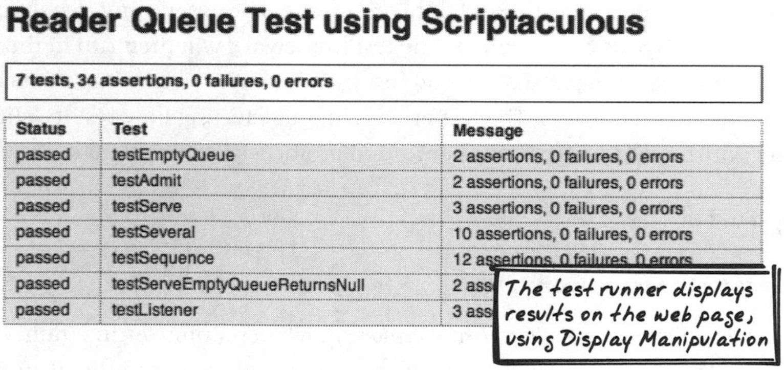

Reader Queue Test using Scriptaculous

7 tests, 34 assertions, 0 failures, 0 errors

Status	Test	Message
passed	testEmptyQueue	2 assertions, 0 failures, 0 errors
passed	testAdmit	2 assertions, 0 failures, 0 errors
passed	testServe	3 assertions, 0 failures, 0 errors
passed	testSeveral	10 assertions, 0 failures, 0 errors
passed	testSequence	12 assertions, 0 failures, 0 errors
passed	testServeEmptyQueueReturnsNull	2 ass
passed	testListener	3 ass

The test runner displays results on the web page, using Display Manipulation

FIGURE 19-3. Scriptaculous Unit Test

An initial test method verifies the queue's initial state:

```
testEmptyQueue: function() { with(this) {
  assertEqual(0, q.size);
  var items = q.items();
  assertEqual(0, items.length);
}},
```

Subsequent methods examine the queue as it's built up:

```
  testSequence: function() { with(this) {
    q.admit("first");
    q.admit("second");
    assertEqual(2, q.size);
    assert(util.membersEqual(["second","first"], q.items()));
    ...
  }},
```

All of this is embedded an HTML file (*http://ajaxify.com/run/reader/queueTest.html*), which, if you visit it, will run the test and report the results. Here's the structure of the HTML file:

```html
<html xmlns="http://www.w3.org/1999/xhtml" xml:lang="en" lang="en">
<head>
  <title>Queue Test</title>
  <meta http-equiv="content-type" content="text/html; charset=utf-8" />
  <script src="/run/Lib/js/util.js" type="text/javascript"></script>
  <script src="prototype.js" type="text/javascript"></script>
  <script src="unittest.js" type="text/javascript"></script>
  <script src="queue.js" type="text/javascript"></script>
  <link rel="stylesheet" href="test.css" type="text/css" />
</head>
<body>
...
<!-- Log output -->
<div id="testlog"> </div>

<!-- Tests follow -->
<script type="text/javascript" language="javascript" charset="utf-8">
  new Test.Unit.Runner({
    q: null,
    setup: function() { with(this) {
      q = new Queue();
    }},
    testEmptyQueue: function() { with(this) {
      assertEqual(0, q.size);
      var items = q.items();
      assertEqual(0, items.length);
    }},
    ...
  });
</script>
</body>
</html>
```

Related Patterns

Service Test

A *Service Test* (see the next pattern) is a good way to complement a Browser-Side Test, since it focuses on the server-side interface rather than the browser application. Testing both is necessary to be confident that all aspects of the system are working.

Logging

Logging (Chapter 18) inside a test can help diagnose problems.

Service Test

Automated, JavaScript, Remoting, UnitTest, TDD, Test, WebService, XMLHttpRequest

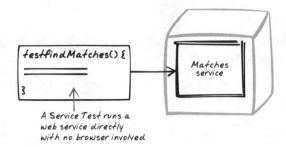

FIGURE 19-4. Service Test

Developer Story

Dave is creating a trading application. On the server, there are services to give quotes and accept orders. To help develop and test the web service, he builds a suite of Service Tests. One test, for example, submits an order and checks that the database registered it. These tests are automated and re-executed every time the project changes.

Problem

How can you test web services?

Solution

Build up automated tests of web services, using HTTP clients to interact with the server as the browser normally would. The browser-server interaction of an Ajax App is usually a sequence of *XMLHttpRequest Calls* (Chapter 6). That's fortunate, because testing the service is usually as easy as simulating the browser—passing a certain request and checking the response. Sometimes, verification might also involve checking what happened on the server, e.g., a database state change or a message to an external system.

The test itself can be built in any language and testing framework you like, because it's completely decoupled from both the browser and the server. The only practical constraint is that you should be able to run it from a script, to allow for continuous integration. Many languages provide an HTTP client library, so it's easy to build a test pass request to the server and make assertions against the response. Indeed, there are client frameworks like HTTPUnit (*http://httpunit.sourceforge.net/*) that are specifically for the purposes of testing web apps. They're typically used for testing conventional applications, where the response contains an entire page, but they work fine for the terse responses usually provided by web services.

A *RESTful Service* (Chapter 9), in particular, should be straightforward to test because it will usually output structured responses which are easily parsed; and there won't be any conversational state to set up and track. A service that outputs an *HTML Message* (Chapter 9) makes tests a bit more fragile; passing in 5+5 will always let you assert 10 as the *Plain-Text Message* (Chapter 9), but not always The <span class="strong">answer</class> is <span class="surprising">10<span>!!! if an HTML Message is used.

Tool Support

Ruby Net::HTTP

Net::HTTP (*http://www.ruby-doc.org/stdlib/libdoc/net/http/rdoc/*) is an HTTP client library for Ruby, shipping with the standard distribution. It's used in the refactoring illustration below.

Jakarta HTTPClient

Jakarta HTTPClient (*http://jakarta.apache.org/commons/httpclient/*) is a richly featured HTTP client framework for Java.

PHP HTTPClient

Simon Willison's HTTPClient (*http://scripts.incutio.com/httpclient/*) is a basic HTTP client framework for Perl.

Code Example: Service Test

The Basic Ajax Pattern Reader (*http://ajaxify.com/run/reader/*) uses some *Simulation Services* to get information from the server. A Service Test was first created against the Simulation Service, and once the Simulation Service passed, the test was used to drive the design of the real services. Earlier, the Solution mentioned that the programming language of the HTTP client is completely independent of the server or browser languages. That's not just theoretical, since some languages (e.g., Ruby and Perl) are particularly well-suited to string manipulation. To prove the point, the example here uses Ruby's Net::HTTP library.

The service being tested is patternSummary.phtml (*http://ajaxify.com/run/reader/patternSummary. phtml*), a pattern text provider that accepts a pattern name and outputs its solution. The test case is very basic—it just requests the *Slider* pattern and checks that the output matches a simple regular expression:

```
require "test/unit"
require "net/http"

class PatternServiceTest < Test::Unit::TestCase

  def test_slider
    sliderResponse = grabPattern("Slider");
    regex = /^\s*<h1><a\ href=\".*?\">Slider<\/a><\/h1>\s*\
            <span\ class=\"summary\">.+?<\/span>.+
            /mx;
```

```
    assert_match(regex, sliderResponse.body);
  end
  ...
  def grabPattern(patternName)
    session = Net::HTTP.new('ajaxlocal', 80);
    response = session.get("/run/reader/logging/realService/" +
                           "patternSummary.phtml?patternName=" + patternName);
    assert_equal("200", response.code);
    return response;
  end

end
```

Related Patterns

Simulation Service

You can sometimes start creating a test against a *Simulation Service* (see earlier), and gradually refactor it into a real service, while evolving the test as well.

Browser-Side Test

A *Browser-Side Test* (see earlier) is a good complement to a Service Test, since the former
tests browser behavior while the latter ensures the server will support the browser in the
correct way.

System Test

Automated, FunctionalTest, JavaScript, PerformanceTest, Regression, Robot, UnitTest, TDD, Test

FIGURE 19-5. System Test

Developer Story

Devi has completed the first cut of a new Ajax App and wants to build an automated test
of the whole thing. With the help of a testing application, she records a typical usage so it
can be played back later. The software takes note of the final state, which will be used for
verification during automated playback.

Problem

How can you test an entire Ajax App?

Solution

Build automated tests to simulate user behavior and verify the results. A System Test exercises a complete system in much the same way as a user would. The most common category of system test is a functional test—verifying the functionality—but system testing also encompass qualities such as performance and robustness. While they are often conducted manually, with users clicking and mousing around, it's highly preferable to automate as much as possible in order to promote continuous integration.

Automated system tests remain somewhat difficult, but tools are improving. They can be broadly categorized as follows:

Browser Controller (Figure 19-6)

A specialized, "robot"-style testing tool will fire up the browser, then use the underlying operating system's API to create the effect of a user interacting with the browser. Several commercial controllers are able to record user actions for later playback.

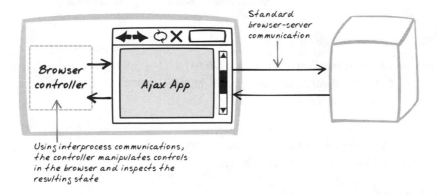

FIGURE 19-6. Browser Controller

Embedded Browser Script (Figure 19-7)

Run the application in a standard browser and embed a *Browser-Side Test* on the page. The test can use some JavaScript trickery to simulate user activity. Don't let the browser aspect put you off, because it's feasible to have a continuous integration tool like Ant coordinate *Browser-Side Tests*, as pointed out earlier in this chapter.

Browser Simulation (Figure 19-8)

The application is executed by a model of a real browser. Typically, the simulation pulls a page from a URL somewhere and builds up a DOM to represent it. The DOM can then be manipulated; e.g. the simulation allows a button click operation to occur or a form to be submitted. While several frameworks like this exist, the important issue for Ajax developers is how well they simulate JavaScript. JavaScript interpreters are implemented in several languages, so it's possible for *Browser Simulations* to incorporate them in order to simulate a realistic Ajax interaction.

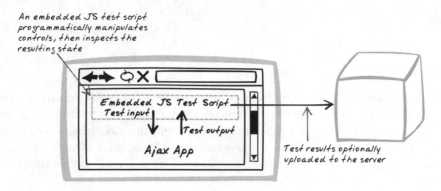

An embedded JS test script programmatically manipulates controls, then inspects the resulting state

Embedded JS Test Script

Test input

Test output

Ajax App

Test results optionally uploaded to the server

FIGURE 19-7. Embedded Browser Script

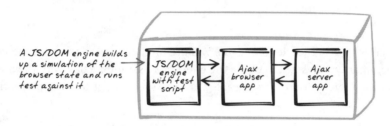

A JS/DOM engine builds up a simulation of the browser state and runs test against it

JS/DOM engine with test script

Ajax browser app

Ajax server app

FIGURE 19-8. Browser Simulation

The first two approaches involve a real browser, which is a more realistic test, but it does imply that the test must run on a machine capable of launching the browser, or of somehow controlling it remotely.

System Tests require not just automation of user behavior, but also automation of result verification. As with other tests, results can be verified with a combination of assertions against the DOM and against server-side state.

Tool Support

GhostTrain

Scriptaculous's GhostTrain (*http://wiki.script.aculo.us/scriptaculous/show/GhostTrain*) is an *Embedded Browser Script* with recording capability. When you start the recording mode, a Scriptaculous test case begins to fill up inside the div. Each mouse and key action becomes a new line of the test case. Later on, you can add your own assertions about the application state. GhostTrain is a very promising work in progress.

Watir

Watir (*http://wtr.rubyforge.org*) follows the *Browser Controller* approach, enabling a Ruby programmer to script browser behavior and interrogate the DOM at any stage. You can easily integrate Watir commands into a standard test case—for example:

```
ie = Watir::IE.start("http://ajaxpatterns.org")
ie.button(:name, "Search").click
```

Watir is IE-specific right now.

Selenium

Selenium (*http://selenium.thoughtworks.com/*) is an open source tool by Thoughtworks developers, an *Embedded Browser Script* framework that works in IE, Mozilla, Firefox, and Safari. A JavaScript Selenium component is embedded inside the browser application under *test*, and it communicates with a server-side component. Interesting, there's flexibility on the location of the server-side component. It can be placed in the web server, to provide a quick summary in the web page being developed. Alternatively, it can be run as a separate server, where the server controls the browser (like a *Browser Controller* would), and the embedded browser component merely transmits server commands to the application.

HTTPUnit

HTTPUnit (*http://httpunit.sourceforge.net/index.html*) is an open source Java testing framework, built on JUnit, and specifically designed for testing web apps. It works as a *Browser Simulator*, converting an HTML page into a Java `HTMLPage` object that wraps a Java DOM model of the original HTML. HTTPUnit simulates JavaScript by delegating to the Rhino JavaScript engine, although support is incomplete.

DojoToolkit

Dojo Toolkit (*http://dojotoolkit.org/docs/compressor_system.html*) is a Java-based *Browser Simulator* that uses Rhino to let you run tests from an Ant task. Given the project's momentum and focus on Ajax, it's likely to evolve into a very solid product.

Code Example: Using Scriptaculous GhostTrain

The Ajax Patterns Reader (*http://ajaxify.com/run/reader/logging/realService/ghost/*) is refactored here to include Scriptaculous's GhostTrain (*http://wiki.script.aculo.us/scriptaculous/show/GhostTrain*), discussed earlier. You can hit `Escape` anywhere in the document to open it up, and then use the buttons to record a test case, which can then be played back (Figure 19-9).

To hook up GhostTrain, the Scriptaculous library files must be included (quite a lot to download, but keep in mind they don't need to be included in production):

```
<script type="text/javascript" src="/run/Lib/js/sc/prototype.js"></script>
<script type="text/javascript" src="/run/Lib/js/sc/controls.js"></script>
<script type="text/javascript" src="/run/Lib/js/sc/effects.js"></script>
<script type="text/javascript" src="unittest.js"></script>
<script type="text/javascript" src="ghosttrain.js"></script>
```

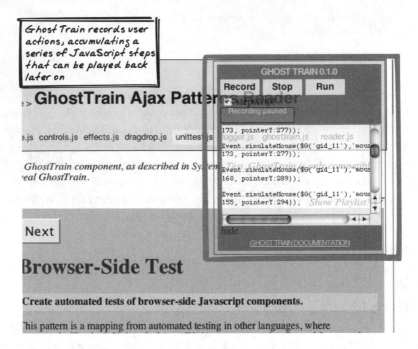

The annotation inside the figure reads:

> Ghost Train records user actions, accumulating a series of JavaScript steps that can be played back later on

FIGURE 19-9. GhostTrain

The only other requirement is to register the GhostTrain object as a keypress handler. The handler will take care of any other initialization:

```
window.onload = function( ) {
    Event.observe(document, 'keypress', GhostTrain.intercept, true);
    ...
}
```

Related Patterns

Browser-Side Test

System Test frameworks that work as *Embedded Browser Scripts* are a form of *Browser-Side Tests* (see earlier).

Simulation Service

For integration tests, you can configure the server to run against a *Simulation Service* (see earlier). That way, you'll have tight control over server behavior, ensuring the final state is deterministic.

Want to Know More?

- A Summary of Functional Testing Frameworks (*http://www.softwareqatest.com/qatweb1.html#FUNC*).

PART SIX

Appendixes

THERE ARE SEVERAL APPENDIXES.

Appendix A, *Ajax Frameworks and Libraries*, is a summary of frameworks and libraries supporting Ajax, ranging across many programming languages and licensing models. Appendix B, *Setting Up the Code Examples*, offers, instructions for setting up the tutorial and demo code on your system. Appendix C, *Patterns and Pattern Languages*, provides a background on patterns, pattern languages, and Ajax Patterns in that context. Finally, Appendix D, *References*, lists the texts that are referenced throughout the book.

Ajax Frameworks and Libraries

AN EXPLOSION OF LIBRARIES AND FRAMEWORKS HAS BEEN ONE OF THE FORTUNATE CONSEQUENCES OF the Ajax phenomenon. They come in all shapes and sizes and in any licensing model you'd care to name. Throughout the Ajax Patterns, the importance of using frameworks and libraries has been emphasized—it's worth knowing the low-level details, but often not worth implementing them yourself. For this reason, the listing here makes a good companion to the Ajax Patterns.

The initial list was published back in June 2005, when I documented what seemed like an overwhelming 20 products. Maintained in an openly editable wiki, it's blossomed to 160-odd products, and doubtless many still to come—stay tuned to *http://ajaxpatterns.org/Ajax_Frameworks* for the latest updates.

Some of these were around long before Ajax was "Ajax," but all are here because they support Ajax development. This section is a lightly edited snapshot of the wiki in January 2006—many of the descriptions come straight from project owners and users. It begins with two sections on pure JavaScript frameworks, where you have to provide your own server-side integration. Following that are frameworks for a large number of server-side environments, many including some JavaScript library API as well as a server-side API.

Note that there's a multilanguage section, since some frameworks address multiple server-side environments. Therefore, consult the multilanguage section in addition to the section for any particular server-side environment you're interested in.

People getting into Ajax often ask me for a "quick-fix" framework to help get started. So at risk of offending many worthy projects, each section points out a few of the frameworks that have generated buzz. This is, of course, a subjective measure, and it is one of popularity more than intrinsic value; do investigate further for any serious development work. In addition, look at the patterns, many of which discuss specific frameworks.

JavaScript Multipurpose Frameworks

These are pure-JavaScript libraries used to achieve a range of functionality in the browser—usually in a manner that protects you from dealing with browser compatibility issues, as described in *Cross-Browser Component* (Chapter 12). The Prototype framework has been very popular for general JavaScript infrastructure, and many frameworks mentioned here build on it. At a higher level, Dojo and Scriptaculous are probably the two best known products here and are good options if you're looking for a multipurpose library. Along those lines, Mochikit and OpenRico have also been popular as well. In the commercial space, there's been a lot of interest in Backbase and Tibco General Interface, though the products here are so varied, it really depends where you look.

AjaxFace (from 2005)

AjaxFace (*http://www.vertexlogic.com*) is an Ajax, JavaScript UI framework.

- High-level JavaScript API for building UI
- Open architecture for updating and retrieving data from the backend
- Automatic synchronization of data and UI
- Easy extensibility
- High performance
- Easy customization of look-and-feel through well-defined stylesheets
- Online demo (*http://www.vertexlogic.com/demo.html*)
- Commercial license by VertexLogic

Backbase (from 2003)

Backbase (*http://www.backbase.com*) is a comprehensive browser-side Ajax framework with cross-browser support. The Backbase Ajax framework is compatible with any server-side platform (e.g., Java, .NET, PHP, or Coldfusion).

- Free community edition for noncommercial/noninstitutional use
- Advanced tooling for .NET developers—Visual Studio 2005 plugin
- Advanced tooling for Java developers—JSF taglib/Eclipse integration

- Over 80 Ajax widgets/components at Backbase Explorer (*http://www.backbase.com/demos/explorer/*)

- Active Ajax developer community at Backbase DevNet (*http://www.backbase.com/#dev/home.xml*)

- Online Ajax demos/starter kits at Check Out (*http://www.backbase.com/#home/pulldown/demos.xml*)

- Commercial license by Backbase (formed in 2003)

Bindows (from 2003)

Bindows (*http://www.bindows.net*) is a software development kit (SDK) that generates highly interactive Internet applications with richness that rivals modern desktop applications using the strong combination of DHTML, JavaScript, CSS, and XML. Bindows applications require no downloads and no installation on the user side—only a browser is required (no Java, Flash, or ActiveX are used). Bindows is probably the leading object-oriented platform for developing Ajax applications.

The Bindows Framework provides you with the following:

- A class-based, object-oriented API

- A complete windowing system with a wide array of supported widgets including menus, forms, grids, sliders, gauges, and more

- The leading toolkit for developing zero-footprint SOA client-side applications

- Native XML, SOAP, and XML-RPC support

- Single-user to enterprise-level support

- Built-in support for Ajax

The Bindows development environment includes:

- Enterprise scale projects support

- Cross-browser, cross-platform support

- Server independent architecture

- Interoperability with new and existing resources

- Uniform development methodology

- Commercial license, by MB Technologies (based in GA, USA, with the main development center in Sweden, formed in 2002)

Dojo (from September, 2004)

Dojo (*http://dojotoolkit.org/*) offers comprehensive widget and browser-server messaging support:

- Extensive deployment support such as dependency-based packaging and compression of required libraries into a single download (see *On-Demand JavaScript* [Chapter 6]).

- Framework for creation of custom JavaScript widgets

- Library of pre-built widgets

- Solid drag-and-drop, effects, and generic animation support

- Browser-server messaging support such as XMLHttpRequest and other mechanisms

- Event management (see *Distributed Events* [Chapter 10])

- Support for bookmarkability and manipulating URLs in the browser

- Open source license (Academic Free License 2.1); led by Alex Russell (*http://alex. dojotoolkit.org/*) of JotSpot (*http://www.jot.com/*)

eBusiness Applications (EBA) Ajax Components (from 2002)

EBA (*http://www.ebusiness-apps.com/*) offers self-contained Ajax components enabling data entry and lookup:

- Library of prebuilt widgets supporting multiple backends (Java, PHP, ASP, and .NET)

- Excel-like data entry and grid tool (see *Data Grid* [Chapter 14])

- Multimode combo box enabling configurable livesearching (Smartsearching, autocomplete, compact, etc.; see *Live Search* and *Suggestion* [Chapter 14])

- Active user community (EBA Developer Forums at *http://forums.ebusiness-apps.com*)

- Online Ajax demos (EBA Grid at *http://developer.ebusiness-apps.com/technologies/ webdevelopment/codeandcomponents/ebagrid/productdemos/griddemos.htm*)

- Commercial license by eBusiness Applications

Engine for Web Applications (from 2002)

Engine for Web Applications (*http://www.imnmotion.com/projects/engine/*) is a framework for building modular components for web applications and separating content from functionality:

- Configurable deployment

- Registry for storing, retrieving, and destroying objects that conform to the common interface

- Message service for intraobject publications and subscriptions

- Transaction service for asynchronous multiobject communication

- Task service for bootstrapping client-side modules of a web application and for creating dependency-based task lists; can load an XML-based task.

- Ability to easily create scoped and redistributable components in XML with automatic event hook-up and containment

- Store and retrieve form field values regardless of whether the form field still exists

- Monitor service for easily creating beacon and Ajax monitoring solutions

- API Documentation (*http://www.imnmotion.com/projects/engine/api/engine_api.html*)

- Demonstrations with source (*http://www.imnmotion.com/projects/engine/demonstrations/*)

- Open source license (custom license) by Stephen W. Cote (*http://www.imnmotion.com/*)

Framework for RESTful JavaScript (Freja) (from 2006)

Freja (*http://www.csscripting.com/freja*) is a JavaScript MVC (Model-View-Controller) framework:

- Geared toward single-screen, zero-latency web applications.

- Excellent scalability (much less server roundtrips).

- True MVC separation.

- True server-side/client-side code separation.

- Very light footprint; only a handful of methods to learn (the framework is 25 KB *uncompressed*).

- Based on Open Standards (XML/XSLT).

- Works with any modern web browser: IE, Firefox, Safari, and Opera.

- Plays well with other JavaScript toolkits and libraries (prototype, Scriptaculous, Dojo, etc.). Freja is not "yet another Ajax library"; it is a Ajax-based, high-level framework. It is not its purpose to provide drag-and-drop functionality or visual effects, but it will let you use your favorite JavaScript library to do so.

- See Tutorials (*http://www.csscripting.com/wiki/index.php?title=Freja#Tutorials*) and Documentation (*http://www.csscripting.com/wiki/index.php?title=Freja_Documentation*).

- Open source license (CC-GPL).

Mochikit (from 2005)

Mochikit (*http://mochikit.com/*) is a highly documented and well-tested suite of JavaScript libraries that will help you get your work done fast. Authors borrowed good ideas from Python, Objective-C, etc., and adapted them to JavaScript.

- MochiKit.Async: manage asynchronous tasks

- MochiKit.Base: functional programming and useful comparisons

- MochiKit.DOM: painless DOM manipulation API

- MochiKit.Color: color abstraction with CSS3 support

- MochiKit.DateTime: "What time is it anyway?"

- MochiKit.Format: string formatting goes here

- `MochiKit.Iter`: itertools for JavaScript; iteration made HARD, and then easy

- `MochiKit.Logging`: we're all tired of alert( )

- `MochiKit.LoggingPane`: interactive `MochiKit.Logging` pane

- `MochiKit.Visual`: visual effects

- Open source license (MIT license or Academic Free License, v2.1) by Bob Ippolito

OpenRico (from May, 2005; based on earlier proprietary framework)

OpenRico (*http://openrico.org/demos.page*) is a multipurpose framework with support for Ajax infrastructure and user interaction.

- An `XMLHttpRequest` response can be routed to one or more callback operations, DOM object, or JavaScript object

- Easy drag-and-drop

- Ajax animation such as scaling and transitions (and presumably the increasingly common idioms such as progress indicators and fading technique)

- "Behaviors," which is essentially a widget library

- External tutorial by Yonah Russ of Mirimar (*http://www.mirimar.net/mailbrowser/*)

- Builds on prototype library

- Open source license; grew from Sabre Airline Solutions internal product, by Bill Scott, Darren James, Richard Cowin, and others (*http://looksgoodworkswell.blogspot.com*)

Plex Toolkit

Plex Toolkit (*http://www.plextk.org*) is an open source feature-complete DHTML GUI toolkit and Ajax framework based on a pure JavaScript/DOM GUI tookit and Ajax framework. Uses the almost identical markup language to PXML (Flex) embedded in ordinary HTML documents for describing the UI. Binding is done with JavaScript.

Pros:

- Full set of widgets such as datagrid, tree, accordion, pulldown menus, DHTML window manager, viewstack, and more (over 60 libraries)

- Markup driven (makes it easy to build the interface)

- Interface components can be easily themed with CSS

- Client side XSLT for IE and Mozilla

- Well-documented with examples

- Multiple remoting transport options such as `XMLHttpRequest` and `IFrame` (an RSLite cookie-based coming soon)

- Back button support (complete history management for all components)
- Support for YAML serialization

Cons:

- No animation framework
- Open source license (GPL, LGPL, or Artistic License; your choice) by Richard Hundt.

Prototype

Prototype (*http://prototype.conio.net/*) makes it easy to use object-oriented concepts like classes and inheritance within JavaScript. It also supports basic Ajax functionality such as web remoting.

- A project run in conjunction with Ruby on Rails, but can be (and certainly is) used independent of Ruby or RoR
- Open source license by Sam Stephenson

qooxdoo (from May, 2005)

qooxdoo (*http://qooxdoo.oss.schlund.de/*) is another ambitious framework with a broad range of UI and infrastructural features being developed.

Infrastructure:

- Portable abstraction of the DOM and event/focus management
- Debugging support
- Timer class for easy scheduling
- Getter/Setter support

UI:

- Widget framework and library of prebuilt widgets
- Layout managers
- Image caching and portable PNG transparency
- Open source license (LGPL) by various contributors

Script.aculo.us (from 2005)

Scriptaculous (*http://script.aculo.us*) builds on the Prototype library to provide a JavaScript with comprehensive Ajax coverage.

- Visual Effects (see *One-Second Spotlight* [Chapter 16]).
- Drag-And-Drop (see *Drag-And-Drop* [Chapter 15]).

- Unit-Testing (see *System Test* [Chapter 19]).

- Open source license by Thomas Fuchs and others. A project run in conjunction with Ruby on Rails, but can be (and certainly is) used independent of Ruby or RoR.

SmartClient (from 2000)

SmartClient (*http://www.smartclient.com*) from Isomorphic Software is a cross-platform Ajax RIA system.

Cross-browser foundation classes and services:

- JSON or XML programming

- Browser abstraction layer

- GUI component services

- Logging and debugging services

- Extensible GUI components

- Navigation and command controls

- Form controls and managers

- Flat, hierarchical, and multidimensional grids

- Containers and layout managers

Data and services stack:

- Client data caches and local operations

- Client data model managers

- Communication and protocol services

Visual development tools:

- Runtime console.

- Log viewer.

- Component inspector and editor.

- Admin console.

- Integrated developer reference.

- SmartClient Ajax applications run on Internet Explorer, Mozilla, Netscape, Firefox, and Safari web browsers, and on Windows, MacOS, Linux, and Solaris operating systems. Unlike other Ajax systems, SmartClient applications are fully functional even when ActiveX is disabled.

- See *www.smartclient.com* for a product brief, live demos, and downloadable SDK.

- Commercial license by Isomorphic Software.

ThyAPI (from end of 2004)

ThyAPI (*http://www.sf.net/projects/thyapi/*) is a library of *DHTML reusable components*. Ajax is only one of its features. Its main purpose is to allow the creation of full desktop-like applications in a browser. ThyAPI is a library based on DynAPI (*http://www.sf.net/projects/dynapi/*), and open source (LGPL).

- Made entirely in DHTML (JavaScript + CSS).

- Totally object-oriented and extensible.

- Follows XMLRPC protocol, for data exchange with the server. Plans to implement JSON-RPC.

- Interface definition entirely in CSS.

- Works in Mozilla Firefox (version 1.0+) (*http://www.mozilla.org*) and Internet Explorer (version 6+).

- A DataSource component, to simplify linking of JavaScript widgets with server methods.

- Cross-browser, cross-platform support (it inherits this characteristic from DynAPI).

- Aimed to provide RAD development of browser-based applications and reuse of custom-made widgets.

- Open source license (LGPL).

TIBCO General Interface (from 2001)

TIBCO General Interface (*http://www.tibco.com/software/business_optimization/rich_internet_applications.jsp*) is a mature Ajax RIA framework that's been powering applications since 2001. In fact, the framework is so mature, that TIBCO General Interface's visual development tools themselves run in the browser alongside the Ajax RIAs as you create them.

- Dozens of extensible GUI components.

- Vector-based charting package.

- Support for SOAP communication (in addition to basic HTTP and XML).

- Full visual development environment.

- WYSIWYG GUI layouts.

- Step-through debugging.

- Code completion.

- Demo in Jon Udell's coverage at InfoWorld (*http://weblog.infoworld.com/udell/2005/05/25.html*).

- The next version of the product and many sample applications at the developer community site (*https://power.tibco.com/app/um/gi/newuser.jsp*).

- Commercial license by Tibco; more info at *http://developer.tibco.com*.

Interactive Website Framework (from May 2005)

Interactive Website Framework (*http://sourceforge.net/projects/iwf/*) is a project aiming to support the various aspects of Ajax infrastructure in the browser.

- Describes itself as a "framework for creating highly interactive web sites using Java-Script, css, xml, and html. Includes a custom xml parser for highly readable JavaScript. Essentially, all the plumbing for making Ajax-based web sites, as well as other common scripts."

- Has a thread-safe XMLHttpRequest implementation.

- Contains a wrapper around the XML document, so you can make more readable code, instead of manual navigation:

    ```
    var node = doc.groceries.frozen[0].pizza[0].size;
    var node = doc.documentElement.firstChild.firstChild.getAttribute("size");
    ```

- Open source license by Brock Weaver (*http://circaware.com*).

Zimbra AjaxTK

Zimbra (*http://www.zimbra.com/*) is a recently released client/server open source email system. Buried deep within this product is an excellent Ajax Tool Kit component library (AjaxTK) written in JavaScript. A fully featured demo of the product is available on zimbra.com that showcases the extensive capabilities of its email client. A very large and comprehensive widget library that was available only in commercial Ajax toolkits is now available to the open source community. Download the entire source tree to find the Ajax directory, which includes example applications.

Pros:

- Full support of drag-and-drop in all widgets. Widgets include data list, wizard, button, text node, rich text editor, tree, menus, etc.

- Build system uses Ant, and hosting is based on JSP and Tomcat.

- Very strong client-side MVC architecture based; architect is ex-Javasoft lead developer.

- Communications support for client-side SOAP, XmlHttpRequest, and IFrames.

- Support for JSON serialized objects and JavaScript-based XForms.

- Strong multibrowser capabilities: IE 5.5+, Firefox 1.0+, latest S.

- High-quality widgets have commercial quality, since this is a commercial open source product.

- Widget library is available as a separate build target set from the main product.

- Debugging facility is built into the library and displays communications request and response.

Cons:

- Does not currently support keyboard commands in menus and in-place datasheet editing.

- Does not support graceful degradation to IFrames if other transports are unavailable.

- Documentation is lacking, but a PDF whitepaper describing widget set and drag-and-drop is available.

- Open source license (Zimbra Ajax Public License ZAPL, derived from Mozilla Public License MPL) by Zimbra.

JavaScript Remoting Frameworks

As many of the Ajax Patterns establish, Web Remoting (Chapter 6) is error-prone, tedious, and broad in functionality, which makes it ideal to encapsulate in a library or framework like those covered here. The multipurpose frameworks covered earlier will do it too, but if you're looking for a standalone simple option, SACK is a popular choice. HTMLHttpRequest is a good option for compatibility as it supports IFrames as well as XMLHttpRequest. A more feature-rich API is offered by Ajax Client Engine (ACE).

AjaxCaller (from May 2005)

AjaxCaller (*http://ajaxify.com/run/Lib/js/ajaxCaller.js*) is a basic, threadsafe wrapper around XMLHttpRequest that is mainly for Ajax newcomers packaged with the Ajax Patterns demos. See TestAjaxCaller (*http://ajaxify.com/run/testAjaxCaller*).

- RESTful calls to the server (GET/POST/PUT/DELETE) with plain-text or XML routed to a callback operation

- Aimed at Ajax newcomers—instead of optimizing performance or footprint, the library aims to be a readable code base and provides debugging support

- Open source license (Creative Commons) by Michael Mahemoff (*http://softwareas.com*), with some ideas from John Wehr and Richard Schwartz

Ajax Client Engine (ACE) (from December 2005)

Ajax Client Engine (*http://www.lishen.name*) is a powerful remoting wrapper.

- Object-oriented API

- Cross-browser support

- Flexible features: request options; request parameter validation; callback argument; callback option; callback timeout; tracing service; caching service; polling service; common callbacks; and exception handling

- Open source license (MIT) by Li Shen

AjaxGear (from November 2005)

AjaxGear (*http://www.ajaxgear.com*) is a simple and cross-platform Ajax toolkit.

- Enables a web browser to make asynchronous call to the web server without the need to refresh the whole page.

- Use the Ajax class to communicate with the web server.

- A complete web site is available for download to see AjaxGear in action.

- Use the *AjaxGear.PageEngine.js* file to learn how a web site can easily use the toolkit.

- Three objects are currently being developed as part of the AjaxGear toolkit—namely, progress bar, autocomplete, and form validator.

- Open source license (MIT) by Allan Spartacus Mangune (*http://www.allanmangune.com*) of ArchCommerce (*http://www.archcommerce.com*).

AJFORM (from June 2005)

AJFORM (*http://redredmusic.com/brendon/ajform/*) is an extremely easy to use Ajax framework. It is designed to be for entry-level Ajax coders. Its single purpose is to send data from any HTML form via XMLHTTP. The AJFORM framework provides you with:

- Three-step setup

- Automatic support for any HTML form

- Ability to implement with little coding knowledge

- Open source license (BSD)

HTMLHttpRequest (from 2005)

HTMLHttpRequest (*http://www.twinhelix.com/javascript/htmlhttprequest/*) also uses XMLHttpRequest and IFrames for improved compatibility.

- Tested and works in IE6, IE5.5, IE5, and IE4 for Windows; Mozilla for Windows; Opera7 for Windows; and in Safari and IE5 for the Mac

- Untested, but probably works in IE4 and Mozilla for the Mac; Opera for other programs; and Konqueror for Linux

- Open source license (LGPL) by Angus Turnbull of Twin Helix Designs (*http://www. twinhelix.com/*)

JSMX (from Aug 2005)

JSMX (*http://www.coldfusion-ajax.com*) is a very simple Ajax implementation for ColdFusion Developers (or any language that can easily build JavaScript Strings). This API does not return XML but String representations of JavaScript expressions.

- Using WDDX and the toScript( ) function within ColdFusion makes converting your ColdFusion objects to JavaScript a snap!

- Smaller packet sizes over the wire (JavaScript versus XML).

- Reduced latency due to less parsing of the responses.

- Parameters can be sent to the server in multiple formats, including strings, objects, and entire forms, without having to build extra logic to handle each type.

- API has no server-side components, which makes it more portable.

- Extremely simple syntax shortens the learning curve and speeds up development:

```
params = document.myForm;
http( "POST" , "remote.cfc?method=dosomething", my_callback , params );
```

- Open source license (Creative Commons Attribution-ShareAlike) by Todd Kingham.

LibXMLHttpRequest (from June 2003)

libXmlRequest (*http://www.whitefrost.com/reference/2005/09/09/libXmlRequest.html*) is a thin wrapper around XMLHttpRequest.

- Synchronous and asynchronous getXML() and postXML( ) methods

- Pooling of XMLHttpRequest objects

- Response caching

- XSL and XPath utilities

- setInnerXHTML utility for copying XML nodes into an HTML document

- Source protected by standard copyright by Stephen W. Cote (*http://www.imnmotion.com/*)

MAJAX (from August 2005)

MAJAX (*http://unips.sourceforge.net/devblog/?p=6*) is yet another *very* thin wrapper for XMLHttpRequest. The idea is to have a really simple interface to send and receive ASCII content.

- Provides handy callback interface for doing actions—e.g., upon server response

- Open source license (GPL or LGPL) by "Peter F"

RSLite

RSLite (*http://www.ashleyit.com/rs/main.htm*) is a thin wrapper around a highly cross-browser compatible transport layer comprised of a JavaScript image object request with a querystring parameter and a cookie response.

- A simple component released as part of Brent Ashley's more comprehensive Remote Scripting work (see "JavaScript Remote Scripting (JSRS) (from 2000)" in the "Multi-language Ajax Frameworks" section)

- Open source license by Brent Ashley

Sack (from May 2005)

Sack (*http://twilightuniverse.com/resources/code/sack/*) is a thin wrapper around `XMLHttpRequest`.

- Caller can specify callback function or callback DOM object. With a callback DOM, the response text is pushed directly into the DOM.
- Open source license (modified MIT license) by Gregory Wild-Smith.

Subsys_JsHttpRequest

Subsys_JsHttpRequest (*http://www.dklab.ru/lib/Subsys_JsHttpRequest/*) is an Ajax framework with `XMLHttpRequest` support and dynamic "script src" generation to emulate Ajax functional for old browsers that are not compatible with `XMLHttpRequest`.

- Open source license (LGPL 2.1 or later) by Dmitry Koterov

XHConn (from April, 2005)

XHConn (*http://xkr.us/code/javascript/XHConn/*) is a thin wrapper around `XMLHttpRequest`.

- Example: `new XHConn().connect("mypage.php", "POST", "foo=bar&baz=qux", fnWhenDone);`
- Open source license (Creative Commons Attribution-ShareAlike License) by Brad Fults

JavaScript Effects Frameworks

Fade Anything Technique (FAT)

FAT (*http://www.axentric.com/posts/default/7*) handles the Yellow Fade Technique (see *One-Second Spotlight* [Chapter 16]).

- Open source license (stated as Creative Commons in the page comments) by Adam Michela

Moo.fx (from Oct 2005)

Moo.fx (*http://moofx.mad4milk.net*) builds on a lite version of the Prototype library to provide an extremely compact effects package.

- Visual effects
- Cookie memory for effects
- 36 KB total file size
- Open source license (MIT) from Volerio Proietti

JavaScript Flash Frameworks

The *Richer Plugin* pattern points out how Flash can benefit Ajax development; these frameworks support Ajax-Flash crossovers.

AMFPHPKit

AMFPHP (*http://amfphp.sourceforge.net/*) is an open source implementation of the Flash Remoting framework.

- Fast, reliable, 100 percent free, and open source. With this new version, we strived to make a product as stable and full-featured as ColdFusion-based remoting (the reference implementation). You also get to use the wonderful NetConnection debugger, which shows you exactly what's being sent between the client and server. Remoting uses AMF, a very lightweight binary format that cuts the bulk out of packets, meaning data exchange is a lot faster than with XML.

- Open source license (GPL) created by Wolfgang Hamann and maintained by various developers.

Flash JavaScript Integration Kit

The Flash JavaScript Integration Kit (*http://www.osflash.org/doku.php?id=flashjs*) allows for the integration of JavaScript and Flash content.

- Enables JavaScript to invoke ActionScript functions, and vice versa.

- All major data types can be passed between the two environments.

- Open source license (modified Apache 1.1) by multiple open source Flash contributors.

Stream (from July, 2005)

Stream (*http://www.stormtide.ca/Stream*) is a bi-directional Ajax platform that brings Flash XML socket support to JavaScript. Also includes an extensible open source stateful socket server and client management platform.

- Plugin API (C# and JavaScript client libraries).

- No more polling (true server-pushed events; not emulated events through polling); see *HTTP Streaming* (Chapter 6).

- Ideal for chat, monitoring, and client interaction systems that would requiring polling.

- Sessions (per-session and per-page state tracking).

- Event monitoring (Interact with mouse events, including maximum fire rate throttling).

- Currently at the Alpha, technology preview, proof of concept stage. Download at *http://beta.stormtide.ca/files/StreamReleases/StreamAlphaGPL20050709.zip?source=ajaxpatterns*.

- Dual license open source (Commercial License and GPL) by StormTide Digital Studios. Full source available.

JavaScript XML Frameworks

These libraries support patterns such as *XML Message, Browser-Side XSLT,* and *XML Data Island.*

Google AJAXSLT (from June 2005)

Google AJAXSLT (*http://goog-ajaxslt.sourceforge.net/*) is a JavaScript framework for performing XSLT transformations, as well as XPath queries.

- Builds on Google Map work
- Open source license (BSD) by Google

Sarissa (from February, 2003)

Sarissa (*http://sarissa.sf.net*) is a JavaScript API that encapsulates XML functionality in browser-independent calls.

- Portable XMLHttpRequest creation
- Portable XPath queries
- Portable DOM manipulation
- Portable XSLT
- Portable serialization to XML
- Open source license (GPL 2.0 or LGPL 2.1, your choice) by various contributors

JavaScript Specialized Frameworks

These are a couple of useful libraries that don't fit well in other sections.

Drag-Drop

Walter Zorn's Drag-Drop library (*http://www.walterzorn.com/dragdrop/dragdrop_e.htm*) is a well-featured drag-and-drop library (see also *Drag-And-Drop* [Chapter 15]).

- Open source license (LGPL 2.1 or later) by Walter Zorn

Giant-Ass Image Viewer (GSV)

GSV (*http://mike.teczno.com/giant/pan/*) lets you place a massive image on the server and allow the user scroll around as if it was all stored locally (like scrolling around Google Maps; see *Virtual Workspace* [Chapter 15]).

- Open source license (custom) by Michael Migurski

Multilanguage Ajax Frameworks

Each library here integrates browser-side JavaScript with several server-side languages. Usually, an individual project will only need to integrate with one server-side language, but the library includes several to make it applicable to a broader market. JSON has had a big impact, because it is as much a popular data format as it is a collection of open source libraries for remoting. SAJAX has also received considerable attention in this area, in part because it supports so many languages. CPAINT is popular as well.

Cross-Platform Asynchronous INterface Toolkit (CPAINT) (from May 2005)

CPAINT (*http://cpaint.sourceforge.net/*) is a true Ajax implementation and a JSRS (JavaScript Remote Scripting) implementation that supports both PHP and ASP/VBScript. CPAINT provides you the code required to implement Ajax and JSRS on the backend, while the returned data is manipulated, formatted, and displayed on the frontend in JavaScript. This allows you to build web applications that can provide near real-time feedback to the user. See *Ajax Stub* (Chapter 9).

- Supports both PHP and ASP

- Unified JavaScript file for all functions

- Supports both remote scripting and XML

- Supports both local and remote functions

- Single or multiple XMLHTTP objects

- Returns backend data as text or as a JavaScript XML/DOM document object

- Can support both POST and GET requests

- Backend proxy functions for accessing remote functions and data

- Tested with all major browsers

- Open source license (GNU, GPL, and LGPL) by various contributors

JavaScript Object Notation (JSON) and JSON-RPC

JSON (*http://www.crockford.com/JSON/index.html*) is a "fat-free XML alternative" and JSON-RPC (*http://www.json-rpc.org/*) is a remote procedure protocol, akin to XML-RPC, with strong support for JavaScript clients. See *JSON Message* (Chapter 9).

- Implementations (*http://www.json-rpc.org/impl.xhtml*) exist for several server-side platforms such as Java, Python, Ruby, or Perl.

- Individual packages and licenses for each platform. Original concept and JavaScript implementation by Douglas Crockford.

JavaScript Remote Scripting (JSRS) (from 2000)

JSRS (*http://www.ashleyit.com/rs/jsrs/test.htm*) routes calls directly from JavaScript into your server-side language and back out again.

- Initially developed back in 2000

- Known browsers: IE4+, NS4.x, NS6.x, Mozilla, Opera7, and Galeon

- Server-side support for ASP, ColdFusion, PerlCGI, PHP, Python, and JSP (servlet)

- Open source license (very flexible custom license) by Brent Ashley (*http://www. ashleyit.com/*)

Rialto: Rich Internet AppLication TOolkit

Rialto (*http://rialto.application-servers.com/*) is a cross browser JavaScript widgets library.

- Because it is technology agnostic, it can be encapsulated in Java/JSP/JSF, .NET, or PHP-graphic components.

- The widgets library includes forms, drag-and-drop, tree, data list with fix header and resizable columns, pop up, and splitter.

- Enables single-page interface-application development.

- Demo available (*http://rialto.application-servers.com/demoRialto.jsp*).

- Open source license (Apache) by multiple contributors.

SAJAX (from March 2005)

SAJAX (*http://www.modernmethod.com/sajax/*) routes calls directly from JavaScript into your server-side language and back out again. So, for example, calling a JavaScript method "x_ calculateBudget( )" will go the server and call an ASP/ColdFusion/Io/Lua/Perl/PHP/ Python/Ruby `calculateBudget( )` method, and then return the value in JavaScript to `x_ calculateBudget_cb( )`.

- As described in *Ajax Stub* (Chapter 9), facilitates mapping from the JavaScript stub function to a backend operation.

- See a demo walkthrough in the "Real-World Examples" of Ajax Stub.

- Capable of stubbing calls to numerous server-side platforms: ASP, ColdFusion, Io, Lua, Perl, PHP, Python, or Ruby.

- Open source license (BSD) by various contributors.

ZK—Ajax/XUL Web Framework

ZK (*http://zk1.sourceforge.net/*) is an Ajax-based, event-driven, XUL-based, all Java framework designed to enable Web applications to have both rich user experiences and a simple programming model.

- With ZK, represent and manipulate RIA in XUL/HTML components that are all running at the server, as has been done for years in desktop applications.

- No JavaScript. No replication of business logic at the clients. No proprietary components. No compilation. ZK works with existent frameworks and technologies, such as JSF and portals. The pace of adapting ZK is all under your control.

- XUL-based components.

- Event-driven model.

- Server-centric processing.

- Script in Java and EL expressions.

- Demo available (*http://www.potix.com/zkdemo/userguide*).

- Open source license (GPL) by Potix Corporation.

C++ Ajax Frameworks

Wt

Wt (*http://witty.sourceforge.net/*) is a C++ widget library, which uses Ajax to render changes to the widget tree when available.

- API inspired by existing GUI libraries. It targets C++ application developers.

- The widget library makes complete abstraction of the underlying technology (JavaScript, HTML, Forms, CGI, Ajax).

- Documentation is at *http://jose.med.kuleuven.ac.be/wt/doc/index.html*.

- Open source license (Affero General Public License) by Koen Deforche.

ColdFusion Ajax Frameworks

AjaxCFC

AjaxCFC (*http://www.robgonda.com/blog/projects/ajaxcfc/*) is a ColdFusion framework meant to speed up Ajax application development and deployment by providing developers seamless integration between JavaScript and ColdFusion. It also provides built-in functions that quickly adapt to any type of environment, security, and help overcoming cross-browser compatibility problems. It contains:

- ColdFusion components following the best practices of object-oriented programming and design patterns. Programming with AjaxCFC involves extending components and creating your own Ajax facades.

- Restricted open source license (free to use in any context but not redistributable) by Rob Gonda.

JSMX (from August 2005)

JSMX (*http://www.coldfusion-ajax.com*) is a very simple Ajax implementation for ColdFusion developers (or for any language that can easily build JavaScript Strings). This API does not return XML but String representations of JavaScript expressions.

- Smaller packet sizes over the wire (JavaScript versus XML).

- Reduced latency due to less parsing of the responses.

- Parameters can be sent to the server in multiple formats including strings, objects, and entire forms without having to build extra logic to handle each type.

- API has no server-side components, which makes it more portable (planned).

- Extremely simple syntax shortens the learning curve and speeds up development:

  ```
  params = document.myForm;
  http( "POST" , "remote.cfc?method=dosomething", my_callback, params );
  ```

- Open source license (Creative Commons Attribution-ShareAlike) by Todd Kingham.

.NET Ajax Frameworks

In the .NET world, all eyes are on Microsoft with their in-progress Atlas framework. It's not yet clear exactly what it covers, how portable it will be, and how it will affect the existing frameworks here. In any event, Michael Schwartz's Ajax.NET is one popular choice, and for a broader-scoped framework, the Monorail project—similar to Ruby on Rails—has a lot of interest too.

Ajax.NET for ASP.NET 1.x/2.0

Ajax.NET (*http://ajax.schwarz-interactive.de/csharpsample/default.aspx*) is an Ajax framework for ASP.NET 1.x/2.0.

- A basic Ajax library for ASP.NET that provides the very basic Ajax capability to make XMLHTTP callbacks. Does not have any Ajax-enabled controls or support for Viewstate, etc.

- Open source license by Michael Schwartz.

Anthem.NET for ASP.NET 1.x/2.0

Anthem.NET (*http://anthem-dot-net.sourceforge.net/*) is Jason Diamonds' new version of a long-established Ajax library, now a SourceForge open source project.

- Athem.NET provides a set of Ajax-enabled controls inherited from ASP.NET server controls, with most Ajax behaviors pre-built, avoiding lots of client JavaScript. It supports Viewstate so that you can actually modify server controls (either Anthem controls or ASP.NET controls inside an Anthem control—e.g., panel) in your server-side code, in C# or VB without having to mess about in JavaScript. Still in its early days (DEC 2005) but promising!

- Open source license by Jason Diamonds.

AjaxAspects

AjaxAspects (*http://www.mathertel.de/AJAXEngine/*) is an engine that uses JavaScript proxies to call server-side web service methods.

- Use Ajax with web services.

- Built upon JavaScript client proxy methods for standard web services. (Just call a regular JavaScript method to call a method on the server.)

- Standard SOAP and WSDL is reused for the communication between client and server.

- No need for special implementations in web services.

- Multiple types, arrays and XML objects are supported as parameters and return values.

- Caching on the client and server.

- Queuing actions.

- Delaying actions.

- Many Ajax controls available that integrate in standard ASP.NET web forms.

- Supporting ASP.NET 2.0.

- Full source code available.

- Demo web site available (*http://www.mathertel.de/AjaxEngine/*).

- Supported by a blog in English (*http://ajaxaspects.blogspot.com/*) and German (*http://ajaxaspekte.blogspot.com/*).

- Open source license (Creative Commons license) by Matthias Hertel (*http://www.mathertel.de*).

Atlas (from late 2005)

Atlas (*http://www.asp.net/default.aspx?tabindex=7&tabid=47*) is Microsoft's in-progress Ajax project. ASP.NET Atlas is a package of new web development technologies that integrates an extensive set of client script libraries with the rich, server-based development platform of ASP.NET 2.0.

- Commercial (license terms unclear at time of writing) by Microsoft

Bitkraft for ASP.NET

Bitkraft (*http://www.tiggrbitz.com*) is a CLR-based (.NET) web framework that allows distributed web content to be created and served in a unique fashion. It is written in C# and compiles for operation under the Microsoft .NET Framework 1.1+ or the .Mono Framework, making it portable to almost any platform.

At its core, the Bitkraft framework extends the ASP.NET architecture to fully support JavaScript-based server callbacks using the XmlHttpRequest object as a transport layer in Ajax.

- Known browsers: IE5+, Firefox1+, and Netscape 6

- Server-side support for ASP.NET, Mono XSP, Cassini, and Apache (modMono) .NET Framework 1.1+

- Attribute driven

- Asynchronous and synchronous methods mapped directly from JavaScript proxy objects to the server

- Supports all .NET types and custom classes mapped to the JSON object on the client

- Uses JSON instead of XML

- Open source library by Wayne Lee-Archer

ComfortASP.NET for ASP.NET 1.1/2.0

ComfortASP.NET (*http://www.comfortasp.de*) is an approach that lets developers rely on pure ASP.NET programming while offering Ajax features. Internally, ComfortASP.NET uses Ajax (using DHTML, JavaScript, XMLHTTP) to implement these features—but the web developer implements only pure server-side ASP.NET!

- Automatically transfer only changes between ASP.NET postbacks, which leads to significantly faster response for low bandwidth connections and less overall HTML traffic (up to 90 percent, depending on new postback data)

- Reduce page reloads and use hidden postbacks instead

- Ajax/DHTML-like client experience (but without programming any Ajax/DHTML directly)

- Keep browser history free of postback entries (the Back button no longer irritates your users)

- Autodisable form and prevent user input while using postback or multiple form postbacks

- Control web client scroll position and focus from the server-side code

- Switch back at all times to original ASP.NET when you need it—even dynamically at runtime

- Open source license by Daniel Zei

MagicAjax.NET (from September 2005)

MagicAjax.NET (*http://www.magicajax.net/*) is an open source framework designed to make it easier and more intuitive for developers to integrate Ajax technology into their web pages, without replacing the ASP.NET controls and/or writing JavaScript code.

- Just make the initial setup, put the controls you want to Ajax-enable inside an Ajax-Panel, and you're done!

- Many other features also available if you really want the advanced features as well.

- Open source license (LGPL) by various contributors.

MonoRail (from May 2005)

MonoRail (*http://www.castleproject.org/index.php/MonoRail*) is a platform for developing C# web applications using templates instead of the webform-based approach.

- Functionally similar to Ruby on Rails

- Generates most or all of the JavaScript for widgets and animation in the browser

- Provides helpers that work with the Prototype JavaScript library (*http://prototype.conio.net/*)

- Functions on the .NET and .Mono platforms on both Windows and Linux

- Open source license by multiple developers

WebORB for .NET (from August 2005)

WebORB for .NET (*http://www.themidnightcoders.com/weborb/aboutWeborb.htm*) is a platform for developing Ajax and Flash-based rich client applications and connecting them with .NET objects and XML web services (see online examples at *http://www.themidnightcoders.com/examples*).

- WebORB includes a client-side library called Rich Client System (*http://www. themidnightcoders.com/rcs/index.htm*). The Rich Client System provides a simple one-line API to bind to and invoke any method on any .NET object or XML web service.

- Supports synchronous and asynchronous method invocations.

- Does not require any modifications on the server-side code, and there is no need for custom method attributes, special signatures, or argument types. Does not require design-time stub generation.

- Synchronous invocations return data from the same invocation (no callback needed). Asynchronous invocations rely on a callback.

- Any server-side method can be invoked synchronously or asynchronously.

- Client application can request special activation modes for the server objects. As a result, objects can easily become stateful without any special programming.

- Provides a special API for handling database query results—server code can return DataSets or DataTables and the client presents it as a special RecordSet JavaScript object. The object provides a way to retrieve column names as well as row data.

- Supports data paging. Client applications can retrieve data in pages, thus streamlining user experience.

- Supports all server-side argument types as well as return values—primitives, strings, complex types, arrays, native .NET collections, and remote references.

- Dual license (standard edition is free, professional is commercial) by Midnight Coders.

zumiPage

With zumiPage (*http://www.zumipage.com*), postbacks to the server are automatically captured on the client side and sent via an XMLHTTP mechanism.

- zumiPage requires no code changes to existing projects, so you can write code for ASP. NET as you always do, using the standard web controls and methodology. zumiPage will take care of the rest. Your web application should be smoother, faster, and more interactive.

- Works with ASP.NET 2.0 and 1.1.

- Fully compatible with Internet Explorer and Mozilla Firefox.

- Save up to 90 percent of the traffic.

- Easy to integrate with existing projects.

- Does not require any use of JavaScript.

- Fast, invisible XMLHTTP postbacks.

- Full control over returned controls on each postback.

- Wait behaviors (for server-loading times).

- Commercial license by Amir Leshem.

Java Ajax Frameworks

Java has always had many wide and varied frameworks. With Ajax, we've seen new ones emerge, and we've also seen add-ons for the earlier projects. Two popular libraries have been the Ajax JSP Tag Library and Direct Web Remoting.

AjaxAnywhere (from September 2005)

AjaxAnywhere (*http://ajaxanywhere.sourceforge.net*) returns any set of existing JSP, JSF, Struts, Spring, etc., components into Ajax-aware components without JavaScript coding. (see the Quick Start Demo at *http://ajaxanywhere.sourceforge.net/quickStart.html*).

- Does not break existing server-side MVC architecture.

- Less JavaScript to develop and maintain. Absence of commonly accepted naming conventions, formatting rules, and patterns makes JavaScript code messier then Java/JSP. It is extremely difficult to debug and unit-test in multibrowser environments. AjaxAnywhere eliminates all these complexities.

- Easy to integrate. AjaxAnywhere does not require changing the underlying application code.

- Graceful degradation. Switch whenever you need to between Ajax and the traditional (refresh-all-page) behavior of your web application. Your application can also support both behaviors.

- Open source license (Apache 2).

AJAX JSP Tag Library

The AJAX JSP Tag Library (*http://ajaxtags.sourceforge.net/*) is a set of JSP tags that simplify the use of Asynchronous JavaScript and XML (Ajax) technology in JavaServer Pages. This library eases development by not forcing J2EE developers to write the necessary JavaScript to implement an Ajax-capable web form. The tags are:

Autocomplete
Retrieves a list of values that matches the string entered in a text form field as the user types.

Callout

Displays a callout or pop-up balloon, anchored to an HTML element with an onclick event.

Select

Based on a selection within a drop-down field, a second select field will be populated.

Toggle

Switches a hidden form field between true and false and at the same time switches an image between two sources.

Update Field

Updates one or more form field values based on response to text entered in another field.

Open source license by multiple contributors.

AJAX Java Server Faces Framework

AJAX-JSF (*http://smirnov.org.ru/en/ajax-jsf.html*) will make any existing Java Server Faces applications use Ajax functionality. Most existing components can be used as is or easily converted to support Ajax.

- See a worked example called MyFaces JSF Tree, with table scroller and a tabbed pane as Ajax components (*http://smirnov.org.ru/myfaces-ajax/ajax.jsf*).

- Minimal differences from JSF specifications. This is proposal to the MyFaces project.

- Open source license (Apache Software License 2.0) by Alexander Smirnov.

Direct Web Remoting (DWR) (from 2005)

Direct Web Remoting (DWR)(*http://www.getahead.ltd.uk/dwr/*) is a framework for calling Java methods directly from JavaScript code.

- Like SAJAX, can pass calls from JavaScript into Java methods and back out to JavaScript callbacks

- Can be used with any web framework: Struts, Tapestry, etc.

- Follows Spring-like KISS/POJO/orthogonality philosophy

- Being incorporated into next WebWork release (*http://www.opensymphony.com/webwork/*)

- Open source license (Apache see *http://www.apache.org/LICENSE.txt*) by Joe Walker (*http://www.getahead.ltd.uk/sg/space/joe/*)

Echo 2 (from March 2005)

Echo 2 (*http://www.nextapp.com/products/echo2/*) allows you to code Ajax Apps in pure Java (see the demo at *http://demo.nextapp.com/InteractiveTest/ia*).

- Automatically generates HTML and JavaScript

- Coordinates messages between browser and server. Provides messaging in XML

- Can hand-write custom JavaScript components if desired

- Open source license (Mozilla Public License or GNU LGPL) by Next App, Inc. (*http://www.nextapp.com/*)

Guise

Guise (*http://www.guiseframework.com/*) provides an elegant server-side component architecture that doesn't require developers to write HTML or JavaScript (see the demo at *http://www.guiseframework.com/demonstration*).

- A true application framework, written completely in Java

- Allows developers to think in terms of component and events instead of HTML generation and DOM programming

- Provides controls, modal dialogs, flyovers, and more

- XHTML-compliant

- Flexible commercial license, with free full-featured development version available for immediate download by Global Mentor Inc.

ICEfaces

ICEfaces (*http://www.icesoft.com/products/icefaces.html*) is a standards-compliant extension to JavaServer Faces (JSF) for building and deploying rich Ajax applications.

- Smooth, incremental page updates with in-place editing and no full page refresh

- User context preservation during page update, including scrollbar positioning and user focus

- Asynchronous page updates driven from the application in real-time

- Fine-grained user interaction during form entry that augments the standard submit/response loop

- Commercial license by IceSoft

JSON-RPC-Java (from April 2004)

JSON-RPC-Java (*http://oss.metaparadigm.com/jsonrpc/*) is an Ajax RPC middleware that allows JavaScript DHTML web applications to call remote methods in a J2EE Application server.

- Transparently maps Java objects to and from JavaScript objects using Java reflection

- Handles marshalling/unmarshalling of arbitrarily complex nested data structures

- Lightweight protocol similar to XML-RPC

- Leverages the J2EE security model with session specific exporting of objects

- Open source license (LGPL) by Michael Clark and others

JSP Controls Tag Library (from December 2005)

JSP Controls Tag Library (*http://jspcontrols.sourceforge.net/*) provides the lifecycle for portlet-like JSP components. The library does not require a portal engine or other central controller. The components built with the Library can be used in any JSP-based application.

- Supports dual-mode components (non-Ajax and Ajax). Therefore, it works even with Netscape 4.

- In non-Ajax mode, components utilize synchronous HTTP request/response cycles via the Redirect-After-Post pattern.

- In Ajax mode, components are updated in place.

- Component reload in non-Ajax mode is completely automatic and transparent.

- Transition between Ajax and non-Ajax mode is undetectable when JavaScript is turned on or off.

- See the demo at *http://www.superinterface.com/jspcontrols/index.html*.

- Open source license (Apache 2.0) by Michael Jouravlev.

jWic

jWic (*http://www.jwic.de*) is a Java-based development framework for developing dynamic web applications with the convenience and familiarity of rich client–style programming.

- Component-based, event-driven programming model.

- Controls are rendered using templates (i.e., Velocity).

- Dynamically updates a control using Ajax mechanisms.

- Open source licence (Apache Licence, Version 2.0) by Florian Lippisch and Jens Bornemann.

Struts-Layout

Struts-Layout (*http://struts.application-servers.com*) is a tag library for Apache Struts that provides easy and fast interface creation. This is achieved by powerful tags that display panels, input fields, tables, treeviews, sortable lists, datagrids, popups, calendars, etc. With those tags customized to your own preference, some of the developers in your team don't have to write or even know HTML.

- The Struts-Layout tag library now allows to put Suggest fields on your web pages (*http://struts.application-servers.com/suggest/index.html*).

- Open source license (Apache 2) by Jean-Noel Ribette and others.

SWATO (from 2005)

SWATO (Shift Web Application TO...) (*http://swato.dev.java.net/*) is a set of reusable and well-integrated Java/JavaScript libraries that give you an easier way to shift the interaction of your web apps through Ajax.

- The server-side Java library can be easily deployed in all Servlet 2.3+–compatible containers.

- The client-side JavaScript library is based on the prototype that can help you code your JavaScript the object-oriented way.

- Uses JSON to marshal the data of your POJOs (Plain Old Java Objects) on the server side.

- Provides a simple interface for your JavaScript code to interact with the remote POJOs exposed to the client side such as RPC or cross domain access.

- Easy and flexible configuration using `<servlet>` and `<filter>` in *web.xml*. Comes with Spring integration.

- Comes with several reusable components (Auto-suggest Textbox, JS Template, JS Logger, etc.) that help you develop your web apps easier.

- Online demo available at *http://swato.throughworks.com*.

- Open source license (Apache) by Zhijie Chen.

Tacos Tapestry Components (from December 2005)

Tacos (*http://tacos.sourceforge.net*) is an Ajax engine/component library for Ajax/DHTML-based applications written in Java for the Tapestry web framework (*http://jakarta.apache.org/tapestry*).

- Written to be completely integrated with the Dojo JavaScript library (*http://dojotoolkit.org*), provides an extensive set of widgets and features.

- Requires little or no JavaScript knowledge to use, though any part of the process can be customized to your liking.

- Provides development tools such as a logging/debug console window for Ajax/other JavaScript-initiated requests that make writing Ajax applications much easier.

- Component library hosts extensive set of production quality code, with a built-in functionality that includes dialogs, floating windows, tons of effects, tree, autocompleter, Inline Editor, etc.

- Extensive form-based Ajax support includes client-side validation, field observers, partial form submissions, etc.

- Open source license (Apache) by multiple contributors.

ThinkCAP JX

ThinkCAP JX (*http://www.clearnova.com*) is designed to build industrial strength transactional business applications.

- Contains Visual Workbench.

- Based on over 20 open source projects, including Struts, Hibernate, JFreeChart, and many more.

- Using three-tier client/server development, this minimizes JavaScript by using a server-side generation library of over 150 methods.

- Handles complex Ajax updates using TransactionSafe. This guarantees no connection leaks and automates complex master-detail updates.

- Rich data-aware controls include Scrollable Updateable DataView Data Grid, Client Sorting, Outlook Bar, Accordion, Tab Panes, Trees, and Autocomplete.

- Smart data binding provides declarative binding to HTTP Request or Session Parms.

- Client and Server Layout Management automatically directs component/Ajax call output to the appropriate default or named areas of a page.

- Dual license (GPL or commercial) by ClearNova.

WebORB for Java (from August 2005)

WebORB for Java (*http://www.themidnightcoders.com/weborb/aboutWeborb.htm*) is a platform for developing Ajax and Flash-based rich client applications and connecting them with Java objects and XML web services. (See online examples at *http://www.themidnightcoders.com/examples*.)

- See the earlier discussion "WebORB for .NET (from August 2005)" for more details.

- Dual license (standard edition is free, professional is commercial) by Midnight Coders.

WidgetServer (from 2004)

WidgetServer (*https://wiser.dev.java.net*) enables you to code Ajax applications in pure Java.

- Automatically generates HTML and JavaScript

- Coordinates messages between browser and server

- Can hand-write custom JavaScript and HTML/CSS components if desired

- Applications run as web, Swing, and Swing client/server Apps

- Dual license (higher-performance commercial version and lower-performance open source version) by Dirk von der Weiden

Lisp Ajax Frameworks

CL-Ajax

CL-Ajax (*http://cliki.net/cl-ajax*) directs JavaScript calls directly into server-side Lisp functions.

- The export function script is as follows:

```
(export-function #'my-function)
```

- Generates a JavaScript stub with arguments.

- Can callback to a JavaScript function or DOM object.

- May be integrated into SAJAX.

- Open source license (custom, very flexible, license) by Richard Newman (*http://www. holygoat.co.uk/*).

Perl Ajax Frameworks

CGI::Ajax—Export Perl Methods to JavaScript for Ajax

CGI::Ajax (*http://pjax.sourceforge.net/*) is a Perl module to make it trivial to write Ajax scripts using Perl. The module is object-based Perl, and creating a link from a JavaScript event to your Perl code is as easy as defining the JavaScript function name to Perl subroutine name mapping.

- Can be used to link any Perl code to an HTML event, including fetching other URLs (using LWP, for example)

- Nestable, so an HTML event can start a chain of Ajax events (e.g., onClick= "do_this( ); now_that( ); finally_this( )")

- Can handle GET or POST

- Not necessary to have your exported subroutines named in a specific way—name them what you want

- Very small overhead—allows you to keep thinking Perl and not get bogged down

- Active development community

- Open source library (Perl and Artistic license) by Brian Thomas

HTML::Prototype—Generate HTML and JavaScript for the Prototype Library

HTML::Prototype (*http://search.cpan.org/dist/HTML-Prototype/*) contains some code generators for Prototype, the famous JavaScript object-oriented library, and the *script.aculous* extensions.

- Basically similar to the Prototype helpers in Ruby on Rails

- Open source license (GPL and Artistic) by multiple contributors

PHP Ajax Frameworks

PHP frameworks tend to focus more on remoting than HTML generation. XOAD is one popular remoting library, as well as CPAINT and SAJAX (covered earlier in "JavaScript Multipurpose Frameworks").

AJASON

AJASON (*http://ajason.sourceforge.net/*) is a PHP-based framework.

- Uses JSON (JavaScript Object Notation) to encode/decode data between server and browser
- Open source license by multiple contributors

AjaxAC (from April, 2005)

AjaxAC (*http://ajax.zervaas.com.au/*) encapsulates the entire application in a single PHP class.

- All application code is self-contained in a single class (plus any additional JavaScript libraries).
- Calling a PHP file or HTML page is very clean. All that is required is creating the application class, and then referencing the application JavaScript and attaching any required HTML elements to the application.
- Built-in functionality for easily handling JavaScript events.
- Built-in functionality for creating subrequests and handling them.
- Allows for custom configuration values, so certain elements can be set at runtime.
- No messy JavaScript code clogging up the calling HTML code—all events are dynamically attached.
- Easy to integrate with templating engine.
- Easy to hook in to existing PHP classes or MySQL databases for returning data from subrequests.
- Extensible widget structure to be able to easily create further JavaScript objects (this needs a bit of work though).
- Open source license (Apache 2.0) by Zervaas Enterprises (*http://ajax.zervaas.com.au/*).

Cajax

Cajax (*http://sourceforge.net/projects/cajax*) is a PHP object-oriented framework that creates and handles server-side requisitions though JavaScript remote calls. Some features are:

- Simple server-side programming
- Almost no client-side programming (less JavaScript writing is possible)
- Handler for server-side events
- A suggest handler like Google's
- Plugin for multiple selects (like country/state/city)
- Remote server calls directly from JavaScript, using an abstraction layer
- Plugin for submitting forms though XMLHTTPRequest

- JavaScript caching
- Open source library (LGPL) by Thiago Pappacena

HTS Web Application Framework

HTSWaf (*http://www.htsdesign.com/index.php?&section=htswaf&page=index*) provides seamless client-to-server event handling.

- The HTS Web Application Framework is a PHP- and JavaScript-based framework designed to make simple web applications easy to design and implement. The framework implements a custom tag engine with an automated JavaScript and/or PHP event model and automates the transfer of data to and from the server.
- Visit the web site for more info and examples (*http://www.htsdesign.com/index. php?&section=htswaf&page=index*).
- Currently in demo stage, by Bert Rosell.

JPSpan

JPSPAN (*http://jpspan.sourceforge.net/wiki/doku.php*) passes JavaScript calls directly to PHP functions.

- Heavily unit-tested
- Open source license

PEAR::HTML::Ajax

PEAR::HTML:Ajax (*http://pear.php.net/package/HTML_AJAX*) is a PHP and JavaScript Ajax library.

- Provides PHP and JavaScript libraries for performing Ajax (communicates from JavaScript to your browser without reloading the page).
- Offers object-oriented (OO) proxies in JavaScript of registered PHP or proxyless operations.
- Serialization of data sent between PHP and JavaScript is provided by a driver model. Currently JSON and Null encodings are provided.
- Open source license (LGPL) by multiple contributors.

Pipeline

The Pipeline framework (*http://livepipe.net*) consists of a simple client-side library and direct integration with the controller. It's main focus is on simplicity, it is not feature rich, and does not use XML. It favors returning HTML or Strings from the controller, or associative arrays that get translated from PHP into JavaScript.

- Open source license with commercial add-ons in development by Picora Pipeworks.

Symfony

Symfony (*http://www.symfony-project.com*) integrates a server-side Ajax layer together with helpers "à la" *script.aculo.us*, to provide an easy way to build Ajax applications in PHP.

- A step-by-step tutorial is available (*http://www.symfony-project.com/tutorial/symfony_ajax. html*) describing the creation of an interactive shopping cart. This demonstrates the tight integration of prototype, *script.aculo.us*, and the MVC model.

- The Advent Calendar initiative (*http://www.symfony-project.com/askeet*) illustrates how to build a real Ajax application in 24 short tutorials, complete with downloadable code. Interactive form submission, Folksonomy, and visual effects are some of the Ajax features of the askeet web site (*http://www.askeet.com*) they are building live. A must see.

- Open source license (MIT License), sponsored by Sensio.

XAJAX

XAJAX (*http://www.xajaxproject.org*) passes JavaScript calls directly to PHP functions.

- Use JavaScript stubs to call functions, object methods, and class methods in a PHP script.

- The response is created using the XAJAX response object, which provides numerous commands, such as assigning HTML to an element, displaying an alert, and more. Custom script output is also supported.

- All browser-specific code (such as using `XMLHttpRequest`) is abstracted, and sending various types of data to the server (including form submission via Ajax) is very easy to accomplish.

- It supports a number of configuration options to allow easy integration with existing web apps and frameworks.

- The JavaScript core is easy to understand and can be overridden to support more advanced JavaScript functionality.

- Well-supported via forums and a new wiki with documentation and tutorials.

- Open source license (LGPL) by J. Max Wilson and Jared White.

XOAD (formerly NAJAX)

XOAD (*http://www.xoad.org*) is a PHP-based Ajax/XAP object-oriented framework.

- It uses *JSON Messages* and native PHP serialized objects to communicate.

- Special attention has been paid to security.

- Supports server-side events (*Distributed Events* [Chapter 10]).

- Supports client-side events (XOAD Events).

- Supports server and client extensions.

- Supports HTML manipulation (extension).

- Supports caching (extension).

- Each class, method and variable is documented.

- Provides easy tutorials to get started using XOAD.

- Provides examples that demonstrate various functionality.

- Won the PHP Programming Innovation Award of August of 2005 (*http://www. phpclasses.org/winners.html*).

- Open source license (PHP 3.0 license) by Stanimir Angeloff.

Python Ajax Frameworks

CrackAJAX

CrackAJAX is a Python framework (*http://www.aminus.org/blogs/index.php/phunt/2005/10/ 06/subway_s_new_ajax_framework*) that does not require JavaScript skills.

- Open source license by Peter Hunt

Turbo Gears

Turbo Gears (*http://turbogears.org*) is a "mega-framework" combining many libraries and frameworks.

- Open source licence (MIT license) and multiple licenses from incorporated frameworks by multiple developers

Ruby Ajax Frameworks

Ruby On Rails

Ruby On Rails (*http://www.rubyonrails.org/*) is a general web framework with strong Ajax support.

- Rails was still in its early days when Ajax hype began, so Ajax may become increasingly important to the Rails framework.

- Generates most or all of the JavaScript for widgets and animation in the browser.

- Supports calling server side.

- Provides scheduling support.

- Open source license [MIT or similar (*http://wiki.rubyonrails.com/rails/show/License*) by David Heinemeier Hansson and contributors (*http://www.loudthinking.com/*).

Setting Up the Code Examples

A SINGLE PACKAGE CONTAINING ALL CODE FOR CHAPTER 2 AND THE AJAX PATTERNS DEMOS AS WELL IS at *http://ajaxify.com/run*. Inside there is a *INSTALL.txt* file containing installation instructions. These instructions are reprinted below, but if you have any trouble, please do check the electronic version as it may include updates.

```
INSTALLING PHP
==============

* If you don't have it already, install PHP5 and integrate with Apache (or
  another web server). The demos rely on the PHP5 OO features, and won't work
  with PHP4 or below.

  There are various installers available that will create an "AMP" (Apache,
  PHP, and MySQL) setup for you (You'll need MySQL for the wiki demo - see
  below). e.g. XAMPP for all major platforms
  (http://www.apachefriends.org/en/xampp.html).  For Apple, consider
  http://www.entropy.ch/software/macosx/php/. For Linux, you may try the
  appropriate Redhat/Debian packages. Alternatively, try the compilation
  instructions at http://dan.drydog.com/apache2php.html.
```

SETTING UP AJAX DEMOS
=====================

* Unzip the package to a temporary location and copy run/, tutorial/, and
  records/ to the apache document root. Assuming the doc root is
  /apache/document/root:

    cp run tutorial records /apache/document/root.

  (Alternatively, if you have sufficient access, set up a new virtual host in
  apache's httpd.conf and point it to the root of the unzipped directory,
  ajaxdemos/).

* Ensure the server can write to (the initially empty) records/ directory. The
  easiest (though not the most secure) way is:

    chmod 777 apache/document/root/records

* Open up run/.htaccess and follow instructions there to set the library path.

* Finished! Visit http://localhost/run/ and http://localhost/tutorial. If you
  can access http://localhost/run/index.phtml but not http://localhost/run/,
  read the following note.

NOTE ON CONFIGURATION: You hopefully won't need any configuration because
run/.htaccess and tutorial/.htaccess contain the relevant settings. But some
apache installations will ignore those settings (depending on the AllowOverride
directive), so be ready to transfer some of the contents of run/.htaccess into
httpd.conf. (run/.htaccess is a superset of tutorial/.htaccess.) Specifically,
modify the existing DirectoryIndex directive to include index.phtml, and add a
new type for phtml as in .htaccess. If the PHP include_path isn't working,
you'll probably need to modify it in php.ini according to the setting in
.htaccess.

SETTING UP THE WIKI DATABASE
============================

NOTE: The wiki demo and its refactorings are the only demos that require a
database. The setup isn't particularly difficult, but if you don't want to mess
with MySQL, you can still run all the other demos.

* Install MySQL if necessary
* Prepare for database access.
  * Enter mysql as power user, e.g.:
        mysql -u root
  * Create "ajaxify_wiki" power user with password "ajaxify_wiki", e.g.:
      GRANT ALL PRIVILEGES ON *.* TO 'ajaxify_wiki'@''localhost'
          IDENTIFIED BY 'ajaxify_wiki';
  * If you'd prefer to use an existing account instead, set the details in
    Model/DAO.php for any wiki demo you wish to run.
* Run run/wiki/Model/freshDB.sh. You only need to do this once, as the tables
  can be shared by all versions of the wiki. NOTE: Ensure your command-line
  path is set up so that "php" will resolve to php5.
* Point your browser at the wiki, e.g. http://localhost/run/wiki/, and you
  should see three fresh messages.

TROUBLESHOOTING
================

If you run into any problems:
* Check the section below, as some demos require some extra setup.
* Try the tutorial demo first. It's less error-prone because there's no library
  path involved.
* Verify file permissions are correct. The easiest way is to run "chmod 755
  document/root". In addition, ensure the records/ directory is writable.
* For the wiki, manually check the database is ready and can be accessed with
  the settings in DAO.php.
* Verify your PHP setup - create a file with "<? php_info ?>" and see if you
  can access it from the browser.
* Ensure you're using PHP 5 (or later).
* Check that you can run a test file, with both .php and .phtml suffixes.
* Check that index.phtml is recognised as a valid directory index. (Check this
  by visiting path/index.phtml instead of just path/.)
* Check that you set the library in .htaccess.
* Check remoting is working as expected with a traffic sniffing tool. (See
  those listed in the Traffic Sniffing pattern).
* Inspect log files. Your PHP log might be different to your Apache error log,
  depending on your setup.
* If problems persist, mail michael@mahemoff.com.

DEMOS REQUIRING EXTRA SETUP
=============================

These demos won't work unless you do some extra setup.

* As mentioned earlier, all the wiki demos (/wiki/..) (but nothing else) require a
MySQL
  database.
* For all portal (/portal/..) and reader (/reader/..) demos, you need net
  access. For the portal synclinks demo (/run/portal/drilldown/syncLinks/), you
  also need to run prepareDrilldown.php first.
* For the shop demo, if you want to run the whole lazy registration process,
  you'll need some form
* For the progress indicator in the Ajaxagram tutorial
  (/tutorial/ajaxagram/..), you either need to run it with net access, or
  change the image source in index.html to point to "/resources/progress.gif".

Patterns and Pattern Languages

ONE SIDE BENEFIT OF THIS PROJECT HAS BEEN TO SEE HOW "PATTERNS" ARE BEING ACCEPTED BY THE development community. Since the Ajax Patterns began to be published, the focus has always been on the "Ajax" and not the "Patterns." For patterns, this is a good thing, and a welcome change from the late '90s, when you not only had to explain the concept but also justify its existence. "Ajax" itself is a pattern—one whose popularity is further evidence for the power of "just a name." For all these reasons, this discussion of patterns and their relationship to Ajax Patterns is kept brief.

Patterns came about in the late 1970s, after Christopher Alexander and colleagues spent years studying the towns and buildings of many diverse cultures. The findings were summarized as 253 distinct patterns, derived from a global pattern describing the division of nations to town-planning patterns such as "Market of Many Shops," all the way down to building patterns like "Soft Tile and Brick." Each pattern is a "thing" you often see in good designs, combined with instructions on making the thing.

Patterns have mostly been confined to academia in their original field, but they have really taken off in software design. Their rise over the past decade has been a great boon to the industry, allowing us to learn about design from real examples and not just vague comments about cohesion, coupling, and encapsulation. The pool of real examples to draw upon has itself risen exponentially, thanks to the Web and the open source movement.

The best-known patterns are software design patterns like Gamma et al.'s *Design Patterns* (1995). But that's not the only domain of software patterns, which have been applied to development processes, deployment practices, and—most important here—usability. Just as the original architecture patterns were fundamentally about improving the experience of inhabitants, usability patterns focus on the people who use—rather than develop—software systems. They have been especially popular for web design (e.g., *The Design of Sites* (Duyne et al., 2003), *A Pattern Language for Web Usability* (Graham, 2003), Martijn van Welie's "Web Design Patterns" at *http://www.welie.com/patterns/*). The Web is ideal for design patterns because examples are readily available for authors to mine and readers to try out.

The Ajax Patterns continue the tradition of web usability patterns, though they focus as much on technical design as on usability. As Alexander et al.'s work shows, it's perfectly possible (desirable, even) for a single language to range across several levels of abstraction. The first three sections of Alexander's work progress from low-level operations to high-level functionality and usability concepts. The fourth section is somewhat separate, as it addresses practices relevant to all those earlier sections, and in that sense is similar to some of the process-oriented pattern languages.

The question has arisen: are these patterns? According to most definitions, these are indeed; each Ajax Pattern shows how real projects have solved a recurring problem. In some cases, there's some speculation involved, but as long as any lack of evidence is declared and the idea is useful, I believe it's worth documenting in the pattern form. Another question here: is this a pattern language, or just a collection of patterns? I'm inclined to say the former, because the patterns are closely linked, filtered according to a consistent set of principles, and generative in that they build on each other. In any event, the most important question here is not about definitions, but about utility: how useful are the Ajax Patterns? I certainly hope the patterns are useful and practical, but I'll let you be the judge of that.

References

THESE ARE REFERENCES CITED THROUGHOUT THE TEXT.

- Buschmann, F., Meunier, R., Rohnert, H., Sommerlad, P., Stal, M. (1996). *Pattern-Oriented Software Architecture*. John Wiley & Sons. See *http://c2.com/cgi/wiki?PatternOrientedSoftwareArchitectureOne*.

- Cooper, A. (1999). *The Inmates are Running the Asylum*. Sams. See *http://www.uidesign.net/1999/books/oct_books1.html*.

- Duyne, D.K., Landay, J.A., Hong, J.I. (2002). *The Design of Sites*. Addison-Wesley Professional. See *http://www.designofsites.com/*.

- Gamma, E., Helm, R., Johnson, R., Vlissides, J. (1995). *Design Patterns*. Addison-Wesley Professional. See *http://c2.com/cgi/wiki?DesignPatternsBook*.

- Graham, I. (2003). *A Pattern Language for Web Usability*. Pearson Education. See *http://www.wupatterns.com/*.

- Norman, D. (2003). *Emotional Design: Why We Love (Or Hate) Everyday Things*. Basic Books. See *http://www.jnd.org/dn.mss/emotional_desig.html*.

Michael Mahemoff has been working with software for 22 years, including 10 years of commercial experience. At the University of Melbourne, he earned degrees in software engineering and psychology, and earned a Ph.D with a thesis on "Design Reuse in Software Engineering and Human-Computer Interaction." He lives in London and consults on software development issues in banking and healthcare. Michael's blog and online projects arc linked from his homepage at *http://mahemoff.com*.

COLOPHON

The cover image is from *Cassell's Natural History*. The cover fonts are Akzidenz Grotesk and Orator. The text font is Adobe's Meridien; the heading font is ITC Bailey.

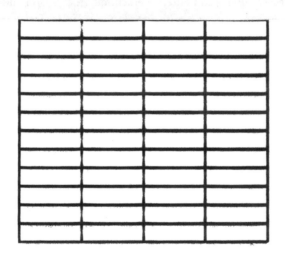

Better than e-books

Buy *Ajax Design Patterns* and access the digital edition FREE on Safari for 45 days.

Go to www.oreilly.com/go/safarienabled
and type in coupon code 5FJG-AVMK-KJ6L-EQLR-CY8M

Search
thousands of
top tech books

Download
whole chapters

Cut and Paste
code examples

Find
answers fast

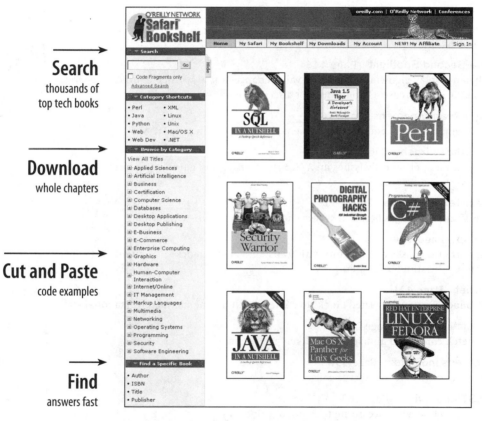

Search Safari! The premier electronic reference
library for programmers and IT professionals.

Ajax Design Patterns

Multi-Stage Download   Page 310
Break content download into multiple stages, so that faster and more important content will arrive first.

On-Demand JavaScript   Page 122
Download and run JavaScript snippets.

One-Second Motion   Page 462
Incrementally move an element from one location to another, or temporarily move it, to communicate an event has occurred.

One-Second Mutation   Page 455
When a page element undergoes a value change or some other significant event, dynamically mutate its shape for a second or so.

One-Second Spotlight   Page 446
When a display element undergoes a value change—or any other significant change— dynamically increase its brightness for a second or so.

Page Rearrangement   Page 78
Add, remove, move, and overlay elements by manipulating the DOM.

Periodic Refresh   Page 215
The browser periodically issues an *XMLHttpRequest Call* to gain new information; e.g., one call every five seconds.

Plain-Text Message   Page 191
Pass simple messages between server and browser in plain-text format.

Popup   Page 401
Support quick tasks and lookups with transient Popups, blocks of content that appear "in front of" the standard content.

Portlet   Page 421
Introduce Portlets—isolated blocks of content with independent conversational state.

Predictive Fetch   Page 297
Pre-fetch content in anticipation of likely user actions.

Progress Indicator   Page 336
Indicate the progress of server calls.

RESTful Service   Page 162
Expose web services according to RESTful principles.

RPC Service   Page 177
Expose web services as Remote Procedural Calls (RPCs).

Rich Text Editor   Page 355
Incorporate a Rich Text Editor widget with easy formatting and WYSIWYG display.

Richer Plugin   Page 149
Make your application "more Ajax than Ajax."

Scheduling   Page 143
Use JavaScript timers to schedule actions.

Server-Side Code Generation   Page 275
Automatically generate HTML and JavaScript from server-side code.